Systems Analysis and Design:

Hoffer/George/Valacich, *Modern Systems Analysis and Design 3/e*

Marakas, *Systems Analysis and Design: An Active Approach*

Valacich/George/Hoffer, *Essentials of Systems Analysis & Design 2/e*

Kendall & Kendall, *Systems Analysis and Design 5/e*

Telecommunications, Networking and Business Data Communications:

Stamper & Case, *Business Data Communications 6/e*

Panko, *Business Data Networks and Telecommunications 4/e*

Security:

Panko, *Corporate Computer and Network Security*

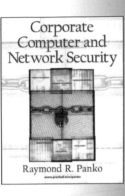

Other Titles:

Awad & Ghaziri, *Knowledge Management*

Marakas, *Decision Support Systems in the 21st Century 2/e*

Marakas, *Modern Data Warehousing, Mining, and Visualization: Core Concepts*

Turban & Aronson, *Decision Support Systems and Intelligent Systems 6/e*

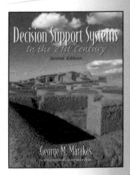

FIRST EDITION

MANAGING THE INFORMATION TECHNOLOGY RESOURCE

Leadership in the Information Age

Jerry Luftman
Stevens Institute of Technology

with

Christine V. Bullen
Stevens Institute of Technology

Donald Liao
Stevens Institute of Technology

Elby Nash
Stevens Institute of Technology

Carl Neumann
Stevens Institute of Technology

PEARSON
Prentice
Hall

Pearson Education, Inc.,
Upper Saddle River, New Jersey, 07458

Library of Congress Cataloging-in-Publication Data

Luftman, Jerry N.
    Managing IT resource / Jerry Luftman.
        p. cm.
    Includes index.
    ISBN 0-13-035126-1 (alk. paper)
    1. Strategic planning—Data processing. 2. Management—Data processing. 3. Information
technology—Management 4. Management information systems. I. Title.

HD30.28.L84 2004
004'.068'4—dc21   2003043368

Executive Editor, MIS: David Alexander
Publisher: Natalie E. Anderson
Project Manager (Editorial): Lori Cerreto
Editorial Assistant: Maat Van Uitert
Editorial Assistant: Robyn Goldenberg
Media Project Manager: Joan Waxman
Senior Marketing Manager: Sharon K. Turkovich
Marketing Assistant: Danielle Torio
Managing Editor (Production): Gail Steier de Acevedo
Production Editor: Vanessa Nuttry
Permissions Supervisor: Suzanne Grappi
Manufacturing Buyer: Natacha Moore
Design Manager: Maria Lange
Cover Design: Bruce Kenselaar
Manager, Print Production: Vincent Scelta
Composition/Full-Service Project Management: Preparé, Inc.
Cover Printer: Coral Graphics
Printer/Binder: Hamilton Printing

Credits and acknowledgments borrowed from other sources and reproduced, with permission, in this textbook appear on appropriate page within text

Pearson Education LTD.
Pearson Education Singapore, Pte. Ltd
Pearson Education, Canada, Ltd
Pearson Education–Japan

Pearson Education Australia PTY, Limited
Pearson Education North Asia Ltd
Pearson Educación de Mexico, S.A. de C.V.
Pearson Education Malaysia, Pte. Ltd

10 9 8 7 6 5 4 3

ISBN 0-13-035126-1

Brief Contents

Contents

Preface

Everyone knows the old adage, "those who can, do; and those who can't, teach." After a notable twenty-two year career at IBM that combined the experience of practitioner (including being a CIO), consultant (including being a manager of consultants), and the last ten years at Stevens Institute as an academic (including being a Professor, Program Director, and researcher), I can comfortably say that I have familiarity with all aspects of an IT career. I trust that there might even be some who would say I was a good CIO, consultant, and Professor. My role as an Executive Vice President of SIM (Society of Information Management) International has provided additional insights regarding the challenges facing Information Technology (IT) organizations. Each of the authors of this text also brings with them a wealth of practical and academic experience. Whether you aspire to become a CIO, consult to a CIO, or prepare graduate students to become a CIO, you will find the IT career demanding and rewarding. This book is intended to be used towards the end of a Masters in Information Systems in giving students the opportunity to understand the strategic, tactical, and operational roles of a CIO.

When I first joined Stevens Institute in 1992 as the Director of Graduate IS Programs, I recognized the need for a course that focused on the strategic, tactical, and operational responsibilities of a CIO. After establishing an IT Executive Board comprised of CIO's from over 35 of the largest companies in the New York–New Jersey metropolitan area, I reviewed the new graduate IS curriculum. This Board also saw the need for a practical course that prepared students to become a CIO, report directly to a CIO, or consult to a CIO. As a result, the course *Managing the IT Resource* was born. The course was built using my experience as a CIO and consultant. I used many current articles, cases, including some of my own research. There was no book that covered the activities that needed to be addressed. The course content was and is continuously reviewed by the Executive Board.

In 1998, I was asked to join a group of leading academics to document and obtain approval for the "Master of Science in Information Systems Status Report from the Joint ACM/AIS Task Force on Graduate IS Curriculum: A Program Designed for the 21st Century." Academia and practitioners alike have approved the program that we documented. A key part of the curriculum was the need to add several courses that integrated many of the lessons learned from the traditional IS graduate courses such as Data Management, Network Management, Analysis and Development of Information Systems, Project Management, Finance, Organization Behavior, and the all-purpose Information Systems. In addition to the important integration course of IT Strategy that places the student in the role of a CIO from a strategic perspective, the group was interested in the integration course that I developed that focused on the tactical and operational perspective of a CIO.

After teaching the course for ten years to practitioners and full time students, the strong demand to comply with the approved ACM/AIS MSIS curriculum, and the many requests to access my syllabus and notes, I decided to write this text.

There are large numbers of articles, books, case studies, and anecdotes that discuss what is being done by IT to affect all aspects of a firm; but still none that adequately address and integrates the strategic, tactical, and operational roles of the CIO.

More and more industries are recognizing that Information Technology can be instrumental in both integrating cross-organizational resources and shaping core business capabilities. Like all transformation, these changes do not come easily. At a minimum, having a harmonious IT-business relationship is key to attaining these benefits. Naturally, the need to align IT and business strategies is fundamental to this text. In fact the Strategic Alignment Maturity Assessment provides the structure to the chapters presented. My book "Competing in the Information Age: Align in the Sand" provides additional insights into this important topic.

The purpose of this book is to provide a set of practical and powerful tools to help ensure that students understand the strategic, tactical, and operational responsibilities of the CIO. Many of these activities are covered in other courses in the graduate IS curriculum. Those that are covered in other courses are not elaborated on here. This book focuses on those activities that are either not addressed elsewhere, or need to be discussed to ensure the student understands how they must be integrated to ensure a successful IT organization.

We have learned a lot from applying the tools presented in this book. Our experiences have helped identify and measure the key elements that lead to a successful IT career. Defining what will be demanded of managers and firms to survive and succeed in the information age remains a major challenge. This book prepares students to meet the challenge.

September 2002 J.L.

▪▪▪ Supplements

This text features a MyCompanion Web site *www.prenhall.com/luftman* where adopters can access password-protected resources including an Instructor's Manual and Test Bank in Microsoft Word. The Test Bank was prepared by Deb Sledgianowski of Stevens Institute of Technology. PowerPoint slides are also available for students and faculty alike.

▪▪▪ Acknowledgements

This book has its origins in research that began in the mid 1980's. Much of the original work has been published and presented around the world. A great deal has changed. A lot has been learned.

The chapters in this book present an evolution of the original research and experience of the authors. As previously discussed the authors have both practical and academic experience. Vita of the contributing authors follows.

While researching, writing, and editing this book, I have become indebted to a large number of individuals and organizations, only a few of whom can be mentioned here. I am greatly appreciative to The Conference Board and Society of Information Systems (SIM) for sponsoring this important research. IBM, especially the Advanced Business Institute, will always be a part of me. Recognition is due to Stevens Institute of Technology for giving me time to research and teach these important ideas to the future leaders of industry, including the participants in the executive information management programs.

Of course a large degree of thanks is due to the hundreds of organizations that have been used in creating, developing, and advancing the application of the strategic alignment model. This includes the thousands of students attending the Stevens graduate programs where thought-provoking discussion has led to many of the new insights.

Thank you to the following faculty for their participation in reviews of this text:

Kregg Aytes, Idaho State University
John Beachboard, Idaho State University
Gerald L. Isaacs, Carroll College
Stephen E. Lunce, Texas A&M International University
William McHenry, University of Akron
John Mendonca, Purdue University
Mary G. Murray, Kennesaw State University
John Newman, Coppin State
Kevin Pauli, Millsaps College
Robert Plant, University of Miami

This book is dedicated to the families of all of the contributors. A major responsibility of a Professor is to prepare the leaders of the future. I especially want to dedicate it to Michael, Melissa L., Valerie, Georgia, Jennifer, Andy, Melissa N., Kathryn, Stefanie, Kristen, Wendy, and little Jack who are well on their way to being the kind of leaders we had always dreamed they would become.

▮▮▮ The Authors

Dr. Jerry N. Luftman is a Professor at the Wesley J. Howe School of Technology Management of Stevens Institute of Technology. He also serves as Program Director, Master of Science in Information Systems (MSIS) for Stevens. After a notable twenty-two year career with IBM, and over ten years at Stevens, Dr. Luftman's experience combines the strengths of practitioner, consultant, and academic. His career with IBM included strategic positions in management (IT and consulting), management consulting, information systems, marketing, and executive education. As a practitioner he held several positions in IT, including a CIO. Dr. Luftman is frequently called upon as an executive mentor and coach. He has published three books and dozens of articles that address areas for improving the IT business relationship.

Christine V. Bullen is a Professor of Management in the Wesley J. Howe School of Technology Management, Stevens Institute of Technology. Her teaching and research focus on understanding how IT enables new business models and processes, strategic planning for the IT function and the impact technology has on people and organizations. From 1976 to1993, she was the Assistant Director of the MIT Sloan School Center for Information Systems Research. Prior to academia, Ms. Bullen spent nine years in industry as a consultant and strategic planner. She received her MS in Management from the MIT Sloan School of Management and is completing her Ph.D. in Information Management at Stevens. Her work appears in numerous papers and books.

Donald Liao is a Ph.D. student in the Information Management program at Stevens Institute of Technology. He was a member of the Master's Degree program for Executives at Columbia University, where he received his MBA in Finance. He obtained his Bachelor of Science in Physics from Stevens. He currently instructs a number of students in the Stevens' executive masters program in information systems (MSIS). He was formerly the school's Director of Financial Systems, and has spent 27 years at MetLife in management positions within Data Administration, Business Controls, Information Technology, and Personal Insurance.

Elby Nash is a Ph.D. student in the Information Management program at Stevens Institute of Technology. He holds a Master's Degree in Computer Science from New

Jersey Institute of Technology and a Bachelor of Electrical Engineering from Pratt Institute. He is Executive Vice President of Knowledge & Information Management Solutions at Taratec Development Corporation, where he provides strategy and knowledge-management related management consulting to the pharmaceutical industry. Mr. Nash is also an adjunct professor at Stevens Institute in the executive master's degree program (MSIS). He was formerly a CIO at Prudential Insurance Company of America's Investment Corporation.

Carl Neumann is a Ph.D. student in the Information Management program at Stevens Institute of Technology. He holds a Master of Business Administration degree and a Master of Science degree from the University of Vermont, as well as a Bachelor of Engineering degree from The Cooper Union. He is the Chief Technology Officer for GeoConcepts, Ltd, where he consults with a wide variety of clients. His firm provides Information Technology services, support, and application development. Mr. Neumann is also an adjunct professor at Stevens Institute's executive masters program in information systems (MSIS). He previously spent 13 years at IBM in various assignments including engineering management as well as systems engineering for IBM midrange systems. He also is a registered Professional Engineer in New York State.

1

Introduction

"The newest computer can merely compound, at speed, the oldest problem in the relations between human beings, and in the end the communicator will be confronted with the old problem, of what to say and how to say it."
—EDWARD R. MURROW, 1964

"I think there is a world market for maybe five computers."
—THOMAS J. WATSON,
Chairman IBM, 1943

Preview of Chapter

The concepts presented in this text revolve around *Strategic Alignment* among the Information Technology (*IT*) and business functions (C. G., Marketing, R & D, Finance) of organizations. Strategic alignment describes an environment in which the business strategy and business infrastructure of an organization are aligned with the Information Technology strategy and infrastructure. It implies that the business functions are integrated with the IT function in the development of business strategies and goals, and that the ultimate success of an organization is dependent on this alignment. This chapter discusses some of the reasons the management of Information Technology has become an important consideration for most organizations.

The ability to assess the current state of alignment among the business and IT functions is the aim of the *Strategic Alignment Maturity Assessment* discussed in the following chapters. This model provides the structure for this text. It describes six categories that can be used to determine how well the business and IT functions are aligned, and how this alignment might be improved. The categories are partnership, scope and architecture, skills/human resources, governance, communications, and competency/value. The important considerations in improving the *maturity* of each of these areas will be the focus of this text.

Much of the material in this text is based on research and experience in large and mid-sized organizations. However, the pervasiveness of Information

Technology has affected many small businesses as well. The implication is that even small organizations must pay attention to the issues discussed in this text. This is complicated by the comparative size of these organizations and the multiple roles management must play in pursuing technology strategies consistent with business strategies. The student should be aware of the difficulties that can arise for these types of organizations in their quest to become larger organizations, or simply to compete with organizations that can maintain larger IT staffs.

This introductory chapter will establish the framework for the importance of the text/course by presenting a broad look at the responsibilities and challenges facing the CIO and senior IT management in today's dynamic environment. Some historical perspective of why IT is important to business will introduce the gaps that currently exist between IT and business organizations. An overview of the chapters of this book will also be presented.

What we will examine in this chapter:

- How has the role of IT evolved over time?
- How does the management of IT differ in scope and complexity from the other business functions?
- Why does the view of IT by IT executives differ from the views of other business executives?
- What has to be done to better manage the IT resource?
- What are some of the key issues in the management of IT organizations?
- Why is the successful management of IT important?

▪▪▪ The Importance of IT and the CIO

The primary purpose of this text is to convey to the student at least two important messages. First, Information Technology is an important and *necessary* component of a successful organization. Second, and more important, is the proposition that the successful *management* of the IT resource is a prerequisite for the success of Information Technology as a source of *competitive advantage* for an organization.

IT can provide and *sustain* competitive advantage for an organization that decides to pursue the use of IT as an integral part of the *business* strategy. Competitive advantage arises out of an organization's ability to attain a superior position relative to its competition. This may be in the area of lower costs, higher quality, leading-edge products and services, etc. Michael Porter describes three primary strategies for organizations to achieve competitive advantage.[1] The three strategies consist of:

1. Cost leadership—competing with lower costs
2. Product differentiation—competing with value
3. Product focus—competing by restricting one's market

Most organizations find that some combination of these three strategies is necessary. This book explores the ability of Information Technology to assist an organization in its goal to achieve competitive advantage. The ability of an organization to create *alignment* among the business functions of an organization and the IT function is discussed throughout this text.

While the formal title of Chief Information Officer (CIO) may not exist in every organization, the roles and responsibilities of such a position need to be addressed for

IT to be successful. This is true regardless of the size and complexity of the organization. The tasks that need to be performed and the roles that IT plays in the organization are the same for any organization that utilizes IT as a key part of its success.

There are many facets to the responsibilities of the CIO and the senior executives of an IT organization. The management of IT requires a broad view of not only technology, but also of business, people, competition, and even global cultures.

The management of IT revolves around three categories: strategic, tactical, and operational. These three categories can be viewed as time horizons. Strategic processes and plans are those that are pertinent to the long-term attainment of goals and visions of the IT function and the business as a whole. The tactical category includes those activities that are needed to achieve the strategic plans and goals—the actions and management functions that produce the changes needed for success. Operational activities are those processes and actions that must be performed to maintain an organization's level of performance on a day-to-day basis.

It is common for many IT management books and journals to place emphasis on the important role of the CIO in an organization's strategic planning and the tactical needs to implement the strategies. However, the operational activities can demand the most attention, and have the greatest impact on the reputation of the CIO and the IT organization; let alone the entire firm. It is the operational set of activities that touch many, if not all, aspects of today's organizations on a daily basis.

The reach of the IT organization into every aspect of an organization's activities underscores the need to adequately prepare today's IT managers. They must be skilled not only in technology, but also in more general *business* skills. Some examples of these skills include:

- **Financial**–budgeting, understanding of the investment decision process (e.g., Return On Investment calculations, financial ratios)
- **Human Resource**–recruiting, retention, motivation, termination, training, corporate culture
- **Relationship Management**–internal and vendor/supplier relationships
- **Legal**–contract management, government regulations
- **Governance**–organizational structure, teams, decision making
- **Marketing**–selling the *value* of the IT function
- **Negotiating**–dealing with external and internal entities to develop mutually beneficial commitments
- **Leadership**–both within the IT organization and the firm as a whole

It is the goal of this text to address these areas as well as others as they relate to the *management* of IT and the achievement of alignment among IT and the business functions. Some of these subjects will only be briefly covered because they are typically covered in other courses. For example, IT architecture is a broad subject and beyond the scope of this text, other than the discussion of the importance of managing emerging technology and developing plans and strategies for architecture. Likewise, project management is considered important enough to warrant a separate course or set of courses. This text, therefore, does not elaborate on these subjects.

The activities discussed in this text are considered the *critical success factors* for the management of IT. John Rockart[2] defines critical success factors as:

> *"The limited number of areas in which results, if they are satisfactory, will ensure successful competitive performance for the organization. They are the few key areas where things must go right for the business to flourish. If results in these areas are not adequate, the organization's efforts for the period will be less than desired."*

"Areas of activity that should receive constant and careful attention from management."

The material presented in this text will provide the student with a foundation on which to build a successful career in IT management; the student is expected to pursue other courses and texts if a focus on specific areas of IT management is required.

The goal of this textbook is to present practical information that will help the student fulfill their career goals of either becoming a CIO, or someone that reports to or consults with a CIO. The activities set forth above are important to attain these goals.

▮▮▮ The Expanding Role of IT

In 1943, the world of computers as we know it today was still the basic material for science fiction writers. As noted in the chapter's second opening quote, even the head of IBM could not foresee the impact of Information Technology on the business world. The impact computers and technology in general has had on our personal lives and our organizations has far exceeded what Mr. Watson was able to imagine.

The evolution of Information Technology can be described as encompassing three primary eras of computing. The first era consisted of the mainframe computer, when computing power resided in a single central computer. This era was followed by the PC era in which computing power was distributed and applications were developed to support individual needs. The era that now exists can be described as one of "pervasive computing."

The progress in microprocessors, telecommunications, application development, and human adaptation to these technologies has contributed to this technological evolution. A comparative view of the co-evolution of these associated technologies is shown in Figure 1-1.

▮▮▮▮▮▮▮▮▮▮▮ FIGURE 1-1 Co-Evolution of Key IT Components.

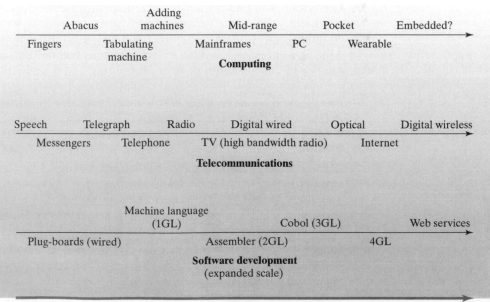

▪ ▪ ▪ ▪ ▪ ▪ ▪ ▪ ▪ ▪ ▪ **FIGURE 1-2** The Ever-expanding Role of IT.

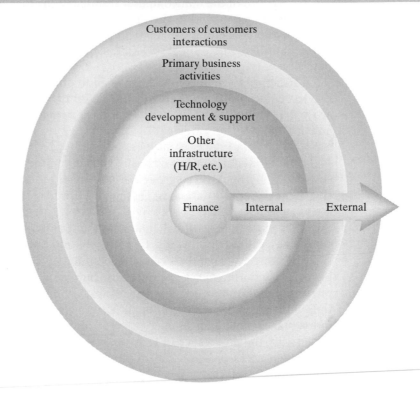

Figure 1-1 presents the technological view of the evolution of Information Technology and related technologies. How does this relate to the changing *impact* of IT on the business functions? When considering the uniqueness of IT relative to the overall running of the business, the impact of IT has increased in terms of *scope*. As illustrated in Figure 1-2, the role of IT over the last 50 years has steadily extended its reach. From the early days of the computer as the simple "number cruncher" supporting the accounting and financial functions in a business, technology has expanded its role and now supports the entire range of business operations, including the external activities that occur in dealing with suppliers and customers. This process should be viewed as a "snowball" rolling down a hill; showing IT's impact on organizations as cumulative over time.

A Historical Perspective

The original role of the computer was for government (the Census) and military (missile trajectory plotting) uses. Organizations then discovered that computers could automate many of the financial processes of the business world, leading to the implementation of systems to perform accounting functions.

Because the primary use was to automate what personnel in the accounting functions were doing, the responsibility for IT (then called Data Processing) fell under the Financial Executive's organization. The responsible manager may have been the Chief Financial Officer, VP of Finance, or Comptroller; but IT was likely to be the responsibility of lower levels of "technical" management. The cost of computers and the perception of them as a back office support tool resulted in the view that they were a cost, not an investment activity that produced a financial return.

As the cost and size of computers shrank, the applications for their use expanded. The emergence of the minicomputer resulted in the development of departmental systems. These systems led to the distribution of computing power and applications to areas of an organization outside the "glass house," where mainframe computers traditionally resided. The term *glass house* stems from the showcase rooms in which computers were typically placed.

As the presence of computers spread to other physical locations, IT organizations had to deal with business people who had different organizational needs. Applications arose that supported and enhanced business *processes*, such as marketing, distribution, and manufacturing. Information Technology staff actually had to start talking to *business people*! Likewise, business people needed to begin to interact with IT staff. Too often IT staff members were still considered the "trolls in the basement," and the interaction between these groups of personnel required the bridging of communications and cultural differences. The need arose for joint understanding of technology issues as well as business issues by all parts of an organization. The management issues raised by this organizational change are addressed from various viewpoints in later chapters (e.g., IT Organization, Governance, and Strategic Alignment).

The appearance of the Personal Computer (PC) as a business tool accelerated the pace of computing pervasiveness. Now individuals had requirements, demands, and problems. There was no longer a central set of applications and hardware. The potential number of unique computing environments could possibly equal the number of individuals in an organization.

Finally, the emergence of local area networks, the Internet and wireless networks, resulted in an IT environment that extended beyond the boundaries of the business organization itself to customers, potential customers, customers of customers, vendors, and competitors. In fact, it has led to the need for technical personnel to deal with business and technical people around the globe.

Information Technology is now becoming pervasive. A computing infrastructure is developing in which the computers themselves become invisible[3]; computing and technology are becoming background systems much like electric power. Arguably, few organizations can compete in today's economy without the use of Information Technology.

E-mail and Internet access are almost a necessity for doing business with other organizations. E-mail addresses are exchanged as frequently as phone numbers were in the past. The telephone, as a tool of business, began a similar journey when it first emerged in the last century. In its infancy, the telephone was seen as useful, but businesses did not become dependent upon the telephone until every other business adapted the technology, thus making it a requirement for conducting business.

The Internet has enabled communications that are independent of time and place. The "asynchronous" nature of e-mail allows for efficient communications between parties that are in different places and that operate on different schedules. The ubiquity of the Internet and the ability to transmit and receive *rich* communications that can include documents, sounds, video, and links to Internet sites serves to extend the nature of communications well beyond that of the traditional telephone.

The evolution of computing, telecommunications, and software development tools and techniques has caused a corresponding shift in the requirements placed on IT management. As IT spread its impact on the organization, the impact of the management of IT became more widespread. As a result, IT staff and managers have faced an increasing need to become more business-savvy. IT managers especially have a need to be generalists more than technologists. The ability to communicate with *all* areas of the business has become increasingly important.

In many organizations today, IT still reports to the financial executive, or may at least be subject to primary oversight by the financial function. A growing number of organizations now have an IT organization with a separate management chain. Generally, a CIO (Chief Information Officer) is the senior executive and reports to an executive outside of Finance, perhaps to the CEO (Chief Executive Officer). In many organizations, the perception still exists that IT is a cost center that must have a return on investment (ROI) that meets the same criteria as purchasing any piece of equipment. This overlooks the reality that in most businesses today, without IT, the organization cannot survive—much as an organization could not survive without telephones. Information Technology, however, has the added potential of enabling or driving business strategies. This topic will be revisited in Chapter 14—The Value of IT.

While an evolutionary model might imply that the prior technologies are *replaced*, that is not the case. The technologies developed during each previous era still exist in many organizations. The integration of these technologies—mainframes, departmental systems, PC networks, mobile computing devices—poses significant challenges for the IT manager. The organizational challenges are also equally important and difficult.

▪▪▪ The Role of IT

The world has gone through profound change. In just the last few years we have experienced economic shifts, terrorism, Enronitis, war, and SARS. All of these have had great impact on business and IT. This section introduces many of the changes that we need to be cognizant of.

As the role of computers in businesses has expanded, how has the role of Information Technology changed in supporting or driving the business? Traditionally, IT had been relegated to a role of supporting the business. Aside from accounting, other back office applications such as billing systems and human resource systems made the role of IT a somewhat unglamorous and seemingly nonintegral part of the business strategy.

However, the impact of the IT organization has changed from being the automated bookkeeper to enabling or driving every facet of some organizations. IT is involved in manufacturing, logistics, marketing, research and development, decision support, forecasting, and intercompany relationships. There are few areas, if any, where IT does not (or at least cannot) play a role.

Figure 1-3 illustrates some of the different issues IT faces in dealing with these "levels" of computer technology within an organization. As the use of IT has increased from a centralized, narrow/focused impact, to affect most or all of an organization's members, as well as customers and suppliers, the complexity for IT management faces dramatically increases.

▪▪▪▪▪▪▪▪▪▪▪ **FIGURE 1-3** Comparison of IT Scope/Concerns/Complexity.

Individual	Departmental	Enterprise	External
• Task-based concerns • Uniqueness of relationships • Potential loss of standards • Potential loss of control over data • Process segmentation	• Process-based concerns • Inter-relationships • Shared data • Collaboration • Information silos	• Relationship concerns • Standardization • Information integration • Easy to control • Difficult to meet individual needs	• Inter-relationship concerns • Adherence to external standards • Information exchange • Security concerns • Rapidly changing needs • Competitive advantage

In the centralized, enterprise role of IT, the primary concerns revolve around the overall functioning of IT as it relates to the organization as a whole. Its support of *relationships* between the various parts of an organization and the ability to *integrate* the information that exists throughout the organization are two important responsibilities. From an enterprise view, standardization and controls can be monitored more easily than in a distributed environment. However, an enterprise approach to computing, with its focus on commonality and standardization, may not meet the needs of any specific business unit or individual.

The departmental, or business unit view of computing focuses more on the *processes* that occur within an organization. Information systems that support specific business functions do so to address the unique characteristics of that function. Departmental information systems tend to be designed to provide a narrower view of the information used and generated by a workgroup. This can result in *information silos*—integration at the enterprise level becomes more difficult.

In supporting individual business units or people within an organization, IT provides a task-based focus. That is, the use of Information Technology by an individual is primarily as a tool in support of specific job requirements. The relationship among individual people is an important part of understanding the needs of the business. This dispersion of computing power also creates some new concerns. IT processes become more fragmented in nature—it is inherently more difficult to control hundreds or thousands of computers than it is to control one.

The expansion of the role of IT into the external interactions between a business and its vendors, customers, and suppliers has added another set of complexities. Relationship issues center around the *inter-relationships* between these various external entities within the business. Dealing with external partners may require adhering to standards that are enforced and controlled by industry organizations, government agencies, or specific partners. Electronic Data Interchange (EDI), for example, is a requirement for conducting business with many large retail chains such as Wal-Mart or Target. This is also an example of the additional complexity for IT in regard to information *exchange* when dealing with external entities.

The integration of Internet presence and internal information systems (the linkage of business systems to a public network) creates security concerns. Organizations must protect important data from external parties who can gain access by exploiting vulnerabilities in systems. IT also faces new sources of requirements that are constantly changing. These requirements come from a wide variety of organizations with an equally wide variety of information systems. Finally, the role of IT in delivering a *competitive advantage* to a business becomes more visible in dealing with the external view of an IT organization.

USAA[4]

The United Services Automobile Association focuses on insurance for military and ex-military personnel. At one time, all of its customer interactions revolved around paper files. If a customer called, the agent receiving the call would need to locate the paper file to resolve any issues. Processing of changes or additions was done in batches of paper. USAA implemented a Document Imaging System that placed all of the company's paper files online as images at the time of receipt in the mailroom.

Now all files were accessible by any service representative. In the words of Robert McDermott, CEO at the time this was implemented, this system *"changed the way we think. Now when you want to buy a new car, get it insured, add a driver, and change your coverage and address, you can make one phone call... In one five minute phone call, you and our service representative have done all the work that used to take 55 steps, umpteen people, two weeks, and a lot of money."*

There are many examples of how IT has been able to *drive* business strategies. Companies such as amazon.com, yahoo.com, and other so-called "dot-coms" have been created solely as a result of Information Technology. However, even before the advent of the Internet, there have been examples of how IT has transformed businesses. The United Services Automobile Association (USAA) is one example of how the implementation of technology (in this case, Document Imaging) resulted in USAA expanding the role of people in the organization, the firm's product offerings, and subsequently the profitability of the business. IT was the impetus to provide a "one-stop-shop" single face to all of its clients.[5]

It is helpful to view the IT organization as having "roles" in relation to an organization's goals. Some of the key roles IT plays in today's organizations follow.

IT as an Enabler of E-business

As many organizations have discovered, the fundamentals regarding IT and the management of IT have not changed as a result of the emergence of the Internet. Whether you are involved in "e-IT" or systems now considered old technology (*legacy systems*), the roles and responsibilities of IT and management are the same.

The major impact of e-business has been to make the good, the bad, and the ugly aspects of IT much more visible to the external stakeholders of an organization as well as the internal stakeholders. Successes and failures of IT can be much more visible when they affect an organization's reputation and the operations that extend beyond the organization's boundaries.

Information Technology can also serve as a "mediator" or link among the various functions of a business, among the business and its customers or suppliers, or among the business and other external organizations. The four primary ways that IT has become a mediator in the business world are through *disintermediation*, *reintermediation*, *hyper-mediation*, and *infomediation*.

Levi Strauss & Co.[6]

In 1995, Levi Strauss launched their Web site with some of the first animated graphics the Web had ever seen. It was an ambitious effort that enabled customers to buy up to 3,000 products directly from the manufacturer. The site design even allowed for recommendations to the customer based on their taste in music and clothing.

Levi Strauss prohibited their brick and mortar channel partners from selling any Levi's products online. By 1999, the online operation was one of the first areas to be hit when Levi Strauss needed to cut costs. After ceasing operations following the holiday season, Levi Strauss decided to sell online only through two of its channel partners—Macys and JC Penney. This served to upset their other partners who had an online presence. In addition, it also gave up control of the customer's online experience of purchasing Levi's products.

Levi Strauss now offers links to a number of retailers who provide online ordering of its clothing line.

One of the best examples of how IT can change the way a business operates is found in the concept of *disintermediation*. This term is used to describe the change in a business model where the "middleman" is essentially eliminated. An example of this is the emergence of electronic stock trading. This phenomenon has served to reduce and/or change the role of the stockbroker and every securities firm. E*trade is one example of a successful Internet venture that has changed the nature of investing.[7] The increased access to investment opportunities such as this has enabled existing firms to focus on service differentiation and to respond with similar offerings for the basic transactional parts of the business.

Disintermediation is not always successful. There are examples of companies retreating from this attempt, including Levi Strauss & Co. This leading manufacturer of jeans and other clothing invested several million dollars in launching its online selling operation. After discovering the amount of sales generated online was insufficient compared to the cost of maintaining the online presence, it decided to abandon the effort.

Reintermediation refers to using the Internet to reassemble buyers, sellers, and other partners in a traditional supply chain in new ways. What else can I sell to the customers with whom I have established relationships? Examples include Philadelphia-based PetroChemNet Inc and ChemConnect, who bring together producers, traders, distributors, and buyers of chemicals in Web-based marketplaces. ChemConnect provides an online "Exchange Floor" where companies negotiate to buy and sell specialized chemicals. For an annual subscription fee, companies can negotiate price, warranties, quality, and shipping.

The largest example of reintermediation is the merging of insurance, banking, and financial services industries. The intent is to provide clients with a single source for all of these services, thus leveraging the previously established relationship and trust. The eBay sidebar describes another innovative example.

eBay[8]

eBay has been one of the best-known success stories of the e-business model. The idea is said to have started as a pet project of its founder, Pierre Omidyar, in response to his (then) fiancé's desire to trade with other collectors Pez dispensers.* It has since grown to become the largest online person-to-person trading community in the world. At the end of the first quarter of 1999, eBay had 3.8 million registered users. By mid-2000, this had grown to 15.8 million, and as of late 2001, stood at 29.7 million registered users. The total amount of transactions for the year 2000 was $5 billion.

The eBay model is an example of reintermediation. It provides a mechanism that brings together buyers and sellers who would otherwise be unlikely to be able to buy and sell goods in the very large marketplace that eBay allows them to reach. It is Information Technology that enables this business model to exist at all.

In May of 1999, eBay experienced server problems that halted auctions for five hours. In June 1999 there was a 22-hour outage that caused $3 million to $5 million in lost revenue. Another outage in August of that year resulted in eBay's stock price falling 10 percent. The fact that eBay's entire business operation depended on the success or failure of its Information Technology became abundantly clear.

*This account of eBay's history has recently been revealed as a myth.

Hypermediation refers to the interactions that can be found in many of the online transactions that occur via the Internet. No longer are transactions just between a buyer and seller, or between those two parties and a broker. Now a transaction might involve wholesalers and retailers, content providers, affiliate sites, search engines, portals, Internet service providers, and software makers. The true "middleman" in these cases is the manager of the integration of the virtual value chain. In hypermediation, organizations provide a complete, seamless, invisible supply chain to their customers, while leveraging many external partners. This is in some ways the opposite of disintermediation.[9] The sidebar "Clicks as Transactions" describes a scenario exemplifying this.

Clicks as Transactions[10]

A simple, everyday example of Internet shopping will show how hypermediation works. Let's say that an occasional Web user—let's call him Bob—becomes interested in the ubiquitous Harry Potter books. He thinks that he'd like to read them, but he wants to learn a little more about them. So he goes onto the Web and, since he's never bothered to change his browser's default home page, he ends up at the Netscape portal. In the search box he types the phrase "Harry Potter," and from a list of available search services he chooses, on a whim, GoTo.com. He's transported to the GoTo site, where his search results are posted. He chooses a promising-sounding site near the top called "Nancy's Magical Harry Potter Page."

Nancy's site, a personal home page with an unsophisticated but friendly design, is full of information that Bob finds useful. There are glowing reviews of the Harry Potter books by Nancy and a few of her friends, detailed plot summaries and character descriptions, and a discussion board where readers share their comments. There's also a link to a special Harry Potter page at eToys. Bob clicks on the link, and he finds that eToys is selling the first book in the series for 50 percent off its list price—just $8.97. He can't resist that kind of a bargain, so he takes out his Visa card and places an order. Three days later, the book is in his mailbox.

This is a fairly routine buying expedition on the Web, right? But consider the complex array of intermediaries that made money off Bob's modest purchase. There are the usual suspects, of course—the retailer eToys, the book distributor that eToys buys from, the bank that issued Bob's Visa card, the U.S. Postal Service. But there are less-obvious players as well. First is Netscape. Netscape puts various search services on its home page and, in return, the services pay Netscape a penny or two every time a visitor clicks through to their sites. So when Bob was transferred to GoTo.com, Netscape received a little money. GoTo, for its part, auctions off its top search results to the highest bidders. Nancy, for instance, agreed to pay GoTo one cent for every searcher who clicks on her link. So when Bob chose Nancy's site, GoTo made a penny. GoTo didn't get to keep all of it, though. Because GoTo contracts with an outside provider, Inktomi, to conduct its searches, it had to pay Inktomi a fraction of that penny for processing Bob's search.

Then there's Nancy herself. Like thousands of other individuals who have personal Web pages, Nancy has signed up to be an affiliate of eToys. When she sends someone to eToys through a link in her page, the e-tailer pays her 7.5 percent of any resulting purchases. So Nancy made a cool 67 cents when Bob bought the book. What's more, eToys doesn't run its own affiliate program. It outsources the job to a company named Be Free. Be Free, in turn, takes a small cut on the purchases it administers. So it, too, got a little of Bob's money.

Add them up, and you'll find that no fewer than nine intermediaries had their fingers in Bob's $8.97 purchase. (And that doesn't even include the people who posted reviews on Nancy's site—they just haven't realized that they could be charging for their words.) In fact, every single time Bob clicked his mouse, a transaction took place: a little bit of value was created, and a little bit of money changed hands. Yes, the money usually amounted to only a penny or two, but it seems a safe bet that far more profit was made by the intermediaries that took those pennies than by eToys when it sold the book for half-price. Bob's transaction is a microcosm of the emerging economic structure of E-commerce: the profits lie in intermediate transactions, not in the final sale of a good.

While this example is imaginary, Web content providers such as Yahoo, Cnet, Excite, ZDNet, and America Online are some real-life examples of starting points for this type of scenario.

Infomediation is the role that IT plays in providing a means for technology users to manage the overwhelming amount of information that exists. An example is the use of search engines or portals that provide meta-information or aggregate information by categories, in an effort to narrow the scope of a search for information.

Data mining technologies play an important part in enabling this IT opportunity. The rapid and accelerating accumulation of information collected, stored, and available for use can result in information overload. Information overload has been defined as

> *"a state where the individual is no longer able to effectively*
> *process the amount of information he or she is exposed to. The result*
> *is a lower decision quality in a given time set."* [11]

Information technologies can help organizations sift through the enormous amount of information, providing insights and clarity not possible otherwise.

The concept of a business model that takes advantage of this wealth of information is presented in *Net Worth*.[12] The accumulation of information about consumers (with their permission, of course) could be used to provide customized services, targeted marketing, and other benefits. The proposed marketplace for these services is in businesses where inefficiencies exist in matching buyers and sellers due to the need for the exchange of information, such as automobile purchases.

IT as a Change Agent

Dynamic Stability describes the ability of IT to support a business environment where dynamic changes in products or services can be made with no change to business processes. The competitive forces in today's economy require organizations that can respond quickly to these demands. They must be able to quickly adapt the organization's products, services, or processes to the constantly changing demands of their customers. Information Technology can create the ability to provide customers and clients with customized products and services with no changes to business processes. This is the definition of dynamic stability—the ability to provide flexible (mass customized) products via fixed business processes.

IT can also provide the means to enable or inhibit incremental as well as radical changes. Innovation in many organizations—such as pharmaceutical firms—is dependent upon the use of Information Technology. The ability of computers to perform complex modeling and computation has driven the rapid advancement of many organizations' product development.

In 1990, for example, McGraw-Hill launched its Primis custom publishing system. This system redesigned the editing, marketing, and distribution processes for college textbooks. The system provides a database of information that allows an instructor to design a customized textbook for a course. These customized books are then distributed electronically to university bookstores where they are printed, bound, and sold. Alternatively, they can be distributed as e-books directly online.

Pearson also has developed an effective vehicle for providing custom textbooks from an extensive database of material. In addition, a broad array of electronic resources are available for instructors to enhance their curriculum.

IT as an Enabler of Globalization

The ability to manage and control the business processes involved in maintaining a global business is enhanced by the success of the IT infrastructure and technologies supporting it. Globalization refers to the impact of organizations expanding their presence beyond the borders of their "home" country. The issues that arise from IT's role in globalization are addressed throughout this text.

The DHL vignette provides an overview of a few of the issues that are important for IT organizations in globalization efforts.

DHL and Global Operations

At DHL Worldwide Express, the attention to cultural issues that arise from dealing globally is considered a key part of the IT effort. Red, for example, is generally a symbol of good luck in China, and some companies use it abundantly in graphics on their corporate Web sites. But smart ones are careful not to write any text in red. The Chinese believe that red is reserved for notes ending a romantic relationship—not exactly a good way to lure potential customers.

Numbers count, too. "Chinese have a lot of superstition about numbers," says Bill Stout, DHL's director of IT operations in Kuala Lumpur, Malaysia. In fact, when DHL set up new account numbers in China, none of them could begin with a four; in both Mandarin and Cantonese, "four" when spoken sounds a lot like the word for "death."

While catering to such local customs can make good business sense, it can also cause headaches for IT managers. Often, they're grappling with such issues on a regional scale, while at the same time trying to meet the objectives of the home office. "How do you satisfy multiple cultures and your chairman at the same time?" asks Alan Boehme, director of customer access at DHL's headquarters in Foster City, California.

DHL does it with a balance of localization and centralization that was achieved only after years of experience. Localization (unique IT products for different countries) lets DHL get close to customers. "The only thing we've standardized on is the firewall," says Boehme, but notes that localization can also make it difficult to handle a single brand image. "Some global customers get frustrated when certain functionality exists in some countries, but not others," Boehme adds.

DHL runs its main corporate Web site, which customers use for tracking deliveries and other important information, from the United States. Nonetheless, operations in dozens of other countries, including South Korea and Australia, have put up their own customized sites for tracking and shipping information. All the company's databases are constantly being refined as the Web matures in those local markets. DHL, which has standardized on Hewlett-Packard 9000 servers and Informix databases, is consolidating back-end operations at data centers in cities such as Hong Kong and Kuala Lumpur.

Some local governments want DHL to become even more localized. Japan and Taiwan, for example, insist that invoices be made out in their local languages, even though that can create problems for packages originating elsewhere. And China, Japan, and South Korea want companies to put screen prompts on applications, as well as storage of data, in their national languages, which goes against DHL's policy of standardizing on English.

DHL's IT executives also watch the macroeconomic trends that can change local business environments, sometimes dramatically. Bert Bertagna, for example, oversees DHL's Latin America regional data center in Fort Lauderdale, Florida, along with all the terminals, PCs, and scanning devices used by some 2,300 employees in nearly 50 countries. But he must also keep up with the activities of Mercosur, a Latin American trade bloc formed by a group of countries interested in coordinating trade and investment rules. Mercosur is developing tariff structures that will affect billing and other applications, and Bertagna has organized some of his IT staff to cover these countries and issues. He says, "We try to work the same way the business and governments work."

IIII The Gap Between IT and "the Business"

If the use of Information Technology has become so pervasive, embedded into so many facets of an organization, why has the Information Technology organization continued to be viewed as such a distinct and separate part of the business? Surveys of organizations, such as that conducted annually by the Computer Sciences Corporation shown in Figure 1-4,[13] invariably rank the lack of alignment between IT and business goals as being a major issue.

Surveys like the one from CSC by academics, research firms, and consultants have identified business/IT alignment as an important (if not *the* most important) issue for over fifteen years. Why has something this important been ranked so high for so long? This will be elaborated on later in this book; but for now...

Educating business management on technology's possibilities and limitations is challenging; so is setting IT priorities for projects, developing resources and skills, and integrating systems with corporate strategy. It's even tougher to keep business and IT aligned as business strategies and technology evolve. There's no silver-bullet solution, but achieving alignment is possible. Alignment has been a concern and an area of research for some time.[14,15,16,17]

Research by Luftman, et al. suggests that both IT executives and business executives express the view that alignment is an important issue. Interestingly, the issues believed to cause this misalignment are also common to both business and IT executives.

The impact of IT in today's environment may be made clearer by considering some of the ways IT can affect the business perspectives it serves. Information Technology can help an organization by being an *enabler or driver* of success or it can hurt an organization by being an *inhibitor*.[18] In the extreme positive case, IT can have a transformational effect on a business; IT can change a business in the areas of process, product, service, management, and even environment.

CSC Survey Rankings

Top IS/IT Issues	2001	2000	1999	1998	1997	1996	1995	1994	1993	1992	1991
Aligning IS and corporate goals	2*	5*	3	1	1	1	1	2	2	1	2
Protecting and securing information systems	2*	NR	NR	NR	NR	NR	NR	NR	NR	NR	NR
Connecting to customers, suppliers and/or partners electronically	6	1	1	4	5	7	7	16	16	20	15
Organizing & utilizing data	4	5*	2	3	2	2	3	3	4	4	5
Optimizing organizational effectiveness	5	3	NR	NR	NR	NR	NR	NR	NR	NR	NR
Developing an e-business strategy	13	4	4	19	NR	NR	NR	NR	NR	NR	NR
Integrating systems with the Internet	10	7*	5*	6*	6	5*	16	8	11	13	9
Optimizing enterprise-wide IS services	1	2	5*	NR	NR	NR	NR	NR	NR	NR	NR
Instituting cross-functional IS	7	9	7	6*	9	3	2	4	4	6	3
Capitalizing on advances in IT	14	12	8	5	3*	5*	15	13	14	19	20
Improving the IS human resource	20	15	9*	2	7	11	5	9	12	5	13
Educating management on I/T	12	13	9*	11	13	13	11	18	18	16	14
Using IT for competitive breakthroughs	16	7*	11	10	3*	4	13	15	15	14	12
Creating an information architecture	18	16	12	8	8	9	8	5	7	3	8
Cutting IS costs	15	14	13	12	12	15	12	12	6	11	11
Improving the systems development process	11	11	14	13*	11	12	10	6	3	9	4
Updating obsolete systems	9	10	15	9	10	8	9	7	8	18	NR
Managing knowledge assets	17	NR	NR	NR	NR	NR	NR	NR	NR	NR	NR
Restructuring the IS function	19	17	17	13*	17	17	NR	NR	NR	NR	NR
Managing complex organizational change	21	NR	NR	NR	NR	NR	NR	NR	NR	NR	NR
Designing the mobile workplace	22	20	NR	NR	NR	NR	NR	NR	NR	NR	NR
Implementing business transformation initiatives	8	18	20	13*	14	10	4	1	1	2	1

* Indicates Tie.

Source: 14th Annual Survey of Critical Issues of Information Management (North America)–CSC 2001.

Alignment can be defined as the application of IT in an appropriate and timely manner, in harmony with business goals, strategies, and needs. Enablers and inhibitors are those characteristics of an organization that serve to either enhance (enable) the alignment of IT and the business goals, or reduce (inhibit) this alignment.

Alignment is a prerequisite for IT to be able to transform the business, and in some cases actually *drive* the business strategy. Therefore, for the student to become a leader, rather than simply a manager in an IT organization, an understanding of this key opportunity is necessary. The issues of alignment among the business and IT organization will be discussed further in Chapters 2 and 3, which discuss Strategic Alignment.

Issues surrounding the gap between business and IT functions may emanate from the technological work performed by IT people. It could be the perception of business people that IT personnel are "geeks" or "trolls in the basement" is propagated by an attitude of "technology for technology's sake" generated by IT people. The IT world may have resisted pressure to learn how its skills and tools impact the organization's goals, and has assumed an attitude of "technology is good and more technology is better." The situation is compounded by the fact that IT people have their own vocabulary, much of it consisting of acronyms, and even acronyms nested within acronyms.

This text will address many of these and other organizational concerns shown in Figure 1-4. These concerns are addressed through the improved *management* of Information Technology and the *resources* brought to bear in providing Information Technology.

E-Nough

Along with the ever-expanding role that Information Technology plays in the modern organization, there is an ever-increasing wealth of knowledge and experience gained by IT professionals. Regardless of this knowledge and experience, IT continues to repeat many of the same mistakes. This text is intended to help reduce the reoccurrence of these mistakes by saying "e-nough"—short hand for "enough is enough." **The student should be able to utilize the material covered in this text and the course it supports to reduce these mistakes—mistakes such as not selling the *value* of IT products and services to the other business units of the organization, ignoring the *strategic* impact of Information Technology on the business goals and strategies, and not addressing the role of IT as a partner to the business rather than as just a service provider to the business.**

One of the most common mistakes repeated over time is not having the right business sponsor and champion take on the appropriate roles to ensure project success. This has been true when IT implemented hierarchical databases, relational databases, client/servers, and Enterprise Resource Planning (ERP). The same problem continues as IT tries to implement any e-commerce application, customer relationship management application, or supply chain management application. The project cannot be successful through IT alone. It must have the right business sponsor and champion. It is not the technology that provides the value; it is the changes that the business makes to leverage the technology that provides the value. The IT-business partnership is key. E-nough is e-nough.

▪▪▪ The Difference between IT and Other Business Functions

It may not be readily apparent yet why IT is viewed as being unique from the other business functions. After all, doesn't manufacturing need to be "aligned" with the business as a whole? Doesn't marketing need to be aligned with manufacturing? What about all of the other functions in the organization? Of course they ALL need to be aligned with each other to create an organization that can rise above the competition.

A key differentiator of IT from the other functions lies in what has already been mentioned—Information Technology activities encompass the entire enterprise. Information Technology cuts across the entire business and extends outside the business boundaries. It can enable, drive, or inhibit every other activity on a daily basis. IT personnel come into contact with every aspect of the business, at every level of management. The business processes are mirrored by—and in some cases embedded in—the Information Systems that support them.

Dell Computer Corporation[19, 20]

While a freshman at the University of Texas, Michael Dell started building computers in his dorm room, selling directly to customers. Once sales reached $80,000 per month, Dell no longer felt compelled to hide his sideline in the bathtub when his parents came to visit him—he simply dropped out of college to form Dell Computer.

Dell's distinction in the PC business was that he took orders directly from the customer, rather than using the traditional distribution chain of retailers, distributors, and resellers. Dell launched its Web site in 1996, allowing customers to configure and order systems online in addition to the existing telephone ordering approach.

Dell has long made use of Information Technology to enable and drive its direct marketing approach. Their entire value chain is driven by their information systems, allowing the turn-around time from customer order to shipment of a completely customized system to regularly average one and a half days. In addition, the selling price of their product has consistently led the market, forcing other manufacturers to lower prices in order to compete.

Even after the sale, Dell makes extensive use of technology to enable its customers to obtain support through online self-help, download updates to system software, and determine the correct upgrade components.

■■■■■■■■■■■ **FIGURE 1-5** Porter's Generic Value Chain.

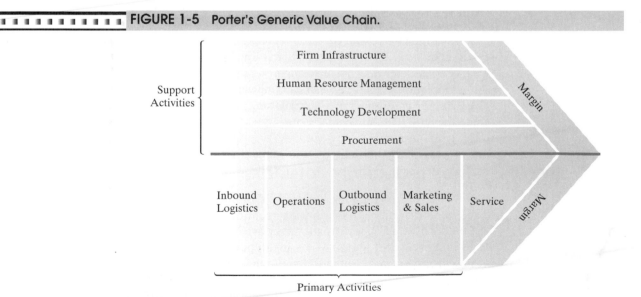

Source: Porter, Michael, *Competitive Advantage: Creating and Sustaining Superior Performance*, Free Press, 1985.

As IT has grown in pervasiveness, its impact has expanded beyond the area of support activities in Porter's Value Chain (Figure 1-5)[21] to encompass every part of the value chain as well as activities that include suppliers and customers. IT can therefore play a greater role in affecting the profitability of an organization than most other functions within the organization.

This situation not only creates unique problems for IT, but it also creates unique opportunities. Few other functions are able to get a view of the overall operation of an organization. No other function owns (or at least controls) ALL the information in the organization. This interaction of IT personnel throughout the organization brings the opportunity to share corporate information and creates some level of synergy between departments.

Once Information Technology is embraced as an instrument of business strategy and enablement, the ability of IT to influence the entire value chain of an organization means that IT can provide strategic advantage. Two examples of this are Cisco and Dell Computer (see sidebars).

Cisco Systems[22]

Cisco Systems produces a wide range of hardware and embedded software that provides much of the backbone for the Internet as well as an organization's internal networks. Started in 1984 by a husband-and-wife team of computer scientists who had designed a network router, Cisco has grown to become the leading manufacturer of equipment handling all forms of communications, including voice, data, and video. Its product range provides a "one stop shop" for an organization's entire network infrastructure. Cisco Systems has a global reach, and has used its own equipment to build a global IT infrastructure.

It has opened the use of its global network to the entire range of its stakeholders, including prospects, suppliers, customers, and employees. Virtually all business and operational information is available to everyone, all the time. Cisco estimated it saved $250 million in servicing costs in 1997 through the use of this global network.

CEO John Chambers based the need for this global network on three assumptions:

- The relationships a company maintains with its key constituencies can be as much of a competitive differentiation as its core products or services
- The manner in which a company shares information and systems is a critical element in the strength of its relationships
- Being "connected" is no longer adequate. Business relationships and the communications that support them must exist in a "networked" fabric

---

▪▪▪ Value of IT—The Productivity Paradox

Over the past three decades, hundreds of billions of dollars have been invested by the business community in information technology to achieve competitive advantage. Computers now pervade virtually every aspect of business life and it is almost impossible to imagine how today's global, highly interconnected, information-intensive business environment could function without information technology. Between 1978 and 1985, capital spending on information technology increased almost three-fold, from 1.8 percent to 7.8 percent of total capital equipment.[23] Penetration of computers in the home has also dramatically increased, with more than half of American households (54 million households) now owning at least one computer.[24] During the period 1984–1997, business use of computers in the U.S. increased from less than a quarter of all employees to almost half of all employees.[25]

Despite these sustained substantial capital expenditures on IT and the penetration of IT into almost every facet of our business and personal lives, the macroeconomic evidence of the effects of IT on business productivity and business transformation is mixed at best and pessimistic at worst. Businesses made extensive investments in IT in the 1980s and 1990s, including ERP (Enterprise Resource Planning) and enterprise procurement software. These investments were made in the expectation of streamlining business processes, reducing costs, and improving information integration for competitive advantage. Instead, IT became merely a "cost of doing business"—easily duplicated by competitors. Extensive surveys of U.S. government productivity statistics found no substantial correlation between IT capital investment and business productivity in either the service sector or the manufacturing sector.[26, 27] Substantial business investment in e-business technologies in the late 1990s yielded similarly mixed results with regard to business transformation. Overhyped predictions of the demise of "brick and mortar" business eventually yielded to the harsh realities of the Internet meltdown of 2000 as it became clear that many online business models were either not competitively differentiating or were easily replicated.

This paradox between the promise of IT to transform business and the reality that the evidence for this transformation is scant can be explained in several ways. One explanation is that the methods used to measure productivity need to be changed; that current methods are based more on production of tangible goods rather than the production of services. Some later studies appear to show that productivity increased in the late 1990s and early 2000s. This apparent increase in productivity has been attributed to the diffusion effect of investment in new technology and the realization of economic benefit—i.e., earlier investments in IT were just being felt in the 1990s as business now concentrated on IT investments that were more "strategic." Some studies done in the mid-1990s by Brynjolfsson and Hitt[28] suggest that the paradox may be more attributable to the services sector than the manufacturing sector. Later research by these authors[29] indicates that when firm-level data is analyzed, the productivity paradox disappears. It would appear from their work that the government's aggregation of data into "industry classifications" might hide the true impact of IT investment.

A more fundamental explanation of the IT-productivity paradox is that business investment in IT has not been sufficiently aligned with the strategic business goals. Business leaders are investing in the wrong things or are too focused on technology. In their seminal paper on the subject of leveraging IT to transform organizations, Henderson and Venkatraman argue that the lack of alignment between the business strategy and the IT strategy of a firm accounts, in part, for the failure of business to realize the true economic potential of IT investment.[30]

If the best IT is applied to ineffective inefficient business processes, the processess will still be ineffective and inefficient. Chapter 14 will expand on the issues surrounding the need for organizations to recognize the value of the IT functions. The real benefits that businesses seek come from changing the *business* processes. Information Technology enables or drives the business process changes that bring value, but does not accomplish it alone. Cisco, Schwab, and Wal-Mart are examples of organizations that depend on IT for their success.

▪▪▪ Overview of the Text: Managing the Information Technology Resource

It is apparent that the rule of CIO and the entire IT organization is challenging, but that is what makes it exciting. It is doable, and the chapters of this text can serve as a vehicle to ensure success. This text will focus on the issues presented in this chapter's introduction and is organized based on Luftman's six components of strategic alignment maturity, described in Chapter 2. These six criteria are:

Communications Maturity
Competency/Value Measurement Maturity
Governance Maturity
Partnership Maturity
Scope and Architecture Maturity
Skills Maturity

Each section of the book contains chapters that describe one of the six components. A brief overview of the contents of these chapters is provided here.

Chapter 2 will present and discuss the Strategic Alignment Model as a way for organizations to assess the gap between the current state of affairs in an organization and the role of IT in reaching the company's objectives—the "To Be." The importance of the need for business and IT people to interact and make joint decisions is discussed. This Model as well as the Maturity Assessment Model presented in Chapter 3 will serve as the foundation for subsequent discussions of the issues the CIO faces in the management of IT.

Chapter 3 goes beyond the Strategic Alignment Model to discuss the Strategic Alignment Maturity Assessment. This model provides organizations with a means to measure the commitment that exists to align business and IT. Similar to the CMM or Capability Maturity Model, the intent is to provide a means of assessing the areas that impact alignment, and to then develop actionable tasks to improve alignment.

Partnership Maturity

A major objective of this book is to show some of the ways IT can affect an organization as a whole, and how the role of the CIO can facilitate this. Business managers in many organizations are assuming some of the traditional responsibilities of IT Management.[31] As the pervasiveness of computing has increased, so has the dispersion of the management of those assets. **Chapter 4** discusses the role of the CIO and other IT managers in this environment, the skills and attributes of a successful CIO, as well as the role of the CIO relative to the business as a whole.

Scope and Architecture Maturity

Chapter 5 will discuss the processes that exist within the IT organization. These processes are grouped into strategic, tactical, and operational processes. Strategic processes generally have a longer-term impact on the organization. Tactical processes tend to have a shorter time frame in which they affect the organization. The majority of a CIO's resources and time are spent on tactical processes. Operational processes are those that tend to be taken for granted. They make up the day-to-day activities of the IT organization. When they become problems, they become visible much more quickly than the strategic or tactical processes. The ever-changing technology landscape requires that the CIO and IT staff continuously monitor the environment for the impact new technology might have on the organization.

Many decisions made today might become useless in several months because of business and technological changes. Yet it is still important for the IT organization to develop flexible strategic plans. Plans might include pilot projects for emerging technology and plans to develop training programs, as well as the traditional project plans. In **Chapter 6**, the importance of this and the IT organization's role in strategic business planning, *as well as the business organization's role in these IT planning processes* will be described.

Chapter 7 will discuss the challenges surrounding the management of emerging technology. It will address questions such as:

- Should our organization be a pioneer, leader, or follower?
- When is the best time to adopt a new technology?
- Which technology, and with what vendor, should we commit to?
- How can we appropriately apply and introduce the technology?

Skills Maturity

Chapter 8 will address the impact of various organizational choices. Business structures can be described as centralized, decentralized, matrix, federated, geographic, skill-based, and so on. This chapter will look at how the IT organization must fit into the business organization to foster a "partnership" relationship. Business strategy, industry, culture, trust, and politics are just a few of the additional factors to consider in designing the IT organization structure. The role of outsourcing in managing the IT function will also be discussed.

Chapter 9 will focus on the Human Resource activities of IT. Hiring, firing, retention, motivation, assessing, training, communications, and knowledge management are some of the responsibilities that are part of the management of IT resources in the form of *people*. The ability of a CIO and the management team to align IT with the other business functions is extremely dependent on the ability to build a framework that creates a team mentality within their own areas of responsibilities.

Chapter 10 discusses one of the more difficult challenges faced by any manager, whether they are a manager of a business function or the IT function—the management of change. What are the unique challenges faced by IT? IT managers and staff are both "changers" and "changees" in today's dynamic environment. Both technical and organizational changes that arise out of the application of IT will be discussed.

Governance Maturity

In **Chapter 11**, the topic of IT Governance will be described. Governance goes beyond simple structure or organization—it involves the manner in which the IT organization manages itself and interacts with external and internal business partners. Some of the important questions addressed will include:

- How are IT decisions made and who makes them?
- How are priorities determined?
- How much resource should be allocated to IT?
- How should strategic partners be managed?

Communications Maturity

Effective exchange of ideas and a clear understanding of what it takes to ensure successful strategies are high on the list of enablers and inhibitors to alignment. Too often there is little business awareness on the part of IT or little IT appreciation on the part of the business. Given the dynamic environment in which most organizations find themselves, ensuring ongoing knowledge sharing across organizations is paramount.

Many firms choose to draw on liaisons to facilitate this knowledge sharing. The key word here is facilitating. Often the authors have seen facilitators whose role is to serve as the sole conduit of interaction among the different organizations. This approach tends to stifle rather than foster effective communications. Rigid protocols that impede discussions and the sharing of ideas should be avoided. **Chapter 12** describes ways to improve IT-business communications.

Competency/Value Measurement Maturity

With all of the challenges the CIO faces, how do they know what is happening on a daily, weekly, or monthly basis? How is the IT organization performing relative to others in the same or different industries? Are the expectations of the "business" being met? **Chapter 13** addresses some of the mechanisms for determining how the IT organization is performing. This chapter addresses the questions:

- Why are measurements important?
- What should be measured?
- Who owns measurements?
- How should they be measured?
- When should measurements be done?
- What should be done with the measurements?

This chapter will focus on the internal measurements of IT, and the daily responsibilities to meet commitments to the organization as a whole.

While the CIO and the IT staff may understand their value to the organization, this is not enough. Building on the prior chapter, the CIO must be able to demonstrate this value to the business executives in *business* terms. The ability to provide *external* measurements is important in demonstrating the value of IT's contribution to the business. In **Chapter 14**, the ways this might be done are addressed, including who needs to demonstrate such value. The difference between demonstrating value and simply measuring and reporting it is addressed. Finally, what happens to the IT organization if it cannot show value to the business?

The Appendix includes supplemental material to support some of the topics addressed throughout the book.

REVIEW QUESTIONS ▪ ▪ ▪ ▪ ▪ ▪ ▪ ▪

1. What are some of the major ways Information Technology has become more important to organizations?
2. What are some other examples of disintermediation, reintermediation, hypermediation, and infomediation?
3. How does Porter's Value Chain demonstrate the changing nature of IT's involvement in the overall business operation over time?

DISCUSSION QUESTIONS ▪ ▪ ▪ ▪ ▪ ▪ ▪ ▪

1. What would you consider some of the key changes in technology over the last 50 years that have had the most impact on organizations?
2. How are companies you know about, or your own company, organized in terms of the IT function? Who does the top IT executive or CIO report to?
3. What are some examples of business models that have changed as a result of Information Technology?
4. What would you consider the most important factor in improving the ability of IT to play a larger role in an organization?
5. What are some of the issues IT faces in the global economy?
6. In reviewing some of the other concerns within organizations shown in Figure 1-3, what role does IT management play? What role does business management play?
7. What contributes to the difficulties IT organizations have in demonstrating the value technology brings to the business goals and results? What is the role of the business function in these difficulties?
8. How will the role of the CIO continue to change in the future? What is the role of the CTO relative to the CIO?
9. How do the concepts of this text apply to current changes apparent in your own organization? How will they shape your own career?

AREAS FOR RESEARCH ▪ ▪ ▪ ▪ ▪ ▪ ▪ ▪

1. Critical Success Factors. Read John Rockart's paper on the use of CSFs.[32]
2. Alignment of IT and business functions—research the history of this problem from an academic and practical perspective.
3. What are some other examples of the role IT plays as a "mediator"? Research the topics of disintermedia-tion, infomediation, reintermediation, and hypermediation.
4. The ability to identify the contribution of IT to improving productivity is important. Research the "Productivity Paradox" discussed in this chapter.

CONCLUSION ▮▮▮▮▮▮▮

This introduction has attempted to provide a brief, yet broad overview of the role of the IT function in most organizations. As discussed, technology is now pervasive in most organizations in the industrialized world. Managing IT well is extremely important to the success of these organizations.

The next chapter will provide more detail on the Strategic Alignment Model. This material will serve as a foundation for the chapters that follow.

REFERENCES ▮▮▮▮▮▮▮

[1] Porter, Michael, *Competitive Advantage: Creating and Sustaining Superior Performance*, Free Press, 1985.

[2] Rockart, John F., *Chief Executives Define Their Own Data Needs*, Harvard Business Review, March-April, 1979.

[3] Grimm, Robert, and Davis, Janet, et al., *Systems Directions for Pervasive Computing*, University of Washington.

[4] Based on the USAA Case Study by Harvard Business School (9-188-102, 9/23/1992).

[5] Luftman, Jerry N. (Editor), *Competing in the Information Age,* Oxford University Press, 1996.

[6] Kirsner, Scott, *Scaredy Pants*, Darwin, Aug/Sept 2000.

[7] Barber, Brad M., and Odean, Terrance, *The Internet and the Investor*, Journal of Economic Perspectives, Volume 15, Number 1, Winter 2001.

[8] Porter, Kelley A., *eBay, Inc.,* (Harvard Business School Case Study # 9-700-007), Harvard Business School Publishing, 1999.

[9] Carr, Nicholas G., *Hypermediation: Commerce as Clickstream,* Harvard Business Review, Jan/Feb 2000.

[10] Carr, Nicholas G., *Hypermediation: Commerce as Clickstream,* Harvard Business Review, Jan/Feb 2000.

[11] Eppley, Martin, MCM Institute, University of St. Galen, 1999.

[12] Hagel, John and Singer, Marc, *Net Worth*, Harvard Business School Press, 1999.

[13] 14th Annual Survey of Critical Issues of Information Systems Management (North America)—CSC 2001 (available at *www.csc.com/features/2001/40.shtml*).

[14] Henderson, J. and Venkatraman, N., *Strategic Alignment: A Model for Organizational Transformation via Information Technology*, Working Paper 3223-90, Cambridge, MA; Sloan School of Management, MIT, 1990.

[15] Earl, M. J., *Corporate Information Systems Management*, Homewood, IL, Richard D. Irwin, 1993

[16] Luftman, J., Lewis, P., and Oldach, S., *Transforming the Enterprise: The Alignment of Business and Information Technology Strategies*, IBM Systems Journal, 32(1), 1993.

[17] Papp, R., *Alignment of Business and Information Technology Strategy: How and Why?*, Information Management (11), 3/4.

[18] Luftman, J., Papp, Raymond, and Brier, Tom, *Enablers and Inhibitors of Business-IT Alignment*, Communications of the Association for Information Systems, Volume 1, Article 11, March 1999.

[19] Rivkin, Jan W., Porter, Michael E., *Matching Dell*, (Harvard Business School Case Study # 9-799-158), Harvard Business School Publishing, 1999.

[20] Smith, Scott S., *Dell On…*, Entrepreneur, April 1999.

[21] Porter, Michael, *Competitive Advantage: Creating and Sustaining Superior Performance*, Free Press, 1985.

[22] Eizenberg, Michael I., Gallo, Donna M., Hagenbuch, Irene, and Hoffman, Alan M., *Cisco Systems, Inc. (1998)*, SMPB–7th Edition.

[23] Kominski, Robert, *Computer Use in the United States: 1989*, Series P-23, No. 171 (U.S. Department of Commerce, Bureau of the Census, Current Population Reports, March 1991).

[24] Newburger, Eric, *Home Computers and Internet Use in the United States: August 2000*, Series P-23, No. 207 (U.S. Department of Commerce, Bureau of the Census, Current Population Reports, September 2001).

[25] Newburger, Eric, *Computer Use in the United States: 1997*, Series P-20, No. 522 (U.S. Department of Commerce, Bureau of the Census, Current Population Reports, September 1999).

[26] Roach, Steven, *Economic Perspectives*, Morgan Stanley, January 1991.

[27] Loveman, Gary, *An Assessment of the Productivity Impact of Information Technologies*, MIT Sloan School of Management, working paper 90s: 88-054.

[28] Brynjolfsson, Erik and Hitt, Lorin M., *"Information Systems Spending Productive? New Evidence and New Results",* Proceedings of the International Conference on Information Systems, Orlando, Florida, December 5-8, 1993, p. 47-64.

[29] Brynjolfsson, Erik, and Hitt, Lorin M., *Beyond the Productivity Paradox,* Communications of the ACM, August 1998.

[30] Henderson, J. C. and Venkatraman, N., *Strategic Alignment: Leveraging Information Technology for Transforming Organizations*, IBM Systems Journal, 32(1), 1993.

[31] Boynton, Andrew C., Jacobs, Gerry C., and Zmud, Robert W., *Whose Responsibility is IT Management?*, Sloan Management Review, Summer 1992.

[32] Rockart, John F., *Chief Executives Define Their Own Data Needs*, Harvard Business Review, March-April, 1979.

2

IT Strategy

"Strategy is the craft of the warrior. Commanders must enact the craft, and troopers should know this Way."
—MIYAMOTO MUSASHI (1584–1645)

"If we do not learn from history, we shall be compelled to relive it. True, but if we do not change the future, we shall be compelled to endure it, and that could be worse."
—ALVIN TOFFLER

Preview of Chapter

The effective management of IT organizations in the dynamic business environment of the 21st century demands that senior IT managers work with senior functional (e.g., marketing, R&D, finance) managers to develop IT strategies that are aligned with the firm's business strategy for sustainable competitive advantage. IT management must be continuously aware of the opportunities to transform the firm. The process for developing strategy must demonstrate the opportunity for IT to enable or drive business strategy, and operational effectiveness and efficiency. This chapter will discuss the concept of Strategic Alignment as the key framework for creating effective IT strategies and review in detail the steps management should consider in creating aligned IT-business strategies. Alignment addresses both how IT is in harmony with the business, and how the business should, or could, be in harmony with IT.

What we will examine in this chapter:

■ The influence of the 21st century business environment on IT strategy
■ Some definitions of strategy in general, and IT strategy in particular
■ The role of IT strategy in your firm
■ The concept of Strategic Alignment and the Strategic Alignment Model
■ The processes and considerations involved in developing an IT strategy

▪▪▪ Introduction

One of the most important missions for IT management in the 21st century is to be *architects* of alignment linking business and IT. The metaphor of architecture is chosen because IT strategy is *not* just about technology—it is about the purposeful creation of *integrated* environments that leverage human skills, business processes, organizational structures, and technologies to transform the competitive position of the business. Naturally, offering new products and services via information technology is another important transformational vehicle. Considerable recent research has shown that the effectiveness of the linkages relating IT and business domains are critically important to sustaining competitive advantage in today's hyper-competitive global markets.[2, 3, 4] When these domains are aligned—i.e., mutually supporting—a company's ability to respond to increasingly uncertain and evolving markets (the external environment) is significantly enhanced; sometimes to the level where companies can define entirely new markets or set the standard of excellence in their industry.

As architects of alignment, IT management plays a pivotal role, as they have responsibility to consider the organization across functional and process boundaries. These boundaries should be expanded to external partners and customers. In this role, IT managers need to:

- Be knowledgeable about how the new IT technologies can be integrated into the business as well as among the different technologies and architectures
- Be privy to senior management's tactical and strategic plans
- Be present when corporate strategies are discussed, and
- Understand the strengths and weaknesses of the technologies in question and the corporate-wide implications.[5]

It is important for the IT manager to understand that alignment is about the evolution of a relationship between business and IT, and how the organization can leverage information technology. Alignment is a process that is enabled or inhibited by a number of factors that are experienced every day. Recent research into the factors that enable or inhibit alignment based on survey responses from senior business and IT managers show that there are six key enablers to alignment as well as six corresponding inhibitors to alignment (Table 2-1).[3, 4] IT managers should especially note that several of the attributes that enable alignment also show up as inhibitors to alignment. The enablers and inhibitors identified in the original research have not changed, as the research continues.

Achieving and sustaining alignment requires conscious attention and focus by IT and functional (e.g., marketing, R&D, finance) management to enhance the enablers of alignment and minimize alignment's inhibitors. Alignment is a consequence of sound practices and evolving human relationships that embrace mutual understandings of goals, value, culture and capabilities that leverage the development of strategies that

TABLE 2-1 Enablers and Inhibitors to Alignment[3, 4]

	Enablers	*Inhibitors*
1	Senior executive support for IT	IT/business lack close relationships
2	IT involved in strategy development	IT does not prioritize well
3	IT understands the business	IT fails to meet commitments
4	Business—IT partnership	IT does not understand business
5	Well-prioritized IT projects	Senior executives do not support IT
6	IT demonstrates leadership	IT management lacks leadership

can ultimately co-adapt to changing circumstances. IT strategies that focus merely on technology and ignore the partnership and communications aspects of the business–IT relationship inevitably fail. Alignment is an ongoing process.

Today's Business Environment

To better understand why the alignment of business strategy and IT strategy is critical not just for competitive advantage, but for business *survival*, organizations need to understand the forces that shape the business environment. Today's business environment can be best characterized as one of increasing globalization, increased competitive pressure, frequent mergers, rapidly changing technology, and evolving patterns of consumer demand. Change is now the norm rather than the exception. Organizations must learn to quickly adapt to these changes or face extinction (at worst) or assimilation (at best) by competitors who can emerge anywhere in the world. In short, the predictability of the business environment has dramatically declined while its complexity (the number of connections to other organizations) has simultaneously accelerated due to the proliferation of technology and its ability to enable networked organizations and individuals.

Competitive advantage in this turbulent environment is no longer about having the best products or the lowest prices, but about having:

- Unsurpassed relationships with one's customers and suppliers
- Unique and adaptable business processes
- The ability to harness the information and knowledge of the firm's employees to continuously create new, hard to duplicate products and services

Organizations need to become "change leaders" merely to survive in the 21st century business environment.[1]

Strategy—a Definition

The word *strategy* is derived from Greek, where it means "the art of the general." Until recently, even in the English language, strategy was a military term. It has only been since the 1960s that the business world has adopted the term.

Strategies are business decisions taken at particular points in time by different people in response to sets of perceived environmental factors. Strategy is about making *choices* that include:

- The selection of business goals
- The choice of products and services to offer
- The design and configuration of policies that determine how the firm positions itself to compete in its markets
- The appropriate level of scope and diversity (e.g., specialization)
- The design of organization structure, administrative systems, and policies used to define and coordinate work

The integration and *coordination* of the choices make them a strategy. Integration and coordination of the choices is key to survival of the enterprise.[6] In essence, an organization's strategy reconciles how to apply its resources for maximum impact against its competitors.

Another definition of strategy is offered by Drucker: "Every organization operates on a *Theory of the Business*—a set of assumptions as to what its business is, its

FIGURE 2-1 Vision, Mission, and Strategy.

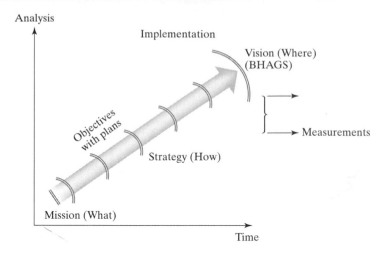

objectives, how it defines and measures results, who its customers are, and what its customers value and pay for. A business strategy converts this *Theory of the Business* into action by enabling an organization to achieve its goals *in an increasingly unpredictable business environment.*"[1]

The formulation of strategy can be thought of as having three key elements—vision, strategy, and mission—each of which has an important relationship to time and the level of analysis required to articulate each element (Figure 2-1):

1. Vision ("Where Do We Want To Go?"). Effective strategies begin with the creation of a vision—a concise, measurable statement of where the company wants to go and what it aspires to be. Ideally, this vision should be clear, compelling, and exciting to everyone in the firm. There is ample research to show that visionary companies—companies that are widely admired in their industry groups for having made a sustained significant impact—have substantially outperformed their peers in the ratio of cumulative stock returns to the general market. Some excellent examples of visionary companies include Wal-Mart, Amazon, GE, Dell, Cisco, Microsoft, and SABRE to name but a few. Visionary companies often use

How Important Is "The Vision Thing"?

Although the concept of creating and nurturing a corporate "vision" may seem to be academic, it is instructive to note the response of financial analysts to AT&T's recent strategic woes that have led to the proposed sale of its Basking Ridge, NJ corporate headquarters facilities, its failure to develop DSL services after acquiring Northpoint Communications in early 2001, potential layoffs of 30% of the staff of some business units, and the announced sale of its broadband cable facilities.

Said one industry analyst: "*Michael Armstrong (AT&T's CEO) does not have a clear vision that is able to be executed for the long haul. He may have a clear vision at times, but it's very short term ... we had no faith in the future direction of the firm.*"[10]

bold statements of their vision—what we call "BHAGs" (short for "Big Hairy Audacious Goals" and pronounced "bee-hags")—to stimulate progress and excitement and to challenge people to achieve something they may have initially thought impossible.

An excellent example of a BHAG was President John F. Kennedy's public statement in early 1961 that the United States "... *should commit itself to achieving the goal, before this decade is out, of landing a man on the moon and returning him safely to earth.*" Given that the United States was still struggling with successfully launching unmanned satellites at the time and had yet to develop any of the required rocket hardware, software, launch or tracking facilities, this statement was not merely bold, but outrageous to some. Yet this BHAG stimulated the collective energies and imaginations of the people involved in what became the Apollo program to meet the audacious challenge of the vision to land a man on the moon before 1970. Similarly, for a company like GE, Jack Welch established BHAGs that were clear, compelling and audacious:[8]

- "Become #1 or #2 in every market we serve and
- Revolutionize this company to have the speed and agility of a small enterprise"

An effective vision is:

Imaginable: Conveys a picture of what the future will look like
Desirable: Appeals to the long-term interests of employees, customers, stockholders, and others who have a stake in the enterprise
Feasible: Comprises realistic, attainable goals
Focused: Is clear enough to provide guidance in decision making
Flexible: Is general enough to allow individual initiative and alternative responses in light of changing conditions
Communicable: Is easy to communicate; can be successfully explained within five minutes
Measurable: Stakeholders will clearly see that they have attained the goal

---

Some Real-Life Examples of Visions For IT Strategy

Example 1:

- Anyone can get any information (site, geographic area, or global level) at any time, anywhere, any way, given the proper security constraints
- The end user does not have to know the location of the data
- Maintain data in only one master place within the organization
- Implement systems to enhance end user productivity
- Systems are able to support competitive business demands with immediate response to quickly changing business needs
- Information Systems adds a competitive edge to the company's product line

Example 2:

- Have delighted customers (users)
- Proactively address business needs
- Provide competitive advantage to the company
- Be recognized in the industry as a world-class Information Systems organization
- Have Information Systems employees with a passion and commitment, people who carry the fire and love their job
- Provide enterprise-wide business solutions

- Have a superior functioning team
- Simplify, standardize, automate, and integrate

Example 3: We will have Business Systems that:

- Take advantage of global "sameness"
- Are purchased whenever practical
- Have integrated data that is entered only once
- Provide consistent definitions of information
- Support functional and cross-functional business processes
- Deliver the *right* information, at the *right* place, at the *right* time, in the *right* format
- Are flexible enough to support changing environments
- Can be accessed by office, home, and mobile workers
- Provide capabilities to external customers and suppliers

2. **Strategic Objectives ("How will we achieve this vision?").** Strategic objectives articulate *how* the vision (or BHAG) will be accomplished over the time period identified in the vision. Effective strategies use mechanisms of phased implementation or checkpoints to allow for "midcourse corrections" and also incorporate measurements or benchmarks to check the effectiveness of the strategy and its implementation. Most importantly, an effective strategy is aligned with the mission and core values of the company and provides the "architectural bridge" between the mission of the company and the vision. The elements of the strategy architecture will be described in the section of this chapter titled "The Strategic Alignment Model".

Some Examples of Strategic Objectives Developed by Different Companies

- Implement solutions in partnership with the business units. Business Sponsor and Champions each project (business-requested project, not infrastructure projects) by business management to ensure that business issues drive technical solutions
- Align information systems projects and priorities with business priorities and direction. Likewise, the strategic direction of the company will determine the strategic direction of Information Systems
- Provide responsiveness and flexibility to address changing business requirements rather than simply utilizing technology
- Meet external customer requirements and assist in solving our customers' business issues
- Maximize productivity and reduce costs throughout the business
- Provide real information for business decisions (as opposed to endless amounts of data). Information must be available anytime (24 hour access), anywhere in the world, in any way (flexible formats), for any one (with security)
- Support worldwide information requirements and business objectives

3. **Mission ("What are we?").** Strategy formulation is not a single step or a stand-alone process, but begins with the mission of the IT function; the reasons the IT function exists. A **mission statement** for Information Technology is a concise

statement of what business the group is in. It is a statement of why the Information Technology group exists and the purpose and function it provides for the company. The company mission should be reviewed to identify ideas or themes for the IT mission. The mission of the company defines why it exists, what its purpose is, and what its core values are. These core values are relatively stable over time and provide an underlying system of shared beliefs and principles that guide the behavior of the organization as a business entity. IT strategies that are formulated that are inconsistent with the mission or the core values of their company run a very high risk of failure.[9]

To realize business value, an effective business strategy coordinates the choices made by management that address the "fit" of these choices to the external environment and aligns these choices with its internal processes, organization, resources, and competencies (including technological competencies). Effective business strategy is also not static—it must continuously change to reflect changes in the business environment.

Some Examples of Information Systems Missions Developed by Different Companies

- "The mission of Information Systems, in partnership with the business units, is to facilitate the availability of timely and accurate information needed to manage the day-to-day and strategic direction of the company by the deployment of systems and tools. This information will assist the company in achieving its objectives and becoming one of the top-ten in the marketplace"
- "The mission of Information Systems in partnership with the business community is to develop, implement, and maintain worldwide business system solutions that provide secure collection, storage, and access to information. We will accomplish this by matching the business requirements with the appropriate technology"
- "The mission of Information Systems is to develop, implement, and maintain high-quality efficient and effective business systems that provide the information needed to support the daily operation and strategic business direction of the business at a level superior to the competition with customer satisfaction as the end goal"
- "Our mission is to facilitate improvements in operating efficiency and effectiveness by delivering worldwide integrated business systems and services. We will drive or enable business strategies to ensure that our contributions provide the highest value to the corporation"

▪▪▪ IT Strategy

IT strategy is therefore a set of decisions made by IT and functional senior management that either *enable* or *drive* the business strategy. It leads to the deployment of technology infrastructure and human competencies that will assist the organization in becoming more competitive. IT strategy must be concerned not just about technology choices, but also about the *relationship* of technology choices to business strategy choices. The selection of appropriate technologies can, in many situations, have substantial influence on or even drive the transformation of the business strategy. As will be extensively discussed in the chapter on "The Value of IT"

(Chapter 14), it is not the technology alone that brings these benefits. It is the business processes that are changed by leveraging information technology that provide the business value. That is why a strong IT–business partnership is critical. Neither IT nor the business can do it alone. Their strategies must be aligned.

Wal-Mart Integrates Its Value Chain

Discount giant Wal-Mart has developed an IT strategy that emphasizes operational efficiency between itself and its suppliers—to the point where, if a firm wants to do business as a supplier to Wal-Mart, it must meet *their* requirements for electronic information exchange. This gives Wal-Mart an enormous competitive advantage over its rivals. In response to this requirement, Procter & Gamble and GE Lighting decided to coordinate their IT strategies with Wal-Mart so that these vendors receive daily sales information about their products in each store and, in response, can continuously replenish Wal-Mart's shelves with their products on an "as-needed" basis. In turn, P&G and GE Lighting supply Wal-Mart with electronic shipping and billing information. Both parties benefit from this arrangement:

1. Inventory costs are lowered for P&G and GE Lighting
2. Wal-Mart needs fewer staff to handle invoices and shipping
3. Wal-Mart is assured its supply of product is always on the shelf for customers
4. Wal-Mart's customers can reap the savings passed on thanks to the operational efficiencies

Source: Davenport, T., "Information Ecology"[11]

The development of an aligned IT strategy is critical in today's business environment for several reasons:

1. Regardless of whether the business is in the manufacturing or service sector, most business is information-based. Information has become the glue that binds organizations with their customers, suppliers, and partners. No business today can effectively compete without an intimate understanding of its customers and their evolving needs. Similarly, organizations have learned that sharing information with their suppliers and customers (e.g., Wal-Mart, Cisco, Baxter Healthcare) can dramatically improve operational efficiency as well as position these firms to anticipate needs rather than merely react to them. The greater the organization's ability to obtain information about the external environment (i.e., its customers, suppliers, partners, and competitors) the less uncertainty it will have regarding its strategic decisions. Information technology is uniquely positioned to enable business strategies that leverage information that spans organizational boundaries for competitive advantage. Business strategy—and changes to business strategy—implies changes to an organization's information environment. Information Technology provides the best tools available for enabling or driving change to these information environments.[11]

2. The ubiquity of IT in manufacturing and services throughout the world has made the market value of physical products and processes less important than the knowledge and information embedded in them. This phenomenon, called "dematerialization," describes a situation that faces all firms today. Competitors can emerge from any part of the globe, thanks to the presence of microprocessor hardware and software, and networks. Even third world countries have access to

information technology, making it more important than ever for firms to develop innovative and aligned business and IT strategies that place a premium on managing and growing the knowledge- and information-based assets of the firm.[13]

A good example of "dematerialization" is in the semiconductor industry, where product lifecycles are estimated in months rather than years. According to Michael Kenney's research into the time-related aspects of knowledge creation in information-based economies,[13] a semiconductor sold in 1997 lost more than 50% of its value by 2000. This accelerated depreciation of the knowledge component of the product (i.e., the integrated circuit) is due to the ability of competitors to quickly replicate the design and form of the component through the use of information technology-based design and manufacturing tools.

3. A turbulent business environment demands organizations that have adaptive processes—processes that are not merely flexible, but also aligned with the changing information requirements of the organization and the external environment. Maintaining competitive advantage requires business to continuously innovate *strategically relevant* new processes.[14] Process innovation refers to the radical design of new processes that include new approaches to work, new organizational structures, and new relationships with customers, suppliers, partners, and employees. Information Technology is the primary enabler of process innovation because all business processes have information content. As an example, the strategically relevant processes for USAA are the outstanding customer contact services that define their identity. USAA's senior management recognized the potential of IT as an enabler for radically improving the level of customer intimacy by integrating customer databases in what became the forerunner of Customer Relationship Management ("CRM") technology. Similarly, Federal Express' *identity processes* are those that are related directly to guaranteed overnight delivery and reliability.

Cisco Becomes "Net Ready" for Competitive Advantage

Cisco Systems is the acknowledged global leader in providing networking products for the Internet. It sells products in over 100 countries through a complex network of direct sales, value-added resellers, distributors, and system integrators. One key element of Cisco's business strategy was to outsource the manufacture of many of the key components it sells under the Cisco label.

Cisco embraced the Web as an over-arching IT-driven business strategy that enabled it to seamlessly link its customers, prospects, sales force, distributors, and employees to such an extent that, regardless of where a Cisco component is manufactured, customers view Cisco as one entity for questions on orders, support, and network configuration. Furthermore, most of Cisco's internal business processes have been Web-enabled to drive the sharing of, and access to, critical customer and production-related information.

What is especially important to note is that, thanks to this transforming strategy, 80 percent of customer requests for technical support are electronically fulfilled, and at levels of customer satisfaction that far surpass the days when these requests were manually handled. The money Cisco saves on providing technical support actually eclipses the dollars its nearest competitor spends on R&D!

Source: Hartman and Sifonis, *Net Ready—Strategies for Success in the E-conomy*, McGraw-Hill, 2000.

4. Business processes are *coordinated* activities that involve people, procedures, and technology.[14] Organizations make choices about which parts of their operations (i.e., processes) they will handle internally and which processes they will outsource according to one theory of why firms exist.[15] Make-or-buy decisions are central to the formulation of strategy as they affect not only the internal processes an organization chooses to focus on, but also the external partnerships and alliances it will need to outsource. The costs associated with coordinating internal activities (processes) can be dramatically reduced by the deployment of IT because of its ability to bridge large distances and reduce the number of process steps and personnel. The coordinating potential of IT is evident in collaborative groupware technologies, knowledge management portals, and the growing use of data interchange technologies. See the sidebars on Cisco, Wal-Mart, and Baxter for excellent examples of how the coordinating power of IT can be leveraged for competitive advantage.

IT and Business Transformation

Baxter/American Hospital Supply Set The Standard for Coordination for Competitive Advantage

In the mid-1970s American Hospital Supply Corporation (AHSC) introduced the first system that allowed its hospital customers to electronically order supplies by telephone. This system, called "ASAP," allowed hospital purchasing managers to enter orders by touch telephone. As ASAP evolved, purchasing managers could directly enter orders into AHSC's computers through terminals, PCs, or their own mainframe computers. ASAP automatically reserved inventory and generated packing lists for each customer. AHSC managed to achieve significant advantage over its competitors, thanks to the customized information flow generated via ASAP.

In 1985 Baxter Travenol acquired AHSC and partnered with GE Information Services to create a new version of ASAP that became the forerunner of Web-based e-marketplaces for medical supplies. ASAP has now evolved to the point where many of AHSC's former competitors now participate in what has become an electronic infrastructure for the hospital industry. Baxter's IT strategy has deliberately focused on the value of the information related to each interaction with the customer, to the point where Baxter provides services to hospitals to manage their own inventory ("vendor-managed inventory") because Baxter understands the needs of the customer better than the customers themselves! Through service excellence, Baxter has also raised the costs to the customer of switching to another service to an unacceptably high level.

In the formulation of an IT strategy, Information Technology can drive business transformation as well as enable transformation. The evidence that IT can transform business has been amply documented.[2, 12, 14, 17] In the role of *transformation driver* the IT strategy *becomes* the business strategy; offering novel and competitively differentiating ways of doing business. In its role as *transformation driver* IT can create and exploit new markets, link customers more tightly to the firm, and define new standards of operational excellence for the industry. Examples of firms that have used IT as a transformation driver (in this case, Web-enabling their businesses) include Dell, Cisco, and Amazon.com—all of whom have established the operational process "bar" over which all potential competitors must now jump to even consider competing in their markets. Another, earlier example of IT as a transformation driver is the Sabre Group—formerly the American Airlines reservation system. Initially a proprietary reservation system for American Airlines flights, Sabre's accommodation of flight information from other airlines eventually opened the way for it to become a flight booking system for the airline and travel industry. Sabre's value grew to the point where the value of its information content—and the driving information technology—exceeded the value of American's flight operations assets. Eventually, Sabre Group was formed as a company independent of American Airlines, with Sabre firmly established as an industry standard.

In its role as an *enabler of transformation*, IT's capabilities to interconnect people and processes, span organizational (and inter-organizational) boundaries, and quickly bridge geographical distances can help organizations explore new markets and customer segments, create new processes, and provide a critical supporting role in the implementation of business transformation strategies. An excellent example of IT as an enabler of transformation is Federal Express' use of IT to track packages; supporting its revolutionary concept of airline hubbing for overnight package delivery. This process innovation redefined the small package delivery business and put the U.S. Postal Service at a severe competitive disadvantage. Another example of IT as a transformation enabler is *USA Today's* use of new communications technologies and graphics information management technologies to support what is now a national newspaper. *USA Today* ® transformed the processes involved with producing, printing, and distributing a daily newspaper to a national and international readership through the deployment of IT.

Unfortunately, IT can also be an inhibitor to business transformation. This situation occurs through several mechanisms:

- *When the IT strategy is not aligned with the business strategy*: just as sound business strategy must take into account both external positioning in the marketplace as well as the internal arrangement of its organizational structure and competencies, IT strategy must also reflect a firm's positioning in the external IT marketplace and the configuration of its internal IT infrastructure and architecture.[18]
- *Over-emphasis by IT management and business management on technology*: can misdirect the focus of transformation away from changing and *transforming* critical business processes to the implementation of technology infrastructure for its own sake. Part of this is due to communications issues between the different "cultures" of management. Schein believes that there are three "sub-cultures of management" in companies that each have their own perspectives on how the firm operates and how it should be run:[19]

  - The "executive" culture is focused on maintaining an organization's financial health and deals with boards of directors, investors, and markets. The "executive" culture is focused outside the organization and as they are promoted into roles of increasing scope, they become more impersonal, seeing people as a cost rather than as an asset to the organization.
  - The "engineering" culture represents the people who work with the various technologies of the organization and how those technologies are to be used. Engineers, whose focus is outside the organization, share common educational, work, and job experiences. The "engineering" culture tries to design humans out of any business processes and sees them as a source of potential error.
  - The "operator" culture evolves locally in an organization or business unit and is based on human interaction. Their focus is inward—towards each other—rather than outward. The "operator" culture believes that it best understands the "real" workings of the organization and may use their learning ability to thwart management's efforts to improve productivity. These cultures often

don't communicate well and frequently operate at cross-purposes. Davenport also points out that companies also tend to focus too narrowly on technology when trying to manage information.[11]

- *Failure of IT and business management to recognize that effective use of IT requires business process change*: leading proponents of IT's value as an enabler of transformational change also stress that sustainable competitive advantage is only achieved when IT is used in conjunction with business process change.[2, 11] It is important to also remember that business process change includes changes to the human component of processes!

▪▪▪ Strategic Alignment

The concept of strategic alignment stresses the harmonization of the goals and implementation plans of IT with the goals and organizational structure of the business. Since 1985, one of the major concerns of key business leaders has been the alignment of business goals and IT goals. Today's IT executives must concern themselves not just with technology, but also must understand the strategic goals of the business in a dynamic and uncertain environment. IT executives must also understand how their organizations are positioned within an equally dynamic and uncertain technology marketplace so that their choices of technology support the delivery of services and products to support the strategic choices of the business *that will enhance competitive advantage*. Strategic alignment refers specifically to the coordination of an organization's external business and IT goals and its internal business and IT organizational infrastructures. Earlier in this chapter, the integrative and coordination characteristics of strategy were introduced. Strategic alignment specifically addresses the processes of coordination among the internal and external domains of business and IT. This chapter emphasizes the importance of the Henderson-Venkatraman Strategic Alignment Model[20] (see Figure 2-2) as an architecture for the *formulation* of a viable IT strategy.

▪▪▪▪▪▪▪▪▪▪▪ **FIGURE 2-2   The Strategic Alignment Model.**

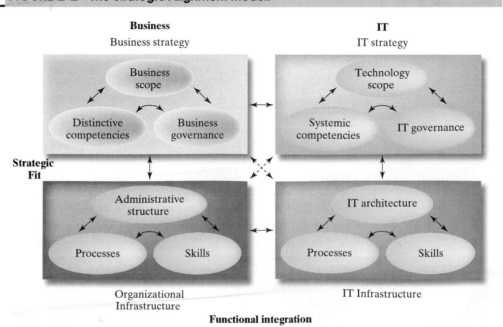

Henderson, J.C. and N. Venkatraman, *Strategic Alignment: Leveraging Information Technology for Transforming Organizations*, IBM Systems Journal, 32(1), 1993.

▮▮▮ Strategic Fit

The concept of strategic alignment is based on two fundamental assumptions:

1. **Strategic Fit.** Any strategy must address both the external environment and the internal environment of an organization. Strategic choices made to address these environments (or "domains") must be consistent—they must "fit" each other and they must be dynamic; that is, the strategic choices must be ones that are amenable to change. The external domain is concerned with those strategic choices and decisions that relate to:

   a. **The Scope of the Firm's Business.** Its customers, products, markets, and its competitors. As an example: for USAA, its customers would be current and former U.S. armed forces officers and warrant officers and their dependents; its products would include life and property and casualty insurance, banking services, financial (asset management) services, various buying services (e.g., automobiles, jewelry, etc.); its markets would be U.S. armed forces personnel stationed anywhere in the world; and its competitors would include financial services companies such as Prudential, Travelers, and Met Life.

   b. **The Distinctive Competencies.** This includes both the core competencies and critical success factors that provide competitive advantage. Core competencies are those activities that differentiate the organization from its competitors. It is the reason why customers choose a particular organization over its competitors. It is why competitors fear another firm. Critical success factors describe those activities the organization must do to succeed.

   Again, as an example, USAA's unparalleled knowledge of its policyholders and its ability to integrate this customer knowledge across its product lines to provide seamless and reliable service to policyholders at all times are distinctive competencies. Its customers have consistently rated USAA among the most esteemed companies for decades. This is due, in large part, to its understanding of the culture of its customers (i.e., military servicemen and women) as well as to USAA's ability to not merely respond to, but *anticipate* customer needs (e.g., a policyholder's dependent turning 16 years of age will prompt USAA to ask if the dependent needs auto insurance coverage), thanks to their distinctive competence in the use of technology.

   c. **The Governance of the Firm.** The impact of regulatory agencies on its strategic choices, how and who makes decisions regarding strategies and plans, and how its partnerships and alliances are managed are all important considerations.

   Governance is becoming increasingly important as companies pursue alliances and partnerships to obtain additional competencies and capabilities for competitive advantage (e.g., Ford Motor Company is aggressively pursuing alliances with Internet portals such as Yahoo and AOL to boost its online car sales). Companies that are in highly regulated industries such as pharmaceuticals and healthcare can, in turn, be strategically constrained by regulatory requirements or changes to existing regulations (e.g., the federal regulations governing electronic signatures and records in the pharmaceutical industry can impose constraints on the choices of technologies available to IT managers).

   These external concerns are reflected in the Strategic Alignment model (Figure 2-2).

   In contrast, the internal domain is concerned with choices and decisions about the firm's:

- **Administrative (Organizational) Structure.** Whether the firm has chosen a functional, matrix, decentralized, process-based, geographic organization structure or some form of hybrid organizational structure. For an excellent discussion of the types of organizational structures and their implications, students are referred to recommended books by Robbins (*Organization Theory—Structure, Design and Applications*, Prentice-Hall, 1990) and Daft (*Organization Theory and Design*, South-Western College Publishing, 7th Edition, 2000).

- **Critical Business Processes.** The architecture of its "salient" business activities or tasks; that is, those activities that are most relevant to a firm's identity (e.g., marketing, R&D, manufacturing, logistics). The identification of which processes are truly salient (and which are merely background processes) can determine a company's ability to successfully implement strategy.[15] One only has to observe the recent struggles of former telecommunications powerhouse AT&T to draw conclusions about its ability to identify its critical processes.

- **Human Resource Skills.** The acquisition and development of the skills of the people required to manage and operate the firm's key business activities. For example, a pharmaceutical company will have key skills that are focused on advanced degrees in medicine, biochemistry, and statistics and will accordingly value these skills when formulating strategy. Other human resource activities (e.g., recruiting, termination, training, retention, culture, assessing) are also considered.

2. **The Dynamic Nature of Strategic Fit.** A firm's competitors will eventually imitate any strategic choice, thereby rendering temporary any competitive advantage obtained from a specific technology or suite of applications. From an IT management perspective, strategic fit implies the need for the organization to develop and sustain capabilities that leverage IT to generate sustainable competitive advantage. Strategic fit also implies that IT management cannot make 'strategic bets' on any one particular technology or application, as IT lowers barriers to competitive imitation. An effective IT strategy is dynamic; it must not merely accept change, it must embrace the fact of change.

Business literature and research persuasively argue that to achieve *sustainable* economic performance, the fit and ability to quickly adapt between the strategic dimensions of external positioning and internal arrangement is essential.

▪▪▪ The Strategic Alignment Model

The Strategic Alignment Model (see Figure 2-2) extends the concept of internal and external business strategy domains to IT strategy. In the Strategic Alignment Model, IT strategy is defined in terms of an external domain (concerned with how the firm is positioned in the external IT marketplace) and the internal domain (how the firm's IT infrastructure and administrative processes are organized). In the external domain, IT strategy needs to be concerned with choices and decisions about:

a. **Scope of the Firm's Technology.** The *critical* technologies and suite of applications that *impact and support business strategy decisions and initiatives*. Critical technologies for a company may include (but are not limited to) data mining, neural networking, data visualization, CRM, the Internet, sales force automation, collaborative software, imaging systems, relational DBMS, etc. For example, the Internet and the technologies associated with it are critical technologies for Amazon. Critical technologies do *not* include support technologies such as e-mail or office productivity software (e.g., the Microsoft Office suite). Similarly, the suite of critical applications should include those that have a direct impact or focus on the critical dimensions of competitive positioning: customer intimacy, product excellence, or process excellence. An example of a critical applications suite would be the customer order management, warehouse management, and invoicing systems that Amazon deploys to manage orders from its customers.

b. **Systemic Competencies.**   Analogous to a firm's distinctive business competencies, these are technology capabilities (e.g., connectivity, customer information) that can have a major positive impact on the execution of the firm's business strategy or support ongoing initiatives. For USAA, its competencies with respect to interconnecting customer information databases for seamless access by service representatives to work with policy holders exclusively by telephone provides USAA with a critical competitive advantage. Systemic competencies are the bedrock upon which strategic options should be founded.

c. **IT Governance.**   Analogous to the choices of business strategic alliances or external relationships (e.g., vendors and consultants), these are choices and decisions about the relationships and alliances that will be pursued to obtain key IT competencies. IT governance also determines how decisions are made with respect to the prioritization of IT initiatives and how funds are allocated to these initiatives. For example: the establishment of a Steering Committee with business and IT management representatives to prioritize IT initiatives is a fairly common form of IT governance in many companies. Although often overlooked as a critical component of IT strategy, the establishment of effective IT governance mechanisms is a prerequisite for consistent decisions about the deployment of IT and the formulation and implementation of IT strategy. The topic of IT governance will be extensively covered in Chapter 11.

As with the internal domain of the business, the internal IT strategy domain is concerned with decisions and choices that affect:

a. **IT Architecture.**   The principles that guide choices and decisions about the selection of technology (hardware, software) and infrastructure as well as the structures and models used to define data and information, networks, applications, and systems. These principles drive the creation of policies and standards that govern technology infrastructure choices and are analogous to the choices made by the business with respect to its administrative structure. For example, Cisco and Dell decided that the IT architecture for their own systems—including their internal administrative systems such as payroll—would be based on the Internet.

b. **IT Organizational Processes.**   The activities and tasks that are critical to the operation of the IT organization such as systems development or IT operations (e.g., data center) management. These activities are analogous to the critical business processes that define and support the strategic initiatives and identity of the firm. The 38 IT processes are covered in Chapter 5.

c. **IT Skills.**   The acquisition and development of the people needed to manage, operate, and design the IT infrastructure of the firm. This is analogous to the firm's key business skills. Other human resource considerations, specific to IT (e.g., hiring, firing, retention, training, assessing) are also considered.

These twelve components of strategic alignment are summarized in Table 2-2.

It cannot be overstressed that, in its formulation of an IT strategy, IT management needs to be concerned with both the external and internal domains of strategic alignment. IT strategy has traditionally focused only on the internal domain of IT infrastructure and

TABLE 2-2 Strategic Alignment Model (SAM) Components[3]

I. Business Strategy

1. Business Scope   Includes the markets, products, services, groups of customers/clients, and locations where an enterprise competes as well as the competitors and potential competitors that affect the business environment.

2. Distinctive Competencies   The critical success factors and core competencies that provide a firm with a potential competitive edge. This includes brand, research, manufacturing and product development, cost and pricing structure, and sales and distribution channels.

3. Business Governance   How companies set the relationship between management, stockholders, and the board of directors. Also included are how the company is affected by government regulations, and how the firm manages its relationships and alliances with strategic partners.

II. Organization Infrastructure and Processes

4. Administrative Structure   The way the firm organizes its businesses. Examples include centralized, decentralized, matrix, horizontal, vertical, geographic, federal, and functional.

5. Processes   How the firm's business activities (the work performed by employees) operate or flow. Major issues include value added activities and process improvement.

6. Skills   H/R considerations such as how to hire/fire, motivate, train/educate, and instill corporate culture.

III. IT Strategy

7. Technology Scope   The important information applications and technologies.

8. Systemic Competencies   Those capabilities (e.g., access to information that is important to the creation/achievement of a company's strategies) that distinguishes the IT services.

9. IT Governance   How the authority for resources, risk, conflict resolution, and responsibility for IT is shared among business partners, IT management, and service providers. Project selection and prioritization issues are included here.

IV. IT Infrastructure and Processes

10. Architecture   The technology priorities, policies, and choices that allow applications, software, networks, hardware, and data management to be integrated into a cohesive platform.

11. Processes   Those practices and activities carried out to develop and maintain applications and manage IT infrastructure.

12. Skills   IT human resource considerations such as how to hire/fire, motivate, train/educate, and culture.

processes and the components of these domains. This inward-looking focus ignores the imperative of an outward-looking focus to meet the demands of a changing, turbulent business and IT marketplace. Traditional IT strategies, with their inward focus, have failed to meet the needs of business. Another, related model—Luftman's Strategic Alignment Maturity Assessment Model (discussed in the next chapter)—will be referenced with regard to mechanisms of IT strategy *implementation capability*.[3]

▪▪▪ Functional Integration

A second, and equally important dimension of strategic alignment is the concept of functional integration. Ideally, the choices made in the IT strategic domain will shape and support the business' strategic choices. Given the potential of IT to offer competitive business advantage, the linkage among the externally focused choices made by IT management and the strategic choice made by senior business management needs to be explicitly accounted for. In the Strategic Alignment Model, the linkage between the IT strategy domain and the business strategy domains is called *strategic integration*.

In similar fashion, the internal domains of business and IT need to be integrated such that the capabilities of the IT infrastructure support the requirements and expectations of the business' organizational structure and processes. This level of linkage is called *operational integration*.

Figure 2-2 illustrates the Strategic Alignment Model and the relationships among the domains of strategic fit and functional integration. Ideally, any IT strategy planning process needs to take into account both these dimensions.

▪▪▪ Planning IT Strategy

The objective of the remainder of this chapter will be to describe a process that can be used by IT management to envision and plan an aligned IT strategy. The process is heavily grounded in the concepts underlying the Strategic Alignment model and has the objective of providing the tools and techniques to assist IT management in formulating an IT strategy that can enable or drive the transformation of the business. As an aid to students, Appendix A of this chapter includes a case study of a fictitious financial services organization. This case study will be used in this chapter and the chapters on Strategic Alignment maturity and IT governance to illustrate how to use the frameworks and concepts discussed in these chapters.

At a high level, the model in Figure 2-3 describes the IT strategy formulation process using the context of the Strategic Alignment Model framework.

At a high level, the IT strategy formulation process can be described as a sequence of activities that transforms the current alignment state to the envisioned future alignment state. The future alignment state has the required condition that it enables sustainable competitive advantage. In addition, the benefits obtained from this envisioned future state of strategic alignment must be amenable to measurement in business terms.

The process of transforming the firm's state of strategic alignment—and the consequent formulation of IT strategy—is done through the following set of activities, some of which are iterative. It must be stressed that these activities require the active commitment and participation of senior business and IT management to be effective. One important precondition for success before using these techniques, however, is that firms should have developed or be in the process of developing a vision and strategy that defines and communicates where the firm is headed. Ideally, the creation of this vision and strategy should involve the IT organization and its senior management. Organizations that actively involve IT staff in the development of a vision and strategy for future markets, products, and services strengthen the degree of strategic alignment among business and IT and better prepare their firms for acceptance of the process innovations that must necessarily follow in order to successfully compete in today's turbulent markets.[14, 3]

▪▪▪ IT Strategy Planning Activities

1. **Obtaining An Executive Champion/Sponsor.** It cannot be emphasized too strongly that the sponsorship of a senior executive is essential to the successful formulation of IT strategy. The first step in the formulation of a viable IT strategy is obtaining the sponsorship of a senior business executive for the effort (Figure 2-4). Establishing harmony among IT and business strategies is a key

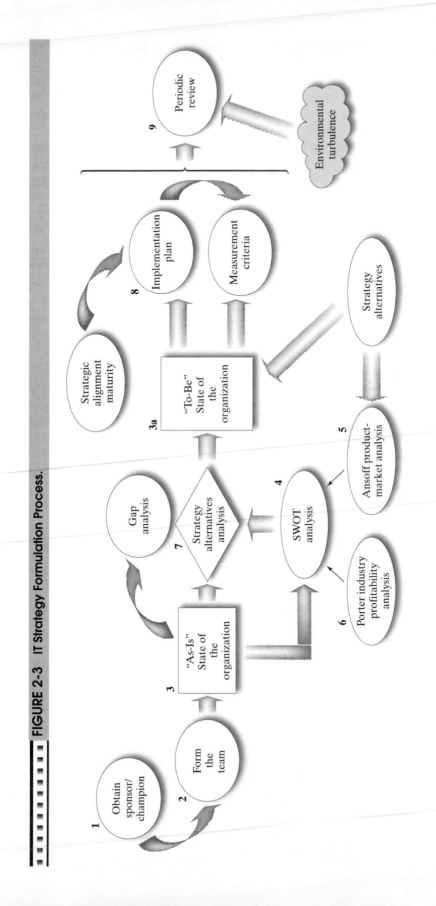

FIGURE 2-3 IT Strategy Formulation Process.

41

FIGURE 2-4 Obtaining an Executive Sponsor/Champion.

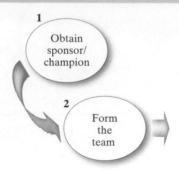

objective of the firm; having the *right* senior executive sponsor is essential for successful IT strategy formulation. Ideally, the champion/sponsor should have many of the following attributes:

- **Power:** The organizational power to legitimize the change with targets
- **Pain:** A level of discomfort with the status quo that makes change attractive
- **Vision:** A clear definition of what change must occur
- **Resources:** A thorough understanding of the organizational resources (time, money, people) necessary for successful implementation and the ability and willingness to commit them
- **The Long View:** An in-depth understanding of the effect the change will have on the organization
- **Sensitivity:** The capacity to fully appreciate and empathize with the personal issues major change raises
- **Scope:** The capacity to understand thoroughly the size of the group to be affected by the change
- **A Public Role:** The ability and willingness to demonstrate the public support necessary to convey strong organizational commitment to the change
- **A Private Role:** The ability and willingness to meet privately with key individuals or groups to convey strong personal support for the change
- **Consequence Management Techniques:** Preparation to reward promptly those who facilitate acceptance of the change or to express displeasure with those who inhibit it
- **Monitoring Plans:** The determination to ensure that monitoring procedures are established that will track both the transition's progress and problems
- **Willingness to Sacrifice:** The commitment to pursue the transition, knowing that a price will most often accompany the change
- **Persistence:** The capacity to demonstrate consistent support for the change and reject any short-term action that is inconsistent with long-term change goals.

Although the terms are sometimes used interchangeably, it is important to note here the difference in roles between a champion and a sponsor:

- A *champion* describes a person—typically a senior business executive—who has the compelling vision of the "To Be" state of affairs. They serve as the project evangelist, and are trusted and respected by the organization implementing the change. This person is willing to lend his/her organizational credibility and reputation to the idea being advocated and communicates this vision of a future state to all levels of the organization. Ideally, a champion has the "power" and "vision" attributes described above. Champions tend to be more focused on communicating the vision and driving the organization to embrace his/her vision.

- A *sponsor* describes a person—typically a business executive—who uses his/her organizational influence to obtain the resources needed to implement the champion's vision. Sponsors tend to be more focused on the aspects and details of strategy execution, including monitoring of progress against objectives. They typically are the source of funding and play an important role in ensuring cross-organizational change.

2. **Forming the Team.** IT management should form a team of senior *decision-makers* from the corporate IT and (if applicable) business unit IT organizations as well as senior business management from the business units. Minimally, the corporate CIO and respective divisional or business unit CIO's should be part of this team. It is also strongly recommended that the team include the corporate systems architect if the organizational structure accommodates this role. It is strongly recommended that the team be constrained in size to about a dozen members for effectiveness. Once formed, the team and the sponsor/champion must quickly establish a joint understanding and commitment to the goals and objectives of IT strategy formulation and its outcomes.

3. **Describing the "As-Is" State.** This activity describes the current state of the firm in terms of the components of the Strategic Alignment Model (see Figure 2-5 and Table 2-2). The "As-Is" description of the firm needs to specify both the business strategy and organization infrastructure and process domains as well as the domains that pertain to the IT organization (i.e., IT strategy and IT infrastructure and processes). An example of an "As-Is" description of the Financial Resources Management Firm, Inc. (a fictitious investiment management firm) is provided in the example at the end of this chapter (see also the sidebar earlier in this chapter titled, *"Baxter/American Hospital Supply Set the Standard for Coordination for Competitive Advantage."*

   The "As-Is" becomes a baseline for senior business and IT management for articulating the firm's strategic positioning in the marketplace for the business as well as understanding the firm's strategic positioning in the IT marketplace. The "As-Is" also reveals relationships among the components of the firm's business and IT strategies that are usually not well understood or taken for granted. For example, IT governance is a component of strategic alignment that is very important to the effective execution of an aligned IT strategy, yet this component is often a source of misalignment through the effects of culture on governance mechanisms.

▪ ▪ ▪ ▪ ▪ ▪ ▪ ▪ ▪ ▪ ▪ **FIGURE 2-5** Describing the "As-Is" state of the organization.

■■■■■■■■■■■ **FIGURE 2-6** Performing the SWOT Analysis.

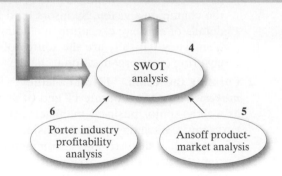

The creation of the "As-Is" is best done in a series of facilitated interactive workshop sessions that include no more than 10 to12 participants from senior business and IT management. Ideally, business participants should include the CEO, COO, President, CFO, and the heads of the strategic business units or divisions of the firm. From the IT organization, attendees in these sessions should include the CIO, Enterprise IT Architect, Chief Knowledge Officer (if the firm has designated a CKO) and CIO's of the respective divisions or SBU's. This team will become the core of the "Strategic Management Team" that will drive the formulation of an aligned IT-business strategy.

4. **"SWOT" Analysis.** This set of activities is designed to generate a detailed analysis of the strengths, weaknesses, opportunities, and threats confronting the firm (see Figure 2-6). The SWOT analysis identifies factors that may affect desired future outcomes for the company. The SWOT model is based on identifying the organization's internal strengths and weaknesses, and threats and opportunities of the external environment. These, along with considerations of company values and culture, lead to the creation, evaluation, and choice of an aligned IT strategy.

The SWOT's objective is to recommend strategies that ensure the best alignment between the external environment and internal situation. The SWOT analysis is informed by several important analysis methods that will influence the analysis and selection of strategy alternatives. The SWOT Analysis is usually presented in the format illustrated by the case study in Appendix 2A with representative examples for illustrative purposes only:

The *"Strengths"* component of the "SWOT" analysis is formed by two important components from the "as-is" description of the firm:

- **Distinctive Competencies.** The critical success factors and core competencies that provide a firm with a potential competitive edge. These include brand, research, manufacturing and product development, cost and pricing structure, and sales and distribution channels.
- **Systemic Competencies.** Those capabilities (e.g., access to information about customers) and critical success factors that are important to the creation/ achievement of a company's strategies and that distinguish the IT services of the firm.

Agreement by the Strategic Planning team on the strengths of the firm is essential to creating an effective strategy, because these *differentiating possibilities* of strengths can be leveraged to generate sustainable competitive advantage. A firm's strengths can include:

- Ability to control distribution of products
- Ability to drive or influence industry standards
- Ability to innovate (and continuously innovate)
- Brand and reputation
- Customer intimacy and customer knowledge
- Enabling of new strategies
- First to market or proprietary products
- Price and cost leadership
- Proprietary technology
- Skilled employees

The *"Weaknesses"* component of the SWOT analysis comes from observation of the existing business and IT problems of the firm. Weaknesses (gaps) will also emerge from observation of the gaps that exist between the desired state of IT-business alignment (the "To-Be" state) and the current state of IT-business alignment (the "As-Is" or current state). As with the strengths, the weaknesses that need to be recognized are concerned with those that affect a firm's strategic positioning and its ability to compete effectively. Some examples of the weaknesses the Strategic Planning Team needs to catalog in this exercise include:

- Ability to withstand risk
- Adequately trained staff
- Change management
- Decreasing demand for products or services
- Inadequate finances
- Narrow product line (or a product line that's too broad)
- Obsolete products, facilities or processes
- Poor brand image or quality
- Poor skills
- Price and cost laggards
- Vulnerability to price changes or suppliers
- Weak market share or distribution system
- Weak management team

As the SWOT analysis also examines opportunities and threats from external sources, two other frameworks are used to populate the "SWOT." They will influence IT management's evaluation of strategy alternatives: the Ansoff "Product/Market Matrix" and Porter's "Five Forces" Model of Industry Profitability (see Figure 2-7).[21, 22]

5. The *"Opportunities"* component of the SWOT analysis is completed by using the Ansoff Matrix—a model that examines the competitive positioning of a firm based on the relationship between new and current products (or services) in new

▪ ▪ ▪ ▪ ▪ ▪ ▪ ▪ ▪ ▪ ▪ ▪ FIGURE 2-7 The Porter and Ansoff analyses as inputs to the SWOT.

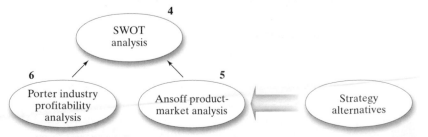

▪▪▪▪▪▪▪▪▪▪▪ **FIGURE 2-8   The Ansoff Product/Market Matrix.**

	Present product	New product
Present market	Market penetration 1.	Product development 2.
New market	Market development 3.	Diversification 4.

Ansoff, I., *Strategies for Diversification*, Harvard Business Review, September-October 1957, pp. 113–124.

and current markets. The Ansoff Matrix (illustrated in Figure 2-8) is especially useful in examining growth strategies and becomes the starting point in the IT strategy planning process for examining strategic alternatives and the enabling impact of IT on these strategies.

As seen in Figure 2-8, each quadrant of the Ansoff Matrix can be described as a different market positioning strategy for the company (Table 2-3). When examining each of these market positioning strategies, senior IT management and its business counterparts should consider the following questions regarding growth strategies:

- Where should we look for the next wave of profitable growth opportunities, and where might they lead?
- How should we select from the several different opportunities before us today?

TABLE 2-3   Ansoff Matrix Positioning Strategies[21]

Market Positioning Strategy	*Strategy Objectives/Implications*
Market Penetration (current products, current markets)	• Use where there is still potential for an existing product/service in the current marketplace • Deepen and broaden relationships with existing customers to sell more of what the organization currently sells to them
Market Development (current products, new markets)	• Taking existing products/services into a new geographical or market sector • Developing understanding of where existing products or services may meet the needs of new customers
Product Development (new products, current markets)	• Useful for selling new products/services to a strong existing customer base; Reintermediation • Anticipating the needs of the existing customer base by building greater customer intimacy
Diversification (new products, new markets)	• High risk, 'new business' approach where the organization does not have the strength of a known customer base or track record in the new product/service • Defining new markets or market niches with innovative new products

▪▪▪▪▪▪▪▪▪

- What defines our business boundaries, and what is the measure of leadership that we strive to attain?
- Is it time to consider redefining fundamentally some of the elements of our core business, and how should we go about doing that?

Each quadrant of the Ansoff Matrix should be populated to comprehensively examine strategic options available to the firm. As an active partner in establishing an aligned IT-business strategy, IT management must play an active, credible role in formulating IT strategic options appropriate to each quadrant. To do this, IT management should use established credible methods, models, or frameworks to help guide and stimulate thinking about various strategy options.

As only one example of a strategic method or framework that can be used to explore strategic options for the Ansoff Matrix, the "Delta Model"[23] is especially useful as a method that examines strategic options around the basis of how a firm competes—either through "Best Product," "System Lock-in," or "Customer Economics" (making it easier for the customer to do business with the firm). The "Delta Model" envisions these strategic options as the apexes of a triangle (see Figure 2-9). A firm's decision to position its business strategy close to a particular apex of the triangle (e.g., "Customer Solutions") will demand specific responses in the domains of IT strategy and related IT infrastructure and processes that will "fit" the required changes in the firm's organizational infrastructure. For example, the firm's decision to position itself near the "Customer Solutions" apex of the Delta Model implies an IT strategy that will enhance linkages to customers— anticipating customer needs and working jointly with customers to develop new products and services that meet specific customer needs.

IT strategies that enable this strategic positioning would be oriented towards integrated Supply Chain Management ("SCM") and Customer Relationship Management ("CRM") or collaborative planning and forecasting using Web-based technologies. Supply chain transparency (allowing customers to schedule products on a "make to order" basis) might be one outcome of this strategic position as would vendor-managed inventory allowing the supplier to manage the customer's warehouse and inventory, thus enabling the supplier to gain invaluable knowledge about the customer's needs.

▪▪▪▪▪▪▪▪▪▪▪ **FIGURE 2-9   The Delta Model.**

Competition based on system economics: complementor lock-in, competitor lock-out, proprietary standard

System lock-in

Customer solutions
Competition based on customer economics: reducing customer costs or increasing profits

Best products
Competition based on product economics: low cost or differentiated position

Source: Wilde and Hax, Sloan Management Review, Winter 1999.

The Delta Model is only one of many models, frameworks, and methods that can be used by IT management as tools to assist in the generation of possible IT strategies. Some selected examples of other models and frameworks are included in this text in Table 2-4 for reference, but the reader should recognize that these are merely a fraction of the models available for use to address real-world strategic issues. Before using any model or framework it is recommended that the model or framework be thoroughly researched from the original source (i.e., the original book, research paper, or other source). Excellent sources of frameworks and models include peer-reviewed journals such as *Sloan Management Review*, *IBM Systems Journal*, *Harvard Business Review*, *MIS Quarterly*, *California Management Review*, *Academy of Management Review*, *Communications of the Association of Information Systems*, and publications of similarly high academic reputation. Books by respected management or strategy authors (e.g., Mintzberg, Porter, Drucker, to name but a very few) are also excellent sources for frameworks and models that can assist the process of exploring strategic options.

TABLE 2-4   Selected Examples of Strategy Frameworks and Models

FRAMEWORK OR MODEL CLASSIFICATION (Business or IT strategy issue being addressed)	*NAME OF FRAMEWORK OR MODEL*	*AUTHOR(S)*	*APPLICABILITY*
Business Strategy	BCG Matrix[26]	Boston Consulting Group	Allows a multidivisional organization to manage its portfolio of businesses by examining the relative market share position and the industry growth rate of each division
	Generic competitive strategies[27]	Porter	Identifying and thinking about the fundamental ways in which an organization may compete
	Types of competitive advantage being pursued[28]	Strickland, Thompson	Classifies types of strategies by market target and product focus
	Reinventing core strategies[29]	Hamel	Examines the question of whether an organization can re-invent its strategy
E-Business Strategy	E-Business value matrix[30]	Hartman, Sifonis	Categorize e-business strategies by examining criticality to the business vs. "newness" of strategy or practice
	Stages of supply chain optimization[31]	Poirier	Examines internal and external factors influencing the evolution and optimization of supply chains through four stages
	Building an infomediary business[32]	Hagel, Singer	Model for building an e-business based on information as the principal generator of value
Human Resources	People Capability Maturity Model (PCMM)[33]	Carnegie-Mellon, Software Engineering Institute	Model for integrating and maturing organizational workforce practices
	Six leadership styles at a glance[34]	Goleman	Characteristics of leadership styles in organizations and their impact

(continues on the next page)

TABLE 2-4 (continued)

FRAMEWORK OR MODEL CLASSIFICATION (Business or IT strategy issue being addressed)	NAME OF FRAMEWORK OR MODEL	AUTHOR(S)	APPLICABILITY
IT Strategy	Product-Process Change Matrix[35]	Pine	Examination of mass customization as an emerging manufacturing paradigm and implications for IT strategy
	Framework for assessing the strategic importance of an IT system[36]	McFarlan, Cash	Application prioritization and application portfolio management
	The generic value chain[37]	Porter	Understanding relationship between technology development and components of the business value chain
	IT strategic alignment based on STROBE-STROIS[38]	Chan, Huff	Relationship between business and IT strategic orientation and business-IT strategic alignment
	Corporate goals for IT[39]	Tallon, Kraemer, Gurbuxani	Examine the focus of IT in organizations relative to strategic goals and effectiveness
	Seven sources of innovation[40]	Drucker	Examines generic sources of innovation for competitive advantage
Measurement	Balanced score card[41]	Kaplan, Norton	Method for creating strategy-focused measurements for success
	Benchmarking process steps[42]	Camp	Identifies the steps required to establish and run a benchmarking program
Organizational Change	Organization change process[43]	Belasco	Process for creating and sustaining change in organizations
	Seven organizational change propositions[44]	Segars, Dean	Explores organizational change as a function of organizational/ technological discontinuity

▮▮▮▮▮▮▮▮▮

6. The "*Threats*" portion of the SWOT analysis employs an expanded model of "Porter's Five Forces Model of Industry Profitability" to identify the threats facing a firm from external sources (see Figure 2-10).[22] Porter argues through the model that industry profitability is a function of five distinct external forces that shape competition, and not just a function of the traditional rivalry between firms. Identifying and understanding the five forces that influence competition within a firm's industry provides powerful insight regarding the strategic positioning a firm should consider in countering external threats. Briefly, the threats are:

- **Rivalry Between Existing Firms.** This is usually the strongest of the threats. Market growth, the number of competing firms in the industry, or commodity-like products are just some of the factors that effect rivalry among industry competitors. Each firm employs its own strategy in an effort to gain competitive advantage. IT management, working with its business partners, should identify the firms that it considers to be its current competitors as well as identify the strategic threats each one of these traditional rivals poses to the firm. The "As-Is" competitors in the Business Strategy, Business Scope components of the Strategic Alignment Model is a source for this information. As an example, if the firm being analyzed is part of the financial services sector, existing

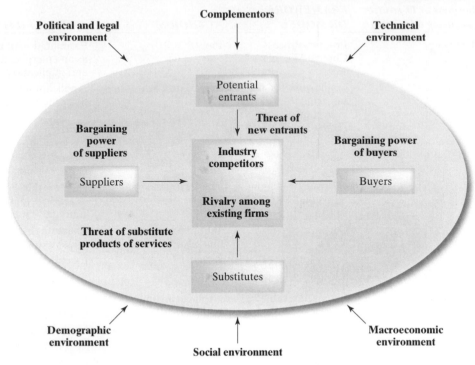

The five competitive forces that determine industry profitability

Porter, M., *Competitive Strategy and Competitive Advantage,* Free Press, 1980.

industry rivals would include companies such as Citigroup, JP Morgan Chase, Fidelity, Prudential Financial, etc. Each of these firms employs IT as a means of enabling competitive strategy, and the identification of these traditional rivals as well as the broad outlines of their competitive strategy (including their IT strategy) is an important element of assessing threats to any organization.

- **The Risk of New Entrants.** New entrants to a market bring new production capacity, new business models, a desire to establish a secure place in the market, and (sometimes) substantial resources with which to compete. More importantly to existing firms, new entrants have the potential to transform entire industry sectors because they do not carry the organizational and administrative "baggage" of existing business models with them. In planning IT strategy, IT management should be aware that IT tends to lower barriers to entry into new markets, thus making the firm potentially vulnerable to this form of competition. Examples of new entrants that changed the basis of competition in their industry sectors include Dell, Cisco, and Amazon.com, all of whom leveraged IT to reduce barriers to entry into what had been stable, predictable markets. Conversely, an IT strategy that is based on the use of proprietary technology that is hard to duplicate may give a firm a window of opportunity to temporarily exploit weaknesses in an established industry.
- **The Power of Buyers.** Buyers are a strong competitive force when they are large and purchase a sizeable portion of a firm's output, when they buy in large volumes, when *their* costs of switching are low, when they can purchase from

several sellers, or when the industry's product is standardized or commoditized. Buyers become even stronger when they can exert leverage over price, quality, service, or other terms and conditions of the sale. The As-Is customers in the Business Strategy and Business Scope components of the Strategic Alignment Model are a source for this information.

- **The Power of Suppliers.** Suppliers are a strong competitive force when it is costly for the firm to switch suppliers, when suppliers have an excellent brand reputation, when switching suppliers may affect the quality of the firm's products or services, when they do not have to contend with substitutes, or when the demand for their products is high. Delivery reliability is also a key indicator of the strength of suppliers. The As-Is Governance in the Business Strategy, Distinctive Competencies component of the Strategic Alignment Model is a source for this information.

- **The Threat of Substitutes.** Represents the likelihood of a customer being able to substitute the firm's product for another—completely different—product or service from a company *outside the industry*. The strength of competition from substitutes is affected by the ease with which a buyer can change over to the substitute. In the mid '90's would anyone pay for a bottle of water instead of Coke? Another example of a substitute product or service for package delivery services might be self-organized delivery or artificial sweeteners substituted for sugar. IT managers should respond to the threat of substitutes by raising the costs (or the perceived costs) to the customer of switching products. One way of raising perceived switching costs is to adopt IT strategies that raise intimacy levels with the customer so high that the customer finds it difficult or undesirable to disentangle themselves from the firm's processes. IT strategies based on the concepts of Integrated CRM/SCM and collaborative forecasting, planning, and scheduling (CPFAR) are one approach to raising switching costs.

It is also important for an organization to consider the impact of its environment on any strategy it is considering. Environmental factors that should be considered (see Figure 2-10) include:

- **Political and Legal Environment.** The regulatory, political, and legal environment can have substantial impact on an organization's markets and its customers. Strategy alternatives need to factor in such considerations as the stability of governments (especially important when considering strategies that involve globalization), the strength of legal institutions and business law (especially troublesome in the former Soviet Union and African nations), the impact of regulatory requirements on producing or distributing certain products (e.g., pharmaceutical regulatory requirements in the U.S. may restrict what can be produced or marketed if the product has a therapeutic purpose). Health and environmental regulations may also have substantial impact on the assessment of a strategy alternative. Trading agreements between nations or supranational organizations such as the WTO may help or hamper a strategy.

- **Macroeconomic Environment.** Strategy alternatives need to consider the state of the overall economy in short and long terms, especially when considering alternatives that involve international scope. Considerations such as the direction of interest rates, the availability of capital, the level of inflation, the state of the industry sector, long-term prospects for the Gross Domestic Product and recent trends of the equity and bond markets may substantially impact the choice of a strategy alternative.

- **Social Environment.** Planners must consider the social implications of a strategy alternative, especially when considering other countries. Considerations such as the dominant religion, prevailing attitudes on the use of foreign products and services, the impact of language on the diffusion of the product or service into the local economy, the amount of leisure time consumers have (and how they spend it), the roles of men and women in the society, and the attitudes of countries and people on environmental ("green") issues can play an important part in the acceptance or rejection of a product or service. For example: how will a society that is used to haggling over the price of a product respond to a "no haggle" Web site?

- **Technical Environment.** Technology is critical for competitive advantage and is a major driver of globalization. In evaluating strategy alternatives one needs to consider whether technology (not just IT) can drive the development and distribution of products faster and more cheaply; whether it can offer customers access to products and services that are more innovative and flexible; how distribution mechanisms may be changed by technology (e.g., Amazon.com); or how technology may effect improved communication between organizations and their customers and suppliers. One also has to consider the availability or ubiquity of technology in certain target markets and how its absence may impact the delivery of products or services to customers (e.g., how effective might a Web-based strategy be if an important target market has poor telecommunications infrastructure).

- **Demographic Environment.** The different stratifications of the consumer population should also be taken into account for any strategy alternative. Considerations such as the expected lifetimes of the consumer, distribution of wealth, religious preference (and its impact on product acceptance), distribution of age groups and their preferences, birthrate trends, etc., can dramatically influence the success of an organization's strategy. For example: a globalization strategy alternative for a major toy distributor should consider the impact of falling birth rates in western Europe and Japan before it makes major investments in physical infrastructure in these countries.

7. Strategy Alternatives Analysis. This step in the IT Strategy Formulation Process involves several discrete activities (Figure 2-11):

▪▪▪▪▪▪▪▪▪▪▪ FIGURE 2-11 **Strategy Alternatives Analysis.**

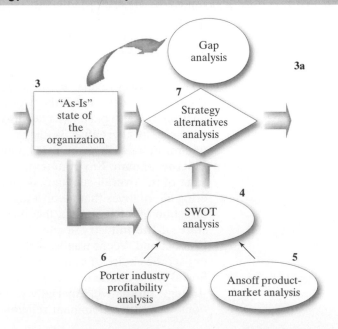

    a. The threat posed by each one of these forces should be ranked on a scale of 1 (weak) to 5 (strong) to determine the role each competitive threat plays in the IT strategies identified in the Ansoff Matrix. In general, a company whose strategy and market position provide a good defense against the forces can earn above-average profits even when some or all of the five forces are strong.

    b. The most promising 3-4 IT strategies identified in the Ansoff Matrix should be identified as those having:

        1. The lowest potential vulnerabilities to the threats identified in the Competitive Forces analysis

        2. The highest potential ability to leverage the strengths identified in the SWOT Analysis

        3. The highest potential to close the gaps identified between the "As-Is" and "To-Be"

        4. The highest potential to mitigate the weaknesses identified in the SWOT Analysis

    c. Articulating the potential costs and benefits of each of the alternative IT strategies. This should not be an exhaustive time-consuming exercise, but should attempt to quantify broad dimensions of cost and benefit (and dependencies) for each IT strategy such that reasonable conclusions can be reached about the attractiveness of a particular approach.

    d. Another technique that can be used to evaluate alternative IT strategies is scenario planning. Scenario planning involves mapping each gap identified in comparing the "As-Is" state of the firm to the "To-Be" envisioned state of the firm on a 2 by 2 matrix that examines the "Probability of Occurrence" of each scenario against its "Potential Impact to the Firm" (see Figure 2-12). Strategy scenarios that have high probability of occurrence (e.g., product obsolescence) and a high impact on the firm (e.g., customers leaving because of substitute products) are those that demand the firm's immediate attention in the form of a transforming (and aligned) IT-business strategy. The mechanisms and structures of IT governance and the processes involved in making decisions about IT investments directly influence how the scenario planning is translated to action. Chapter 11 addresses the subject of IT governance and its impact on the management of IT organizations.

8. IT Strategy Implementation Planning. Much to the distress of strategy theorists, who focus on the *formulation* of strategies, surveys of strategy practioners have revealed that less than 10 percent of effectively formulated strategies are actually implemented! Further analysis on the failure of CEO's concluded that their failures were due less to the formulation of brilliant strategies than it was to the lack of ability of their firms to *execute* the strategy.[24]

▪▪▪▪▪▪▪▪▪▪▪ **FIGURE 2-12 Scenario Planning Grid.**

Impact on firm

		High	Medium	Low
Probability of occurrence	High	High priority		
	Medium		Medium priority	
	Low			Low priority

▪▪▪▪▪▪▪▪▪▪▪ FIGURE 2-13   IT Strategy Implementation Planning.

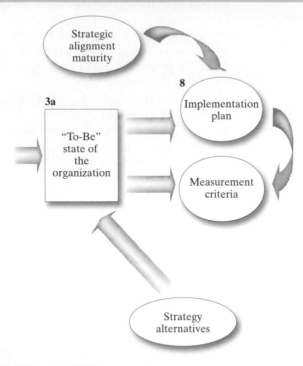

The ability of a company to *execute* strategy can, in many cases, be more important than the strategy itself. Why is this the case?

The implementation of an aligned IT strategy (see Figure 2-13) is contingent on several factors, foremost among them being the active commitment and engagement of senior business management, the "strategic maturity" of the organization (which will be extensively discussed in Chapter 3—Strategic Alignment Maturity) and the implementation of effective tools for measuring the impact of those strategies. Considerations on planning for the implementation of an IT strategy include:

- **Commitment and engagement of senior business management.**   This is an absolutely essential component and precondition for the successful implementation of an aligned IT strategy. Extensive studies on the enablers and inhibitors to strategic alignment have repeatedly identified support of senior management as the leading enabler to achieving strategic alignment. It is equally important to note that the *absence* of close relationships with IT is the leading *inhibitor* to strategic alignment![4] It is therefore critical for IT management to have secured the active commitment of senior business management throughout the process of formulating the IT strategy, that is, *prior to* the implementation planning. Securing the commitment of senior management to an IT strategy that has transformational potential *cannot* happen through after-the-fact presentations of charts, graphs, and analyses. Commitment and active engagement are emotional in nature, and can only happen if IT management and senior business management have shared a common journey through the strategy formulation process. Having partnered in the creation of a shared strategy vision, enlisting the support and championship of senior business management to implement the IT strategy should not be an issue.
- **Strategic Alignment Maturity.**   This concept, to be discussed in greater detail in Chapter 3, addresses the ability of organizations to adapt their IT and

▪▪▪▪▪▪▪▪▪▪▪▪ **FIGURE 2-14** **Measurement and Periodic Review.**

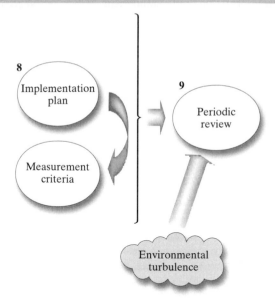

business strategies in a harmonious fashion. Early research on the topic of Strategic Alignment Maturity[3] has shown that organizations that demonstrate a high level of alignment maturity appear to be more capable of executing strategy as critical enablers of strategic alignment such as effective partnership, communications, and governance manifest themselves through business–IT relationships and practices.

- **Adoption of Measurement Criteria.**   The execution of strategy must be measurable in meaningful business terms, and the most effective measurement systems and criteria are those that can measure the effects of implementing strategy in several different dimensions. The Chapters on "The Value of IT" (Chapter 14) and "Measuring and Controlling" (Chapter 13) contain extensive discussions of this important area.

9. Periodic Review.   All strategies need to be periodically reviewed (see Figure 2-14) to ensure that:

- The initial assumptions made about markets and external forces are still correct, especially if the company exists in an environment of significant uncertainty
- Implementation plans are on schedule and meeting established milestones
- Measurements are being captured and reported and that these measurements support ongoing alignment of IT strategy with the business

These reviews are part of the IT Governance considerations that will be described in Chapter 11.

REVIEW QUESTIONS ▪▪▪▪▪▪▪

1. Describe the concept of Strategic Alignment and its importance to a company.
2. What are the major domains of the Strategic Alignment Model and their components?
3. What are the domains of the Strategic Alignment Model and how are they interrelated?
4. Name some examples of enablers and inhibitors to Strategic Alignment.
5. Name some symptoms of lack of alignment between IT and the business.
6. What are "distinctive competencies" and "systemic competencies" and why are they important to the formulation of an IT strategy?
7. How might a company use IT to drive its business strategy?

8. What are the forces that affect profitability in any industry? Why is it important to understand them?

9. What techniques or tools might be used to measure the effectiveness of an IT strategy?

10. How can the maturity of an organization's strategic alignment impact its ability to execute an IT strategy?

DISCUSSION QUESTIONS ▪▪▪▪▪▪▪

1. Why isn't a business strategy sufficient for a company to determine how it can leverage IT for competitive advantage?

2. Does your company have an IT strategy? Has it been published or otherwise communicated? What are its strategic goals and objectives?

3. What do you think are your company's distinctive competencies?

4. Does your IT function have systemic competencies? What are they?

5. What do you think are the main external threats facing your company?

AREAS FOR RESEARCH ▪▪▪▪▪▪▪

1. Read Henderson and Venkatraman's paper on the concept of Strategic Alignment.[20]

2. Business strategy challenges of the 21st Century— Read Drucker's book on looming strategic challenges for business and IT management.[45]

3. IT as an enabler of strategic transformation—read Davenport's book on the innovation of new processes (with IT as a strategic enabler).[14]

CONCLUSION ▪▪▪▪▪▪▪

This chapter has discussed the concept of Strategic Alignment as the key framework for creating effective IT strategies and the importance of creating an aligned IT strategy for competitive advantage. This chapter has also underscored the importance of IT as an enabler of business transformation—providing business with the capa-bility to enter new markets or create dramatically new products or services. This chapter has also provided an approach grounded in the concepts of the Strategic Alignment Model for IT management to consider using in generating aligned IT-business strategies.

REFERENCES ▪▪▪▪▪▪▪

[1] Drucker, Peter, *Peter Drucker on the Profession of Management*, Harvard Business School Press, 1998.

[2] Luftman, J., Lewis, P., and Oldach, S., *Transforming the Enterprise: The Alignment of Business and Information Technology Strategies*, IBM Systems Journal, 32(1), 1993.

[3] Luftman, J., *Addressing Business-IT Alignment Maturity*, Communications of the Association for Information Systems, December 2000.

[4] Luftman, J., Papp, R., and Brier, T., *The Strategic Alignment Model: Assessment and Validation*, In Proceedings of the Information Technology Management Group of the Association of Management (AoM) 13th Annual International Conference, Vancouver, British Columbia, Canada, August 2-5, 1995, 57-66.

[5] Rockart, J., Earl, M., and Ross, J., *Eight Imperatives for the New IT Organization*, Sloan Management Review, (38)1, 43-55, (1996).

[6] Rumelt, R., Schendel, D., and Teece, D., *History of Strategic Management*, Chapter 1, Fundamental Issues in Strategy, Harvard Business School Press, 1994.

[7] Collins, J., and Porras, J., *Built to Last—Successful Habits of Visionary Companies*, Harper Collins, 1994.

[8] Slater, R., *The New GE*, Homewood, IL: Richard D. Irwin, 1993.

[9] Kaplan, R., and Norton, D., *The Strategy Focused Company*, Harvard Business School Press, 2001.

[10] May, J., *Analysts Are Predicting Doom of AT&T*, Sunday Star-Ledger, November 25, 2001.

[11] Davenport, T., *Information Ecology*, Oxford University Press, 1997.

[12] Hartman, A., and Sifonis, J., *Net Ready—Strategies for Success in the E-conomy*, McGraw-Hill, 2000.

[13] Kenney, M., *The Temporal Dynamics of Knowledge Creation in the Information Society*, in "Knowledge Emergence," ed. by I. Nonaka and T. Nishiguchi, Oxford University Press, 2001.

[14] Davenport, T., *Process Innovation: Reengineering Work Through Information Technology*, Harvard Business School Press, 1993.

[15] Keene, P., *The Process Edge*, Harvard Business School Press, 1997.

16 Coase, R., *The Nature of the Firm*: Origins, Evolution, and Development, eds. Oliver Williamson and Sidney Winter, Oxford University Press, 1993.

17 Earl, M. J., *Corporate Information Systems Management*, Homewood, Ill: Richard D. Irwin, Inc., 1993.

18 Henderson, J. C., Venkatraman, N., and Oldach, S., *Aligning Business and IT Strategies*, in "Competing in the Information Age—Strategic Alignment in Practice," ed. by J. Luftman, Oxford University Press, 1996.

19 Schein, E., *Three Cultures of Management: The Key to Organizational Learning*, Harvard Business Review, Sloan Management Review, 38(1), Fall 1996.

20 Henderson, J. C. and Venkatraman, N., *Strategic Alignment: Leveraging Information Technology for Transforming Organizations*, IBM Systems Journal, 32(1), 1993.

21 Ansoff, I., *Strategies for Diversification*, Harvard Business Review, September-October 1957, pp. 113–124.

22 Porter, M., *Competitive Strategy and Competitive Advantage*, Free Press, 1980.

23 Hax, A., and Wilde, D., *The Delta Model: Adaptive Management for a Changing World*, Sloan Management Review, Winter 1999.

24 Charan, R., and Colvin, G., *Why CEO's Fail*, Fortune, June 21, 1999.

25 Luftman, J., *Competing in the Information Age— Strategic Alignment in Practice*, ed. by J. Luftman, Oxford University Press, 1996.

26 Boston Consulting Group, *Perspectives on Experience*, Boston, MA: The Boston Consulting Group, 1974.

27 Porter, Michael E., *Competitive Advantage: Creating and Sustaining Superior Performance*, The Free Press, 1985.

28 Thompson, A., and Strickland, J., *Strategic Management: Concepts and Cases, Eleventh Edition*, McGraw-Hill, 1999.

29 Hamel, G., *Leading the Revolution*, Harvard Business School Press, August 2000.

30 Hartman, A., and Sifonis, J., Ibid.

31 Poirier, C., *Advanced Supply Chain Management*, Berrett-Koehler Publishers, 1999.

32 Hagel, J., and Singer, M., *Net Worth*, Harvard Business School Press, 1999.

33 Carnegie Mellon Software Engineering Institute, *www.sei.cmu.edu/products/publications/sei.series.html*.

34 Goleman, D., *Six Leadership Styles at a Glance*, Harvard Business Review, 2000.

35 Pine, J., *Mass Customization—The New Frontier in Business Competition*, Harvard Business School Press, 1993.

36 McFarlan, W., and Cash, J., in Ward, J., Griffiths, P., and Whitmore, P., *Strategic Planning for Information Systems*, Wiley, 1990.

37 Porter, Michael E., Ibid.

38 Chan, Y., Huff, S., *Investigating Information Systems Strategic Alignment*, Proceedings of the International Conference on Information Systems, December 1993.

39 Tallon, P., Kraemer, K., Gurbaxani, V., *Executives' Perceptions of the Business Value of Information Technology: A Process Oriented Approach*, Journal of Management Information Systems, Spring 2000.

40 Drucker, P., *Innovation and Entrepreneurship*, HarperBusiness, 1993.

41 Kaplan, R., and Norton, D., Ibid.

42 Camp, Robert C., *Business Process Benchmarking: Finding and Implementing Best Practices*, ASQC Quality Press, 1995.

43 Belasco, J., *Teaching the Elephant to Dance: Empowering Change in Your Organization*, Plume, 1991.

44 Segars, A., and Dean, J. in Zmud, R., *Framing the Domains of IT Management*, Pinnaflex Educational Resources, 2000.

45 Drucker, P., *Management Challenges for the 21st Century*, HarperBusiness, 1999.

Appendix 2A

▪▪▪▪▪▪▪▪ **Case Study** ▪▪▪▪▪▪▪▪
Financial Risk Management, Inc.

Background

Financial Risk Management, Inc. ("FRM" as it is known on Wall Street) is a boutique asset management company headquartered in New York City. Established in 1982, it manages over $200 billion of assets for wealthy individuals (individual portfolios must be greater than $10 million) and institutions. FRM is highly profitable and has a reputation for disciplined research and a rigorous approach to risk management. FRM's investments include assets in fixed income securities (e.g., bonds and mortgages), equity (e.g., stock) and derivatives (e.g., options). FRM is a private company and employs 5,000 people in offices in New York, London, Boston, Chicago, San Francisco, Miami, and Phoenix. FRM's assets under management have grown at a compound annual rate of 17% over the last five years and its founders—all former Stanford University graduates—have been prominently featured in publications like *Fortune*, *The Wall Street Journal*, and *The Economist* for their expertise in applying chaos theory-based algorithms to the area of investment risk management.

FRM's principal expertise is in the area of fixed-income products such as mortgages, loans, bonds, and securitized instruments (e.g., "privately placed" fixed income securities that represent loans made to corporations). FRM's ability to "pick the winners" among the thousands of products offered on the capital markets is based on their Risk Management Division's services and the technology-based tools they use to perform advanced analysis. FRM's risk management analysis capabilities are so advanced and so well regarded that FRM now provides fee-based risk management analysis services to other financial institutions with aggregate assets of over $1 trillion. FRM's success was even more notable given the highly competitive asset management market that had become dominated by giants such as Citigroup, Goldman-Sachs, and Morgan Stanley-Dean Witter.

FRM is headquartered in New York and is organized into several operating divisions:

- Risk management services
- Investment research
- Product development
- Marketing
- Trading services (institutional and individual)
- Operations administration (i.e. the "back office")
- Client services
- Finance and systems
- Administrative services

FRM had a culture of granting a significant level of autonomy to the heads of the divisions that generated revenue. Division heads often managed to their own profit and loss statements (P&L's) and were responsible directly to the Executive Committee (headed by the three founders of FRM) for identifying revenue and profit "bogies"(targets) and establishing and executing the plans needed to meet those targets. FRM's founder encouraged innovative thinking and risk-taking by the division heads, but held them accountable for success (and failure).

FRM's senior management recognized the potential of its risk management tools to generate additional revenue for the firm, but senior management also acknowledged that despite their success in this particular niche, FRM's name recognition was not high, especially in Europe and the emerging Asian and Eastern European markets. Bud Weisman, the head of the Risk Management Division for FRM, was a believer in the power of information technology as a driver of FRM's current success. Weisman also believed that FRM had significant opportunity to tie itself closer to its existing customer base of large U.S. asset management firms using IT to provide integrated trading services with advanced risk management analytics capability using FRM's unique risk management algorithms. He also believed that these capabilities would provide FRM with a compelling "hook" to market FRM's services to new overseas markets.

FRM decided that the best course of action, given FRM's name recognition issue (i.e., "branding") and the capital investment required to develop, launch, and service a new IT-based investment product to a global market was to partner with another firm. Ideally, this partner should bring several critical capabilities to the table for the partnership to be effective:

- A well-recognized name or "brand" in the financial markets FRM wants to penetrate
- Expertise in the development and support of financial services and IT products
- Global presence
- Expertise in the subject matter areas of asset management, risk management, trading systems development, IT product development, and customer support

After a search and negotiations that lasted the better part of 2001, FRM consummated an alliance with BigRock Financial Services, Inc., a global financial services company with assets under management of over $3 trillion for individual and institutional clients. BigRock Financial offered its clients a wide range of products and services including group and individual insurance, annuities, brokerage, underwriting of corporate securities, private placements (securitized corporate loans) and risk management. BigRock employed over 5,000 people in offices in the Americas, Asia, and Europe and was aggressively opening new offices in the emerging Pacific Rim nations.

BigRock found FRM's offer to partner in an IT-based solution to provide integrated trading and risk management tools to institutional investors highly attractive, as BigRock's own risk management services had not met industry benchmarks for reducing various measures of investment risk. BigRock, in fact, had drawn considerable negative press when it failed to adequately estimate environmental and regulatory risks associated with mining and paper products investments several major clients were considering in the Amazonia region of South America. BigRock felt that a partnership with FRM would give BigRock access to FRM's risk management analytic tools as part of a co-branded product and enhance their own reputation as a provider of integrated asset management services.

Information Technology at FRM, Inc.

FRM's founders—Drs. John Symon, Steven Mollen, and Ram Mohan—were true believers in the power of technology to transform the business. All three were intimately familiar with information technol-

ogy, including the use of advanced computational and statistical algorithms, relational databases, super computers and advanced networking technologies. Each had advanced degrees in business, statistical analysis, and investment theory and all were enthusiastic about applying IT to create a competitive edge. Each of the founders took a keen interest in applying technology to further the strategic interests of FRM and they were not shy about offering their opinions to anyone about the latest advances in information technology. All three often spoke at professional conferences about FRM's innovative use of technology as an enabler of FRM's business model.

FRM had established a formal CIO function in 1998, which reports to the chief financial officer. Charles Moone, the current CIO, was hired from a prestigious Wall Street investment banking firm. Moone was brought in to bring formal IT management discipline to FRM's technology practices. FRM's executive management had finally realized that the cost of IT had reached unsustainable levels. FRM's executive management had earlier commissioned a leading management-consulting firm to benchmark their IT costs against industry norms. The consulting firm reported that FRM's proportion of spending on IT-related services was twice as high as comparable industry benchmarks. The consultants also reported that they were concerned about FRM's ability to respond to their client's increasing demands for services that were Web-enabled or that relied on other emerging technologies such as wireless.

IT investment decisions at FRM are typically made by the division heads, who have their own application development and support staff, and are informally discussed among the division heads and the founders at each Monday's executive management meeting. The CFO is part of the Executive Committee, but the CIO is not. It was notoriously difficult to obtain consensus concerning decisions regarding enterprise-wide IT projects, as their funding had to come from each division head's budget.

IT infrastructure (e.g., shared servers, telecommunications equipment, shared applications such as word processing, e-mail services and spreadsheet software, mainframe computers, etc.) is the province of the Office of the CIO, which sets standards for its acquisition and use and is responsible for its operation. The divisions, however, have considerable latitude with respect to selecting, installing, and operating hardware and software that meets "local" requirements for use. It was not uncommon to see Sun Microsystems equipment (and associated infrastructure) being used in the trading and investment research divisions while the marketing division used Macintosh and the "back office" used IBM mainframe equipment.

Moone found the IT staff generally upbeat about working for FRM as their compensation had reflected FRM's favorable profitability, but turnover was higher than Moone expected it to be. Digging deeper after some "one on one" sessions with the staff and IT management, Moone uncovered issues he knew would have to be addressed. These issues included IT career paths (there were no formal career paths), IT's position in the "pecking order" at FRM (many felt that unless one had an MBA in investment management from a prestigious school they were treated as "second class citizens"), the view by many in the business that IT was a "cost of doing business" and not a strategic player, and the difficulty IT had getting decisions on major cross-divisional initiatives.

Despite these issues, IT had a strong track record for providing service to FRM's divisions. Major applications included:

- **TOPS.** Real-time trade order processing
- **MAPS.** Money management application
- **RiskMan.** Advanced risk management processor (FRM's proprietary risk analysis algorithms and database)
- **ClientView.** An integrated customer relationship database that allowed FRM to see all client relationships across all products and divisions
- **OneFRM.** FRM's integrated Customer Relationship Management (CRM) system and call center

FRM's IT staff had strong technology skills in Oracle database management, statistics (and statistical algorithms), data mining and modeling software, and CRM technology. Many IT staff also had developed a strong working knowledge of the business (or at least the functions of the divisions they were part of). UNIX was the principal operating system in use for many of the servers used by FRM, but Linux was coming on strong for some of the more esoteric risk management analysis applications. FRM's IT staff was well-versed in Web-based technologies as well, having developed and implemented a proprietary Web portal on the FRM intranet to facilitate the sharing of risk management data and analytics among the various FRM offices and risk management analysts over FRM's wide area network (WAN).

Using This Case

The information contained in the "FRM" case has been used to populate the analysis frameworks discussed in this chapter as components of developing an IT strategy. This case will also be used in the chapters on Strategic Alignment Maturity and IT governance.

The reader should be aware that while the case is fictitious, the issues discussed in the case are real and have been observed (unfortunately, too often) by the authors and are not merely exaggerations for illustrative purposes.

The "As-Is" for FRM, Inc.

The "As-Is" for both the business and IT components of the organization reflect the *current* state of the organization (see Table 2A-1).

TABLE 2A-1   "As-Is" for FRM, INC.

	Business As-Is
Business Scope	• *Products/Services*: Manages over $200 billion of assets for wealthy individuals and institutions • *Direct Customers*: Wealthy individuals with assets over $10 million Risk managers of financial institutions (e.g., other asset management firms) with assets under management of $1 trillion or more • *Indirect Customers*: Pension plans (they use asset management companies to manage their investments) • *Competitors*: Citigroup, JP Morgan Chase, Goldman-Sachs, Prudential Financial, Deutsche Bank, BigRock Financial Highly competitive, fragmented marketplace—giant firms as well as small boutiques
Distinctive Competencies*	• Outstanding brand reputation in its current client base • Proprietary risk management analysis algorithms • Excellent risk management track record
Business Governance	• Privately owned • Board of Directors: increase revenues by 6% annually • Executive committee for operations and capital decisions • SEC • ERISA • Deloitte & Touche—auditors • Autonomous business units
Administrative Structure	• Divisional structure—9 operating divisions by product • Decentralized—high degree of autonomy of revenue-generating division heads
Key Processes	• Financial planning • Risk management analysis • Risk management data collection • Investment portfolio • Marketing • Customer relationship management
Human Resources	• Large number of MBAs in management • Advanced financial planning • Statistical analysis • Substantial founder influence on existing operations and culture

▪▪▪▪▪▪▪▪▪

* These should be taken directly from the "Strengths" component of the "SWOT" analysis

TABLE 2A-2   The Information Technology "As-Is" for FRM, Inc.

Information Technology As-Is

Technology Scope

Key Applications:
- **TOPS.** Real-time trade order processing
- **MAPS.** Money management application
- **RiskMan.** Advanced risk management processor (FRM's proprietary risk analysis algorithms and database)
- **ClientView.** An integrated customer relationship database that allowed FRM to see all client relationships across all products and divisions
- **OneFRM.** FRM's integrated Customer Relationship Management (CRM) system and call center

Key Technologies:
- IBM parallel-processor mainframe
- Sun SPARC stations
- Oracle RDBMS
- Intranet Web portal for analytics
- Wide area network (Cisco routers)
- Advanced data mining and modeling software for risk analysis
- CRM

Systemic Competencies
- Integrated information about clients and product preferences
- Founders' comfort level with IT as an enabler of business value

IT Governance
- Decentralized IT
- Weak corporate IS function—primarily responsible for non-revenue-generating functions
- CIO reports to CFO
- CIO not part of executive management committee
- Application development staff report to divisions
- IT capital investment decisions made by division heads and approved by executive management
- IT perceived as a cost of doing business by many

IT Architecture
- Mainframe-parallel processor for corporate functions and heavy analysis
- WAN linking all offices
- Web-based information portal for limited knowledge sharing
- Heterogeneous web and client-server based architectures supporting divisional requirement
- Common CRM platform
- Heterogeneous data mining and statistical analysis tools used by divisions

Key Processes
- Application systems development
- Application systems enhancement/maintenance
- Statistical analysis programming
- Data modeling, design and database support
- All 38 IT processes (see Chapter 9)

Human Resources
- Technology management
- Data mining
- Statistical applications development and support
- Customer support
- Customer training

Swot Analysis for FRM, Inc.

TABLE 2A-3 SWOT Analysis for FRM, Inc.	
Strengths	*Weaknesses*
• Outstanding brand reputation in its current client base • Strong revenue and profitability picture • Proprietary risk management analysis algorithms • Excellent risk management track record • Integrated information about clients and product preferences • Founders' comfort level with IT as an enabler of business value	• Poor brand recognition outside current client base • Lack of presence in overseas markets • Private company—may lack sufficiently "deep pockets" for major capital investments • Weak enterprise IT standards and architecture • Perception by many managers that IT is a "cost of doing business" • CIO reports to the CFO, reinforcing "IT as a cost" image • CIO not a part of executive management • IT investment decisions made locally and without discussion with CIO • Client perception that FRM is slow to adopt new technologies • Low IT employee morale • Lack of experience in developing and supporting global IT-based products
Opportunities	*Threats*
FRM's opportunities should be reflected in the Ansoff analysis (illustrated later in this appendix). They are partially summarized here for illustrative purposes: • Enhance global presence via a partnership with an existing firm for risk management products • License risk management algorithms to other firms • Create and market an artificial intelligence tool for asset portfolio management • Provide customized online risk management analysis services for existing publications and newsletters	Threats to FRM should be reflected in the Porter diagram (illustrated later in this appendix). They are partially summarized here for illustrative purposes: • Turbulent financial markets • Concern about impact of terrorism on equity investments • Unfamiliarity with potential overseas market cultures and investment management needs • Other firms with deep(er) pockets may copy FRM's offerings

Ansoff Analysis for FRM, Inc.

TABLE 2A-4 Ansoff Analysis for FRM, Inc.		
	Current Products	*New Products*

Current Markets	• Offer incentives and promotions to current individual and institutional customers:
	• Targeted discounts to customers based on volume of business
	• Television promotions on Sunday morning news and "talking head" programs
	• Sponsorship of financially oriented programs and TV stations:
	    Wall Street Week
	    CNBC
	    CNN Financial
	• Risk management seminars for individuals
	• License proprietary risk management algorithms to other firms
		• Risk analysis newsletters customized to individual risk tolerances
		• Risk analysis consulting services
		• Web hosting of risk management capability (i.e., become an "ASP")
		• Alliance with prestigious insurance companies in profitable niche markets (e.g., USAA)
		• Offer risk management and statistical analysis education through an alliance with a major university
		• Alliance with major asset management company to offer integrated trade entry/risk management product in U.S.

New Markets	• Alliances or partnerships with asset management firms in EU and Asian markets • Go " downscale" to market current services to individuals with less than $10 million in assets • Alliances or partnerships with major financial services firms seeking to create an asset management/risk management offering (e.g., Schwab) • Expand into EU and Asia-Pacific with current products	• Alliance with major asset management company to offer integrated trade entry/risk management product • Develop own integrated trade entry/risk management product for EU and Asia • Offer risk management data collection and data mining services to global asset management firms

▪▪▪▪▪▪▪▪▪

TABLE 2A-5 Expanded Porter Industry Profitability Analysis for FRM, Inc.

Dimension	*Factors*
Traditional Competitors	• Full-service broker-dealers: 　　Merrill Lynch 　　Morgan Stanley Dean Witter 　　AXA Financial 　　UBS Paine Webber • Insurance/Financial Services Companies: 　　Prudential Financial 　　Charles Schwab 　　BigRock Financial 　　AIG • Banks/Investment Management Companies: 　　Citigroup 　　Goldman Sachs 　　Solomon Smith Barney 　　JP Morgan Chase
Suppliers	• Technology Suppliers: 　　IBM 　　Microsoft 　　Sun 　　Dell 　　Cisco 　　Telco's (e.g., Verizon, AT&T) • Consultants/auditors (subject matter experts): 　　"Big 5" such as KPMG, Deloitte & Touche • Exchanges/trading institutions: NYSE, NASD, AMEX
Buyers	• Wealthy individual investors • Taxable and tax-exempt institutional investors • Certified financial planners
Substitutes	• Publicly available risk management algorithms • Proprietary risk management strategies • Texts on risk management
Potential New Entrants	• Microsoft • Reuters • Bloomberg • AIG
Political and Legal Environment	• Increased concern about risk-adjusted investment performance • Increased focus by SEC and media on accounting practices • Impact of terrorism on risk tolerance of clients
Demographic Environment	• Untapped individual investor market in emerging "power" economies (e.g., South Korea) • Anticipated drain on 401k assets starting in 2010 due to "baby boomers" retiring
Complementors	• Market desire for integrated investment product suites

(continues on the next page)

TABLE 2A-5 (continued)

Dimension	Factors
Technical Environment	• Growing adoption of data mining and other advanced analytics technologies • Steady growth and penetration of Web-based applications as a de facto "standard" for inter-organizational interface • Technically sophisticated individual clients
Social Environment	• Turbulent times—fear of investment loss due to uncontrollable events (e.g., terrorist attack) • Reduced tolerance for risk
Macroeconomic Environment	• Turbulent market conditions—mixed signals regarding growth or recession in almost all markets • Flight to "risk free" or reduced risk investments

Readers should refer to the chapter on Strategic Alignment Maturity (Chapter 3) for a completed Strategic Alignment Maturity Analysis.

The "To-Be" for FRM, Inc.

The "To-Be" for both the business and IT components of the organization (Table 2A-6) reflect the envisioned *future* state of the organization. As such, only those things that have changed from the "As-Is" state are reflected in order to highlight the changes. The changes reflected in each matrix are the result of decisions made by executive management with input from the CIO.

TABLE 2A-6 "To-Be" for FRM, Inc.

	Business To-Be
Business Scope	• Provider of integrated trading and portfolio management product to institutional investors as part of an alliance with BigRock Financial Services • New offices in Tokyo, Hong Kong, Singapore, and Seoul
Distinctive Competencies*	• Unique ability to provide clients with integrated real-time trading and risk analytics capability • Integrated client relationship management across FRM and BigRock client base
Business Governance	• Alliance with BigRock Financial Services • Foreign regulations governing financial services in new Asian offices
Administrative Structure	• New trading and risk analytics products division
Key Processes	• Alliance (partnership) management • Contract negotiation • Contract monitoring
Human Resources	• New emphasis on entrepreneurial skills (business development)

* These should be taken directly from the "Strengths" component of the "SWOT" analysis

The Information Technology "To-Be" for FRM, Inc.

TABLE 2A-7   The Information Technology "To-Be" for FRM, Inc.

Information Technology To-Be	
Technology Scope	*Key Applications:* • TRAPS—integrated investment portfolio management, risk analytics and trading applications suite *Key Technologies:* • Data mining/OLAP (Online Analytics and Processing) • Advanced risk management analytics • RDBMS • The Web
Systemic Competencies	• Integration of client trading and portfolio history with real-time data mining • Knowledge management (of client preferences, history) • Personalization of applications

I/T Governance	• Technology and development alliance with BigRock Financial
	 • CIO part of the executive management committee meetings
	 • CIO reports to CEO or President
	 • Formal IT steering committee
	 • Formal career path for IT professionals
	 • Divisional IT staff have reporting line to CIO:
	     Career path
	     Professional development
	 • Establishment of IT architecture and standards group
	 • Establishment of emerging technologies group
	 • IT support established for new Asian offices

I/T Architecture	• Oracle RDBMS • Web-based infrastructure (hardware and software) to facilitate communications
Key Processes	• Alliance management (i.e., with BigRock) • Systems integration
Human Resources	• Emphasis on data mining and analytics skills • Rotational assignments of IT professionals into business

CHAPTER 3

Strategic Alignment Maturity

"Maturity is when your long-term intentions shape your short-term focus"
—ANONYMOUS

"Maturity is the capacity to endure uncertainty."
—J. FINLEY

Preview of Chapter

As discussed in Chapter 2, strategic alignment focuses on the activities that management performs to achieve cohesive goals across the IT (Information Technology) and other functional organizations (e.g., finance, marketing, H/R, manufacturing). Therefore, alignment addresses both how IT is in harmony with the business, and how the business should, or could, be in harmony with IT. Alignment evolves into a relationship where the function of IT and other business functions adapt their strategies together. Achieving alignment is evolutionary and dynamic. It is a process that requires strong support from senior management, good working relationships, strong leadership, appropriate prioritization, trust, and effective communication, as well as a thorough understanding of the business and technical environments. Achieving and sustaining alignment demands focusing on maximizing the enablers and minimizing the inhibitors that cultivate alignment. Once the maturity of business-IT alignment is understood, an organization can identify opportunities for enhancing the harmonious relationship of business and IT.

What we will examine in this chapter:

- The importance of IT and business alignment
- Enablers and inhibitors to alignment
- The concept of alignment maturity and the importance of alignment maturity
- The five levels of Strategic Alignment Maturity
- The six criteria that characterize each level of Strategic Alignment Maturity
- Assessing Strategic Alignment Maturity
- Strategic Alignment as a process

▪▪▪ Introduction

Business-IT alignment refers to applying Information Technology in an appropriate and timely way, in harmony with business strategies, goals, and needs. It is still a fundamental concern of business executives. This definition of alignment addresses:

1. How IT is aligned with the business, and
2. How the business should or could be aligned with IT.

Mature alignment evolves into a relationship where IT and other business functions adapt their strategies together. When discussing business-IT alignment, terms like *harmony*, *linkage*, *fusion*, and *integration* are frequently used synonymously with the term *alignment*. It does not matter whether one considers alignment from either a business-driven perspective or from an IT-driven perspective; the objective is to ensure that the organizational strategies adapt harmoniously. The evidence that IT has the power to transform whole industries and markets is strong;[1-10] good examples of this have been Amazon.com, Dell, Cisco, and Fed Ex to name but a few organizations. Important questions that need to be addressed include the following:

- How can organizations assess alignment?
- How can organizations improve alignment?
- How can organizations achieve mature alignment?

The purpose of this chapter is to present an approach for assessing the maturity of a firm's business-IT alignment. Until now, none was available. The alignment maturity assessment approach described in this chapter provides a comprehensive vehicle for organizations to evaluate business-IT alignment in terms of where they are and what they can do to improve alignment. The maturity assessment applies the previous research that identified enablers/inhibitors to achieving alignment,[10, 11] and the empirical evidence gathered by management consultants who applied the methodology that leverages the most important enablers and inhibitors as building blocks for the evaluation. The maturity assessment is also based on the popular work done by the Software Engineering Institute, Keen's "reach and range," and an evolution of the Nolan and Gibson stages of growth.[12-14]

▪▪▪ Why Alignment Is Important

The importance of alignment has been well known and well documented since the late 1970s.[10, 15-23] Over the years, it persisted among the top-ranked concerns of business executives. Alignment seems to grow in importance as companies strive to link technology and business in light of dynamic business strategies and continuously evolving technologies.[2, 24] Importance aside, what is not clear is how to achieve and sustain harmony between business and IT, how to assess the maturity of alignment, and what the impact of misalignment might be on the firm.[25] The ability to achieve and sustain this synergistic relationship is anything but easy. Identifying an organization's alignment maturity provides an excellent vehicle for understanding and improving the business-IT alignment process.

Alignment continues to be important today as companies strive to link technology and business. Alignment addresses both:

- Doing the right things (effectiveness), and
- Doing things right (efficiency).[2, 10, 24]

In recent years, a great deal of research and analysis focused on the linkages among business and IT,[2, 3, 10, 11, 26] the role of partnerships among business and IT management,[13,27] and the need to understand the transformation of business strategies resulting from the competitive use of IT.[28,29] Firms need to change not only their business scope, but also their infrastructure as a result of IT innovation.[30-32] Much of this research, however, was conceptual. Empirical studies of alignment[22,34-35] examined a single industry and/or firm. Conclusions from such empirical studies are potentially biased and may not be applicable to other industries. It was the lack of consistent results across industries, across functional position, and across time that was the impetus for defining a vehicle for assessing business–IT alignment maturity. The components of the strategic alignment model were discussed in the previous chapter.

Alignment maturity evolves into a relationship where the function of IT and other business functions adapt their strategies together. Achieving alignment is evolutionary and dynamic. IT requires strong support from senior management, good working relationships, strong leadership, appropriate prioritization, trust, and effective communication, as well as a thorough understanding of the business and technical environments. Achieving and sustaining alignment demands focusing on maximizing the enablers and minimizing the inhibitors that cultivate the integration of IT and business.

Alignment of IT strategy and the organization's business strategy is a fundamental principle advocated for over a decade.[8,40,41] IT investment has been increasing for years as managers look for ways to successfully manage and integrate IT into the organization's strategies. As a result, IT managers need to:

- Be knowledgeable about how the new IT technologies can be integrated into the business and its different technologies and architectures
- Be privy to senior management's tactical and strategic plans
- Be present when corporate strategies are discussed, and
- Understand the strengths and weaknesses of the technologies in question and the corporate-wide implications[41]

Several proposed frameworks assess the strategic issues of IT as a competitive weapon. They have not, however, yielded empirical evidence; nor do they provide a roadmap to assess and enhance alignment. Numerous studies focus on business process redesign and reengineering as a way to achieve competitive advantage with IT.[36-39] This advantage comes from the appropriate application of IT as a driver or enabler of business strategy.

▮▮▮ Strategic Alignment Maturity

The concept of alignment *maturity* as a necessary precondition for an organization's ability to implement its strategy emerged as a concept in the late 1990s. It became increasingly evident that organizations were, by and large, failing to successfully execute nominally well-defined strategic objectives (see Chapter 2). Why was this the case? Early research into this issue[43] hypothesized that an organization's ability to successfully implement strategy was related to the "level" of strategic alignment between IT and the business. Both the dynamic nature and the process of alignment reflect key organizational practices which enable (or inhibit, in their absence or misapplication) alignment.[10,43] A model of alignment maturity emerged from this research that exhibits these concepts. As Figure 3-1 illustrates, the *Strategic Alignment Maturity* model involves the following five conceptual levels of strategic alignment maturity:

1. **Initial/Ad Hoc Process.** Business and IT not aligned or harmonized
2. **Committed Process.** The organization has committed to becoming aligned
3. **Established Focused Process.** Strategic Alignment Maturity established and focused on business objectives

▪▪▪▪▪▪▪▪▪▪▪▪ **FIGURE 3-1** Strategic Alignment Maturity Summary.

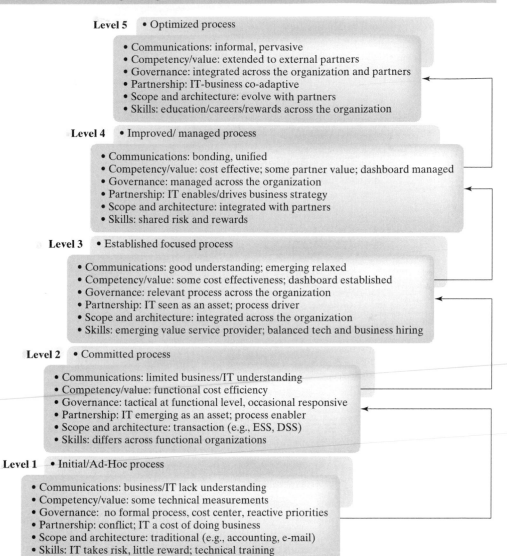

Level 5 • Optimized process

- Communications: informal, pervasive
- Competency/value: extended to external partners
- Governance: integrated across the organization and partners
- Partnership: IT-business co-adaptive
- Scope and architecture: evolve with partners
- Skills: education/careers/rewards across the organization

Level 4 • Improved/ managed process

- Communications: bonding, unified
- Competency/value: cost effective; some partner value; dashboard managed
- Governance: managed across the organization
- Partnership: IT enables/drives business strategy
- Scope and architecture: integrated with partners
- Skills: shared risk and rewards

Level 3 • Established focused process

- Communications: good understanding; emerging relaxed
- Competency/value: some cost effectiveness; dashboard established
- Governance: relevant process across the organization
- Partnership: IT seen as an asset; process driver
- Scope and architecture: integrated across the organization
- Skills: emerging value service provider; balanced tech and business hiring

Level 2 • Committed process

- Communications: limited business/IT understanding
- Competency/value: functional cost efficiency
- Governance: tactical at functional level, occasional responsive
- Partnership: IT emerging as an asset; process enabler
- Scope and architecture: transaction (e.g., ESS, DSS)
- Skills: differs across functional organizations

Level 1 • Initial/Ad-Hoc process

- Communications: business/IT lack understanding
- Competency/value: some technical measurements
- Governance: no formal process, cost center, reactive priorities
- Partnership: conflict; IT a cost of doing business
- Scope and architecture: traditional (e.g., accounting, e-mail)
- Skills: IT takes risk, little reward; technical training

Luftman, J., *Addressing Business–IT Alignment Maturity*, Communications of the Association for Information Systems, December, 2000.

4. **Improved/Managed Process.** Reinforcing the concept of IT as a "Value Center"

5. **Optimized Process.** Integrated and co-adaptive business and IT strategic planning

Each of the five levels of alignment maturity focuses, in turn, on a set of six criteria based on practices validated with an evaluation of "*Fortune 500*" companies. At this time over fifty Global 2000 organizations have participated in formally assessing their IT business alignment maturity.

The six IT–business alignment criteria are illustrated in Figure 3-2 and are described in the following section of this chapter. These six criteria are:

1. **Communications Maturity.** Ensuring ongoing knowledge sharing across organizations

▮▮▮▮▮▮▮▮▮▮▮ **FIGURE 3-2** Strategic Alignment Maturity Criteria.

Communications	**Competency/value measurements**	**Governance**
• Understanding of business by IT • Understanding of IT by business • Inter/Intra organizational learning/education • Protocol rigidity • Knowledge sharing • Liaison(s) effectiveness	• IT metrics • Business metrics • Balanced metrics • Service level agreements • Benchmarking • Formal assessments/reviews • Continuous improvement	• Business strategic planning • IT strategic planning • Organization structure • Budgetary control • IT investment management • Steering committee(s) • Prioritization process

IT Business Alignment Maturity Criteria

Partnership	**Scope and Architecture**	**Skills**

• Business perception of IT value
• Role of IT in strategic business planning
• Shared goals, risk, rewards/penalties
• IT program management
• Relationship/trust style
• Business sponsor/champion
	• Traditional, enabler/driver, external
	• Standards articulation
	• Architectural integration:
	  – Functional organization
	  – Enterprise
	  – Inter-enterprise
	• Architectural transparency, agility, flexibility
	• Manage emerging technology
		• Innovation, entrepreneurship
		• Cultural locus of power
		• Management style
		• Change readiness
		• Career crossover training
		• Social, political, trusting interpersonal environment
		• Hiring and retaining

Luftman, J., *Addressing Business–IT Alignment Maturity*, Communications of the Association for Information Systems, December, 2000.

2. **Competency/Value Measurement Maturity.** Demonstrating the value of IT in terms of contribution to the business
3. **Governance Maturity.** Ensuring that the appropriate business and IT participants formally discuss and review the priorities and allocation of IT resources
4. **Partnership Maturity.** How each organization perceives the contribution of the other; the trust that develops among the participants and the sharing of risks and rewards
5. **Scope and Architecture Maturity.** The extent to which IT is able to:
   - Go beyond the back office and into the front office of the organization
   - Assume a role supporting a flexible infrastructure that is transparent to all business partners and customers
   - Evaluate and apply emerging technologies effectively
   - Enable or drive business processes and strategies as a true standard
   - Provide solutions customizable to customer needs
6. **Skills Maturity.** Going beyond the traditional considerations such as training, salary, performance feedback, and career opportunities are factors that enhance the organization's cultural and social environment as a component of organizational effectiveness

▪▪▪▪▪▪▪▪▪▪ **FIGURE 3-3** Convergence of Strategic Alignment Gaps.

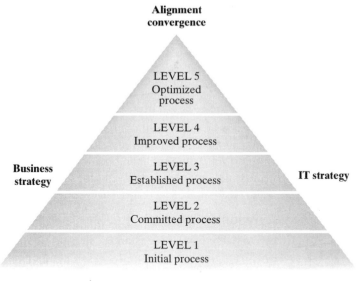

Alignment convergence

LEVEL 5
Optimized process

LEVEL 4
Improved process

Business strategy   LEVEL 3
Established process   **IT strategy**

LEVEL 2
Committed process

LEVEL 1
Initial process

Alignment gap

Luftman, J., *Addressing Business–IT Alignment Maturity*, Communications of the Association for Information Systems, December, 2000.

Knowing the maturity of its strategic choices and alignment practices make it possible for a firm to see where it stands with respect to its "alignment gaps" (see Figure 3-3) and how it can close these gaps. Once the maturity is understood, the assessment method provides the organization with a roadmap that identifies opportunities for enhancing the harmonious relationship of business and IT. The alignment process is described later in this chapter.

▪▪▪ The Six Strategic Alignment Maturity Criteria

This part of the chapter describes each of the six criteria (see Figure 3-2) that are evaluated in deriving the level of strategic alignment maturity. Examples taken from actual assessments illustrate the kinds of insights that can be identified.

Most organizations today appear to be at a Level 2+. That means that average results of the formal assessments to date (more than 50 mid-sized to large organizations) are at a Level 2 with some attributes of Level 3. This is similar to what has been found by the Carnegie software development process model that identifies the comparable stage of application development. Naturally, the objective of the Strategic Alignment Maturity model is to identify opportunities to move the organization to a higher level (i.e., Level 3 or higher) of Strategic Alignment Maturity. Keep in mind that it is not the maturity level that is the primary objective of the assessment. The primary objectives of the assessment are to understand where IT and business executives:

- agree that a criteria needs to be improved
- agree that a criteria is good, but can be better
- disagree with how good/bad a criteria is
- desire to focus their efforts to improve

When there is agreement among the participants regarding the criteria assessment, the model can be used as a roadmap to identify how alignment can be improved.

Where there is disagreement, the key stakeholders need to understand the respective perspectives of the participants and come to an agreement regarding the criteria. Then the group can proceed to use the model as a roadmap. Hence, it is not the maturity "number" that is important. It is what the organization does as a result of identifying how they can work together to improve alignment.

In the next six sub-sections we discuss each of the Strategic Alignment Maturity criteria in more detail and include examples of how they manifest themselves in organizations. These examples have been abstracted from recent research done with a number of major U.S. and global organizations.[11]

As this research is still ongoing it is not possible to share the specific names of the participating organizations. However each section illustrates specific issues of Strategic Alignment Maturity that have been uncovered in the research and identifies the industry of the participating organizations.

1. Communications

Effective exchange of ideas and a clear understanding of what it takes to ensure successful strategies are high on the list of enablers and inhibitors to alignment. Too often there is little business awareness on the part of IT or little IT appreciation on the part of the business. Given the dynamic environment in which most organizations find themselves, ensuring ongoing knowledge sharing across organizations is paramount.

Many firms choose to employ people in formal inter-unit "liaison" roles or cross-functional teams to facilitate this knowledge sharing. The key word here is "*facilitate.*" Some organizations have facilitators whose role is to serve as the sole conduit of interaction among the different units of the organization. This approach tends to stifle rather than foster effective communications. Rigid protocols that impede discussions and the sharing of ideas should be avoided.

For example, a large aerospace company assessed its communications alignment maturity at Level 2. Business-IT understanding is sporadic. The relationship between IT and the business function could be improved. Improving communication should focus on how to create the understanding of IT as a strategic business partner by the businesses it supports rather than simply a service provider. The firm's CIO made the comment that there is "no constructive partnership". However, in an interview with the firm's Director of Engineering and Infrastructure, he stated that he views his organization as a "strategic business partner." One way to improve communications and, more importantly, understanding, would be to establish effective business function/IT liaisons that facilitate sharing of knowledge and ideas.

In a second case, a large financial services company's communication alignment maturity placed it in Level 2 with some attributes of Level 1. Business awareness within IT is through specialized IT business analysts, who understand and translate the business needs to other IT staff (i.e., there is limited awareness of business by general IT staff). Awareness of IT by the firm's business functions is also limited, although senior and mid-level management is aware of IT's potential. Communications are achieved through bi-weekly priority meetings attended by the senior and middle level management from both groups, where they discuss requirements, priorities, and IT implementation.

In a third example, a large utility company's communication alignment maturity places it at a Level 2–. Communications are not open until circumstances force the business to identify specific needs. There is a lack of trust and openness between some business units and their IT team. The lack of cooperation among business-IT partners tends to create bottlenecks in meeting commitments. The poor performance of the IT team in previous years left scars that have not healed.

2. Competency/Value Measurements

Too many IT organizations cannot demonstrate their value to the business in terms that the business understands. Frequently business and IT metrics of value differ. A balanced "dashboard" that demonstrates the value of IT in terms of contribution to the business is needed.

Service levels that assess the commitment of IT to the business often help. However, the service levels have to be expressed in terms that the business understands and accepts. The service levels should be tied to criteria (see Criteria 4—Partnership, below) that clearly define the rewards and penalties for surpassing or missing the objectives.

Frequently organizations devote significant resources to measuring performance factors. However, they spend much less of their resources on taking action based on these measurements. For example, an organization that requires a Return on Investment (ROI) analysis before a project begins, but that does not review how well objectives were met after the project was deployed provides little value to the organization. It is important to assess these criteria to understand (1) the factors that lead to missing the criteria; and (2) what can be learned to improve the environment continuously.

For example, a large aerospace company assessed its competency/value measurement maturity to be at a Level 2. IT operates as cost center. IT metrics are focused at the functional level, and Service Level Agreements (SLAs) are technical in nature. One area that could help to improve maturity would be to add more business-related metrics to SLAs to help form more of a partnership between IT and the business units. Periodic formal assessments and reviews in support of continuous improvement would also be beneficial.

A large software development company assessed its competency/value measurement maturity at Level 3. Established metrics evaluate the extent of service provided to the business functions. These metrics go beyond basic service availability and help desk responsiveness, evaluating such issues as end-user satisfaction and application development effectiveness. The metrics are consolidated onto an overall dashboard. However, because no formal feedback mechanisms are in place to react to a metric, the dashboard lacks effectiveness in maintaining an open communication path between business and IT.

At a large financial services company, IT competency/value was assessed at a Level 2 because they use cost efficiency methods within the business and functional organizations. Balanced metrics are emerging through linked business and IT metrics, and a balanced scorecard is provided to senior management. Service level agreements are technical at the functional level. Benchmarking is not generally practiced and is informal in the few areas where it is practiced. Formal assessments are done typically for problems and minimum measurements are taken after the assessment of failures.

3. Governance

The considerations for IT governance were defined briefly in Figure 3-1. Ensuring that the appropriate business and IT participants formally discuss and review the priorities and allocation of IT resources is among the most important enablers/inhibitors of alignment. This decision-making authority needs to be clearly defined.

For example, IT governance in a large aerospace company is tactical at the core business level and not consistent across the enterprise. For this reason, they reported a Level 2 maturity assessment. IT can be characterized as reactive to CEO direction. Developing an integrated enterprise-wide strategic business plan for IT would facilitate better partnering within the firm and would lay the groundwork for external partnerships with customers and suppliers.

A large communications manufacturing company assessed its governance maturity at a level falling between 1 and 2. IT does little strategic planning because it operates as a cost center and, therefore, cost reduction is a key objective. In addition, priorities are reactive to business needs as business managers request services.

A large computing services company assessed their governance maturity at a Level 1+. A strategic planning committee meets twice a year. The committee consists of corporate top management with regional representation. Topics or results are not discussed nor published to all employees. The reporting structure is federated with the CIO reporting to a Chief Operating Officer ("COO"). IT investments are traditionally made to support operations and maintenance. Regional or corporate sponsors are involved with some projects. Prioritization is occasionally responsive.

4. Partnership

The relationship that exists between the business and IT organizations is another criterion that ranks high among the enablers and inhibitors. Giving the IT function the opportunity to have an equal role in defining business strategies is obviously important. However, how each organization perceives the contribution of the other, the trust that develops among the participants, ensuring appropriate business sponsors and champions of IT endeavors, and the sharing of risks and rewards are all major contributors to mature alignment. This partnership should evolve to a point where IT both enables AND drives changes to both business processes and strategies. Naturally, this demands having a good business design where the CIO and CEO share a clearly defined vision.

For example, a large software development company assessed their partnership maturity at a level of 2. The IT function is mainly an enabler for the company. IT does not have a seat at the business table, either with the enterprise or with the business function that is making a decision. In the majority of cases, there are no shared risks because only the business will fail. Indications are that the partnership criterion will rise from a Level 2 to 3 as top management sees IT as an asset, and because of the very high enforcement of standards at the company.

Partnership for a large communications manufacturing company was assessed at Level 1. IT is perceived as a cost of being in the communications business. Little value is placed on the IT function. IT is perceived only as help desk support and network maintenance.

For a large utility company, partnership maturity was assessed at a level of 1+. IT charges back all expenses to the business. Most business executives see IT as a cost of doing business. There is heightened awareness that IT can be a critical enabler to success, but there is minimal acceptance of IT as a partner.

Partnership for a large computing services company was assessed at Level 2. Since the business executives pursued e-commerce, IT is seen as a business process enabler as demonstrated by the Web development. Unfortunately, the business now assigns IT with the risks of the project. Most IT projects have an IT sponsor.

5. Scope and Architecture

This set of criteria tends to assess information technology maturity. The extent to which IT is able to:

- Go beyond the back office and into the front office of the organization
- Assume a role supporting a flexible infrastructure that is transparent to all business partners and customers
- Evaluate and apply emerging technologies effectively
- Enable or drive business processes and strategies as a true standard
- Provide solutions customizable to customer needs

Scope and Architecture was assessed at a level of 2+ at a large software development company. This is another area where the company is moving from a Level 2 to a Level 3. ERP systems are installed and all projects are monitored at an enterprise level. Standards are integrated across the organization and enterprise architecture is integrated. It is only in the area of Inter-enterprise that there is no formal integration.

A large financial services company assessed their scope and architecture at Level 1. Although standards are defined, there is no formal integration across the enterprise. At best, only functional integration exists.

6. Skills

Skills were defined in Figure 3-1. They include all of the human resource considerations for the organization and go beyond the traditional criteria of training, salary, performance feedback, and career opportunities. Also considered is the cultural and social environment of the organization. Is the organization ready for change in this dynamic environment? Do individuals feel personally responsible for business innovation? Can individuals and organizations learn quickly from their experience? Does the organization leverage innovative ideas and the spirit of entrepreneurship? These are some of the important conditions of mature organizations.

For example, a large aerospace company assesses their skills maturity at a Level 2. A definite command and control management style exists within IT and the businesses. Power resides within certain operating companies. Diverse business cultures abound. Getting to a non-political, trusting environment between the businesses and IT, where risks are shared and innovation and entrepreneurship thrive, is essential to achieve improvements in each of the other maturity tenets. Organizational behavior research has demonstrated that sharing information that is based on expertise is often the most successful approach to influencing others to cooperate and trust one another.[45]

Skills maturity at a large computing services company is assessed at a level of 1. Career crossover is not encouraged outside of top management. Innovation is dependent on the business unit, but in general is frowned upon. Management style is dependent on the business unit, but is usually command and control. Training is encouraged but left up to the individual employee.

Amazon.com—Alignment Maturity Enables Strategic Transformation

"I buy books from Amazon.com because time is short and they have a big inventory and they're very reliable."
—BILL GATES

"I cannot live without books."
—THOMAS JEFFERSON

By now, everyone knows the brand Amazon.com and its transformation of the staid world of selling books via the Internet. Even the phrase "*being Amazoned*" has entered the business lexicon as synonymous with being blindsided by an unexpected competitor that uses e-business as an enabler of strategic transformation of the business (not to mention the industry). Could Amazon.com have impacted its industry as it did without a high level of Strategic Alignment Maturity? Let's look at some facts about Amazon—using the Strategic Alignment Maturity criteria discussed earlier in this chapter—that might support the hypothesis that a high level of Strategic Alignment Maturity contributed to Amazon's ability to transform the book sales industry:

- **Communications.**   Jeff Bezos, the founder and CEO of Amazon, understood the power of IT to transform the business of selling books. Understanding of the enabling power of IT by the business (and vice versa) is part of the "warp and woof" of how Amazon operates. Without IT, there is no Amazon.com! Amazon also continuously reinforces its entrepreneurial culture with messages to its employees from Bezos and the executive team about Amazon's vision and philosophy ("being able to buy anything, anytime, anywhere at the greatest store on Earth."). Employees understand that being with Amazon is about making history.
- **Competency/Value Measurements.**   Amazon passionately focuses on the metrics of excellent customer service and the effectiveness of its advertising strategy. For example, Amazon produces a weekly report that shows the effectiveness of *each* online advertisement placed in terms of the customer traffic that was generated and the revenue for each customer visit to Amazon's site. Given the intense competition from other Web retailers, Amazon continuously monitors its performance against its rivals and adjusts business processes to set the pace rather than react to changes in the environment.
- **Governance.**   Amazon has divided its business into three segments: 1) "Mature" businesses such as books, music, and DVDs that have to "pay their way"; 2) "Early-Stage" businesses such as games, consumer electronics, and home improvement that need nurturing and feeding; and 3) Amazon's EU-based businesses. This governance model defines how decisions will be made regarding the investment Amazon will make in its IT portfolio and how that investment will be funded (i.e., self-funded or funded from outside investment). It is also clear that Jeff Bezos and a small, tightly-knit group of executives make the key strategic business and IT decisions as IT strategy *drives* the business of Amazon.com.
- **Partnership.**   It is clear from Amazon's business model—which is enabled through IT—that IT is valued as the engine of industry transformation. The high level of partnership between business and IT is driven by the vision of the CEO—Jeff Bezos—and continuously reinforced by Amazon's ability to co-adapt its IT architecture to an evolving business model. Amazon has also heavily invested in other online retailers (members of its "Commerce Network") to extend its retailing capabilities to other products such as jewelry, consumer electronics, etc.
- **Scope and Architecture.**   The scope of Amazon's business and its IT architecture is driven by the external expectations of its customers. Amazon has implemented standard IT architectures around personalization features and order fulfillment that ensure consistent service to customers around the world.
- **Skills.**   Amazon is known in the industry as a firm that aggressively recruits people who are bright, energetic, entrepreneurial, and customer-centric. Amazon's focus on hiring people who are skilled at personalization technologies and other "customer experience" technologies strengthened their brand and their reputation as being "absolutely fanatical about our

customers". Amazon also developed deep expertise in fulfillment technologies ("picking, packing, and shipping") that are essential to delivering against high customer expectations of service.

In the discussion in the next section of this chapter we look at the different levels of Strategic Alignment Maturity using the above criteria. What alignment maturity level would you assign to Amazon.com and why?

Source: Harvard Business School Case Study 9-897-128, April 9, 1998; Harvard Business School Case Study 9-800-330, September 5, 2000

▪▪▪ Levels of Strategic Alignment Maturity

Level 1—Initial/Ad Hoc Process

Organizations that are at Strategic Alignment Maturity Level 1 can be characterized as having the lowest level of Strategic Alignment Maturity. For example: in the "Communications" criteria of the model, understanding of the business by IT is very low (see Figure 3-4). Similarly, the attribute called "Understanding of IT by business" is also very low for an organization at Level 1 maturity.

It is highly improbable that these organizations will be able to achieve an aligned IT business strategy, leaving their investment in IT significantly unleveraged. See Figures 3-4, 3-5, and 3-6 for the specific criteria for Level 1.

▪▪▪▪▪▪▪▪▪▪▪▪ **FIGURE 3-4** Level 1 Strategic Alignment Maturity Criteria (communications and competency/value measurement).

Communications	
Attribute	**Characteristics**
• Understanding of business by IT	Minimum
• Understanding of IT by business	Minimum
• Inter/intra-organizational learning	Casual, ad-hoc
• Protocol rigidity	Command and control
• Knowledge sharing	Ad-hoc
• Liaison(s) breadth/effectiveness	None or ad-hoc

Competency/value measurements	
Attribute	**Characteristics**
• IT metrics	Technical; not related to business
• Business metrics	Ad-hoc; not related to IT
• Balanced metrics	Ad-hoc unlinked
• Service level agreements	Sporadically present
• Benchmarking	Not generally practiced
• Formal assessments/reviews	None
• Continuous improvement	None

Luftman, J., *Addressing Business–IT Alignment Maturity*, Communications of the Association for Information Systems, December, 2000.

▮▮▮▮▮▮▮▮▮▮▮ **FIGURE 3-5** Level 1 Strategic Alignment Maturity Criteria (governance and partnership).

Governance	
Attribute	**Characteristics**
• Business strategic planning	Ad-hoc
• IT strategic planning	Ad-hoc
• Reporting/organization structure	Central/decentral; CIO reports to CFO
• Budgetary control	Cost center; erratic spending
• IT investment management	Cost-based; erratic spending
• Steering committee(s)	Not formal/regular
• Prioritization process	Reactive

Partnership	
Attribute	**Characteristics**
• Business perception of IT; value IT	Perceived as a cost of business
• Role of IT in strategic business planning	No seat at the business table
• Shared goals, risk, rewards/penalties	IT takes risk with little reward
• IT program management	Ad-hoc
• Relationship/trust style	Conflict/minimum
• Business sponsor/champion	None

Luftman, J., *Addressing Business–IT Alignment Maturity*, Communications of the Association for Information Systems, December, 2000.

▮▮▮▮▮▮▮▮▮▮▮ **FIGURE 3-6** Level 1 Strategic Alignment Maturity Criteria (scope and architecture and skills).

Scope and architecture	
Attribute	**Characteristics**
• Traditional, enabler/driver, external	Traditional (e.g., accounting, e-mail)
• Standards articulation	None or ad-hoc
• Architectural integration:	No formal integration
– Functional organization	
– Enterprise	
– Inter-enterprise	
• Architectural transparency, flexibility	None

Skills	
Attribute	**Characteristics**
• Innovation, entrepreneurship	Discouraged
• Locus of power	In the business
• Management style	Command and control
• Change readiness	Resistant to change
• Career crossover	None
• Education, cross-training	None
• Social, political, trusting environment	Social, political, trusting
Interpersonal	Minimum
Environment	Minimum
• Attract and retain best talent	No program

Luftman, J., *Addressing Business–IT Alignment Maturity*, Communications of the Association for Information Systems, December, 2000.

Level 2—Committed Process

Level 2 organizations can be characterized as having committed to begin the process for Strategic Alignment Maturity. For example, in the "Competency/Value Measurements" criteria of the model, IT metrics (an "attribute") are focused on cost and efficiency (see Figure 3-7). Similarly, in the "Partnership" criteria of the model, the business perception of IT (again, another "attribute") is that IT is emerging as an asset to the organization.

This level of Strategic Alignment Maturity tends to be directed at local situations or functional organizations (e.g., marketing, finance, manufacturing, human resources) within the overall enterprise. However, due to limited awareness by the business and IT communities of the different functional organizations' use of IT, alignment can be difficult to achieve. Any business-IT alignment at the local level is not typically leveraged by the enterprise, but the potential opportunities are beginning to be recognized. See Figures 3-7, 3-8, and 3-9 for the specific criteria for Level 2.

Level 3—Established Focused Process

This level of Strategic Alignment Maturity concentrates governance, processes, and communications towards specific business objectives. The reason for this focus is because:

- The organization needs better decision-making processes (governance) around which business processes are able to invest scarce IT dollars
- The organization wants to focus on those business processes that generate the most long-lasting competitive advantage (and presumably, profitability), and
- The organization has to effectively communicate its vision and get "buy-in" from all employees and management

████████████████ **FIGURE 3-7**　Level 2 Strategic Alignment Maturity Criteria (communications and competency/value measurement).

Communications	
Attribute	**Characteristics**
• Understanding of business by IT	Limited IT awareness
• Understanding of IT by business	Limited business awareness
• Inter/intra-organizational learning	Informal
• Protocol rigidity	Limited, relaxed
• Knowledge sharing	Semi-structured (some formal processes) for sharing knowledge
• Liaison(s) breadth/effectiveness	Limited tactical technology based

Competency/value measurements	
Attribute	**Characteristics**
• IT metrics	Cost efficiency
• Business metrics	At the functional organization
• Balanced metrics	Business and IT metrics unlinked
• Service level agreements	Technical at the functional level
• Benchmarking	Informal
• Formal assessments/reviews	Some, typically for problems
• Continuous improvement	Minimum

Luftman, J., *Addressing Business–IT Alignment Maturity*, Communications of the Association for Information Systems, December, 2000.

▮▮▮▮▮▮▮▮▮▮▮ **FIGURE 3-8 Level 2 Strategic Alignment Maturity Criteria (governance and partnership).**

Governance

Attribute	Characteristics
• Business strategic planning	Basic planning at the functional level
• IT strategic planning	Functional tactical planning
• Reporting/organization structure	Central/decentralized, some co-location; CIO reports to CFO
• Budgetary control	Cost center by functional organization
• IT investment management	Cost-based; operations/maintenance focus
• Steering committee(s)	Periodic organized communication
• Prioritization process	Occasional responsive

Partnership

Attribute	Characteristics
• Business perception of IT value	IT emerging as an asset
• Role of IT in strategic business planning	Business process enabler
• Shared goals, risk, rewards/penalties	IT takes most of the risk with little reward
• IT program management	Standards defined
• Relationship/trust style	Primarily transactional
• Business sponsor/champion	Limited at the functional organization

Luftman, J., *Addressing Business–IT Alignment Maturity*, Communications of the Association for Information Systems, December, 2000.

▮▮▮▮▮▮▮▮▮▮▮ **FIGURE 3-9 Level 2 Strategic Alignment Maturity Criteria (skills and scope and architecture).**

Skills

Attribute	Characteristics
• Innovation, entrepreneurship	Dependent on functional organization
• Locus of power	Functional organization
• Management style	Results consensus-based
• Change readiness	Dependent on functional organization
• Career crossover	Minimum
• Education, cross-training	Minimum
• Social, political, trusting, interpersonal	Primarily transactional environment
• Attract and retain best talent	Technology focused

Scope and architecture

Attribute	Characteristics
• Traditional, enabler/driver, external	Transaction (e.g., ESS, DSS)
• Standards articulation	Standards defined
• Architectural integration:	
– Functional organization	Early attempts at integration
– Enterprise	Early attempts at integration
– Inter-enterprise	Early concept testing
• Architectural transparency, flexibility	Limited

Luftman, J., *Addressing Business–IT Alignment Maturity*, Communications of the Association for Information Systems, December, 2000.

IT is becoming embedded in the business. Level 3 leverages IT assets on an enterprise-wide basis and applications systems demonstrate planned, managed direction away from traditional transaction processing to systems that use information to make business decisions. The IT *"extrastructure"* (leveraging the inter-organizational infrastructure) is evolving with key partners. For example: in the "communications" criteria of the model, the sharing of knowledge (an "attribute") tends to be structured around key processes (see Table 2A-1). Similarly, in the "governance" criteria of the model, the prioritization process (again, another "attribute") tends to be reactive. See Figures 3-10, 3-11 and 3-12 for the specific criteria for Level 3.

Level 4—Improved/Managed Process

Organizations at Level 4 leverage IT assets on an enterprise-wide basis and the focus of applications systems is on driving business process enhancements to obtain sustainable competitive advantage. A Level 4 organization views IT as an innovative and imaginative strategic contributor to success. The enterprise-wide emphasis of Level 4 organizations breaks down the "process silos" that exist between business units in lower level organizations in order to capitalize on the information and knowledge embedded in an organization's business processes and practices. Level 4 organizations also utilize IT "hard" (i.e., hardware and software) and "soft" assets (e.g., knowledge and information about customers, competitors, products, and employee skills) by consciously deploying enterprise-wide architectures. One example of such architecture might be an enterprise intranet portal for collecting, categorizing, and sharing customer/product information as well as unstructured information (e.g., Web URLs, journal articles, etc.) about competitor products.

▪▪▪▪▪▪▪▪▪▪▪▪ **FIGURE 3-10** Level 3 Strategic Alignment Maturity Criteria (communications and competency/value measurement).

Communications	
Attribute	**Characteristics**
• Understanding of business by IT	Senior and mid-management
• Understanding of IT by business	Emerging business awareness
• Inter/intra-organizational learning	Regular, clear
• Protocol rigidity	Emerging relaxed
• Knowledge sharing	Structured around key processes
• Liaison(s) breadth/effectiveness	Formalized, regular meetings

Competency/value measurements	
Attribute	**Characteristics**
• IT metrics	Traditional financial
• Business metrics	Traditional financial
• Balanced metrics	Emerging business and IT metrics linked
• Service level agreements	Emerging across the enterprise
• Benchmarking	Emerging
• Formal assessments/reviews	Emerging formality
• Continuous improvement	Emerging

Luftman, J., *Addressing Business–IT Alignment Maturity*, Communications of the Association for Information Systems, December, 2000.

▮▮▮▮▮▮▮▮▮▮▮▮ **FIGURE 3-11** Level 3 Strategic Alignment Maturity Criteria (governance and partnership).

Governance

Attribute	Characteristics
• Business strategic planning	Some inter-organizational planning
• IT strategic planning	Focused planning, some inter-organizational
• Reporting/organization structure	Structure central/decentralized, some federation; CIO reports to COO
• Budgetary control	Cost center; some investments
• IT investment management	Traditional; process enabler
• Steering committee(s)	Regular clear communication
• Prioritization process	Mostly responsive

Partnership

Attribute	Characteristics
• Business perception of IT value	IT seen as an asset
• Role of IT in strategic business planning	Business process enabler
• Shared goals, risk, rewards/penalties	Risk tolerant; IT some reward
• IT program management	Standards adhered
• Relationship/trust style	Emerging valued service provider
• Business sponsor/champion	At the functional organization

Luftman, J., *Addressing Business–IT Alignment Maturity*, Communications of the Association for Information Systems, December, 2000.

▮▮▮▮▮▮▮▮▮▮▮▮ **FIGURE 3-12** Level 3 Strategic Alignment Maturity Criteria (skills and scope and architecture).

Skills

Attribute	Characteristics
• Innovation, entrepreneurship	Risk tolerant
• Locus of power	Emerging across the organization
• Management style	Consensus; results based
• Change readiness	Recognized need for change
• Career crossover	Dependent on functional organization
• Education, cross-training	Dependent on functional organization
• Social, political, trusting interpersonal environment	Emerging among IT and business
• Social, political, trusting environment	Emerging valued service provider
• Attract and retain best talent	Tech/business focus; retention program

Scope and architecture

Attribute	Characteristics
• Traditional, enabler/driver, external	Expanded scope (e.g., business process enabler)
• Standards articulation	Emerging enterprise standards
• Architectural integration:	Integrated across the organization
– Functional organization	Integrated for key processes
– Enterprise	Emerging enterprise architecture
– Inter-enterprise	Emerging with key partners
• Architectural transparency, flexibility	Focused on communications

Luftman, J., *Addressing Business–IT Alignment Maturity*, Communications of the Association for Information Systems, December, 2000.

This level of Strategic Alignment Maturity demonstrates effective governance and services that reinforce the concept of IT as a value center. For example, in the "communications" criteria of the model, the sharing of knowledge (an "attribute") is institutionalized. Similarly, in the "scope and architecture" criteria of the model, the organization has established enterprise standards. See Figures 3-13, 3-14 and 3-15 for the specific criteria for Level 4.

FIGURE 3-13 Level 4 Strategic Alignment Maturity Criteria (communications and competency/value measurement).

Communications

Attribute	Characteristics
• Understanding of business by IT	Pushed down through organization
• Understanding of IT by business	Business aware of potential
• Inter/Intra-organizational learning	Unified, bonded
• Protocol rigidity	Relaxed, informal
• Knowledge sharing	Institutionalized
• Liaison(s) breadth/effectiveness	Bonded, effective at all internal levels

Competency/value measurements

Attribute	Characteristics
• IT metrics	Cost effectiveness
• Business metrics	Customer-based
• Balanced metrics	Business and IT metrics linked
• Service level agreements	Enterprise-wide
• Benchmarking	Routinely performed
• Formal assessments/reviews	Formally performed
• Continuous improvement	Frequently

Luftman, J., *Addressing Business–IT Alignment Maturity*, Communications of the Association for Information Systems, December, 2000.

FIGURE 3-14 Level 4 Strategic Alignment Maturity Criteria (governance and partnership).

Governance

Attribute	Characteristics
• Business strategic planning	Managed across the enterprise
• IT strategic planning	Managed across the enterprise
• Organizational reporting structure	Federated; CIO reports to COO or CEO
• Budgetary control	Investment center
• IT investment management	Cost effectiveness; process driver
• Steering committee(s)	Formal, effective committees
• Prioritization process	Value add, responsive

Partnership

Attribute	Characteristics
• Business perception of IT value	IT is seen as a driver/enabler
• Role of IT in strategic business planning	Business strategy enabler/driver
• Shared goals, risk, rewards/penalties	Risk acceptance and rewards shared
• IT program management	Standards evolve
• Relationship/trust style	Valued service provider
• Business sponsor/champion	At the HQ level

Luftman, J., *Addressing Business–IT Alignment Maturity*, Communications of the Association for Information Systems, December, 2000.

▪▪▪▪▪▪▪▪▪▪▪▪ **FIGURE 3-15** Level 4 Strategic Alignment Maturity Criteria (skills and scope and architecture).

Skills	
Attribute	**Characteristics**
• Innovation, entrepreneurship	Enterprise, partners, and IT managers
• Locus of power	Across the organization
• Management style	Profit/value based
• Change readiness	Programs in place at the corporate level
• Career crossover	Across the functional organization
• Education, cross-training	At the functional organization
• Social, political, trusting interpersonal environment	Achieved among IT and business
• Social, political, trusting environment	Valued service provider
• Attract and retain best talent	Formal program for hiring and retaining

Scope and architecture	
Attribute	**Characteristics**
• Traditional, enabler/driver, external	Redefined scope (business process driver)
• Standards articulation	Enterprise standards
• Architectural integration:	Integrated with partners
– Functional organization	Integrated
– Enterprise	Standard enterprise architecture
– Inter-enterprise	With key partners
• Architectural transparency, flexibility	Emerging across the organizations

Luftman, J., *Addressing Business–IT Alignment Maturity*, Communications of the Association for Information Systems, December, 2000.

Level 5—Optimized Process

Level 5 organizations leverage IT assets on an enterprise-wide basis to extend the reach (the IT extrastructure) of the organization into the supply chains of customers and suppliers. It is often difficult to determine if a Level 5 organization is more a technology company than it is a securities, insurance, travel, or retail company (e.g., "Travelocity" or Amazon.com).

A sustained governance process integrates the IT strategic planning process with the strategic business process. For example, in the "communications" criteria of the model, "understanding of the business by IT" and "understanding of IT by the business" (two "attributes") are pervasive. Similarly, in the "skills" criteria of the model, "innovation and entrepreneurship" are the norm for the organization. See Figures 3-16, 3-17 and 3-18 for the specific criteria for Level 5.

▪▪▪ Assessing Strategic Alignment Maturity

An essential part of the assessment process is recognizing that it must be done with a team including both business and IT executives. The convergence on a consensus of the maturity levels and the discussions that ensue are extremely valuable in understanding the problems and opportunities that need to be addressed to improve business-IT alignment. As previously discussed, the most important part of the process is the creation of recommendations addressing the problems and opportunities identified. The most difficult step, of course, is actually carrying out the recommendations. This section ties the assessment metrics together. The examples and

FIGURE 3-16 Level 5 Strategic Alignment Maturity Criteria (communications and competency/value measurement).

Communications

Attribute	Characteristics
• Understanding of business by IT	Pervasive
• Understanding of IT by business	Pervasive
• Inter/Intra-organizational learning	Strong and structured
• Protocol rigidity	Informal
• Knowledge sharing	Extra-enterprise
• Liaison(s) breadth/effectiveness	Extra-enterprise

Competency/value measurements

Attribute	Characteristics
• IT metrics	Extended to external partners
• Business metrics	Extended to external partners
• Balanced metrics	Business, partner, and IT metrics
• Service level agreements	Extended to external partners
• Benchmarking	Routinely performed with partners
• Formal assessments/reviews	Routinely performed
• Continuous improvement	Routinely performed

Luftman, J., *Addressing Business–IT Alignment Maturity*, Communications of the Association for Information Systems, December, 2000.

FIGURE 3-17 Level 5 Strategic Alignment Maturity Criteria (governance and partnership).

Governance

Attribute	Characteristics
• Business strategic planning	Integrated across and outside the enterprise
• IT strategic planning	Integrated across and outside the enterprise
• Organizational reporting structure	Federated; CIO reports to CEO
• Budgetary control	Investment center; profit center
• IT investment management	Business value; extended to business partners
• Steering committee(s)	Partnership
• Prioritization process	Value added partner

Partnership

Attribute	Characteristics
• Business perception of IT value	IT co-adapts with the business
• Role of IT in strategic business planning	Co-adaptive with the business
• Shared goals, risk, rewards/penalties	Risk and rewards shared
• IT program management	Continuous improvement
• Relationship/trust style	Valued partnership
• Business sponsor/champion	At the CEO level

Luftman, J., *Addressing Business–IT Alignment Maturity*, Communications of the Association for Information Systems, December, 2000.

■■■■■■■■■■■ **FIGURE 3-18** **Level 5 Strategic Alignment Maturity Criteria (skills and scope and architecture).**

Skills

Attribute	Characteristics
• Innovation, entrepreneurship	The norm
• Locus of power	All executives, including CIO and partners
• Management style	Relationship-based
• Change readiness	Proactive, anticipate change
• Career crossover	Across the enterprise
• Education, cross-training	Across the enterprise
• Social, political, trusting interpersonal environment	Extended to external customers and partners
• Social, political, trusting environment	Valued partnership
• Attract and retain best talent	Effective program for hiring and retaining

Scope and architecture

Attribute	Characteristics
• Traditional, enabler/driver, external	External scope; business strategy driver/enabler
• Standards articulation	Inter-enterprise standards
• Architectural integration:	Evolve with partners
– Functional organization	Integrated
– Enterprise standard	Enterprise architecture
– Inter-enterprise	With all partners
• Architectural transparency, flexibility	Across the infrastructure

Luftman, J., *Addressing Business–IT Alignment Maturity*, Communications of the Association for Information Systems, December, 2000.

experiences provided in the preceding section on the Six Strategic Alignment Criteria, together with the procedure described in the next section, served as the vehicle for validating the model.

Each of the criteria and levels are described by a set of attributes that allow a particular dimension to be assessed using a 1 to 5 Likert scale, where:

1. this does not fit the organization, or the organization is very ineffective
2. low level of fit for the organization
3. moderate fit for the organization, or the organization is moderately effective
4. this fits most of the organization
5. strong level of fit throughout the organization, or the organization is very effective

Different scales can be applied to perform the assessment (e.g., good, fair, poor; 1, 2, 3). However, whatever the scale, it is important to evaluate each of the six criteria with both business and IT executives to obtain an accurate assessment. The intent is to have the team of IT and business executives converge on a maturity level. Typically, the initial review will produce divergent results. This outcome is indicative of the problems/opportunities being addressed.

The relative importance of each of the attributes within the criteria may differ among organizations. For example, in some organizations the use of SLAs (Service Level Agreements) might not be considered as important to alignment as the effectiveness of liaisons. Hence, giving SLAs a low maturity assessment should not significantly impact the overall rating in this case. However, it would be valuable if the group discusses why the organization does not consider a particular attribute (in this example, SLAs) to be significant.

Using a Delphi approach with a group decision support tool often helps in attaining the convergence.[44] Experience suggests that "discussions" among the different team members helps to ensure a clearer understanding of the problems and opportunities that need to be addressed.

Keep in mind that the primary objective of the assessment is to identify specific recommendations to improve the alignment of IT and the business. The evaluation team, after assessing each of the six criteria from Level 1 to Level 5, uses the results to converge on an overall assessment level of the maturity for the firm. They apply the next higher level of maturity as a roadmap to identify what they should do next. A trained facilitator is typically needed for these sessions.

Early research into Strategic Alignment Maturity via an assessment of 25 Fortune 500 companies indicates that over 80 percent of the organizations are at Level 2 maturity with some characteristics of Level 3 maturity. As additional research is done and the number of companies assessed grows, it is anticipated that exemplar benchmarks based on factors such as industry, company age, and company size will be factored into the research to obtain their effect on alignment maturity.[43]

■■■ Strategic Alignment as a Process

Attaining and sustaining business-IT alignment must first focus on understanding the current level of Strategic Alignment Maturity. Next, steps must be taken that concentrate organizational energy on maximizing alignment enablers and minimizing inhibitors. This process embraces the following[10] (see Figure 3-19):

1. **Set the Goals and Establish a Team.** Ensure that there is an executive business sponsor and champion for the assessment. Next, assign a team of both

■ ■ ■ ■ ■ ■ ■ ■ ■ ■ ■ ■ **FIGURE 3-19** Strategic Alignment as a Process.

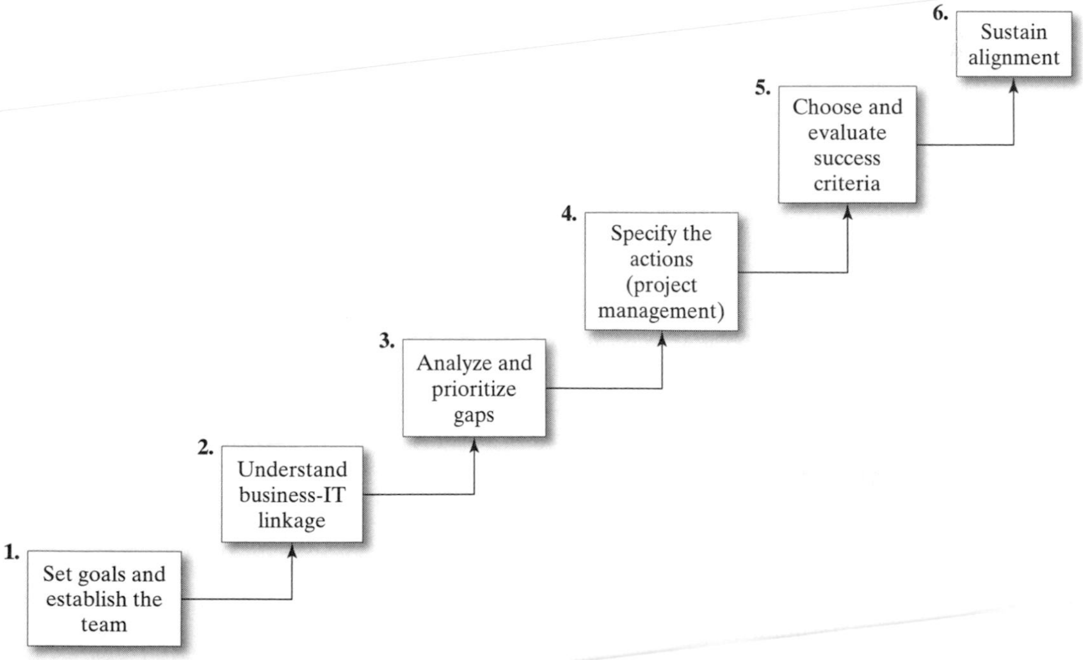

Luftman, J., *Addressing Business–IT Alignment Maturity*, Communications of the Association for Information Systems, December, 2000.

business and IT leaders. Obtaining appropriate representatives from the major business functional organizations (e.g., marketing, finance, R&D, engineering) is critical to the success of the assessment. The purpose of the team is to evaluate the maturity of the business-IT alignment. Once the maturity is understood, the team is expected to define opportunities for enhancing the harmonious relationship between business and IT. Assessments range from three to 12 half-day sessions. The time demanded depends on the number of participants, the degree of consensus required, and the detail of the recommendations to carry out.

2. **Understand the Business-IT Linkage.** The Strategic Alignment Maturity assessment is an important tool in understanding the business-IT linkage. The team evaluates each of the six criteria. This can be done via executive interviews, group discussion, a questionnaire, or a combination. A trained facilitator can be valuable in guiding the important discussions.

3. **Analyze and Prioritize Gaps.** Recognize that the different opinions raised by the participants are indicative of the alignment opportunities that exist. Once understood, converge on a maturity level. The team must remember that the purpose of this step is to understand the activities necessary to improve the business-IT linkage. The gaps between where the organization is today and where the team believes it needs to be in the future are the gaps that need to be prioritized. Apply the next higher level of maturity as a roadmap to identify what can be done next.

4. **Specify the Actions (Project Management).** Naturally, knowing where the organization is with regard to alignment maturity will drive what specific actions are appropriate to enhance IT-business alignment. Assign specific remedial tasks with clearly defined deliverables, ownership, timeframes, resources, risks, and measurements to each of the prioritized gaps.

5. **Choose and Evaluate Success Criteria.** This step necessitates revisiting the goals and regularly discussing the measurement criteria identified to evaluate the implementation of the project plans. The review of the measurements should serve as a learning vehicle to understand how and why the objectives are or are not being met.

6. **Sustain Alignment.** Some problems just won't go away. Why are so many of the inhibitors IT related? Obtaining IT-business alignment is a difficult task. This last step in the process is often the most difficult. To sustain the benefit from IT, an "alignment behavior" must be developed and cultivated. The criteria described to assess alignment maturity provides characteristics of organizations that link IT and business strategies. By adopting these behaviors, companies can increase their potential for a more mature alignment assessment and improve their ability to gain business value from investments in IT. Hence, continuing to focus on understanding the alignment maturity for an organization and taking the necessary action to improve the IT-business harmony are of key importance.

▮▮▮ Conclusions

Achieving and sustaining IT-business alignment continues to be a major issue. Experience shows that no single activity will enable a firm to attain and sustain alignment. There are too many variables. The technology and business environments are too dynamic. The research to derive the business-IT alignment maturity assessment has just begun and the tools and processes are still being refined. Much work still needs to be done to refine hypotheses around Strategic Alignment Maturity and to measure its impact on organizations and their ability to execute strategy.

REVIEW QUESTIONS ▮▮▮▮▮▮▮▮

1. Describe the concept of Strategic Alignment Maturity and its importance to a company.
2. What are the five levels of the Strategic Alignment Maturity model?
3. What is the significance of each level?
4. How do the six criteria of the Strategic Alignment Model impact alignment maturity?
5. Do you believe any of the six criteria are more important than the others? Why?
6. Name some examples of enablers and inhibitors to strategic alignment.
7. What processes should one consider in maintaining strategic alignment?
8. How can the maturity of an organization's strategic alignment impact its ability to execute an IT strategy?
9. Name three present-day firms that you believe have an alignment maturity level above Level 3 and explain why.

DISCUSSION QUESTIONS ▮▮▮▮▮▮▮▮

1. Why is the state of alignment maturity important to an organization?
2. How might you describe the state of Strategic Alignment Maturity for your own organization? Why?
3. What aspects of Strategic Alignment Maturity do you believe are most problematic for your organization?
4. Why do organizations appear to rate so low on the maturity of their Strategic Alignment?
5. Would your organization welcome an assessment of Strategic Alignment maturity?

AREAS FOR RESEARCH ▮▮▮▮▮▮▮▮

1. Read Chan and Huff's paper on "Strategic Information Systems Alignment,"[22] and identify two ways that IT is adding *business value* to your organization.
2. Relating IT infrastructure to Strategic Alignment—read Weill and Broadbent's book, *Leveraging the New Infrastructure*.[32] How might your own organization better leverage its IT infrastructure for competitive advantage?
3. Considering IT as an enabler of strategic transformation—read Keen's book, *Shaping the Future*.[30] Can you identify three key processes that your organization might change using IT as a transforming agent?
4. Suggested project: Using the six Strategic Alignment Maturity criteria, construct a survey tool/questionnaire that could be used to assess your own organization's maturity level.
5. Read the Amazon.com case study on page 77. Use the Strategic Alignment Maturity criteria to assess Amazon's current level of Strategic Alignment Maturity. At what level do you think they are? Why?

SUMMARY ▮▮▮▮▮▮▮▮

This chapter has discussed the concept of Strategic Alignment Maturity as a critical enabler to an organization's ability to execute its strategic objectives and has explored the concepts of a model that can be used to assess alignment maturity for any organization. We have also explored the concept of strategic alignment as an ongoing process and reviewed a series of activities that organizations should consider in measuring and sustaining business-IT alignment.

REFERENCES ▮▮▮▮▮▮▮▮

[1] King, J., "Re-engineering Focus Slips," *Computerworld*, March 13, 1995.
[2] Luftman, J., *Competing in the Information Age: Practical Applications of the Strategic Alignment Model*, New York: Oxford University Press, 1996.
[3] Earl, M. J., *Corporate Information Systems Management*, Homewood, IL: Richard D. Irwin, Inc., 1993.
[4] Earl, M. J., "Experience in Strategic Information Systems Planning," *MIS Quarterly*, 17(1), 1–24, 1996.
[5] Luftman, J., Lewis, P., and Oldach, S., "Transforming the Enterprise: The Alignment of Business and Information Technology Strategies," *IBM Systems Journal*, 32(1), 198–221, 1993.
[6] Goff, L., "You Say Tomayto, I Say Tomahto," *Computerworld*, (Nov. 1, 1993), page 129, 1993.
[7] Liebs, S., "We're All In This Together," *Information Week*, October 26, 1992.
[8] Robson, W., *Strategic Management and Information Systems: An Integrated Approach*, London: Pitman Publishing, 1994.
[9] Luftman, J., Papp, R., and Brier, T., "Enablers and Inhibitors of Business-IT Alignment,"

Communications of the Association for Information Systems, (1) 11, 1999.

[10] Luftman, J. and Brier, T., "Achieving and Sustaining Business-IT Alignment," *California Management Review*, No. 1, pp. 109–122, Fall 1999.

[11] Luftman, J., Papp, R., and Brier, T., " The Strategic Alignment Model: Assessment and Validation," In *Proceedings of the Information Technology Management Group of the Association of Management (AoM) 13th Annual International Conference*, Vancouver, British Columbia, Canada, 57–66, August 2–5, 1995.

[12] Humphrey, W.S., "Characterizing the Software Process: A Maturity Framework," IEEE Software, Vol. 5, No. 2, pp. 73–79, 1988.

[13] Keen, P., "Do You Need An IT Strategy?" in J. N. Luftman (ed.), *Competing in the Information Age*, New York: Oxford University Press, 1996.

[14] Nolan, R.L., "Managing the Crises In Data Processing," Harvard Business Review, March 1, 1979.

[15] McLean, E., and Soden, J., *Strategic Planning for MIS*, New York: John Wiley & Sons, 1977.

[16] IBM, *Business Systems Planning Guide*, GE20-0527, White Plains, NY: IBM Corporation, 1981.

[17] Mills, P., *Managing Service Industries*, New York: Ballinger, 1986.

[18] Parker, M., and Benson, R., *Information Economics*, Englewood Cliffs, New Jersey: Prentice-Hall, 1988.

[19] Brancheau, J., and Wetherbe, J., "Issues In Information Systems Management," *MIS Quarterly*, 11(1), 23–45, 1987.

[20] Dixon, P., and John, D., "Technology Issues Facing Corporate Management in the 1990s," *MIS Quarterly*, 13(3), 247–55, 1989.

[21] Niederman, F., Brancheau, J., and Wetherbe, J., "Information Systems Management Issues For the 1990s," *MIS Quarterly*, 15(4), 475–95, 1991.

[22] Chan, Y., and Huff, S., "Strategic Information Systems Alignment," *Business Quarterly* (58),1 pp. 51–56, 1993.

[23] Henderson, J., and Venkatraman, N., "Aligning Business and IT Strategies," in J. N. Luftman (ed.), *Competing in the Information Age: Practical Applications of the Strategic Alignment Model*, New York: Oxford University Press, 1996.

[24] Papp, R., *Determinants of Strategically Aligned Organizations: A Multi-industry, Multi-perspective Analysis*, (Ph.D. Dissertation), Hoboken, NJ: Stevens Institute of Technology, 1995.

[25] Papp, R., and Luftman, J., "Business and IT Strategic Alignment: New Perspectives and Assessments," In *Proceedings of the Association for Information Systems, Inaugural Americas Conference on Information Systems*, Pittsburgh, PA, August 25–27, 1995.

[26] Henderson, J., Thomas, J., and Venkatraman, N., *Making Sense Of IT: Strategic Alignment and Organizational Context*, Working Paper 3475-92 BPS, Cambridge, MA: Sloan School of Management, Massachusetts Institute of Technology, 1992.

[27] Ives, B., Jarvenpaa, S., and Mason, R., "Global Business Drivers: Aligning Information, 1993.

[28] Boynton, A., Victor, B., and Pine II, B., "Aligning IT With New Competitive Strategies" in J. N. Luftman (ed.), *Competing in the Information Age*, New York: Oxford University Press, 1996.

[29] Davidson, W., "Managing the Business Transformation Process," in J. N. Luftman (ed.), *Competing in the Information Age*, New York: Oxford University Press, 1996.

[30] Keen, P., *Shaping the Future*, Boston, MA: Harvard Business School Press, 1991.

[31] Foster, R., *Innovation: The Attacker's Advantage*, New York: Summit Books, 1986.

[32] Weill, P., and Broadbent, M., *Leveraging the New Infrastructure*, Cambridge, MA: Harvard University Press, 1998.

[33] Henderson, J. and Thomas, J., "Aligning Business and Information Technology Domains: Strategic Planning In Hospitals" in *Hospital and Health Services Administrative*, 37(1), pp. 71–87, 1992.

[34] Broadbent, M. and Weill, P., "Developing Business and Information Strategy Alignment: A Study in the Banking Industry," *IBM Systems Journal*, (32), 1, 1993.

[35] Baets, W., "Some Empirical Evidence on IS Strategy Alignment in Banking," *Information and Management*, Vol. 30:4, pp. 155–77, 1996.

[36] Rockart, J., and Short, J., "IT in the 1990's: Managing Organizational Interdependence," *Sloan Management Review*, 30(2), 7–17, 1989.

[37] Davenport, T., and Short, J., "The New Industrial Engineering: Information Technology and Business Process Redesign," *Sloan Management Review*, Vol. 31, No. 4, 11–27, 1990.

[38] Hammer, M., and Champy, J., *Reengineering the Corporation: A Manifesto For Business Revolution*, New York: Harper Business, 1993.

[39] Hammer, M., and Stanton, S., *The Reengineering Revolution*, New York: Harper Business, 1995.

[40] Rogers, L., "Alignment Revisited," *CIO Magazine*, May 15, 1997.

[41] Rockart, J., Earl, M., and Ross, J., "Eight Imperatives for the New IT Organization," *Sloan Management Review*, (38) 1, 43–55, 1996.

[42] Wang, C., *Techno Vision II*, New York: McGraw-Hill, 1997.

[43] Luftman, J., *Addressing Business-IT Alignment Maturity*; Communications of the Association for Information Systems, December 2000.

[44] Luftman, J., *"Align in the Sand,"* Computerworld, February 17, 1997.

[45] Greenberg, J., Baron, R., *Behavior in Organizations*, Upper Saddle River, NJ: Prentice Hall, 1997.

▪▪▪▪▪▪▪ Case Study ▪▪▪▪▪▪▪
Sample Strategic Alignment Maturity Assessment

Using the "FRM, Inc." case study in Appendix 2A of Chapter 2, the following Strategic Alignment Maturity Assessment template (see Table A3-1) was developed to illustrate how the assessment template is utilized as a tool as part of the IT strategy formulation process. Compare the results of this assessment against the Amazon.com "mini case" described earlier in this chapter. How would they differ? As the preceding chapter has pointed out, the principal value of the Strategic Alignment Maturity assessment is not the assessment itself (or the assessment levels), but the implications of the levels attained by the organization.

Note: the Strategic Alignment Maturity Assessment is done on the "As-Is" state of the organization.

TABLE A3-1   Sample Strategic Alignment Maturity Assessment

Assessment Criteria	Score	Justification for Score	Implication of Score
Communications	1+ or 2–	• Pockets of understanding of business by IT in FRM's divisions • Limited understanding of IT by the business • Some appreciation by senior management of role IT can play in the business • Informal communications • No formal knowledge-sharing mechanisms • No formal liaison roles established	• Effective exchange of ideas and a clear understanding of what it takes to ensure successful strategies are high on the list of enablers and inhibitors to alignment • Given that FRM is proposing an alliance with BigRock to develop and roll out a technology-based business product, effective communications between business and IT and with FRM's partners will be paramount for success
Competency/Value Measurements	2	• Business benchmarking appears to be *ad-hoc* (not an institutional practice) • Business metrics likely to be customer-based • No discussion of IT metrics in the case, but can assume they are cost-based given FRM's culture • Likely presence of CRM or Call Center-related metrics	• An alliance or partnership will demand attention to developing and monitoring Service Level Agreements (SLAs) with BigRock. This competency will have to be developed
Governance	1	• No formal strategic planning approach • IT spending erratic or based on informal relationships between business managers • CIO reports to CFO • IT viewed as a cost center—budget is primary means of control	• Ensuring that the appropriate business and IT participants formally discuss and review the priorities and allocation of IT resources is among the most important enablers/inhibitors of alignment • Decision-making authority for IT investment needs to be clearly defined

(continues on the next page)

TABLE A3-1 (continued)

Assessment Criteria	Score	Justification for Score	Implication of Score
Partnership	1+	• Limited perception of IT as having business value • No formal role for IT in strategic business planning • Selective business sponsorship of key initiatives • Business drives the vision—not shared	• Risk of conflicting goals and objectives for new initiatives • Lack of trust between IT and the business can result in misunderstanding and delay of important activities • Loss of productivity and knowledge sharing for competitive advantage

Scope and Architecture	2+	• Transactionally-based architectures
		• Some enterprise standards around non value-added technologies
		• No formal emerging technology function
		• Some limited attempts at integration
			• IT will have difficulty in:
			    Going beyond the back office and into the front office of the organization
			    Assuming a role supporting a flexible infrastructure that is transparent to all business partners and customers
			    Evaluating and applying emerging technologies effectively
			    Providing solutions customizable to customer needs

Skills	2	• Innovation and entrepreneurship exist in the business • IT skills are primarily technology-based, but some pockets of business acumen exist • Minimal career cross-over	• Use of the potential for creating new knowledge for competitive advantage not capitalized • Potential for high turnover and loss of valuable skills and knowledge
Overall	1.71		The level of Strategic Alignment Maturity for FRM implies that a technology-enabled or technology-driven business strategy will be difficult to execute unless the inhibitors to alignment are actively managed and eliminated as part of a change management program.

▪▪▪▪▪▪▪▪▪

CHAPTER 4

The Role of the CIO

"Leaders are visionaries with a poorly developed sense of fear and no concept of the odds against them."
—ROBERT JARVIK

"Leaders have to act more quickly today. The pressure comes much faster."
—ANDY GROVE

"Management by objective works—if you know the objectives. Ninety percent of the time you don't."

"Management is doing things right; leadership is doing the right things."
—PETER F. DRUCKER

"Don't follow where the pathway goes, lead instead where there is no path and leave a trail."
—SUN TZU IN *THE ART OF WAR*

Preview of Chapter

CIO has been humorously described as meaning "Career Is Over" or "Crisis Is Ongoing," among others. Why is this a challenging position in most companies? In this chapter the overall function of the CIO is described as it relates to the business at large and to their own area of responsibility. The issues that a CIO faces and deals with in today's challenging world are discussed. Included is a description of the skills and attributes that a successful CIO must possess.

While some readers of this text may aspire to the position of CIO, others may not. In either case, the roles and responsibilities of the CIO can affect the success or failure of anyone who reports to or consults with this person. The purpose of this chapter is to review the role a CIO plays in the support and direction of an organization's strategy. In addition, the chapter addresses the dependency a CIO and their organization have on the CEO, as well as the impact of the perception of the IT organization as a whole. Anyone in an IT organization should understand these issues for them to contribute to the success of the IT organization and the overall corporation.

What we will examine in this chapter:

▪ What is the role of the Chief Information Officer in an organization?

▪ How has this role changed over time?

▪ What are the key characteristics of effective CIOs?

▪ What is the relationship of the CIO to the need for *alignment*?

▪▪▪ Introduction

Dana Deasy, the CIO of Siemens, describes his job as "part psychologist, part politician and, of course, part bird."[1] The psychologist refrains from giving mandates that people can resist, but rather uses diplomacy and "self-realization." The politician treats the staff and managers like constituents and lobbies for desired outcomes. Why a bird? The bird spends most of its time flying to all parts of the organization networking and communicating face-to-face. Sounds exhausting, but these are only a few of the various roles of the Chief Information Officer in most organizations.

The title *CIO* is only used in some environments, but the roles and responsibilities of a CIO are everywhere. Some organizations prefer *Vice President of Information Systems* or *Director of IT*. It does not matter what the title is—the individual has a complex role combining managerial and technological skills.

A generic CIO performance plan is presented in Figure 4-1. Some of the job requirements are discussed in other chapters, but the overall *role* of the CIO encompasses these requirements, and more. The requirements keep changing and expanding, as discussed in this chapter.

▪▪▪ The Chief Information Officer

The Beginnings

The position of a CIO as a title arose at the beginning of the 1980s, and has been attributed to Synott and Gruber.[2] As recently as 1985, Synott was suggesting:

"The traditional data processing manager will be replaced by the chief information officer (CIO) by 1990. This position will be created by business because the CIO will: 1. manage information resources as a vital corporate asset, 2. bring systems into the

▪▪▪▪▪▪▪▪▪▪▪▪ **FIGURE 4-1** A CIO Performance Plan.

- Participate in development of corporate *strategies*
- Foster business–IT *relationship and confidence*
- Demonstrate business *value* of IT
- Maintaining *technology competency*
  - Applications
  - Data, information, knowledge
  - Network
- Attract, retain, and develop talented *people*
- Meet *project* commitments
- Practice sound *financial* principles
- Facilitate *change*
- Build a *governance* framework
- Continuous improvement of *IT processes*
- Manage external contractors, vendors, and partners

competitive marketplace, 3. manage and coordinate increasingly decentralized information resources, 4. manage end-user computing so that it serves the corporation's needs, and 5. be a catalyst for corporate change."[3]

It is interesting to note the focus on *management* in four of the five areas mentioned above. Since the CIO position was the evolution of prior titles, such as DP Manager, VP of Information Systems, or Director of Information Systems, it is reasonable that the management of IT was considered a major aspect of a CIO's job. However, the role of the other "chiefs" in an organization tends not to be primarily that of management. The Chief Executive Officer, for example, is more frequently associated with the role of a *strategist*, not a manager. Any management attributes related to the CEO are usually couched in terms that are ascribed to *leadership* rather than management. The difference between management as compared to leadership will be discussed as a key differentiator between effective and ineffective CIOs.

The Evolution of the CIO

Ross and Feeney[4] describe how the role of the CIO has changed over time as the primary architecture of the Information Technology has changed. Their description of the architectural evolution parallels the discussion in the introductory chapter and centers on the interaction with three intermediate forces, as depicted in Figure 4-2.[5] The role of the CIO has evolved in response to the associated changes in executive attitudes toward IT as a whole. The evolution also has to do with the CIO's role, the dependence of the organization on IT as a result of the changing application set, and the influence of the suppliers' products and services that determine the available technologies. These forces interact not only with the CIO and their role, but also with each other. A supplier's access to business executives can affect the executive's attitudes toward IT. The attitude of executives can affect the success or failure of the application portfolio, as well as the selection of the application set. Finally, the dominant supplier(s) can influence the early adoption and acceptance of technologies. A key point made by Ross and Feeney is that these forces are not one-way. The influence of the CIO *on* the forces determines the *effectiveness* of the CIO.

▪▪▪▪▪▪▪▪▪▪▪▪ **FIGURE 4-2   Forces Influencing the CIO Role.**

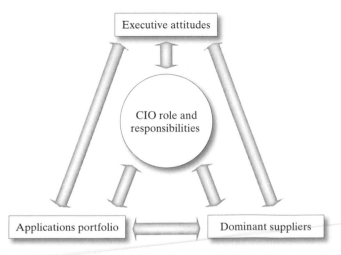

Source: Ross, J.W. and Feeney, D.F., "The Evolving Role of the CIO," in R.N. Zmud (ed.), *Framing the Role of IT Research: Glimpsing the Future Through the Past*, Cincinnati, OH: Pinnaflex Educational Resources, Inc., 1999.

Mainframe Era

During the mainframe era of computing, the role of the CIO (although they still may have been called DP Manager) was primarily that of an operational manager. With IBM (the dominant supplier) having great influence on business executives and the application portfolio available, the IS leader's tasks revolved around delivery of systems on time and within budget. As the size of projects and the range of functions the applications covered expanded, the skills demanded of the IS leader changed from technical aptitude to management and communication skills.

Distributed Era

During the distributed computing era, the applications portfolio began to target knowledge workers in a more individual and specialized nature. IT began to be seen as a means for enhancing business processes and providing competitive advantage. The business press began to influence executive attitudes in raising the expectation that IT should be aligned to business strategy.

The reality of over-commitment by IT and the declining reliability that arose during this era created the divergent view of IT as a liability in some organizations and an asset in others. Outsourcing emerged during this time period, raising the question of whether IT was a core competency that was better staffed by suppliers specializing in IT. The dominant suppliers of this era reflected the growing complexity of IT. There was a fragmentation of suppliers into more specialized areas. Intel and Microsoft dominated the desktop arena; IBM, EDS, CSC, and Anderson emerged as the key outsourcing firms; SAP, PeopleSoft, Oracle, and others provided the enterprise-level applications.

The role of the CIO during the distributed era changed as dramatically as the nature of IT. Four major roles emerged for the CIO:

Organizational Designer. As the nature of the IT architecture changed, the appropriate design for the IT organization changed. The organizational choices available to a CIO are discussed further in Chapter 8 as well as in Chapter 11 on IT governance. Chapter 12 also discusses the role of steering committees, such as those utilized by Kathy Hudson at Kodak (see sidebar, Kodak) in implementing her organization design for managing outsourcing.

Kodak[6]

Kodak's CEO, Colby Chandler, appointed Kathy Hudson as head of the Corporate Information Systems division in 1988 and charged her with making major changes to the IT organization to improve Kodak's competitive position and lower costs. Her decision to outsource major aspects of the IT organization resulted in significant changes with long-term consequences.

One consequence that emerged was the importance of managing alliance partners and vendors for IT managers today. By outsourcing to multiple vendors, the need to create mechanisms to manage the inter-relationships between these vendors became evident and was dealt with. Hudson's approach was to create steering committees to manage the complex relationships that arose. Her participation in these committees served to underscore the impact management had on the relationships across the overall business.

It is significant that Hudson had little IT experience when accepting the position. With this in mind, she chose Henry Pfendt to lead the group that would define the organization to enable this outsourcing initiative. Pfendt was an experienced IT person, and respected by both IT and the business functions. The combination of Hudson's business acumen and Pfendt's cross-functional IT knowledge and prestige resulted in what many regard as the first successful foray into large outsourcing projects.

Strategic Partner. The expanding influence of IT across the organization served to increase the importance of the strategic nature of the CIO position. The increasing body of literature surrounding the need to *align* business and IT strategy underscored the need for the CIO to understand the business strategy as well as how to connect the IT strategy and the business strategy. Many of these issues have been discussed in earlier chapters, specifically Chapters 2 and 3, and will be further discussed in Chapter 11 on IT governance.

Technology Architect. The increased complexity brought on by more hardware and software architecture choices, more vendor choices, and more influence across the business resulted in the need for more understanding of how to integrate the technology and the business. The importance of scanning for emerging technologies increased as the source of those technologies moved from a single primary vendor to multiple vendors and also emergent vendors.

Informed Buyer. The new choices available to the CIO relative to vendors, organization, and whether to outsource IT or not, affected the decision making process for the CIO. The CIO needed to understand the relative risks and benefits of these choices to deliver the most effective and efficient combination of resources. The CIO's role, like that of IT, expanded beyond the boundaries of the organization to include vendor management.

Web-based (Pervasive) Era

The current era of computing brings with it new responsibilities for the CIO. As discussed in other chapters, the extension of IT's role outside the organization to encompass suppliers and customers through the applications themselves increases the impact that IT can have. The relatively recent movement of IT into this era means that there is minimal research to support the definition of any long-term shifts in the CIO role. There is little reason to believe any changes will *replace* the roles already mentioned, as the CIO in many organizations must support an IT environment that consists of all three eras. That is, many organizations maintain information systems that consist of mainframes, distributed systems, client/server systems, Internet and intranet systems as well as emerging wireless-enabled systems. Instead of any responsibilities of the CIO being replaced, it is likely new roles will be added to the already complex functions that the CIO performs.

Business executives affected by the Web-based era look to their CIOs to help them determine the correct strategy to implement any e-commerce projects. The dependence on IT serves to increase the influence of the CIO on the business; it also serves to make the CIO's position more risky. The list of dominant suppliers continues to expand; network and equipment companies that supply the important components of Internet presence such as Sun and Cisco have been added. The ease of substitution and the range of major suppliers raise the question whether dominance by one or more suppliers is an important factor.

The impact of these changes on the role of the CIO is still in question. Certainly, the importance of the role of strategist has expanded to become a necessary part of *business* strategy. There are researchers who have begun to question whether the range of responsibilities for this position has increased to a level that is too much for a single person.

The CIO's Resume

As the role of the CIO has evolved, the requirements for the skills, education, and experience of the CIO also have evolved. A brief comparison of the CIO of 1985 as compared to today is shown in Figure 4-3.[7]

Luftman and Brier, in their work at the IBM Advanced Business Institute, continue to survey business and IT executives on their views of a CIO's qualifications. Their findings are presented in Figure 4-4. It is important to note that two qualifications are viewed by 80 percent or more of the executives questioned as key to the CIO job from both the IT and business function (e.g., finance, marketing, R&D)

▪▪▪▪▪▪▪▪▪▪▪ **FIGURE 4-3   The CIO Resume.**

1985	Today
• Hierarchical kingpin	• Visionary leader
• Dictator	• Relationship manager
• Technology guru	• Marketer
• Mainframe bigot	• Open systems-oriented
• 20 years at IBM Laboratories	• 20 years in LOB mgt. jobs
• COBOL, PL1, FORTRAN, C	• French, German, Japanese
• Ph.D., MIT	• Masters, Harvard Business

Source: Real Decisions, A Gartner Group company.

▪▪▪▪▪▪▪▪▪▪▪ **FIGURE 4-4   What Is the Number One Qualification for a CIO?**

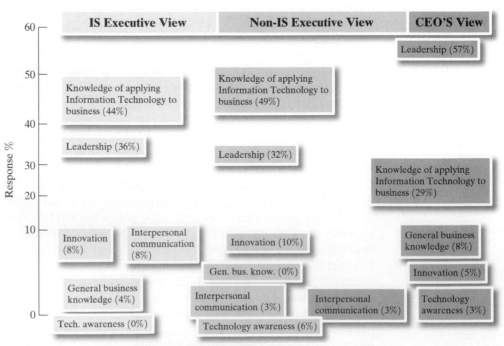

Source: Luftman and Brier, IBM Advanced Business Institute. White Paper, 1997

perspective. The first is knowledge of applying IT to the business; and the second is leadership. CEOs view *leadership* as the primary qualification for a CIO.

The Current View of the CIO

Turnover

Why is it important to focus on the role the CIO plays in today's organizations? In informal surveys of a number of organizations, nearly two-thirds of the CIOs have been replaced within the prior two years. In following up on the careers of CIOs nominated for CIO of the Year by *Information Week* during the past seven years, over half have left their job within three years of receiving their recognition. This mobility (whether voluntary or involuntary) of people in the CIO position is a key reason why someone considering advancing to the level of a CIO may want to understand the CIO role in more depth.

It is apparent that CIOs are under extraordinary pressure to perform, and to perform quickly. The impact of IT on today's organizations requires the CIO to deliver effectively and rapidly on the promise IT makes to business.

The Real CIO

What do practicing CIOs think their job entails? A view of the current concerns facing them sheds some light on the key issues. Figure 4-5[8] presents a recent ranking of the top eight concerns of the CIO. This list provides additional insight into the primary skills a CIO must bring to their job if they are to be successful.

Where do CIOs Come From?

As is already evident, the CIO must be a well-rounded individual, technically astute, people-oriented, with excellent business skills. Current statistics indicate that the majority of CIOs and IT executives continue to come primarily from IT backgrounds. Approximately two-thirds of CIOs have IT backgrounds from a professional education and experience perspective (see Figure 4-6[9]). In Figure 4-7,[10] the Korn/Ferry results have been expanded to indicate other business function backgrounds CIOs may have if they are not career IT professionals.

The CIO and the Value of IT

In Chapter 14 of this text, the importance of describing the value IT brings to an organization will be discussed. What role does the CIO play in this important issue? Earl and Feeny's research led them to state: "...the CIO's ability to add value is the

▪▪▪▪▪▪▪▪▪▪▪▪ **FIGURE 4-5 What Concerns CIOs the Most?**

- 94% Enhancing customer satisfaction
- 92% Security
- 89% Technology evaluation
- 87% Budgeting
- 83% Staffing
- 66% ROI analysis
- 64% Building new applications
- 45% Outsourcing hosting

Source: CIO Insight Attitute Survey/What Concerns CIOs the Most?

▮▮▮▮▮▮▮▮▮▮▮ **FIGURE 4-6** **What Is your Professional Background?**

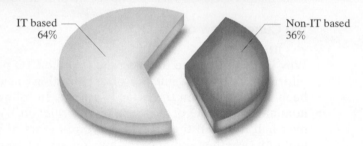

Source: "The Changing Role of the CIO," Korn/Ferry International, 1998 (in conjunction with the *Financial Times* (available at *www.kornferry.com/Sources/Pdf/PUB_008.pdf*) What is your professional background?

▮▮▮▮▮▮▮▮▮▮▮ **FIGURE 4-7** **CIO Career Plan: What Organization Is the Source of CIOs?**

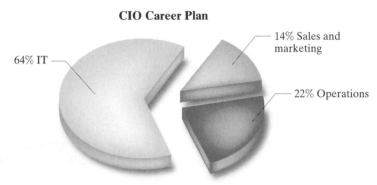

Source: Korn/Ferry, Creative CIOs. *(www.industryweek.com)* (available at *http://www.industryweek.com/CurrentArticles/asp/articles.asp? ArticleID=562*)

biggest single factor in determining whether the organization views IT as an asset or a liability."[11]

Earl and Feeny summarized several projects that studied the relationship of the CEO and CIO, the factors that contributed to the survival of CIOs, and the experience and learning gained by CIOs over a five-year period. Table 4-1 presents how various questions posed to members of an organization might be answered depending on the view of IT as an asset or a liability.

The CIO can affect the perceived value of IT in a number of ways. First, the CIO needs to focus on the business needs as they relate to the IT organization. Also, the CIO should become an educator to the business executives by relating stories of external IT successes, illustrating how IT can add value to the business. The role of educator provides a means to demonstrate the importance of IT and foster more interaction, thereby increasing the communications channels with the business community.

Another focus for the CIO adding value is to communicate the successes and value of IT to the business. This needs to be accomplished in a manner that does not require the CIO's personal time. The desired results can be gained by using subordinates and procedures that provide feedback from and to the business about IT processes and actions. The CIO should also involve the business in maintaining the correct focus of IT development efforts as another way to provide value. If the CIO has a good understanding of the business vision, they will then be able to concentrate the development efforts on the goal of a shared IT-business vision.

TABLE 4-1   Perception of IT[12]

Issue	*IT is a Liability*	*IT is an Asset*
Are we getting value for the money?	ROI is difficult to measure, and the organization is generally unhappy with IS as a whole.	ROI is difficult to measure, but the organization believes IT is making an important contribution.
How important is IT?	Stories of strategic use of IT are dismissed as irrelevant to "this" business.	Stories of strategic use of IT are seen as interesting and instructive.
How do we plan for IT?	IT plans are made by specialists or missionary zealots.	IT thinking is subsumed within business thinking.
Is the IS function doing a good job?	There is general cynicism about the track record of IS	The performance of IT is no longer an agenda item.
What is the IT strategy?	Many IT applications are under development.	IT efforts are focused on a few key initiatives.
What is the CEO's vision for the role of IT?	The CEO sees a limited role for IT within the business.	The CEO sees IT as having a role in the transformation of the business.
What do we expect of the CIO?	The CIO is positioned as a specialist functional manager.	The CIO is valued as a contributor to business thinking and business operations.

The contribution of the CIO to *general* business thinking and operations is also an important way to improve the perception of IT and the CIO's role. As discussed in the Introduction chapter of this text, IT is able to "see" across the business functions. In the words of Michael Earl and David Fenny,

"...the nature of IT is such that the CIO gets a view across the business; the job requires the CIO to have a curiosity about 'how things work.' CIOs are well placed to understand the connections and interrelationships between functions and organizational units, and it is by improving these linkages that the greatest opportunities for business improvements often occur."[13]

This *cross-functional* view of the business is a key factor in the role the CIO can play in *transforming* the business. The nature of IT as the enabler of communication channels and information flow among an organization's functions and beyond its boundaries provides significant opportunity to enable changes in business processes and models.

The Global CIO

Figure 4-3 indicates a shift from computer-based to people-based languages that a CIO now needs to know. Today's global economy requires the CIO of many organizations to deal with factors that are affected by the organization's operations in, and exposure to, other nations. These factors include working with business units, customers, and vendors located around the world. Education and experience in dealing with people of other nationalities and cultures can have a major impact on the successful implementation of technology across national boundaries. This globalization increases the need for the CIO to be knowledgeable about cultural differences, geography, and history, for example, to more successfully implement global information systems.

For example, overseas outsourcing has become a common way to reduce cost and turnaround time for larger-scale development projects. Today's CIO requires the ability to manage projects across time zones and effectively deal with the language and cultural differences such projects bring with them. Chapter 11 discusses other issues related to global management.

▪▪▪ Strategic Alignment

The CIO

In Chapter 1 and Chapter 2 on Strategic Alignment, the enablers and inhibitors found to be among the major factors involved in achieving alignment were presented and discussed. This list is repeated in Table 4-2 for ease of discussion:[14]

The list of enablers and inhibitors mirrors many of the insights of Ross and Feeney's work discussed earlier. The influence of the executive relationship with the CIO is seen in the impact senior executive support has on alignment. The role of the CIO as strategic partner is supported by IT's involvement in strategy as an enabler and its failure to understand the business as an inhibitor. The consequences of delivering or not delivering on projects are associated with the role of the CIO as a manager. The remaining factor— that of leadership—is implied by the role the CIO can play in *influencing* the forces rather than *being influenced* by them.

It was mentioned previously, in the discussion about Synott's prediction in 1985, that the *management* (as opposed to leadership) responsibilities of the CIO should have a smaller role than other responsibilities. The enablers and inhibitors suggest this also. The management of IT is among the top five enablers in the area of project prioritization, but is an inhibitor through poor prioritization and inability to make commitments. The implication here is not that management is unimportant. The original role of the IT executive was to effectively manage the IT organization. However, this does not mean that the primary responsibility for IT management needs to be *performed* by the CIO.

A slightly different way of looking at the issue of management is that a shift must take place from a focus on managing *technology* to managing its *use*.[15] This is a more concise way of restating the thought presented in Chapter 1—IT-oriented professionals have developed a stereotype that "technology is good, more (and increasingly more complex) technology is better." While this thought process might be beneficial in many organizations, it should not be followed without focusing on how this increasing complexity improves the business and fits the business strategy. *Managing technology* refers to the tendency to focus on technology for technology's sake, while *managing its use* refers to the focus on connecting the implementation of technology to the organization's goals and strategy. This is another way of saying that IT and business strategies should be aligned.

TABLE 4-2 Enablers and Inhibitors	
Enablers	*Inhibitors*
Senior executive support for IT	IT/business lack close relationships
IT involved in strategy development	IT does not prioritize well
IT understands the business	IT fails to meet its commitments
Business—IT partnership	IT does not understand business
Well-prioritized IT projects	Senior executives do not support IT
IT demonstrates leadership	IT management lacks leadership

▪▪▪▪▪▪▪▪▪

Luftman, Papp, Brier (1999)

Two considerations for the alignment between IT and the business relative to the CIO are the position of the CIO in the organizational chart, and whether or not the CIO serves on an organization's internal management board. Figures 4-8 and 4-9 reflect recent statistics. As evidenced by Figure 4-8, many IT organizations still report to the financial function. As discussed later in regards to the CEO relationship, this alone is not necessarily indicative of a problem, as long as there is a *relationship* with the CEO and the high-level business executive team. Figure 4-9[16] shows that the CIOs are members of their organization's internal board in only half the companies surveyed. A further consideration even in those cases is the role played by the CIO as a member of that board. The CIO must be an *active, participating, and contributing* member in order to effectively improve the alignment between IT and the business functions.

The CEO

If the alignment of IT strategy and business strategy and the partnership between IT and business are key factors in the success of the CIO, the role of the business executive(s) in this success is critical. The research of Fenny et al.[17] in the relationship between the CIO and CEO suggests that successful relationships result in success for IT in several areas—strategic IT planning, business/IT partnerships, and CEO involvement in IT management. Their findings pointed to the following attributes of excellent CIO/CEO relationships:

▮▮▮▮▮▮▮▮▮▮▮ **FIGURE 4-8** To Whom Does Your Top IS Manager Report?

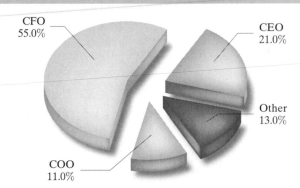

CFO 55.0%

CEO 21.0%

Other 13.0%

COO 11.0%

▮▮▮▮▮▮▮▮▮▮▮ **FIGURE 4-9** Do You Sit on Your Company's Internal Board?

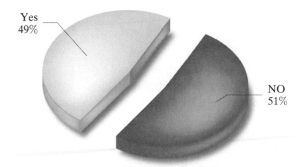

Yes 49%

NO 51%

Source: "The Changing Role of the CIO," Korn/Ferry International, 1998 (in conjunction with the *Financial Times* (available at *www.kornferry.com/Sources/Pdf/PUB_008.pdf*) What is your professional background?

CEO ATTRIBUTES

- General management and/or marketing background
- Change-oriented leadership
- Attended IT "awareness" seminars
- Experience IT project success
- Perceives IT as critical to the business
- Positions IT as agent of business transformation

ORGANIZATIONAL ATTRIBUTES

- Personal/informal executive style
- Executive workshops on strategic issues
- CIO accepted into executive team

CIO ATTRIBUTES

- Analyst background and orientation
- Promotes IT as agent of business transformation
- Contributes beyond IT function
- Accurate perception of CEO views on business and IT
- Integrates IT with business planning
- Profile stresses consultative leadership and creativity

USAA[18]

"Systems and communications technologies are strategic weapons and it is imperative that we take full advantage of the opportunities that new and emerging information processing technology will offer to us over the next few years. Our success and even survival, will be closely tied to how well we will be able to compete in the marketplace on technological grounds.

We are not just an insurance company anymore. Our success has been brought on by diversification and expansion into products and services which meet our members' changing needs."

GENERAL MCDERMOTT, CHAIRMAN AND CEO—USAA

The experience of USAA was first mentioned in the introductory chapter. The attitude of their CEO at the time of this case is something CIOs may wish for or may dread. Certainly General McDermott was a willing sponsor and even a champion for the use of IT in his organization. This focus on the use of IT to drive business strategy also increases the intensity of the spotlight shining on the IT organization. His commitment to transforming USAA's business through his vision of the "paperless environment" played a major role in making his CIO a key player on the USAA management team.

It is significant that the role of IT was viewed as having key importance to the CEOs in this study, and that this perception of the role of IT was shared by the CIO and CEO. The study also found that the inclusion of the CIO as part of the top management team from an activity-based and communications point of view appeared more important than a formal reporting structure that included the CIO as a member of the top executives. Once again, the emphasis on communications and inclusion in strategy would seem to contribute to the goal of aligning IT and Business strategy.

Figure 4-10[19] presents the view that the CEO's role is to *believe* in the importance of IT to the business.

▪▪▪▪▪▪▪▪▪▪▪ **FIGURE 4-10**   Diagnosing the CEO Who Is Fit for the Information Age.

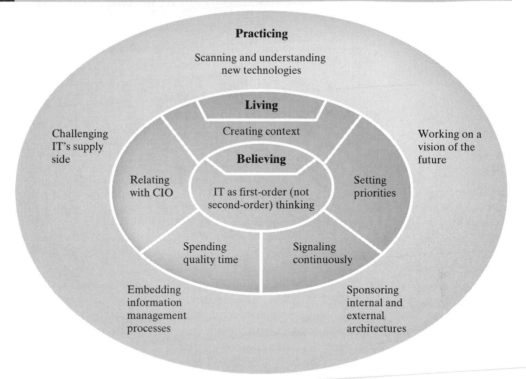

Source: Earl, Michael, and Feeny, David, "How to be a CEO for the Information Age," *Sloan Management Review*, Winter 2000/Diagnosing the CEO Who is Fit for the Information Age.

For a CEO to demonstrate a belief in IT, the CEO must *live* this belief by:

Creating Context.   The CEO must create a context of change in the organization that supports the need for successful exploitation of technology.

Setting Priorities.   The CEO needs to establish a core group of business priorities that drive the need for continuous enhancement of the technology infrastructure.

Signaling Continuously and Positively.   The CEO's belief in IT must be a public matter. Sending signals about the positive value of IT and the importance of IT to the organization creates an atmosphere of support for IT.

Spending Quality Time.   "Believer" CEOs spend time focusing on IT issues in a proactive manner. They insure they are well read in IT issues in order to better understand them.

Relating with the CIO.   A two-way relationship between the CEO and CIO must exist. The relationship itself is important, not whether it is formal (as in direct reporting) or informal.

General McDermott, the CEO or USAA, clearly demonstrated these beliefs.

Living the Information Age suggests a number of subtle behaviors that the believer CEO follows. Of equal importance are a number of more active behaviors that deal with business strategy.

Scanning and Understanding New Technologies.   Believer CEOs take an active role in scanning and understanding the implications of new technologies for businesses.

Working On a Vision of the Future. The business vision and the IT vision are crafted into a coherent strategy for the future state of the business. The believer CEO does not support implementation of technology for technology's sake, but understands it is a component of the overall strategy.

Sponsoring Internal and External Architectures. The believer CEO is involved in shaping the architectures required to pursue the business strategy. The internal IT architecture that supports the business processes, as well as the external architectures that support the vendor and customer linkages, are understood and sponsored by the CEO.

Embedding Information Management Processes. The CEO who believes in IT includes the three key IT management processes in the overall set of business processes driven by the CEO. The three processes are: IT strategy development, IT investment decisions, and IT project implementation and governance.

Challenging IT's Supply Side. Being a believer in IT does not mean the CEO avoids the decision to outsource those IT processes or functions when it makes good business sense.

▪▪▪ How to Be a CIO

The Effective CIO

There is evidence that the role of the CIO has changed in response to the needs discussed above. Stephens, et al. found evidence that practicing CIOs have acquired more of an executive role than a functional manager role.[20] This study (and others, such as Ives and Olsen's[21]) describes some attributes of CIOs that seem to contribute to effectiveness. They are:

Delegation of Operational Tasks. This seems to support the contention that management of technology is not an important role for the CIO to perform; a lower level of management or staff can perform it.

Seize Expenditure Authority. The CIO's authority is less apt to be questioned by other business functions if he or she has financial authority. Requesting approval for expenditures from other executives reduces the believability of the CIO as a top executive.

Avoid Adversarial Positions. Skill at reading situations and cultivating relationships are important factors for an effective CIO. This is an important component of leadership.

Initiate Contacts Outside the Information Technology Unit. The creation of relationships with business peers is an important factor in advertising the value of IT.

Use Language Carefully. As first mentioned in Chapter 1, it is important to avoid the use of technology jargon. For the CIO especially, this can contribute to the impression of IT as a separate, unique function. Recasting IT language into mainstream business terms supports the notion that IT is another *business* function.

Top 10 Requirements of the CIO Position[22]

10. Ability to hire, develop, and retain high quality IT professionals
 9. International or global experience
 8. Knowledge of, and experience in, a specific industry
 7. Ability to create and manage change

6. Communication skills
5. Management skills
4. Relationship skills
3. Business savvy
2. Expertise in aligning and leveraging technology for the advantage of the enterprise

And the number one requirement for the position of Chief Information Officer is:

1. Leadership

A profile developed in the Feeny et al. study[23] indicates the "ideal" CIO has the following characteristics:

Honesty, Integrity, Sincerity, Openness. The CIO is as willing to report problems as they are to talk about successes. These attributes are also considered important traits of the effective leader.[24]

Business Perspective, Motivation, Language. The CIO speaks in business terms rather than technical jargon.

Communicator, Educator, Motivator, Leader, Politician, Relationship Builder. The CIO serves as a mediator between IT and the business functions/executives. These also are traits of effective leaders.

Continuously Informed on Developments in IT, Able to Interpret their Significance to the Business. The CIO must correctly select the technology that is most appropriate for the business and ensure that it can be deployed in a timely manner.

Change-Oriented Team Player, Catalyst to Business Thinking. The CIO needs to be a neutral player in the executive team, able to commit to the appropriate direction rather than the power base within an organization.

Skills

The descriptive literature is useful to understand the nature of the CIO's role in an organization, but it is also important to understand the *skills* needed to be a CIO and to perform the job well. The roles and attributes discussed above point to the ideal CIO as possessing a combination of business, technology, and leadership skills.[25]

As Applegate and Elam point out,[26] this combination may be difficult to locate. Someone with a purely business background may not be able to manage the technology nature of the job, while a purely technology-oriented person may lack business skills. Leadership skills may be lacking in either background, and someone from outside the organization may be challenged by the organizational knowledge and relationships necessary to be effective.

In Chapter 1, the following list of nontechnology related skills was presented as being important to the CIO's job:

- financial skills—budgeting, understanding of the investment decision process (e.g., Return On Investment calculations and other financial ratios)
- human resource skills—recruiting, retention, motivation, termination, training, corporate culture
- relationship management—vendor/supplier relationships
- legal—contract management, government regulations

- governance—organizational structure, teams, decision making
- marketing—selling the *value* of the IT function
- negotiating—dealing with external and internal entities to develop mutually beneficial commitments
- leadership skills

The issues of marketing and financial skills are discussed in Chapter 13 on measuring, reporting, and controlling and Chapter 14 on the value of IT. The human resource skills required are addressed in Chapter 9, while Chapter 11 discusses IT governance. Legal skills are beyond the scope of this text, and are likely to be delegated to professional counsel in practice. The remaining skills (relationship management, negotiating, and leadership) are all associated with social and personal skills. Leadership skills may be considered as a "wrapper" for the other two skill sets. Negotiation and relationship management skills both consist of many of the skills needed to be an effective leader.

This "mix" of skills required for IT management changes as the level within the organization changes. If the skills are categorized into technical, interpersonal, and administrative/conceptual skills, this mix changes as diagrammed in Figure 4-11.

As an IT manager or any functional manager moves up the organizational ranks, the importance of their technical skills as well as interpersonal skills declines. The suggested decrease in interpersonal skills may be surprising. However, the importance of interpersonal skills declines as the manager needs to interact with a lesser variety of people. The higher a person moves in the executive ranks, the lower the variety of viewpoints and goals in other people that they deal with. Human resource issues tend to be delegated to the management levels below.

The legend on the right in Figure 4-11 refers to the primary role of someone as they move to higher management levels. Staff and first-level managers play primarily a technical role—that is, a person at these levels is still mainly responsible for *performing* tasks. As a person moves up the managerial ladder, the primary role changes to selling the importance of the sub-organization. The manager becomes a spokesperson for the function being managed. At the next level, the role becomes one of responsibility for the ability of the functional area to change and keep pace with the needs of the business. At the executive level, the primary role is one of a *peer* manager or *partner* with the other executives in obtaining the organizational objectives.

▪▪▪▪▪▪▪▪▪▪▪ **FIGURE 4-11** The IT Managerial Skill Mix.

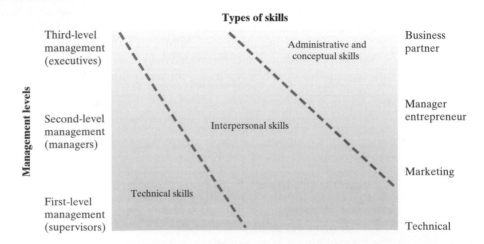

▪▪▪ Leadership versus Management

As implied by the discussion and lists above, management and leadership are NOT the same. The results produced by the two components of many executives' roles in organizations can be quite different, as indicated in Figure 4-12.[27]

A recurring theme in the discussions above has been *leadership*. If in fact leadership is a primary role and skill of the CIO position, then perhaps this may contribute to an explanation of why many CIOs fail. Business and technical knowledge are relatively easy to obtain through experience or by surrounding oneself with people who have the requisite knowledge. Leadership, however, cannot be delegated.

What Makes a Manager?

Mintzberg described ten roles for a manager.[28] The ten roles can be grouped along the managerial activities that relate to interpersonal behavior, information-processing behavior, and decision-making behavior.[29]

Information Processing Roles:

Disseminator   Managers are the recipients of information not readily available to subordinates. This activity requires the manager to interpret and edit before passing it on.

Monitor   This role consists of the activities a manager performs as a consumer of information. A manager must analyze the information available to ascertain problems and to keep informed of activities outside the manager's subunit.

▪▪▪▪▪▪▪▪▪▪▪▪ FIGURE 4-12   Management versus Leadership.

Management	Leadership
• Planning and budgeting: establishing detailed steps and timetables for achieving needed results, then allocating the resources necessary to make it happen.	• Establishing direction: developing a vision of the future—often the distant future—and strategies for producing the changes needed to achieve that vision.
• Organizing and staffing: establishing some structure for accomplishing plan requirements, staffing that structure with individuals, delegating responsibility and authority for carrying out the plan, providing policies and procedures to help guide people, and creating methods or systems to monitor implementation.	• Aligning people: communicating direction in words and deeds to all those whose cooperation may be needed so as to influence the creation of teams and coalitions that understand the vision and strategies and that accept their validity.
• Controlling and problem solving: monitoring results, identifying deviations from plan, then planning and organizing to solve these problems.	• Motivating and inspiring: energizing people to overcome major political, bureaucratic, and resource barriers to change by satisfying basic, but often unfulfilled, human needs.

HOW	WHAT
• Produces a degree of predictability and order and has the potential to consistently produce the short-term results expected by various stake-holders (e.g., for customers, always being on time; for stockholders, being on budget).	• Produces change, often to a dramatic degree, and has the potential to produce extremely useful change (e.g., new products that customers want, new approaches to labor relations that help make a firm more competitive).

Source: Kotter, J. P. *A Force for Change: How Leadership Differs from Management.* New York: Free Press, 1990/Management vs. Leadership

Spokesperson Just as managers pass on information to subordinates, they also act as the source of information about their subunit to superiors and to other organizational units. In addition, this encompasses the activities that "sell" the capabilities and value of the manager's organization.

Decision-Making Roles

Entrepreneur The manager "owns" his organizational subunit. The design of the structure of that unit and the processes utilized by the unit can be changed. This change capability is part of the entrepreneurial role of the manager.

Disturbance Handler The manager is responsible for dealing with conflict and crises that arise in the operation of the organization.

Resource Allocator The manager is responsible for controlling the resources within the organization. This includes the budgetary, staffing allocation, scheduling, and equipment responsibility.

Negotiator Part of a manager's responsibilities includes the negotiation of the commitments made relative to resources or conflict resolution.

Interpersonal Roles

Liaison This role consists of the activities required for a manager to maintain relationships with other organizational units.

Figurehead This role consists of the formal obligations that come with a managerial title. An activity such as document signature as part of the formal authority is one example.

Leader Although leadership has come to be considered a separate role for most executives, Mintzberg considered this to be a role of every manager. This responsibility encompasses the requirement for managers to make their organizational subunit operate as a whole while pursuing the business unit's goals. This role includes the human resource activities of management.

What Makes a Leader?

What then, defines leadership? Kotter[30] defined an effective leader as having the following characteristics:

- Broad business and organizational knowledge
- Broad set of relationships in the firm and the industry
- Excellent reputation and a strong track record in a broad set of activities
- Keen mind and strong interpersonal skills
- High integrity and personal values
- High level of motivation (energy and drive to lead)

Much research has been conducted attempting to identify the characteristics of effective leaders related to learned traits (first three items in list) versus personal traits (last three in list). Most researchers now subscribe to the notion of the *contingency theory* that suggests the traits for effective leadership are context-specific, so that an effective leader requires different approaches and traits in different organizational situations. However, the context—that is, the organizational situation a leader is faced with—tends to remain stable as long as the organization remains stable.[31]

Effective Leadership

As stated previously, much of the research regarding leadership has been unsuccessful in ascertaining one particular set of traits that determine an effective leader. Nonetheless, there are certain fundamental characteristics of leadership that have arisen out of this research. They can be summarized as the following "Laws":[32]

1. **A Leader has Willing Followers.**   No leader exists without gaining the support of others. Followers must be willing participants in the relationship for someone to become a leader.
2. **Leadership Is a Field of Interaction—a Relationship Between Leaders and Followers.**   Leadership is not a person, but the combined artifact of leader and follower.
3. **Leadership Occurs as an Event.**   The relationship between leader and follower is temporal in nature. The acceptance of a person as a leader occurs over time and the accumulation of specific actions or events.
4. **Leaders Use Influence Beyond Formal Authority.**   Managers rely on formal authority and influence. Leaders arise out of influence based on relationships.
5. **Leaders Operate Outside the Boundaries of Organizationally Defined Procedures.**   Leaders operate outside organizational policies and procedures. They are thus better able to deal with unknown territory than people who are simply managers.
6. **Leadership Involves Risks and Uncertainty.**   This law is the consequence of the fifth law.
7. **Not Everyone Will Follow a Leader's Initiative.**   Not everyone is a follower, no matter how charismatic, convincing, or important a leader may be.
8. **Consciousness (Information Processing Capacity) Creates Leadership.**   Leaders think in ways that others do not. Their ability to influence others to believe in their way of thinking or paths to solutions is what creates leadership.
9. **Leadership Is a Self-Referral Process.**   Followers must see the world in the same way as the leader for leadership to occur.

Leadership is primarily concerned with direction, goal setting, support, and encouragement. The focus for leaders is on *getting things done*, not with *doing things*.

Another comparison between leaders and managers is presented in Figure 4-13. Leaders define *what* their team or organization does, with a sense of why. This is

FIGURE 4-13   Leaders versus Managers.

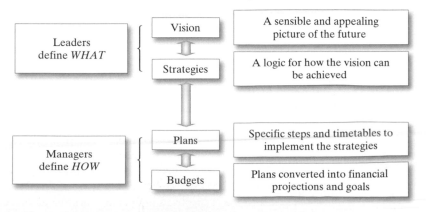

Vision, Strategies, Plans, and Budgets versus Leaders and Managers

Leaders define *WHAT*

Vision — A sensible and appealing picture of the future

Strategies — A logic for how the vision can be achieved

Managers define *HOW*

Plans — Specific steps and timetables to implement the strategies

Budgets — Plans converted into financial projections and goals accomplished through the communication of visions and strategies. The goal here is to develop a common set of goals for the organization. Managers define *how* the tasks of the team or organization are achieved. This can be best accomplished by controlling, through plans and budgets, the *means* by which the task is completed.

■■■ Where Is the Role of the CIO Heading?

Organizational Changes

Several factors are at work to bring the role of the CIO into question. As IT organizations have moved from centralized to decentralized to federated organizations, line managers have gained an increasing amount of responsibility for managing IT.[33] While IT managers are still involved—due to their technical knowledge and abilities—the IT function is often *managed* by business line managers.

There are inherent dangers in allocating too much responsibility for managing IT to line management. First, some loss of the overall IT strategy will result from the more parochial view of a line manager. Second, technical knowledge is important for scanning and evaluating emerging technology. Boynton et al.[34] propose that organizations apportion management responsibilities by taking into consideration four factors:

- The extent of the organization's need for *networking resources* to exchange information among business units or external organizations
- The firm-specific requirements to *share data elements* among business units or with external firms
- The extent to which applying *common application systems* across the firm is desirable
- The requirements for *specialized human resources* related to IT

Associated with these factors are five critical IT management processes:

- setting strategic direction
- establishing infrastructure systems
- scanning technology
- transferring technology
- developing business systems

Organizations may apportion these processes among IT functions or business functions depending on their needs. The result may be a lesser role or need for a CIO.

Functional Changes

Associated with the organizational changes that reduce the *management* function of the CIO is the renewed focus on the *strategist* role of the CIO. The CIO will be "*at the center of operations for strategy pertaining to technology and its implementation.*"[35] The importance of general business skills will continue to increase. The CEO of Charles Schwab, Dawn Lepore, believes that an increasing number of CEOs will need technology skills and many future CEOs will have held IT management or CIO positions.[36]

Jack Rockart believes that the continuing outlook for changes in business and technology will create a continued demand for the role of a CIO, but with a focus on being a technology executive who acts as a counselor for the business executives.[37] Michael Earl suggests that the role of the CIO may be split into two jobs owing to the ever-increasing complexity of the role.[38] One possible scenario is the CIO being given responsibility for strategy, change, and information resources, while a Chief Technology Officer (CTO) is given responsibility for technology policy, infrastructure planning, and operations.

▪▪▪ Tips for the New CIO

The following list provides some thoughts a new CIO should consider when arriving at his or her new position. It would also be useful for an *existing* CIO to review on occasion.

- **Get a Seat at the Table.** As suggested by most research, the CIO is ineffective if there is no relationship with the business executives. Whether this is a formal or informal relationship, it must exist to enable an understanding of the business needs and to communicate the value of IT.
- **Regular One-to-One Communications with the CEO.** In addition to acting as a forum to discuss issues with peers, the ability to interact with the CEO can play a major role in the CIO's success. Starting out in a position that does not include regular interaction with the CEO can mean a quick end to a CIO.
- **Create a Partnership with Peers.** Approach the position from the beginning as an equal partner in the business strategy. Focusing on the business advantages of the CIO role for the business is more effective than focusing on the technology.
- **Study the Corporate Culture.** The culture of an organization can have a significant impact on the success or failure of the IT organization. Understanding the history of the organization, the power bases, and what groups are critical as political allies is an important first task for a CIO.
- **Understand the Business Model.** Organizations in similar businesses or industries do not necessarily follow the same business model. There can be differences in marketing approaches, primary target customers, regional effects, etc.
- **Define Current Commitments.** Taking over a position does not "reset the clock" for existing IT commitments. The new CIO needs to understand what the organization has committed to and ensure follow-through. This can help make a lasting first impression.
- **Establish Credibility First through Small Things.** It is not necessary to pursue a major success right away. Accumulating small successes can garner credibility and will likely be easier to attain.
- **Build a Personal Board of Directors.** There is no need to "go it alone." Create an informal team of advisors from the business functions as well as within IT. Portraying a style that exhibits a willingness to listen helps build support.
- **Listen and Talk.** While it is important to avoid starting out too aggressively, the new CIO needs to quickly display the ability to contribute ideas and knowledge appropriate to the business needs. Listen to what others view as problems; then, turn them into opportunities.
- **Be Accessible and Responsive.** Being available to listen to others demonstrates a willingness to be a team player. However, it is important to respond to the needs presented.
- **Set Realistic Goals.** Although the new CIO has existing commitments to meet, the fact that the CIO was replaced may indicate these were impossible commitments. Reevaluate these commitments and look for achievable results to establish credibility.
- **Take Inventory (People, Applications, Technology, Services).** Knowing what the assets of the IT organization are is necessary for understanding the capabilities of the organization.
- **Assess your People.** As discussed in this chapter, management and leadership is context-dependent. There may be hidden capabilities in the organization that the former CIO was unaware of.

- **Understand the Value and Threat of Outsourcing.** Outsourcing is a common occurrence in the current environment. There may be value in outsourcing, but until many of the above suggestions are implemented, it will be difficult to assess. It is important to understand the business view of this to determine whether it is an immediate threat to the IT organization.

REVIEW QUESTIONS ▪▪▪▪▪▪▪

1. What are some of the key differences between management and leadership?
2. How have technology changes influenced the changing roles of the CIO?
3. What are the primary roles of a CIO?
4. What are the key *management* skills and responsibilities of the CIO?
5. What are the key *leadership* traits that are important for an *effective* CIO?

DISCUSSION QUESTIONS ▪▪▪▪▪▪▪

1. How has the Internet Age affected the role of the CIO?
2. What is the primary role of the CIO in your organization? Is it primarily one of management or leadership?
3. Does the size of an organization affect the roles of the top IT management position, regardless of title?
4. Do you think the CIO MUST report to the CEO to be effective?

AREAS FOR RESEARCH ▪▪▪▪▪▪▪

1. What are the roles of some of the other technology "chiefs," such as Chief Technology Officer or Chief Knowledge Officer?
2. Research techniques for delegation. What are some of the issues for technology-driven people in delegation?

CONCLUSION ▪▪▪▪▪▪▪

This chapter has presented an overview of the role of the CIO. The CIO position has developed into a key factor in demonstrating and delivering on the value of IT. The importance of the CIO in shaping and enabling business strategy has increased as the impact of IT has expanded into more business processes and beyond the organizational boundaries. This has caused a transition from a management role for the CIO to roles that require leadership traits in order to be successful.

In Chapter 5, the IT processes that a CIO is responsible for will be presented. As discussed above, these processes may not need to be *managed* by the CIO directly. The CIO, however, is still *responsible* for their effective and efficient delivery.

"If we do not change our direction, we might end up where we are headed."
—CHINESE PROVERB

REFERENCES ▪▪▪▪▪▪▪

[1] Deasy and Villano, "The World According to Deasy," *CIO Magazine*, December 15, 2000/January 1, 2001.
[2] Synott, W.R., Gruber, W.H., *Information Resource Management*, John Wiley and Sons, New York, NY, 1981.
[3] Synott, W.R., *Combating Corporate Chaos: Why Companies Need a CIO*, Management Technology, May 1985.
[4] Ross, J.W. and Feeney, D.F., "The Evolving Role of the CIO," in *R.M. Zmud (ed.) Framing the Domain of IT Research: Glimpsing the Future Through the Past*, Cincinnati, OH: Pinnaflex Educational Resources, Inc., 1999.
[5] Ross, J.W. and Feeney, D.F., "The Evolving Role of the CIO," in R.M. Zmud (ed.) *Framing the Domain of IT Research: Glimpsing the Future Through the Past*, Cincinnati, OH: Pinnaflex Educational Resources, Inc., 1999.
[6] Based on the Harvard Business School Case Study (9-192-030, 9/29/1995) "Eastman Kodak Co.: Managing Information Systems Through Strategic Alliances."
[7] Real Decisions: a Gartner Group Company.

8 CIO Insight Attitude Survey.

9 "The Changing Role of the CIO" Korn/Ferry International, 1998 (in conjunction with the Financial Times (available at *http://www.kornferry.com/Sources/ PDF/PUB_008.pdf*).

10 Korn/Ferry, *www.industryweek.com*, 6/7/99 (*http://www.industryweek.com/CurrentArticles/asp/ articles.asp?ArticleID=562*).

11 Earl, Michael J., Fenny, David F., *Is Your CIO Adding Value?*, Sloan Management Review, Spring 1994.

12 Earl, Michael J., Fenny, David F., *Is Your CIO Adding Value?*, Sloan Management Review, Spring 1994.

13 Earl, Michael J., Fenny, David F., *Is Your CIO Adding Value?*, Sloan Management Review, Spring 1994.

14 Luftman, J., Papp, Raymond, Brier, Tom, *Enablers and Inhibitors of Business-IT Alignment*, Communications of the Association for Information Systems, Volume 1, Article 11, March 1999.

15 Marchand, Donald A., Davenport, Thomas H., Dickson, Tim, *Mastering Information Management*, Prentice Hall, 2000.

16 "The Changing Role of the CIO" Korn/Ferry International, 1998 (in conjunction with the Financial Times (available at *http://www.kornferry.com/Sources/ PDF/PUB_008.pdf*).

17 Feeny, David F., Edwards, Brian R., Simpson, Keppel M., *Understanding the CEO/CIO Relationship*, MIS Quarterly, December 1992.

18 *Based on the USAA Case Study by Harvard Business School (9-188-102, 9/23/1992)*.

19 Earl, Michael, Feeny, David, *How to be a CEO for the Information Age*, Sloan Management Review, Winter 2000.

20 Stephens, Charlotte S., Ledbetter, William N., Mitra Amitava, Ford, F. Nelson, *Executive or Functional Manager? The Nature of the CIO's Job*, MIS Quarterly, December 1992.

21 Ives, B., Olson, M.H., *Manager or Technician: The Nature of the Information Systems Executive Job*, MIS Quarterly, December 1981.

22 Polansky, Mark, in *CIO*, September 15, 2001.

23 Feeny, David F., Edwards, Brian R., Simpson, Keppel M., *Understanding the CEO/CIO Relationship*, MIS Quarterly, December 1992.

24 Yukl, Gary, *Leadership in Organizations*, Prentice Hall, New Jersey, 2002.

25 Applegate, Lynda M., Elam, Joyce J., *New Information Systems Leaders: A Changing Role in a Changing World*, MIS Quarterly, December 1992.

26 *Ibid*.

27 Kotter, J.P. *A Force for Change: How Leadership Differs from Management*. New York: Free Press, 1990.

28 Mintzberg, H., *The Nature of Managerial Work*, Harper & Row, New York, 1973.

29 Yukl, Gary, *Leadership in Organizations*, Prentice Hall, New Jersey, 2002.

30 Kotter, J.P., *The Leadership Factor*, The Free Press, New York, NY, 1988.

31 Pfeffer, J. *The Ambiguity of Leadership*, Academy of Management Review (2:1), January 1977.

32 Blank, Warren, *The 9 Natural Laws of Leadership*, American Management Association, New York, 1995.

33 Boynton, Andrew C., Jacobs, Gerry C., Zmud, Robert W., *Whose Responsibility is IT Management?*, Sloan Management Review, Summer 1992.

34 *Ibid*.

35 McAteer, Peter, Elton, Jeffery, *Are CIOs Obsolete?*, Harvard Business Review, March-April 2000.

36 Lepore, Dawn, *Are CIOs Obsolete?*, Harvard Business Review, March-April 2000.

37 Rockart, J., *Are CIOs Obsolete?*, Harvard Business Review, March-April 2000.

38 Earl, Michael J., *Are CIOs Obsolete?*, Harvard Business Review, March-April 2000.

5

IT Processes

"All parts should go together without forcing. You must remember that the parts you are reassembling were disassembled by you. Therefore, if you can't get them together again, there must be a reason. By all means, do not use a hammer."
—IBM MAINTENANCE MANUAL, 1925

Preview of chapter

This chapter will discuss 38 IT processes. IT processes are the fundamental activities/tasks that IT performs. The actual names, amount of resource devoted, and total number might vary from one firm to another, based on the organization's emphasis. However, they are all required for IT to deliver effective and efficient service. All 38 must be performed whether you are a Global 2000 organization or if you are managing a single PC in the home. Many IT processes are covered elsewhere (e.g., other chapters of this book, other graduate courses, and journals of special interest groups). For example, you learned about IT processes in Chapter 2 in the discussion of developing IT strategies and there will be added discussion of improving IT measurements, including SLA, in Chapter 13. Improving IT management of emerging technologies will appear in Chapter 7, and managing change is discussed in Chapter 10.

Of special note: the IT processes have been segmented into two types of processes for clarity. This chapter will focus on IT implementation and execution processes, while IT planning processes will appear in Chapter 6—IT Planning Processes. That chapter has extended information on all planning processes and is designed to present the IT processes not covered elsewhere.

What we will examine in this chapter:

- How many processes are there in IT?
- What is the strategic layer of IT processes?
- What is the tactical layer of IT processes?
- What is the operational layer of IT processes?
- Why is planning important?
- Which processes are most important in light of their contribution to achieving our critical success factors?

■ Who owns each of these process containers?

■ How much resource should be applied to each of these processes?

■ How effective are each of these processes today?

■ What priority should be placed on improving each of these processes?

▪▪▪ Introduction

IT processes are the functions and duties that IT performs. These activities range from development and maintenance of applications, supporting infrastructure (e.g., hardware, systems software, and networks), to managing human resources. While all these activities have some dependence on each other, this chapter will review the 38 processes described in Figure 5-1 individually and will provide some insight on their relative importance.

To address the IT processes in a coherent fashion, the processes have been categorized in three main layers for added clarity. The first layer is the strategic layer. The IT processes associated with the strategic layer focuses on the long-term goals of the firm and how IT can enable their achievement. The second layer is the tactical layer. The tactical layer consists of IT processes that work towards achieving the strategic goals. The third layer is the operational layer. The IT processes that comprise this layer deal with day-to-day production activities. These processes affect the maintenance and monitor-

▪▪▪▪▪▪▪▪▪▪▪▪ **FIGURE 5-1** Information Technology Management Process Overview.

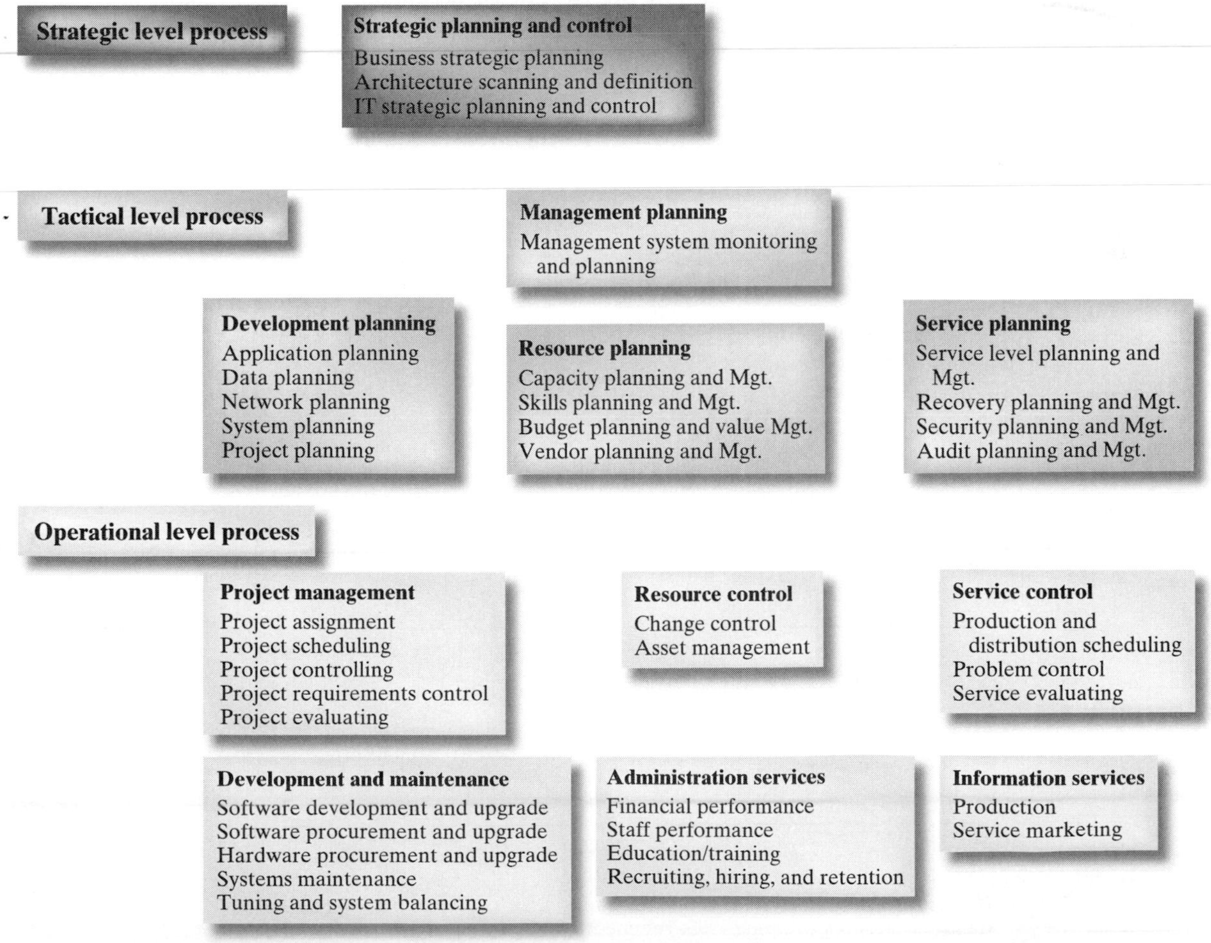

1.

Strategic level process

Strategic planning and control
Business strategic planning
Architecture scanning and definition
IT strategic planning and control

2.

Tactical level process

Management planning
Management system monitoring
and planning

Development planning
Application planning
Data planning
Network planning
System planning
Project planning

Resource planning
Capacity planning and Mgt.
Skills planning and Mgt.
Budget planning and value Mgt.
Vendor planning and Mgt.

Service planning
Service level planning and
Mgt.
Recovery planning and Mgt.
Security planning and Mgt.
Audit planning and Mgt.

3.

Operational level process

Project management
Project assignment
Project scheduling
Project controlling
Project requirements control
Project evaluating

Resource control
Change control
Asset management

Service control
Production and
distribution scheduling
Problem control
Service evaluating

Development and maintenance
Software development and upgrade
Software procurement and upgrade
Hardware procurement and upgrade
Systems maintenance
Tuning and system balancing

Administration services
Financial performance
Staff performance
Education/training
Recruiting, hiring, and retention

Information services
Production
Service marketing

ing of systems, applications, and networks. Processes that involve training, staffing, accounting, scheduling, and administration are included here. Chapter 6 expands on the description of strategic, tactical, and operational. This list of 38 processes comprises all of the planning, organizing, and administering processes required to effectively and efficiently manage IT. See Figure 5-1 for a detailed look at the layers and how the processes are distributed within each layer.

By categorizing the IT processes in these three layers, it will be easier to see the codependencies between many of the IT functions. For example, it will be apparent that the strategic layer will impact the tactical layer by changing the technologies, tools, and methodologies that will be used in the tactical processes. As an additional consequence, new technologies, tools, and methodologies will also impact the operational level by changing the requirements of staff, their training, and job functions. As the tactical processes are completed and moved to production, the impact on the operational layer is visibly altered in adding or subtracting schedules, changes, and maintenance processes. It will also be easy to see the codependencies of IT processes in the same layer. For example, processes such as problem control, change control, production scheduling, and service evaluating may find that problems in production areas require interactions between those processes to resolve the issues.

▪▪▪ How Many Processes Are There in IT?

Surveying the leading management-consulting firms (i.e., Ernst & Young, Price Waterhouse Coopers, et al.) or asking the Society of Information Management (SIM), what number of IT processes exist would give different responses. Ernst & Young have presented 70 IT processes while PricewaterhouseCoopers use 62. The Society of Information Management (SIM) has listed 40 IT processes and in Figure 5-2,[1] David

▪▪▪▪▪▪▪▪▪▪▪ **FIGURE 5-2   Another View, Looking at Nine Core IT Processes.**

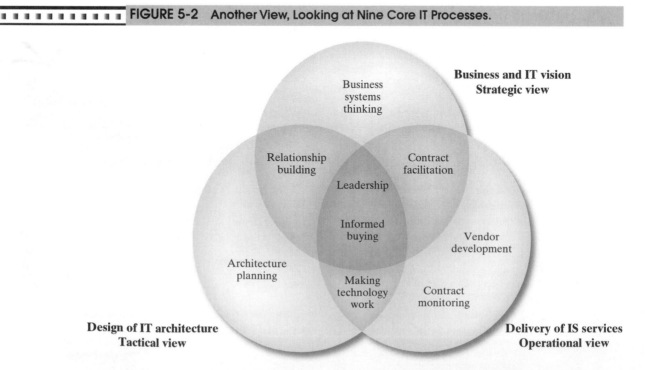

Source: David F. Feeney (1998) "Core IS Capabilities for Exploiting Information Technology" MITSloan Management Review, Spring 1998, Volume 39, Number 3, pp. 9–21.

Feeney lists nine major (core) categories of IT processes. In Feeney's view of the IT processes, categories overlap between strategic, tactical, and operational layers.

Continuous research, discussion, and development of IT Governance and Control issues are being performed today by the CobiT Project. The CobiT project is supervised by a Project Steering Committee formed by international representatives from industry, academia, government, and the security and control profession. Overall project guidance is provided by the IT Governance Institute and has been supported by experts from the Gartner Group and PricewaterhouseCoopers. This industry group has developed their own list of IT processes. In Figure 5-3[2]—The CobiT and the IT Governance Institute display 34 IT processes.[3] They differ from our model in that they

▪▪▪▪▪▪▪▪▪▪▪ **FIGURE 5-3   CobiT Framework—34 IT Processes.**

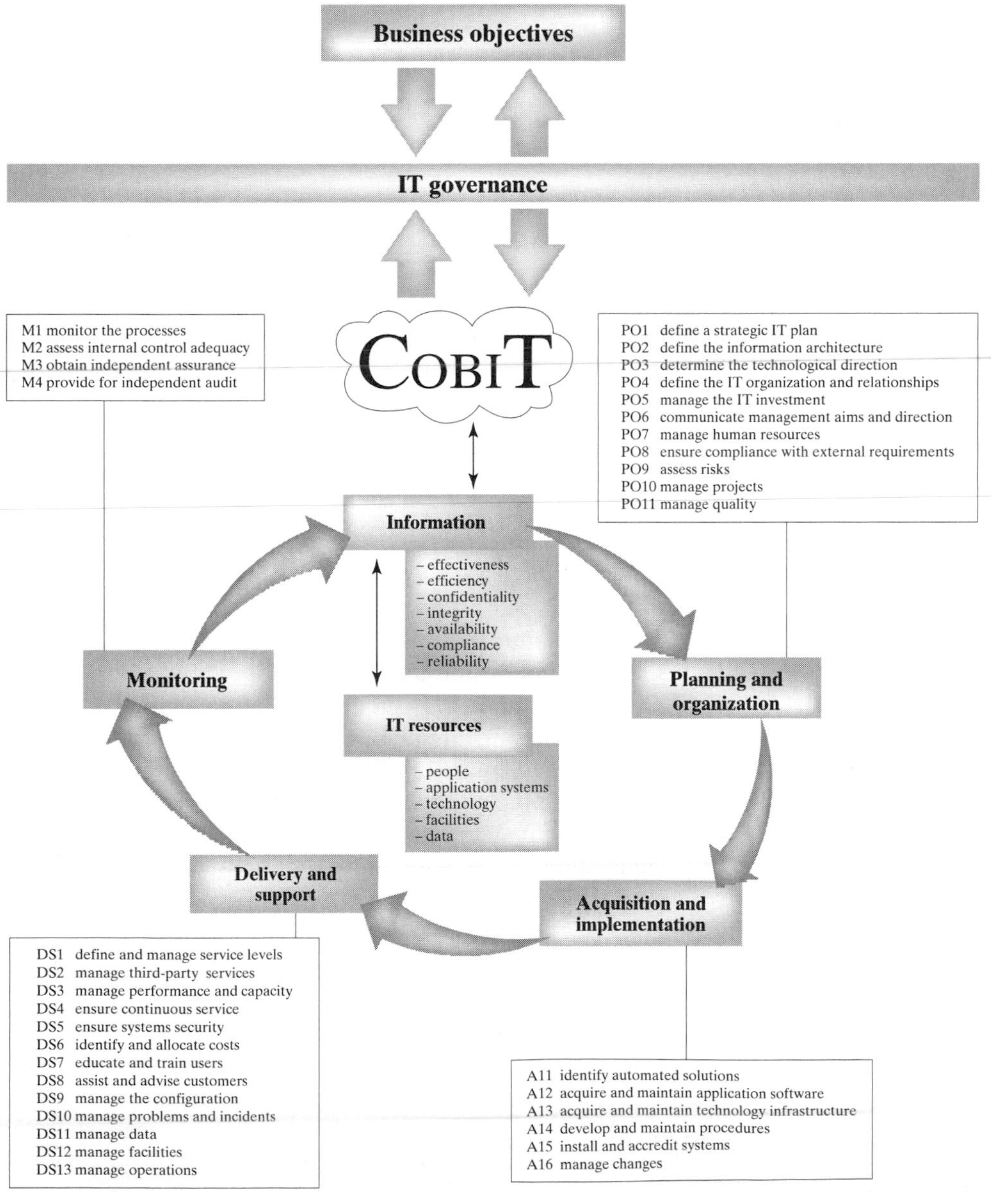

Business objectives

IT governance

CobiT

M1 monitor the processes
M2 assess internal control adequacy
M3 obtain independent assurance
M4 provide for independent audit

PO1   define a strategic IT plan
PO2   define the information architecture
PO3   determine the technological direction
PO4   define the IT organization and relationships
PO5   manage the IT investment
PO6   communicate management aims and direction
PO7   manage human resources
PO8   ensure compliance with external requirements
PO9   assess risks
PO10 manage projects
PO11 manage quality

Information
– effectiveness
– efficiency
– confidentiality
– integrity
– availability
– compliance
– reliability

Monitoring

Planning and organization

IT resources
– people
– application systems
– technology
– facilities
– data

Delivery and support

Acquisition and implementation

DS1   define and manage service levels
DS2   manage third-party services
DS3   manage performance and capacity
DS4   ensure continuous service
DS5   ensure systems security
DS6   identify and allocate costs
DS7   educate and train users
DS8   assist and advise customers
DS9   manage the configuration
DS10 manage problems and incidents
DS11 manage data
DS12 manage facilities
DS13 manage operations

A11 identify automated solutions
A12 acquire and maintain application software
A13 acquire and maintain technology infrastructure
A14 develop and maintain procedures
A15 install and accredit systems
A16 manage changes

Source: CobiT: Control Objectives for Information and Related Technology, "Control Objectives," *Information Systems Audit and Control Foundation (ISACF) and IT Governance Institute, 2000*.

list six major categories and they do not distinguish between a strategic, a tactical, or an operational layer viewpoint.

In this chapter, the number of processes that the CIO faces in the management of an IT organization will be 38 IT processes as shown in Figure 5-1. This effort is not to take argument with the other lists, but it is an attempt to consolidate the various views.

Long term—Strategic

Figure 5-1 lists 38 IT processes grouped into three layers: strategic, tactical, and operational. Strategic level processes are those processes that will have a long-term impact on the enterprise. Decisions made in these processes will consider a longer time horizon to implement and may take a long time before benefits are attained. Strategic processes can create competitive advantage, deliver cost efficiencies, and introduce major improvements to business processes within the firm. The processes are:

1. Business strategic planning
2. Architecture scanning and definition
3. IT strategic planning and control

Short term—Tactical

Tactical level processes are those processes that have an intermediate or short-term impact on an organization. Quite commonly, a tactical level process will respond to a competitor's threat (where a competitor has created a competitive advantage) or provide intermediate (until the next round of strategic developments are introduced) improvements to existing operations. The majority of the IT staff are involved in these IT processes and these areas tend to receive the largest budgets.

The processes are:

4. Application planning
5. Data planning
6. Network planning
7. Systems planning
8. Project planning
9. Service level planning and management
10. Recovery planning and management
11. Security planning and management
12. Audit planning and management
13. Capacity planning and management
14. Skills planning and management
15. Budget planning and value management
16. Vendor planning and management
17. Management systems planning and monitoring

Day-to-day—Operational

Operational level processes are typically taken for granted. These activities cover many day-to-day functions such as production, scheduling, maintenance, resource control, and administrative services. These activities are sometimes the most critical, however, because a failure in this area will be visible to external clients/customers and partners, and internal partners (end users). So unlike application development and strategic planning, it is often unheralded, and attention is only given upon lack of or poor performance.

The processes are:

18. Project assignment
19. Project scheduling

20. Project controlling
21. Project requirements control
22. Project evaluating
23. Change control
24. Asset management
25. Production and distribution scheduling
26. Problem control
27. Service evaluating
28. Software development and upgrade
29. Software procurement and upgrade (contract and vendors)
30. Hardware procurement and upgrade (contract and vendors)
31. Systems maintenance
32. Tuning and systems balancing
33. Financial performance
34. Staff performance
35. Education and training
36. Recruiting, hiring, and retention
37. Production
38. Service marketing

An Overview of the 38 IT Processes

1. Business Strategic Planning *

This process defines a business strategy that is enabled/driven by IT. It defines the enterprise demands of its IT function through the strategic plan period and the opportunity IT has in meeting these demands.

Chapter 2 on Strategic Alignment also covered this process as well and is a cornerstone of a typical course offered in Masters in Information Systems programs such as "Strategic Management of Information Technology."

2. Architecture Scanning and Definition

Using the information obtained in the business strategic planning process and considering the whole enterprise, this process re-defines, in IT terms, the architectural goals of the IT organization. The creation of an architectural definition provides a common understanding of the path to be followed for the members of the IT staff. This was introduced in Table 2–2.

Architecture scanning and definition consists of:

• Defining the data, information, and knowledge architecture for the enterprise
• Defining the application architecture for the enterprise
• Defining the IT technology (e.g., networks, computers, et al.) architecture for the enterprise
• Integrating architectures

See Appendix 5A at the end of this chapter for a closer view of this process. A course such as "Integration of Information Systems Technology" offered in many Masters in Information Systems programs would also provide additional insights.

*[Note that Chapter 6—IT Planning Processes has additional information for all planning processes. All processes denoted with an asterisk (*) will be discussed further in Chapter 6. Refer to that chapter for detail.]

3. Information Technology Strategic Planning and Control*

Based on the goals of the firm and IT, this process defines the general direction regarding how to attain these goals, via an IT strategic plan.

Chapter 2 on Strategic Alignment and Chapter 11 on IT Governance also cover this process in more detail, as well as would a typical course such as "Strategic Management of Information Technology" offered in many Masters in Information Systems programs.

4. Application Planning*

The application plan is a portfolio and schedule of applications to be built or modified within a set period of time.

This process would also be covered in more detail through typical courses such as "Analysis and Development of Information Systems," "Enterprise Systems Management," and "Integration of Information Systems Technology" offered in many Masters in Information Systems programs.

5. Data Planning*

The data planning process reviews the application plan and determines what the data needs will be for the applications that are planned.

This process would be covered in more detail through typical courses such as "Analysis and Development of Information Systems," "Data Management," "Enterprise Systems Management," and "Integration of Information Systems Technology" offered in many Masters in Information Systems programs.

6. Network Planning*

The network planning process focuses on the network connectivity demands of the enterprise.

This process would also be covered in more detail through typical courses such as "Network Management," and "Integration of Information Systems Technology," offered in many Masters in Information Systems programs.

7. System Planning*

The comprehensive system plan is a translation of the enterprise's strategic goals and directions into a scheduled update of the enterprise's hardware, software, network, and facilities to enable applications to meet the strategic goals of the enterprise.

This process would also be covered in more detail through typical courses such as "Analysis and Development of Information Systems," "Data Management," "Network Management," "Enterprise Systems Management," and "Integration of Information Systems Technology" offered in many Masters in Information Systems programs.

8. Project planning*

The project planning process is to define technically feasible and manageable projects that will reflect the enterprise's strategic goals and direction and translate all of the plans into manageable projects.

This process would be covered in more detail through typical courses such as "Project Management," "Analysis and Development of Information Systems," and "Enterprise Systems Management" offered in many Masters in Information Systems programs.

9. Service Level Planning and Management*

The service level planning process defines and negotiates individual service level agreements (SLA) using the service volume forecasts and service charge rates established by the service marketing planning process. Also see Chapter 13 for a more detailed view of the Service Level Agreement (SLA) process.

10. Recovery Planning and Management*
The recovery planning process works to ensure that there will be a continuation of business operations in the event of technology failure or disaster.

11. Security Planning and Management*
The security planning process builds an overall plan to ensure that agreed levels of security for systems and services are met.

12. Audit Planning and Management*
The audit planning process builds an overall plan to ensure that the agreed levels of audit and compliance for systems, applications and services will continue to be met.

13. Capacity Planning & Management*
The capacity planning process uses a forecast load from new projects or from the evolution of existing services; this process defines how systems resources will support the demand.

A course such as "Integration of Information Systems Technology," offered in many Masters in Information Systems programs would also provide additional insights.

14. Skills Planning and Management*
The skills planning process uses the requirements identified in the project and service plans to define the manpower the enterprise needs to compete in this tactical time horizon. Skills can be obtained from existing staff and by hiring new staff, outsourcing, or acquiring an organization. The process also needs to identify education plans for existing staff that would enable the enterprise to meet the skills requirement of the near future. Also see Chapter 9 on IT human resources for additional insights.

This process would be covered in more detail through typical courses such as "Organizational Behavior," "Organizational Theory," and "Human Resources Management of Information Systems" offered in many Masters in Information Systems programs.

15. Budget Planning and Value Management*
The budget planning process converts individual plans into financial terms and identifies how funds will be obtained and allocated. Chapter 14 on Value of IT should also be reviewed.

This process would be covered in more detail through typical courses such as "Financial Management," offered in many Masters in Information Systems programs.

16. Vendor Planning and Management*
Vendor planning and management process deals with the outsourcing of IT services and coordination of IT vendors. It must also measure and monitor performance against the service level agreements and contracts to determine if any corrective action is necessary. Chapter 11 on IT Governance has an extended discussion of vendor management.

17. Management Systems Planning and Monitoring*

The management systems planning process uses the strategic processes and an assessment of the existing IT plan to define a new prioritized portfolio of projects and plans. It improves the management system through a project management approach.

This process is discussed in Chapter 8—Organizing IT, Chapter 11—IT Governance, and Chapter 14—IT Value. It would be covered in more detail through a typical course such as "Strategic Management of Information Technology" offered in many Masters in Information Systems programs.

18. Project Assignment

This process defines the project scope, leadership, and business partner involvement necessary to ensure successful project completion. The project definitions are placed in a project organization and objectives document based on the tactical plan that was created in the "tactical plan management" process.

Important components of this process are the selection of a project leader, defining IT and business involvement, and obtaining management commitment for the completion of this project.

This process would be covered in more detail through typical courses such as "Project Management" and "Analysis and Development of Information Systems" offered in many Masters in Information Systems programs.

19. Project Scheduling

This process prepares a detailed project plan including objectives, resources, time scale, tasks, organization, and deliverables. This process must use the project organization and objectives document that was prepared in the process "project assignment."

This process also obtains approval from the project team, sponsor, and IT management team. Components of this process are:

- define deliverables
- define tasks
- estimate project time and costs
- schedule resources
- finalize a detailed project plan

This process would be covered in more detail through typical courses such as "Project Management" and "Analysis and Development of Information Systems" offered in many Masters in Information Systems programs.

20. Project Controlling

This process monitors the project through its phases; conducting reviews, resolving any developmental problems, and documenting its life cycle. The process uses the detailed project plan developed in the project assignment.

This process will include the submission of change requests to move the deliverable to the system inventory. Components of this process include:

- tracking progress against the plan
- reporting status
- conducting project reviews
- resolving development problems
- reviewing any make/buy decisions
- submission of change requests

This process would be covered in more detail through typical courses such as "Project Management" and "Analysis and Development of Information Systems" offered in many Masters in Information Systems programs.

21. Project Requirements Control

This process accepts or rejects requests for changes and adjusts the detailed project plan as necessary. These changes result from modified objectives, new procedures, new technology, or errors in the original project scope. Components of this process include:

- receipt of requests for requirement changes from users and other sources
- analysis of specifications of new requests including the impact on the project
- acceptance or rejection of the requests
- revising the project plan (if necessary)

This process would be covered in more detail through typical courses such as "Project Management" and "Analysis and Development of Information Systems" offered in many Masters in Information Systems programs.

22. Project Evaluating

This process documents the completion of a project and ensures that all promised deliverables were actually furnished. This process uses the detailed project plan developed in "Project Assignment" and the project history that was produced during project development.

It compares actual and planned results and identifies reasons for variances. Components of this process include:

- documentation of the final status of the project and the deliverables
- comparison of project achievement with the project plans
- identification and reporting the reasons for variances
- obtaining approval to terminate the project and report its completion

This process would be covered in more detail through typical courses such as "Project Management" and "Analysis and Development of Information Systems" offered in many Masters in Information Systems programs.

23. Change Control

This process identifies, assesses, coordinates, groups, and monitors all changes to information systems resources and procedures in such a way that there is either minimal impact on the IT operation or minimal risk.

This process makes use of change requests, as these change requests trigger resource and data inventory updates. Components of this process include:

- recording change requests
- prioritizing and grouping changes based on a technical assessment
- prioritizing and grouping changes based on a business assessment
- scheduling, deferring, or rejecting changes
- monitoring testing
- monitoring installation
- reporting and controlling the status of all recorded changes

See Appendix 5B at the end of this chapter and Chapter 10 for a closer view of this process.

24. Asset Management

This process manages and monitors inventories of all IT resources (including hardware, software, personnel and financial resources.) This process relies on change information. Components of this process include:

- identification of systems, applications, data, personnel, supplies, and financial resources

- updating of inventory status
- maintenance of the security of these resources
- administration of access to these resources (e.g., disk space allocation, password administration)
- reporting and controlling the status of the inventories

See Appendix 5C at the end of this chapter for a closer view of this process.

25. Production and Distribution Scheduling

This process translates planned service agreements into a schedule of work and performance measurement for production and distribution. This process uses the tactical plan developed in the "tactical plan" process and the inventory from "resource and data performance control." Components of this process include:

- planning production and distribution service workload
- developing a maintenance and measurement schedule
- developing a current work schedule
- negotiation of any deviations from the service agreements with users
- publishing work, maintenance, and measurement schedules
- monitoring and modifying schedules (as necessary)

This process also schedules jobs, transactions, information, and data through the distribution network on a minute-to-minute basis to meet the agreed-upon service levels. It monitors the progress of information movements against the schedule and takes corrective actions, typically based on the 1–90-day schedule established in production and distribution scheduling. It also includes receiving, storing, and shipping of data and information through the distribution network. Components of this process include:

- translating data into machine-readable form
- receiving, registering, and validating input from all sources
- packaging, distributing, checking, and registering outputs
- monitoring progress of distribution work against the production and distribution schedules and taking corrective action (if necessary)
- executing predefined or emergency distribution procedures for bypass, recovery, security and/or performance
- reporting distribution status, incidents, actions taken, and results

This process would be covered in more detail through typical courses such as "Analysis and Development of Information Systems," "Data Management," "Distributed Information Systems Management," "Enterprise Systems Management," and "Integration of Information Systems Technology" offered in many Masters in Information Systems programs.

26. Problem Control

This process receives problems and monitors their resolution by requesting bypass actions and/or projects (maintenance or tuning). It informs the service evaluating process of the service impact of the problems. Components of this process include:

- recognizing the problems
- reporting/logging of the problems
- determining the nature, impact, and true extent of the problem
- selecting predefined bypass and recovery procedures
- initiation of action to resolve the problems
- reporting and controlling the status of all problems on hand

See Appendix 5D at the end of this chapter for a closer view of this process.

27. Service Evaluating

This process translates the performance status and the problem impact reports into business terms and compares them with service agreements. It also identifies and reports any variances to users and management. Components of this process include:

- translating operational data (production, distribution, performance, and problem) into service-level terms
- assessing user ratings of the service
- evaluating compliance to service agreements
- identifying and reporting reasons for variances
- reporting service status and new service requests

This process also provides an interface with the business to understand their expectations and to help and guide them in realizing these expectations. Components include:

- publishing support service offerings including contact person and telephone number
- providing user help offerings for appropriate services (e.g., information center, development center, and user help desk)
- forwarding all problems to the appropriate function

See Appendix 5E at the end of this chapter and Chapter 13 or a closer view of this process.

28. Software Development and Upgrade

This process develops and upgrades applications, operating systems software, other support software, and all related documentation within the framework of a project. Components of this process are:

- defining detailed requirements (including recovery, security, and audit)
- designing externals of the application
- designing internals of the application
- structuring data
- negotiating design compromises with users
- developing and testing programs
- integrating and testing applications including procured modules
- installing software

This process would be covered in more detail through typical courses such as "Project Management," "Analysis and Development of Information Systems," "Enterprise Systems Management," and "Integration of Information Systems Technology" offered in many Masters in Information Systems programs.

29. Software Procurement and Upgrade (Contracts and Vendors)

This process procures and modifies applications, operating systems software, other supporting software, and all related documentation within the framework of a project. The process controls the basic "buy" cycle. Components of this process include:

- defining detailed requirements for ideal system
- reviewing the integrity and performance of available offerings including promised vendor modifications
- negotiating compromises with vendors and users
- confirming or amending "buy" decisions and selecting systems
- defining system recovery for operating environment
- generating system and executing provided tests

- publishing instructions for integrating into the operating environment
- integrating and testing application/software including supplied modules
- installing application software

Chapter 11 on IT governance has an extended discussion of this process. Refer to that chapter for more detail.

30. Hardware Procurement and Upgrade (Contracts and Vendors)

This process selects, installs, removes, modifies, and upgrades information systems hardware and facilities within the framework of a project. Components of this process include:

- defining detailed requirements
- selecting hardware/network/facility
- laying out physical planning
- defining hardware, network, and facility recovery
- testing new units
- testing complete systems
- installing hardware, network, or facility

Chapter 11 on IT governance has an extended discussion of this process. Refer to that chapter for more detail.

31. Systems Maintenance

This process corrects defects in hardware, applications, software, and facilities (including engineering changes and temporary program fixes) within the framework of a project. Components of this process include:

- revalidating the cause of the problem
- understanding the environment of the suspect component
- diagnosing suspect components
- determining the fix for failing components
- testing fixes
- changing management review
- installing fixes

This process would be covered in more detail through typical courses such as "Analysis and Development of Information Systems," "Data Management," "Distributed Information Systems Management," and "Integration of Information Systems Technology" offered in many Masters in Information Systems programs.

32. Tuning and System Balancing

This process tunes the systems resources to ensure proper performance of individuals or groups of resources within the framework of a project. This process includes periodic regression testing to ensure that new changes have not caused undesired performance results in existing resources. Components of this process include:

- defining detailed requirements
- developing solutions
- executing testing of new or modified units
- testing complete systems
- changing management review
- installing new systems

This process would be covered in more detail through typical courses such as "Analysis and Development of Information Systems," "Data Management," "Distributed

Information Systems Management," and "Integration of Information Systems Technology" offered in many Masters in Information Systems programs.

33. Financial Performance

This process applies service rates to systems resources to determine total costs applicable to individual business units (including IT), accumulates these costs, charges them to the individual user organization (where appropriate), and matches them against the budget. The process also includes maintaining contractual agreements for project work, hardware and software leasing, and other supportive efforts. Components of this process include:

- calculating charges due for services when applicable
- administering vendor and other contracts
- executing cost accounting procedures
- purchasing equipment, supplies, and services
- reporting accounting and financial status
- tracking vendor performance

This process is discussed in Chapter 14—The Value of Information Systems Technology, and would be covered in more detail, through courses such as "Financial Management" offered in many Masters in Information Systems programs.

34. Staff Performance

This process tracks staff performance and reports productivity. This process consists of:

- collecting data on absences, accidents, and attendance
- collecting data on job performance
- comparing and reporting productivity

Appraisal of staff performance will require the training of many managers. For example, if the activity of telecommuting should be implemented in IT, managers will need training in the evaluation and appraisal of telecommuters. As new technologies, methodologies, and tools are introduced, most activities will need to be reviewed. A re-examination of procedures and polices will be necessary to determine how the activity can be tracked and managed.

This process would be covered in more detail through typical courses such as "Organizational Behavior," "Organization Theory," and "Human Resources Management in Information Systems" offered in many Masters in Information Systems programs. See Chapter 9 for additional information on this process.

35. Education and Training

This process educates business and IT personnel on Information Technology-related topics through job training or formal education. Components of this process include:

- performing training for information systems services and other needs
- performing education for information systems services and other needs
- developing and maintaining education documentation (course guides, etc.)
- maintaining an education and training profile for all IT staff.

This process would be covered in more detail through typical courses such as "Organizational Behavior," "Organizational Theory," and "Human Resources Management in Information Systems" offered in many Masters in Information Systems programs. See Chapter 9 for additional information on this process.

36. Recruiting, Hiring, and Retention

This process focuses on the activities necessary to acquire and maintain an effective, motivated, and competent workforce to enable Information Technology to meet the needs of the business. Most large IT organizations will have their own human resource unit to work with them. This process is successful if the policies and practices of the firm are sound, fair, and appealing to management and staff alike. This process must focus on the following:

- recruitment and promotion
- training and qualification requirements
- cross-training and job rotation
- hiring and firing
- measuring performance
- responding to technical and market changes
- balancing internal and external demands for staff and special skills
- succession plan for key staff

This process would be covered in more detail through typical courses such as "Organizational Behavior," "Organizational Theory," and "Human Resources Management in Information Systems" offered in many Masters in Information Systems programs. See Chapter 9 for additional information on this process.

37. Production

This process schedules and executes jobs, transactions, and data through the hardware and software to meet the agreed-upon service levels. It monitors the progress of work against the schedule and takes corrective actions (based on the 1–90-day schedule defined in production and distribution scheduling). Components of this process include:

- receiving jobs, transactions, and input data from distribution
- setting up, initiating, and running jobs and transactions
- making jobs, transactions, and output data available for distribution
- monitoring progress of production work against the production and distribution schedules and taking corrective action (if necessary)
- executing predefined or emergency production procedures for bypass, recovery, security and/or performance
- recording and reporting information on status, incidents, actions taken, and results

This process would be covered in more detail through typical courses such as "Analysis and Development of Information Systems," "Data Management," "Distributed Information Systems Management," "Enterprise Systems Management," and "Integration of Information Systems Technology" offered in many Masters in Information Systems programs.

38. Service Marketing

This process markets services to business partners and identifies needs for future services. This includes the sale of any product, resources, or service developed and/or owned by IT. Components of this process include:

- selecting service offerings to fit client needs
- marketing these offerings appropriately
- reporting user needs for new services
- initiate actions to provide services
- executing public relations activities on behalf of the I/S organization

This process also provides an interface among IT and the business to facilitate the understanding of expectations and to help and guide them in realizing future needs and expectations. Components include:

- publishing support service offerings including contact person and telephone number
- providing user help offerings for appropriate services (e.g. information center, development center, and user help desk)
- forwarding all problems to the appropriate function

Chapter 11 on IT Governance covers this process in more detail.

Which Processes Are Most Important?

All IT processes are important. Each process will contribute to the effective management and performance of IT. However, if they are examined from the perspective of the business, depending on the environment and demands, many of the processes have a more important contribution critical to the firm's success. For example, application development is typically considered most visible to developing competitive and strategic advantage. The project management-related processes are the essential processes that enable the completion of application development. Strategy, architecture, and the planning processes further enable IT to manage, anticipate, and assemble technologies and methodologies to assure a stable and continuously improving IT environment.

Security and recovery planning have gained greater stature because of the new threats to the stability of systems. Vendor management has also increased in importance, as many firms are outsourcing more of their activities. These processes are prominent because the business can see direct linkages between the activity of these processes and the activity of the business. Does this reduce the importance of the remaining processes?

If focus is not placed on the remaining processes, it is often because they are done well, so they tend to be taken for granted. These processes would be attracting greater attention if they were done poorly. For example, if change control, problem control, or asset management were to fail, there would be financial consequences and they would indirectly affect the production processes. When the production processes are affected, the business would suffer and the processes would be noticed.

As with business process, IT processes should be assessed based on their relative importance (e.g., impact on the critical success factors of the business), and their relative effectiveness (e.g., good, fair, poor). Hence, processes that are critical to the success of the business but in poor condition should be improved first. On the other hand, those processes that are not critical to the success of the business and in relatively good condition can be left unchanged.

Who Owns Each of These Process Containers?

IT processes are the domain of IT, so it is clear that IT must take ownership of their process containers. The ownership of the processes means that IT must be responsible for ensuring that each process is done efficiently and effectively. Each process varies in complexity, so active management is required to ensure that a quality product is delivered at the best cost. Best cost is not necessarily lowest cost, but includes taking into account: financial conditions, services, relationships, reliability, and so forth.

Some processes may be considered for outsourcing. If outsourcing is considered, care must be taken to ensure that ownership is not forgotten. The consequences of the lack of ownership will be the loss of responsibility in assessing the level of quality and performance of the activity. Lack of ownership will jeopardize the long-term success of the outsourced activity. This will be discussed more in Chapter 11—IT Governance.

▪▪▪ How Much Resource Will Be Applied to Each Process?

The amount of resources that are applied to each process varies a great deal depending on the relative importance and complexity of the process. Of the 38 IT processes discussed in this chapter, 21 processes were placed in the operational level. These processes account for more than 60 percent of the activity within Information Technology, but fewer than 40 percent of the IT staff work on operational activities. What enables IT to use fewer people in this area can be explained by the proliferation of many automated processes and tools that assist IT in maintaining equipment, networks, and production applications. Considerable effort was made in the 1980s and 1990s to develop scheduling tools, version control systems, and library maintenance applications, the use of which makes it easier for IT to handle operations with minimal staff.

The bulk of IT staff concentrates on application development and other planning tasks associated in the tactical layer. Historically, it was easy to establish funding for hiring and maintaining staff who were supporting new business projects and applications. This too is changing, as IT applies new ways to increase the productivity of individual programmers and analysts. In the past decade, dozens of new Computer Aided Software Engineering (CASE) tools, Rapid Application Development (RAD) methodologies, and the introduction of object-oriented programming languages have all helped to increase productivity while decreasing staff. Now the focus is on improving the strategic processes and achieving alignment with the business to improve the firm's bottom line profits as well as create strategic and competitive advantage.

▪▪▪ How Effective Are Each of These Processes Today?

Over the past three decades, IT has continuously improved many of the 38 processes. The project management related processes (assignment, scheduling, controlling, requirements control, and evaluating) have successfully evolved from mainframe-based development solutions to client/server and Web-based development solutions. Production and distribution scheduling, tuning and system balancing, production, and system maintenance are fairly stable across corporate IT data and computer centers.

Most IT processes can always be improved and made more effective and efficient by introducing new tools and methodologies. There are known troubling issues in IT processes, however, such as unevenness in their execution. For example, the hardware and software procurement and upgrade processes vary widely across many corporate implementations. In addition, asset management, change control, problem control, service evaluating, and service marketing are processes that are implemented very differently from one firm to another. Unlike those processes that have standard operating procedures, as in project management, these processes do not have the uniform standards and methodologies that are generally accepted. Support services for many of these processes are fragmented because there is a great variety of vendors that supply different products. Also, major corporations have built their own homegrown systems to support these processes. It is these operational level processes that require review to assess the prospect of improvement.

▪▪▪ What Priority Should Be Placed on Improving Each of These Processes?

Improving the IT processes can always occur, but is it worth the cost? Over the past several decades, IT executives have had to manage their organizations very closely because their budgets were always tight. This is not a trend that will likely go away. The business will always look to either reduce overhead costs or spend their money on IT investments that have the best opportunity to be profitable. Making improvements to any IT process requires IT to present a business case. The financial gain must be quantifiable to get support from the business. Many of the IT processes that are considered to be troubling remain that way because they lack the priority to be fixed. It would be good to upgrade the change control or problem control process, but if the same money could be used to build better applications and expand into new markets, it would be difficult to convince the business that the IT process should have a higher priority. What needs to be marketed is the impact that these improved processes could have on new applications or market expansion.

Improving the asset management process has often demonstrated a major reduction in losses of assets while also reducing clerical and overhead expense. Upgrading service evaluation has also improved performance of the vendors and internal suppliers of services. A change to the hardware and software procurement process has often saved companies a great deal of money. In summary, establishing priority to improve or upgrade an IT process will require the same cost-benefit analysis that would be needed to establish a new application. An IT process improvement is not unlike any other project needing funding, but there need to be quantifiable results that will justify the expense for the job.

REVIEW QUESTIONS ▪▪▪▪▪▪▪

1. Differentiate between strategic, tactical, and operational processes.
2. What are the components of IT architecture?
3. How has productivity increased in application development?
4. How can operational layer processes be performed with much a smaller staff than comparable tactical layer processes?
5. Are there processes that span more than one layer? If so, identify them.

DISCUSSION QUESTIONS ▪▪▪▪▪▪▪

1. How might a CIO get more involved in the strategic processes of the business functions in an organization?
2. What is the role of organizational politics and power in enabling or inhibiting the strategic processes of an IT function?
3. Why have disaster recovery processes and security processes gained prominence in our economy?
4. Why is planning important for IT processes?
5. What are some of the organizational issues that impede the development and implementation of effective means of appraising performance?
6. How do the three layers, strategic, tactical, and operational, differ from each other?
7. Why do the names and number of processes differ from one company to another?

AREAS FOR RESEARCH ▮▮▮▮▮▮▮

1. Discuss IT strategic processes and how they will have an impact on the pace of technological change in an enterprise.
2. What is the role of IT architecture in aligning the business and IT functions of an organization?
3. How are service level agreements handled in your firm?
4. Can IT be outsourced? If so, which parts? Explain.
5. Have some of your IT processes been outsourced?
6. What IT processes can be co-owned with their business partners?

CONCLUSION ▮▮▮▮▮▮▮

This chapter reviewed three layers of IT processes: strategic, tactical, and operational. The focus of this chapter was on the importance of information systems being prepared for many eventualities and to improve its overall effectiveness and efficiency in a continuous manner. Today, it is more vital that the IT processes are continuously improved and adjusted because of the rapid change in emerging technologies, methodologies, and tools, and because of the direct impact that IT has on the success of the business.

As will be discussed in later chapters, great emphasis is placed on measuring and demonstrating the value of these processes to the firm and its stakeholders. IT needs to establish processes that will enable IT to help the firm to meet its strategic objectives while also delivering the day-to-day services. By regularly reviewing and improving the 38 processes described in this chapter, the opportunity for IT to be considered a valued contributor to business success is greatly enhanced.

Appendix 5A

▮▮▮▮▮▮▮ Focusing on IT Architecture ▮▮▮▮▮▮▮

How do you develop an IT architecture?

The components of IT architecture will include:

- Knowledge, Information and Data Storage
  - Accessibility—how can end users easily retrieve important information?
  - Security—how can unauthorized users be kept away from the confidential data?
  - Accuracy—how can the end users be assured of data integrity?
  - Viability—how can applications be built that will permit timely, accurate, and easily accessible information derived from multiple sources and processed in a unique and effective manner to provide end users with the elements necessary to create knowledge?
- Security
  - Protection against viruses, unauthorized entry, denial of service attacks, hackers, destruction of applications, screens, and data from within
  - Protection of the interfaces with other systems (in-house, private, or public networks) from similar attacks
  - Monitoring of the hardware and software for auditing and financial accounting

- Network Communications and Data Transport
  - Obtaining successful network communications
  - Exchanging data in multiple environments
  - Using multiple platforms, such as the Internet, intranet, client server, LAN, WAN, mainframe, etc.

- Computer Systems
  - Providing adequate hardware to handle existing and future applications
  - Providing cost-effective systems as opposed to bleeding-edge equipment that costs more than necessary
  - Providing systems that are easy to learn and easy to use
  - Providing systems that are easy to maintain and upgrade.

- Interfaces
  - Connecting applications to internal and external systems
  - Connecting applications to the Internet, intranet, LAN, and WAN
  - Connecting applications and systems to new devices and appliances

- Application/Data Transformation
  - Building applications with traditional and newer programming languages
  - Building applications with CASE tools and/or Object-Oriented Programming Systems (OOPS)
  - Implementing/using Enterprise Resource Planning (ERP) systems
  - Implementing/using Customer Relationship Management (CRM) systems
  - Implementing/using Application Service Providers (ASP) via the Internet
  - Using multimedia/Real Player/video/DVD/Media Player for business applications
  - Implementing/using/upgrading operating systems (e.g., Windows XP, 2000, NT/ UNIX/ Linux)
  - Implementing/using/upgrading off-the-shelf systems (e.g., Microsoft Office XP/2000, Star Office 5.2, Corel WordPerfect, Lotus SmartSuite)
  - Implementing/using Internet development languages, such as JAVA, C++, XML, Visual Programming, FrontPage

All of these components must be defined with an emphasis on developing an integrated solution with clearly defined standards. They must be integrated so that new systems can communicate with existing systems with little difficulty. IT needs to enable the integration of the business to be able to speak easily across organizations, systems, and technologies. Standards are necessary because the cost of maintaining skilled staff familiar with many technologies and languages is extremely expensive, and recruiting such skilled personnel if difficult as well.

When developing the IT architecture, the following questions are raised:

- Are the right technologies being used and are they integrated properly?
- What levels of information sharing, security, and access should be supported?
- Which applications will be developed versus which will be bought?
- Are applications, tools, and data easy to upgrade, update, and maintain?
- Who will upgrade, update, and maintain the applications, tools, and data?
- Who will assess whether the architecture will meet the firm's needs?

- Will the horizontal architecture support the horizontal processes of the firm?

Vertical structures of the firm are illustrated by an example of departments or divisions that are separated functionally in typical corporations. Departments like finance, marketing, manufacturing, legal, sales, human resources, etc. are often thought of as separate vertical functional groups. Horizontal structures are those units formed to support a product line or business segment. The structure would form teams that extend across functional areas. For example, the team would include members of finance, legal, marketing, sales, manufacturing, human resources, and IT. The horizontal structures would foster great synergy, as all team members would be focused on the success of the product line or business.

In a vertical structure, it would be obvious that having a standardized set of tools, software, data, and hardware would be essential to facilitate communications, sharing, and working together. However, it has been observed that standardized tools, software, data, and hardware are not always established across the different functional departments. The weakness of this becomes apparent when the department is unable to effectively participate in the horizontal processes; that is, support of new products and business segments. The issues of standards will be raised again when attempting to formalize an effective IT organization.

IT Architecture Imperatives

IT architecture must enable a certain set of imperatives to effectively support the enterprise. The following is a partial list of these imperatives:

- Minimize cost and maximize responsiveness
- Enable vastly improved and increased communication
- Put "information" in the hands of decision makers
- Enable process integration
- Establish improved customer linkages
- Support learning

In many enterprises where there is a lack of control in the organization, IT architecture decisions may be made by:

- Application developers based on their skills and not on what is best for the long term or in the interest of integration within the enterprise

▪▪▪▪▪▪▪▪▪▪▪ **FIGURE 5A-1** Developing an IT Architecture.

Developing an IT architecture

Integration and standards

- **Knowledge, information and data storage**
  - Accessibility   Viability
  - Security   Accuracy
- **Security**
- **Network communications and data transport**
  - Obtaining
  - Exchanging
  - Client Server
- **Computer systems**
- **Interfaces**
- **Application / data transformation**
  - Traditional / 3rd Generation / 4th Generation   ERP
  - CASE   OOPS   ASP
  - KBS   Visual Programming
  - Multimedia   Internet / intranet / extranet   Virtual Reality

- The data center based on its capabilities and its current resources, not on future issues of security/recovery/backup/integration
- Any end user who is allowed to purchase software on his own, disregarding any corporate/department/workgroup standard

In Figure 5A-1, the complexity of developing the IT architecture is shown. All of the various components of the architecture must be integrated and working harmoniously to assure the firm that IT is optimized for the future. In addition, developers of IT architecture would seek to adopt standards that would balance the following concerns:

- Volume and capability—the products and technologies would be able to meet requirements now and in the near future; the product has been thoroughly tested and is reliable, scalable, and easy to use in development; the product must be easy to maintain.
- Strategic opportunities, i.e. the opportunity to partner with vendors, develop alliances with competitors and non-competitors in piloting new technologies and products; take advantage of special offers, discounts, and special opportunities, such as beta testing.
- Governance—regulatory issues, governmental policies, SEC, IRS, laws and ordinances, licenses, copyrights, trademarks, etc.
- Technical opportunities—emerging technologies that are generational leaps in sophistication; major gains in productivity that are measurable and can be quantified.

- Business implications—the communication between the different departments, functions, and locations, and across organizations with customers and partners would be greatly improved; efficiencies, such as shared databases, shared applications, and single sources of key data, would increase productivity and minimize the duplication of effort in many areas.

E-business Implications on IT Architecture

In Figure 5A-2,[4] Web architecture is shown to be just as challenging to design and integrate. The Internet has influenced IT architecture by introducing new tools and languages, but there are other implications as well. The first issue is that the advent of the Internet has enabled end user access to e-business enterprise systems 24/7/365. In other words, end users can and do gain access to an organization's Web sites at any time of day or night. This implies that:

- Facility planning will be much more expensive because it must perform to a higher level of service.
- The mindset of people in the organization has changed; there is an expectation that IT will provide a higher level of service quality.
- System design and engineering will require complete fault tolerance in order to maintain the maximum uptime for 24/7/365 service.
- Technology operations are more complex as well as more intense.

▮▮▮▮▮▮▮▮▮ **FIGURE 5A-2** Web Services Actors, Objects, and Operations.

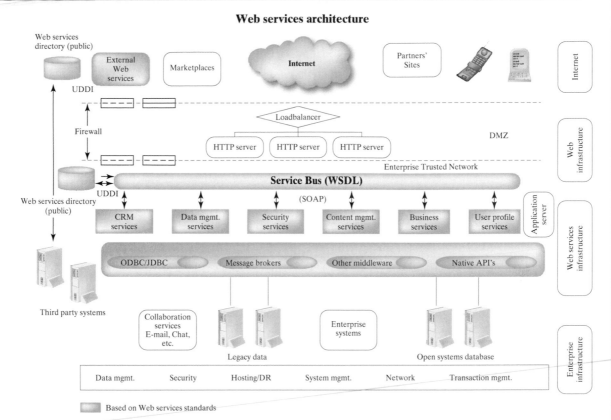

Web services architecture

Source: Gottschalk, K. et al., "Introduction to Web Services Architecture," *IBM Systems Journal*, vol 41, no. 2, (2002), pp. 171.

- Processes and procedures must be highly effective, well planned, and able to meet the needs of almost every customer.
- Maintenance of the application, operating environment, hardware, and network must be made as simple as possible while being maintained with minimum effort.
- Backup/recovery/business continuity planning/outsourcing/key processes must all be performed with great care. Customers will not return if they feel that your operation is unreliable and ill-managed.

The bottom line is that e-business customers will demand a lot and they have many competitors to choose from. Disappointment with one service can lead them to look elsewhere.

In Figure 5A-3, the issue is "Can the firm's facilities support e-business? "(i.e., the data centers.) Facilities that support e-business must be more densely populated with servers and networking equipment. Rack-mounted server clusters are popular today and as a consequence, the amount of power required to keep all these data centers up and running has been rising steadily. More power usage results in more heat generated and thus, the need for more air conditioning facilities. Generators, switches, routers, hubs, etc. require more power, more heat, more cooling, and so on. Fire control, disaster recovery, and telecom backups all require careful planning and administration. Careful planning and anticipation of needs is vital to doing the right things.

In summary, the job of building IT architecture is complex, demanding, and yet crucial to the firm. The success or failure of the process will have a dramatic and long-lasting impact on the firm's business and its competitive position in the marketplace. The people who can do this job will be very valuable and will represent the greatest assets to the firm.

▪▪▪▪▪▪▪▪▪▪ **FIGURE 5A-3** Demands of a Web Economy on Architecture.

Demands of a Web Economy on Architecture

Infrastructure Readiness – 7 × 24 × 365

Is your facility capable of supporting e-business operations?

- Data centers are more densely populated
- Racks are requiring more power - 2 Kva/rack
- Power generates more heat – requires more cooling
- Generators, switchgear, UPS, HVAC, infrastructure
- Fire suppression – can't wait for refills
- Telecom – multiple providers, CO's, SONET

Construction $700 to $1,000/sq.ft. raised floor

Appendix 5B

▪▪▪▪▪▪▪▪ Focusing on Change Control ▪▪▪▪▪▪▪

Change control is a formal organized process that enables the requests for updates to production activities to be carried out. This process must be done accurately because it will affect all users of the production environment. Errors made in this process can negatively reflect the production process by causing 1) unpredictable and incorrect results; 2) systems crashes or premature stops; 3) incorrect information to be transmitted or received; and 4) systems that interface with the production system to fail as well. Many companies use a very rigid and structured approach to manage this activity because of the high impact and risk that exists. In Figure 5B-1, a typical change control process is exhibited in the form of a flow diagram.

In the flow diagram, a change request is submitted by the business area, providing exact details as to the nature of change, reason for the change, and extent of the change. An evaluator must perform an impact analysis and make a recommendation to do or not do the change. The evaluator sends the analysis to the change control board that has the ultimate decision-making authority to approve or reject the change request. If it is decided that the change should not be done (i.e., not a good business case, too expensive, or not reasonable, etc.), then the request is rejected and sent back. On the other hand, if the request is approved, it is assigned to a modifier. The modifier is responsible for handling the change, making changes to the code or process, testing, and installing the fix. At any point during this period, the change can still be cancelled by either the business or by IT.

Once the change has been completed through the coding, testing, and installation phases, there are some cases where another person or group would review the change to ensure it was done correctly. When the change has been thoroughly reviewed it will then be logged and the change request will be filed in the closed case file. Again, this process documents a typical change process. Many firms will have a process customized to meet the special needs of their company.

Figure 5B-2 illustrates a job description of a change control coordinator, providing information on what the job entails and what kind of person should hold that responsibility.

Figure 5B-3 shows a sample request form (from Chubb, Inc.) that is generally filled out by the business when they wish to upgrade or fix an

▪▪▪▪▪▪▪▪▪▪▪ **FIGURE 5B-1** Change Request Flow Diagram.

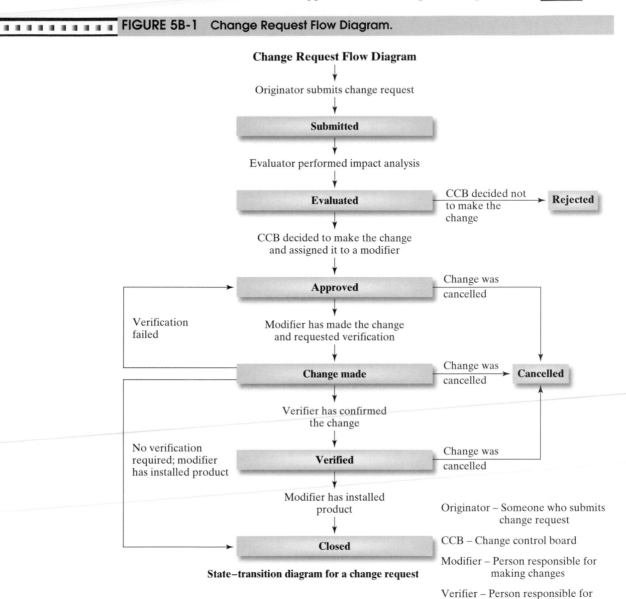

Change Request Flow Diagram

↓

Originator submits change request

↓

Submitted

↓

Evaluator performed impact analysis

↓

Evaluated → CCB decided not to make the change → **Rejected**

↓

CCB decided to make the change
and assigned it to a modifier

↓

Approved → Change was cancelled

↓

Verification
failed

Modifier has made the change
and requested verification

↓

Change made → Change was cancelled → **Cancelled**

↓

Verifier has confirmed
the change

↓

No verification
required; modifier
has installed product

Verified → Change was cancelled

↓

Modifier has installed
product

↓

Closed

State–transition diagram for a change request

Originator – Someone who submits change request

CCB – Change control board

Modifier – Person responsible for making changes

Verifier – Person responsible for determining if the change was made correctly

existing production process. The form provides space for the business to use to inform the evaluator about the business necessity for this change. Every change, other than government-mandated changes, will have a different cost associated with the fix. Each change should be evaluated on a business case framework to assure that the change merits the cost of the fix.

▪▪▪▪▪▪▪▪▪▪▪ FIGURE 5B-2 Sample Job Description for Change Control Coordinator.

Overview of Responsibilities

- Analyzes each change request to ensure that no conflicts exist with other requests
- Interacts with IS personnel to develop a scheduled date for each change request
- Monitors all change requests to ensure timely implementation
- Is a member of, and reports any conflicts to, the change control committee
- Is responsible for the maintenance of change files and production libraries

Detailed Responsibilities

- Coordinates all changes in the production environment concerning online and batch systems through the use of appropriate forms
- Monitors and logs progress of changes to ensure that scheduled dates are met; if a scheduled date cannot be met, ensures that all affected areas are notified of any schedule changes
- Reviews all change requests to ensure that the requested dates are feasible; schedules requests that have little impact on the production environment; reports to the change control committee for scheduling of those changes that conflict with other requests or that significantly affect the production environment
- Maintains the change file to ensure that all historical data is correct and up-to-date
- Ensures that all change request entries are removed from the change file when implemented
- Provides special reports to the change control committee or management on request
- Moves all test programs to production libraries on the scheduled date and controls the production libraries' passwords
- Forwards to the change control committee all problem reports resulting from a previous change request
- Interacts with the technical standards group (if one exists) when a change request warrants a technical announcement bulletin

Qualifications

- Ability to communicate and work effectively with all levels of IS, communications, and user personnel
- Strong oral and written communication skills
- Three to five years experience in information systems, including at least one year of hands-on JCL experience
- Working knowledge of procedures for maintaining computerized files and databases
- Understanding of the user community and its use of, and dependence on, computing services

▪▪▪▪▪▪▪▪▪▪▪▪ **FIGURE 5B-3** Sample of Typical Change Request Form.

Change Request Form

Document Preparation Information (To be completed by preparer)

Change Request/Problem Log Number: Prepared by: Phone: Date Prepared:

Change Information (To be completed by preparer)

Proposed Change:

Business purpose: – Easier to do Business with Chubb   – Reduce/Manage Expenses
                    – Domestic/Overseas Growth   – Better/More Timely
                    – Increase Productivity   – Reduce Losses or Loss Expenses
                    – Employee Skill/Knowledge Improvement   – Regulatory Mandates
                    – New Market/New Products   – Senior Management Directive
                    – Competitive Position   – Other (explain)

Reason for Change/Description of Problem:

Request Implementation Date: /Priority:

Change Impact Assessment (To be completed by the I/T)

Describe the impact of the Change on the Project, including all components affected (Design, Database design; System, Subsystem, or process impact; conversion, etc.) as well as any organizational impacts.	Quality effort: days, weeks, months:	Impact assessed by:

Provide Release and/or date this change could be implemented

Approval for Impact Assessment

Change Request Control Number (Provided by Project Manager)	Client Project Representative/Date Approved	Project Manager or I/T Representative/Date Approved

Assigned to

Assigned to:	Date Assigned:	Date Completed:

QA testing

Assigned to:	Date Assigned:	Outcome/Sign off date:

Approval for Implementation

Date and Release Number for Delivery:	Date Approved:	Date implemented to production:

Appendix 5C

▭▭▭▭▭▭▭ Focusing on Asset Management ▭▭▭▭▭▭▭

This process focuses on building, securing, accessing, and managing the inventories of all IT resources and includes all hardware, software, and networks, as well as personnel and financial assets. Asset management requires the identification of all systems, applications, data, personnel, supplies, and financial resources. Reporting and control status of the inventory of these resources must be kept up-to-date and secure. Lastly, asset management also has the responsibility of administrating access to these resources (including data set space allocation and password administration).

In Figure 5C-1,[5] it is clearly seen that the administration of asset management extends across all processes within IT. Every IT processes is dependent on some asset that asset management is monitoring and protecting.

Asset management covers the entire life cycle of all products used within IT, from requisition to retirement. Figure 5C-1 illustrates that many units within the organization and their associated IT processes must assist in tracking each asset as it is passed from one stage to another in the product's life cycle.

One important aspect of Asset Management is the opportunity to conserve money by spending less or saving more. In Figure 5C-2,[6] seven ways to save are suggested by the Gartner Group.

There are other issues that asset management must resolve. What should be done with old obsolete PCs and other hardware? Should they be given to charity, given to employees for home use, or sold to PC recyclers? How can software distribution be handled in the office? What kind of penalties should be enforced when employees use unlicensed software at the office? How can the use of software by employees in the office be effectively monitored without causing undue resentment while still ensuring that the company is protected from copyright violation? Asset management must address all these problems and uphold the corporate culture while doing it.

▮▮▮▮▮▮▮▮▮▮▮▮ **FIGURE 5C-1** Asset Management Practices.

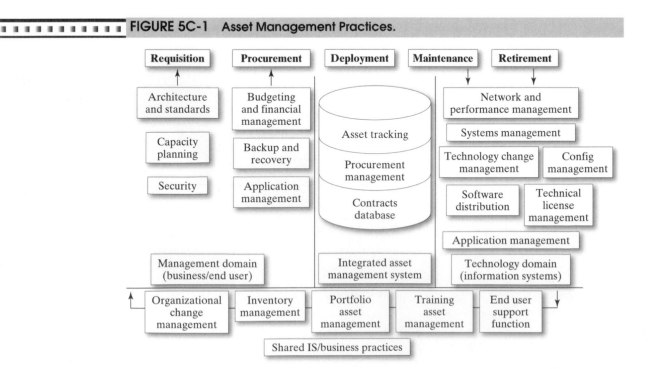

Source: Gartner Group.

▪▪▪▪▪▪▪▪▪▪ **FIGURE 5C-2   IT Asset Management Implementation.**

IT Asset Management Implementation – Seven Ways to Save

1. Software volume licenses
  • Aids implementing standards
  • Increase discounts by 10 percent to 15 percent
  • Savings of 25 percent

2. Consolidated procurement
  • Reduce the number of buying centers
  • Acquire equipment faster
  • Save as much as 10 percent annually

3. Maintenance contracts
  • Differentiate user profiles for maintenance contracts
  • Save 10 percent to 20 percent on per-seat maintenance payments

4. Property tax
  • Accurate inventory reduce tax bills
  • Savings may reach 20 percent of property tax bill

5. Help desk
  • Inventory reduces diagnosis and response time
  • Cut technician time by 50 percent
  • Savings as high as 57 percent over worst case

6. Electronic software distribution
  • Save 2,000 hours labor
  • Invest $100,000 first year
  • Save 55 percent on software distribution costs

7. Software metering
  • Most effective when on current use is at 20 percent to 40 percent
  • Invest $50,000 first year
  • Save 27 percent on PC software budget

Source: Gartner Group.

Appendix 5D

▪▪▪▪▪▪▪ **Focusing on Problem Control** ▪▪▪▪▪▪▪

Problem control is the process that addresses trouble reports, performance problems, and user complaints and monitors their resolution by requesting bypass actions and/or projects. Actions that are initiated might attempt to provide a workaround, repair, or tune a process, software, or hardware device. Problem control will also inform the service evaluating process of the service impact of the problem.

The key factors in this process are the logging and recording of the initial complaint, understanding the problem so that it can be explained to others, assessing the impact of the problem, finding a temporary solution until the problem can be fixed, and initiating the fix and monitoring the process until resolution. Unfortunately, the complexity and severity of problems are so wide-ranging that the process can be overwhelming at times.

The main objective of problem management is to "minimize the impact of problems on IT services by focusing attention and responsibilities on identifying problems." When problem management is successful, there are 1) fewer and shorter outages; 2) improved IT-user relationships; 3) enhanced productivity; 4) environment for growth; and 5) stronger management control.

In 1999, Comdisco prepared a vulnerability study to illustrate the causes of unplanned application downtime. That study showed that 40 percent of the time it was the application that failed; 20 percent of the time it was a hardware or technology fault; but more significantly, the remaining 40 percent of the time it was operator error. That seems to indicate that a large percentage of the time, the downtime could have been avoided!

▪▪▪▪▪▪▪▪▪▪ **FIGURE 5D-1** Relative Occurrence of Outage Incidents.

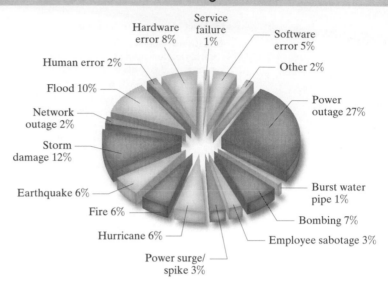

Source: Contingency Planning Research, Inc.

In Figure 5D-1,[7] Contingency Planning Research did a statistical mapping of relative occurrence of outages and it is clear that there is a wide variety of reasons why outages occur, which will make it difficult to anticipate and prepare for every possibility.

Problem management must also support the help desk. The help desk becomes the frontline of activity when things go wrong within IT. The help desk will get calls from the business when their applications are not running and they will get calls from IT staff who cannot fix problems themselves, especially network problems and hardware failures.

In Figure 5D-2,[8] the Meta group analyzed key help desk statistics.

As activity is rising in IT customer service centers and help desks, many firms are moving towards a more structured environment. This is done because as the volume of calls rises, not all issues can be handled at once. This means that a procedure must be created to handle the different callers and provide a differentiation between each caller so that the callers with the greatest problems are handled first. In Figure 5D-3, an example of a four-tier breakout between levels of severity is shown. This process is similar to how hospitals address patients

▪▪▪▪▪▪▪▪▪▪ **FIGURE 5D-2** Helping the Help Desk.

In its Service Management Strategies report, the **Meta Group** analyzed some key characteristics of the help desk usage.

- 15% to 35% of help desk call volumes were password resets.
- 25% to 35% of call volume is from new service requests or status checks.
- Average number of calls to the help desk, per end-user:
  - 1.75 calls per month
  - Estimated for 2003: three calls per month (20% annual increase)
- Help desk queries via Internet: 6%; By 2003–2004, over 20%
- By next year, 40% of IT help desks will migrate to IT customer service centers.

Source: Meta Group.

▪▪▪▪▪▪▪▪▪▪ **FIGURE 5D-3 Help Desk Severity Levels.**

Emergency (Severity 1) Critical
Many customers affected (Server/line down, poor server performance, host application unavailable or poor performance).

High (Severity 2) Urgent
Specific to one customer, problem prevents customer from continuing with a critical task (Forgotten/revoked password, general protection faults, virus, terminal timing out).

Normal (Severity 3) Important
Workstation is functional but a problem exists which prevents the completion of a non-critical task (PC software problems and questions, application specific questions, report distribution, hardware repairs).

Low (Severity 4) Not urgent
Request for information that does not prevent the user from performing (e.g., report request, information, have someone paged).

Source: Jerry Luftman/Meta Group.

in emergency rooms, where treatment is provided to the most serious problems first.

Problem management will remain challenging because there is complexity, great variety, and unknown variations and mutations of problems that could occur. How a firm can best staff a help desk has been a daunting question. Should an organization distribute trouble tickets or should it have the help desk try to help callers? If the firm wants to have the help desk personnel help, what skills do they need? With the wide variety of issues, can anyone be fully trained and qualified to help while still keeping the process economical?

Appendix 5E

▪▪▪▪▪▪▪ **Focusing on Service Evaluating** ▪▪▪▪▪▪▪

In this section, the focus is on reporting service status and preparing new service requests. If a process is managed by a service level agreement, reporting service status requires translation of production, distribution, problems, and performance data into service level terms. That means that since there is a binding contract that defines the expected level of service, there must be an explicit demonstration of variance between the expected performance and the actual performance. It is important to include the user assessment of the service in this variance review. The service evaluating team needs to review these findings and report to management on the success or failure to comply with the terms of the service level agreements. The service evaluating team would need to attempt to discover any circumstances or reasons for variances between the provisions of the agreement and the actual performance.

In Figure 5E-1,[9] there are systems management tools that will assist in tracking performance, production, distribution, and problems. The Gartner Group and Dataquest did the research.

The other process is to prepare new service requests based on the requests of users for additional services or fixes to existing systems or processes. As was mentioned in the previous appendix, some of the requests will be generated from problem control. These requests will be for fixes to existing applications or processes. Other requests can be generated from new business, government regulation, competitive issues, cost savings initiatives, etc. These requests may have an impact on the existing service level agreement and will need to be addressed or may lead to a new service level agreement that will be established to augment a new service.

▪▪▪▪▪▪▪▪▪▪ **FIGURE 5E-1 Tools for Service Evaluating.**

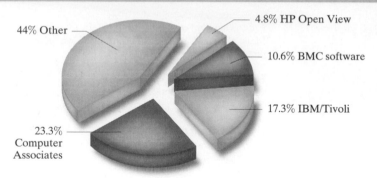

The service management tools

Source: Dataquest/Gartner Group.

In Figure 5E-2[10] The Gartner group introduces a Service Desk Toolkit that helps integrate the various problem/change/call tracking and inventory management issues so that service evaluating can review the need for new services against multiple criteria. Since new services represent an increase in cost, this evaluation process is a way to measure the service across many dimensions and verify that the costs are justified.

There are many issues concerning measuring, monitoring, planning, and managing service level agreements that have not been discussed here. Measuring and monitoring are discussed in Chapter 13—Measuring, Reporting, and Controlling. Planning service level agreements is discussed in Chapter 6—IT Planning. Managing service level agreements and vendors will be discussed in Chapter 11—IT Governance.

▪▪▪▪▪▪▪▪▪▪ **FIGURE 5E-2 Toolkit for Service Evaluating.**

The service desk toolkit integrates:

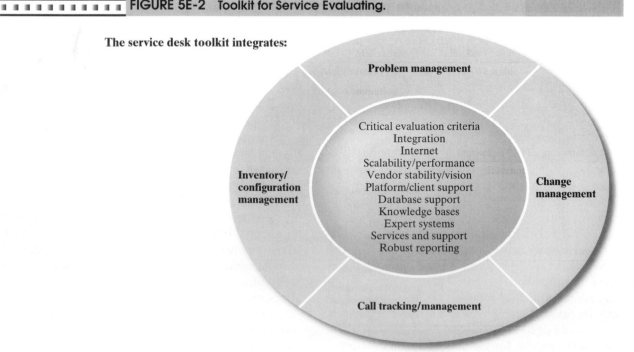

Source: Gartner Group.

REFERENCES

[1] David F. Feeney (1998) "Core IS Capabilities for Exploiting Information Technology" MITSloan Management Review, Spring 1998, Volume 39, Number 3, pp. 9–21.

[2] CobiT: Control Objectives for Information and related Technology, "Control Objectives," *Information Systems Audit and Control Foundation (ISACF) and IT Governance Institute, 2000.*

[3] CobiT: Control Objectives for Information and related Technology, "Control Objectives," *Information Systems Audit and Control Foundation (ISACF) and IT Governance Institute, 2000.*

[4] Gottschalk, K. et al., "Introduction to Web Services Architecture", IBM Systems Journal, vol 41, no. 2, (2002), pp. 171.

[5] Gartner Group.

[6] Gartner Group.

[7] Contingency Planning Research, Inc.

[8] Meta Group.

[9] Dataquest/Gartner Group.

[10] Gartner Group.

6

Planning-Related IT Processes

"It is a bad plan that admits of no modification."
—PUBLILIUS SYRUS

"What we plan we build …"
—PHOEBE CARY

Preview of Chapter

This chapter provides a more detailed discussion of the 16 IT planning-related processes that are part of the 38 general IT processes discussed in Chapter 5. IT planning describes the formal activities and processes associated with the allocation of organizational resources (e.g., capital, human, hardware, software) and time as they relate to the accomplishment of specific business and/or IT objectives. This chapter further discusses the three levels on which IT planning occurs:

- Strategic
- Tactical
- Operational

The differences each level has on both the IT planning process and the contents and execution of those plans are also described. Last, concepts and empirical evidence of what constitutes a successful plan, as well as the issues IT management must manage in each level of planning to avoid problems in plan execution, are discussed.

The intent of this chapter is to provide the IT manager with general guidance and an overview with respect to the types of plans and related processes that require the organization's attention. Entire books have been written on the details of performing many of the planning processes described in this chapter. The reader is encouraged to discover what these authors have to say on each of these types of plans.

Readers should also refer to Chapter 7—Managing Emerging Technologies for a detailed discussion on planning activities related to identifying and incorporating emerging technologies into the organization's IT strategy, technology architecture, infrastructure, business processes, and culture.

What we will examine in this chapter:

■ Why planning is important to the management of IT organizations and why it is different from other types of business planning

■ The levels of IT planning in organizations and the implications of each level

■ Strategic-level IT planning

■ Tactical-level IT planning

■ Operational-level IT planning

■ Global considerations in IT planning

▪▪▪ Why Is IT Planning Important?

It would seem self-evident to most IT managers that planning is an important component of the management of IT organizations. After all, IT managers are routinely involved in planning activities; from developing or reviewing software development plans to planning the acquisition of new hardware or software. Planning (or the activities that *behave* like planning) is part of the role and responsibilities of IT managers from the operational through the strategic levels of the organization. While planning for IT-related activities is an almost daily occurrence, the process of conceptualizing the requirements of the different types of plans, and their linkage with each other and to the organization's business objectives, is not always well understood.

First, why is IT planning different from other kinds of planning? One important difference stems from the fact that, unlike most other organizational functions, the IT function must look across all the other functions that comprise the enterprise. IT must be able to integrate the business perspectives of the other organizational functions into an enterprise IT perspective that addresses strategic (outward-facing) and internal technology (architecture and infrastructure) requirements. In addition to this integrative role across the enterprise, the IT function must also be able to "drill down" into the business functional organizations to support specific business requirements at strategic, tactical, and operational levels for those business units. While other organizational functions (e.g., marketing, finance) may have a similar role with respect to a cross-functional perspective, it is unlikely that a marketing function in an organization would be tasked with supporting the back office of a major securities firm or defining—or even needing to understand—the linkage between that back office's functions and the role and impact of an enterprise marketing program.

Another critical difference with respect to IT planning is that it must deal with two environments that can best be described as turbulent and dynamic: the ever-changing and unpredictable external business marketplace as well as the IT environment itself. Changes in both the business environment as well as the IT environment are coming at an ever-increasing pace and the impact of these changes on the company—and on each other!—must be taken into account. Unlike most other forms of business planning, IT plans need to accommodate both environments if IT is to be effectively aligned with business to deliver competitive advantage (see Chapter 2—IT Strategy for a more detailed discussion about strategic alignment). This complexity is sometimes seized upon as an excuse by some IT managers for not planning, but as discussed in the chapter on IT strategy, not planning is merely a formula for letting the winds of change batter the company against the rocks of competition.

Why plan at all? Without plans, the coordinated activities required to build and deliver new things to customers—products, services, knowledge—becomes much more difficult, if not impossible. Planning is an essential process that facilitates communication and enhances understanding among the stakeholders. In large, complex, and increasingly global organizations, planning (and communication) is essential for marshalling the required people, capital, technology, and procedural resources (this includes knowledge) to achieve important organizational goals over timeframes that are becoming ever more critical to economic success. "Muddling through" or "making it up as we go along" simply won't work as a substitute for sound IT planning practices in the complex, turbulent, interdependent and knowledge-intensive environment that now characterizes 21st century IT organizations.

How, then should IT managers think about IT planning? How many types of plans should IT managers be concerned with? What should be the objectives and characteristics of these IT plans? What things should IT management be concerned with to improve the chances for success of their plans?

Lastly, what is meant by "strategic," "tactical," or "operational" level IT planning? Envision that organizations have three "layers" of management focus (see Figure 6-1):

- **Strategic.** This level of the organization is focused on the external environment and making decisions about the allocation of resources for competitive advantage. Time frames and planning horizons are typically longer-term (years) and information requirements focus on the organization's ability to monitor environmental change and track trends. Refer to Chapter 2 to review a prior discussion of IT strategy. This domain is typically the province of senior management—CEOs, CIOs, CFOs, etc. From an IT planning standpoint, the types of planning activities at this level are:
  - Business strategic planning
  - IT strategy planning

- **Tactical.** This level is focused on the external environment to address short-to-medium timeframe organizational responses to competitive threats. It is also focused on the internal organizational environment over the same timeframe to address operational or organizational management issues or improvements. This domain tends to be the province of "middle management," which is principally concerned with coordinating information and processes between the strategic and operational layers of the organization and developing plans for the execution of

▪▪▪▪▪▪▪▪▪▪▪▪ FIGURE 6-1 Layers of Management Focus (Adapted from Robert N. Anthony).[1]

Information content	Management level	Information characteristics
Policies Plans Budgets Objectives	Strategic	External source Wide scope Ad hoc Unscheduled Future-oriented Infrequent Summarized
Measurement Schedules Revenues Profits Costs	Tactical	
Performance Services Goods	Operational	Internal source Narrow focus Pre-specified Scheduled Historical Frequent Detailed
	Responsibility/ authority	

Source: Anthony, Robert N., *Management Control Systems*, McGraw-Hill, 1997.[1]

strategic objectives. From an IT planning standpoint, the primary types of plans formulated and managed at this level are:

- Application planning
- Data planning
- Systems planning
- Network planning
- Project planning
- Service level planning
- Recovery planning
- Security planning
- Audit planning
- Capacity planning
- Skills planning
- Budget planning
- Vendor planning
- Management systems planning

- **Operational.** This level is focused on day-to-day concerns of running the IT infrastructure or executing plans developed at the "tactical" and "strategic" layers of the organization. At the operational level, plans are typically implemented or executed rather than formulated.

Chapter 5 introduced the 38 processes and described the non-planning processes that are also categorized by strategic, tactical, and operational levels.

▖▖▖ Strategic IT Planning

The principal types of planning addressed at the strategic level of the organization are business strategic planning and IT strategy planning.

Business Strategic Planning

This process assists senior management by defining the enterprise demands of its IT function through the strategic plan period and the freedom IT has in meeting these demands. For this process to be successful, it must use all available inputs from the enterprise (both formal and informal) to be able to arrive at accurate definitions.

Components of business strategic planning include:

- Defining the IT mission based on the enterprise's mission and objectives
- Defining IT policies to carry out its mission
- Defining business processes, information, and information flows of the enterprise
- Defining the enterprise requirements for information throughout the strategic time period

Although the CIO will make major contributions to this plan, the senior business executives should be the owners of this process and will provide their vision, processes, information flows, goals, and future business needs. The CEO, CFO, and senior officers representing the various functional departments must be the owners of this process. Chapter 2—IT Strategy provides a more detailed discussion of the processes involved in strategy formulation and alignment of IT strategy and business strategy.

IT Strategy Planning

Based on the goals of information systems and the constraints of the enterprise, this process provides the general direction on how to attain these goals, via an information systems strategic plan. It specifies the sequence in which the key activities of the enterprise will be addressed and how the existing services provided will evolve. The plan also ensures coherence and consistency of this direction against tactical achievements.

Steps toward developing an information systems strategic plan include:

- Evaluating alternate implementation of services, applications, and infrastructure, including business justification and risk assessment
- Defining and prioritizing the strategic objectives within the information systems policies
- Obtaining approval for the information systems strategic plan
- Controlling the information systems strategic plan against the tactical performance

The owners of this process are the senior managers within IT. The CIO is considered the owner of the overall process and the other senior managers will have a major impact on implementation and maintenance of the plan.

Chapter 2—IT Strategy and Chapter 11—IT Governance cover this process and the details of the components of an information systems strategic plan in more detail.

IIII Tactical IT Planning

Tactical IT planning activities address issues that have a time horizon generally bounded or strongly influenced by the budget cycle of the organization (12–24 months). The principal types of IT planning activities at this level of the IT organization are described in detail in the following subsections of this chapter.

Application Planning

The application plan is a schedule or forward-looking map of applications to be built or modified within a set period of time. The time period spans the business planning cycle or what is referred to as the tactical period. For the application plan to be successful, the application plan must address each key function of the enterprise within the tactical period. To do this, as part of the application planning process, the strategic goals and direction of the enterprise are considered, and there is a review of all existing and proposed applications to determine if all goals have been successfully translated to an existing or new application activity. The principal inputs to this activity are the business strategic plan and the information systems strategic plan (see the preceding section on strategic IT planning).

During this review period, the application architecture may be expanded as well to include:

- Emerging technologies
- Integrated processes, and/or
- Improved standards in development or maintenance

Chapter 7—Managing Emerging Technologies will provide a detailed discussion on planning activities related to emerging technologies.

The end result of the application planning process will be an updated plan for the tactical time period that will enable the enterprise to reach as many strategic goals as possible in the business planning cycle.

In the current economic climate of continuous and unpredictable change, IT management should approach applications planning with several important points understood:

1. Traditional approaches to application planning based on long-term stability of the business environment need to be abandoned.

2. Alignment with the strategic *business* objectives of the organization is paramount.

3. Applications being considered for new investment of capital or resources should demonstrate:

   a. *Salience*: they should support business processes that contribute directly to the organization's identity.

   b. *Worth*: they should demonstrate tangible business benefit that exceeds the true cost of development and implementation.[2]

A critical first step in application planning is the development of a portfolio view of the organization's current applications. The portfolio view characterizes the organization's applications along two dimensions (see Figure 6-2, and Chapter 14—Assessing the Value of IT):

- The organization's dependence on the application (i.e., how important is the application to the organization's daily operation?), and
- The strategic impact of the application (i.e., does the application provide competitive advantage or distinctiveness?)

The combination of the above two dimensions in the Application Portfolio Matrix allows IT management to characterize its portfolio of applications in four categories:

1. Support—applications with low strategic impact and on which the organization has a low level of dependence. Examples of such applications might be payroll, general ledger systems, accounting systems, etc. These applications are also potential candidates for outsourcing.

2. Factory—applications with low strategic impact, but on which the organization is highly dependent for its day-to-day functions. Examples of such applications might be manufacturing process control systems, inventory management systems, airline reservation systems, Enterprise Resource Planning (ERP) systems such as SAP, J.D. Edwards, etc.

3. Strategic—applications with high strategic impact, and on which the organization is highly dependent for daily operation. Examples of these applications might be Amazon.com's "one-click" technology or Wal-Mart's warehouse and inventory management systems.

4. Turnaround—applications that have high (or potentially high) strategic impact, but on which the organization has low day-to-day dependence. These

▪▪▪▪▪▪▪▪▪▪▪▪ **FIGURE 6-2** Application portfolio matrix (adapted from F. Warren McFarlan and James Cash).

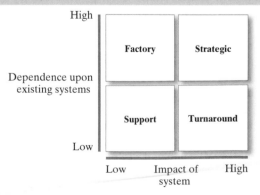

Source: Ward, John, Griffiths, Pat, and Whitmore, Paul, *Strategic Planning for Information Systems*, John Wiley & Sons, 1990.

applications may be "organizational experiments" or new systems that have the potential to open or define new markets or radically transform how the organization competes, but have not yet been proven effective. Applications in this category need to be nurtured and evaluated, but ruthlessly weeded out if they do not demonstrate their ability to move into the "strategic" category.

Developing and populating such a matrix (assuming, of course, that IT management has maintained a current inventory of applications!) for current and *proposed* applications is one method IT management can employ to plan its applications portfolio to deliver business value (see Chapter 14—Governance). Ideally, the applications identified as "strategic" in the matrix are directly linked to the strategic business initiatives and IT strategic initiatives identified in the business strategic plan and the information systems strategic plan.

Once the application portfolio matrix has been populated and alignment with business and IT strategic objectives has been verified, IT management can perform additional planning related to the implementation sequence of applications (i.e., prioritization). Prioritization at the application level should consider two critical dimensions:

- Business impact—the ability of the application to deliver business benefit
- Ease of execution—how many resources the application will consume; how difficult it will be for the organization to implement the application

For the proposed applications identified in each quadrant of the Application Portfolio Matrix, IT management can map business impact and ease of execution (see Figure 6-3) to assist planning of application development sequence. By using this matrix IT management can identify the applications that have the most business impact attractiveness and the highest likelihood for successful implementation.

The most attractive applications are those that are relatively easy to implement and yield relatively high business benefit ("quick wins"). IT management should strongly consider these applications for funding first. IT management should likewise consider the applications that also yield relatively high business benefit but may be relatively difficult to implement ("must haves"). These applications should be evaluated with respect to the level of business benefit provided to the organization and whether that benefit provides competitive distinctiveness or enables the organization to stay competitive. If so, a case may be made for funding applications in this category.

▪▪▪▪▪▪▪▪▪▪▪▪▪ **FIGURE 6-3** Application prioritization matrix (adapted from Hartman and Sifonis).[3]

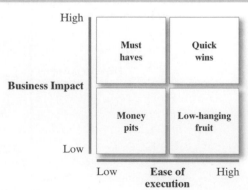

Source: Hartman, A., and Sifonis, J., *Net Ready—Strategies for Success in the E-conomy*, McGraw-Hill, 2000.[3]

Applications that are difficult to implement and have low business benefit are "money pits" and should not be considered for funding. Conversely, those applications that are relatively easy to implement and have low-medium business benefit can be considered "low-hanging fruit" and may be considered for funding if surplus resources exist, but only after IT management has identified applications that are in the upper two quadrants.

In Chapter 11, the section on prioritizing projects and Figure 11-1 (Scenario Planning Grid) provide another useful framework for planning projects.

Data Planning

The data planning process is very dependent on the outcome of the application plan. The data planning process reviews the application plan and determines what the data needs will be for the applications that are proposed for implementation. Because the application plan has translated the strategic goals of the enterprise into required applications to be developed, meeting the data needs of the application plan must translate to providing the data to meet the strategic goals of the enterprise.

The data architecture may be expanded if the application architecture has been shifted or updated. Or, the data architecture may change to include:

1. Emerging data storage technologies
2. Changes to the database architecture by the vendor
3. Integrated data processes, or
4. Improved standards in development or maintenance of data

Chapter 7—Managing Emerging Technologies will provide detailed discussion on planning activities related to emerging technologies.

The end result of the data planning process will be an updated plan for the time period that will enable the enterprise to meet the application planning goals. The objectives of data planning are threefold:

1. Facilitate the cost-effective and timely transformation of raw data into productive information
2. Facilitate the reuse of data and information across the organization
3. Protect the organization's data and information assets

Critical success factors in developing a data plan that accommodates these objectives are:

1. Developing data models of the organization's key processes. In this context, "organization" represents a strategic business unit or major organizational function (e.g., marketing, manufacturing, HR, etc.) and not the entire enterprise.
2. Defining the underlying shared data used by the organization's key processes, a key assumption being that many of the organization's key processes use a "core set" of common data. Although compelling cases have been made for developing enterprise data models, empirical evidence appears to show that the implementation of enterprise data models and data architectures is fraught with problems.[4]
3. Developing common definitions of "core" data and sharing these with functional groups.
4. Developing common information/data models for key organizational processes as part of an overall "data architecture."
5. Identifying how the proposed applications identified in the applications plan create new data (and where that data will be stored), use or modify existing data (and where that data comes from), or archive data. Planning priority should be given to applications that create new data or use data that is externally focused

(e.g., customer data, market data). Note that this places a requirement on the applications plan to define the data requirements for proposed applications.

6. Applying the appropriate governance for data management to proposed applications (i.e., data "ownership"), security and confidentiality requirements, archiving and recovery planning requirements, and physical location and distribution rules.

The end result of the data planning process should be a *data* architecture that will correlate the organization's data and information to its key business processes, applications, and technology infrastructure to enable, among other things:

- Improved understanding of customer and supplier interactions with the organization
- Consistency of information across the organization for improved decision-making, and
- Enhanced reuse of data, information, and applications for improved productivity

System Planning

The system planning process uses the results from the application planning process and the data planning process to create a comprehensive system plan. The comprehensive system plan is a translation of the enterprise's strategic goals and directions into a planned update of the enterprise's hardware, systems software, network, and related IT infrastructure facilities to enable applications to meet the strategic goals of the enterprise.

The objectives of the system plan are to:

1. Document *which* systems are planned for development
2. Document the justification for developing those systems (e.g., alignment with corporate strategic objectives)
3. Identify the time frames for developing those systems
4. Document the impact on the organization's IT architecture of developing those systems
5. Document any implications on the organization's disaster recovery plan

The systems architecture may be expanded in relation to any changes introduced by changes to the application architecture or data architecture. Or, the systems architecture will change, just to include:

- Emerging operating systems technologies
- Integrated systems processes, or
- Improved standards in planning systems resources or in the maintenance of the facilities

Again, Chapter 7—Emerging Technologies—will provide a detailed discussion on planning activities related to emerging technologies.

The end result of the system planning process will be an updated plan for the time period that will enable the enterprise to meet the application planning goals.

Network Planning

Network planning addresses how telecommunications technologies facilitate the needs of the organization. Telecommunication is an essential ingredient of 21st century organizations and the products and services they provide. The IT organization has responsibility for continually maintaining and upgrading its physical and software telecommunications infrastructure to cope with ever-increasing demands. The requirement for sound network planning is even more important as the demand for web-enabled services and applications grows both internally and externally. End-users and customers today have expectations that the organization's communications network will support fast downloads of data and graphics. Furthermore, the explosion of the use of non-PC related devices (PDAs, wireless and mobile devices, etc.), the renewed interest (post-9/11) in teleconferencing, the growing use of remote e-learning capabilities, and the expectation that knowledge workers will have connectivity to the organization and its data assets *anytime* or *anywhere*, place special demands on IT management for network plans that anticipate turbulent environments. Given the modern organization's need to move data and information rapidly across geographic boundaries—especially as e-business operational models proliferate—it can be reasonably argued that the communications network is as important, if not more so, than the computing devices connected to it!

What, then, should IT management consider in developing a network plan? Some important considerations that a robust network plan should address are:

a. Impacts of recent mergers or consolidations on network capacity and future demand
b. The impact on current network capacity and infrastructure (hardware, software) of proposed Web-enabled or remote access applications
c. Opportunities to standardize network components or services across the enterprise
d. Opportunities to consolidate existing services and infrastructure to enhance network:
   - Reliability
   - Availability (including the network's reach and range)
   - Service responsiveness
   - Security
   - Scalability
e. Security of the network against external and internal threats
f. Recovery of the network from natural or man-made catastrophes
g. Identification and repair of network performance issues
h. Customer service (e.g., "help desk")
i. Vendor management and service agreements
j. Cross-border issues
k. Hardware upgrade plan
l. Software upgrade plan
m. Capital investment plan

Project Charters

Some organizations have begun to call project plan documents "Project Charters" to avoid confusion with the detailed resource/time allocation documents more commonly referred to as "project plans." Regardless of what they are called—project charters or project plans—these documents typically share important components:

1. Introduction
   1.1 Business problem/opportunity
   1.2 Summary project recommendations
2. Scope and objectives
   2.1 Business objectives and timeline
   2.2 Project dependencies
   2.3 Project context
   2.4 Stakeholder list

> **2.5** Project organization
> **2.5.1** Roles and responsibilities
> **2.5.2** Project structure
> **2.6** Controls strategy
> **3.** Project approach
> **3.1** Constraints and assumptions
> **3.2** Delivery strategy
> **3.2.1** Recommended delivery option
> **3.2.2** Proposed technology infrastructure
> **3.2.3** Initial cost benefit analysis
> **3.3** Impact and risk assessment
> **4.** Current environment
> **4.1** Architectural impact
> **4.2** Current system profile
> **4.3** Current technology infrastructure
> **4.4** IT policies
> **5.** Preliminary project plan
> **6.** Glossary

The end product of the network planning process will be an agreed-upon set of architectural principles and a course of action for the organization's telecommunications infrastructure and applications (see Project Charters sidebar). This network plan should govern the selection, deployment, use, and control (including security) of telecommunications-related services across the entire organization.

Project Planning

The project planning process uses the results from the application, data, network, and systems planning processes, and translates all of these plans into manageable, clearly defined, and well-documented projects. The aim of project planning is to define technically feasible and manageable projects that will reflect the enterprise's strategic goals and direction. The project plans will include the specifications of the resources, time frames, and service level requirements (especially recovery, security, and audit requirements) that each project will need.

The project plans will also need to explain any unique control requirements and financially justify and prioritize any and all facets of the project. They must also justify the use of any nonstandard resources, hardware, software, network and database management tools. If the project needs to span periods larger than the tactical time horizon, that need would have to be justified as well.

Service Level Planning and Management

The service level planning process negotiates individual service agreements using the service volume forecasts and service charge rates, established by the service marketing process (see Chapters 4 and 5). During the tactical time horizon, the individual service agreements define the respective Information Systems organization and end-user commitments. It also identifies individual requests for recovery, security, and audit ability, and creates an overall service plan which incorporates consolidated recovery, security and audit plans. Service level planning includes the negotiation of service agreements (especially recovery, security, audit, and charges), as well as forecasting the level and volume of service agreements for users. The process also develops a preventive maintenance plan to help keep costs down and reviews current existing service level agreements ("SLAs") to ensure that they continue to be cost-effective.

IT managers need to be cautioned, however, that while the implementation of SLAs is often cited as a best practice, the planning, execution, and administration of SLAs has not been widely adopted. This appears to be because of the difficulty many IT organizations have in managing the administrative costs and complexities involved in defining and monitoring a uniform set of service level contracts and associated metrics—essentially, contract management for internal customers. Refer to Chapter 5—IT Processes, which provided a more detailed discussion of the SLA process, including a detailed review of the components of effective service level agreements.

Recovery Planning and Management

The recovery planning process works towards a way to ensure that there will be a continuation of business operations in the event of failure or disaster. Recovery planning has assumed even more importance for organizations and IT management after the 9/11 terrorist attacks and continuing threat of damage or contamination to business organizations and infrastructure.

As IT management begins to develop recovery plans, one learns that there is a wide range of potential failures and levels of disaster that could occur and need to be addressed. Therefore, preparation of multiple contingency plans rather than one single plan to address potential disaster scenarios becomes necessary. This brings to the forefront the concept of scale. The recovery planning process needs to be scalable, meaning that the plan must be flexible enough to handle a localized failure of hardware, software, or network, or capable of encompassing the problems precipitated by a major disaster of great loss, such as complete loss of a data center or worse.

Whereas major catastrophes have fortunately been very rare, the potential for great loss has been well documented (see Figure 6-4). In the past, natural disasters such

FIGURE 6-4 Major IT Disasters 1987–2001.

Date	Type of Disaster	Location(s)	Affected
08/14/1987	Flood	Chicago	64
05/08/1988	Network outage	Hinsdale, IL	175
05/11/1988	Pakistani virus	Nationwide	90+
11/02/1988	Internet virus	Nationwide	500+
10/17/1989	Earthquake	San Franscisco	90
08/13/1990	Power outage	New York	320
04/13/1992	Flood	Chicago	400
05/01/1992	Riot	Los Angeles	50
08/24/1992	Hurricane Andrew	Southeast	150
03/15/1993	Blizzard	East coast	50
02/26/1993	World Trade	NYC	150 comp. out of business
09/15/1999	Hurricane Floyd	Northeast	NJ $250M
09/15/1999	Earthquake	Taiwan	Compaq chips
09/11/2001	Terrorists	NYC; DC	$ 15.8 B

Source: University of North Texas Emergency Administration and Planning,
http://www.unt.edu/eadp/info.html.

as floods, hurricanes, earthquakes, tornadoes, and blizzards have been the greatest source of concern; now, man-made disasters have become increasingly as dangerous. Man-made disasters, such as power outages, fires, riots, hacker attacks,computer viruses, and terrorism (including bombing, chemical, and biological attacks), have made the world a much more dangerous place. All of these disasters require much more vigilance and planning to cope with future needs.

When beginning to plan for recovery, there are four major tasks that must be completed:

1. Consolidate the recovery requirements for all service agreements.
2. Define the business and IT recovery-operating environment.
3. Identify variances between operating environments and agreements, and
4. Develop an overall recovery plan.

Let's look at each of these tasks in more detail.

First, the need to consolidate the recovery requirements of all service agreements is important to establish the scope of the business that must be maintained, regardless of the size and nature of the disaster. Whether these service agreements are to provide for computing strength, financial or transactional services, or network connectivity, they all provide a picture of the required operations and services that must be continued for business operations. This becomes the baseline measure of what areas need to be addressed in the recovery planning process.

What Happens When Business Doesn't Want to Spend Enough for Disaster Recovery?

What happens if the business is unwilling to spend what is necessary to ensure business continuation? Surveys have shown that if a business was unprepared when a major disaster struck, only 6 percent of those organizations survived, 51 percent closed their doors within two years, and an astounding 43 percent never even reopened their doors. For a clearer understanding of the importance of disaster recovery, ask your business partners, "What would it cost us per day if we were unable to continue business operations?" Once they have researched how other companies have been fiscally hurt by business interruption, they will be less hesitant to sponsor recovery planning. Conversely, have them research the success of companies like American Express, Cantor Fitzgerald, and Morgan Stanley, who were able to return to business within days of a severe and devastating catastrophe.

Lastly, what if a firm considers itself too small to provide for the kind of recovery plan an AT&T, American Express, or a Morgan Stanley can provide? In reality, there are many more choices available for developing disaster recovery options. Firms like IBM, GE Disaster Recovery, and SunGard are providing off-site recovery options for the small and medium-size business. By taking advantage of these kinds of options, an effective recovery plan should be in reach of every business.

Secondly, defining the business and IT recovery-operating environment is important to enable one to establish a benchmark for the minimum level of service that needs to be provided. This must be done, working with the organization's business partners, to ensure business continuation (see "What Happens When Business Doesn't Want to Spend Enough for Disaster Recovery?" sidebar). It must be clear here that an absolute minimum requirement needs to be set to provide a service level that would enable business continuation at a modest level. The organization's business partners must be informed that in a major catastrophe, business demands will be at much-reduced levels, and customers would understand if business was not continued at the original pace. The question would be what would represent this minimum level to provide to customers?

Third, identifying the variances between operating environments and agreements would allow the organization to perform a gap analysis to determine the areas that need attention. In building an effective recovery plan, IT management needs to know where the gaps are before problems can be remediated. Once the gaps are identified,alternative solutions to close those gaps can be proposed and prioritized (e.g., finding or building alternate data centers for operations, obtaining back-up power generation, offsite back-up of critical data, etc.).

Finally, development of an overall recovery plan is crucial for success. An overall recovery plan is based on assembling the three issues: 1) what services the business and IT needs to provide; 2) the minimum operating environment level that the business needs to perform at during the crisis; and 3) what areas the firm needs to address to enable the business to continue. The gap analysis gives form to the plan by forcing the business to take action now, before a disaster strikes.

What are the consequences of not having a disaster recovery plan? A frequently quoted study performed by the University of Texas[7] revealed some sobering facts:

- About 85 percent of organizations are totally or heavily dependent on computer systems.
- On average, by the sixth day of an outage, companies experience a 25 percent loss in daily revenue; by the 25th day it is 40 percent.Financial and functional loss increases rapidly after the onset of an outage.
- Within two weeks of the loss of computer support, 75 percent of organizations reach critical or total loss of functioning.
- Of the 43 percent of companies that experience a disaster but have no tested business continuity plans in place, only one in 10 are still in business two years later.

What elements, then, should a disaster recovery plan address? Minimally, disaster recovery plans should address:

- Data recovery
- Technology (infrastructure) recovery
- Business-process recovery
- Crisis management (how will the organization act *during* the actual crisis/disaster?)
- Customer-support operations
- Facilities
- Human resources
- Procedures for key suppliers and partners
- Public relations and damage control
- Protection of intellectual property (this last item has emerged in importance after a fire at a Silicon Valley biotechnology company in early 2002 not only completely destroyed the data related to several years' experiments but also damaged their ability to claim intellectual property rights as well.)

Ownership and creation of a corporate recovery and management plan in many organizations is the responsibility of the CEO, CFO, COO or other corporate executives, with maintenance (including testing) of the plan falling to the CIO or senior IS executive (see "Nine Steps to Promote Business Continuity Planning" sidebar).

FIGURE 6-5 Elements of a Business-Continuity Plan.

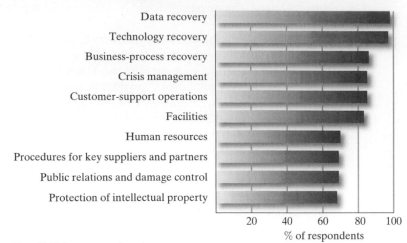

Which elements are included in your company's *business-continuity* plans?

Note: Multiple responses allowed
Base: 245 companies with business-continuity plans
Data: Information Week Research Business-continuity survey of 350 Business-technology managers.

Source: Information Week.

Sponsorship of the recovery plan, however, is typically the province of the CIO given its heavy technology focus.

IT managers should consider the following checklist as a guide to the basic types of information required in a business continuity plan:

- Description of departmental operations
- Functions that support department operations
- Peak operating times
- Impact of department downtime
- Recovery priorities and time frames for departmental functions
- Staffing requirements under normal circumstances and in an emergency
- Computer support for both departmental operations and individual functions (This should cover both centralized and decentralized computer operations)
- Site requirements for both normal and emergency operations
- Equipment needed (and the vendors of that equipment)
- Availability of office and other supplies (and their vendors)
- Critical records needed and their backup and recovery requirements
- Priority ranking of departmental functions
- Name and address of alternative site vendor
- List of responsibilities and home telephone numbers of key personnel
- Emergency telephone numbers (e.g., local fire and police departments)
- Critical forms (number, names and average use)
- Special equipment specifications
- Area user list
- Vendor backup contracts
- Critical functions and assumptions (e.g., individuals might assume that they will have access to backup files)
- Minimum equipment and space requirements

Recovery and management plans should be tested at least annually or twice yearly, with performance gaps identified and actively managed for remediation.

Nine Steps To Promote Business Continuity Planning

1. **Visualize** the business functions (top-down approach)
2. **Itemize** the tasks involved (bottom-up approach)
3. **Prioritize** work only on critical functions until they are substantially complete
4. **Categorize** and organize the problems into manageable pieces of work
5. **Minimize** the risk—the ultimate goal of business continuity planning
6. **Organize** staff to react to emergencies as they occur
7. **Rehearse** events so that staff is familiar with the planned responses
8. **Sponsor/Champion** participation to demonstrate and communicate the importance of the recovery plan
9. **Vigilant Monitoring** of supply chain and partners' plans

Source: Giga Group.

Lastly, IT management needs to be aware and make senior management aware of the fact that disaster recovery plans and business continuity plans can be a legal requirement depending on the industry sector and the country/economic region where the organization does business. For example, financial services organizations must be in compliance with Federal Reserve, FDIC, and OCC (Office of the Comptroller of the Currency) regulations regarding the establishment, maintenance, and testing of such plans according to the 1996 FFIEC IS Examination Handbook. Similar regulatory requirements exist for the Bank of England (Bank of England Surveillance # S&S/1996/6 Part 3), Hong Kong (Securities and Futures Commission), Canada (Toronto Securities Exchange) and other jurisdictions, all promulgated by major governmental regulatory authorities. IT management is accountable to the organization to ensure that the business is in compliance with local regulations regarding disaster recovery and business continuity (see "Websites for Disaster Recovery Information" sidebar).

Web Sites for Disaster Recovery Information

www.Drie.org: Disaster Recovery Information Exchange
www.Drj.com: Disaster Recovery Journal
www.Isaca.org: The Information Systems Audit and Control Association and Foundation

Security Planning and Management

The security planning process builds an overall plan to ensure that agreed-upon levels of security for systems and services are met. The building of an overall security plan begins with the consolidation of security requirements of all service agreements. Once the security requirements are known, the plan establishes the business and information systems security-operating environment. The plan must contain what is identified as the variances between the current environment and what the future environment must be to support the service agreements. What must be added, updated, or modified in the systems environment becomes a significant part of the overall security plan.

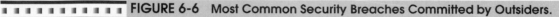

▪▪▪▪▪▪▪▪▪▪▪ **FIGURE 6-6** Most Common Security Breaches Committed by Outsiders.

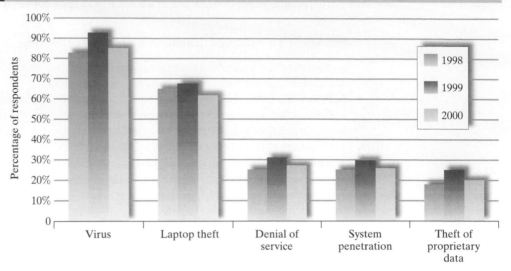

Source: Computer Security Institute, "*Computer Security Issues and Trends: 2000*"; CSI/FBI Computer Crime and Security Institute, San Francisco (*www.gocsi.com*).

In a recent survey of businesses, a majority of them did not have a company-wide security policy,[5] yet all companies that have a network and a Web site are subject to a number of potential security threats. Some of the better-known security issues are:

1. Unauthorized access to systems
2. Unauthorized access to confidential data
3. Virus attack
4. Denial of service attacks on Web sites and e-mail system
5. Illegal or unwanted use of computer systems and equipment
6. Illegal use or monitoring of e-mail systems and the Internet, and
7. Possible physical or virtual destruction of financial and/or administrative databases, Web sites, applications, computer systems, equipment, and networks

Because the development of an overall security plan is such a daunting task, IT managers need to prioritize which areas to work on first. The best way to start is to review those operational areas that have the greatest financial impact on the firm. Evaluate what would happen if the system, application, Web site or database were disabled, damaged, hacked, or destroyed. Impact estimates should span time frames that range from hours to a number of weeks to months. Consider the extreme case in which the data or information could not be recovered at all. Could the business survive that kind of loss? Examine the costs of replacing the systems, applications, Web sites and databases after the fact. Then begin looking at alternative ways to keep the systems, applications, Web sites and databases going in the event of a catastrophe.

Insider Damage Assessment

Should organizations be more concerned about security threats from outside or inside the organization? A brief sample of security problems below suggests that the greatest threat may be from those "inside the walls":

1985. A brokerage firm clerk alters computer records and changes the ownership and price of 17,000 shares of Loren Industries stock.

1989. A former employee of Southeastern Color Lithographers Inc. destroys billing and account information worth $400,000.

1996. A computer operator at Reuters Group PLC in Hong Kong sabotages the dealing systems for five investment-bank clients.

1997. A temporary employee working as a computer technician at *Forbes* magazine is charged with crashing the company's network and causing more than $100,000 in damage.

1998. A disgruntled programmer at defense contractor Omega Engineering Corp. sets off a digital "bomb," destroying $10 million in data.

2001. Robert Hanssen, a career FBI agent with access to counter-intelligence databases, is charged with spying for Russia since 1985.

This is the beginning stage of developing an overall recovery plan. Starting with the possible loss potential, IT management will be able to build a business model to determine what amount would be considered affordable to spend on ensuring business continuity. Using business economic models, IT management can construct the expectation of loss for a major catastrophe. Insurance companies do this to determine what premiums they should charge for a risk they would take. IT management and its business partners must do a similar process of assessment of risk to determine what they should spend to protect their systems and applications. Upon completion of this process, they will have established a rough idea of the cost they might be willing to bear to improve IT security.

If the economic threat to the organization is severe enough, IT management may wish to consider creating and staffing a formal IT management position that is exclusively focused on information security (see "Insider Damage Assessment" sidebar). This role would have overall responsibility for:

- Developing, presenting, and managing the dissemination of information security awareness and training materials.
- Evaluating their effectiveness efficiency and compliance with existing information security control measures.
- Recommending control measures to improve information security (including evaluating and selecting products and services.
- Monitoring developments in the information security and information processing fields to identify new opportunities and new risks.
- Interpreting information security requirements emanating from external bodies, such as government agencies and standards-setting groups.
- Investigating alleged information security breaches and, if necessary, assisting with disciplinary and legal matters associated with such breaches.
- Developing security policies, standards, guidelines, procedures, and other elements of an infrastructure to support information security.
- Coordinating and monitoring information security activities throughout the organization, including the preparation of periodic status and progress reports.
- Serving as a liaison between various groups dealing with information security matters (e.g., with the legal department and the insurance department).
- Preparing implementation plans, security product purchase proposals, staffing plans, project schedules, budgets, and related information security management materials.
- Representing the organization on information security matters to external groups (e.g., participating in meetings to establish technical standards).

- Providing information security system administrative support (e.g., to maintain data bases for password access control systems).
- Performing research on new and improved ways to properly protect the organization's information research assets.
- Providing consulting assistance on implementing information security controls (e.g., encryption system deployment and secure application system development procedures).

Once a new or upgraded security policy is generated, the next important step is to immediately inform employees that it exists and that it will be enforced. Employees may require assistance in meeting some of the new security measures that are developed to safeguard your systems, applications, Web site, and databases. IT management might consider offering to publish manuals, issue notices, institute training classes, or hold meetings to discuss any changes in policies or procedures. Helpdesk facilities will need to address an increase in the volume of calls that they will receive. Employees, customers, managers, and executives may experience delays or inconveniences in attempting to comply with the new security polices. All of these factors require as much communication as possible before, during, and after the rollout of new security measures.

Top 10 Factors That Could Trigger Unethical Employee Behavior

1. Efforts to balance work and family
2. Poor internal communications
3. Poor leadership
4. Work hours, work load
5. Lack of management support
6. Need to meet sales, budget, or profit goals
7. Little or no recognition of achievements
8. Company politics
9. Personal financial worries
10. Insufficient resources

Audit Planning and Management

The audit planning process builds an overall plan to ensure that the agreed levels of audit and compliance for systems, applications, and services will continue to be met. The process begins by consolidating the audit requirements of all service agreements. Once the audit requirements are known, the plan establishes the business and information systems audit-operating environment. The audit plan identifies the variances between the current environment and what the future environment must be to support the audit and compliance for all of the service agreements. What must be added, updated, or modified in the systems environment becomes a significant part of the overall audit plan.

The main mission of the audit is to evaluate and ensure the adequacy of the internal systems of controls for financial and administrative transactions and functions. This is also to be alert to possibilities of fraud, bribery, and illegal access to confidential data, theft of property, or other forms of larceny. The auditors must also review the laws (state, federal, municipal, foreign, etc.) as well as legislation (tax codes, reporting, etc.) that may affect the firm's operation in order to ensure legal compliance with them. It is further recognized that the audit must be an objective, independent review of the firm's operation. This review is required to be reported to management, and these findings generally become available for review in the public domain.

The Securities and Exchange Act of 1934 was amended by the 1977 Foreign Current Practices Act to require all publicly held companies to keep accurate records and maintain internal control systems to safeguard assets. The courts have defined assets to include the computer systems and all the data they contain. Critical records and original documents are assets that should be protected as well.

Fair Information Practices Principles

1. There should be no personal record systems whose existence is secret.
2. Individuals have rights of access, inspection, review, and amendment to systems that contain information about them.
3. There must be no use of personal information for purposes other than those for which it was gathered without prior consent.
4. Managers of systems are responsible for their reliability and security and can be held accountable and liable for the damage done by systems.
5. Governments have the right to intervene in the information relationships among private parties.

Privacy Policy

Recent legislation has been passed to ensure that every individual has a right to keep his or her personal information private. This legislation has translated into a requirement for all commercial entities to establish a formal written policy concerning how each company would handle an individual's personal information. This legislation further required the commercial entities to send a copy of this policy to all individuals on which the firm held personal information. This provides an opportunity to individuals who do not like the privacy policy to "opt out" and remove their information from the company. This has severely curtailed a number of efforts by companies to sell mailing lists and marketing data (see Figure 6-7).

Another type of audit that IT management should consider in its overall audit plan is a corporate responsibility audit. These audits are designed to ensure that the organization is fulfilling its mission statement—i.e., auditing an organization's core practices to close the "rhetoric-reality gap.[6]"

Steps in Developing a Corporate Responsibility Audit

- Gain CEO commitment.
- Appoint a steering committee to guide the audit.
- Appoint an auditing team (auditors, key managers, and organizational development experts) that will develop questions to be used in examining the firm.
- Diagnose the corporate culture and investigate designated functional areas, such as employee relations and human rights, community relations (the company's social impact), quality programs, and environmental practices.
- Analyze the mission statement and look for circumstances when the stated mission/goals and actual company performance do not coincide.
- Seek fundamental or underlying reasons that performance and goals are not consistent.
- Collect relevant industry information, existing benchmark studies, and available information on competitors and industry standards in each designated functional area.

▪ ▪ ▪ ▪ ▪ ▪ ▪ ▪ ▪ ▪ ▪ **FIGURE 6-7   Recent U.S. Privacy Legislation.**

Representative U.S. Federal Privacy Legislation

Legislation	Content
Privacy Act of 1974	Prohibits the government from collecting information secretly
	Information collected must be used only for a specific purpose
Privacy Protection Act of 1980	Provides privacy protection in computerized and other documents
Electronic Communications Privacy Act of 1986	Prohibits private citizens from intercepting data communication without authorization
Computer Security Act of 1987	Requires security of information regarding individuals
Computer Matching and Privacy Act of 1988	Regulates the matching of computer files by state and federal agencies
Video Privacy Protection Act of 1988	Protects privacy in transmission of pictures
Fair Health Information Practices Act of 1997	Provides a code of fair information
Consumer Internet Privacy Protection Act of 1997	Requires prior written consent before a computer service can disclose subscribers information
Federal Internet Privacy Protection Act of 1997 (H.R. 1367)	Prohibits federal agencies from disclosing personal records over the Internet
Communications Privacy and Consumer Empowerment Act of 1997(H.R. 1964)	Protects privacy rights in online commerce
Data Privacy Act of 1997 (H.R. 2368)	Limits the use of personally identifiable information and regulates spamming
Computer Security Enhancement Act of 2000	Policy on digital signature
Financial Services Modernization Act of 1999	Bans dissemination of consumer information without consumer consent

- Interview relevant stakeholders who are involved in each functional area (e.g. customers, employees, federal and local environmental officials, local community officials) about their perceptions of the firm's socially responsible performance.
- Compare internal data and external stakeholder perceptions.
- Write final report for company managers and the audit steering committee.

Capacity Planning and Management

The capacity planning process uses a forecast load from new projects or from the evolution of existing services; this process defines how resources will cover the demand. It also proposes alternatives to managers (such as changing the number of work shifts, decreasing services, altering systems plans, etc.) The process must translate service requirements into a load forecast of hardware, network, software, facilities, and supplies. Capacity of existing and planned resources must be identified. The load forecast is then compared against the identified capacity and the variance is noted. When a gap is established, it is identified and evaluated, and a proposal must be made to provide alternate load forecasts and capacity. Once this is completed, the capacity plan must be documented and distributed to the management system planning team.

Capacity planning is important for several reasons:

- It reduces customer dissatisfaction: Proper capacity planning can help identify potential bottlenecks before they occur, preventing most performance-related problems. It reduces productivity decline: If your systems cannot handle the expected peak throughput, productivity will suffer. Employees may spend a significant portion of their day waiting for results from a query.

- It reduces budgetary constraints: With proper capacity planning, upgrades can be budgeted ahead of time.
- It improves stability: By identifying potential problem areas and capacity limitations, stability problems can be avoided, or at the very least predicted.

The process of capacity planning combines the monitoring of current IT resources with forecasts of future service requirements and expectations of growth of existing systems. The data gathered is compared against existing IT infrastructure capacity and translated into a projection of future demands for IT services. Implications for IT organizations include:

- Budgets
- Disaster recovery/business continuation
- Service level agreements
- Effective use of resources
- Business growth
- New services
- Performance management
- Integration

Alternative approaches to capacity planning are highlighted in Figure 6-8

▪ ▪ ▪ ▪ ▪ ▪ ▪ ▪ ▪ ▪ ▪ **FIGURE 6-8** Capacity Planning.

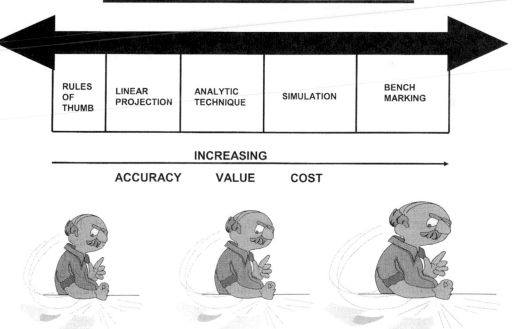

IT management needs to be aware that the cost of capacity planning is high in today's highly complex, heterogeneous, and distributed environments. Organizations need to consider the value of the investment obtained by doing a capacity plan; the value derived from the plan depends on the maturity of the organization's capacity planning process (see Table 6-1). The lower the maturity level of the organization's capacity planning process, the lower the value obtained from the organization's investment in the process.

TABLE 6-1   Organizational IT Capacity Planning Maturity and Characteristics

Capacity planning process maturity level	Characteristics
Level 1	**Reactive**; firefighting
Level 2	**Efficient**; professional and sophisticated firefighting
Level 3	**Fewer fires**; analysis of problems, start of process improvement
Level 4	Process includes **procedural improvement**
Level 5	Process becomes **self-correcting**

Source: Gartner Group

Skills Planning and Management

The skills planning process uses the requirements identified in the project and service plans to define the manpower the enterprise needs to compete in this tactical time horizon. The process also needs to identify education plans for existing staff that would enable the enterprise to meet the education and skills requirements of the near future.

To create a complete plan, the skills planning process must:

- Define the manpower requirements to support the systems plan
- Consolidate manpower required to support the project and systems plans, as well as develop formal career paths
- Identify existing and planned manpower skills requirements

▪▪▪▪▪▪▪▪▪▪▪▪ **FIGURE 6-9   Balancing IT Skills.**

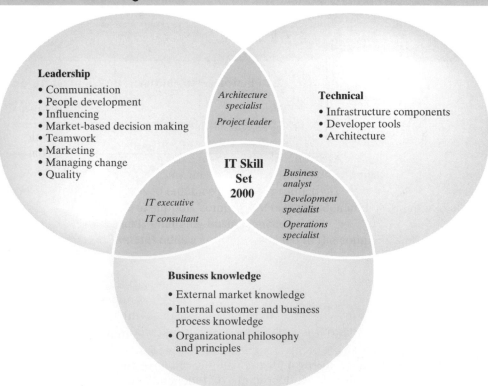

Source: The Gartner Group.

▪▪▪▪▪▪▪▪▪▪▪▪▪ **FIGURE 6-10** What Skills Do Companies Need for Successful IT?

Process knowledge	Project management	Technical knowledge
• Sales, marketing, customer service, best practices • B2B • B2C	• Enterprise program management • Project control • Issue resolution • Risk management • Leadership • Expectation management	• Client/server and Web technologies • Performance/benchmarking • Network • Middleware • E-mail routing systems

 People, Process, and Technology

Product expertise	Change management	Industry knowledge
• Application knowledge • Architecture knowledge • Project management	• Job analysis and redesign • Training and documentation • Team building • Stakeholder management	• Best practices • Industry issues • Industry-specific solutions

Source: PriceWaterhouseCoopers.

- Establish and evaluate alternate manpower plans, including sources of manpower
- Define an effective education plan, and
- Document manpower and education plans

In developing an IT skills management plan, organizations need to achieve a balance between leadership skills, technology skills, and business knowledge in their employees (see Figure 6-9).

What types of skills, then, should a skills management plan address to be successful? At a minimum, a robust skills management plan should identify what skills the IT organization *currently* has, what skills it *needs* to have (based on the information systems strategic plan and the systems lan), *when* those skills are required, and *how* those skills will be obtained. Empirically, successful IT organizations tend to group required skill sets around six knowledge areas (see Figure 6-10):

- Process knowledge
- Project management
- Technical knowledge
- Product expertise
- Change management
- Industry (or business) knowledge

Refer to Chapters 8–10 of this book for further discussion regarding skills considerations for the IT organization.

Budget Planning and Value Management

The budget planning process converts systems plans into financial terms and identifies how funds will be obtained and allocated to organizations (and organizational subunits). The budget planning process is a basic aspect of IT governance (see Chapter 11). The budget planning process must translate the system, service, project, capacity, manpower, and education plans for the tactical time horizon into financial terms for the organization. The budget plan must reconcile all sources of funds earmarked for IT projects, then establish and evaluate alternate budgets. Once the evaluation is complete, the budget plan must be documented and returned to all departments for their review. This process often becomes an iterative process as the values of the projects are weighed against the cost of the projects.

The principal caveat regarding budget planning for IT management is to avoid making the budget planning process synonymous with strategic planning. Organizations naturally tend to link the development of information strategic plans and systems plans with the development of budgets. Unfortunately, many organizations then drift into the mode of thinking that the budget *is* the strategic plan; with some significant negative consequences:

- Budget cycles tend to be year-to-year while not all technology initiatives (especially strategic initiatives) are begun, end, or coincide with the budget cycle.
- Budgets are financially focused and induce managers to "use it" or "lose it"—thus creating the dynamic of IT managers scrambling at year-end to launch underfunded systems projects for the remainder of the year to prevent "losing" budget spending authority for the next year.
- Budget cycles are intensely time-driven and managed top-down; the pressures of the process itself (e.g., rapid turn-around of budget versions, assessing the impact of mandated "cuts," etc.) sometimes run counter to the deliberative planning that took place on the strategic level of the IT organization.

The general injunction is, wherever possible, to decouple the budget planning process from the strategic planning process. Chapter 14—Assessing the Value of IT provides a more detailed discussion on the value of IT.

Vendor Planning and Management

The vendor planning and management process deals with the hardware, software, network and outsourcing products and services used by IT. It must also measure and monitor performance against the service level agreements and contracts to determine if any corrective action is necessary. This process is almost an art form, as it attempts to balance both internal and external resources (service, project, capacity, manpower, education, budget, system, application, and data) so that these processes will be optimum for the firm. Once the contracts are approved, an internal team will need to continuously measure and report the activities of the contractors of outsourced projects. The business function must assist IT in measuring the performance of the vendors, and IT must not assume that if the business users do not complain, the process must be going well.

The vendor planning and management process must also continuously monitor the entire service level agreement, comparing the actual with the plan estimates and analyzing the variances. Readjustments frequently occur, requiring reviews of the plan and additional feedback from business management. Certainly, if readjustments require new rules for enforcement, the service level agreement would need to be renegotiated and agreed to by all the parties. If the business users are unhappy with the level of service they receive, enforcement of the contract must be instituted. The penalties for noncompliance to the service level agreement should never be so debilitating that the vendor would suffer irreparable harm and would have no incentive to even partially fix the problems. See Chapter 11—IT Governance for a more detailed discussion on vendor management.

Management Systems Planning and Monitoring

The management systems planning process uses strategic guidance and an assessment of existing management processes (and the current management systems plan) to define an improved set of IT management processes. It improves the IT management system through a project management approach that relies on a structured methodology. This process looks across all 38 processess (horizontal view) to ensure cohesiveness.

The process takes the information systems model and relates it to the local situation. It defines the information systems organization and its objectives. It examines the information system processes and lists those who have organizational responsibility. The process then defines the requirements for standards, procedures, and methodology to enhance the management system and thus increase the effectiveness and efficiency of the information systems processes. The process then highlights those projects that are both technically feasible and manageable while also supporting the management system. The management system is not complete until it defines the project resources and time frames, as well as justifying and prioritizing the entire management systems plan.

The effectiveness of the current management system in an iterative process can also be assessed using feedback from all the Information Systems planning processes. This assures that the IS planning processes will be enhanced, as necessary.

Components of this process include:

- Collect and summarize IT organization performance data
- Compare the results to the IT organizational objectives and standards
- Diagnose deviation or substandard performance, and
- Analyze variance and initiate effectiveness/efficiency improvements in the organization, standards, procedures, and methods

This process also develops and modifies management standards, procedures, and methods for use in the information systems organization within the framework of a project. It also develops methods to measure their effectiveness and efficiency. Components of this process include:

- Defining detailed requirements based on enterprise policies
- Evaluating alternative standards, procedures, and methodologies
- Designing solutions,
- Publishing instructions for use of these standards, procedures, and methodologies
- Testing solutions in limited environments, and
- Installing solutions

For more discussion and detail on the process, see Chapters 8, 11, 13, and 14.

▪▪▪ Operational Level IT Planning

By definition, the operational level of the IT organization is concerned with the day-to-day administration and execution of processes and plans. As such, any plans at this level are very transient in nature and concerned only with execution of the immediate tasks and activities required as components of strategic-level or (much more likely) tactical-level plans.

One of the more important types of plans created and executed at this level of the organization is project-related plans. These are the types of plans most familiar to project managers of applications development, IT infrastructure deployment, or other related activities. These plans are created to effect the implementation of the requirements contained in the plans developed at the strategic and tactical levels of the IT organization.

Effective project planning and execution at the operational level is a complex and rigorous discipline that has evolved since the late 1960s when the Project Management Institute™ ("PMI") was founded. PMI has embodied the best practices of project management in a guide and framework titled *A Guide to the Project Management Body of Knowledge*© [8] (abbreviated as the "PMBOK" and pronounced "pim-bok"), which is widely used as a best practices guide for establishing and managing projects. PMI conducts professional certification programs in project management (e.g., "Project Management Professional"), which are increasingly viewed by organizations as valuable credentials for advancement. Readers are encouraged to visit the PMI website at *www.pmi.org* for more information about PMI, its publications, and its certification programs.

Chapter 5—IT Processes provided a more detailed discussion of all IT processes, including those at the operational level.

▮▮▮ Global Considerations and IT Planning

Twenty-first century IT organizations are increasingly global regardless of where they are headquartered. Chapter 11—IT Governance discusses the impact of global considerations on IT governance and planning.

REVIEW QUESTIONS ▮▮▮▮▮▮▮

1. Describe the types of plans formulated at the strategic level of the organization.
2. What is the purpose of a business systems plan?
3. How would you develop an applications portfolio?
4. What techniques might you use to prioritize applications identified in your applications portfolio?
5. What are the major elements of a project plan?
6. Why is recovery planning important?
7. What is IT management's role in developing a business continuation plan?
8. Describe the major security threats to IT organizations and outline potential mitigation approaches.
9. How should IT organizations plan for required skills?

DISCUSSION QUESTIONS ▮▮▮▮▮▮▮

1. How does your organization perform strategic-level IT planning?
2. Do you know what your organization's business systems plan says?
3. Have you ever read your organization's information systems plan?
4. Where does your organization most need improvement in its tactical-level planning?
5. How often has your IT management formally assessed its management systems plan?
6. What forms of security planning, business continuity planning, and privacy planning is your organization *mandated* by law to perform and test?

AREAS FOR RESEARCH ▮▮▮▮▮▮▮

1. Review Jon Toigo's book on disaster recovery planning (*Disaster Recovery Planning: Strategies for Protecting Critical Information Assets*, 2nd Edition, by Jon William Toigo, Prentice Hall PTR, 2000).
2. Review your organization's mandatory requirements for business continuity, privacy, and security.

Further Readings On Information Security

War By Other Means: Economic Espionage in America, by John J. Fialka, W.W. Norton.

Corporate Espionage, by Ira Winkler, Prima Publishing.

Spectacular Computer Crimes, by Buck BloomBecker, Dow Jones-Irwin.

The Cuckoo's Egg, by Clifford Stoll, Doubleday.

DCE Security Programming, by Wei Hu, O'Reilly & Associates.

Information Warfare: Chaos on the Electronic Superhighway, by Winn Schartau, Thunder's Mouth Press.

Information Security: An Integrated Collection of Essays, Edited by Marshall D. Abrahams, Sushil Jajodia, Harold J. Podell, IEEE Computer Society Press.

Computer Security Basics, by Deborah Russell and G.T Gangemi Sr., O'Reilly & Associates.

Building Internet Firewalls, by D. Brent Chapman and Elizabeth D. Zwickey.

Web Security: A Matter of Trust, by C. Bradford Biddle, Simson Garfinkel, John Gilmore, Rohit Khare, Crickey Liu and Lincoln Stein, O'Reilly & Associates.

Computer Security for Dummies, by Peter T. Davis and Barry D. Lewis, IDG Books.

Authentication Systems for Secure Networks, by Rolf Oppliger, Ph.D., Artech House.

Complete Book of PC and LAN Security, by Stephen Cobb, Windcrest/McGraw-Hill, Inc.

Netware to Internet Gateways, by James E. Gaskin, PrenticeHall, Inc.

Network and Internetwork Security, by William Stallings, PrenticeHall, Inc.

Network Security, by Steven L. Shaffer and Alan R. Simon, AP Professional.

LAN Times: Guide to Security and Data Integrity, by Marc Farley, Tom Stearns, Matt Arnett, McGraw-Hill.

Issue Update on Information Security and Privacy in Network Environments, Diane Publishing Co.

Computer System and Network Security, by Gregory B. White, Eric A. Fisch, and Udo W. Pooch, CRC Press, Inc.

LAN Security Handbook, by Ellen Dutton, M&T Books

Secure Data Networking, by Michael Purser, Artech House, Inc.

Securing Client/Server Computer Networks, by Peter T. Davis (Editor), McGraw-Hill, Inc.

Network Security: PRIVATE Communications in a PUBLIC World, by Charlie Kaufman, Radia Perlman, and Mike Speciner, PrenticeHall, Inc.

Firewalls and Internet Security, "Repelling the Wily Hacker," William R. Cheswick and Steven M. Bellovin (Addison-Wesley).

CONCLUSION ▪▪▪▪▪▪▪

We reviewed three layers of IT planning: strategic, tactical, and operational. Without effective planning, IT management cannot be adequately prepared for many eventualities and cannot continually improve its overall effectiveness.

Today, it is more vital that IT planning processes are continuously improved and adjusted because of the rapid change in emerging technologies, methodologies, and tools that are made available each year.

REFERENCES ▪▪▪▪▪▪▪

[1] Anthony, Robert N., *Management Control Systems*, McGraw-Hill, 1997.

[2] Keene, P., *The Process Edge*, Harvard Business School Press, 1997.

[3] Hartman, A., and Sifonis, J., *Net Ready—Strategies for Success in the E-conomy*, McGraw-Hill, 2000.

[4] Goodhue, D.L., Kirsch, L.J., and Quillard, J.A., "*Strategic Data Planning: Lessons From the Field*," MIS Quarterly, March, 1992.

[5] Cosgrove-Ware, L., "*Survey: Companies More Aware of Security Risks, but Many Are Still Open to Attack*," CIO Magazine, August/2001.

[6] Waddock, S., "*Corporate Responsibility Audits: Doing Well by Doing Good*," Sloan Management Review, Winter 2000.

[7] University of North Texas Emergency Administration and Planning, *www.scs.unt.edu/depts/eadp/*

[8] Project Management Institute, *www.pmi.org*

7

Managing Emerging Technologies

"The phonograph is not of any commercial value"
—THOMAS EDISON, 1880

"Prediction is very difficult, especially if it's about the future."
—YOGI BERRA

Preview of Chapter

The ever-changing technology landscape requires that the CIO and IT staff continuously monitor the environment to identify the impact new technology might have on their organization. The pace of technological development continues to increase. There is no guarantee that a new technology will bring any benefit at all to an organization. However, delaying the adoption of what may become a *disruptive* technology (one which greatly alters the fundamental business model) can result in a major setback for an organization. Conversely, being on the leading edge of implementing such a technology can catapult an organization into becoming the leading competitive force in an industry. This would obviously have some benefit for the CIO, IT, and the firm as a whole. As discussed in other chapters, it is changes to the business processes that are enabled/driven by the new technology that bring business value.

While this text focuses on Information Technology, it is important to consider that technologies from different domains can at times *converge* to create seemingly new technologies and new opportunities that become an important factor in the management of Information Technology. For example, until recently, telephone systems and information systems were considered separate systems from a management viewpoint—telephones were considered part of the facilities management function. With the emergence of digital PBX systems and then VOIP (Voice Over IP), the management of these systems is more frequently in the domain of the CIO.

In addition to management issues, at times new technology can be *disruptive*. A disruptive technology is one that can cause upheaval in a company or an entire industry. The Internet, for example, can be viewed as a disruptive technology due to its ability to lower the barrier of entry for competitors, create new business models, and to change existing business models. The CIO and the

IT and business management team must be aware of and understand this to be able to minimize the reaction time to these changes and to be proactive in *leading* their organization to adopt and adapt to new technologies.

Chapters 5 and 6 reviewed the *processes* involved in the management of IT. This chapter will discuss the issues surrounding the management of emerging technology. This aspect of an IT executive's job directly affects and can be affected by some of the processes discussed in these earlier chapters. Business strategic planning and IT strategic planning can drive the search for emerging technologies. The reverse may also be true in that emerging technology may form the foundation for strategic plans and require significant changes to the IT and business strategy.

The tactical processes also must take emerging technologies into account. Application, data, systems, network, skills, and budget plans need to incorporate the role of new technologies, and must take into account the role these plans can play in encouraging and enabling the search for emerging technologies. These processes include architecture, capacity planning, recovery, maintaining storage levels, and skills. Chapter 11—IT Governance is also relevant to the management of emerging technologies.

What we will examine in this chapter:

- ■ Why is it important to understand emerging technologies?
- ■ Should an organization be a pioneer, leader, or follower?
- ■ When is the best time to adopt a new technology?
- ■ How can a new technology be introduced and appropriately applied?

▪▪▪ An Introduction to Emerging Technology

Emerging technologies is a relative term. What might seem to be emerging to one organization might be viewed as old by another. Technology seen as emerging by the second organization might be considered old by the first. The relative newness is important to understand. If a certain technology was new to a business unit but old in the firm at large, it would be helpful to learn from the experience of the other business units so their experience can be leveraged (a great opportunity for an internal knowledge system). If a technology was new to a firm but not new in the industry, the source of expertise would come from external IT professionals in the industry. If the technology were new to industry, the primary source of expertise would then come from vendors.

The Automatic Teller Machine (ATM)

The ATM provides a well-known example of a technology that has passed through the four life cycle phases in a relatively short period of time. When Citibank first introduced this technology, it was a pioneer in its use. The ability to provide banking services 24 hours a day depended on at least two other technologies whose development converged to enable the ATM-communications network and transactional information systems. This initial introduction as a customer service technology was subsequently adopted by other banks, and quickly moved into the key technology phase as customers used the availability of an ATM as a reason for choosing their bank. Today, the interconnection of ATMs that allows customers to utilize any ATM to access their own bank accounts makes the ATM a base technology. All banking institutions provide access for their customers throughout the country and from most foreign countries. It is now a commodity.

Emerging technologies are typically defined as those technologies that are just coming out of research and development labs and are becoming available for implementation in an organizational setting. This does not imply that the technology in question is practical, profitable, ethical, or sustainable. These are the questions that must be addressed to decide the proper course of action concerning technologies that are emergent.

The Technology Life Cycle

Technologies, much like products, have a life cycle. A traditional description of this life cycle (see "The ATM" sidebar) describes technologies as passing through four phases:

1. **Emerging Technology.** In this phase, a technology is considered an innovation and is still developing in terms of capability or capacity. Its potential marketplace has not yet accepted it as a technology that will be useful, useable, cost effective, or a viable substitute for a technology (or service) it could replace.
2. **Pacing Technology.** In this phase, the technology is beginning to grow in acceptance. Multiple competing organizations may be implementing or evaluating the technology. The technology has been identified as having benefits that exceed its cost, or is viewed as one that has a competitive advantage that cannot be ignored.
3. **Key Technology.** Once a technology reaches this phase, it has become a technology that provides a *competitive differential*, that is the use of this technology enables/drives the business and/or is a major reason the organization is more successful than its competitors.
4. **Base Technology.** This final phase of a technology's life cycle is reached when the technology becomes a *required technology* for an organization. If an organization is to remain viable, it cannot avoid using the technology.

The net benefit of a given technology varies during its life cycle. As shown in Figure 7-1, a given technology may or may not have the potential for providing a competitive advantage to an organization. During the emergent phase, the achievable benefits are not fully known, so some organizations may choose to experiment with or adopt technologies based on hype or calculated risk. Some technologies will subsequently be abandoned or they may prove to be marginally beneficial. Organizations already having investments in these technologies will continue to utilize them, while others choose not to. Once the benefits are understood and are deemed to be positive, they become pacing technologies. As more organizations implement a given technology, it then becomes a major driver to maintain a competitive posture. At this stage, the technology still provides a competitive advantage, but its adoption is driven more by the need to maintain this advantage than to gain the advantage first. Finally, once a technology has been established and becomes a necessary part of doing business, it becomes known as a base technology and provides little competitive advantage.

▮▮▮▮▮▮▮▮▮▮▮▮ **FIGURE 7-1** The Technology Life Cycle.

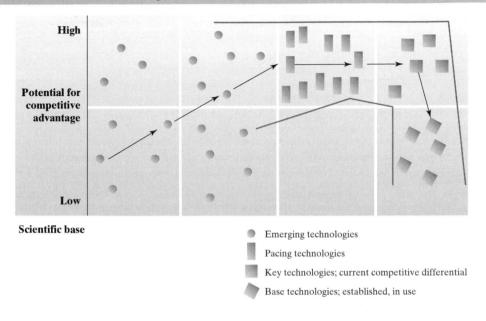

Scientific base

● Emerging technologies

▮ Pacing technologies

▮ Key technologies; current competitive differential

◆ Base technologies; established, in use

Experts?

"We are at great haste to build a magnetic telegraph line from Maine to Texas. But Maine and Texas have nothing to talk to each other about."
—HENRY DAVID THOREAU, 1854

"It will appear that we have reached the limits of what is possible to achieve with computer technology, although one should be careful with such statements, as they tend to sound pretty silly in five years."
—JOHN VON NEUMANN, 1949

"I have traveled the length and breadth of this country and talked with the best people, and I can assure you that data processing is a fad that won't last out the year."
—PRENTICE HALL BUSINESS BOOKS EDITOR, 1957

"There is practically no chance that space satellites would improve telephone service."
—T.A.M. CRAVEN, FCC COMMISSIONER, 1961

"Long before the year 2000, the entire antiquated structure of college degrees, majors and credits will be in shambles."
—ALVIN TOFFLER

"A computer will not defeat a chess-master until 2010."
—GARRY KASPOROV, 1995

"The Internet will catastrophically collapse in 1996."
—ROBERT METCALFE

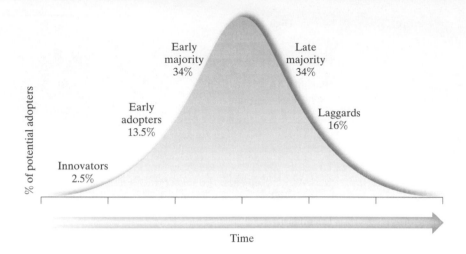

Adoption of Technology

In addition to the inherent lag in the identification of benefits to a new technology, there are human characteristics that affect the rate at which technologies are adopted. A key model in understanding this is found in the theory of diffusion of innovations.[1] This model suggests that technologies are adopted at rates that follow a normal distribution as shown in Figure 7-2. This diagram presents the implementer's point of view of technology as opposed to the technology point of view.

The categorization of these adopter types is as follows:

1. **Innovators:** Organizations or people that are willing to take higher risk, have "deeper pockets" (i.e., are able to finance projects more readily), or have experience in evaluating/piloting projects based on emerging technologies. There is a possible negative viewpoint of people or organizations in this category—it includes people and organizations that embrace technology "for technology's sake" rather than selecting only technologies that provide sustainable benefits. This adopter type would likely implement a technology during the emerging phase.
2. **Early Adopters:** Organizations or people that are more visionary. There is some assurance of the potential returns from adopting a technology, but its visibility is not yet widespread, or only these adopters see its application. These adopters would implement emerging or pacing technologies.
3. **Early Majority:** Adopters who waited until there was more assurance for the success of the technology. Other firms, perhaps competitors, have already proven that the technology can be successful and there is an understanding that the technology will eventually become a key and base technology. These adopters would likely implement technologies only after they have become pacing technologies.
4. **Late Majority:** This category includes the organizations that have realized they will have to adopt the technology to stay competitive. These are the conservative organizations, which prefer low risk or have low investment capability. The pressure to adopt the technology to remain competitive has risen to a level where the technology cannot be ignored. These adopter types would most likely only adopt a technology that has reached key status.
5. **Laggards:** These are the true skeptics. The technology is likely to have become a base technology and the main benefit to adopting it is to stay in the market. The

▪▪▪▪▪▪▪▪▪▪▪▪ **FIGURE 7-3** Moore's Landscape of Technology Adoption Life Cycle.

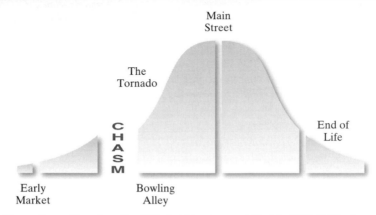

Source: The Chasm Group Encyclopedia of Market Development Models (2001 Edition).

risk in being a laggard is that the cost of implementation may now be greater than the economic benefit.

In *Inside the Tornado*,[2] Geoffrey Moore relabels these categories as:

1. Technology enthusiasts
2. Visionaries
3. Pragmatists
4. Conservatives
5. Skeptics

Moore provides a look at technology innovation from a product *provider* point of view. His approach is useful in providing the supplier's view of the customer in the adoption of new technology. The adopter categories above can be generalized into two larger components. The first is the *early market*, made up of the enthusiasts and the visionaries. The second component is the *mainstream market*, where the technology has been accepted and adoption begins to accelerate. The *chasm* is found between these two phases. Technologies that never become viable or accepted fall into this chasm. These are the technologies that never achieve any competitive potential.

As shown in Figure 7-3,[3] the Technology Adoption Life Cycle can be extended with the addition of two phases ignored by the initial description above. Moore identifies these phases as zones. Table 7-1 lists Moore's definition of these zones in the left column. The right column presents the view a CIO might have, relative to the phase a technology is in.

▪▪▪ Why Not Just Wait?

It would appear from the above discussion that there is great risk in being an early entrant into the adoption of a new technology. Since many technologies fall into the "chasm," what benefit is there in expending resources in evaluating emerging technologies? It is just as important to ask what is the *risk* of *not* expending resources.

In a 1998 survey by A.T. Kearney, 213 CEOs were asked what the implications were of not keeping pace with technology change. The results are shown in Figure 7-4.[4] Maintaining competitive advantage is a primary reason for a focus on technology change.

TABLE 7-1   Moore's Product Provider View of Technology Innovation

Moore's (supplier's) view	Organization's (CIO's) view
The Early Market (emerging technology phase), a time of great excitement when customers are technology enthusiasts and visionaries looking to be first to get on board with the new paradigm.	A time when the technology is the latest "toy." The true visionary may see the potential for value, but there is great potential for failure
The Chasm (not identified in initial model), a time of great despair, when early-market's interest wanes but the mainstream market is still not comfortable with the immaturity of the solutions available.	A time when the CIO and staff may need to back away from a technology and perhaps abandon pilot projects. Continuing with a new technology when the marketplace is questioning it requires serious thought.
The Bowling Alley (pacing technology phase), a period of niche-based adoption in advance of the general marketplace, driven by compelling customer needs and a willingness of vendors to craft niche-specific whole products.	This time period may consist of the formation of alliances with the technology supplier to develop focused applications of the technology, or to craft a shared-risk/reward approach to creating a more mature technology. This may be a period when the technology is *adapted* rather than *adopted*. The ability of the technology to satisfy a niche application is the "pin" that is knocked down to make it viable.
The Tornado (key technology phase), a period of mass-market adoption, when the general marketplace switches over to the new infrastructure paradigm.	This period spans the shift of a technology into that of a key technology. Organizations begin adopting the technology in increasing numbers. The benefits of the technology are apparent. The leading supplier of the technology may become the standard. Additional applications for the technology become apparent and a period of rapid growth in its use (the Tornado) begins.
Main Street (base technology phase), a period of aftermarket development, when the base infrastructure has been developed and the goal now is to flesh out its potential.	During this period, IT looks for other applications of the technology, ways to leverage its knowledge of the technology into other areas of the organization or into new business strategies for the organization.
End of Life (ignored and presumed in original model), which can come all too soon in high tech because of the semiconductor engine driving price/performance to unheard levels, enabling wholly new paradigms to come to market and supplant the leaders who themselves had only just arrived.	Eventually, most if not all technologies become obsolete. They primarily become obsolete because of substitution of newer technology. The cost of maintaining obsolete technology may grow beyond the cost of implementing the substitute technology.

▪▪▪▪▪▪▪▪▪

Source: Moore, Geoffrey A., *Inside the Tornado*, HarperBusiness, 1995.

▪▪▪▪▪▪▪▪▪▪▪▪ **FIGURE 7-4   Implications of Not Keeping Pace with Technology.**

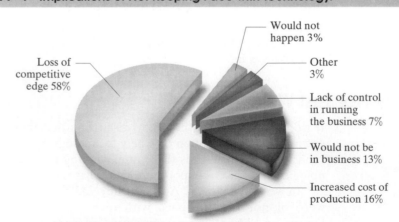

Source: "Strategic Information Technology and the CEO Agenda." A.T. Kearney survey of 213 CEOs and senior executives, 1998.

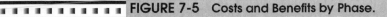

▪▪▪▪▪▪▪▪▪▪▪ FIGURE 7-5   Costs and Benefits by Phase.

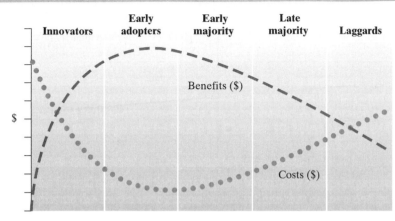

Source: Adapted from Arthur Anderson Report by Konsynski, 1991.

Figure 7-5[5] demonstrates the relative benefits versus costs of a given technology over the technology's life cycle. As shown in this figure, the risk in delaying the adoption of a technology is that the total return will decline as implementation is delayed. The total return in this figure consists of the volume bounded by the vertical lines denoting the implementation of the technology and the abandonment of the technology, and the benefit and cost lines. This is meant to provide a generic view of the costs and benefits over time—the actual shape and size varies by technology, and of course this example presumes the technology being considered has a positive benefit. The largest gap between benefits and costs is in the early adopters segment. By following the innovators, early adopters learn from and improve on the earlier experience.

The area at the left of the chart (the fishtail in the innovators phase) includes those projects that were aborted. The area at the far right of the laggards phase represents legacy systems that cost more than the value delivered. In this case it is important to recognize that systems are approaching this legacy state, and prepare strategies and plans to address this problem.

▪▪▪ Organizational Aspects of Technology Development

The various stages of the technology life cycle can be characterized based on several attributes. These organizational characteristics, as shown in Figure 7-6, can be used to assess the organization's timing in adopting a technology.

Organizations that tend to place a greater emphasis on R&D are much more likely to adopt new technologies during the initial stages of its application. The culture of these organizations allows for experimentation and accepts failure. Laggard organizations tend to emphasize production, which leads to an aversion to any change that can impact daily stable operations.

Different organizations exhibit different *couplings* between functions or groups within the organization (i.e., the key relationships are found between different functions depending on the view relative to technology). In the innovators organization, it is more likely that the tightest couplings will be between R&D and the systems within the organization. As the primary couplings shift from a technology-oriented basis to an end-user and production basis, the willingness to adopt technology before it is proven declines.

FIGURE 7-6 Strategies for Technology Development.

	Innovator "pioneer"	Early adopter	Late majority	Laggards "me too"
Emphasis on:	Research and development	Development	System design and engineering	Production
Couplings:	R&D and systems	R&D and end users	Systems and users	Production and users
Technical abilities:	State of the Art	High	Moderate	Low
Features:	R&D risk	Competitive intelligence, responsive	Minimize costs	Quick copy delivery performance
Style:	Technical enthusiasts, visionaries	Pragmatists	Conservatives	Skeptics

Organizations that have greater *technical abilities* will tend to be more willing (and able) to evaluate and implement technologies earlier in their life cycle. This technical ability is not generic, however; technical ability is measured in relation to the technology under consideration.

Organizations tend to develop strategies that vary in their basic *features*. The innovator will more frequently accept risk as a normal part of strategy. Early adopters will consider the competitive environment as an important part of developing their technology strategy, and respond to the developments taking place in the marketplace. The focus of the late majority is to minimize costs so this group usually enters the life cycle once a technology has become accepted and the apparent cost of the technology has bottomed out. Once a technology has been proven and is optimized, the laggard will then adopt the technology since the strategy of this organization focuses on delivering the goods.

Finally, the organizational *style* mirrors the definition of the adopter categories, ranging from the *visionary* innovators to the *skeptical* laggards.

The S-Curve

A discussion of life cycles would not be complete without the use of the S-curve. While the normal distribution describes the rate of adoption of technologies, the S-curve describes the cumulative adoption. There are several implications relative to this cumulative effect of technology adoption over time.

It is important to remember that successive technologies overlap. As a technology moves into its obsolescence phase, replacement technology is likely to exist side-by-side. *Sunsetting* refers to this time period during which a technology is earmarked to be discontinued, but exists alongside the new technology.

Figure 7-7 describes the cumulative adoption of a given technology. The left-most end of the curve corresponds to the time period that innovators adopt the technology, whereas the laggards will be adopting the technology only when the majority of users have done so, as depicted at the right-most end of the curve.

▪▪▪▪▪▪▪▪▪▪▪ **FIGURE 7-7**   Diffusion Curve.

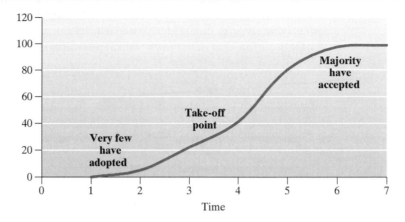

Change Along the Curve

There are implications for change management relative to the diffusion curve, as indicated by Figure 7-8.[6] During the initial phases of the technology life cycle, the business and IT management needs to build the awareness of the emerging technology. During this stage, the selection of experts to be associated with the technology is made.

As the early and late majority begins to adopt a technology, more people need to be skilled in the technology. The change affects more people and the need to gain more acceptance of the technology grows. Users and supporters need to be *invited* to embrace the technology.

Finally, when a technology has become a base technology, and an organization must adopt the technology, change becomes a requirement. Management needs to shift from persuasion and encouragement to more direct methods of insuring the acceptance of the technology.

In considering the implications and impact of an emerging technology, IT and business management needs to consider the scope of any changes that will be caused by the technology. Minor, incremental changes in technology carry a far different result than a *disruptive or discontinuous* change in technology.

▪▪▪▪▪▪▪▪▪▪▪ **FIGURE 7-8**   Managing Change.

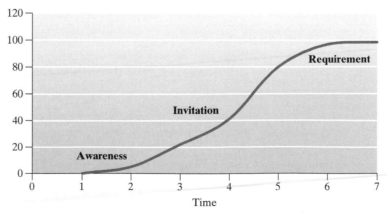

Source: Frances Horibe.

"Discontinuous change is qualitatively different from incremental change. It requires a break with the past, perhaps even the deliberate destruction of certain elements of the current system. It raises fundamental issues of values and basic vision. It is frequently uncertain, incomplete, and headed toward a future that is unclear. It is traumatic, painful, and demanding on the organization and its people"[7]*

One of Nadler, Shaw, and Walton's key differences between incremental change and discontinuous change that is of major importance to the firm is that discontinuous change *cannot* be delegated to lower levels of the organization. Due to the impact of such changes, the CEO or the senior management team of the organization must lead it. Such leadership becomes critical for the success of any technological changes of this scope.

Moore[8] identifies two types of discontinuities that shape the technology life cycle discussed earlier. *Paradigm shock* is the effect experienced by end users or the infrastructure supporting them. The greater the impact on stakeholders relative to the level of "newness" in terms of ideas, investments, and behaviors, the greater the paradigm shock.

Application breakthrough comes about as a result of dramatic changes in the roles of the end user of a technology. These changes cause significant improvements in returns from the technology investment. Application breakthrough is thus the driver for adoption of new technology, whereas paradigm shock is the inhibitor. Chapter 10 – Managing IT Change will provide more insight into the issues surrounding the management of change.

Learning Along the Curve

Figure 7-9 illustrates the demands for learning within an organization relative to technology change. Early in the life of a technology, the number of people knowledgeable about a technology is relatively small, but as its adoption rate begins to increase, the need for more knowledgeable staff (both users and technical support) grows.

As the adoption rate reaches the fastest rate of growth, the need for learning is likewise at its peak. Once a technology enters the obsolescence phase, there is a decline

❚❚❚❚❚❚❚❚❚❚❚ **FIGURE 7-9** The Learning S-Curve.

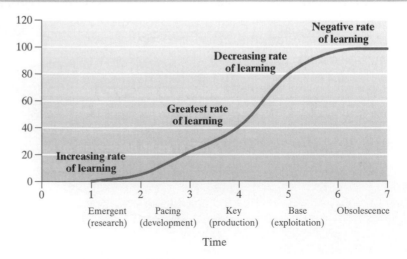

Time

*Nadler, David A., Shaw, Robert Bruce, and Walton, A. Elise, *Discontinuous Change*, Jossey-Bass (1995).

▪▪▪▪▪▪▪▪▪▪▪ **FIGURE 7-10** Three Strategic Postures.

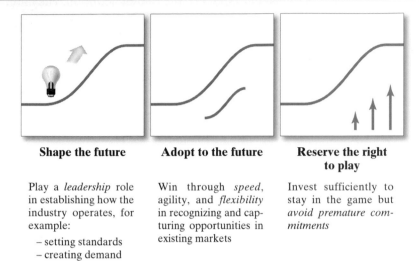

Shape the future	**Adopt to the future**	**Reserve the right to play**
Play a *leadership* role in establishing how the industry operates, for example: – setting standards – creating demand	Win through *speed*, agility, and *flexibility* in recognizing and capturing opportunities in existing markets	Invest sufficiently to stay in the game but *avoid premature commitments*

in the available knowledge as people move on to the next new technology. This is an important phase for managers to consider. There is a risk that the pool of available knowledge will decline faster than the technology's use. This contributes to the rising cost of technology in the later years of the life cycle as discussed earlier.

Strategy and the S-Curve

The technology S-curve also has implications for the strategic posture that a new technology can create for an organization as shown in Figure 7-10. Innovators and early adopters can play a greater role in shaping the subsequent use of a technology. This can have a compounding effect on the competitive potential of the technology. The organization that participates in *shaping* the future will have greater influence in driving the marketplace.

Adopters that fall into the middle range of the curve—the majority (primarily the early majority)—are those who *respond* to their environment. Their strategy is to be flexible enough to *adapt* to their circumstances, yet avoid some of the risks inherent with adopting a technology too soon.

The late majority and laggards maintain a strategic posture where investment in technology is made as late as possible. They remain competitive (sometimes barely), while avoiding most or all of the risk of adopting new technologies. The risk for this strategy is "getting into the game" too late.

▪▪▪ Innovation Diffusion (Reprise)

How do organizations *apply* the S-curve discussion above? Of what use is this seemingly theoretical and abstract notion that technology follows some kind of adoption rate? To help to understand this, a review of the foundations of the theory of innovation diffusion and more recent research follows.

Everett Rogers formed much of the framework for the concepts of innovation diffusion. This work built upon the anthropological and social science theories regarding diffusion. *Diffusion* is defined as *the process by which an innovation is communicated, over time, through certain channels to members of a social system.*[9] *Innovation* is considered as synonymous with "technology." Rogers identified five characteristics of innovations that influence the rate of adoption. They are:

- **Relative Advantage.** This attribute considers the degree to which the innovation is perceived to be better (more advantageous) than the technology it replaces.
- **Compatibility.** A higher level of compatibility with the values and needs of the potential adopter is considered to improve the chances of adoption.
- **Complexity.** Technology that is difficult to learn, use, or implement will have a slower rate of adoption.
- **Trialability.** Technology that can more easily be experimental will have a better chance of being adopted.
- **Observability.** The degree to which an innovation can be "seen" by other users and adopters will affect the rate of adoption.

These five characteristics can be weighed to analyze the potential for a technology's rate of adoption or assess whether it will be adopted at all.

Much of the research in innovation diffusion has been based on the context of decision making by the adopters as an *independent*, *binary* process. That is, it presumes that innovators are not influenced by others (such as management) and that technology implementation is simply a yes/no decision (as opposed to a degree of implementation).[10] Classical innovation diffusion theory does not address the impact of organizational influences, knowledge issues, and interdependencies with other adopters of the technology as primary factors affecting adoption.

Additional insight can be gained by evaluating a technology from the perspective of *economics of technology standards*.[11] This approach includes the characteristics of technology adoption that contribute to *increasing returns to adoption*. This refers to technologies whose benefits depend a great deal upon the size and timing of the community of other adopters of the technology. Fichman and Kemerer use major software-oriented technologies as the basis for their work since the historical improvements in hardware provide few well-known examples of "bad" choices of adoption. Several software technologies exist, however, that provide examples of significant differences in rates of adoption that are not predicted by Innovation Diffusion Theory alone.

There are three primary sources of increasing returns to adoption mentioned by Fichman and Kemerer: learning by using, positive network externalities, and technological interrelatedness. *Learning by using* refers to the increase in the benefit a technology brings as the community of adopters accumulates experience and knowledge of its use. *Positive network externalities* refer to the benefits brought by the *number* of users of a technology. The greater the number of users, the greater the benefit of the technology. Finally, *interrelatedness* refers to the existence of compatible products that serve to increase the likelihood of a larger base of adopters.

The adoption of complex technologies within organizations can be impeded by the need for learning. This "knowledge barrier" can inhibit innovation diffusion.[12] In the face of these *knowledge barriers*, there are several characteristics of organizations that are more likely to become early adopters of such technologies:[13]

- An ability to amortize the costs of learning
- An ability to acquire any given amount of new knowledge with less effort
- A higher level of initial knowledge about a given technology

An outgrowth of research into innovation diffusion has been the recognition that acquisition of technology does not necessarily equate to implementation. An example of this discrepancy is that of "shelf-ware." It is not uncommon for technology-oriented organizations to purchase products simply because they are the "latest and greatest"

▪▪▪▪▪▪▪▪▪▪▪ **FIGURE 7-11** The Assimilation Gap.

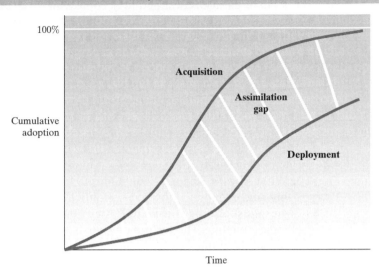

Source: Fichman, Robert G., Kemerer, Chris F., *The Illusory Diffusion of Innovation: An Examination of Assimilation Gaps*, Information Systems Research, Vol. 10, No. 3, September 1999.

only to find these products are not necessarily better than the existing product it replaces. These products then stay on the shelf, leading to their nickname.

This lag between the acquisition of a product and its actual implementation, whether it is a temporary lag or a permanent difference, has been described as the *assimilation gap*.[14] This gap between the apparent adoption of a technology when using acquisition of a technology as a guideline as compared to the deployment of the technology in actual use can have a significant impact on decision-making. It has been proposed that increasing returns to adoption along with the knowledge barriers to adoption discussed above contribute to this assimilation gap (see Figure 7-11[15]).

This "gap" can provide important information to a firm assessing the viability of a technology. It highlights the importance of disregarding marketing "hype" as reason to pursue a technology. The sales revenue associated with any particular technology as reported by a technology's vendor must be tempered with an assessment of the actual *use* of the technology.

▪▪▪ Identifying Emerging Technologies

With this background of the life cycle of technologies and the generic potential risks and benefits in hand, how does an organization identify technologies to consider? There are four basic questions to ask as a starting point:

1. **What *Can* Happen?** As mentioned earlier, prior to a technology being classified as "emerging" it must first have been developed in an R&D lab, an inventor's garage, or arise out of the *convergence* of existing technologies. Science (and in some cases, science fiction) provides the foundation for this. Keeping abreast of developments occurring in the high-technology labs of the world through newspapers, journals, or networking can provide the basic background for reducing the element of surprise when a technology emerges as a product. Large firms can negotiate with their vendors to visit their labs to get a peek into the future.

2. **What *Will* Happen?** Not every new technology development that comes out of a lab or garage is destined to become a viable product. Engineering hurdles must be crossed. For example the equipment needed to produce a product in volume may require innovation also, delaying the ability to produce the product. A new process or technology may not be reproducible in a manufacturing environment. For example, crystalline structures that have been grown in space cannot easily be produced on earth.

   Economic factors may play a role in accelerating or slowing the emergence of a technology. The price of oil in the 1970s spurred renewed interest in many existing and new technologies. There are many alternate forms of energy that exist (fuel cells, wind, solar, wave, etc.), but remain in the labs or as pilot projects simply because of the economics involved.

3. **What *Should* Happen?** In addition to the "hard" facts about science, engineering, and economics, the social, political, and ethical issues surrounding technologies must also be considered. An example from the non-IT world is that of biological cloning. The technology exists to clone human beings, yet the ethical and moral dilemma this has created will most likely prevent this technology from being used for some time to come.

   Occasionally, these factors can spur technology. One of the best examples would be the social and political goal expressed by President Kennedy in 1960 (which was discussed in Chapter 2) to send a man to the moon by the end of the 1960s. The focus created by this governmental program accelerated the pace of technology development and created technologies that otherwise may never have occurred or been significantly delayed.

   Also, just because a technology is effective does not mean that it will be accepted as a standard. In the early days of consumer adoption of video cassette recorders, the Betamax standard was pitted against the VHS standard. While the Betamax standard was considered technically superior in certain ways, VHS became more widely accepted through more effective marketing and licensing.

4. **How *Will* it Happen?** This question is the main topic of this chapter. The decisions made by a firm form the basis for the success of evaluating and/or implementing emerging technologies. Frequently, how R&D envisions a product being used is far different than how it is actually applied.

Encyclopedia Britannica

Some companies ignore the technology happening around them. Encyclopedia Britannica seemed to ignore what was happening with the Internet and personal computers until it was almost too late. This company, now over 200 years old, decided to continue selling the $1500 print version of its encyclopedia in the late 1980s and early 1990s, while Microsoft partnered with Funk & Wagnall to produce *Encarta* in 1993 for under $100. When it became apparent to Encyclopedia Britannica in 1999 that it was nearly doomed by technology, it decided to post the entire contents of their encyclopedia on the Web and provide free access! It decided on an unproven business model of generating income through advertising on its Web site. The initial inactivity on the site was almost disastrous. The company survives, but it took only 10 years to nearly force a 230-year old company into extinction, simply because they ignored emerging technology that was unstoppable.

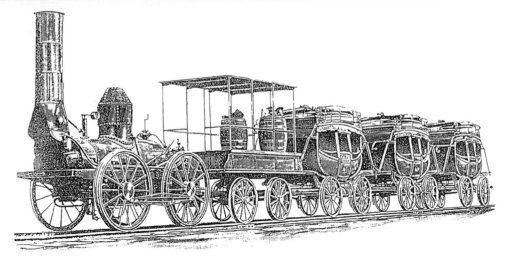

Source: http://pchs-fsm.org/westpointfoundry/galleryartifacts/the_dewitt_clinton.html.

Identifying the Application

Another element of the identification of emerging technologies is the corresponding identification of the *application* for the technology. Historically, there are many significant examples of how emerging technologies were implemented in a way that incorrectly identified the true benefit, or was merely an adaptation of the existing technology. For example:

- Steam engines initially pumped water into water wheels (which the engine eventually replaced) to provide power.
- Early motion pictures (movies) looked like stage plays that were filmed.
- Initial television shows were like radio shows on screen. They were simply television broadcasts of people talking.
- The "horseless carriage" looked like a horse should pull it.
- Some of the first railroad cars (Figure 7-12[16]) looked like stagecoaches.
- The radio was thought of as a wireless telegraph.

Adner and Levinthal[17] describe this phenomenon as *speciation*; they consider most applications of emerging technologies to be an evolutionary event. As they state: "Technological speciation is not usually the result of a sudden technological revolution. The revolution is in the application." The application of a technology or set of technologies shifts from one domain to another, possibly resulting in a technology application considerably different from what was originally intended.

▪▪▪ Inhibitors to Embracing Emerging Technologies

There are many traps faced by organizations in identifying and pursuing emerging technologies. George Day and Paul Schoemaker identified four sequential traps.[18] They are delayed participation, sticking with the familiar, reluctance to fully commit, and lack of persistence. These traps exist because of the inherent conflict and ambiguity that is created when organizations evaluate emerging technologies. Managers should be aware of these effects when evaluating technologies.

Delayed Participation

Managers of organizations create their own mental models of their business. Past experiences contribute to create a model of the organization that is helpful for enabling incremental improvements, but not necessarily helpful for disruptive or sudden changes or improvements. The current state of an emerging technology should not deter the implementation of the technology. A longer-term outlook on the potential of the technology is necessary.

Factors That Slow Adoption of New Technologies[19]

- The offering does not provide substantial *performance advantages* over current solutions.
- Target customers are currently quite *satisfied with current* solutions.
- Those customers who will benefit most from the offering *do not control* the purchasing decision.
- The final offering needs to undergo a significant *regulatory* approval process.
- The customer's perception of value will be dependent on the *backing* of other parties.
- The sale of the product will depend on the efforts and resources of other parties, such as *distributors*.
- Adoption of the offering will require users, customers, or distributors to change expensive *embedded systems*.
- Target markets will have to be *educated* in how to use the offering.
- Target markets will have to radically change their *usage patterns*.
- The technical *standards* in this industry are not yet clearly set.
- The purchasing decision will be *risky* for target customers.
- Significant sales are unlikely until a *critical mass* of products is in use.
- *Infrastructure* or technology must be developed in parallel to get the offering to the market.

Sticking with the Familiar

In some cases more than one emerging technology may be available as alternatives. In this case the possibility of selecting the wrong one may come about because of a particular technology's similarity with past successes. It is also possible that a competing technology may have skill requirements similar to those already existing and thus become a favored choice.

Reluctance to Fully Commit

This trap comes about when an emerging technology is pursued, but then the pursuit is half-hearted. This occurs primarily due to competing forces within an organization. For example, existing projects and technologies are usually the primary focus. The decision to apply resources to new and possibly low- or no-return projects when priorities are constantly shifting can be a difficult one to make. Day and Schoemaker also propose a paradox in risk-taking among managers—the tendency to make bold forecasts, but timid choices.

Visionaries?

"I think there is a market for about five computers."
—THOMAS J. WATSON, CHAIRMAN IBM, 1943

"Computers in the future may weigh no more than 1.5 tons."
—POPULAR MECHANICS, 1949

"But what is it good for?" (The microchip)
—ENGINEER AT ADVANCED COMPUTING SYSTEMS

"There is no reason for any individual to have a computer in their home."
—KEN OLSEN, PRESIDENT DIGITAL EQUIPMENT, 1977

"640K ought to be enough for anybody."
—BILL GATES, 1981

Lack of Persistence

This trap is created by the unwillingness of organizations to endure the trials of implementing technologies that have high risk. The emphasis on quarterly returns that exists in most organizations spills over onto projects that may take time to produce results.

The Establishment

Utterback[20] points out one of the inherent dangers in today's service-based economy. In industries where Information Technology serves as the backbone for many business processes, the danger is that:

"Industry outsiders have little to lose in pursuing radical innovations. They have no infrastructure to defend or maintain and... they have every economic incentive to overturn the existing order."

Existing organizations, on the other hand, have large investments in their current infrastructure and technology. Maintaining the status quo or enabling marginal improvements can consume the majority of a firm's resources. There is little incentive emotionally or organizationally to make radical change.

▪▪▪ Human Resource Considerations

The management of emerging technologies includes managing the human resource problems and opportunities that arise in the course of evaluating and implementing new technologies. These issues include availability of talent, resource allocation, motivation, and knowledge management.

Availability of Talent

Assuming an emerging technology has been identified as having potential benefit to an organization, the organization must then acquire the personnel who can best implement the technology. Before this step, the organization must determine if it has the best talent to evaluate the technology. Given some of the difficulties in adequately identifying and evaluating technologies, consideration should be given to whether existing talent is strategically sound.

These concerns lead to the proposition that managing emerging technologies needs to be viewed as a unique function. In the event an emerging technology is selected for pursuit, it is important that personnel with the right skills do the job, which in most cases will require the use of outside resources on at least a temporary basis to transfer the requisite skills to the organization. Where the experience resides depends on the relative newness of the technology. Does another business unit in the organization have experience? Are there available external resources to hire? Is there a need to partner with the vendor?

Resource Allocation

As discussed above, it can become difficult for IT management to remain fully committed to implementing an emerging technology. This implies that there is a benefit to dedicating resources to the evaluation and implementation of emerging technologies. Managing this important part of the IT function as a process separate from the daily operations can reduce the potential for diverting resources away from this function. This may be done in combination with outside resources as mentioned earlier. This "center of competence" or "center of excellence" approach will be described in Chapter 8—Organizing IT.

Motivation

Whether the staff members involved in emerging technologies are organized as a separate function or intermingled with the rest of the IT operation, motivation of those team members can be an important concern. First, it is important that the risks inherent in managing emerging technologies be considered when dealing with failures. Project failures must not be used as vehicles to punish staff. The possibility that project failure may create self-imposed punishment by staff involved in that project should also be considered and guarded against.

Perhaps more important is the issue of what to do with staff members who participate in successful projects. The knowledge gained in this case can easily make the people involved more valuable to other companies, including competitors who wish to implement a successful technology. In this case, organizations need to address the need to motivate employees to remain with the organization. The issue of motivation is discussed further in Chapter 9—Human Resource Considerations.

Knowledge Management

There are several dimensions to knowledge management as it pertains to emerging technology (see "Technology Convergence" sidebar). First, as a follow-on to the motivation issue, project failures as well as successes should be considered learning experiences. An environment that fosters sharing of "lessons learned" (good or bad) can benefit future projects.

Technology Convergence: McGraw-Hill's Primis[21]

As 1990 approached, McGraw Hill began to see a decline in market share. The decline was to due to the used book market as well as educators' development of their own course material made up of selected materials from books, articles, and other writings. The *convergence* of several technologies paved the way for the creation of the Primis system. This system made use of an online database of material, remote access to the database index, and the implementation of a new Electrobook printing press that allowed for variable book quantity runs. The existence of these various technologies *converged* in a way that their combined capabilities could be used to allow customers (professors, for example) to select material from a variety of sources and assemble them into custom textbooks that met their own unique requirements. Had any one of these technologies (a database that stored Postscript-based data, telecommunications for remote access and printing, or the digital Electrobook printing press) been unavailable, the Primis concept could not have been launched.

Second, there may not be any existing knowledge required to either evaluate or implement an emerging technology. In this event, the utilization of outside consultants to evaluate and/or initiate emerging technology projects may be necessary. This source of talent should then be used to transfer knowledge into the organization.

Finally, this "new" knowledge may need to be protected, especially if the technology implemented proves to be a competitive advantage and is not yet implemented by the competition. Organizations need to consider this in structuring agreements with outside consultants and in relation to their own IT staff.

In any event, it is important to share the experience gained with other business units.

▪▪▪ Technology Scanning

Technology scanning refers to the process of keeping abreast of developments and potential developments in the technology arena. Some examples of sources that can be used to stay informed are:

- Books and periodicals
- Formal studies
  - Interviews
  - Surveys/questionnaires (Delphi method)
  - Scenario planning
  - On-site observations
- Personal contacts/network
- Professional organizations/workshops/conventions
- R&D organizations
- State and federal departments
- Universities
- Vendors and consultants
- Early adopters

Technology forecasting is a process that might be thought of as less scientific or formal in nature. In regard to the distant future, the prognoses and forecasts of experts must be used as an indicator of general trends. The tendency of technologies to emerge over years, rather than simply bursting on the scene, reduces the need for forecasting to one of awareness—it is rarely critical that one knows the nature of technologies that will be available more than a few years in the future.

Two methods that are available to assess possible future developments include the Delphi method and the scenario planning method. The Rand Corporation developed the Delphi method in the 1950s. The methodology uses a multiround survey approach with feedback. Experts in a particular field or area are utilized and through the feedback within the group, a consensus is reached after several rounds of questions and answers. The premise with this approach is that the answer(s) converged on over the survey iterations carry the highest probability of being correct.

Royal Dutch Shell developed the scenario planning method in the 1970s. This method examines a given scenario (possible new technology, environmental change, etc.) and evaluates the probability of it occurring versus the impact the development would have on an organization. Scenarios that have both a high impact and a high probability of occurring become high priority issues. This method was discussed in Chapters 2 and 3 on IT strategy.

▪▪▪ Factors Affecting Successful Introduction of Emerging Technologies

As with any Information Technology project, the implementation of a new technology requires an approach that will increase the likelihood of success. Since implementing a technology that has a significant level of uncertainty carries greater risk, it is important to be certain that the following factors be addressed:

1. Identify the problem and opportunity that the technology addresses. There must be a *business linkage* and the technology must be of *value* to the business. These factors can be utilized to obtain a *sponsor* for implementation of the technology.
2. Identify and empower a *champion*. A project's success is much more likely if there is a person or group that believes in the value of the project. In the case of emerging technologies, a champion from a business function can enhance the likelihood of acceptance by others, and reduce the fallout from project failure.
3. Create a cross-functional, dedicated, and accountable team. Communications among the team are important, along with top management support and a strong team leader.
4. Build an environment that will support the introduction of the technology. This environment includes the organizational factors, tools, and expertise to support the technology.
5. Identify and address the risks associated with the new technology. Few, if any emerging technologies are free from risks. Be as prepared as possible to address risks. Constant communications can help identify risks when they occur.
6. Manage the project. Set reasonable goals and schedules. Develop standards for abandoning the project, if possible. Approach the project as an R&D venture, where a negative outcome does not necessarily imply failure.

▪▪▪ The ET Function

As suggested earlier in this chapter, one approach to managing emerging technology is through the creation of a dedicated function within the IT organization responsible for technology scanning, evaluation, selection, and implementation. Hamel and Prahalad's[22] research indicates that in most organizations, less than 3% of senior management's time is spent building a future perspective. They indicate that in their experience, a senior management team should devote 20 to 50% of its time for a period of several months to building this view of the future, and then revisit that view on a continuous basis.

While this viewpoint is focused primarily on the business strategy, the nature of technology and its impact on many of today's firms implies a similar need for senior management's attention to the technological future of the organization. By dedicating resources to focus on emerging technology, organizations can improve their chances of selecting those technologies—at the right time—that will provide the most competitive advantage.

▪▪▪ The Technology Assessment Process[23]

Figure 7-13[24] presents an iterative process that can be applied to reduce the uncertainties that arise out of traditional static approaches to evaluating emerging technology. Each component of the process is interrelated. The four steps of the process are:

1. **Scoping.**   In this step, the capabilities of the firm and the potential threat or opportunity from the technology are analyzed to establish the scope and domain of the technology search. Additional learning about the firm and the technology is a continuous process; the scope will change along with this learning process.

    The business strategy of the organization is an important consideration during this step of the process. The business needs and the ability of the organization to adopt the technology are also issues to evaluate. In some cases, the business scope and strategy may be expanded in response to the consideration of a new technology. An example of this is the decision made by Barnes & Noble to compete via the Internet.

2. **Searching.**   The organization must screen technologies and search for signs of emerging technology and determine if they have commercial viability. The

▪▪▪▪▪▪▪▪▪▪▪▪ **FIGURE 7-13** The Technology Assessment Process.

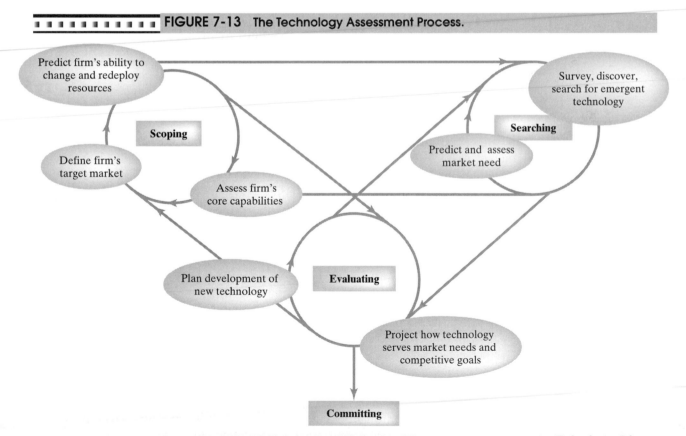

Source: George Day, P. Shoemaker, and E. Gunther, *Wharton on Managing Emerging Technologies*, John Wiley & Sons, Inc. 2000.

information and technology sources to monitor, the procedures that need to be followed, and the organizational arrangements that will allow this to occur must be determined.

Possible sources for identifying emerging technologies have been identified previously in the section entitled "Technology Scanning." The organization itself can also be a source for possible technologies. Brainstorming sessions, R&D groups, and other divisions of larger firms can produce potential innovations to evaluate. Reviewing patent disclosures may also be a source for discovering technologies that warrant tracking.

3. **Evaluating.** This step consists of identifying and prioritizing technologies that are considered potentially viable and evaluating them based on the organization's technical abilities, the needs of the organization, and the competitive opportunities of the organization.

The impact of the technology relative to financial, competitive, and organizational considerations needs to be analyzed. The risks involved in implementing (or not implementing) should be weighed as well as the benefits. Information developed about technologies that are not considered viable for commitment should be retained, as these technologies may become viable in the future.

4. **Committing.** Scoping, searching, and evaluating assist in the determination of whether a technology should be considered. The commitment step considers *how* it should be pursued and implemented. A technology that reaches the commitment step is considered viable with the potential to provide some level of advantage to the organization.

The firm may choose strategies of various levels of commitment depending on the associated risk. An organization may not choose to implement at this stage due to uncertainty, but may choose to continue to invest resources in monitoring the technology. The organization may decide to fully commit to a technology that provides significant advantages with little risk.

▪▪▪ Managing Emerging Technology Checklists[25]

The nature of evaluating and implementing technology that may have uncertain value is fraught with risks. This technology can have a major impact on an organization in that there is no failsafe prescription for managing it. There are key elements to this CIO responsibility that can be addressed using the following suggestions when considering emerging technology.

How to Sell New Technology to Senior Executives

- Focus on selling a business *solution* to a problem or opportunity, not selling technology. There must be a linkage between the technology being considered for adoption and the *business need* for the technology.
- Identify *value* to the organization. Value can take many forms as discussed in Chapter 14—The Value of IT.
- Compare the new technology to the existing technologies. Explain in business terms why the new technology is better or more attractive than the existing technology.
- Consider a range of alternatives to be evaluated. Unless an organization falls into the "laggard" category of adopters, there are usually competing technologies to evaluate.
- Create champions throughout the organization. Having supporters within the business functions of an organization when implementing a new technology can improve the chances for success and/or acceptance of failures.

- Manage expectations. Create clear milestones so that "bailing out" is possible. The earlier in a technology's life cycle that adoption is attempted, the higher the probability of failure. Determining objectives in advance can help reduce the risk of "sticking with" a bad decision for too long. This must be balanced against the "lack of persistence" caution mentioned previously.
- Start small to mitigate risk, then strengthen your credibility over the life of the initiative. In more common terms, "avoid biting off more than you can chew."
- Look to other industries with similar business models to see how technology is changing their industry.
- When you are on the forefront (the *bleeding* edge), be sure you (and the senior executive) understand the iterative/evolutionary nature of new technologies.
- Underpromise, but not so much that you avoid attention. If a technology has not yet been proven, avoid repeating the marketing hype, but embrace the possibility that some of the hype is possible.
- Be honest when things go awry. Contribute to resolving the problem. Learn from failures rather than burying them.

How To Prioritize and Focus on the Right Emerging Technology

- Prototype, demo, and show the business users the technologies. Involving the ultimate users and beneficiaries of the technology as early as possible will improve the chances of success if adoption proceeds.
- Become intimate with business drivers—the attributes of a business environment and/or organization that are the critical success factors of the organization's strategy. The more in-depth the knowledge of business drivers and strategy held by IT personnel, the more likely the identification of a valuable and viable emerging technology will be.
- Understand business requirements. IT cannot determine the applicability of a technology without knowledge of the business requirements.
- Highlight the benefits of the technology, such as increased revenue and productivity.
- Weigh the risks. This is another area where the involvement of business personnel is important. Identification of *business* risks is as important as explaining the technology risks.
- Identify technologies that will enable new business (breakthrough technologies). Emerging technologies do not only improve or affect existing business processes: they also create new ones.
- Identify technologies that can be easily integrated with existing architecture. Emerging technologies do not arise and get adopted in a vacuum. Existing systems and prior (or concurrent) choices are an important factor in selecting technologies.
- Measure the risks in the context of your organization's ability to absorb failure/success. Risk acceptance is contextual. It must be weighed in light of the current organizational ability to absorb risk in financial, political, and cultural terms.
- Understand the organization's culture and its fit with the emerging technology.
- Set aside money for changing priorities throughout the year. Emerging technology selection and IT strategy development are not annual activities. They are continuous processes.

Developing the Business Case for Emerging Technology

- Identify the *business* need. New technologies should be selected for their business benefit, not for their technology hype. Involving the business functions in the review of emerging technology can aid in this.

- Identify how it fits into the current *business* priorities. Business priorities change quickly and need to be reviewed frequently. The basis for a business case may change, sometimes requiring changing or halting the implementation of a technological change.
- If replacing current business technology, identify areas that will be impacted. Recognition and acceptance that a technology may impact the business in unanticipated ways is important.
- Identify the benefits to and impact on the bottom line. Although qualitative benefits are important, IT still needs to address the impact on financial measures.
- Identify the competitive landscape and any potential cost of *not* pursuing the technology.
- Identify the assumptions and justify them.
- Utilize proof of concepts/prototypes.
- Work with a business function collaborator to add validity to proof of concept and identify impact to *business function*.
- Evaluate implementation options such as in-source versus outsource.
- Evaluate fit with existing architecture.
- Ask for feedback from potential customers.
- Identify a project champion that has credibility and line responsibility.

How to Decide When to Deploy Emerging Technologies, Minimizing Risks but Not Getting Left Behind

- Look at industry trends. Benchmark. Evaluate the apparent adoption rate or current level of assimilation of a technology under evaluation. This may be done in many cases through review of academic, industry, or business publications. Technical conferences can also provide some insight into the real level of implementation of a specific technology.
- Evaluate when the risk of not doing it is greater than the risk of doing it.
- Pilot technology to validate proof of concept/direction.
- Utilize outside consultants to evaluate. The knowledge barrier of emerging technology can be reduced through the use of outside consultants, as they may have experience in implementing a technology in other industries or firms.

▪▪▪ Lessons From the Past

The earlier discussion about the ultimate use of a new technology and the opening quotes of this chapter illustrate that while emerging technologies come about because of science, the management of ET is *not* science. Just as scientists make use of history to develop new technologies founded in past learning and experiences, the IT manager can also look to past experiences as a way to understand and accept the potential surprises that are inherent in adopting new technologies. What are some of the lessons of the past to consider?

1. "Expert" predictions are fallible. Even though IT managers need to resort to the use of experts on occasion, managers should not ignore their own experiences, knowledge, and intuitions relative to an emerging technology.
2. Timing is relevant—iterate and review frequently. Technologies that appear to be of little use at one point in time may suddenly mature when a supporting technology emerges. For example, the basic technologies for the fax machine date back to 1843, and the first electrical apparatus that transmitted images was patented before 1900.
3. Which new technologies become adopted is hard to predict. If the inventor of the phonograph became disenchanted with his own product, how can the IT manager be confident the choice of technology is correct? Adopting a technology does not

mean all other potential technologies are abandoned. The manager needs to continue to evaluate the decisions made; this is a primary reason for piloting, using experts, and carefully assessing the risks.

4. Organizational consequences of adopted new technologies take a long time to become evident.

■■■ "Rules" and "Laws" of Technology

A number of oft-quoted (and occasionally misquoted) laws exist that were developed by members of the Information Technology community over the past several decades. Some of these laws are listed here. Note that they lean toward the hardware focus of technology, while many of the current issues surrounding emerging technology are software and organizational issues.

- **Bigger Computers Are Better (Grosch's Law).**[26] *Computing power increases with the square of its cost.* Herbert Grosch was an IBM employee and subsequent head of the U.S. National Bureau of Standards. While this "theory" was never published, and subsequently disproved, it was an accepted guideline for IBM's pricing of its computer product line and capacity planning.
- **Smaller Computers Are Better (Moore).** *Transistor density on a manufactured semiconductor doubles about every 18 months.* This "law" is often misinterpreted to imply that computing *power* doubles every 18 months for the same cost. While there is some correlation, the other components of computer systems (disks, memory, etc.) also affect "power."[27]
- **Connected Computers Are Better (Metcalfe).** *The value of a network grows as the square of the number of its users.* This simply means that the more users of a network there are, the more value it brings to the users.[28]
- **Machines May Leap, But Programs Creep (Wirth).** *Software gets slower faster than hardware gets faster.*[29]
- **Networks Will Triple Every Year (Gilder).** *For the foreseeable future, the total bandwidth of communications systems will triple every 12 months.*

■■■ The Benefits of Technology?

Even successful technologies may bring about unintended consequences. As discussed earlier, the long-term consequences of a technology are seldom known in the early stages of the technology's development. Sometimes decades may pass before all the consequences are known or before associated technologies are developed that modify the original benefits (or costs) of the technology.

As an interesting wrap-up to this chapter, what might the original inventors of some of the most basic technologies in use across the world today think of the consequences of their technologies?

Inventor	*Consequences*
Henry Ford (automobile)	Traffic, hot rods, strip malls, drive-through fast food, insurance
Alexander Graham Bell (telephone)	Telephone credit cards, Home Shopping Network, electronic funds transfer, fax, World Wide Web, video conferencing
Thomas Edison (electrical distribution/lightbulb)	Night baseball and football, radio, TV, computers
Wright Brothers (airplane)	Frequent flyer programs, airports/hubs, B2 bomber, Stealth fighter

REVIEW QUESTIONS ∎∎∎∎∎∎∎

1. Why is emerging technology important to organizations?
2. What do you consider the major differentiator(s) between incremental technology changes and discontinuous technology changes?
3. Describe some of the major stumbling blocks to introducing a new technology into an organization.
4. Why is the management of emerging technology of greater importance today than it was 50 years ago?

DISCUSSION QUESTIONS ∎∎∎∎∎∎∎

1. What would you consider some of the key emerging technologies of today?
2. What are some of the emerging technologies of five years ago? Ten years? Which were successful, and which unsuccessful?
3. How is emerging technology managed in your organization?
4. What are some organizations that were affected in major positive or negative ways by disruptive technology changes?
5. Describe some other technologies that have had unintended consequences or resulted in the development of other new technologies.
6. Relate the concepts discussed in the chapter about the value of IT to concepts you might need in managing ET.

AREAS FOR RESEARCH ∎∎∎∎∎∎∎

1. Scenario Planning. Research the methodology and discover some examples of its use.
2. Research the concept of technology convergence. Identify past, current, and possible future technologies that depend on this concept.

CONCLUSION ∎∎∎∎∎∎∎

This chapter has presented an overview of emerging technologies and discussed the key management issues faced by the CIO and the IT management team. One of the key aspects of managing ET is the implementation of new technologies. The impact that technologies can have on an organization can be fairly dramatic. This makes the management of the *change* created by such implementation an important consideration. The importance of this management responsibility is explained in Chapter 10—Managing IT Change.

Another key issue mentioned only indirectly in this chapter but an important consideration is the need to demonstrate the *value* a new (or existing) technology brings to an organization. As this need is not specific to ET, and applies equally to *any* technology project or existing system, this discussion is contained in Chapter 14—Assessing the Value of IT.

REFERENCES ∎∎∎∎∎∎∎

[1] Rogers, Everett. (1995). *Diffusion of Innovations*. Fourth Edition. New York, NY: The Free Press.

[2] Moore, Geoffrey A. (1995), *Inside the Tornado*, HarperBusiness.

[3] The Chasm Group Encyclopedia of Market Development Models (2001 Edition), *http://www.chasmgroup.com/publications/sampleslides.htm*.

[4] "Strategic Information Technology and the CEO Agenda." A.T. Kearney survey of 213 CEOs and senior executives, 1998.

[5] Adopted from Arthur Andersen Report by Konsynski, 1991.

[6] Frances Horibe.

[7] Nadler, David A., Shaw, Robert Bruce, Walton, A. Elise, (1995), *Discontinuous Change*, Jossey-Bass.

[8] Moore, Geoffrey A.(1995), *Inside the Tornado*, HarperBusiness.

[9] Rogers, Everett (1995), *Diffusion of Innovations*, Fourth Edition, The Free Press, New York.

[10] Fichman, Robert G. (1992), *Information Technology Diffusion: A Review of Empirical Research*, Proc. Thirteenth International Conf. On Information Systems, Association for Computing Machinery, Dallas, TX.

[11] Fichman, Robert G., Kemerer, Chris F., *Adoption of Software Engineering Process Innovations: The Case of Object Orientation*. Sloan Management Review, Winter 1993, Cambridge, MA.

[12] Attewell, P. (1992), *Technology Diffusion and Organizational Learning: The Case of Business Computing*, Organization Science, 3,1.

[13] Fichman, Robert G., Kemerer, Chris F., *The Assimilation of Software Process Innovations: An Organizational Learning Perspective*, Management Science, Providence, Oct. 1997.

[14] Fichman, Robert G., Kemerer, Chris F., *The Illusory Diffusion of Innovation: An Examination of Assimilation Gaps*, Information Systems Research, Vol. 10, No. 3, September 1999.

[15] Fichman, Robert G., Kemerer, Chris F., The Illusory Diffusion of Innovation: An Examination of Assimilation Gaps, Information Systems Research, Vol. 10, No. 3, September 1999.

[16] Found at: *http://pchs-fsm.org/westpointfoundry/galleryartifacts/the_dewitt_clinton.html*.

[17] Adner, Ron and Levinthal, Daniel A. (2000), *Technology Speciation and the Path of Emerging Technologies*, "Wharton on Managing Emerging Technologies," John Wiley & Sons.

[18] Day, George S., Schoemaker, Paul J. H., Gunther, Robert E. (2000), *Avoiding the Pitfalls of Emerging Technolgies*, "Wharton on Managing Emerging Technologies," John Wiley & Sons.

[19] McGrath, Rita Gunther, Macmillan, Ian C. (2000), *Assessing Technology Projects Using Real Options Reasoning*, Research Technology Management 43(4), July-August 2000.

[20] Utterback, James M. (1996), *Mastering the Dynamics of Innovation*, Harvard Business School Press.

[21] *The College Textbook Marketplace in the 1990s*, A Case Study by N. Venkatraman, Boston University School of Management, 1997.

[22] Hamel, Gary, Prahalad, C.K. (1994), *Competing for the Future*, Harvard Business School Press.

[23] Doering, Don, Parayre, Roch; Day, George S., Schoemaker, Paul J. H., Gunther, Robert E. (ed.) (2000), *Identification and Assessment of Emerging Technologies*, "Wharton on Managing Emerging Technologies," John Wiley & Sons.

[24] George Day, P. Shoemaker, and E. Gunther, Wharton on Managing Emerging Technologies, John Wiley & Sons, Inc.

[25] Adapted from Session Notes of a Gartner Group Symposium held Monday October 16, 2000 entitled *Managing Emerging Technologies for Business Gain*.

[26] Strassman, Paul A., *Will Big Spending on Computers Guarantee Profitability?*, Datamation, February 1997.

[27] Dragan, Richard V., *The Meaning of Moore's Law*, PC Magazine, June 12, 2001, Vol. 20, Issue 11.

[28] Hayes, Frank, *'LAWS' to Work By*, Computerworld, September 3, 2001, Vol. 35, Issue 36.

[29] *http://www.sysprog.net/quotlaws.html*, May 3, 2002.

CHAPTER 8

Organizing IT

"All are born to observe order, but few are born to establish it."
—JOSEPH JOUBERT

"We trained hard…but every time we formed up teams we would be reorganized. I was to learn that we meet any new situation by reorganizing. And a wonderful method it can be for creating the illusion of progress while producing confusion, inefficiency and demoralization."
—PETRONIUS ARBITER, 22-66 A.D.

"In any great organization it is far, far safer to be wrong with the majority than to be right alone."
—JOHN KENNETH GALBRAITH

Preview of Chapter

This chapter examines the question of how IT should be organized. It is not a prescriptive chapter but rather a descriptive chapter on the many ways that IT can be organized and what the keys are for IT to be effectively managed. How the business itself is organized varies from company to company by subtle differences in some cases, or by dramatic proportions in other cases. This chapter will review the major formal business structures that have been commonly employed and will suggest how the IT organization can be designed to structure its function within the overall firm.

There is no one "right" structure for the firm or for IT. Every organization will be different, in terms of its industry, type of business, business strategy, culture, politics, size, stakeholders, etc. How the firm is organized and managed will reflect the complex interactions of those factors. The IT organization is equally influenced by the complexity of these factors and also by the structure of the firm itself. The organization of the firm will also evolve often to reflect changes in market forces, management thinking, trends in business, and even for the sake of change itself. In recent years, it has become quite common for businesses to announce and implement reorganizations every 18 to 24 months. While many of the reorganizations are minor, affecting only small units within the organization, many others will be more encompassing.

What we will examine in this chapter:

- ■ What is Organization Theory and how can it be applied?
- ■ What are the classical organizational structures common to business firms?
- ■ What are the common ways that businesses are organized today?
- ■ What are the common ways that IT is organized today?
- ■ What is the federalist IT model?
- ■ How do you determine the best organizational structure for the IT organization?
- ■ Can the appropriate organizational structure improve IT and the firm?

▪▪▪ Introduction

A great deal of study has focused on determining if there is an optimum structure for a successful business. Each researcher has sought to find a general pattern or formula to predict the best organizational structure. The theories evolve as a direct reflection of the societal values of the times. As society (and the environment) changes, organizational theories evolve to include these new beliefs or, if the changes are extreme, a new theory emerges.

Organizational theories emerge, become dominant, and decline. However, they rarely disappear. Therefore many approaches to organizational design exist side-by-side. This chapter reviews the relevant theory and discusses its application to the design of IT organizations. The appendix of this chapter discusses organization theory

▪▪▪ The Changes to the Environment upon Entering the 21st Century

The 21st century brings with it an astonishing array of information technology that is distinguishing this period from previous ones. The success of the Internet, Webcams, wireless computing, Web-enabled cell phones, and dozens of other new technologies raise questions, such as: How does an organization handle this much change? How does an organization effectively manage the technology? How will the organization be affected by the new technologies? How does the organization manage the employees using all this new technology? How does the technology *drive* organization change and design? Naturally, the business and environmental changes bring additional considerations. Chapter 10 discusses change management considerations.

One important impact of the rise of telecommunications technology is that the firm has been freed to adopt any organizational design it chooses, ranging from fully centralized to the idea of a virtual organization or an "e-lance" economy,[32] where there are only a few full-time employees in the firm. IT enables worldwide communication facilitating this flexibility of organizational design. However, the range of possibilities has also increased the complexity of the design decision. One key aspect is how the roles of managers and subordinates may change in different organizational designs.

Figure 8-1 illustrates how typical hierarchical organizations place authority in the hands of managers, while flatter organizations and networked organizations tend to give subordinates more latitude.

These effects raise questions about where and how managers gain latitude and workers gain discretion and become empowered to make wider-ranging decisions.

▪▪▪▪▪▪▪▪▪▪▪ **FIGURE 8-1   The Roles of Managers and Subordinates in the Different Types of Organizations.**

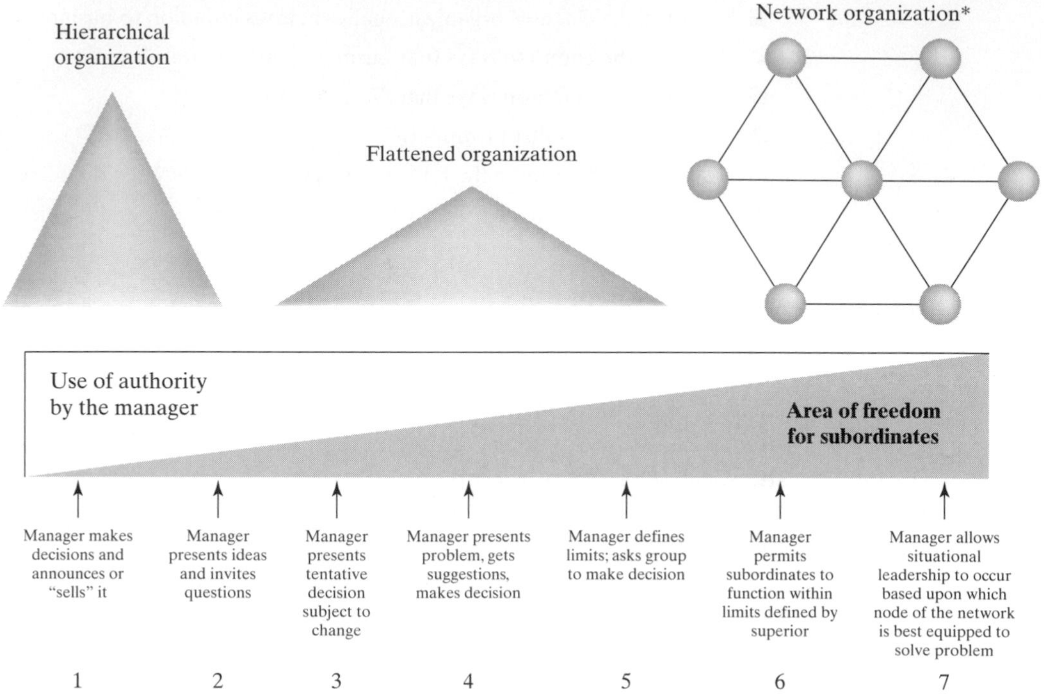

Hierarchical organization

Flattened organization

Network organization*

Use of authority by the manager

Area of freedom for subordinates

Manager makes decisions and announces or "sells" it	Manager presents ideas and invites questions	Manager presents tentative decision subject to change	Manager presents problem, gets suggestions, makes decision	Manager defines limits; asks group to make decision	Manager permits subordinates to function within limits defined by superior	Manager allows situational leadership to occur based upon which node of the network is best equipped to solve problem
1	2	3	4	5	6	7

* Multiple networks exist in organizations.

Looking at specific examples will illustrate some of the considerations. If an organization is willing to adopt a new technology, like wireless computing, then this technology permits workers to work from home or at the beach or at a remote site or on a business trip. The impact on the organization and the workers and their managers is significant. By virtue of having the computer available 24/7/365 (24 hours a day, 7 days a week, 365 days a year), the home (in fact, the world) becomes an extension of the office. Conceptually, the worker becomes available 24/7/365. Management must decide how to use the opportunity that IT provides for flexibility, in concert with maintaining a rational work schedule for the individual. Workers may choose working at home to allow flexible hours because they cannot work the typical 9 to 5 period. The organizational design must accommodate this flexibility while ensuring that the workers' colleagues and supervisors can also accomplish their tasks within the new schedule. When workers use the flexibility enabled through these technologies, an organizational design must be created to allow all the components of the organization to work together. This is a particularly challenging aspect of organizational design in today's IT enabled firm.

As another example, the Internet has enabled organizations to reach customers, clients, vendors, and employees worldwide. This provides a wonderful opportunity for organizations to improve communications among all their stakeholders. If they were successful, it would mean that they could possibly have customers all around the world. A business must dramatically increase support staff to meet this exceptional growth and provide 24/7 call centers. Managing the growth requires managing the organizational structure as the firm's size increases. Global considerations further complicate the organizational choices. Globalization is covered in Chapter 11, as part of IT governance.

Some theorists have suggested that size is an important determinant of organizational structure; thus, a larger bureaucracy would be required for this growth. The

growth is complicated by geographic distribution, requiring a plan for global coverage. One strategy for handling this kind of growth today is using outsourcing. Outsourcing is a solution enabled by information technology to make it possible for worldwide customer support to be handled by a firm dedicated to this service.

Emerging video technologies (e.g., Webcams and digital cameras) are becoming increasingly affordable, making it possible to have richer worldwide communication for all staff. Video can be used to enhance tasks ranging from customer service to team meetings. Technology here is an enabler, providing a business function where there was none. Video technology raises more questions about how to organize to take advantage of these capabilities and enhance the performance of the firm.

▪▪▪ What Can Be Learned from Organizational Theory?

The application of new information technology presents the firm with an almost infinite array of choices for designing the organization. While organizational theories (see chapter appendix) often lead to different specific design outcomes, they have commonalities as well:

- Organization is important to the firm. Without organization, there would be chaos and an inability to achieve the goals of the firm.
- There is not one correct organizational structure that will apply to a particular situation.
- The organization and its structure will be influenced by technology, power, politics, culture, size, history, industry, and competition.
- The workers within the organization have an impact on how the organization will be managed. Workers' ethics, skills, and maturity will affect their response to management initiatives.
- Organizations are finding in the 21st century that if they are not quick to adapt to market and competitive changes and become responsive to their key customers, they, like the dinosaur, will become extinct.

These commonalities help to define the basic factors that must be considered when designing organizational structures. Two views of structure help to define the outcome of organizational design: organizational infrastructures and organizational types. They are described in the next sections.

Organizational Infrastructures

Organizational infrastructures provide a broad view of the nature of an organization, determined by factors such as design parameters and situational characteristics. These are not organizational forms, but rather, descriptions of the "personality" of the organization. Figure 8-2[33] summarize a number of common organizational infrastructures:

A *simple structure* can be defined as a basic organization that is hierarchical in nature. An owner heads the firm, as seen in examples like a family business or a single proprietary business. Additional levels of management may evolve as the organization matures and supervisors and managers are added to lead the growing number of lower-level employees. In many small businesses, the owner and the other managers often wear multiple hats (i.e., one person could be responsible for accounting and billing, account receivables, taxes, etc., and another could be responsible for marketing, sales, and customer service). Another aspect of a small business is that there are fewer formal rules and responsibilities. In that way, each employee has a greater stake in the success or failure of the business. This infrastructure is seen most often in young and small companies. Typically, the IT "department" in a simple structure would consist of one IT professional (perhaps it is one of many responsibilities) who handles all aspects of the function.

▪▪▪▪▪▪▪▪▪▪▪ **FIGURE 8-2** Organizational Infrastructure Model.

Configuration	Simple structure	Machine bureaucracy	Professional bureaucracy	Divisional form	Adhocracy
Key coordinating mechanism	Direct supervision	Standardization of work	Standardization of skills	Standardization of outputs	Mutual adjustments
Key part of organization	Strategic apex	Techno structure	Operating core	Middle line	Support staff
Design parameters					
Specialization of jobs	Little specialization	Much horizontal and vertical specialization	Much horizontal specialization	Some horizontal and vertical specialization (between divisions and headquarters)	Much horizontal specialization
Training	Little	Little	Much	Little	Much
Indoctrination	Little	Little	Little	Some of divisional managers	Some
Formalization of behavior, bureaucratic organic	Little formalization organic	Much formalization, bureaucratic	Little formalization, bureaucratic	Much formalization (within divisions), bureaucratic	Little formalization, organic
Grouping	Usually functional	Usually functional	Functional and market	Market	Functional and market
Unit Size	Wide	Wide at bottom, narrow elsewhere	Wide at bottom, narrow elsewere	Wide (at top)	Narrow throughout
Planning and control systems	Little planning and control	Action planning	Little planning and control	Much preferential control	Limited action planning
Liaison devices	Few liason devices	Few liaison devices	Liaison devices in administration	Few liaison devices	Many liaison devices throughout
Decentralization	Centralization	Limited horizontal decentralization	Horizontal decentralization	Limited vertical decentralization	Selective decentralization
Situational factors					
Age and size	Typically young and small (first stage)	Typically old and large (second stage)	Varies	Typically old and very large (third stage)	Often young
Technical systems	Simple not regulating	Regualting but not automated, not very sophisticated	Not regulating or sophisticated	Divisible, otherwise typically like machine bureaucracy	Very sophisticated often automated or else not regulating or sophisticated
Environment	Simple and dynamic, sometimes hostile	Simple and stable	Complex and stable	Relatively simple and stable, divesified markets (especially products and services)	Complex and dynamic, sometimes disparate
Power	Chief executive control, often owner managed, not fashionable	Technocratic and external control, fashionable	Professional operator control, fashionable	Middle-line control, fashionable (especially in industry)	Expert control, very fashionable
Implied planning style	Bottom-up	Top-down /bottom-up	Bottom-up /top-down	Multiple	Multiple

Source: Adapted from Mintzberg, Henry, *Power in and Around Organizations*, Prentice Hall, 1983.

A *machine bureaucracy* would be a much larger organization than most simple structures. The organization finds itself with a more formal organization, where technology has affected the nature of the firm greatly. Mechanization of operations and manufacturing has increased the complexity of producing, assembling, and distributing products to the firm's customers. There is a lot of horizontal and vertical specialization in job responsibilities and management roles. This increase in specialization has often led to improvements in productivity and quality. This infrastructure is typical of large, older firms that have not reached a level of complexity requiring the creation of divisions. Machine bureaucracies have a great deal of vertical and horizontal specialization. Typically, the IT department would be a centralized function servicing the entire organization.

A *professional bureaucracy* is best described as an organization that consists of doctors, lawyers, or accountants. These firms or practices employ these professionals in a partnership organizational model. In these practices, the organization is generally quite flat and skills of the individuals will be quite high. The individuals would be specialists, concentrating on specific areas; for example, there are doctors that specialize in surgery, internal medicine, psychiatrics, gynecology, etc., or lawyers specializing in criminal defense, accident and injury, real estate, etc. The IT organization within most professional bureaucracies is centralized to provide shared services for all the individual professionals.

A *divisional form* is best described as a major corporate form of organization. Large companies like financial institutions (i.e., banks, life insurance companies, brokerage houses) often have a hierarchical structure and contain many divisions within the structure. There is a lot of bureaucracy and formalization in the firm, and it is often an older form of a machine bureaucracy yet larger and diversified. Often function, product, or customer separates the divisions. Many of the Global 2000 companies are considered to be of this form. The IT function within a divisional firm can take on many different organizational forms depending on the needs of the firm and marketplace. For example, IT can be centralized, serving all divisions, or decentralized where they report directly to each division. Discussion of the pros and cons of these different forms comes later in this chapter.

An *adhocracy* is a relatively new form of infrastructure, but fast becoming a more dominant form. An adhocracy can be defined as an organization that has banded together for a special purpose, and upon completion of the purpose, the group can be disbanded, or placed in reserve, until another special purpose or project is identified. Examples include using consultants, producing a Hollywood movie, and constructing a building. The adhocracy form is employed within many other formal organizational designs. An adhocracy can be internal or external to the firm. The use of a temporary team to address an emergency, often referred to as a SWAT team (taken from the police term "special weapons and tactical" team), and groups that leverage the skills/talents of a group for a project, often referred to as "centers of excellence" or "centers of competency" are examples of internal adhocracies. The IT organization itself uses the adhocracy infrastructure when it outsources functions such as the development of a new application. What makes adhocracy a popular organizational infrastructure is the benefit of paying for services only on an as-needed basis. There is no commitment to the staff employed once the job is complete.

Organizational Types

Organizational types describe the actual, physical ordering of a company's responsibilities and people. This is the picture seen on an organizational chart. This section describes the common organizational types found in most firms.

The organization types in Figure 8-3 are descriptive of many typical corporate forms. For example:

The *vertical functional stovepipe* is generally found in a *centralized organization* and often describes the divisional form of infrastructure (defined in the preceding section) that has been common in many large firms. Each vertical stovepipe represents a function or business unit, such as IT, marketing, finance, human resources, R&D, etc.

▬▬▬▬▬▬▬▬▬▬▬ FIGURE 8-3   Organization Types.

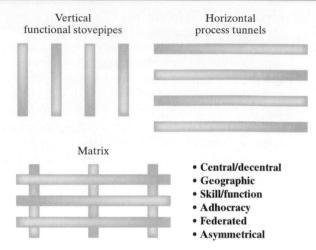

The major benefits of this centralized structure are: 1) the expertise is shared among all organizations within the firm. Entry-level staff can converse with experienced managers easily because they belong within the same work unit. 2) There are clear career paths and training programs because the career and salary paths are easy to identify or build within the work unit. 3) There is back up because of the redundancy of skills within the work unit. Staff can be moved between different projects if there are emergencies or turnovers. 4) Managers familiar with the jobs and tasks perform staff performance evaluations. 5) A centralized organization can more easily establish standards that can be used across the entire firm. For example, standards in accounting, programming, application developing, testing, and training can be more readily dictated. Standards in what products, tools, and methodologies can be used can also be enforced as well.

The drawbacks are: 1) each stovepipe is a self-contained bureaucracy and has often become an autonomous unit, separating it from the other units in the firm. 2) This separatist mentality is problematic because it leads to the thinking that troubles in other parts of the firm do not affect the department. 3) There are often failures in communication with the other functions resulting in one hand not knowing what the other is doing. 4) Business priorities and measurements may not be the same as the group's priorities. Because everyone reports hierarchically, the division, not the business as a whole, sets the priorities. And 5) the business unit may believe that the projects are not what they wanted. If they have no ownership, they have no stake in getting it done right. The bottom line is that stovepipe suborganizations optimize for local efficiency and effectiveness, which usually leads to suboptimal value for the organization as a whole. The story of Nortel in the following sidebar describes how a company can have successfully operated with a stovepipe organization for many years, when a change in the marketplace suddenly makes this design a severe liability.[34]

Nortel

Nortel was incorporated in 1895 as The Northern Electric and Manufacturing Company Limited. As an affiliate of AT&T for 43 years, Nortel enjoyed access to technology and research at the forefront of innovation in the industry. In the 1970s it was a leader in digital technologies, producing a full line of digital communications equipment.

In the 1990s Nortel realized that changing technology had altered the market. Nortel's customers were no longer buying individual switching systems or wireless transmission equipment. Instead the demand was for an integrated set of products which could address specific business needs. To be successful in such a market meant that the company had to present a single, unified face which could offer customized, integrated solutions to the customer needs, drawing components of those solutions from many different areas of the business or even beyond it. Clearly this represented a significant challenge to a company that traditionally had a decentralized, product-focused structure with all of its implicit fragmentation.

Nortel had to move away from the product stovepipe organization and into one where the business units had a direct view of the customer and total solutions necessary for customer satisfaction. They chose to move to a divisional organization with information systems providing the integrating link between divisions. They also instituted the process owner model, using this to focus on the total solution for the customer.

The *matrix* organization attempts to marry the vertical stovepipes, thereby reducing a number of disadvantages that would be found. The matrix organization would have workers in cross-functional teams with two bosses. Each worker would have a dotted line or direct line to both a product manager and a functional manager. The product manager would be responsible for managing priorities and assessing daily tasks. The functional manager would be responsible for work evaluations, providing training, and insuring standardization of the work produced. The idea of rotating workers and awarding promotions would be a joint task of the product and function managers together.

The major drawback of this arrangement is that workers often experience difficultly in reporting to two or more bosses. Their performance reviews are determined by multiple managers, which can frustrate the individual. More frequently there are the differences in direction or priority that exist among the mangers, which places the employee in an awkward position. There always exists the chance that there will be internal conflicts that will go unresolved because it is not clear whose responsibility it is to clear them up.

The *Horizontal Process Tunnels* are often found in *Decentralized Organizations* and describe those units of the firm that have been created to focus on a particular business area (product, process, or projects) in an independent fashion. In this case, an organization usually reserves corporate-wide functions to be in a headquarters organization, while products or services are decentralized into more autonomous suborganizations. In banking firms, there might be a division focused on retail banking, another on corporate customers, and another on government and municipal clients. In insurance firms, there are separate divisions that solely work on personal insurance lines, pension plans, casualty insurance, health insurance, and group insurance clients. This divisional structure is horizontal in the sense that each product line will require many functions, such as sales, marketing, finance, accounting, IT, legal, human resources, etc.

The horizontal process tunnel can also be scaled down to a task force level. Cross-functional teams can be created as well within a firm to address new single product rollouts, such as an IRA product or a new consumer product like soap or soup. The cross-functional team would be a microcosm of a division and would be able to accelerate the product's delivery to market. Some organizations have imple-

mented the ultimate decentralization and spun off their units to form separate subsidiaries. For example, the telephone provider Verizon took their cell phone subunit
and created Verizon Wireless to focus the entire organization on this new business
area. As an independent subsidiary, Verizon Wireless went on to acquire several
smaller wireless phone service providers and build a national company. Another
example is Citibank which, located in New York City, decided to spin off its credit
card subunit into a separate company called Citicard located in South Dakota. Both
of these examples highlight the specialized nature of the subunits in a horizontal
process tunnel. This specialization means that IT is contained within the subunit to
provide dedicated, specialized services.

The major benefits are: 1) rather than having priorities set by individual functions,
the priorities are based on the needs of the products, process, or project. Everyone
is measured by the success of the group. Many firms have seen great results in reducing
time to market and greater responsiveness to clients and customers. 2) Communication
among functions increases dramatically as the multiple groups work as a team. And 3)
there is great opportunity for staff to be knowledgeable about multiple aspects of the
product and process because sharing of information and knowledge across functions is
widely available.

The drawbacks are: 1) the perception that there are limited upward career paths in
the horizontal organization, 2) evaluation of job performance may be done by individuals not experienced in the nature of the work, 3) there is often lack of back-up personnel available when vacancies occur or when emergencies arise. And 4) there may be
no synergy in the firm. Everyone is doing it their own way, leading to redundancy and
duplicated efforts. Lack of standards becomes the usual by-product.

The *federated* organizational structure uses as its model the U.S. federal government. The concept is that there are some responsibilities that are best handled by a
strong centralized unit because they have an impact on the organization as whole
(Think about the U.S. federal government). At the same time, there are responsibilities
that the local decentralized units can best handle, usually because of the specialized
nature of the issue (Think about the U.S. state governments). It is a blend of the centralized and decentralized organizational model. The federal government, under the
CEO called the President, sets direction, policy, and priorities. The state government
focuses on local issues and concerns, but operates within the overall structure built by
the federal government.

In a firm, the CEO formulates the direction, policy, and priorities for the firm (i.e.,
standards for accounting, IT application development, tools, and practices). The local
units have great latitude in how they achieve their goals and objectives while working
within the overall umbrella structure of the firm.

The federated structure often attempts to eliminate redundancy in areas that
would benefit from a single central organization to perform basic tasks. Besides having
central units to define standards, many federated organizations have included or
adopted units that serve the entire corporate interest, such as development centers
(e.g., centers of excellence), centralized IT departments responsible for infrastructure
and common systems, centralized accounting, taxation and finance departments,
human resource training and recruiting centers, legal and medical service centers, and
many others. Each decentralized unit must be responsible to follow the corporate standards and they do so because the centralized part of the organization controls the ultimate funding of each unit.

The benefits of a federated structure are the sum of the benefits of both the
centralized and decentralized structures. The individual workers report to one
manager and the senior managers of the unit are accountable for performance
and compliance.

▮▮▮▮▮▮▮▮▮▮▮▮ **FIGURE 8-4**   Virtual Organization or the Extended Enterprise.

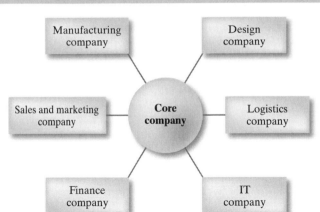

And finally there is the *adhocracy type* (see Figure 8-4.) Previously the term *adhocracy* was used as an example of a way of operating. Here it is being used to describe an actual physical organization that is completely composed of temporary, project-oriented work groups. This organizational form can scale from a simple project with three or four staffers to a major department of hundreds of staff working towards the completion of a major initiative. Adhocracy simply allows staff to work on a project-by-project basis. Staff can be rotated within projects, and through the extensive use of consultants, needed skills can be provided through temporary employment. The use of SWAT teams, centers of excellence or centers of competency are examples of internal adhocracies. An adhocracy where nonemployees are carrying out tasks can evolve to a virtual organization where most of the people do not belong to the host firm.

Calyx & Corolla

The fresh flower industry wasn't! Because of the fragmentation in the distribution channels, it was extremely inefficient. Therefore "fresh flowers" were usually seven to ten days old before they became available for sale to the consumer. Ruth Owades, the founder and CEO of Calyx & Corolla, saw an opportunity to dramatically improve this distribution process by having the flowers go directly from the growers to the consumers. She created an organization that was the marketing intermediary to link the two. Owades understood the idea of a virtual organization early on when she created partnerships to provide the enterprise services that she needed. For example, she worked with the flower growers to train them to package their product for delivery to the end customer. Previously they bulk-shipped their flowers to distributors and florist shops. They had to be convinced that they could change their traditional operation to work with C&C. Owades invested a great deal of time teaching and educating to create a solid partnership with all the growers.

Owades also worked with Federal Express to create a delivery mechanism designed to protect the delicate product during shipping. In fact, Owades is credited with helping FedEx to understand that they had a great business potential in becoming the distribution arm of many of their shipping customers. They then went on to use this approach in marketing and were very successful. Owades said, "I envisioned a table with three legs, and Calyx and Corolla was only one of them. The second was the best flower growers available, and the third was Federal Express, the number one air carrier." Owades also partnered with credit card companies to handle all payment and reporting tasks.

Thus, C&C is a pure example of a virtual company. The only thing C&C does is market the product to the consumer and coordinate order and delivery.

As previously discussed, construction, entertainment, and consulting industries are illustrations of adhocracy. The Internet revolution has spawned numerous examples of adhocracy/virtual organizations. Using the enabling power of electronic communications, companies have been able to link to business partners who provide temporary services (e.g., application development).

One of the pioneering virtual companies is Calyx and Corolla. The story is described in the sidebar[35] and provides a textbook example of the virtual organization; however there are many others today, including those that outsource some of their services to providers who are experts in the area. For example, customer service and help desk services are often provided by outside call centers; firms outsource payroll and accounting to specialized providers like ADP; market research on the Web is provided by DoubleClick, etc.

Corporations have evolved adhocracy to include outsourcing. With outsourcing, instead of managing temporary corporate employees for a project, the work is performed by people from outside the firm. The greatest allure for this style of organization is that the unwelcome obligation to carry employees beyond the project completion date is gone. It is the ultimate pay as you go plan: use and pay for only what you need. The rise in popularity of this organizational form has been dramatic, as many corporations have used consultants, temporary workers, and outsourcing firms. Naturally, this approach is effective when there is a skills shortage.

What are reasons that adhocracy can fail? One of the issues is that when nonemployees perform work outside the company, any expertise developed in the process is lost to the firm. If the work is temporary, then even the nonemployee is no longer available for consulting. Firms that outsource IT work often plan to regain the expertise as part of the project. Additional drawbacks include 1) consultants and temporary employees are often not loyal to the firm. However, they develop loyalties to their profession. Malone and Laubacher's research (described in the following paragraph) suggests that these employees will coalesce into guilds that become professional centers providing a peer group and benefits not provided by the employers (e.g., health and retirement).[36] Therefore this may be less a drawback and simply a change of perspective. 2) Turnover may be more prevalent and therefore incur the additional costs related to bringing in replacements in the course of a project. 3) Outside vendors have a reputation of doing a "bait and switch," having brought experienced and skilled workers to work in a project in the early stage, only to recall them later for other assignments and replacing them with unskilled workers. This tactic has annoyed many corporations but more importantly, they are stunned to find no contractual obligation for the agency to keep the skilled workers on board. And 4) maintenance can be very difficult because no one who has experience in developing the project has remained to provide continuity. This can be frustrating for the company; however, steps taken during the course of the project to ensure training for in-house personnel can alleviate this problem.

The concept of virtual organizations taken to the extreme is explored in the work of Malone and Laubacher.[37] They propose a future where everyone is an "e-lancer" or electronic freelancer. Companies do not employ anyone full time, but rather bring together the talent and skills they need for every task undertaken. The electronic aspect of this idea is that people find their work electronically, often carry it out electronically, and then move on to the next job. For the e-lance economy to succeed, the electronic communications must be reliable and broadband. The concept of the corporation becomes one of an entity that pulls together the talent necessary to achieve a specific goal and then moves on. This is a radical notion, but one with intriguing benefits. In fact, there is a lot of work that is accomplished this way today as increasing numbers of firms pull in outside talent when they need it as opposed to employing it full time.

Tapscott et al., discusses another intriguing organizational concept in the book *Digital Capital*.[38] The authors focus on the value that firms gain today from capital that is not part of their organization, but accessed electronically. The best example of this is Amazon.com. Amazon started by selling books. One of the important factors in their quick success was the reviews and comments made by customers on the books they had read. Amazon succeeds in selling its product through the value contributed by nonemployees who post reviews on the web site. This is an example of human capital in the book. When a firm can leverage customers and partners to help it succeed, it is benefiting from digital capital in today's electronic world. This is the model that is followed by Cisco, Dell, eBay, and others that are enabled by electronic communications.

It is interesting that virtual organizations and digital capital are organizational concepts that cannot succeed without the enabling mechanism of information technology. The role IT currently plays in facilitating organizational design, whether considering traditional centralized and decentralized forms or the e-lance economy, is significant and will only gain in value in the future. Choosing an organizational structure is not easy. Often it is a combination of structures.

▬▬ How Can IT Be Organized?

The IT function should choose to organize in any way deemed to deliver the most value to the firm. These options have been increased since the introduction of electronic communications as discussed earlier.

Traditional IT Organizational Forms

This section examines some of the more traditional ways in which firms have chosen to design their IT organizations.

Figure 8-5 illustrates a traditional IT functional organization. This is conceptually identical with the functional organization design of the business. There are staff departments like finance and administration as shown in the diagram (other examples include human resources and training), and line departments, which carry out the business of the IT organization: working with business partners to design and implement systems. The three line areas, shown in the diagram are:

1. **Consulting.**   This area covers the planning and managing of projects and services with the business.
2. **Development.**   This area includes the design, programming, and delivery of systems.
3. **Service Units.**   This area includes the operational elements such as data centers, telecommunications, customer service, and help desks.

▪▪▪▪▪▪▪▪▪▪▪ FIGURE 8-5 Traditional IT Functional Organization.

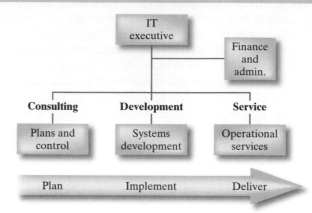

The organizational design question becomes how these functions are arranged for the most efficient and effective delivery of services. IT as an organization can be structured like any other organizational unit, applying any of the constructs described in this chapter. IT can be organized as a centralized structure, decentralized structure, federalized structure, and increasingly with aspects of an adhocracy (internal or outsourced). The following are examples of IT organizations.

Centralized IT

As a centralized entity (as shown in Figure 8-6), IT can be managed in a conventional formal hierarchical structure with the senior management position headed by the CIO (or senior officer title.) One of the defining elements of a centralized organization is that the head, in this case the CIO, manages all IT resources. The CIO determines what work will be carried out and who will do it. Mechanisms can be established, such as alliances, liaisons, or relationship managers to facilitate the relationship. However, the fundamental nature of the centralized organization places the CIO as the ultimate gatekeeper of the entire IT organization.

The benefits of a centralized IT organization are the same as those discussed previously for any centralized structure:

- The single IT group provides a mechanism for sharing expertise and learning among all the IT staff. This provides each IT professional with knowledgeable colleagues and a ready peer group for problem solving.
- There are clear career paths and training programs. The career ladder is visible and available to every IT professional.
- There is managed skill redundancy with staff capable of substituting for each other, which guarantees support and consistency. This facilitates the handling of emergencies or unexpected turnovers.
- Managers who are experts in information technology and familiar with the projects carry out employee evaluations. Each IT professional knows that someone who knows the field is doing the evaluation.
- Standards can be readily defined and promulgated throughout the organization.

Colgate Palmolive is an excellent example of a centralized IT organization. Ed Toben recognized the need to centralize to reduce redundancies, disseminate standards, and maintain close control over IT resources. Colgate Palmolive implemented a worldwide ERP system to help achieve the standardization. Toben was asked to provide IT value to the firm for a reasonable cost and found this centralized approach best. The return on investment has been excellent and the firm is very pleased with the centralized organization.

▪▪▪▪▪▪▪▪▪▪▪▪ FIGURE 8-6 Centralized IT Functional Organization.

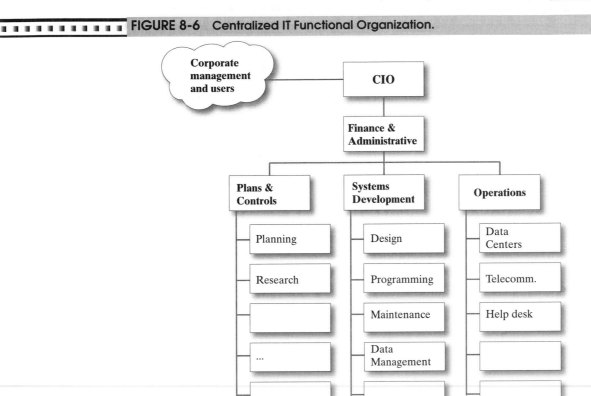

Source: Christine Bullen.

The major criticisms of a centralized organization are:

- The centralized organization is unresponsive to individual business unit needs. There is a sense that the centralized IT organization's first priority is to technology and the business must stand in line.
- Measurement objectives are different for IT and business units.
- There is no one in the centralized organization who really understands the business area. There are no functional experts. Everyone is a technical specialist and a business generalist.
- The centralized organization can become insular and unaware of the world outside its borders, yet still within the firm. It has a language and culture of its own.
- There is a tendency to form an "ivory tower" mentality because the IT professionals become focused on perfection rather than solving the business problems.

A talented CIO can manage many of these criticisms; however, the perceptions linger and can often damage the relationship between the IT organization and the line managers.

Decentralized IT

In a totally decentralized IT organization (Figure 8-7), the IT professionals do not reside in the IT organization. In this structure there are duplicate IT organizations that report to each business function. In a fully decentralized design this is true of both corporate functional areas and business units. The CIO at the headquarters level does not necessarily have a dotted line responsibility, but rather is more of an advisor to the decentralized IT departments. The strength of the responsibility line between

■■■■■■■■■■■ **FIGURE 8-7** Decentralized IT Functional Organization.

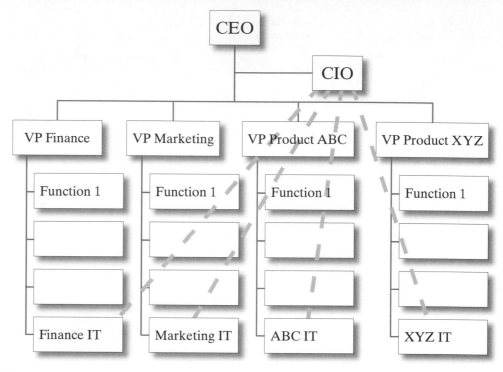

Source: Christine Bullen.

the CIO and the decentralized IT areas varies within the design and governance (see Chapter 11—IT Governance) of a particular firm.

The defining element in the decentralized IT organization is that the individual business areas own, fund, and determine the priorities of their own IT departments. This benefit directly addresses a major criticism of the centralized model that IT is not responsive to the local area needs. There is no issue since the business area controls its own IT.

Additional benefits include:

- The IT professionals are experts in the business area.
- Priorities are set within the business unit.
- Funding is provided by the business unit.
- There is a potential career path within the business and out of IT.
- Measurements and objectives are the same for IT and business.

There are also criticisms of this model:

- The decentralized IT departments create huge redundancies without the associated value of backing up each other.
- The career path within IT is limited.
- The IT department will optimize for its local business area, which may be suboptimal for the firm as a whole.
- Integration and adhered to standards are more difficult.
- Loyalties develop to the business area and not to the firm.

The fully decentralized IT organization is somewhat uncommon today, although one industry that has maintained this design is the pharmaceutical industry. A typical firm will likely have product line divisions, each with their own IT organizations (e.g., consumer products, pharmaceutical products, veterinary products). This design has worked well for pharmaceuticals because of the specialized ways in which IT has been employed to support each area. For example, the pharmaceutical R&D organization applies computers in research functions, while the consumer products area focuses on marketing.

Federal or Hybrid IT

The more common form of decentralized IT organizations is a variation that combines the pros of both centralized and decentralized organizations while eliminating many of the criticisms. The goal of a federated structure is to incorporate the strength of centralized architecture, standards, procedures, common systems, etc., while decentralizing ownership and control of specific application development efforts.

In this model (Figure 8-8) the functions that benefit from central control, like standards, common systems, and architecture, remain centralized. The functions that benefit from decentral control like the application development functions report to the business unit managers.

ABC Television uses this structure in their IT organization. Technology has become embedded in every aspect of television broadcasting, from traditional functions such as accounting, reporting, and e-mail to specialized technology that supports the entire broadcast value chain. As a result, it is important for the business unit to have a very close relationship with the IT staff who support it. Each IT development group is dedicated to its respective business unit.

▪ ▪ ▪ ▪ ▪ ▪ ▪ ▪ ▪ ▪ ▪ **FIGURE 8-8** Federal IT Functional Organization.

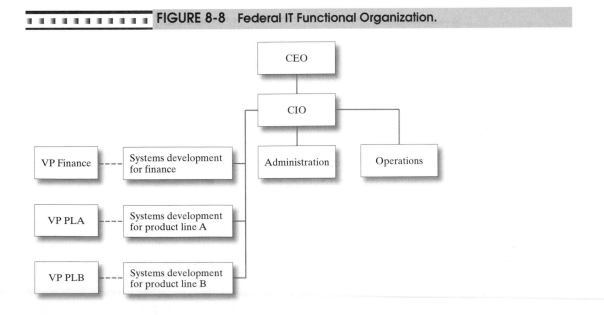

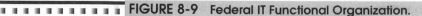

FIGURE 8-9 Federal IT Functional Organization.

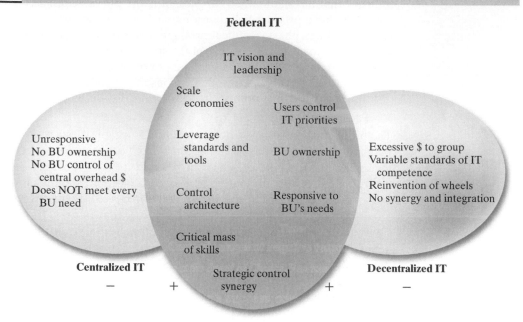

Benefits of the Federal IT Model

Figure 8-9 shows how the federal model captures the benefits of both the centralized IT model and the decentralized IT model. When managed by a skillful CIO, this approach can successfully deliver the strategic alignment needed for the most effective use of IT for the organization. It maintains the close interaction with the business, while creating the control needed for corporate-wide functions like architecture, standards, and data center operations. It also provides the IT professionals with a large and talented peer group that enhances each person's growth and development.

Strategic alignment among IT and line management is the goal. The Federal model facilitates this goal by helping to eliminate the negative criticism of IT that line organizations often have, such as the unresponsiveness of centralized IT and the excessive cost of decentralized IT. If the Federal model can focus the IT area on using the technology to enable the competitive positioning for the business, then this model fosters excellence through strategic alignment. However, without an effective IT governance process (see Chapter 11), even a well thought-out organization structure will have difficulty succeeding. Remember all six components of strategic alignment maturity must be addressed.

Adhocracy (Internal or Virtual) Organization Concept

The notion of the adhocracy organization (Figure 8-10) can be applied to any of the three dominant models above. For example the use of centers of competency/excellence or SWAT teams can be leveraged with centralized, decentralized, or federated structures. Also, as IT organizations increasingly use external providers of services they move toward more virtuality. For example, the outsourcing of the help desk function makes this a virtual function within IT. For many, this is not a temporary solution, but a permanent one that brings better customer service. Another example would be hiring contract programmers to accomplish the creation of new software. This could be a temporary

▪▪▪▪▪▪▪▪▪▪▪ **FIGURE 8-10 Adhocracy.**

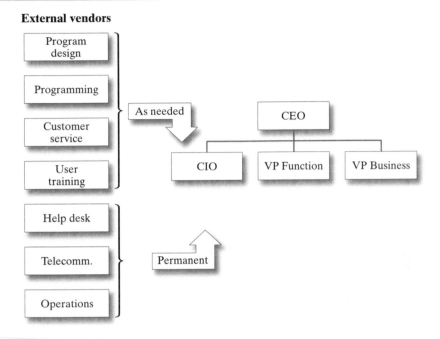

approach to increasing either the number of IT professionals or the skill set needed to accomplish the goal.

Dell provides another interesting example. For their best customers, Dell provides inventory tracking and maintenance for all hardware. This is a valuable benefit to the customer and aides Dell in marketing new equipment to replace aging computers. In this case, the virtual organization carries out a small segment of the management process for the hardware.

As experience and success with the adhocracy approach for segments of the IT organization grows, more CIO's are willing to increase the tasks that are managed this way. However, there is a skill to managing relationships with staff that do not formally report to an organization, and people must acquire this skill before this trend can grow to the concept of a full-blown adhocracy, where employees (internal or external) working on a temporary basis carry out all projects. Outsourcing is discussed further in Chapter 11, IT Governance.

▪▪▪ Is There a Proper Fit for IT in a Business Organization?

Previous sections have described common organizational structures that many businesses use. Various IT organizational structures were explored as well and it was shown that the IT choices are the same as the firm's choices. If the business is structured in a centralized fashion, must IT be centralized as well? If the business is decentralized, should IT be decentralized? The answer to both questions is "perhaps." IT organizations can be centralized when the business is decentralized and vice-versa.

In Figure 8-11, IT is a decentralized organization within a functional vertical business structure. A firm may choose this approach to ensure that IT is completely responsive to these functional business area needs. This sometimes happens when IT

▪▪▪▪▪▪▪▪▪▪ FIGURE 8-11 Functional Business Unit Structure.

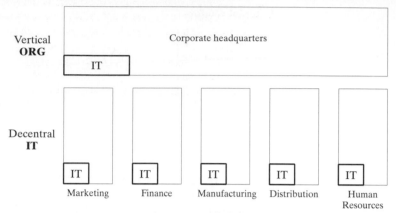

What IT responsabilities reside where?

has been centralized in the past and the line managers have been unhappy with the responsiveness of IT. This form can also come about by accident when each line business area finds it has personnel with IT expertise who can develop systems for the area. This was common in the past. When spreadsheet programs like Excel and Lotus 123 were first introduced, people in the finance area immediately grasped the value these tools could provide them in creating financial analyses and reports. The tools were simple to use, so the finance experts learned them and proceeded to create the analyses they needed without any aid from IT professionals. This resulted in people becoming the local experts to whom everyone in the department would go for their IT skills. Ultimately this led to IT expertise within the business area. Some organizations then formalized this approach.

Figure 8-12 and 8-13 show two different horizontal, decentralized business organizations with decentralized IT organization support.

Both the divisional and SBU structures follow the traditional decentralized IT model with the benefits described previously: creating IT organizations that are completely responsive to their business units, funded and controlled by the business unit managers, and experts in their business areas.

▪▪▪▪▪▪▪▪▪▪ FIGURE 8-12 Divisional Structure.

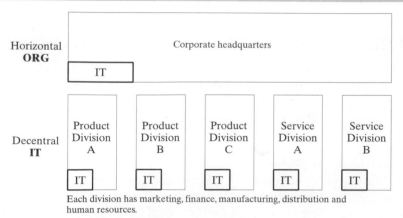

Each division has marketing, finance, manufacturing, distribution and human resources.

What IT responsibilities reside where?

▮▮▮▮▮▮▮▮▮▮▮ FIGURE 8-13 Strategic Business Unit Structure.

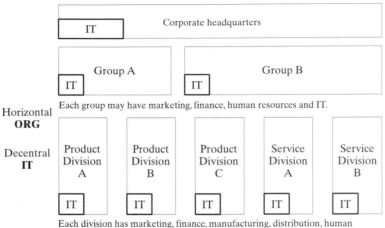

What IT responsibilities reside where?

The IT organizations shown in Figures 8-11 through 8-13 could also be federated depending on what functions are provided by headquarters and what functions are provided by the business unit.

A variation not shown is a decentralized business organization with a centralized IT organization.

Ultimately the organization of IT should not be dependent on the structure of the firm, but rather on the market forces and competitive nature of the business environment. The form of the IT organization is an important factor in supporting the overall organization's ability to respond to market forces and compete effectively. The benefits and weaknesses for each IT organizational structure have been described earlier in this chapter. The driving force behind which organizational form to choose should be which design facilitates strategic alignment and improves the firm's position on the alignment maturity scale (Chapter 3). The key to success goes beyond just having a good organization structure. A good structure works to strengthen all six components of alignment maturity: communications, competency/value, governance, partnership, scope and architecture, and skills.

▮▮▮ Strategic Alignment and Organizational Structure

The key to deciding which organization structure to employ is to understand which structure delivers the most effective strategic alignment. This requires that the firm understand 1) how market forces are affecting its relationship with its customers, and 2) how IT can best relate to the line business functions to enable the strategic application of technology. Figure 8-14 summarizes the market forces that drive toward a centralized or decentralized structure.

A focus on cost reduction will tend to drive a firm toward a centralized IT organization where costs can be closely controlled, and technical skills focused on the critical projects.

If responsiveness, flexibility, and ownership are the primary objectives, decentralization of IT is the appropriate organizational structure. And if the requirements are mixed or balanced, implementing the federal model may be the best answer for many situations.

▪▪▪▪▪▪▪▪▪▪ **FIGURE 8-14** Fitting IT Structure To Business Needs.

Market forces
– Increasing cost reduction focus
– Establishing the critical mass to tackle major enterprise initiatives
– Driving toward a single view of the customer

Market forces
– Increasing business autonomy
– Need for rapid response and flexibility
– Market fragmentation

Centralized	Decentralized
Strengths	**Strengths**
– Easier implementation of cross-business unit applications and architectures	– Faster decision-making on IT priorities
– Ability to drive economies of scale	– Stronger operating unit alignment
– Deeper specialization through critical mass	– Improved business knowledge and understanding
– Technical career mobility	
Limitations	**Limitations**
– Tougher to stay aligned with business in turbulent times	– Tougher to implement common architecture
– Cultural separatists	

▪▪▪ Why Adopt the Federal IT Model?

A major benefit of the federal model is that it can typically best achieve strategic alignment. Figure 8-15 illustrates how the federal model provides IT with the ability to effectively communicate with each aspect of the business. This equates to providing a strong 1:1 relationship among IT and its business partners. The objective is to ensure the business that IT is keeping its activities in line with strategic business objectives. In both the

▪▪▪▪▪▪▪▪▪▪ **FIGURE 8-15** Strategic Alignment in the Federal Structure.

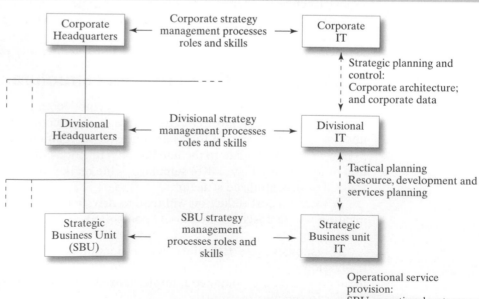

centralized and decentralized forms, as illustrated in Figure 8-9, there are negatives associated with each that prevent the aligned relationship that will deliver the most value.

The federal model presents the best structure for enhancing alignment by clarifying the relationship between IT organizations and their corresponding line organizations. This clarity supports the overall organization in its journey toward alignment maturity.

▪▪▪ How Does a Firm Prosper If the IT Organization Is Right?

The early organization theorists believed that there are universal laws of organizational theory that would permit companies to plan for greater wealth or business longevity. In some ways they have been proven right. Environmental situations (i.e., competitive forces, industry, culture, size, etc.) will have a major impact on a corporation, and the firm must choose an effective management and organizational structure. Many businesses have been successful in reorganizing their structure over the years and most businesses will continue to do so, to remain fresh and effective in the years to come.

The IT organization needs to be effective as well, and this is achieved by aligning the IT organization with the business in a strategic manner. The marketplace environment will have the greatest impact on how to best organize IT. This chapter has focused on the benefits of each organizational model that appear to drive the organization toward strategic alignment. The federal model is outstanding as a strong organizational form for achieving strategic alignment.

If the appropriate IT organization is in place, it means IT will be in a better position to provide the most effective and efficient services to the overall firm. Again, all six components of alignment maturity must be addressed. In today's environment, information technology enables most critical business functions and provides valuable competitive advantage. The firm must focus on the best organizational form to gain the greatest value from its information technology function.

REVIEW QUESTIONS ▪▪▪▪▪▪▪

1. What are the major differences between machine bureaucracy and professional bureaucracy?
2. How are roles of managers affected by organizational structure?
3. What are the benefits and drawbacks of a centralized organizational structure?
4. What are the benefits and drawbacks of a decentralized organizational structure?
5. What are the benefits and drawbacks of a federalist organizational structure?
6. What are the benefits and drawbacks of an adhocracy?
7. What is a vertical functional stovepipe?
8. What is a horizontal process tunnel?
9. What are the benefits and drawbacks of a matrix organization?
10. What should be the determining factor in how IT should be organized?

DISCUSSION QUESTIONS ▪▪▪▪▪▪▪

1. What would you consider some of the key considerations in organizing IT?
2. Why is the way IT is organized so important to the entire organization?
3. Why is the way business is organized so important to the IT organization?
4. Can IT be organized centrally while the business is organized decentrally? And vice-versa?
5. What are the merits and drawbacks to adhocracy? Why is adhocracy so popular?
6. What impact does the current organization of the business have on how IT should be organized?
7. Why do organization theorists believe that they can find universal laws that can be applied to management of firms?
8. Are there any laws about organizational structures that make sense? Explain.
9. Why do companies reorganize their business so often? How could reorganizing help a firm?
10. How does IT improve if it adopts standards in development, procedures, testing, etc.?

AREAS FOR RESEARCH ▪▪▪▪▪▪▪

1. Read Jay Galbraith, *Designing Complex Organizations*, Addison-Wesley, 1973, and more recent publications by Galbraith, for more information about his communication and coordination theory.
2. Read Malone and Laubacher's paper, "The Dawn of the Elance Economy," *Harvard Business Review*, September-October 1998 for a better understanding of the e-lance concept.
3. Read Morabito, J., Sack, I., and Bhate, A., *Organizational Modeling: Innovative Architectures for the 21st Century*, Upper Saddle River: Prentice Hall, (1999) to gain a thorough understanding of organizational theory.
4. Read Robbins, S.P., *Organization Theory: Structure, Design and Applications* (1990) for more depth in the OT structure area.
5. Read Shafritz, J.M. and Ott, J.S., *Classics of Organization Theory*, New York: Harcourt Brace & Company, (1994) for an historical review of the field.
6. The impact of Taylor's theories has been of great significance in organizational design. Read his original work, Taylor, F.W., *The Principles of Scientific Management* (1911) for a thorough understanding of what he did.

CONCLUSION ▪▪▪▪▪▪▪

This chapter has covered organization theory, popular organizational structures for businesses, and popular organizational structures for IT. It is worthwhile to repeat that organizing the business or IT is complex and there are no simple answers as to how it should be done. Most businesses rely on experimentation, trying different structures and organizations. Some firms reorganize each 18 to 24 months. As the quote from 210 B.C. indicates, the problems of reorganization are not a new phenomenon, but one mankind has been suffering with for a long time.

The chapter discussed the merits and pitfalls of common organizational structures. An organization needs to examine possible structures and decide whether it is right for them with the goal of enhancing strategic alignment. The firm needs to look at the benefits and costs, the current market environment, their competitors, their clients, their own corporate culture, etc., and try to optimize their competitive position.

Effective organization structure alone will not guarantee a firm's success, but rather will facilitate its ability to interact with its customers and enhance trust and creditability within the firm. Finding the best way to relate the IT organization to the business organization is a key factor in success in today's marketplace. All aspects of alignment maturity must be assessed. Information technology is embedded in many aspects of the firm and underlies its competitive advantage in numerous ways. Every organization must strive to achieve strategic alignment between IT and the line functions. Doing so will put the organization on the road to a successful outcome in the marketplace.

A p p e n d i x   8 A

▪▪▪▪▪▪▪ Organization Theory: ▪▪▪▪▪▪▪ Early History

When did organization theory first evolve? The "List of Organization Theory Highlights from Early World History" sidebar presents a list of examples of organizational concepts from early world history.[2] These few highlights demonstrate that people have been concerned about understanding the best way to organize large groups of people for a long time; possibly since humans first began to build artifacts.

Classical organization theory has its foundation in over three thousand years of observation and analysis of these early theorists, philosophers, and scientists, Division of labor, unity of command, basic principles of administration, and planning were of labor, unity of command, basic principles of administration, and planning were already recognized as a foundation for scientific management. The industrial revolution and subsequent progress through the 19th century served to focus attention on organizational issues. A new generation of scientists, dedicated to improving the efficiency and effectiveness of organizations, founded the first school of classical organization theory.

A List Of Organization Theory Highlights from Early World History[2]

It is believed that Egyptians must have had a clearly defined hierarchy to manage the construction of the pyramids and build their great "wonders of the world."

The first conclusive written evidence (circa 1491 B.C.) is documented in the Bible when Jethro advised Moses to delegate authority among his followers so that Moses did not have to rule over his multitudes alone.[3]

Simultaneously in early China and ancient Greece (circa 500 to 400 B.C.), Sun Tzu realized there was a need for hierarchical organization, interorganizational communications, and staff planning in *The Art of War*,[4] while the philosopher Socrates suggested that the universality of management is an art unto itself. Xenophon recorded the activity of a Greek shoe factory and a description of the advantages of the division of labor.[5]

For nearly 2,000 years, the Roman Catholic Church has served as an enduring model of hierarchical management, where 400,000 clergy are in one of five rungs: pope, cardinal, archbishop, bishop, or priest.

Muslim scholars (circa 1377 A.D.) introduced principles of administration, described formal and informal organizations, and argued that methods for organizational improvement can be developed through the study of the science of culture.[6]

Machiavelli (circa 1513 to1521) offered the principle of unity of command in *The Discourses*.[7]

Adam Smith reinforced the advantages of division of labor in 1776 when he discussed the optimal organization of a pin factory in *The Wealth of Nations*.[8]

Charles Babbage delivered his "basic principles of management," a precursor to the scientific management movement in *On the Economy of Machinery and Manufactures,* published in 1854.[9]

Daniel McCallum wrote of his six basic principles of administration in his annual report as superintendent of the New York and Erie Railway Company in 1855.[10]

In 1885, Captain Henry Metcalf stated that there is a "science of administration" that can be discerned from careful observation in *The Cost of Manufactures and the Administration of Workshops, Public and Private*.[11]

Organization Theory Entering into the 20th Century

It was thought, in the 20th century, that an organization theory although an art form, if based on proper observation and analysis, would yield basic principles of management that would have universal application. In the latter half of the 1890s, a number of theorists began refining their thoughts on organizational theory.

Considered the founding father of the school of classical organization theory, Frederick Winslow Taylor (a graduate of Stevens Institute of Technology) wrote *Shop Management* in 1903 and *Principles of Scientific Management* in 1911. These works were the results of his experiments with workers, in which Taylor proposed that significant improvements in productivity would occur if four principles,[12] would be followed:

1. The application of rule-of-thumb methods for determining each element of a worker's job with scientific determination
2. The scientific selection and training of workers
3. The cooperation of management and labor to accomplish work objectives, in accordance with the scientific method
4. More equal division of responsibility between managers and workers, with the former doing the planning and supervising, and the latter doing the execution.

Taylor was looking at the organization of work at the lowest level of the organization, appropriate for a shop steward or foreman. This work is still applicable to mass production processing activities, in which there is a lot of routine activity and low complexity. Taylor was able to demonstrate that managers, who carefully assess the one best way for each job to be done, would be able to maximize efficiency. It would then be management's job to explicitly select, train, and motivate workers to ensure that the best way was followed.

In France, Henri Fayol was developing his own general principles of management. This work was mostly ignored, until Constance Storr translated it into English in 1949. *General and Industrial Management* contained fourteen principles that Fayol maintained were universally applicable and could be taught in schools and universities. This differed from Taylor in that it was aimed at the general managers and executives rather than at the unit level manager. Fayol wrote these principles based on his many years of experience as a practicing business executive:[13]

1. Division of work
2. Authority and responsibility for managers
3. Discipline of employees
4. Unity of command
5. Unity of direction
6. Subordination of individual interest to the general interest
7. Remuneration of personnel
8. Centralization in decision-making
9. Scalar chain (line of authority)
10. Order in resources
11. Equity in treatment of individuals
12. Stability of tenure of personnel
13. Initiative
14. Esprit de corps

Fayol and Taylor had a profound effect on the fields of business and public administration, but it was not until 1910 that the phrase "scientific management" was coined. Louis Brandeis, before he became a Supreme Court justice, went to court against railroad companies requesting a rate increase from the Interstate Commerce Commission. When a consultant testified that the railroads did not need a rate hike if they systematized operations, Brandeis argued that they could save a million dollars a day by using "scientific management" methods. Scientific management emerged as a national movement, leading to the encouragement of many more associates to advocate scientific management as the centerpiece of organization theory. Unfortunately scientific management has been interpreted by many to mean that there is one best way to manage an organization, and thus implies that it can be found with thorough study and experimentation. This notion has had a significant influence on organizational design and has been particularly strong in organizations where the work is scientific (e.g., in IT areas). The perception has also fueled the belief that the right organizational design will solve all problems. The following discussion of succeeding schools of organizational design shows how researchers tried to introduce factors other than pure scientific reasoning. While this is not a text on organizational theory, and will not cover the field in depth, it is useful to look at those areas that have had an influence on the IT area.

A Discussion of Succeeding Organization Theories

The researchers who presented the following approaches to organizational theory (OT) were reacting to the purely scientific reasoning that had dominated the traditional organizational theory work. It is amusing to observe that because the world of OT deals with people and their relationships, the attempt to structure and understand organizations was also an attempt to make the messy, non-scientific aspects more ordered through scientific reasoning. The subsequent schools of thought reacted to this by finding ways to reintroduce the human aspects to the research. In other words, you cannot subtract the human emotions and behavior from OT by pure reasoned thinking.

Human Relations Organizational Theory

Human relations theory (also called neo-classical theory) modifies and somewhat extends the classical theory by focusing on the motivation and involvement of the employee. It is also called the "humanistic school" of behavior theory.

One key researcher in this field was Herbert A. Simon, who challenged the tenets of classical theory by criticizing general principles of management as being inconsistent, conflicting, and inapplicable to many administrative situations facing managers.[14] Simon introduced the ideas of span of control and unity of command as important factors that must be considered in organizational design. Other prominent human relations theorists include:

- Chester Barnard, who introduced the idea of incentives to gain employee cooperation[15]
- Douglas McGregor, who is the author of the famous Theory X/Theory Y concept, which describes how managers motivate employees[16]
- Philip Selznick, who describes the issues related to cooptation and the misalignment of individual goals with those of the firm[17]

All of these contributors recognized that factors uniquely related to humans and their capabilities had to be considered when designing an organization. These ideas are reflected in IT organizations in the use of small, specialized project teams, creative incentives (e.g., exercise breaks, casual dress, snack areas, napping tents), reviews based on mutually defined objectives.

Modern Structural Organizational Theory

In 1922, Max Weber developed the "ideal" organizational structure, calling this structure a *bureaucracy*. It is characterized by a division of labor, hierarchical decision-making, a high degree of formal procedures and regulations, and impersonal relationships.[18] The bureaucracy is the archetype for the structure of today's large organizations.

Although the word *bureaucracy* today conjures visions of hopelessly snarled red tape and inefficiencies, at the time it was proposed it brought structure to the organization that protected employees from arbitrary management behavior and enforced consistency in a firm's relationships with its customers. Modern structuralists[19] are focused on organizational efficiency and rationality that will increase the production of wealth in terms of real goods and services. The organization chart is the ever-present "tool" of a structural organization theorist.

Some researchers have predicted that bureaucracy would die out because it would be unable to adapt to rapidly changing environments, rise of democracy in organizations, and alienation of employees. However, bureaucracy appears to be holding on, because of its efficiency and its promotion of equity and representation. It is also interesting to observe that the existence of the bureaucracy or structure does not require there to be a lack of humanistic concerns. This is part of the reason why the bureaucratic structure survives well today. IT organizations often reflect this basic structure in logically dividing the area by job function and in the chain of command that directs how decisions are made. The development of formal procedures for how customers request and get approval for their IT needs also demonstrates these principles.

Power and Politics Organizational Theory

In all of the schools discussed, it is accepted that the organization uses rational thought in developing objectives, accomplishing established goals, and designing and managing the organization for maximum effectiveness and efficiency. The "power and politics" school of thought rejects those assumptions as being untrue because where individuals are involved, there are often conflicts of interest, personal agendas, and selfish attitudes. There is the perception that managers make decisions based on what is best for them rather than what is best for the firm. For example, when units compete for resources in an organization, the conflicts between the units within the organization are not over the resource but over their different goals.[20] When managers fight for budget and headcount they are exhibiting the behavior described here. IT managers develop expert skills in these areas to ensure they get the resources they need for getting their work done. They also learn to network among the powerful line managers to create a power position of their own.

Systems Theory

Systems theory, also called "organizational economics," posits that the organization is an open system, where everything is related to everything else; therefore, the key elements of success in organizing are flexibility, responsiveness, individual and group empowerment, and customer service. This movement, arising in the 1970s and 1980s, was driven by fear of the loss of competitiveness in industry as well as in global economics. It is tied to the importance of quality and productivity, ideas that date back to the work of Dr. W. Edwards Deming[21] in the 1950s. Deming's work focused on improved quality control and statistical analysis was ignored in the U.S. Japanese managers adopted Dr. Deming's techniques and in a period of twenty or thirty years, Japan achieved great success in improving both quality and product. The key message here is that an organization must make changes if it wants to survive. This theory is represented in Peter Senge's work on learning organizations,[22] and in the IT context, on business process reengineering (BPR) described by Hammer and Champy[23] and Davenport.[24] Firms use BPR to apply information technology in the redesign of organizational processes. Many traditional processes grew through history and accident: BPR is an attempt to scrutinize processes, recognizing the interrelatedness of processes throughout the enterprise.

Institutional Organizational Theory

Institutional organizational theory, also called "organizational culture[25] and sense-making," refers to the culture that exists in an organization; something akin to a societal culture. It is comprised of many intangible things such as values, beliefs, assumptions, perceptions, behavioral norms, artifacts, and patterns of behavior. The essence of culture is that it be may be ingrained deeply into the fabric of the organization, where the individuals within the corporation are unaware that it even exists.

Institutional OT seeks to encompass a number of theorists from both the systems school and the power school by including them in a contingency framework where all schools of thought apply to some degree. Karl Weick, a leading researcher in this field, concluded that many organizational behaviors[26] and decisions are almost predetermined by the patterns of basic assumptions that are held by members of an organization. Those patterns lead people to make decisions that worked in the past for the organization, contributing to organizational resistance to change. A discussion of culture and its role in resistance to change can be found in Chapter 10, Management of Change.

Forces That Have an Impact on Organizational Design

In addition to the formal schools of thought on how to actively design organizations, there are those who discuss the forces acting upon organizations that cause a design to emerge.

Impact of Technology on Organizational Theory

OT researchers[27] agree that technology refers to the information, equipment, techniques, and processes required to transform inputs to outputs in the organization. That is, technology looks at how the inputs are turned into outputs. There is also agreement that the concept of technology, despite its mechanical or manufacturing connotation, is applicable to all types of organizations.

In 1965, Joan Woodward focused on production technology in an attempt to discover if technology was a main determinant of structure.[28] Woodward's conclusion was that there were distinct relationships between these technology classifications and the subsequent structure of the firms, and the effectiveness of the organizations was *related to* the fit between technology and structure, thus demonstrating a link between technology, structure, and effectiveness. Charles Perrow proposed an alternative to Woodward's study looking at knowledge technology rather than production technology.[29] Perrow argued that the more routine the technology is, the more highly structured the organization should be and conversely, the more complex and unfamiliar the tasks are, the more flexible and informal the structure of the organization should be.

In 1967, James Thompson's contribution lies in demonstrating that technology determines the selection of a strategy for reducing uncertainty. He identified long-linked technology (characterized by sequential interdependence), mediating technology (which performs an interchange function linking units that are otherwise independent), and intensive technology (which represents a customized response to a diverse set of contingencies.[30])

This school of OT appears to center around complexity of tasks and formalization of structure, where routine activity will allow a high level of formalization and non-routine activity permits a low level of formalization for success in managing the technology. As the Internet emerged as a new technology force in organizations, most firms did not understand it very well. As a result these firms often set up small independent groups to chart the course for Internet use. These "skunk works," as they are often called, are examples of flexible, informal structures dealing with new complex technology.

Communication and Coordination

One organizational theorist, Jay Galbraith, proposed the idea that the key purpose for the existence of firms is the need for communication and coordination.[31] He states that organizational structures are designed to foster communication and coordination among the people and processes to achieve the purpose of the firm (i.e., the production of goods or the delivery of services). Prior to the telecommunications revolution, colocating people who had the most interaction associated with a product or service accomplished this communication. Thus firms organized around product lines (e.g., the automobile industry), geographical areas (e.g., this is the way IBM was organized for many years), or customer groups (e.g., this is a traditional approach for computer manufacturers like Dell). This approach leads directly to the stovepipe phenomenon (described later in this chapter) where very independent subunits develop within an organization in pursuit of a specific function, product, or service goal. The communication and coordination need drives the organization to bring together and closely associate the people involved both physically and culturally.

REFERENCES ▪ ▪ ▪ ▪ ▪ ▪ ▪

[1] Shafritz, J.M. and Ott, J.S., *Classics of Organization Theory* (pp. 30 and 31), New York: Harcourt Brace and Company, 1994.

[2] adapted from Shafitz, J.M., and Ott, J.S., *Classics of Organization Theory* (pp. 11–21) and Robbins, S.P., *Organization Theory: Structure, Design and Applications* (pp. 32–34), Upper Saddle River, NJ: Prentice Hall, 1990.

[3] Exodus 18:14–23, *http://www.biblegateway.com,* (circa 1491 B.C.).

[4] Sun Tzu, *The Art of War,* *http://classics.mit.edu/Tzu/artwar.html,* (circa 500 B.C..)

[5] Xenophon, *The Memorabilia of Socrates,* (translated by Rev. J. S. Watson), New York: Harper and Row, 1869.

[6] ibn Khaldun, *The Muqaddimah: An Introduction to History,* 1377.

[7] Machiavelli, Niccolò, *Discourses on the First Ten Books of Titus Livius, 1513–1521,* *http://www.lucidcafe.com/library/96may/machiavelli.html*

[8] Smith, Adam, *Wealth of Nations,* *http://www.bibliomania.com/2/1/65/112/frameset.html,* 1776.

[9] Babbage, Charles, *On the Economy of Machinery and Manufactures, http://www.cbi.umn.edu/exhibits/cb.html,* 1854.

[10] McCallum, Daniel, "Connections Tick Tock," *Scientific American,* August 1998.

[11] Metcalf, Henry, *The Cost of Manufactures and the Administration of Workshops, Public and Private,* 1885.

[12] Taylor, F.W., *The Principles of Scientific Management,* 1911.

[13] Fayol, H., *General and Industrial Management,* translated by Storr, C. (1949), 1916.

[14] Simon, Herbert A., *Administrative Behavior: A Study of Decision-Making Processes in Administrative Organizations,* Free Press; ISBN: 0684835827; 4th edition (April 1997), first published by Macmillan, 1947.

[15] Barnard, Chester, *The Functions of the Executive.* Cambridge, MA: Harvard University Press, 1938.

[16] McGregor, Douglas, *The Human Side of Enterprise,* New York:McGraw-Hill, 1960.

[17] Selznick, Philip, *TVA and the Grass Roots.* University of California Press, 1949.

[18] Morabito, J., Sack, I., and Bhate, A., *Organizational Modeling: Innovative Architectures for the 21st Century* (pp. 19), 1999.

[19] Shafritz, J.M. and Ott, J.S., *Classics of Organization Theory,* New York: Harcourt Brace and Company (pp. 205–207), 1994.

[20] See authors such as Jeffrey Pfeffer (on power in organizations), John French, Jr. and Bertram Raven (on five bases of social power), Michael Cohen and James March (on the role of a university president), Rosabeth Moss Kanter (on productive power) and Henry Mintzberg (on power games and players).

[21] Deming, W. Edwards, *Out of the Crisis,* Cambridge, MA: M.I.T. Press, 1986.

[22] Senge, Peter, *The Fifth Discipline,* Currency/Doubleday, ISBN: 0385260954; 1st edition, January 15, 1994.

[23] Hammer, Michael and Champy, James, *Reengineering the Corporation,* HarperBusiness, ISBN: 0066621127, June 5, 2001.

[24] Davenport, Thomas, *Process Innovation: Reengineering Work Through Information Technology,* Harvard Business School Press, ISBN: 0875843662, October 1992.

[25] Shafritz, J.M. and Ott, J.S., *Classics of Organization Theory,* New York: Harcourt Brace and Company (pp. 420–421), 1994.

[26] Weick, Karl E., *Administering Education in Loosely Coupled Schools,* Phi Delta Kappan, pp. 673–676, June 1982.

[27] Robbins, S.P., *Organization Theory: Structure, Design and Applications,* Englewood Cliffs, NJ: Prentice Hall (pp. 176–177), 1990.

[28] Woodward, Joan, *Industrial Organization: Theory and Practice,* London: Oxford University Press, 1965.

[29] Perrow, Charles, *A Framework for Comparative Analysis of Organizations,* American Sociological Review, pp. 194–208, April 1967.

[30] Thompson, James D., *Organizations in Action,* New York: McGraw-Hill, 1967.

[31] Galbraith, Jay, *Designing Complex Organizations*, Addison Wesley, 1973.

[32] Malone, Thomas P. and Laubacher, Robert J., "The Dawn of The Elance Economy," *Harvard Business Review*, September-October, 1998.

[33] Adapted from Mintzberg, Henry, *Power in and Around Organizations*, Englewood Cliffs, NJ: Prentice Hall, 1983.

[34] Volkoff, Olga, and Newson, E.F. Peter, "Nortel—Re-inventing Information Systems," Ivey Management Services, Richard Ivey School of Business, University of Western Ontario, 9-97-E001, 1997.

[35] Wylie, David, "Calyx and Corolla," Harvard Business School Case 9-592-035, October 1995.

[36] Malone, Thomas P. and Laubacher, Robert J., "The Dawn of The Elance Economy," *Harvard Business Review*, September-October, 1998.

[37] *Op. Cit.*, Malone.

[38] Tapscott, Don, Ticoll, David, and Lowy, Alex, *Digital Capital*, Harvard Business School Press, ISBN: 1578511933; (May 2000).

Human Resource Considerations

"Do not hire a man who does your work for money, but him who does it for love of it."
—HENRY DAVID THOREAU (1817–1862)

"People who work sitting down get paid more than people who work standing up."
—OGDEN NASH (1902–1971)

Preview of Chapter

A critical issue in the management of IT organizations is the management of IT human resources. The people and their skills are the heart of the organization. In the past, there has been a focus on the technical skills needed to manage and develop the technical components of the IT organization. Today the skill requirements are considerably broader, including general management skills and deep business knowledge. This chapter will discuss the state of human resources within the IT organization and review the critical elements that must be carefully managed by every CIO.

What we will examine in this chapter:

- The market for IT professionals
- What IT professionals are seeking in a position
- Characteristics of the IT environment that contribute to the HR complexity
- The future for IT professionals
- Skills required for a successful future in IT
- The retention of IT talent
- Stress in the workplace
- IT career development

▪▪▪ Introduction

The market for IT professionals, like the market for most corporate positions, will vary with the economy, trends in business strategy, world events, and availability of skills. The first few decades of IT (starting in the 1950s in terms of business application) brought steady growth in IT professional positions. Government reports and private research trumpeted the glory of an IT career. IT professionals were in demand as businesses expanded the ways in which technology became embedded in products and services. The Information Technologies Executive Survey of Critical Issues in 1998[1] ranked retention programs for IT talent as the number 2 issue facing IT management. Companies experienced a 25% turnover rate with a full-time employee retention period of less than 25 months.[2] In the late 1990s, as the dot-com start-ups grew in number, specific IT skills became extremely valuable (e.g., knowledge of networking, Web page design skills, security). There were not enough people to fill the requirements in corporations, non-profits, and government positions.

Then came the dot-com debacle, with small companies failing at record-breaking rates and established companies scaling back on their efforts in the Internet marketplace. These failures had a significant impact on Web-related IT skills and a smaller impact on general IT professionals. However, businesses maintained their interest in finding and keeping IT professionals in selected areas, as the following salary chart shows. *Computerworld* reports in its 2001 salary survey issue:

"As the list of fizzled start-ups grows, so does the pool of talented IT professionals in need of a new gig. But even in the midst of an economic downturn, corporations are still aggressively pursuing business objectives that have an emphasis on technology. And as a result, IT salaries are gaining a little ground this year.

Still, gone are exorbitant bonus plans. Say goodbye to wide-scale sign-on and retention bonuses, rapid hiring sprees and mushrooming baseline compensation. Instead, salary increases have been moderate this year—just less than 6%—and bonuses have been restricted to key members of the IT team"[3]

The *Computerworld* Salary Chart for 2001 (Figure 9-1)[4] illustrates the average salaries for various IT positions organized by geographic location.

The IT job categories command excellent salaries from entry level to CIO. In May 2002, the Information Technology Association of America (ITAA) reported, "Companies are optimistic about future hirings over the next twelve months. They project an aggregate demand for IT workers of 1,148,639 in 2002, of which they expect 578,711 positions to go unfilled due to a lack of qualified workers, referred to as the "gap" in IT workers."[5] Last year, the ITAA said there were 900,000 openings for IT workers.

The economic downturn that continues through 2003 presents a challenge to all businesses, forcing cutbacks in many areas, including IT. However, the critical role technology plays in business helps to maintain the need for IT skills even in the face of an economic slowdown. The specific skills may change. For example, the need for Web design fades as dot-coms fail, but the need for application maintenance, knowledge management, and security increases in the aftermath of September 11th. As companies explore new technologies such as wireless, the field will advance, increasing the need for skills in wireless networking and protocols. One of the most significant challenges for IT management is retaining the critical talent and understanding the mix of skills that are needed as the business strategy evolves. No matter what is happening in the economy or with the technology sector specifically, managing the IT human resource remains an important issue for every organization. One important aspect of aligning the business and IT strategies is understanding the skills that will be required.

▪▪▪▪▪▪▪▪▪▪▪▪ FIGURE 9-1   Total IT Compensation by Region, 2001.

Total IT compensation (salary plus bonuses) by region				
Job title	National average	New England	Middle Atlantic	East North Central	West North Central
CIO/vice president of IT	$165,100	$176,100	$191,600	$126,200	$147,500
Director of IT/IS/MIS	$108,200	$109,400	$114,500	$107,100	$96,100
Project manager	$88,200	$103,400	$100,800	$84,300	$86,300
Database manager	$84,800	$88,900	$88,100	$84,700	$70,900
Senior systems analyst	$72,300	$75,600	$75,600	$74,400	$74,000
Senior systems programmer	$68,900	$74,100	$70,000	$68,700	$66,500
Web application developer	$61,700	$60,500	$59,800	$54,800	$66,300
Network administrator	$60,000	$65,400	$62,300	$57,600	$57,200
Programmer/analyst	$55,100	$50,700	$56,400	$51,900	$52,400
Help desk operator	$39,700	$39,000	$39,200	$35,700	$36,600

Job title	South Atlantic	East South Central	West South Central	Mountain	Pacific
CIO/vice president of IT	$135,300	$149,300	$198,500	$144,500	$211,800
Director of IT/IS/MIS	$104,100	$112,100	$119,000	$99,900	$118,000
Project manager	$84,800	$67,600	$89,800	$75,500	$93,700
Database manager	$78,900	$78,300	$89,400	$103,400	$93,900
Senior systems analyst	$68,500	$54,800	$73,600	$60,300	$78,300
Senior systems programmer	$66,500	$47,800	$66,700	$65,100	$78,200
Web application developer	$59,000	$59,300	$66,800	$60,900	$66,500
Network administrator	$57,200	$40,900	$71,100	$54,000	$63,200
Programmer/analyst	$54,500	$41,300	$57,700	$49,200	$61,800
Help desk operator	$44,400	$27,000	$37,600	$42,500	$42,900

Source: Computerworld. http://www.computerworld.com/careertopics/careers/recruiting/story/ 0,10801,76080,00.html.

▪▪▪ What Do IT Professionals Say They Are Looking For?

The 2001 Job Satisfaction Survey from *Computerworld*[8] looks in detail at what IT professionals seek in their working environments. The overall results of the survey indicate that the majority of respondents were generally satisfied. In addition, 60% are very satisfied with IT as a career choice. But looking at the specifics there are some very troubling areas:

1. More than 50 percent of the respondents believe they do not have opportunities for advancement within their current companies. This indicates that while they are satisfied with their jobs, half of the IT professionals believe they must change

employers to advance their careers. If the IT career path stalls within the IT area, which all studies described later in this chapter indicate is unlikely, IT professionals may be forced to look toward general management for advancement within their firms. They may not want to "advance out" of IT. They may not have or want to get a Masters degree in another area of business but have no choice. Companies face losing a huge number of people simply because the career path opportunities within IT have not been laid out or made clear to the staff. This churn rate saddles the average firm with burdensome recruiting and termination costs.

2. About 50 percent of the respondents think they earn less in their salary and bonus than they deserve. Research indicates that job satisfaction is more important than salary, but this statistic clarifies how rampant the feeling is among IT professionals that they are not being paid what they are worth. Coupled with the first issue, this compounds the pressure on an individual to change employers to remedy the salary and advancement issues.

3. Two thirds of the sample report that they understand the business goals and strategies of their companies, but only one third believe they are empowered to have an effect on the company's success. An important part of job satisfaction is the feeling of contributing in a significant way to the success of the organization. This is one of the intangibles that work to make people feel useful and productive. If this sense is missing in a large percentage of IT professionals, then the industry as a whole has a significant issue to remedy.

4. About 60 percent appreciate flexible hours, but would rather telecommute. As the technology improves to allow effective job performance from any location, the pressure increases for organizations to enable telecommuting. Clearly, the IT professionals will be aware of the enabling characteristics of the technology long before the general population. They will seek the alternative work style and become disenchanted if the organization denies this or awards telecommuting as a perk only to favored employees.

5. Almost half are dissatisfied with their ability to discuss career goals with their management. The likely scenario here is that IT management, traditionally low on the people skill scale, has not opened up the communication lines that their staff need to feel comfortable discussing career issues. Most IT managers have not been trained to help foster their staff's careers. Give them a technology problem to tackle and they are off and running, but bring up a personnel issue and many IT managers feel ill-prepared to manage their employees' needs.

6. About 40 percent believe they have too burdensome a workload. IT, like other areas in the firm, has been downsizing. This trend has resulted in all employees feeling their individual work loads have increased. The technical nature of the work that IT staff undertake makes this a serious concern. Mistakes in the design or implementation of technology can have disastrous effects. If the burdensome workload leads to an increase in errors, the IT manager will have an escalating problem to manage.

7. About 45 percent believe there is not enough company-sponsored training and seminars. The nature of IT as a technical area dictates the need for constant upgrading of staff skills. At the same time, a burdensome workload means that time for upgrading is limited. The IT manager must aggressively monitor this issue to ensure that the staff has the best opportunities for upgrading their skills and improving their career opportunities.

8. About 80 percent report their jobs are stressful, with more than 50 percent saying this is an increase over a year ago. Putting all seven of the previous concerns together, one can easily surmise that the stress of the environment in IT has increased. There is more work, less time for skills upgrading, less opportunity for advancement, a sense of not being valued, and the need to resign in order to improve the situation.

Despite these serious issues, there are positive results from the survey:

- Almost 60 percent believe they have job security and have a satisfying relationship with their managers.
- About 50 percent report good communication with their managers, and report receiving recognition.
- About 75 percent believe they have a good relationship with their IT peers and almost as many report a good relationship with their users.

There is clearly room for improvement in job satisfaction with the IT career. And results such as these underline areas where the IT manager can enhance the jobs of the employees and begin to manage the retention issue.

▪▪▪ Characteristics of the Environment Contribute to the Complexity of Human Resource Management

Characteristics of the IT environment contribute to the complexity of this issue. There is constant pressure to master the new technology (software, hardware, or telecommunications) brought on by the pace of change in the industry and the rate of adoption of the new innovations. Basic materials research and advances bring about significant changes in hardware. Software vendors push expanded and improved versions of their products, resulting in releases that introduce huge disruptions in service and integration complexities. The telecommunications industry is buried in standards battles that maintain a lack of coherence in wireless technology. At the same time organizations have significant legacy systems requiring traditional IT skills and knowledge, and a commitment to long-term maintenance and support.

The need for both constant learning of new technologies and maintaining the old ones can create a two-class society within the IT organization: those who get to work on the new and exciting stuff and those who must remain with the "vanilla-flavored" legacy technologies. One distinct challenge for the CIO is keeping these two groups of staff content and productive.

The pie chart in Figure 9-2 shows that as much as 50 percent of IT staff may be involved in maintenance and support activities (e.g., programming and software

▪▪▪▪▪▪▪▪▪▪▪▪ **FIGURE 9-2   IT Staff Deployment.**

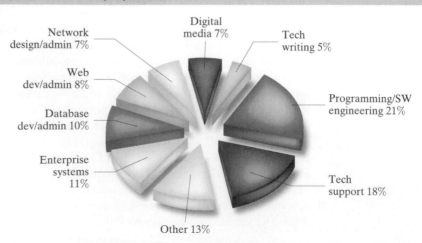

Source: Information Technology Association of America, "*Bouncing Back: Jobs, Skills and the Continuing Demand for IT Workers,*" ITAA, 2002, p. 13.

engineering, tech support, and enterprise systems).[7] This is the category of deployment where CIOs find the most discontent. It is important to have creative incentives for this large percentage of the staff. Specific management plans are discussed later in this chapter, but this source of staff discontent must be red-flagged for aggressive management attention.

In addition to the technical requirements of the position, IT staff is under pressure to relate to the business in increasingly significant ways. As IT enables business processes and becomes an integral part of the competitive positioning of an organization, IT staff must enhance their business and industry knowledge to play an effective role. Some of this knowledge comes from experience working with the business areas; some comes from in-house education sessions; and, increasingly, this knowledge is coming from IT staff seeking formal education through graduate management degrees. They are recognizing that it takes more than technical knowledge to have a successful career in IT.

■ ■ ■ Is There a Future Working in Information Technology?

Reports from the U.S Bureau of Labor Statistics along with those from private research organizations all list IT positions as the fastest-growing occupations. Figure 9-3[8] illustrates that the category of systems analyst leads in total jobs added in the 10-year period from 1998 to 2008, with a 94 percent growth. In addition, the top five jobs in percentage of growth in that same 10-year period are all IT professions:

- Computer engineer—108 percent
- Computer support specialist—102 percent
- Systems analyst—94 percent
- Database administrator—77 percent
- Desktop publishing specialist—73 percent

■ ■ ■ ■ ■ ■ ■ ■ ■ ■ ■ **FIGURE 9-3** Jobs of the Future.

Top five in total jobs added, 1998–2008			Top five in percentage growth, 1998–2008		
	Jobs added	Percentage growth		Jobs added	Percentage growth
System Analyst	577,000	94%	**Computer Engineer**	323,000	108%
Retail Salesperson	563,000	14%	**Computer Support Specialist**	439,000	102%
Cashier	556,000	17%	**System Analyst**	577,000	94%
General Manager	551,000	16%	**Database Administrator**	67,000	77%
Truck Driver	493,000	17%	**Desktop Publishing Specialist**	19,000	73%
Overall	20,300,000	14%	**Overall**	20,300,000	14%

By 2006 50% of the U.S. workforce will be employed by either companies in the IT industry or companies that are intensive users of IT.

Source: U.S. Bureau of Labor Statistics, *http://stats.bls.gov/emp/home.htm#outlook.*

FIGURE 9-4   Fastest-Growing Occupations, 2000 to 2010.

Occupation	2000	2010	Percent Increase
Computer software engineers, applications	380	760	100
Computer support special ists	506	996	97
Computer software engineers, systems software	317	601	90
Network and computer systems administrators	229	416	82
Network systems and data communications analysts	119	211	77
Desktop publishers	38	63	67
Database administrators	106	176	66
Personal and home care aides	414	672	62
Computer systems analysts	431	689	60
Medical assistants	329	516	57

Source: U.S. Bureau of Labor Statistics, *http://stats.bls.gov/news.release/ecopro.t06.htm.*

In additional analyses from the U.S. Bureau of Labor Statistics, IT areas dominate the top 10 fastest-growing occupations as shown in Figure 9-4[9]. IT positions fill the first seven slots and then appear again in slot nine.

The data verifies that IT is a good profession to choose for the foreseeable future. What is also interesting is that the variety of areas within IT is rich, including highly technical jobs, those that require organizational skills, and those that need an element of design and artistic ability. As technology invades all aspects of business, the jobs and associated skills become varied, allowing people with many different talents and interests to find a home under the IT umbrella.

The reputation of IT as a good career choice presents the IT executive with a dilemma. On the pro side, the good reputation means that there should be a steady stream of talent from which to choose IT staff. On the con side, the good reputation means that the challenge of retaining quality IT staff continues as companies compete for people offering the best skills. Additionally, the effects of this increased supply of IT staff means there will be a large pool of educated and talented but inexperienced workers who may demand high salaries. The potential is there for salary compression issues within IT departments.

Skills Required To Have a Successful Future In IT

The career of a professional in Information Technology requires a broad set of business technology and interpersonal skills. Gone are the days when being a "computer nerd" qualified you for a lucrative career in information systems. Because IT has become an integral part of every business function in the modern corporation, IT professionals have become business generalists with IT skills. Work experience in IT alone will not guarantee success in today's corporate world.

Skills for the Recent Graduate

The knowledge any individual acquires comes from two primary sources: education and experience. For a recent graduate from a master's level program in management or business administration, a potential employer would consider the following *general management skills* (in alphabetical order) important when recruiting an information systems professional:

- Business analysis—the ability to understand the business issues and describe the processes
- Change management—skills needed to lead an organization through change to new processes and procedures, including the use of IT
- Communication—the ability to both listen clearly and speak effectively to convey ideas
- Finance—every manager must have basic financial skills, such as budgeting and assessing projects costs and benefits
- Project management—the ability to run an effort from conception to implementation and evaluation, tracking time and budget milestones
- Leadership—the ability to inspire people to follow
- Managing value—managing to budget is no longer adequate; a manager must be able to harness the value of the function for the good of the organization
- Marketing—the ability to spotlight achievements and talent to inspire organizational support
- Mentoring/career development—managers need to foster the careers of their staff through caring advice, skills improvement opportunities, availability of experience and advancement potential, selflessly supporting others
- Stakeholder management—the ability to understand the influences of people and other areas on the work of IT, and managing those pressures to allow IT to flourish
- Team building—a complex set of skills to inspire people to work together and excel in achieving their goals
- Training—the ability to teach

These general management skills are extremely important in today's IT organization because of the critical need for the IT function to be well aligned with the business functions of the organization. There are many characteristics of strategic alignment discussed throughout this book but the simple message here is that IT professionals need general business management skills just as much as any beginning manager in the organization. In an interview, the CIO of Wal-Mart, Kevin Turner, was asked to comment on how he helped his people to truly understand the business:

"In any development effort our IS people are expected to get out and do the function before they do the system specification, design or analysis. The key there is to do the function, not just observe it. So we actually insert them into the business roles. As a result they come back with a lot more empathy and a whole lot better understanding and vision of where we need to go and how we need to proceed.

We've learned some hard lessons in our stores, clubs and distribution centers when we developed something and people didn't use it, and they chose to find other ways to get the job done. We are working hard to develop systems that are easy to use. That puts an awesome responsibility on that developer to get out and understand the business. That's one of our key things: We're merchants first and technologists second."[10]

Many firms would consider this commitment to understanding the user side of the business extreme. However, as every system becomes a critical business enabler and an expensive undertaking, the effort put into getting the right information service before starting to design becomes the key part of the approach. Wal-Mart is admired by many in a variety of industries for its application of IT to improve business processes. It would seem that their approach works. Michael Schrage, writing in *MIT Technology Review* proposes that Wal-Mart's use of IT matters because it delivers:

"In terms of sheer economic impact, the single most important, dynamic, defining technological innovation in America hasn't been the silicon cliché of Moore's Law; it's the relentless promotional promise of "everyday low prices." Sure, Microsoft, Intel, Cisco and Dell may be terrific companies, but the true corporate leader driving productivity improvement over the past decade has been Wal-Mart. When it comes to managing high-impact innovation, there is no contest—Sam Walton still matters more than Bill Gates.

The reason is simple. Wal-Mart is by far the commercial world's most influential purchaser and implementer of software and systems. It is the 800-pound gorilla in a retail jungle of bonobos and howler monkeys. Microsoft and Cisco may set technical standards; Wal-Mart sets business process standards."[11]

The graduate intending to become a manager in the information systems area will also need competency in general technology skills, such as:

- Application software
- Databases
- Hardware infrastructure/architecture
- Knowledge of general IT management issues
  - Career development
  - Organizational forms
  - Strategy and planning
- Networks and networking architectures
- Systems development and programming
- Integration within and across all architectures

There are additional technology skills associated with specific areas such as e-business, telecommunications, and database management. Anyone seeking a specialized position in IT would seek training in that particular area. Many certificate programs can provide specific technology training. For example, Microsoft's MCSE and the more basic A+ certification are available from professional training organizations like The Chubb Institute and New Horizons, and can be a valuable supplement to an MBA or MSIS in pursuing a technical position.

Recent graduates often run into a situation where IT managers want to find new employees with experience. This is the traditional "Catch-22" issue of needing experience to get experience. Managers must recognize this problem and understand the value of investing in less-experienced new employees. When a company hires a new graduate and provides experience and training, not only does the organization get to shape the training, but the individual is often more loyal to the company, remaining with the company for a longer time. The IT manager should also recognize the value of internships, part-time positions, and volunteer work that provide the recent graduate with experience. Individuals should consider the value of these situations as well while they are in the process of getting their formal education.

Skills for Experienced IT Professionals

Beyond the initial position after graduation, organizations seek individuals with industry-specific and firm-type-specific (e.g., pharmaceutical, financial, retail, accounting, manufacturing, consumer product) experience in addition to their academic training:

- Industry knowledge
  - Best practices
  - Industry issues
  - Industry-specific solutions
- Firm-type-specific knowledge
  - Business processes
  - Generalized business strategies
  - Influencing decision-making
  - Markets

What this means is that both the individual and the manager must focus on improving this knowledge as part of the normal aspect of working in IT. It is too easy to get caught up in the day-to-day problems and responsibilities of a position and not find the time for improving one's overall experience. The individual should be constantly seeking to broaden his or her industry and firm knowledge. The IT manager should be facilitating this broadening experience as part of the career development responsibility all managers have for their employees.

For individuals seeking promotion within their current firm, skills indicating a depth of knowledge about the specific company and general managerial skills are highly valued. These skills include

- Ability to communicate across business disciplines
- Ability to employ consulting skills
- Ability to influence decision-making
- Information about business process
- Understanding organizational philosophy
- Understanding the strategic goals and objectives

With each added year of employment, the experience-based skills grow. In addition, general management skills like those above need to expand through both experience and education. IT managers should seek to provide their employees with educational programs that enhance their general managerial skills. It is also important for the technology skills to continue to expand and change as the technology evolves. It is therefore critical for information systems professionals to focus on increasing their own technical skill levels throughout their careers. This is why the job satisfaction survey from *Computerworld* is disturbing: almost 45 percent of the respondents felt they did not have enough company-sponsored training and seminars. Some companies fear that if they train their employees too well, they will leave for a more lucrative position elsewhere. However, if increasing technical skills is on the critical path to success for the IT professional, then companies must make such programs available to their employees. If companies do not provide both managerial and technical training, the employees will become disenchanted and leave anyway.

Becoming a First-Line Manager

Each individual position has characteristics and challenges specific to its environment. For example, Figure 9-5 illustrates the challenges associated with a first-line management position in information technology. For many, the shift in nature from being man-

▪▪▪▪▪▪▪▪▪▪ **FIGURE 9-5   The Challenge of First-Line Management.**

- Becomes responsible for the output of other people, usually for the first time

- Acts as a leader rather than a "boss"

- Stays informed on technical issues, but realizes that this is no longer the primary focus of the job, nor the primary determinant of success or failure

- Acquires many new and unfamiliar administrative duties, that may relate to personnel, procedural, and budgetary issues

- Deals with employees and their problems, but no longer as a coworker

- Faces many new situations in which the action to be taken is unclear and requires a judgment call rather than reference to a rule

aged to being a manager creates anxiety and concern. It is important to understand what to expect and to recognize the new position as one of the many educational experiences involved with career development. For those who have graduated from a masters level program, most of the issues in a first-line manager position have been studied in the classroom. While this is not the same as the real experience, it helps to ease the anxiety. But for those who are promoted to this management position without the degree experience, it can be a daunting challenge.

As with many life experiences, each person will be stronger after working through it. However, having some guidelines can be valuable. The recommendations in Figure 9-6 can be useful in avoiding common mistakes and planning for a successful experience. One of the most important is being willing to ask for help. People often assume that because the management responsibility has been given to them, they must succeed or fail on their own.

▪▪▪▪▪▪▪▪▪▪ **FIGURE 9-6   Important Considerations for First-Level Managers.**

First-level managers should consider the following:

- **Pitfalls to Avoid**

  – Trying to be "popular" instead of effective.
  – Failing to ask for advice.
  – Overlooking the role of supportive problem solver.
  – Failing to keep employees informed.
  – Micro-managing by overemphasizing policies, rules, and procedures.
  – Acting like "the boss" rather than a coach.

- **Training Suggestions**

  – Network with other FLMs.
  – Identify a potential mentor.
  – Participate in FLM development workshops and seminars.
  – Register for FLM courses at local colleges and universities.
  – Subscribe to periodicals and FLM training journals and magazines.

- **Basic Success Strategies**

  – Admit mistakes rather than attempting to cover them up.
  – Show consideration.
  – Provide details to all members of the team.
  – Exhibit confidence and belief in your team members.
  – Provide ongoing feedback, praise, and recognition.

This is never true, not even at the highest levels of management. Management today is a complex, fast-paced job. The best managers do not "do it all" themselves, but rather know how to facilitate a strong team of peers and employees who work together to accomplish the organizational goals.

Another common pitfall is getting carried away with the inherent power of being the "boss." This is never a good tactic. Feeling useful and appreciated is what motivates people; not being bossed around by a dictator. There is a traditional theory about management formulated by Douglas McGregor[12] called Theory X, Theory Y.

Theory X and Theory Y is one of the most famous distinctions in the history of management theory. McGregor says,

"Behind every managerial decision or action are assumptions about human nature.

Behind Theory X, are the assumptions that people dislike work, will avoid it if they can, must be coerced, controlled and directed and threatened with punishment to get results; have little ambition and desire security most of all.

Behind Theory Y, are the assumptions that work is as natural as play, self-direction and self-control are equally natural, that motivation results from self-esteem and a sense of achievement; that most people seek responsibility. Theory Y also holds that imagination is present in most people and that organizations use only a tiny part of the intellectual capacity of their workforce."[13]

The view of the manager will often determine the behavior of those managed. Thus the manager who espouses the beliefs of Theory X will find people lazy and difficult to manage. Theory Y managers, on the other hand, create a motivating environment for their workers.

The basic success strategies in Figure 9-6 come from a Theory Y approach and provide an excellent guide for the new manager.

▪▪▪ Recruiting and Retention of IT Talent

Turnover of IT personnel is a management problem on many levels. First it is difficult to know how to plan to use human resources without knowing what skills you have to manage. Second, it is very disruptive to the organization and has a negative impact on the morale of those who remain when talented coworkers depart. Third, the real costs to the organization of losing a skilled employee and replacing that person are staggering. The estimates vary, but all describe considerable value loss:

- $30,000 to $50,000 according to *Accelerating Change Newsletter*
- 1 to 2 1/2 times annual salary according to the Hewitt and Saratoga Institute
- $200,000 to $300,000 according to *Fast Company*

These costs are hard to pin down because different firms value the process in different ways. However, the costs generally come from a combination of the direct costs associated with recruiting (e.g., advertising, recruiting, selecting, training, paying recruiter fees) and the indirect costs such as the impact on employee morale, impact on customer satisfaction, and ramp-up time of a new employee.

Recruiting

Recruiting strategies vary across firms and evolve with the times. Figure 9-7[14] illustrates the various approaches that companies reported using for finding IT talent in 1999.

The traditional methods, such as classified ads, search firms, word of mouth and internal listings account for 89 percent of the recruiting strategies. A growing percentage comes from the use of the Internet and Web job sites: "The Web is one of the

▪▪▪▪▪▪▪▪▪▪▪ **FIGURE 9-7   How IS Talent Is Recruited.**

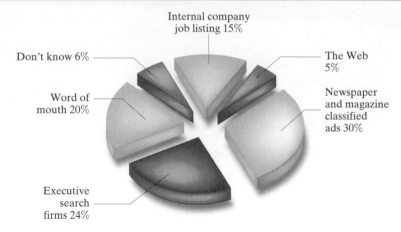

Source: Lee Hecht Harrison, Inc., *http://www.lhh.com/us/rsrchinfo/res&info.html.*

most explosive mediums I've seen in years for recruiting," says Chad Theule, manager of recruitment technology at Murray Hill, N.J.-based Lucent Technologies Inc. "It helps us find out what talent is out there and enables us to distribute [résumés and job postings] quickly around the globe."[15] By 2002 the use of electronic means to recruit had increased dramatically: Lee Hecht Harrison reports that 56 percent of companies that they surveyed used the Internet for recruiting and 43 percent used their own Web site.[16] While a list of current Web sites is always risky given the longevity of dot-coms, the following three have weathered many storms and seem to be established locations for both those seeking positions and companies listing positions: Monster.com, Vault.com and Hotjobs.com. Executive search firms continue to be popular despite their expense, because of the prescreening services they provide. Generally candidates brought in via a search firm are a good fit due to excellent background checks. Companies who use Web sites must perform all the prescreening tasks themselves.

Figure 9-8[17] highlights the importance of personal networking. Companies fill 70 percent of their openings with known candidates. This category includes current employees and those brought in through personal recommendations of employees and acquaintances.

Individuals seeking new positions are turning to the Web to research typical salaries and career paths. A number of well-recognized industry publications and sites carry out surveys and maintain the results on their websites. Several examples are *www.computerworld.com*, *www.informationweek.com/itsalaryadvisor*, *www.brint.com/jobs.htm#salary*, and *www.execunet.com*. Companies cannot ignore the role of the Web in current hiring practices. Those seeking employment use the resources provided by the Internet to understand the job market, salary and position options, and to take advantage of the online resume options. Those hiring must also learn to use the Internet resources for advertising positions, searching resumes, and prescreening applicants.

Retention

Concerns about turnover have led firms to create employee retention programs. Some firms have also established specialized HR departments for the IT area. These programs are designed to focus on what IT employees are seeking in order

▪▪▪▪▪▪▪▪▪▪▪▪ **FIGURE 9-8**   Avenues to Employment.

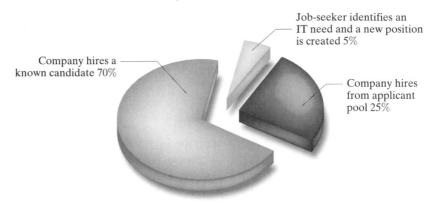

**If you're going for the highest probability of a paycheck,
turn to your network of contacts.**

Job-seeker identifies an
IT need and a new position
is created 5%

Company hires a
known candidate 70%

Company hires
from applicant
pool 25%

Source: Lee Hecht Harrison, Inc., *http://www.lhh.com/us/rsrchinfo/res&info.html.*

to keep them satisfied and avoid the disruption and expense of a high turnover rate. The Gartner Group[18] has recommended guidelines for a successful retention program:

Compensation
- Pay within 10 percent of market rates
- Integrate human resource and IT functions for a stronger, more proactive partnership and allow IT functional managers greater flexibility in determining salary and compensation levels
- Build defensive intelligence sources and survey often
- Set aside money for training that vests over a period of time that employees collect as they stay with their organizations
- Offer time- and performance-based bonuses that pay out over a three to five year period
- Stock options

Benefits
- Health, dental, and vision are a "given"
- Financial benefits include matching 401-K, pension plan, employee stock purchase plans, and tuition/education reimbursement
- Lifestyle benefits, including casual dress, telecommuting, flexible hours, and sabbaticals

Training
- Organizations that invest less than 3 percent of payroll in training and upgrading skills see twice the staff turnover than those that invest 10 percent

Work Environment
- Provide IT professionals with the chance to work with new technologies through conscious job-rotation programs
- Make the working environment fun (e.g., "Walk-up massage," napping tents)
- Recognition programs

Eliminate Burnout Through Staffing and Time Off

- Staff to meet objectives, renegotiate service levels, co-opt user support or increasingly outsource after-hours premium support
- Offer time-off to employees who have put in long hours for an extended period of time

Poll Employees

- Ask for employee satisfaction data once a year; address concerns
- Use a 360-degree review process[19] for managers to better understand how their staffs perceive them and the work environment
- Implement "skip-level lunches" to gain insight into regional or departmental problems

Hire the Appropriate Profile

- Everyone wants aggressive go-getters, but these people are most likely to "go get" the next best opportunity
- Understand a person's cultural fit within the organization and the role for which that individual might be best suited in the long term
- Assign mentors

Open Career Paths

- Do not place artificial boundaries on career ladders. Allow an IT professional to grow in compensation and influence within a chosen career path
- Allow people to have the opportunity to build process management skills, even if they are not suited for people or project management jobs

These guidelines directly address the complaints that many employees report during their exit interviews. The enlightened organization wants to know what employees are troubled about long before the exit interview! There are a variety of ways that firms have used to get feedback from employees about their satisfaction with their job and with the firm. These range from formal written surveys to informal brown bag lunch events. Figure 9-9[20] shows the range of methods for obtaining employee feedback along with the percentage of organizations using each method.

▪ ▪ ▪ ▪ ▪ ▪ ▪ ▪ ▪ ▪ ▪ ▪ **FIGURE 9-9** Methods Used to Understand the Needs and Desires of IT Employees.

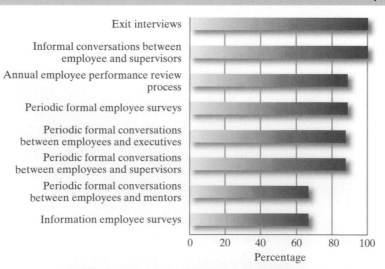

Source: American Productivity and Quality Center, Houston, TX, *www.apqc.org.*

▪▪▪▪▪▪▪▪▪▪▪▪ **FIGURE 9-10** Career Path Choices.

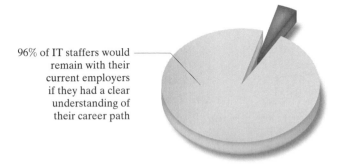

96% of IT staffers would remain with their current employers if they had a clear understanding of their career path

Source: Personnel Decisions Inc., Minneapolis, MN, *www.personneldecisions.com.*

Exit interviews are a universal approach in business today. This approach comes, however, when it is too late to have an impact on the individual who is leaving. The other methods allow for "mid-course" corrections and may save a valuable employee who has experienced some difficulties in the working environment. Most of the value of these approaches comes from the actual experience of the event. Both employee and supervisor or mentor must feel at ease with the conversation, or there is no real value. Formal surveys are often anonymous and therefore allow each respondent to be completely honest without fear of retribution. However, the anonymity makes it impossible to know who is expressing the discomfort and needs help. Formal surveys are more valuable as indicators of overall satisfaction in a working environment.

One of the most important aspects of retaining employees is making sure they understand their career path. Figure 9-10[21] illustrates the results of a survey done by an HR consulting firm. 96 percent of the respondents indicated that career path understanding is the most important reason for staying in their positions. Two other important factors are whether the individual understands the expectations of his/her supervisor and whether there are good opportunities for communication relevant to working conditions.

Successful employee retention begins with the first day of employment and the impression that the new hires garner from their introduction to the organization. Figure 9-11 illustrates the key points in planning an effective orientation for a new employee. Beginning with a genuine welcome is an important first step. The individual has made a commitment to a particular firm and IT position, and should be made to feel that their presence has been anticipated with positive enthusiasm. It is also important to make sure the new person is properly introduced to coworkers. Taking the time to do this shows the individual that the ritual is important to the supervisor and to the coworkers. It is also critical that the orientation includes an explicit statement of work responsibilities.

Maintaining motivated employees to increase productivity and reduce turnover involves a series of factors that must be actively managed by the IT supervisor. Some of these factors are particularly relevant to the IT organization because the technical nature of the job requires the individuals to maintain their expertise and professional contacts. The following are key factors[22] to consider in motivating IT staff:

1. Allow people to learn new technologies as they emerge.
2. Give people the resources they need to do their jobs well.

▮▮▮▮▮▮▮▮▮▮▮ **FIGURE 9-11   Planning an Effective Orientation.**

- A genuine, warm welcome from supervisors and coworkers (there should be room for fun and celebration)
- Preparation of coworkers (at least a telephone call in advance of introduction)
- Introduction to coworkers and other employees in the organization
- Overview of job setting, including tour of facility
- Assigning a volunteer mentor
- Providing an employee manual/handbook–enough information without overload:
    - Brief history of organization
    - Organizational overview
    - Other items included by personnel department
- List of specific job requirements:
    - Job responsibilities
    - New employee's position in organization
    - Work values
    - Work expectations of the employees
    - Critical facilities (e.g., restroom, copy machine, parking, etc.)
    - Working hours and breaks
    - Pay and performance appraisal policies

Source: Personnel Decisions Inc., A human resources consulting firm in Minneapolis Exhibit 8.

3. Be competitive in terms of salary and benefits; consider annual salary surveys to keep abreast of salary levels.
4. Provide for workers' personal development; for example, 1) allow people to attend technology conferences and 2) give them a clearly defined career path.
5. Provide strong leadership during periods of rapid and random change.
6. Make certain that people perceive that what they do on the job is meaningful work.

Aggressive management of these factors will help the IT staff stay competitive in their knowledge, remain productive contributors, and ensure that they are getting the personal development in their careers that will keep them at the firm.

▮▮▮ Organizational Examples

The following examples illustrate how some organizations are managing their human resource assets.

The story of Skandia, a 144-year-old Swedish insurance and financial services firm, illustrates how a company that is serious about managing and measuring the value of its human resource asset can attack the issue (see "Skandia Insurance Company Ltd." sidebar). Skandia has a U.S. subsidiary called American Skandia where the software developed in Sweden is used to drill down to understand the performance and growth of each employee. Through its efforts to develop systems to manage the human resource, Skandia has been recognized as the uncontested leader in the field of measuring human capital.[23]

The Georgia Merit System, personnel department for the state of Georgia, uses a competency research process called Strategic Assessment Research to identify the value of the state's collective human capital, says Senior Human Resources Consultant,

Charlie Brooks. The process involves measuring the performance of each employee to identify the high performers, then conducting a series of behavioral interviews with each employee to determine how the most productive employees work. Brooks conducts behavioral interviews to find out what the high performers have in common. He asks employees to tell him the precise details of how they do their jobs, and he documents the high performers' attitudes, rules of thumb, and methods. When interviewing for new hires, Brooks looks for the qualities that have been shown to be an asset on the job. And perhaps more important, he trains existing agents to adopt some of the high performers' work practices.[24]

Skandia Insurance Company, Ltd.

The leaders of the company recognized that they had a lot of invisible assets that simply were not recognized by the marketplace, and they wanted to find a way to assess and communicate that value. They developed a matrix known as the Skandia Navigator, a tool to identify and improve the intellectual capital in the company's Assurance Financial Services (AFS) division. The Navigator looks at how human capital—in combination with customer capital, internal processes and the company's capacity for innovation—creates financial value for the company. Used as a business-planning model, the Navigator provides big-picture perspective on the company's past (financial focus), its present (customer focus, process focus, and human focus) and its future (renewal and development focus).

At the individual level, American Skandia, the company's U.S. division, uses the Navigator to drill down on the performance and growth of each employee. Employees are measured on critical success factors that tie into the company's strategic direction and values. For example, if the company decided that it needed to improve its investment on employee training, the Navigator could look at the number of hours of training that an individual receives and the dollars spent on training that employee. The employee could also access the Dolphin program on Skandia's intranet to see what courses they would be expected to complete in the next six to 12 months. In addition, the Navigator can provide performance feedback, record achievements, and identify future renewal and development objectives.

At the corporate level, Skandia tracks the value of its human capital through use of an empowerment index that reflects employee motivation, loyalty, and competence. The company also looks at employee turnover, training costs per employee, average years of service, and average education level to paint a clearer picture of the state of its human capital.

Alabama Gas Corp., or Alagasco, as the division of Energen Corp. is called, has twice been named by *Fortune* as one of the best companies to work for. Much of that honor is due to the work the company has put into measuring the attitudes employees have toward their jobs and creating programs that measure and build on those impressions. The company tracks employee satisfaction diligently because it sees customer satisfaction as a direct outgrowth of employee happiness.

In the early 1990s, Michael Warren, chairman and CEO of Alagasco, was looking for ways to improve the employee experience at the company. Research revealed that the organizations that are widely regarded as the best places to work also tended to be top performers in their industries. The company launched a series of programs designed to enhance the employee experience at Alagasco. For example, the company implemented the Temporary Reassignment Program, which lets employees try out job roles that are completely different from their own. The goal is to give employees a chance to develop new skills as well as enlarge their overall scope of experience. When employees are seen in roles that they might never assume in their regular duties, it builds not only their confidence in their own capabilities but also the trust and respect of managers and coworkers.[25]

▮▮▮ Stress in the Workplace

The chart in Figure 9-12 indicates that the greatest source of workplace stress for IT professionals is "increasing workloads." As the new century began, the effects of the technology market downturn, plus the terrorists attack on New York, and an overall slowing economy combined to create a situation where firms laid off IT staff or did not recruit to fill vacancies. To increase the workload by reducing staff size in an environment that already has a heavy workload due to the constant need to update technical skills presents the average IT professional with a stressful environment. The IT manager must strive to relieve the pressure of the stressful workload. The next two most significant sources of workplace stress are "office politics" (24 percent) and "issues of work/life balance" (12 percent).

All three of the stress factors need to be recognized and managed through stress-reduction techniques. Employing some of the following techniques[26] can do this:

1. Bring in outside contractors to reduce workloads—The quality of outside contractors is excellent and there is always someone to whom the IT manager can outsource a particular project. This provides a temporary solution by reducing the workload burden on in-house employees. Outsourcing must be carefully managed to gain all the benefits and, most importantly, must not be seen as threatening by the in-house staff.

2. Improve communications and encourage team building to defuse office politics—Nothing fosters paranoia better than a lack of communication. When IT staff (or any staff for that matter) do not understand what is happening in their area, they assume the worst alternatives. It is critical for the IT manager to promote

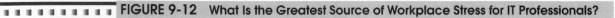

▮▮▮▮▮▮▮▮▮▮▮▮ FIGURE 9-12   What Is the Greatest Source of Workplace Stress for IT Professionals?

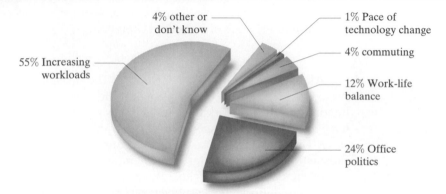

4% other or don't know

1% Pace of technology change

4% commuting

55% Increasing workloads

12% Work-life balance

24% Office politics

Source: RHI Consulting Survey, IntelligentEnterprise.com, *Stress Anyone*, July 17, 2000, Volume 3, No. 12.

understanding through clear and open communications. The application of team building techniques will also help to defuse politics (see Chapters 10 for a discussion on team building techniques).

3. Involve employees in decisions about managing workloads—They may have new, creative solutions. Often the workers involved at the detail level have the most creative solutions but they are sometimes ignored or there is no mechanism for soliciting their ideas. The IT manager should seek ways to gather input to help solve the workload problems.

4. Plan and promote outside activities to break up the workplace monotony and give people a chance to bond and have fun—Introducing an element of fun or games into the work environment can often serve to relieve stress. This involves setting aside a discrete amount of time to break up the workday with other activities such as exercise equipment, changing locations, team sports, napping tents (areas where workers can lie down to rest with some privacy), etc.

The successful IT manager is aware of these challenges and works to solve the workplace stress issue. Doing so will create a better environment and increase productivity for everyone, and thereby increase the success of the department as a whole.

There are techniques that can help manage employee stress. A manager who sees the indications of stress in an employee needs to work with that person and provide training for self-management as well as provide a better environment. Figure 9-13 is adapted from the Stress Management and Counseling Center and indicates steps that an IT executive can take to help manage stress with employees.[27] Many of these suggestions are good, wholesome ideas for living, such as proper diet and exercise. These habits become even more important when the individual is in a stressful

▪▪▪▪▪▪▪▪▪▪▪▪ **FIGURE 9-13   How the IT Executive Can Help IT Staff Manage Stress.**

- Keep staff regularly *updated on the status* of projects
- Make sure each person knows *what's expected* and when it's due
- *Set priorities* for projects to help each person schedule work
- Manage *deadlines*
- Make sure the staff *takes breaks regularly* to avoid physical problems associated with working at computer stations
- Make sure IT staff learns about latest *developments in the field*
- Arrange for *massages and exercise* time, especially in periods of high stress to meet deadlines
- Arrange for food to be available that constitutes a well-balanced diet
- Encourage staff to work with *"stress buddies"* who can encourage stress-reducing practices
- Ask staff to keep a *"stress diary"* to help identify ways to reduce high-stress situations
- When staff appear highly stressed, encourage them to take *time off* whether a walk around the block or an extended vacation
- Encourage staff to ask for *help* when they need it
- Make sure the work area includes *ergonomic* equipment, proper lighting, and good ventilation

Source: Elkin, Allen, *Stress Management for Dummies*, Wiley, 1999.

situation. The human body reacts to stress in a very primitive way and cannot always distinguish the source of it. Medical reports have shown that a single stressful event can require nine months for the body to fully recover. Finding ways to mitigate the stress, whether having a massage or taking a quiet walk, become essential to an employee's health and productivity.

Physical problems can also occur due to stress. Repetitive Stress Syndrome (RSS) and Carpal Tunnel Disease involve nerve damage due to repeated motions under stress. RSS can often be cured through rest and exercise, but Carpal Tunnel symptoms often require surgery to relieve the pressure on the nerve in the wrist caused by swollen tissue surrounding it. Backache, neck ache, headaches, and eyestrain have all been reported as resulting from working under stress at a computer workstation.

Figure 9-13 provides suggestions for managers to help identify and manage a stressful workplace. Everyone needs to be concerned about avoiding physical or emotional injury that will ultimately result in lower productivity, poor performance, lost work time, or loss of a valued employee.

▪▪▪ Career Development

An important function of the IT manager is to ensure the personal career development of IT employees through education and training. The Conference Board[28] reports that workplace education programs improve employee morale and esteem. This was the number one benefit in 87 percent of the companies they surveyed. Other benefits include:

- Increased quality of work—82 percent
- Improved capacity to solve problems—82 percent
- Better team performance—82 percent
- Improved capacity to cope with change in the workplace—75 percent
- Higher success rate in promoting employees within the organization—71 percent
- Increased output of products and services—65 percent
- Increased employee retention—40 percent

These results would indicate that education programs have beneficial effects far beyond the education itself. And, even more importantly, the programs appear to counteract some of the stress-induced problems and enhance employee retention.

The IT manager must evaluate education programs to determine the right amount to be invested and the right mix of delivery mechanisms. Industry surveys indicate that within the IT organization, 17 to25 percent of the IT operating budget is being allocated for education. In terms of delivery, the programs may vary from computer-based training to in-house training to outside classes at professional and academic institutions. As mentioned previously, education should encompass the full range of informational opportunities that an IT professional needs for career development. This includes general managerial skills, communication skills, and technical skills. Individuals respond differently to various forms of education. The IT manager will need to weigh the opportunities for different employees and develop a formal evaluation to measure the effectiveness of the various educational programs.

Many companies provide tuition reimbursement for individuals seeking higher degrees such as masters degrees in IS or business administration as well as doctoral degrees in these areas. It is not uncommon for firms to require a commitment of several years of employment in exchange for providing tuition reimbursement. Most IT staff are willing to make this commitment in order to gain the higher degree, which will be important for their careers.

Ethical Conduct and Data Management

An important part of education in today's corporate world is training in ethical conduct. Scandals associated with the top management of Enron, Tyco, and WorldCom underline how important it is to understand the rules of ethical behavior and actions. The IT organization is in the unique position of building systems that can bring visibility to all information. In a way, the IT manager has the power to enforce ethical conduct on the management of a firm through the handling and monitoring of the firm's data and information. Kevin Turner, in an interview in *CIO Magazine,* responded to a question about this significant responsibility:

"My job as the chief information officer for Wal-Mart is to bring visibility to all of our information, to eliminate the blind spots, to not wait to be asked to develop controls and balances but to be the champion for the information."[29]

Training in ethical conduct and decision making comes from both formal education and on-the-job experiences working with ethical people. The head of the IT area is a role model for all of the IT staff. This person must be especially focused on ethical behavior.

Ethical behavior covers a broad range of activities, from treating coworkers with respect to honesty in financial dealings, using corporate assets appropriately, or building software that works properly. The topic cannot be thoroughly covered here; however, there are several key areas that merit discussion.

Commitment to Building Quality IT

As information technology is embedded in an increasing number of products, the quality of that technology becomes increasingly critical. IT staff must understand the role they play in enabling that quality through their work.

There are numerous anecdotes about systems that were developed with "bugs" in them in order to meet deadlines. These products range from operating systems to voting machines. In almost every case, someone raised the question of the ethics associated with releasing a product with known errors in it. Someone else made the decision to do so. Employees must learn how to handle these situations. Ethical actions will strengthen the profession, while unethical ones will cultivate mistrust.

There are also instances of software errors that were unknown and very dangerous. The horror story extreme of the critical nature of software design is the Therac-25, a computer-controlled radiation machine.[30] Patients treated with this machine were sometimes given lethal doses of radiation when a specific series of keys were pushed in error. This instance is one of poor quality and design. It is not uncommon for products with embedded software to be "pushed" out the door to meet deadlines despite concerns about the quality of the product. When the product involves safety, its lack of quality becomes an ethical decision. The Therac-25 story serves to underline the critical nature of an IT professional's job in some circumstances.

The issue of the increasing criticality of quality software is explored in an excerpt from an article in *Wired Magazine* as shown in "The Bugs in the Machine" sidebar.[31] The bottom line is that as more software becomes embedded code, we become more dependent on its working perfectly, all the time. To date, IT failures account for $293 billion a year in lost productivity. IT executives must focus on developing staff who commit themselves to quality and ethical solutions in the development of IT products and services.

The Bugs in the Machine

By Brendan I. Koerner Ed Yourdan was sitting in a jet on a tarmac in Pittsburgh when he got a glimpse of the coming software hell. His New York shuttle had been cleared for takeoff when the pilot pulled a U-turn and headed back to the gate. The flaps were stuck. "We're going to have to power down and reboot," the pilot announced. It was the aeronautical equivalent of Ctrl+Alt+Delete. "Makes you think," says Yourdan, author of *Byte Wars*, "Maybe they had Windows 95 underneath the hood."

He's not necessarily joking. The so-called embedded systems crammed into jets, cars, and "smart" appliances increasingly rely on the same bug-ridden code that corrupts PowerPoint slides, freezes Ultima games mid-quest, and costs corporate America $293 billion a year in lost productivity.

The problem is built into the software industry. There are five to 15 flaws in every 1,000 lines of code, the Software Engineering Institute estimates. So laptops crash, government servers botch Medicaid requests, and the occasional NASA robot goes haywire on Mars—*c'est la vie digitale*, right? Except that buggy software is creeping into systems where failure can't be dismissed with curses and a sigh. Consider: DARPA is using wearable computers designed to beam tactical information to the "data visors" of combat troops. The devices run Windows 2000, an OS so flawed that its bug-cleansing "service packs" run to 100 megabytes. A sniper-filled valley near Mazar-i-Sharif would be a particularly lousy spot to encounter a Runtime Error pop-up.

Ethical Management of Data

The question of ethical data management is becoming increasingly important in the aftermath of some corporate fiascos in the misuse of data. Critical questions arise: Who owns the data? Who is responsible for its management? Who is the guarantor of its integrity? "Electronic data about customers, partners and employees has become corporate America's most valuable asset. But the line between the proper and improper use of this asset is at best blurry… Since the CIOs are responsible for the technology that collects, maintains and destroys corporate data, they sit smack in the middle of this ethical quagmire." These comments are from an article in *CIO Magazine* where Six Commandments of Ethical Data Management are proposed (see Figure 9-14).[32] While

▪▪▪▪▪▪▪▪▪▪▪▪ **FIGURE 9-14** The Six Commandments of Ethical Data Management.

The Commandments

1. Data is a valuable corporate asset and should be managed as such, like cash, facilities, or any other corporate asset.

2. The CIO is steward of corporate data and is responsible for managing it over its life cycle–from its generation to its appropriate destruction.

3. The CIO is responsible for controlling access to and use of data, as determined by governmental regulation and corporate policy.

4. The CIO is responsible for preventing the inappropriate destruction of data.

5. The CIO is responsible for bringing technological knowledge to the development of data management practices and policies.

6. The CIO should partner with executive peers to develop and execute the organization's data management policies.

Source: Berinato, Scott, "Take the Pledge," CIO Magazine, July 1, 2002, pp. 57–63.

the responsibility is proposed for the CIO in all of these, it is clear that ethical data management becomes the responsibility of the entire IT organization and therefore has an affect on every individual employee.

Ethical Use of Corporate IT Assets

Another aspect of the ethical considerations is that companies are beginning to take more active roles in monitoring employees' use of IT, especially related to the use of the Internet. Any machine that belongs to a company is a corporate asset that the firm can choose to monitor. While most companies inform employees that they might be monitored, this is not a requirement. People often resent this intrusion on their "privacy;" however, firms have the right to do so and to judge someone's behavior unethical or inappropriate for the work environment. Such a judgment can result in dismissal. Firms are using sophisticated software to monitor employees' activity. According to Karen Bannan:

"More than 14 million Americans are under continued electronic surveillance by their employers, who not only watch email, chats, and Web traffic but also look into employee files ... 27 percent of companies have dismissed employees for misuse of the Internet or e-mail ... More than 77 percent of companies record and review employee telecommunications ... 63 percent of companies monitor employee Internet connections."[33]

This data underlines the importance of understanding what constitutes ethical conduct. Most people do not wish to be "caught" doing something inappropriate, especially if they do not know they are acting in an unacceptable manner. There needs to be a clear statement and education for everyone on generally accepted ethical conduct.

There is an old adage for measuring the ethical appropriateness of an action. It consists of two questions: 1) How would I feel if my actions were reported in a headline on the front page of the *New York Times*? and, 2) How would I feel if my mother found out what I was doing? These are simple questions that represent a powerful way to judge one's conduct. Managers at all levels should be asking themselves these questions on a regular basis.

Every IT manager should have a human resource plan for the IT department. Some organizations have HR specialists within the IT organization to manage this aspect of the business. The education programs should enhance and advance the HR plan. Is progress being made over time to create the world-class IT organization that the HR plan is intended to create? Formal evaluation techniques can help the IT manager keep the educational programs on track.

Figure 9-15 illustrates some key strategies for career success. Each step represents an important goal to have as one climbs the career ladder. Some of these are for personal achievement, such as "promote your successes" and "assess your skills." But others focus on an individual's actions towards others: "be an ethical leader" and "become a mentor." Career success involves both of these aspects. While it is important to be focused on your own achievements, it is also critical to be aware of your relationship with others. Your own advancement is often accelerated when you are helping your peers to do well.

In the end, individuals must manage their own careers to achieve the position, experience, and knowledge that are desired. This is true at all levels of the organization, from the new hire to the CIO. In the process the individual should also establish a record to be proud of in terms of ethical behavior and the treatment of others. Climbing the ladder of success does not mean stepping on others to advance. One

▪▪▪▪▪▪▪▪▪▪ **FIGURE 9-15** Career Success Strategies.

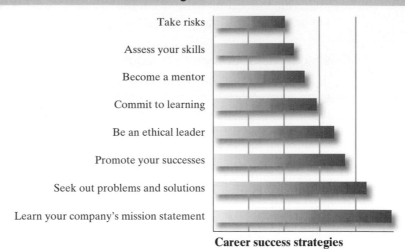

Source: RHI Consulting Survey, IntelligentEnterprise.com, Stress Anyone, July 17, 2000, Volume 3, No. 12.

never knows when a co-worker may be in a position to determine one's future success. It is important to never "burn bridges" as one ascends the corporate hierarchy.

Nor does climbing the ladder mean producing shoddy work to make deadlines. As information technology becomes embedded in every aspect of the modern firm, the critical nature of the systems that are developed increases. The corporation fortunes and sometimes people's lives depend on information technology that operates effectively. The IT professional should strive to always be proud of his or her body of work.

Review Questions ▪▪▪▪▪▪▪

1. What are the most important characteristics of a position that IT professionals are seeking?
2. How does the IT environment contribute to the complexity of managing IT professionals?
3. What skills are required for the recently graduated IT professional?
4. What are important features of a retention plan for IT personnel?
5. Describe the key elements that contribute to stress in the workplace.
6. How can the IT manager develop the careers of IT professionals?

Discussion Questions ▪▪▪▪▪▪▪

1. Does your company have an explicit career development plan for IT professionals?
2. Does the HR organization contribute in a positive way to the development of personnel in your firm?
3. If you were pursuing a career as an IT professional what skills would you seek to acquire?
4. Does your organization have any programs for managing stress in the workplace?

Areas for Research ▪▪▪▪▪▪▪

1. Read Douglas McGregor's *The Human Side of Enterprise* for a better understanding of Theory X and Y.[34]
2. For more description on what motivates people in the work place, read about Abraham Maslow's
"Hierarchy of Needs" in *Toward a Psychology of Being*.[35]
3. Read Kling's *Computerization and Controversy* for an in-depth look at the conflict and social choices associated with IT.[36]

CONCLUSION

This chapter has discussed the elements of managing human resources in the IT organization. While managing human resources well is a consistent challenge across any organization, the particular aspects presented by doing so in an environment where the technical skills are dynamic and short lived adds a new complexity to the task. In addition, the traditional mobility of IT professionals results in a highly competitive market place. The combination of these two factors presents the organization with the difficult process of both recruiting and retaining the IT skills and experience needed. The chapter illustrates current approaches for attracting IT professionals, developing successful retention programs, and creating a motivational environment for their employment. The chapter also focuses on the importance of stress management programs and career development planning.

REFERENCES

[1] Saharia, Aditya, "The Information Technologies Executive Survey of Critical Issues", unpublished research, 1998.

[2] Bullen, Christine, Minutes of Fordham CIO Roundtable meeting, 11/11/98.

[3] Copeland, Lee, "More for the Money," *Computerworld*, 9/3/01.

[4] *http://www.computerworld.com/careertopics/careers/ recruiting/*

[5] Information Technology Association of America, "Bouncing Back: Job Skills and the Continuing Demand for IT Workers," ITAA, May 2002, p. 8.

[6] Cohen, Sacha, "2001 Job Satisfaction Survey: Desperate for Direction," *Computerworld*.

[7] Continuing Demand for IT Workers," ITAA, May 2002, 13.

[8] *http://stats.bls.gov/emp/home.htm#outlook*

[9] *http://stats.bls.gov/news.release/ecopro.t06.htm*

[10] Lundberg, Abbie, "The IT Inside the World's Biggest Company," *CIO Magazine*, July 1, 2002, pp. 64–70.

[11] *http://www.technologyreview.com/articles/ schrage0302.asp*

[12] McGregor, Douglas, *The Human Side of Enterprise*, McGraw-Hill, 1960.

[13] *http://managementlearning.com/ppl/mcgrdoug.html*

[14] Lee Hecht Harrison, Inc., *http://www.lhh.com/us/rsrchinfo/res&info.html*

[15] *http://www.cio.com/archive/enterprise/091598_hr.html*

[16] Lee Hecht Harrison, Inc., *http://www.lhh.com/us/rsrchinfo/res&info.html*

[17] Lee Hecht Harrison, Inc., *http://www.lhh.com/us/rsrchinfo/res&info.html*

[18] Gartner Group, *http://www4.gartner.com/Init*

[19] A 360-degree review process allows each individual to review his or her supervisor as well as be reviewed by them.

[20] *http://www.apqc.org*

[21] *http://www.personneldecisions.com*

[22] Zawacki & Associates, Colorado Springs, Colorado.

[23] *http://www.cio.com/archive/enterprise/ 111599_human.html*

[24] *Ibid.*

[25] *Ibid.*

[26] RHI Consulting survey, www.IntelligentEnterprise.com, Stress Anyone, Volume 3, No. 12, July 17, 2000.

[27] Elkin, Allen, "Stress Management for Dummies," Wiley, 1999.

[28] The Conference Board, *http://www.conference-board.org*

[29] Lundberg, Abbie, "The IT Inside the World's Biggest Company," *CIO Magazine*, July 1. 2002, p. 70.

[30] Kling, Rob, editor, "Safety-Critical Computing: Hazards, Practices, Standards and Regulations," *Computerization and Controversy*, Academic Press, Second Edition, 1996, Section VII.

[31] Koerner, Brendan I., "The Bugs in the Machine," *Wired*, 08/2002, pp. 27–28.

[32] Berinato, Scott, "Take the Pledge," *CIO Magazine*, July 1, 2002, pp. 57–63.

[33] Bannan, Karen, "Watching You, Watching Me," *PC Magazine*, July 2002, pp. 100–104.

[34] Op. cit., McGregor.

[35] Abraham H. Maslow *Toward a Psychology of Being*, D. Van Nostrand Company, 1968 Library of Congress Catalog Card Number 68-30757.

[36] Kling, Rob, editor, "Safety-Critical Computing: Hazards, Practices, Standards and Regulations," *Computerization and Controversy*, Academic Press, Second Edition, 1996.

10

Management of Change

"It is not the strongest of the species that survives, not the most intelligent, but the one most responsive to change."[1]
—CHARLES DARWIN

"Let it be noted that there is no more delicate matter to take in hand, nor more dangerous to conduct, nor more doubtful in its success, then to be set up as a leader in the introduction of changes. For he who innovates will have for his enemies all those who are well off under the existing order, and only lukewarm supporters in those who might be better off under the new."[2]
—MACHIAVELLI, 1513

Preview of Chapter

The management of change is a responsibility that many managers fear, misunderstand, and have very little training to handle. Yet for the IT executive, managing change is a critical skill because the implementation of new systems always involves change. In this chapter we will examine the issues associated with change management and discuss techniques that IT managers can use to successfully manage change.

What we will examine in this chapter:

- Change is a complex organizational concept.
- Why do people resist change?
- How is IT a player in change management?
- What is involved in successful planning of change?
- What are the global factors in change management?

▪▪▪ Introduction

The ability for an organization to change, while understood as important for decades, has always been difficult to undertake and therefore has always presented a dilemma to managers trying to bring about change. It is inherent in the nature of humans to resist change. People find comfort in the way things have always been and been done. Disrupting this comfort through change, creates fear: fear of the unknown, fear of personal inability to learn, fear of the investment of time necessary to succeed. As a result, successfully managing an organization through a change process is a challenging task for a manager. In the best of circumstances, change will degrade peoples' productivity for a period of time. This will have a negative impact on the organization's ability to deliver its product or service. One of the most important goals for a manager of a change effort is to minimize these dual burdens. The manager does this by careful planning for the total time involved in the change process, minimizing the downtime of the people and shielding the product or service during the process.

Managing change is discussed here because the implementation of IT almost always involves putting people through organizational change. In fact, texts in IT define an information system as including hardware, software, processes, and people. The complex interaction of these elements has always provided the major challenge in the implementation and use of technology. It is often difficult to understand whether problems stem from the technology or the way people use the technology. The interaction of IT with institutional and cultural contexts has been termed social informatics by Rob Kling, one of the leading researchers in this area:

"Social informatics (SI) is the systematic, interdisciplinary study of the design, uses and consequences of information technologies (IT) that takes into account their interaction with institutional and cultural contexts. Thus, it is the study of the social aspects of computers, telecommunications, and related technologies, and examines issues such as the ways that IT shape organizational and social relations, or the ways in which social forces influence the use and design of IT... One of the key concepts of SI is that IT are not designed or used in social or technological isolation. From this standpoint, the social context of IT influences their development, uses, and consequences. Consequences can be very indirect and may be most visible over periods of years and decades rather than over months. From an SI perspective, IT applications may be viewed as "socio-technical networks," that is, systems that include many different elements, such as IT hardware, software, legal contracts and people in relationship to each other and other system elements... Non-SI perspectives on the uses and effects of IT focus almost solely on technical characteristics (such as a computer's information processing features), and posit specific effects due to those features. This position is called technological determinism. These perspectives overlook many important elements, such as the social and organizational contexts of the technologies and the people who use them. Such perspectives also make faulty assumptions, such as assuming that an IT application has the same meanings for all who use it and will have similar consequences for all."[3]

Social informatics focuses in-depth research on the complexities of relationships surrounding organizational use of technology. For our purposes, what is important to understand is the need for organizational change in concert with IT implementation, and the consequent need for change management to be part of the plan for every IT implementation. IT can change how people work and people can interpret the use of IT in ways that the designers never anticipated. These issues must be addressed in a change management plan.

A basic motivation for applying information technology to a business process is to improve the functioning of the process, usually by changing how it is accomplished. The definition of business process reengineering (BPR) or, "redesign," given by most experts includes the implementation of IT as part of the reengineering. In fact, many of the challenges of BPR were those of managing change rather than managing technology. Many of the failures of BPR were not technology failures, but change management failures. Organizations undertaking BPR today better understand the critical role that people and organizational change play in the implementation of technology.

One of the gurus of organizational behavior is Edgar Schein. He explains that organizational culture is a significant force in resisting change. He defines organizational culture as "A pattern of shared basic assumptions that the group learned as it solved its problems of external adaptation and internal integration that has worked well enough to be considered valid and, therefore, to be taught to new members as the correct way to perceive, think, and feel in relation to those problems."[4] Cultures are pervasive and complex and based on deep-seated assumptions. One of the difficulties in change management is bringing these assumptions to the surface so that they can be understood.

A basic model of the change process was put forth by Lewin and Schein[5] and it involves three distinct phases of change: unfreezing, change, and refreezing. What this simple model signifies is that there must be a concerted effort to unfreeze a process before attempting to change it. As obvious as this may sound, it is a difficult task. People do not easily abandon procedures and habits they have adopted for existing in an organization and getting their work done. So while they may appear to be open to learning a new way or applying new tools, they may be unconsciously clinging to the previous process. This resistance makes it both difficult to learn a new way and difficult to let go of the old way. Therefore, the first step in planning a change is to address the issues involved in *unfreezing*. The second step, *change*, involves introducing the new process through education and training. The third step, *refreezing*, signifies that the new process has become the norm, and that the individuals will not revert to the original way of doing things.

The Lewin-Schein model will be used in discussing the change management issue and the role of IT in managing change. Figure 10-1 summarizes the areas to be discussed in each phase of the model. Since the primary focus in a change management plan is to persuade people to accept the new way of doing things, an aspect of resistance to change is part of each of the three phases. For example, in the unfreezing

▪▪▪▪▪▪▪▪▪▪▪▪ **FIGURE 10-1** Using Lewin-Schein for Managing Change Through IT.

Unfreezing	Change	Refreezing
• Motivation for change – Pain – Real improvement – Charismatic leader • Impediments – Complex interaction between IT and culture – Reaction to change	• Well-defined objective • Communication • Plan – Leadership – Right people – Team building – Resources • Stakeholder management • Plan for resistance to change	• Institutionalize change • Overcome lingering resistance to change

Source: Adapted from Lewin and Schein, Christine Bullen.

phase, one must understand people's reaction to change and how that can be an impediment to unfreezing. In the change phase, it is important to have a plan for how to overcome resistance, and in the refreezing phase, the change manager must be prepared to deal with lingering resistance to change.

▥ Unfreezing

Pain As a Motivator

What makes people want to try something new? One of the strongest motivators for unfreezing is "pain." When it becomes clear that an organization is failing or about to be failing in the marketplace, or missing potentially advantageous opportunities, then the proverbial light bulb goes on and management is ready to try something new. A common mistake change managers make is believing that making the value of a new approach self-evident will convince people to adopt it. This could not be further from the truth. Without a stimulus, like pain, people prefer to go on as they have been.

In the case of information technology, the pain may come from an inability to see critical information about business trends, competition, or customer accounts. (See the "Nortel" sidebar) This lack of information leads to difficulties with decision-making and ultimately with the success of the business. A particularly strong pain occurs when a manager discovers that the competition has information technology that provides the kind of data being sought. Nothing is as powerful in the pain category as hearing "the competition has it!" When a business customer initiates the contact with IT, this is a critical signal that unfreezing has occurred and an important opportunity is presenting itself. IT needs to be ready to seize such an opportunity.

Nortel[6]—Reinventing Information Systems

Nortel is an old and respected manufacturing company (1895) who led the digital technology revolution in the communications industry in the 1970s. They produce a full range of digital communications equipment.

The changing marketplace for telecommunications prompted Nortel to recognize that in order to compete effectively, "it had to reorient itself as the 'provider of solutions' to customers who might require an integrated package of various products and who might need considerable assistance in designing that package." Their traditional organizational structure was decentralized with product-focused silos. They needed to drastically change this organizational strategy to provide for more integration across the business units.

The decision was made to embark on a major business process redesign (BPR) effort having an impact on procedures, systems, and technology. A major component of the integration effort was the role that IT would play in leading the reengineering of corporate-wide processes.

There were three challenges associated with this change effort: 1) IT had traditionally served in a support role, being more tactical than strategic; 2) IT itself needed realignment and restructuring; and 3) BPR efforts were being highly criticized as fads or fancy names for down sizing.

Nonetheless, Nortel proceeded to train their managers in BPR and undertake an aggressive change effort. The CIO realized that while the business managers were paying enthusiastic lip service to the change, few were taking ownership of the process. He decided that a radical move to unfreeze everyone and gain support for the change program was needed. He felt he should create a discontinuity, his version of pain, to get people's attention and support for the new approach. He commented, "Changing the structure first would certainly throw us into a state of chaos for some period of time… On the other hand natural human resistance to change could doom a more measured approach … This approach could move us faster or it could kill us. One thing it will ensure is success or failure—nothing in between."

Another form of pain may come directly from a customer or partner request. If two organizations are integrating their information through an extranet or other communication system, it can become urgent for the business manager to implement technology to support the exchange. This is a highly sensitive area since IT will be working directly with the customer or partner. The pressure is on IT to have the knowledge, both business and technical, necessary to bring this project to a successful conclusion.

A particularly searing pain results from the need to integrate disparate systems resulting from an acquisition or merger. A well-developed plan for the change is critical here and must anticipate the political realities of this scenario. In most instances, top management has not considered the systems problems resulting from combining two organizations with different technology standards. In addition to the expected change management issues, this systems integration and change is fraught with the politics associated with power and influence. Each IT department believes its technology is the better solution. The competition among the managers for who ranks higher in the ultimate organization is fierce. These entanglements prolong the merger of the systems and can lead to serious personal relationship problems, resentment, loss of key personnel, and a generally unpleasant experience.

A simple form of pain comes from individuals' inability to perform their work because of IT constraints such an antiquated technology. This pain results in direct requests to the IT department to work with the user area to upgrade hardware, software, telecommunications, etc. The need, coming from the user, starts the unfreezing and puts IT in a good position to manage the change. Usually the major obstacle in this example is that IT is too overloaded to respond in the time frame that the user needs. However, it is important for the IT executive to manage such requests and respond quickly before the opportunity becomes an unpleasant situation.

While these examples are all motivated by managerial pain, they can in fact become huge opportunities for the IT organization. They present business management, unfrozen and seeking change. They open the door to valuable strategic alignment conversations between IT and line management. Very often they coincide with ideas that the CIO and top IT management have wanted to implement, but could not because they could not get business management's attention. In these instances the unfreezing step has been easy.

Real Job Benefits As a Motivator

A second motivation for change is seeing that one's own job will benefit from the new processes and technologies. People are not altruistic in the sense that they will do something "that is in the best interests of the organization as a whole." Rather, people will adopt a change that will directly benefit them. In the early days of groupware systems, Bullen and Bennett[7] studied groups where calendaring systems were being introduced. The primary reason why users resisted these systems is summed up in the following quote: "Why should I spend my time to enter my calendar information in the group calendar when the person who benefits is the boss's secretary setting up meetings for the group?" The respondents saw the work as 1) redundant, since they wanted to maintain a portable paper calendar, and 2) demeaning, as they equated it with "keypunching." Without a direct benefit, the individual will not invest effort in a process even if the process benefits the organization or firm as a whole. The benefits gained must balance or outweigh the invested resource.

Information technology that improves the way an individual carries out a job can range from something as simple as a new interface for an old system to total system integration through an ERP system. This form of motivation rarely presents itself at the CIO's door. Rather the IT professionals realize the opportunities for the business because they are current on the new developments in technology that can enable better business processes. The job of unfreezing becomes a difficult one for the CIO who finds that demonstrating the benefits of a new way to do things runs right into all of the cultural and human resistance tendencies discussed above.

A Charismatic Leader As a Motivator

A third impetus for change is the impact of a charismatic leader. If the champion of the change is highly respected, others may follow simply because they come to believe in the vision for change. This motivation is not to be confused with a direct hierarchical order to effect change. A decree "from on high" does not always mean it will be adopted and followed, and is a coercive form of management that often results in failure. Resistance may come in passive ways that include subtle sabotage of new procedures. Keen, in a classic paper from 1980 entitled "Information Systems and Organizational Change,"[8] describes the "counterimplementation" techniques that can be adopted consciously and unconsciously. Also, see the "Classic Resistance to Change" sidebar.

Classic Resistance to Change

To: President Andrew Jackson

The canal system of this country is being threatened by the spread of a new form of transportation known as "railroads." The federal government must preserve the canals for the following reasons:

> One: If canal boats are supplanted by "railroads," serious unemployment will result. Captains, cooks, drivers, hostlers, repairmen, and lock tenders will be left without means of livelihood, not to mention the numerous farmers now employed in growing hay for horses.
> Two: Boat builders would suffer and tow-line, whip and harness makers would be left destitute.
> Three: Canal boats are absolutely essential to the defense of the United States. In the event of the expected trouble with England, the Erie Canal would be the only means by which we could move the supplies so vital to waging modern war.

For the above mentioned reasons the government should create an Interstate Commerce Commission to protect the American people from the evils of "railroads" and to preserve the canals for posterity.

As you may well know, Mr. President, "railroad" carriages are pulled at the enormous speed of 15 miles per hour by "engines" which, in addition to endangering life and limb of passengers, roar and snort their way through the countryside, setting fire to crops, scaring the livestock, and frightening women and children. The Almighty certainly never intended that people should travel at such breakneck speed.

—MARTIN VAN BUREN
Governor of New York
January 31, 1829

IT As Changer and Changee

Change associated with IT is also complicated because there are times when IT brings the change to the organization and there are other times when IT is the object of change brought about by organizational decisions. Figure 10-2 illustrates this dual role as *changer* and *changee*. As a changer IT introduces new technologies in the form of hardware, software, and telecommunications. These new systems often result in process and personnel changes on both the IT side and the line side of the organization. Thus the people using these systems find themselves faced with not only new technology to learn, but also process and procedural changes that bring up all the fears discussed earlier in the chapter: fear of the unknown, fear of their inability to learn; fear of the changes in their job.

When IT is the changee, this is often the result of a major business crisis. These are the unfreezing forces like a merger or acquisition, customer demands, or competitive challenge. Sometimes the impetus for change stems from a corporate layoff and the ensuing push to do more with technology to support the smaller work force. Regulatory changes such as tax law revisions can pose a burden on IT to respond. And clearly, corporate changes in strategy will have ripple effects on processes and systems that support them. Sometimes these change forces require IT to acquire and learn entirely new technologies. The extreme example of this is the introduction of the Internet as a business phenomenon. Most companies did not have in-house skills or technologies to implement Internet access, Web site development, security, etc., associated with this dramatic move in the marketplace.

Positive and Negative Response to the Idea of Change

Conner discusses the stages that people go through in responding to change.[9] There is a positive cycle leading to satisfaction with change. There is also a negative cycle that will eventually result in the acceptance of change. These cycles come from research observing people handling change situations. It is difficult to predict which cycle will occur with an individual, since some of the reactions are tied to personality. However, it may be possible to guide people toward the positive cycle by carefully planning the introduction of change to lessen the surprise element, and thus the shock that can precipitate the negative cycle. However, if an individual is threatened by the change, the negative cycle may present a more difficult situation than the IT manager envisioned

▪▪▪▪▪▪▪▪▪▪▪ **FIGURE 10-2** Changers and Changees.

IT as changers
- Targets:
  - hardware
  - systems software
  - application software
  - connected information/Networks
  - personnel
  - processes

IT as changees
- Anticipate or react to opportunities or problems:
  - change in objectives, processes, regulation, economy, "innocent" bystander
  - scarcity of labor, raw materials, etc.
  - mergers and acquisitions
  - customer demands
  - actions of competitors
- New IT

in the change management plan. An understanding of these cycles illustrates the importance of knowing the target population and being aware of the potential impact of the proposed change. Ultimately, knowledge of these cycles can prepare the change agent to manage the effect of change once the cycle has been observed.

Figure 10-3 illustrates the positive cycle, with five phases:

- **Uninformed Optimism.** This is the state at the beginning of a change effort where pessimism is low and people are certain that they will succeed in the effort. This is uninformed because people know very little about what is going to be required in the effort. They are beginning the journey assuming everything will go as planned.
- **Informed Pessimism.** This occurs a little farther along in the process where people have some experience and begin to learn how difficulties are creeping into the effort and presenting hurdles to achieving the goal. It is informed because the doubt and concern are a result of actual experience with the change effort.
- **Hopeful Realism.** This occurs when enough time has passed and the ideas have been "tested" within and outside the organization and have received support. This provides the hope necessary to carry the project through to completion. It is realistic because there has been visible progress and support from the environment.
- **Informed Optimism.** This phase in the cycle occurs in the home stretch when participants can see the end goal in sight. Confidence is built as the change effort moves toward conclusion.
- **Completion.** Completion of the process brings the satisfaction of having succeeded in getting to the objective.

As Figure 10-3 illustrates, this is a healthy cycle, providing the energy and enthusiasm to progress through all the phases even when there are doubts about ever succeeding. The IT manager plays an important role in managing information and communication about the change throughout this cycle. When participants understand the strategic alignment value of the change, it can help move them into the "hopeful realism" and "informed optimism" phases. They can understand the process improvement and implementation of IT as useful tools in enhancing the competitive

▪▪▪▪▪▪▪▪▪▪▪ **FIGURE 10-3** Conner's Stages of Positive Response to Change.

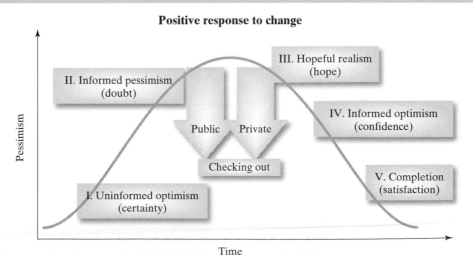

Positive response to change

Conner's stages of positive response to change

Source: Conner, Daryl, *Managing at the Speed of Change*, Random House (1992).

▪▪▪▪▪▪▪▪▪▪▪ **FIGURE 10-4** Conner's Stages of Negative Response to Change.

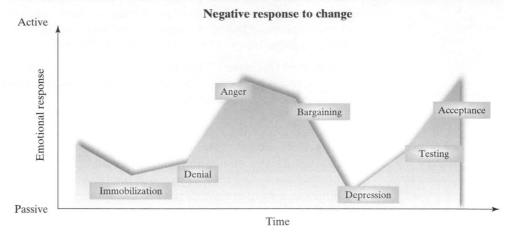

Conner's stages of negative response to change

Source: Conner, Daryl, *Managing at the Speed of Change*, Random House (1992).

position of the firm. Then when success comes, the satisfaction is even stronger having weathered the doubting period.

Figure 10-4 illustrates the negative cycle with seven stages:

- **Immobilization.**   This first stage indicates the inability to move forward that is brought on by information that shocks the system. This is an active emotional response and difficult for many to control. When the announcement of a disruptive implementation of new technology is first made, many people have this emotional response and cannot move forward to embrace the change.
- **Denial.**   This stage is when people assume the position that this new initiative will fade away like so many others. When organizations have endured many change initiatives and new technologies that have not become a part of the standard operating procedures, there is a tendency to believe that the current one is just another in the series. This stage presents a very strong resistance to change that has to be managed.
- **Anger.**   When denial is not well managed and people see the changes being implemented around them, there is a second peak emotional response of anger that results from a feeling of helplessness. The change is viewed as happening *to them* without their ability to control it in any way. Employees need to be aggressively brought into the process at this stage so they become a part of the change and can feel they are helping to direct what is happening to their careers.
- **Bargaining.**   The Anger stage is frequently followed by a stage in which the people attempt to bargain with the organization to mitigate the change. It is a desperate move to halt the planned change and reshape what is heppening to suit their desires. This can be a turning point because dialogue is being initiated by the target population and it may be possible to get them involved in the desired change. But too often it becomes a "venting" exercise leading nowhere.
- **Depression.**   When employees feel they are helpless to change their destiny it can lead to a sense of resentment. The result can be depression. They have tried to influence the effort through immobilization, denial, and anger to no avail. They are being pushed along the path toward the end goal of a change within the organization, process, and style of working.
- **Testing.**   The Depression stage is followed by one in which people test the resolve of the organization to proceed with the change. This is not unlike children testing their parents' limits by exhibiting unacceptable behavior to see if

they will indeed be punished. Employees will try to continue to work in the old ways, pointing out what is wrong with the new process, in the hope that the change can still be scuttled. When these efforts fail, the employees begin to enter the final phase of Acceptance, still harboring resistance and plans for counterimplementation.

- **Acceptance.** Acceptance occurs when people have a positive emotional response to the change. They embrace it and work to support it, understanding that while they have been unable to change the process, it is their destiny to be brought to the new objective.

The negative cycle in Figure 10-4 has three peaks and two valleys making it a more difficult cycle to get through—there are more opportunities to quit the process. The positive cycle involves stages of doubt and questioning, but this negative cycle involves denial, anger, and depression, where the change agent can lose the target population irreversibly, contributing to a failure in change management. Here, even more so than in the positive cycle, it becomes critical that the IT manager maintain open communication about the change, the process, and the technology, and educate the employees about how all of these factors support strategic alignment that will ultimately benefit the competitive position of the firm.

The critical goal of the unfreezing step is to create a climate for change and secure the support of all those involved in the change process. This first step can go a long way to heading off future resistance that often arises when least expected.

▦ Change

The second step of the Lewin-Schein model is implementing the change itself. The overall plan for the change process must be carefully thought out. The needs of and demands on all the stakeholders, political and power implications, timing, adequate education, and adequate time for assimilation are all factors to be considered. These issues are particularly acute in the implementation of information systems, which is an intensely political and technical process. "Information systems increasingly alter relationships, patterns of communication and perceived influence, authority and control," according to Keen.[10] The rollout of information systems threatens people in organizations on many levels. It introduces new procedures that interfere with the organizational norms, new technologies that create fear of the unknown, and new power relationships that upset the hierarchy. As Keen adds, "All in all, human information processing tends to be simple, experiential, nonanalytic and, on the whole, fairly effective. Formalized information systems are thus often seen as threatening and not useful. They are an intrusion into the world of the users who are rarely involved in their development and see these unfamiliar and nonrelevant techniques as a criticism of themselves."[11] While we might argue that today's users are more involved than those of 1980, the behavior pattern remains the same. The problems in implementation of ERP systems in organizations today are a direct result of these political and technical issues.

The tactical nature of the Lewin-Schein model suggests that to succeed in step two it is critical to have well-defined goals and objectives that are clearly communicated to everyone involved. Once the unfreezing has been accomplished, people must be kept involved and aware of the change process in order to remain on board. The manager must be constantly concerned about building consensus and managing the needs of the stakeholders. The timetable must be managed with adequate time for education and training. Tying the change process closely to strategic alignment and competitive positioning of the firm is valuable in this phase.

James Belasco expanded the Lewin-Schein model in his book on change management, *Teaching the Elephant to Dance*.[12] He makes an analogy between the corporation and the elephant that has been conditioned to stay in place with a small bracelet around its leg. Even when the chain is not tethered, the presence of the bracelet causes the elephant to remain stationary: "Like powerful elephants, many companies are bound by earlier conditioning constraints. 'We've always done it this way' is as limiting to an organization's progress as the unattached chain around the elephant's foot."[13] The conditioning of culture is particularly strong and self-propagating, and once it is in place it is very difficult to effect change. Every new employee is "shown the ropes" by existing employees who unwittingly pass along the cultural norms in this process.

Belasco's expansion of the model is shown in Figure 10-5. He calls the unfreezing task, "building a sense of urgency." He then breaks up the second step into two tasks: create a clear tomorrow and develop a migration plan. These two tasks highlight important aspects of implementing change: people in the organization need a clear statement of the goal and a clear direction to follow. Too often the end point in a change process is vague. For example, when a new reporting system is being implemented, the users need to know more than it will produce "better reports." They should be given a sense of how the reporting will be improved and how the new products will look when completed. With this understanding they are much more likely to cooperate and support the process leading to the change. They can become advocates of the procedural changes when they see a goal that will enhance their work.

The third part of Belasco's model, "develop a migration plan," focuses on the need to have a clear path toward the end goal. When there is not a clear direction, employees will begin to lose confidence in the management of the change process. They will see the ship drifting, which will encourage their resistance to the entire project. This can be avoided with a clear work plan that includes a schedule and milestones along the way. This is not to say that the migration plan cannot be revised and updated. To continue the sailing analogy, the ship can change course as long as it is still under control.

Most CEOs and top managers have struggled with managing change and leading their people to innovative goals. Jack Welch, the former CEO of General Electric who is considered one of the leaders in management technique worldwide, believes that

▪▪▪▪▪▪▪▪▪▪▪▪ **FIGURE 10-5** Organization Change Process.

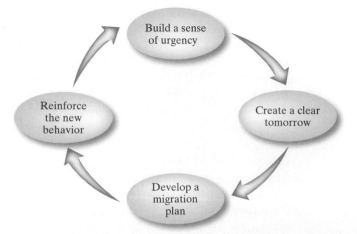

Source: Belasco, James, *Teaching the Elephant to Dance, http://www.belasco.com/elephant.htm*

you must 1) empower people to change; and 2) help them focus their energies on new ways of doing things. He states, "We have found what we believe to be the distilled essence of competitiveness. It is the reservoir of talent and creativity and energy that can be found in each of our people. That essence is liberated when we make people believe that what they think and do is important—and then get out of their way while they do it."[14]

Four Keys to Implementing Change

The change management process is critical and complex. To view it from a high level, the following four overall keys to implementing change are presented:

- Leadership Plus Facilitation
- Get the Right People Involved
- Team Building
- Secure Resources

1. Leadership Plus Facilitation

Leaders create strategies. However, people at all levels need to participate to create the value in the plan. Involving people in all aspects of the plan is an effective way to get both their creativity and their cooperation and support for it. People respond well when their ideas are solicited and respected. Sometimes the front line employees who are those closest to the work have the most innovative solutions to problems. They may not be technology experts, but they are content experts. It is important to listen to their ideas, consider them as alternatives, and envision how the technology can be used to enable their solutions. They are more likely to defend the new direction when their input has been solicited and implemented in determining the outcome.

2. Get the Right People Involved

Choosing the best people to work through the plan and execute the strategies is another key to success. Too often organizations choose the people who are available but not necessarily the best ones to lead the change process. Several years ago, a prominent pharmaceutical corporation lost its CIO in the middle of a major effort to revitalize and change the IT organization. Rather than seek a new, highly qualified CIO, they selected an executive who was nearing retirement and without a portfolio to fill the position. His only qualification was that he was available. He became a placeholder; the change process was set back by a year; and the staff of the IT department lost respect for the corporate management.

Focusing the talent of the best people on the change process results in several benefits:

- project benefits from the creativity and innovation of the people;
- best people provide role models for others in the organization;
- project gains respect throughout the organization by virtue of the talent involved;
- project is more likely to remain on budget and on time;
- successful process becomes a model for others to follow;
- achieved goal is respected.

3. Team Building

An important part of choosing the right people is building the people into a cohesive team. Team building skills are keys to successful management today, since almost every major undertaking in organizations involves managing teams well. These same skills can be applied to the change project as a whole: the entire effort can be seen as managing a very large team of people from initial vision to outcome and product. In the late 1980s Larson and LaFasto undertook a three-year study of teams.[15] Their goal was to identify the characteristics of highly successful teams. Their study included an extremely diverse group of teams ranging from McDonald's Chicken McNugget team to cardiac surgery teams to the 1966 national champion Notre Dame football team. Despite this diversity, the study found unusual consistency in the features of effective teams. These features were then tested on a sample of executive management and project teams from a wide range of industries. The outcome revealed eight characteristics of effectively functioning team leadership or project management that must be actively and aggressively managed to achieve success. These eight characteristics are described in the "Larson and LaFasto" side bar, and provide an excellent checklist for team building in the process of a change management program in conjunction with the implementation of technology.

Larson and LaFasto: Eight Characteristics of High Performing Teams

A Clear Elevating Goal This factor characterized every effectively functioning team. There needs to be a clear understanding of the project objective. The leader/Change Agent must work to keep the vision visible. Goal clarity in some environments can be surprisingly simple. The NASA Apollo project was committed to "placing a man on the moon by the end of the 1960s." Absolutely no ambiguity there! In the implementation of new IT, the clarity of the final goal often involves some ambiguity and therefore the manager must work to give all participants something to shoot for. This ambiguity stems from user requirements that fluctuate during design, changes in budget or deadlines, technology updates occurring during the process, etc. Prototyping final reports and user interfaces can serve to keep the goals clear.

The goal must be elevating. While in the corporate world it may be difficult to find goals that employees can become emotional about, this effect can be achieved through goals that are personally challenging. The goal of a project should stretch the limits of employees' abilities and provide people with an opportunity to prove what they are capable of accomplishing.

What gets in the way of an elevating goal? The answer is usually politics and personal agenda items. If the leadership of the project becomes distracted and loses focus because of personal concerns such as power shifts, the employees will begin to distrust the direction of the project.

Results-Driven Structure Fundamental management ingredients such as communication channels, assigned roles and responsibilities, and clear lines of authority must be established. However, too much or inappropriate structure is as dangerous as too little. "...the significance of structure lies in identifying the appropriate structure for the achievement of a specific performance objective—a configuration that does not confuse effort with results and that makes sense to the team members involved."

An important aspect of team structure is boundary management. This refers to the responsibility that team leaders have to alter their strategy with respect to outside interaction with a team depending on what stage the team is in. In the beginning it is important to protect the team while it is jelling; throughout the process it is important to secure corporate support and the resources required; and toward the end it is important to open the boundaries to display progress and products, and receive external recognition. Boundary management is a subtle combination of protecting and enabling the amount of interaction between the team and its environment. The IBM PC development team was set up outside the IBM organization in an early form of "skunk works." They were insulated from the traditional organizational culture and norms in order to work quickly and create a whole new product line. The same was true for the Chicken McNugget team. Too often managers at McDonald's had seen good ideas fail to develop because they were bogged down by traditional thinking. This team worked outside the hierarchy and was able to achieve their goal quickly. These teams both had the "breathing room" they needed for innovation and fleet development.

Competent Team Members As stated earlier, get the best people for the project. People should be involved who have the right skills and experience to get the quality job done. They also need the personal characteristics to achieve excellence while working with others. This involves being able to resolve issues that often result from a collaborative work environment and not allowing such issues to derail the project. Nothing degrades a group effort more quickly than team members losing respect for their peers. If there is a sense that someone is not skilled enough or cooperative enough, others develop negative attitudes toward the group and their ability to contribute disappears. Team members need to believe in each other and have confidence that the group working together will succeed.

Unified Commitment This is the sense of loyalty and dedication that the team must develop to work together. It's the "team spirit" that distinguishes a champion team from a mediocre one. In highly successful teams this spirit is demonstrated in a sense of excitement, willingness to do anything, and intense identification with the team. Commitment is enhanced through a sense of involvement and feeling of worth. The team leader must value individual contributions. Since the best people have been picked for the team, it is up to management to bring out each person's contribution. The best team leaders encourage the participation of all members and seek consensus for choosing direction. Everyone wants their ideas to be respected even if they are not adopted.

In the case of the implementation of IT, this approach should be extended to all users of the technology. The best way to get everyone to cooperate is to involve them, solicit their ideas, and use the best ones to improve the entire implementation process. Getting users committed to the technology prior to roll-out is a guarantee for success.

Collaborative Climate "Often, when the team exceeds what could be reasonably predicted from a knowledge of the member's abilities, such unusual outcomes are frequently explained in terms of some internal dynamic operating either within the team or between team members and the leader." This is the outcome of a collaborative climate. An important element in collaboration is trust. Trust promotes communication, allows people to remain problem-focused, and improves the quality of the experience. Trust has even been shown to lead to "compensating" (i.e., when one team member picks up another's slack).

Collaboration is built through involvement and allowing people to work autonomously. A leader who "coaches" rather than dictates a course of action promotes collaboration. The best team leaders inspire others to follow without using coercion. They use persuasion, "honey not salt."

Standards of Excellence   Team members need a concrete understanding of the performance requirements necessary for success. In some team activities like mountain climbing, cardiac surgery, or football there are immediate consequences for good or poor adherence to standards. However, in many corporate teams there is more freedom of choice and opinion, and therefore more ambiguity in what signifies success. In these instances, the requirements must be clear and there must be a focus on discipline to achieve them. Three variables enter into this issue: 1) it is necessary to establish a set of appropriate standards; 2) individual team members must require one another to perform according to the standards; and 3) the team must make changes to improve the standards when appropriate.

" ...standards of excellence consist of pressure to perform. While pressure may be exerted in several different ways, it is eventually focused on individual effort, as team performance is ultimately dependent upon how each individual executes assigned responsibilities."

An important part of this characteristic is tracking progress on the standards. Good project management requires milestones and checkpoints to evaluate progress and apply midcourse corrections. The team leader must manage this aggressively. The team members must be provided with periodic reports and updates on their performance, understand the standards being applied, value them as appropriate, and track their own performance.

External Support and Recognition   One clear signal that a team is receiving external support is that it receives the resources it needs to accomplish its job. This factor is discussed later as one of the four keys to implementing change. Another is that an appropriate incentive structure exists to reward individual members and is tied to team performance. Sometimes the recognition reaches beyond the corporate boundaries as when a team gains prominence in its industry for its achievements. Bristol-Myers Squibb undertook a massive project to implement an ERP system. Their success, among the first in the pharmaceutical industry, led to many studies and articles about what they did. The team has been credited with saving the corporation multiple millions of dollars through the use of the technology.

Sometimes support is subtle and its absence is more significant than its presence. When a team feels a lack of support there is a concurrent loss of morale, erosion of confidence, and lack of commitment.

Principled Leadership   The team leader or change agent can add a tremendous amount of value to the collaborative effort. This has been discussed in other areas earlier and emphasis on the leader indicates how significant this role is. Larson and LaFasto list six expectations for team leaders:

"As team leader, I will:

- Avoid compromising the team's objective with political issues.
- Exhibit personal commitment to our team's goal.
- Not dilute the team's effort with too many priorities.
- Be fair and impartial toward all team members.
- Be willing to confront and resolve issues associated with inadequate performance by team members.
- Be open to new ideas and information from team members."

These expectations are particularly important in change management projects. The nature of change management magnifies issues of trust and successful outcomes. The change agent must adhere to principled behavior and good leadership tactics or the project will fail.

At a time when our daily newspapers are filled with reports of unprincipled corporate leadership, these simple guidelines seem to have great strength.

4. Secure Resources

The fourth key is focusing resources on accomplishing the strategy. Too often a grand plan for change is scuttled because not enough resources (time, people, and money) were invested in bringing it about. Once the leadership has made the decision to implement change, a careful study of the resources required is critical to ensuring the allocation of these resources. Here again the ERP example is an excellent one. Implementing ERP is much more than putting new software in place. ERP requires understanding corporate business processes in great detail and in most cases, redesigning those processes to enhance the use of the ERP. The involvement of the business area management and staff as well as the IT department becomes necessary. Effort to redesign the processes is a major element of ERP implementation. Effort to manage the change impact on how things are done and, more importantly, on how individual authority and power are affected is required. The total investment of resources in ERP implementation is rarely calculated or understood until well into the process. This is why so many organizations have deemed their ERP efforts failures: they are over budget, off schedule, and rarely end up handling all the tasks that were anticipated. Leverage business sponsor and champion(s) are critical to the success of these changes.

▪▪▪ Stakeholder Roles in Managing Change

One aspect of planning the management of change is to be sure that you understand all of the people who will be involved in or affected by the change. This is the list of change stakeholders. The first stakeholder is the *change sponsor* who is the person in top management initiating the program of change. As a high level manager this person brings authority to the decision to implement the change. The strong support of a respected sponsor is a key element in the eventual success of the program. The sponsor defends the change to the organization at large and ensures the resources needed are committed to the process.

A second important stakeholder is the *change agent* or *champion*. This is the person responsible for implementing the change, and is generally a manager closer to the actual program of change. Therefore this can be a middle- or lower-level manager. In a project that occurs at very high levels in an organization, this person may be a top-level manager. The change agent/champion plays a strong, hands-on role in the change process. This person serves as a trusted evangelist that facilitates the project success.

Next in the stakeholder list is the *change target*; that is, the individuals or groups who are directly affected by the change. These people need a great deal of attention in the process since they are the ones whose jobs are changing and who will have to learn new approaches and skills. These are the people who need to be involved, whose ideas need to be gathered and applied to the process, and whose behavior must be changed through education, training, and new incentive programs.

Finally, there is the *influencer* who is helping the target through the process of change. This is often someone trained to handle, or experienced in handling, the people issues of the change management process. Organizations employ change specialists, trainers, and anthropologists for this role. In many examples of change management, there is no one to assume this role so it becomes the responsibility of the change agent. If the change agent has a knack for this task, it can work out successfully. But, functioning as an influencer is an important enough task to warrant having an individual specifically assigned to the role.

▪▪▪ Classic Reasons People Resist Change

There are many reasons why people resist change, as we have been discussing in this chapter. The following are among the most common:[16]

- **Loss of Face.**   Fear that dignity will be undermined, a place of honor removed. A new process can change the work enough that an individual feels demeaned by the change. If the change is billed as an improvement, the individual can feel embarrassment because the change may appear as exposure of past mistakes.
- **Loss of Control.**   Anger at decisions being taken out of one's hands. A new process will often result in power shifting to another department or manager. Individuals experiencing this feel that their influence has been undermined or that they have been demoted even if their position and title do not change.
- **Excess Uncertainty.**   A feeling of being uninformed about where the change will lead and what is coming next. This generates a sensation similar to walking off a cliff blindfolded and occurs when there is no clear path to the new state.
- **Surprise.**   Defensive reaction to no advance warning. When the target population has no chance to get ready, they resent the change process and feel they are not respected enough to have been briefed ahead of time.
- **The "Difference" Effect.**   Rejection of the change because it doesn't fit existing mental models, seems strange and unfamiliar, and challenges usually unquestioned habits and routines. This is running up directly against the power of long-established corporate culture. If the change presents a state that is dramatically different from the existing one, human resistance will be strong.
- **"Can I Do it?"**   Concerns about future competence, worries about whether one will still be successful after the change. People take comfort in the usual way of doing things and feel threatened by new ways.
- **Ripple Effect.**   Annoyance at disruptions to other activities and interference with the accomplishments of unrelated tasks. The change process adds work to the normal course of activities and individuals do not have slack time to absorb the disruptions.
- **More Work.**   Resistance to additional things to do, new things to learn, and no time to do it all. Organizations do not allow for the individuals to be relieved of other duties during the change.
- **Past Resentments.**   Memories of past hostilities or problems that were never resolved. The change in procedure may throw together individuals or departments with unresolved historic enmities.

- **Real Threats.** Anger that the change will inflict real pain and create clear losers. A change process is often associated with a layoff of staff. If the goal for the change is improved efficiencies, individuals will fear for their positions.
- **Competing Commitments.** Concern that there will be a negative impact on individuals' existing commitments, resulting in their failure to achieve desired results outside of the change.

Kegan and Lahey address resistance to change and cite a psychological dynamic called "competing commitment" as the real reason for resistance.[17] Their research shows that "Resistance to change does not reflect opposition, nor is it merely a result of inertia. Instead, even as they hold a sincere commitment to change, many people are unwittingly applying productive energy toward a hidden *competing commitment*."[18] Examples include 1) a talented team leader who avoids teamwork because of a fear of the conflict that naturally accompanies any ambitious team effort; 2) a rising star (young manager) who derails an important development effort to avoid success that will change their relationship with their manager; 3) a young black manager who avoids success with a primarily white executive team for fear of threatening their sense of loyalty to their own racial group. Kegan and Lahey emphasize the power of implicit assumptions and how they shape our reality. In one amusing story they describe a woman from Australia, living in the U.S. for a year, who complains about Americans driving on the wrong side of the street and putting the steering wheels on the wrong side of the cars. "One day I was thinking about six different things, and I got into the right side of the car, took out my keys and was prepared to drive off. I looked up and thought to myself, 'My God, here in the violent and lawless United States, they are even stealing *steering wheels*!'"[19] Her implicit assumption about where the steering wheel should be was so strong, that she could not see it immediately to her left.

As strong as the notion of competing commitments is to the individual, groups are also susceptible to its power to resist change. The leadership team of a video production company underwent a planning process leading to a strategy to which they all became committed. However, the strategy was not accomplished despite their enthusiasm to do so. They discovered that their competing commitment was to keep the relationships within the group as they had always been, and that achieving success with the new strategy would alter those relationships.

The article proposes ways to diagnose the hidden dynamic and thus move beyond the behavior that is stalling the change process. (See 'The Real Reason People Won't Change' side bar.) Change agents can use this research as another way to evaluate possible resistance to change and plan for managing through the hidden dynamics.

The Real Reason People Won't Change

Quoted from HBR On Point

By Robert Kegan and Lisa Laskow Lahey.

Use these steps to break through an employee's immunity to change:

Diagnose the Competing Commitment   Take two to three hours to explore these questions with the employee:

> **"What would you like to see changed at work, so you could be more effective, or so work would be more satisfying?"** Responses are usually complaints—e.g., Tom, a manager, grumbled, "My subordinates keep me out

of the loop." **"What commitment does your complaint imply?"** Complaints indicate what people care about most—e.g., Tom revealed, "I believe in open, candid communication."

"What are *you* doing, or not doing, to keep your commitment from being more fully realized?" Tom admitted, "When people bring bad news, I tend to shoot the messenger."

"Imagine doing the *opposite* of the undermining behavior. Do you feel any discomfort, worry or vague fear?" Tom imagined listening calmly and openly to bad news and concluded, "I'm afraid I'll hear about a problem I can't fix."

"By engaging in this undermining behavior, what worrisome outcome are you committed to preventing?" The answer *is* the competing commitment— what causes them to dig in their heels against change. Tom conceded, "*I'm committed to not learning about problems I can't fix.*"

Identify the Big Assumption   This is the worldview that colors everything we see and that generates our competing commitment.

People often form big assumptions early in life and then seldom, if ever, examine them. They're woven into the very fabric of our lives. But only by bringing them into the light can people finally change their deepest beliefs and recognize why they're engaging in seemingly contradictory behavior.

To identify the big assumption, guide an employee through this exercise:

"Create a sentence stem that inverts the competing commitment, then 'fill in the blank." Tom turned his competing commitment to not hearing about problems he couldn't fix into this big assumption: "I assume that if I *did* hear about problems I can't fix, *people would discover I'm not qualified to do the job.*"

Question the Big Assumption   Then help your employee simply observe or analyze themselves in the context of their big assumption—but without yet *changing* their thinking or behavior. For example, ask:

- "What does and doesn't happen because you believe the big assumption is true?"
- "What would cause you to question the validity of the big assumption?"
- "How and when did the big assumption develop?"

Test—and Consider Replacing—the Big Assumption   By analyzing the circumstances leading up to and reinforcing their big assumptions, employees empower themselves to test those assumptions. They can now carefully and safely experiment with behaving differently than they usually do.

After running several such tests, employees may feel ready to reevaluate the big assumption itself—and possibly even replace it with a new worldview that more accurately reflects their abilities.

At the very least, they'll eventually find more effective ways to support their competing commitment *without* sabotaging other commitments. *They* achieve ever-greater accomplishments—and your *organization* benefits by finally gaining greater access to their talents.

Implementing the change is the focus of this second step. Part of this deals with overcoming resistance. In many ways these are intimately intertwined—when the change agent plans well for the implementation, overcoming resistance is part of the methodology. However, the ultimate test appears in step three, refreezing, where hidden resistance can come to light when the new process does not take root.

▪▪▪ Refreezing

The third step is institutionalizing the new processes and systems to the extent that they become the norm for the organization. There are countless examples of information systems that have been introduced into the organization, taught with extensive education, piloted and tested for adequate time periods, and yet, people have reverted to old systems and methods. For example, people update the "official" database, yet maintain their own Excel spreadsheet. Managers contribute to the customer database, but require their secretaries to keep a card file for important customer information.

There are a variety of reasons for these examples of noncooperation. In some cases the information system is not adequate. It does not do the job the manager needs. This is a legitimate criticism of the system and warrants addressing. In other cases, the managers simply do not want to change their old habits. Social inertia is a powerful force. The information system is just a part of a complex process and the manager has succeeded for many years by using the old process.

One of the most emotional reasons for managerial resistance to a change is that the new process threatens the individual's power, status, or income. In some instances, the implementation of a new IT system redirects procedures and unintentionally dilutes a manager's position of power. For example, when IT automates an approval process and removes the delaying step of requiring a manager's signature, the company benefits from a streamlined process, but the manager feels less powerful because the individual approval process has been eliminated. The manager can no longer choose between expedition and delay for specific requests or shuffle charges to improve the appearance of specific accounts. Another example is described in the "Merrill Lynch: Integrated Choice" sidebar where financial consultants were very skeptical of Merrill's entree into online trading.[20]

Merrill Lynch: Integrated Choice

In 1999, Merrill Lynch made the strategic decision to add direct online trading as a product for their customers. The firm had always enjoyed the reputation of a full-service financial consultant with extremely well respected advisors working with individual customers. When they made the strategic decision to create the "Integrated Choice" product, they faced three significant challenges: 1) they had to create the technology to support this effort; 2) they had to convince their financial consultants (FCs) that this was the right strategy for Merrill; and 3) they had to convince their customers that this was a good approach.

Two critical stakeholders, FCs and customers, were resistant to this change. The FCs income and bonuses depended on their individual relationships with their customers. Integrated Choice directly threatened their income and status with Merrill. There was a danger that FCs would walk out the door and take the assets they managed with them.

Merrill was concerned that customers would have a variety of issues: 1) they would be confused by all the choices; 2) they would resent that some customers got their trades handled by Merrill at a discount; 3) they would take their business elsewhere.

To address the FC concerns, Merrill met with all of them to discuss the future benefits to their income and to offer a "compensation bridge" to protect their incomes in the short-term transition. There were also a series of internal communications focused on creating excitement and support for the new strategy. In the end, these approaches to implementing the change worked well: Merrill lost only a few of the top producers.

> To reach customers, Merrill launched an extensive media blitz, including the Internet and direct mail, to promote understanding and enthusiasm within the customer population.
>
> Ultimately the role of FC and the relationship between the FC and the customer had to be redesigned to support the new strategy and refreeze the new approach to business.

Overcoming Resistance to Change

All of the techniques discussed thus far focusing on managing the change deal with aspects of overcoming resistance. It is important to recognize that resistance is natural and inevitable; therefore the change agent must *expect it*. Resistance is often subtle and hidden. People can be very creative about appearing to cooperate while finding ways to not only resist, but even sabotage change efforts. People in the target population will present arguments that mask their true concerns. The change agent must see through the arguments and understand where the resistance is really coming from. Therefore the change agent must *find the resistance*. We have discussed many motivations for resistance. It is critical that the change agent thoroughly *understand the motivations of resistance* in order to work through managing them.

Doing this well involves highly developed skills, such as:

- Listening to what people are and are not saying
- Communicating so that people will feel knowledgeable and involved in the change
- Addressing the concerns so that the real issues of resistance are surfaced and managed
- Applying the 80/20 rule that requires putting the effort into preparing for the change rather than the change itself.

The 80/20 rule can be reinterpreted to apply to managing change in several creative ways:

1. Determine which people in the target population are the top 20 percent business producers.
2. Spend 80 percent of the time you have budgeted for people issues with this top 20 percent.
3. Spend 80 percent of your personnel development budget on the top 20 percent.
4. Study the work and determine what 20 percent of the job results in 80 percent of the return.
5. Train an assistant to do the remaining 80 percent so that the top producer can focus on the top 20 percent of the work.
6. Enlist the top 20 percent to do the on-the-job training for the next 20 percent.

Allocating your effort and resources this way ensures that the goals of supporting the top-level people in the organization are not lost in the complex change process. This approach keeps the change agent's "eye on the ball" throughout the ups and downs of the actual process.

One key to refreezing is the *reward system*. Incentives play an important role in managing the change process. But for the incentives to be effective, the change agent must understand the concerns of the population. Organizations often overlook the conflict between the existing incentives that reinforce behavior from the old way of doing things versus reinforcing the new desired behavior. Therefore, part of the change process is instituting new reward systems and removing those that were based on the old process.

For example, a hospital supply company piloted a system for just-in-time (JIT) surgery kit replenishment with a small number of partner hospitals. Hospitals have a major problem with lack of storage space. They need every square foot for medical procedures and cannot allocate much space for supplies. The strategy behind the JIT kit was that as a surgeon stepped into the operating room, the appropriate kit would be there. What becomes the most important question when the patient is anesthetized and waiting is: does the kit have all the right contents? The hospital supply company rewarded its employees who assembled the kits in the typical piece work manner: those who got the most kits out the door were the best. However, the new goal was not only to produce high quantities but also to assure quality of the final product. The system had to be changed to reward those who got the highest number of *perfect* kits out the door. The supply company soon realized its problem and implemented the appropriate reward system change.

Another key to refreezing is to build in *benefits to the users* in the new ways of doing things. As discussed in "unfreezing" people are not altruistic. They need a personal benefit to embrace a new way of working. This is where IT processes and systems can reinforce the change. The ability to view information in a new way or produce reports that benefit the user's job are both valuable reinforcement tools.

Knowledge is a powerful tool for overcoming resistance. When the target population is kept in the dark about what is happening and why, their instinctual reaction is to resist. As knowledge about the plan, process, and end goal is disseminated, people can better understand the purpose. Information helps dispel uncertainty and, in many cases, the fear that accompanies a move towards the unknown.

The creative change agent plans for *intervention techniques* that will garner support and move the population toward refreezing. Examples include spending one-on-one time with the opinion leaders and influential members of the population; securing an influential champion; and supporting the creation of "skunk works" to foster a new way of introducing innovation.

One of the time-tested techniques for eliciting cooperation is *involvement*. Individuals who are involved in a meaningful way become supportive and spread the positive news about the change. This approach thus multiplies its value by co-opting the involved individuals as well as their cohorts.

At times, there are two somewhat negative mechanisms that must be employed to make progress: *indoctrination and coercion*. Indoctrination can be accomplished by slowly moving parts of the organization. Using "guerilla warfare" implements the change slowly, one "chunk" at a time. After many small wins, the entire organization has been changed. Coercion requires an edict from an authoritarian figure that directs everyone to cooperate. As discussed earlier, these techniques can backfire and create more and stronger resistance. They must be used with care and only when other techniques have failed to effect the cooperation of the target group.

Defining how a new process or task will be reinforced should be part of the change management plan. The organization cannot assume people will be content with adopting new ways of working without building in specific incentives. Without refreezing, the entire change management effort will fail. With well-thought-out incentives and other mechanisms, the new approaches will succeed and will do so more quickly, thus helping to mediate the negative consequences of change.

Brynjolfsson proposes the 90/10 rule as illustrated in Figure 10-6.[21] When an organization embarks on an IT improvement effort, they expect 90 percent of the effort to go into finding or developing the best hardware and software for the solution, and only 10 percent of the effort directed toward management of the change. This perception is the opposite of the reality. The technical solution is usually the easiest part of the job. Getting the organization to embrace it is the difficult part.

▪ ▪ ▪ ▪ ▪ ▪ ▪ ▪ ▪ ▪ ▪ FIGURE 10-6   Why Improvement Efforts Fail.

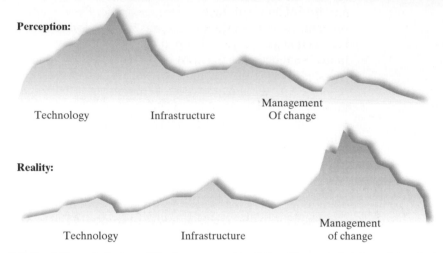

Erik Brynjolfsson: **Software and Hardware account for 10% ... The rest is devising and introducing**

Source: Brynjolfsson, Erik, *http://ebusiness.mit.edu/erik/*

It is important to remember that change is continuous in today's fast-paced, flexible business world. The three phases of unfreezing, change, and refreezing follow each other on a regular basis. In the popular bestseller about change, *Who Moved My Cheese?*,[22] Spencer Johnson discusses the problems people have with embracing change as opposed to resisting it. Using change as a positive force that opens up new opportunities is the goal. Those who do embrace change succeed and people who resist change are left out of the organizational growth. Change will continue to happen: people must adapt and leaders must show the way.

▪ ▪ ▪ Elements of Change Management

It should be clear at this point that change management is a complex managerial task. Researchers have studied it, dissected it, and tried to publish approaches and techniques to help the practicing manager. In this chapter, we have highlighted some of the work that should be useful for the IT manager acting as an agent of change. One author, Kanter, has summarized the elements in the planning of change, as shown in Figure 10-7.[23] In general this is a restatement of the things we have been discussing

▪ ▪ ▪ ▪ ▪ ▪ ▪ ▪ ▪ ▪ ▪ FIGURE 10-7   Eight Elements in the Planning of Change.

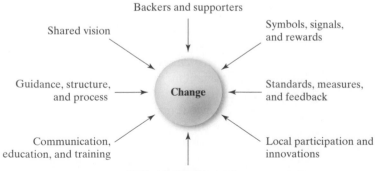

Source: Kanter, Rosabeth Moss, *Evolve!*, Harvard Business School Press, 2001.

in this chapter, with a slightly different view that may be useful for some readers. The figure shows eight elements surrounding the process of change, with each element encompassing key aspects of the change process:

- "Guidance, Structure and Process" shown on the left, incorporates the leadership strategy and process design for the change. This is the beginning of the vision and where the change sponsor and change agent lay out the path to the future reshaped process or organization.
- "Shared Vision" describes the need to involve the target population in the creation of the vision of the end point of the change. This step serves to bring everyone on board by incorporating their ideas into the vision.
- The "backers and supporters" includes the roles discussed in "Stakeholder Roles in Managing Change." A thorough plan includes understanding all the issues various segments of those affected will have. The target population is not explicitly shown in the figure, but is included in the circle of change.
- "Symbols, Signals, and Rewards" addresses the need to explicitly design incentives to encourage the target population to embrace the change. This is a key part of bringing about refreezing.
- "Standards, Measures, and Feedback" defines the need to incorporate an evaluation step in this process as all well-designed projects do. Every change management process should be viewed as a project in the project management sense and carried out with the discipline associated with that approach.
- "Local Participation and Innovations" builds on the advice from Jack Welch about letting your best people alone to carry out their innovative ideas, and emphasizes the importance of involving the target population in all aspects of the change process.
- "Policy and Systems Review" reminds us that the impact of the new procedures must be understood and anticipated as part of the change plan. Areas where people will gain or lose power must be addressed explicitly.
- "Communication, Education, and Training" emphasizes the importance of committing resources to doing this step well, throughout the change process and as part of the refreezing goal.

This summary diagram can serve as a useful checklist against which to measure the plans for a change management process.

▪▪▪ Classic Mistakes in Managing Change

Despite having all the best intentions, senior managers have difficulty in avoiding well-known mistakes in implementing change. The following classic mistakes are adapted from Manzoni.[24]

First, there are many factors involved in why employees resist change. Too often management assumes that employees "know how to behave in the way the company wants, could do so if they wanted, but don't want to."[25] This is an example of addressing the symptoms of a problem without addressing its causes. Managers may be overlooking structural issues related to the new process, to learning technology, to the ever-present social inertia of the existing culture, to the inadequate skill sets of employees, and to the behavior of senior managers which results in inappropriate employee behavior. To focus solely on believing employees do not want to cooperate is a dangerous simplification.

Second, change takes time and managers need to be persistent. This is not unlike raising children. Desired behavior must be reinforced over many years to achieve the result. Companies have to reinforce new behavior repeatedly and may experience people falling back into old patterns even five to ten years after a change has been implemented. "The second major cause of unsuccessful implementation of change is insufficient time and energy given to managing the process and marketing the change to employees."[26]

Third, managers fall into the trap of thinking that if they focus on what is going to be achieved, this will ensure the cooperation of the target population. In so doing they do not invest enough time in setting the clear path to the goal. The employees want to know how to get from Point A to Point B, not how great it is going to be when they get there.

Fourth, the scarcest resource is managerial time. The change plan must allow enough time for those involved to carry out their assigned tasks. If the best managers and people are assigned to too many projects and committees, they may not have the critical mass of time necessary to ensure the success of the change project. Yet, the organization needs the talents and skills of its best people focused on the change.

Fifth, while it is true that human nature resists change, managers who expect a strong emotional response can end up triggering that response through their own behavior. For example, they may exhibit secretive behavior and discuss the change process in a guarded manner. This can backfire and end up encouraging the hostile resistance that they expected. Anticipating resistance is an important part of the plan. However, it is also important to listen to the target population and credit them with having some insight into the issues. It should not be automatically assumed that everyone suffers from the "NIH" ("not invented here") syndrome. The employees need to be brought into the plan because they will have something valuable to contribute.

Sixth, there is a temptation when time is running out to resort to coercive management techniques rather than inclusive ones. Rather than work to get employee cooperation, managers begin to hand down declarations of "Just do it!" This technique invariably backfires. People may appear to be marching in line, but this approach encourages resistance and the creation of counterimplementation plans, as described earlier by Keen. "The only thing such directives achieve is to weaken the credibility of the senior managers who signed them."[27]

Finally, the argument for why a change is being implemented is often supported as a way to increase shareholder value. For most employees the "shareholder" is a very distant concept. As discussed earlier, it is important for employees to see a personal return on their investment of time and energy. Value for employees attempting to accomplish their work must be built into the vision. Nebulous concepts of value and good do not help to convince anyone to buy into the change process.

As change is becoming a way of life in today's organization, it becomes more important that all employees receive education in change management. Businesses need to consider change management as an important element in career development for all employees and especially for managers.

▪▪▪ Transnational Issues

In this discussion so far, we have been addressing change management issues in a general sense and not introducing the complications that accompany change when dealing with more than one nationality and/or culture. There is an entire set of issues that increase the complexity of managing change in transnational organizations.

Transnational organizations are defined as those corporations whose aim is to simultaneously achieve global efficiency, local responsiveness, and learning on a

▪▪▪▪▪▪▪▪▪▪▪ **FIGURE 10-8   Localization Barriers.**

- Languages
- Cultures, values
- Business practices
- Taste
- Competitors
- Proximity to local customer
- Risk
- Cost
- Pace
- Food
- Authority
- National and regional protectionism
- Laws, regulations, tariffs
- Communications weakness
- Labor unions
- Transportation
- Quality of labor
- New technology
- Organization

worldwide basis.[28] These organizations run into countless barriers to communication and cooperation because of the myriad of local cultures included in their corporate families. Figure 10-8[29] presents a list of the localization barriers that organizations must consider when managing change. When the change involves the implementation of IT, the additional fears associated with new technologies will add to the complexity of the event.

There are numerous tales of companies that have introduced products and services in international marketplaces without understanding the local customs. They make amusing anecdotes after the fact, but illustrate how ethnocentric a company can be: McDonald's introducing burgers into the market in India where a large percentage of the population is vegetarian and cows are thought to be sacred; Microsoft using the advertising slogan "Where do you want to go today?" in Japan, where it translates as "If you don't know where you want to go, we'll make sure you get taken." How such large and successful corporations overlook the planning required to introduce new products and ideas into cultures different from their own should be a lesson to all businesses.

Very simple differences, like the traditions associated with the use of colors, can spell disaster when misunderstood. For example, look at the various meanings of the color red in Table 10-1.

TABLE 10-1

Country	Meaning of Color Red
China	Happiness
Egypt	Death
France	Aristocracy
India	Life, creativity
Japan	Anger, danger
United States	Danger

▪▪▪▪▪▪▪▪▪

In China, the traditional wedding dress for the bride is red. What interpretation would people in the United States have if a bride wore red? It is important for organizations to research and understand cultural differences. This is part of the job of the change agent who is laying out the pathway to the vision. In Figure 10-9[30] how different cultures view other cultures is illustrated and provides insight into why negotiations and implementing change can be especially challenging in cross-cultural situations. While many of these views can be judged as stereotypes, it is important to remember that stereotypes can influence how people act. That perception can influence an individual with power equivalent to fact.

The key to understanding the transnational complexity is performing a thorough stakeholder analysis that includes understanding the characteristics of each stakeholder in much more detail than when looking within a company's home culture. While it may seem that these suggestions have taken us far away from the IT organization, this is not true. Transnational firms must be concerned about implementing systems in their locations worldwide. This means they will run into these issues in dealing with a variety of cultures and norms. The IT executive implementing technology outside of his or her "home" country will be well served to focus on the following tasks for each stakeholder.[31]

- Research on the stakeholder's city and country, including geographic context and size;
- Learn pronunciation of names;
- Research political, economic, religious, social, intellectual, and artistic contexts;
- Learn about customs and taboos;
- Learn how foreign executives view and use time;
- Seek advice from others who have interacted with managers from the same location and/or company;
- Find out as much as possible about the individuals you will be dealing with: for example, latest local company issues, position in hierarchy, career path, family (if appropriate);
- Assess your own prejudices about the people and location.

Even in countries where Americans feel comfortable, there can be serious cultural differences. The story of Singapore, the "Gateway to Asia,"[32] shown in the sidebar is an enlightening example. Many U.S. corporations choose to establish their first foothold in the Asian marketplace in Singapore because of its Western ways. But even these can be deceiving because at its core, Singapore is not Western, but rather has very distinct Eastern values.

▪▪▪▪▪▪▪▪▪▪▪▪ **FIGURE 10-9 Cross-Cultural Stereotypes.**

	American	Arab	Chinese	Japanese	Scandinavian
American		Ritualistic	Controlling	Formal	Careful
Arab	Work-oriented		Callous	Consentient	Egalitarian
Chinese	Patronizing	Religious		Participative	Environmental
Japanese	Direct	Pushy	Power-centered		Matter-of-fact
Scandinavian	Profit-centered	Rhetorical	Secretive	Sexist	

Singapore—Gateway to Asia

Singapore has been called the "Gateway to Asia" by many firms interested in doing business in the Asian marketplace. Westerners feel comfortable in Singapore because it is a modern, technology-savvy place:

- 61 percent of homes have a personal computer
- 75 percent of the country is served by cell phones
- 99 percent of households are reached by Singapore One broadband network.

But while Singapore is stable with a largely English-speaking population, sophisticated computer and networking infrastructure, and a heterogeneous population, there are factors that make it challenging for U.S. organizations:

- Skilled labor and available housing are both scarce and expensive;
- There is no street congestion or air and noise pollution because the number of cars and drivers is strictly regulated: you must win a lottery and then pay $10,000 for a driver's license (the average midsized car costs $100,000);
- The government is heavily involved in everything from recruitment to regulation—that is, the government is your business partner, like it or not;
- The business-friendly government is not so friendly in other ways; it restricts expression, entertainment, and political dissent to a degree that feels oppressive to most Westerners.

Appearances can be deceiving—Singapore feels Western but the fact is that doing business there requires careful planning and much adaptation on the part of Western employees.

Thorough preparation will position the change agent to anticipate issues and avoid a serious cultural *faux pas* when implementing change. Nevertheless, the complexity of the change process is multiplied when change is being undertaken in a cross-cultural setting. Organizations should ensure the expertise of those assigned to enact change in a transnational organization. Careful application of the change management techniques and team building concepts will help the sponsor and change agent achieve success in this risky undertaking. The 80/20 rule applies here: 80 percent of the work is done in planning and setting the stage for the change; 20 percent in enacting the change.

▪▪▪ Change—An Inevitable Part of Life and Work

Change is inevitable and resisting change is natural. This dichotomy summarizes the challenges that face any organization in implementing change. The IT manager confronts change management on a daily basis. Technology is the conduit that brings almost constant change to organizations. The implementation of new hardware, software, and telecommunications is a never-ending evolution as organizations strive to have the best tools to support their people and processes. The challenge to every firm is to grab onto change as an opportunity and not as a threat.

The lessons from *Who Moved My Cheese?* endure:

- Change happens (They keep moving the cheese)
- Anticipate change (Get ready for the cheese to move)
- Monitor change (Smell the cheese often so you know when it is getting old)

- Adapt to change quickly (The quicker you let go of old cheese the sooner you can enjoy new cheese)
- Change (Move with the cheese)
- Enjoy change (Savor the adventure and enjoy the taste of new cheese)
- Be ready to change quickly and enjoy it again and again (They keep moving the cheese).[33]

REVIEW QUESTIONS ▪▪▪▪▪▪▪

1. What is change management?
2. What are the negative impacts on an organization during a change management process?
3. Describe the three phases of the Lewin-Schein model.
4. How does pain play a positive role in change management?
5. What factors motivate change?
6. What is meant by the phrase *counterimplementation*?
7. Why is team building an important aspect of change management?
8. What are the eight characteristics of effectively functioning teams?
9. What are the four keys to implementing change?
10. Why is understanding stakeholders an important approach to change management?
11. What are reasons people resist change?
12. Describe the issues of change management in transnational organizations.

DISCUSSION QUESTIONS ▪▪▪▪▪▪▪

1. Does your company provide change management training/education for your employees?
2. Does your company employ change management professionals who assist in change processes?
3. Describe how the implementation of IT involves change management issues.
4. To what extent do implicit models control our thinking?
5. What unique challenges face the transnational organization regarding change management?

AREAS FOR RESEARCH ▪▪▪▪▪▪▪

1. Read Edgar Schein, *Organizational Culture and Leadership* for a better understanding of the Lewin-Schein model.[34]
2. Read James Belasco, *Teaching the Elephant to Dance,* for a good general background on change management.[35]
3. Read Spencer Johnson, *Who Moved My Cheese?*, for an interesting look at resisting change.[36]
4. For a general background in what makes teams successful, read Larson and LaFasto, *TeamWork*.[37]
5. Read Kegan and Lahey for more detail on "competing commitments."[38]

CONCLUSION ▪▪▪▪▪▪▪

This chapter has looked at the challenges associated with the management of change. These challenges reach beyond the IT organization as a pervasive problem organization-wide. However, the IT management must ~~REFERENCES~~ changes in virtually every technology implementation undertaken. Research on techniques for change management was presented, including detail on team building as an important tool for successful change management. The chapter also discussed the special challenges associated with change in transnational organizations.

REFERENCES ▪▪▪▪▪▪▪

[1] Darwin, Charles, *The Origin of the Species*, *http://www.literature.org/authors/darwin-charles/ the-origin-of-species-6th-edition/*
[2] Machiavelli, 1513.
[3] Kling, Rob, "Social Informatics," *http://www.slis.indiana.edu/si/si2001.html*
[4] Schein, Edgar, *Organizational Culture and Leadership,* 2nd Edition, Jossey-Bass (1992) ISBN 1-55542-487-2.
[5] *Ibid.*
[6] Volkoff, Olga and Newson, E.F. Peter, "Nortel— Re-Inventing Information Systems," Ivey Management Services, 1997-05-28.
[7] Bullen, Christine V., and Bennett, John L., "Groupware in Practice: An Interpretation of Work Experience," MIT Center for Information Systems Research Working Paper, no. 205, March 1990.

8 Keen, Peter, G.W., "Information Systems and Organizational Change," MIT Center for Information Systems Research Working Paper, no. 55, May 1980.

9 Connor, Daryl, *Managing at the Speed of Change*, New York: Random House, (1992).

10 Keen, *Op.Cit.*

11 *Ibid.*

12 Belasco, James, *Teaching the Elephant to Dance*, *http://www.belasco.com/elephant.htm*

13 *Ibid.*

14 Welch, Jack: "How Good a Manager?" *Business Week*, December 14, 1987, pp. 38–41.

15 Larson, Carl E., and LaFasto, Frank M.J., *TeamWork: What Must Go Right/What Can Go Wrong*, Sage Publications (1989).

16 *Adapted from Rosabeth Moss Kanter, Evolve!*, Harvard Business School Press (2001).

17 *Kegan, Robert and Lahey, Lisa Laskow*, "The Real Reason People Won't Change," *Harvard Business Review*, November 2001.

18 *Ibid.*, p. 85.

19 *Ibid.*, p. 91.

20 Rangan, V.K. and Bell, M., "Merrill Lynch: Integrated Choice," Harvard Business Case 9-500-090, Revised 3/14/01.

21 Brynjolfsson, Erik, *http://ebusiness.mit.edu/erik/*

22 Johnson, Spencer, M.D., *Who Moved My Cheese?*, G.P. Putnam's Sons (1998).

23 Kanter, Rosabeth Moss, *Evolve!*, Harvard Business School Press, 2001, pp. 256–7.

24 Manzoni, Jean-Francois, "Classic Mistakes in Managing Change," *Financial Times*, 10/12/01.

25 *Ibid.*

26 *Ibid.*

27 *Ibid.*

28 Prahalad and Doz, *The Multinational Mission: Balancing Local Demands and Global Vision*, Free Press, (1987).

29 Luftman, Jerry N., *Competing in the Information Age*, Oxford University Press (1996).

30 Bjerke, Bjorn, *Leadership and Culture*, Edward Elgar, 2001, ISBN1-84064-627-6.

31 Adapted from Deep, Sam and Sussman, Lyle, *Smart Moves for People in Charge*, Perseus Publishing (1995).

32 Field, Tom, "First Stop, Singapore," *CIO Magazine*, July 1, 2001, pp 89–94.

33 Johnson, Spencer, M.D., *Who Moved my Cheese?*, G.P. Putnam's Sons (1998).

34 Schein, Edgar, *Organizational Culture and Leadership*. 2nd Edition, Jossey-Bass (1992) ISBN 1-55542-487-2.

35 Belasco, James, *Teaching the Elephant to Dance*, *http://www.belasco.com/elephant.htm*

36 Johnson, Spencer, M.D., *Who Moved My Cheese?*, G.P. Putnam's Sons (1998).

37 Larson, Carl E., and LaFasto, Frank M.J., *TeamWork: What Must Go Right/What Can Go Wrong*, Sage Publications (1989).

38 Kegan, Robert and Lahey, Lisa Laskow, "The Real Reason People Won't Change," *Harvard Business Review*, November 2001.

CHAPTER 11

IT Governance

"The king reigns but does not govern."
—JAN ZAMOYSKI

"Every cook needs to learn how to govern the state."
—VLADIMIR ILICH ULYANOV ("LENIN")

Preview of Chapter

The complexities of information technology in the 21st century require organizations to make informed decisions about how best to leverage IT. Most importantly, organizations need to ensure that the decisions about deploying IT are aligned with the organization's strategic business objectives (see Chapter 2—IT Strategy for a broader discussion of alignment). Organizations also need to ensure that decisions about the strategic direction and deployment of IT are consistent across the firm and that they are in harmony with the organizational culture. Successful organizations in today's information economy integrate IT and business strategies and leverage customers and partners in a web of relationships that share information. How, then, should organizations make decisions about the deployment of IT? Which projects should be funded? Should organizations "make" or "buy" systems and software? Who should be the decision-maker? How should organizations make decisions about partners and alliances? And lastly, what processes should organizations use to make these critical decisions?

What we will examine in this chapter:

- The definition of IT governance
- Why IT governance is an issue for organizations
- Why formal IT governance mechanisms are needed
- IT governance alternatives
- Forms of governance and leadership roles in cross-functional initiatives
- Steering committees—their composition and critical success factors
- Prioritizing projects and assessing risk
- Global considerations

▥ Introduction

IT governance is the term used to describe the selection and use of organizational processes to make decisions about how to obtain and deploy IT resources and competencies.[1] In short, IT governance is about:

- *Who* makes these decisions (power)
- *Why* they make them (alignment)
- *How* they make them (decision process)

Ideally, business and IT management jointly make these decisions. Underlying the principles of IT governance is the theme of effective and efficient communication between IT and business. This is critical for appropriate decision-making regarding IT.

Business management's expectation of its investment in IT is that it will result in some improvement in the delivery of service to its customers/clients, reduce the cost to manufacture or deliver some product or service to its customers/clients, or shorten the cycle time required to develop and produce some new product or service. In short, business management's expectation is that its investments in IT will produce added business value.

The gap between business' expectations of its return on its IT investment and IT management's tendency to overpromise and underdeliver are evidenced in many organizations as symptoms of misalignment:

- Poor business IT understanding and rapport
- Competitive decline
- Frequently fired IT manager(s)
- High turnover of IT professionals
- Inappropriate resources (HR, $$)
- Frequent IT reorganizations
- Lack of executive interest in IT (absent champion/sponsor)
- Lack of vision/strategy
- No communication between IT and users
- Ongoing conflicts between business and IT
- Unselective outsourcing of the entire IT function
- Productivity decrease
- Projects:
  - Not Used
  - Canceled
  - Late
- Redundancies in systems development
- Absent systemic competencies (key IT capabilities that create competitive advantage)
- Systems integration difficult (e.g., standards, politics)
- Unhappy users/complaints

For many business managers, the promises they hear from IT management versus the reality have led to a substantial credibility gap regarding the value of IT.[2] These considerations are discussed in Chapter 2—IT Strategy, Chapter 3—Strategic Alignment Maturity, and Chapter 14—Assessing the Value of IT. Long lists of symptoms of IT-business alignment problems are a symptom of alignment problems.

Historically, IT management has focused on the promise of new technologies to address discrete business problems, but has failed to marry technology capabilities and resources to the overall needs of the business in an integrated fashion. Without having the commitment of business to actively participate and leverage the technology to change how they do things, IT has little chance of achieving, let alone demonstrating its contribution to, value (see Value of IT—Chapter 14). For example, when IT management of many organizations began to see the potential of the digital revolution and e-commerce to transform business, business management often responded with one or more of the following rationales for not pursuing this important technology as part of the organization's business and IT strategy:

- We're doing too well financially (there is no sense of urgency).
- Change is too difficult, and no one has the appetite for this much change.
- We have too many other priorities.
- We are in the midst of a turnaround and cannot focus on digital innovation.
- E-commerce is just a fad.
- We don't know how to do it.
- It's not in our current business plan.
- It's not in our budget.
- It's not part of our vision.
- We don't want to alienate our existing customers.
- We don't want to upset our sales and distribution channels.
- Our customers are not digital-ready.
- Our employees are not digital-ready.
- We can not afford to spend money on the digital infrastructure.
- Our management team is not digital-savvy.
- We are already too late.

Given this perceived lack of interest on the part of executive business management to embrace the promise of the "digital revolution," IT management often launched initiatives on its own to "Web-enable" business processes—often selling the perceived benefits of going digital to middle managers or local project sponsors.

"Pure Strategic Thinking"

Or so bubbles the "CEO" in the recent television advertisement for a major e-commerce solutions company as he joins a conference room filled with the senior IT management of the firm. He proceeds to enthusiastically tell the IT management team how he's just spent $2 million on "the best bit of strategic thinking our consultants have ever done." Better yet, this executive tells the "IT guys" how this strategy has the "real possibility to transform" their firm. He then asks IT management if they can implement this strategy. After a brief exchange of weary glances among the IT managers, the universal answer is "No!" The CEO looks surprised and disappointed. What surprises *you* most about the situation depicted in this advertisement:

a. That a "transforming" business strategy was developed without input from IT management?
b. That executive business management had no clue about the IT capabilities of their own organization?
c. All of the above?
d. None of the above?

The unfortunate result of many of these IT-sponsored or "local" initiatives (substitute any technology you wish in this example: CRM, document management systems, supply chain management, ERP, etc.—the result is the same) is that they collectively failed to generate the best possible return on the enterprise's overall investment in IT. When decisions about IT investments are made either by business management without active involvement of IT management—or vice versa—the inevitable result is an investment that performs poorly or not at all (see "Pure Strategic Thinking" sidebar). Worse yet, in many organizations the responsibility for setting the strategic direction of IT is not clear.

The common theme of these disconnects between business and IT is governance or the lack of it. The lack of governance affects the organization's ability to make informed decisions about the direction and use of IT. In short, this type of organizational disconnect will exist when the organization's IT governance is not clearly defined, is "immature,"[3] or under some form of political threat by internal constituencies.

In brief, IT governance addresses how to prioritize and select projects, and how to appropriately allocate IT resources (e.g., staff, budget). A list of some IT governance alternatives is provided later in this chapter. Not any one alternative can assure effective business-IT alignment, but the appropriate combination of most of them can lead to sustained alignment. Typically there are separate executive committees that address strategic, tactical, and operational activities. Frequently, it is the assessment of the governance alternatives that becomes the initial charge of a *strategic steering committee*.

To have a strategic steering committee comprised of a group of IT and functional business executives at any of the three levels (strategic, tactical, operational) meeting on a regular basis is considered to be among the best practices for strategic alignment. Successful IT steering committees concentrate their attention on all of the governance alternatives. Gaining the commitment from these executives is difficult. Keeping their commitment is even harder. The critical success factors for effective steering committees, described later in this chapter, are important for all three levels of steering committees (strategic, tactical, and operational). How they are addressed and their relative importance may differ.

To ensure success, appropriate value measurements must be selected and continuously tracked. Stakeholders ought to be aware of the measurements and the actions that will be taken based on their results. IT's value should be demonstrated in terms of their contribution to the business. These measurements should affirm IT's role as an enabler or driver for providing the organization with an opportunity to do something new, or allow the organization to perform better, faster or cheaper. At a minimum IT must understand the priorities of business value measurements and how the business perceives the contributions of IT. The value of IT is discussed in Chapter 14.

▪▪▪ Some Definitions of IT Governance

IT governance is the operating model for how the organization will make decisions about the use of information technology. IT governance addresses decisions about the allocation of resources, the evaluation of business initiatives and risk, prioritization of projects, performance measurements and tracking mechanisms, determinations of cost and their assignment (i.e., how IT costs are allocated), and the assessment of the value of an IT investment.

Also, just as business governance (see Chapter 2) is concerned with make-buy decisions in business strategy, IT governance is also concerned with external relationships for obtaining IT resources. These relationships may embrace mechanisms such as strategic alliances, partnerships, outsourcing, spin-offs, joint ventures (for developing new IT capabilities), and licensing activities.

IT governance involves authority, control, accountability, roles, and responsibilities among organizational units and their management for making decisions about the use of IT. The dynamics of these relationships are crucial to an organization's effective use of IT in an economic climate of increasing uncertainty and the need for ever-more-rapid strategic responses to the uncertainty of the external environment. A well-structured governance model is an important prerequisite in large, complex organizations for making effective and *efficient* decisions about the investment of scarce capital and human resources. In essence, IT governance involves important aspects of organizational power—*who has the authority* to make decisions about IT?

IT governance involves the organization's *processes and methods for making decisions* about IT investments or obtaining IT resources. These processes include the funding model for IT investments, the methods used to evaluate project cost and potential business value, project risk assessment methodologies, the procedures used to identify potential business initiatives, and the processes used to measure the value of IT.

Embedded within governance processes are also judgments about how well a decision about the use of IT enables or drives the strategic direction—the business objectives—of the organization. IT governance, then, addresses important aspects of *alignment* of IT and business—in other words, *why a decision is made about the use of IT*. As discussed in Chapter 2, the alignment of IT with the business (and vice versa) is a critical component of overall business strategic effectiveness.

▪▪▪ Why Is IT Governance an Issue?

Despite the growing evidence that IT has become an integral part of business, IT governance is still an issue for many organizations. While the governance models for marketing or finance are rarely discussed, the governance model for IT for many organizations is still neither well understood nor well executed, and becomes a topic of debate. Why is this?

In part, the reason for this ongoing debate is that the dominant business culture still does not value IT as an integral part of the business. In large measure, governance reflects the importance the executive management of the organization places on the component parts of the organization. Executive culture understands and values financial measures and treats employees as fungible assets rather than as investments to be nurtured.[4] Based on its historically poor performance in delivering or demonstrating business value, and the tendency of the IT management culture to focus on itself (i.e., on the technology profession, and the hardware and software components of technology) and not on the business, executive business management too often tends to view IT as a "support" function rather than as a legitimate partner for generating business value.

Decisions about the use of support functions generally don't require executive business input or involvement, and the governance mechanisms for dealing with support or commodity-like functions are usually relegated to lower administrative levels of the organization's management structure. For example, it would be highly unlikely that the head of a strategic business unit or the CEO of a large organization would be involved in decisions about which cafeteria service company to use or which supplier of electric power should be used for the firm. The governance models for these types of decisions are straightforward and appropriately relegated to middle management or the heads of functional departments responsible for these supporting operations.

This devaluation of the importance of IT as a strategic asset by executive management is evident in many organizations: the absence (or minimal contribution) of the CIO on most executive management committees while the chief financial officer (CFO) and the heads of marketing, product development, or manufacturing sit on these very same committees. Yet, at the same time, the organization must make decisions about the use of IT that cuts across many of these same organizational functions! Dysfunctional governance models are the inevitable result of organizational cultures that do not value IT.[4]

The Business Case Issue

Should business cases be applied to all Information Technology projects? When is a business case not appropriate? Decades have passed. Billions of dollars have been invested. Applying Information Technology (IT) in an appropriate and timely way, in harmony with business strategy, goals, and needs, still remains a key concern of business executives. Of the measurements presented in Chapter 14 –Assessing the Value of IT what should be considered? Is it more practical to just do the IT project or just do the financial analysis? Many managers realize that information is among their company's most important assets. However, many do not know how to leverage their investments in information technology.

Financial methods are important, but not to the exclusion of others. For an organization to perform well it must balance all of its measurements. It must balance its impact on customers/clients (e.g., profits, services, satisfaction, flexibility, differentiation), processes (e.g., time to market, productivity, quality), people (e.g., motivation, morale, job satisfaction, learning, social), and finance (e.g., ROI, activity based costing). For many applications a business case is not even considered. Organizations just do it! Cases in point include:

1. Maintenance, especially fixing application problems. Most of IT's people resource is dedicated to the preservation of the technical infrastructure. How many companies performed a financial analysis to decide whether or not to address Y2K? Albeit, some might have applied portfolio management to select which approach to employ.
2. Government legislation requirements to ensure compliance must be performed (e.g., tax laws and reporting demands).
3. CEO or senior executive has a "hot" idea. These projects receive top priority.
4. Competitor's innovative application of IT. This might be a matter of survival. The second, third, and nth bank considering ATMs did not perform a financial justification.

Typically, important strategic applications do not require traditional financial assessments. Therefore, you might consider the request to prepare a business case on a project to be an indicator that additional marketing must be performed to senior management. IT must comply and prepare a business case when it is requested. But, that does not diminish the need to sell the strategic business implications of the project to the key stakeholders. Consider leveraging the six enablers and inhibitors (see Table 11-1 and discussion in Chapter 2—IT Strategy). Frequent requests to keep IT

TABLE 11-1 Enablers and Inhibitors to Alignment[3]

	Enablers	*Inhibitors*
1	Senior executive support for IT	IT/business lack close relationships
2	IT involved in strategy development	IT does not prioritize well
3	IT understands the business	IT fails to meet commitments
4	Business—IT partnership	IT does not understand business
5	Well-prioritized IT projects	Senior executives do not support IT
6	IT demonstrates leadership	IT management lacks leadership

costs down and continuous treatment of IT as a cost center are other indicators for more effective marketing of the value of IT to the business. Focus on business measurements like profits, time to market, morale, new services, and quality.

Financial executives who are comfortable with accounting data and see project evaluation in traditional accounting and financial terms favor business cases. Traditional financial measurements should be rethought. Senior executives are beginning to reduce their emphasis on cost cutting. They are focusing their attention on business growth. Often, they are seeing the opportunity to leverage IT as the enabler or driver to meet these objectives. IT should strive to be measured in terms of business value, not just financial cost.

Often the problem is that too much attention is placed on the technology itself rather than its links with other business operations, customer value, and management decision-making. Companies race to have state-of-the-art technology without considering how it will impact other components of the business. The benefit does NOT come from the technology. The benefit comes from the new products/services or the enhanced business processes made available from the innovative application of the technology. Chapter 14—Assessing the Value of IT describes an approach that combines portfolio management, options, and value management that has proven very effective. If traditional financial measurements are the primary vehicle applied to ensure that the project focus is on the business, more thought should be given to the business—IT relationship and the measurements being applied.

The long-term implications of technology on the business are difficult to assess. For example, retail banks invested heavily in automatic teller machines (ATMs) in the 1980s, believing them an essential aspect of customer service and critical to maintaining market share. As a result, ATMs rapidly ceased to be a competitive advantage and instead became an added cost of doing business.

The point here is not that any individual bank made an inappropriate decision, but that ROI alone does not always paint the entire picture, let alone an accurate one. It is a story that has parallels in many other industries (e.g., airline, brokerage, retail, petroleum).

The business area, because of their different perspective, may not see ROI the same way as IT does. It is desirous to have the business see the project as a vehicle for competitive advantage rather than solely for financial advantage. In any case, how often does your organization conduct a postproject review to assess the achievement of the ROI? For example, frequently the ROI is defined in terms of reduced headcount. If all of the headcount reductions projected by project plans were taken into account, there would be even more employees downsized.

While addressing the project value, another important consideration is the inability of IT to meet its project deadlines. This is a problem that has plagued businesses since the introduction of the modern computer three decades ago. Too often IT is overwhelmed by all it has to do. Frequent requests changing the requirements of IT projects driven by changing business demands severely hinders a project team's ability to meet commitments. Business executives and end users become increasingly upset that projects are late and over budget. Recent studies by *Forrester Research*™ (suggest that 30 percent of IT projects are cancelled before completion; 50 to 100 percent are over budget, and six to twelve months late. The IT—business relationship that exists plays a major role in addressing this pervasive problem. Should IT be considered a credible business partner in light of its chronic inability to meet its commitments?

How can IT achieve a harmonious relationship with business functions? This crucial question needs to be addressed in order to respond to many of the important issues raised regarding assessing the value of projects. There are known enablers and inhibitors that help and hinder business—IT alignment (discussed in Chapter 2). IT executives experience them daily.

IT and business must work together to define and implement the prioritized projects to meet the competitive demands of the firm. This requires a good relationship (all components of alignment maturity:[3] communications, partnership, skills, value measurements, technology, governance) among the team members. The team needs to work together in business terms to assess a balanced set of measurements. ROI is only one available vehicle. IT must understand the business and be considered a valuable business partner. To do this effectively demands senior executive support. To earn this role, IT must do an effective job in marketing/communicating the business value available from leveraging information technology.

Why Have Governance?

Organizations that cannot structure their IT governance model waste precious resources—capital, time, and human—in an era where time is of the essence, capital is in short supply, and truly qualified IT people are always hard to find.

Diagnosing Poor or "Broken" IT Governance

How do we know when IT governance is a problem? When organizations "present" symptoms of poor or broken IT governance we often see/hear the following comments from business or IT management:

- "We have too many people and organizations making decisions about technology."
- "Business units aren't accountable to corporate IT for any technologies they decide to employ."
- "We have no enterprise architecture because we cannot agree on how it will be established or maintained."
- "We spend too much on hardware and software because we cannot agree on a common sourcing policy."
- "We are measuring our performance, but the business doesn't understand what our measures mean."
- "We do not measure the success of IT. I would not know where to begin."

You be the consultant.

Why do organizations need an IT governance model? The very environment in which IT management must cope gives ample reasons:

- Insufficient resources to meet current and future commitments
- Unreliable delivery schedules resulting from insufficient staff and requirements changes
- Lack of focus on daily operations due to utilizing IT operations and maintenance staff on projects
- Reduced quality of delivered projects
- Potential for working on the wrong things
- Business functions begin to move in their own IT direction to satisfy their own requirements with minimal or no IT support
- Chaotic/nonstandard infrastructure, resulting in poor operational maintainability[5]
- Poor communications and relationships between IT and business

How Critical Is Governance for E-Business?

IT governance is an especially critical issue when considering e-business operating alternatives. Organizations considering various e-business operating models will need to make early fundamental decisions about how the e-business itself is governed (i.e., is it a subsidiary or is it a seamless part of the existing operating model?).[6] Equally important are the IT governance issues that need to be addressed in establishing a viable e-business—especially as the corporate governance models evolve.[7]

- Who makes decisions about which e-business initiatives to fund?
- Who has accountability for e-business IT architecture?
- Who drives e-business initiatives (i.e., marketing, IT, customers, etc.)?
- How are e-business initiatives funded?
- How will we measure the business value of e-business initiatives?
- How will we allocate resources to e-business initiatives?
- Will we outsource any of our e-business operations?
- How will we leverage our strategic alliances, if at all?

Organizations that have addressed these governance issues "up front," such as Cisco, Dell, USAA, and Amazon have consistently demonstrated better alignment between their corporate vision and strategy and their e-business initiatives—and consequently higher business value from their e-business investments.

For IT management to fulfill the promise of information technology to the business, it must:

1. Ensure that decisions about the use of IT are made *jointly*—by business and IT management.
2. Develop *mutual* and agreed-upon expectations among business and IT.
3. Help senior business management understand the costs and risks associated with IT investment and help them make the best possible decisions.
4. Provide the IT capabilities required to implement the decisions made in item 3.
5. Monitor and measure the value of the business' IT investments.
6. Help senior business management understand that this is an *ongoing* process.[5]

This is possible only with a suitably mature and robust IT governance model for the organization.

Governance Alternatives

There are several IT governance alternatives that must be considered, each with its strengths and drawbacks. Large organizations should employ more than one mechanism as part of an overall governance model:

Budget (The "how" and "why" of financial resources which are allocated to projects)—Though this is the most basic governance mechanism, a flaw with this mechanism is that it tends to promote the perception of IT as a "cost center" rather than as a potential "value center" (see Chapter 14—Assessing the Value of IT).

Career crossover (IT staff working in the business unit; business unit staff working in IT)—This is an excellent alternative and is good for "seeding" business or IT organizations with people who have perspectives that can generate empathy and build relationships and understanding.

CIO-CEO   (Reporting structure having lead IT executive report to lead business executive)—Having the CIO report directly to the CEO has the potential to dramatically energize the organization in its ability to leverage IT for strategic business advantage, if the CIO is a business visionary. According to a March, 2002 survey published by *CIO*™ magazine, approximately 50 percent of CIOs now report directly to the CEO, with approximately 11 percent of CIOs still reporting to the CFO.

Communicate/market/negotiate   (IT staff must learn and continuously execute effectively)—Continually "selling" and "marketing" IT's value to internal constituents will help to change perceptions as long as the ability to deliver value is present. This can degenerate, however, into a process of "deal-making" between IT management and business unit management to fund individual projects as a substitute for more formal decision processes regarding the use of IT as a generator of broader business value (see discussion on Portfolio Management in Chapter 14—Assessing the Value of IT).

Competitive enabler/driver—Demonstrating that IT initiatives can be a significant driver or enabler of competitive advantage can strongly influence business management's willingness to move IT away from being treated as a cost center and towards being regarded as an investment center or profit center.

Education/cross-training   (IT must understand the business; business must understand IT)—Institutionalizing formal training for business executives in their roles and responsibilities regarding IT and, in turn, requiring formal training of IT management and key staff in the operational and management aspects of the business will enhance understanding, rapport, and communication between the communities. In turn, this improved communication will result in improved communication of business needs to IT management and a better understanding by IT management of how these needs are aligned with the strategic objectives of the organization. This requires a substantial sustained investment of time and resources by the organization.

Liaison   (Primary point of contact for facilitating IT business relationship)—This person facilitates the business and IT relationship. They understand and communicate well with both IT and business professionals. Their objective is to ensure effective communications among the communities. Too often the role defined may actually impede effective communication between business and IT by defining the liaison as the only person who can communicate between IT and business.

Location   (Physical placement of IT staff and business staff together)—Co-locating the IT resources with the business resources they support is an underappreciated enabler of effective communication and understanding among IT and the business. Doing this introduces the risk, however, that IT staff may identify more strongly with parochial interests of the business unit at the expense of broader IT professional and corporate interests.

Organization—The degree of centralization of the IT function and organizational lines of reporting (e.g., does the CIO report to the CEO or to the CFO?) is a substantial influencing factor in IT governance.

- *Centralized* IT organizations will have decision-making rights concentrated in the office of the CIO or the equivalent, but will tend to have less effective communications with the business community and less feeling of ownership of IT initiatives and investments.
- *Decentralized* IT organizations will have decision-making rights distributed to the various strategic business units and will enjoy improved communications (and

feelings of ownership of IT initiatives and investments) with the business, but run the risk of developing IT architectures and infrastructure that are not aligned with corporate objectives.

- *Hybrid (or "Federal")* IT organizations attempt to balance these competing interests by centralizing decision rights about "common" (enterprise-wide) IT infrastructure (e.g., e-mail, computing hardware, office productivity software, telecommunications, e-business connectivity standards) while decentralizing IT decision rights to the business units to meet local requirements (e.g., applications). This organizational structure requires more coordination than either centralized or decentralized schemes.

Other organizational alternatives include:

- Traditional structures like centralized, decentralized, geographic, horizontal, vertical, etc.
- Federated (hybrid) structure centralizing infrastructure and decentralizing application support
- Centers of competency (COC) or centers of excellence (COE) that leverage specialized skills
- Insourcing/outsourcing decision identifying what functions to keep in-house and what functions to outsource externally to partners

These organizational alternatives are further discussed in Chapter 8—Organizing IT.

Partnership/Alliance management—Partnerships and alliances are becoming a fact of life in the business strategy and IT strategy of leading firms to gain new competencies, share the risk of developing new IT capabilities, move into new markets, or gain access to new resources.[8] The management of these alliances and partnerships needs to take into account the formal and contractual aspects of governance as well as the interpersonal aspects of the relationship to ensure that goals are set and monitored, specific plans are made for joint activities, and that decision rights are clearly understood and communicated to all parties. The risk inherent in partnerships/alliances is that they, like internal partnerships, require formal and informal management of relationships to be effective, a task often overlooked.

Process (The team structure and approaches that are defined and applied to define strategies, plans, priorities, and make IT decisions)—Many organizations adopt some form of project approval process, which tends to be tied to the budget cycle. Other organizations have developed business systems planning processes that require business units to tie their IT initiatives to specific business plans. Still other organizations have instituted formal processes for making decisions about capital investments in IT. Clearly understood and well-communicated governance processes are a necessary prerequisite to a robust IT governance model, with the risk being that the processes—*rather than the reasons behind the decisions*—may become the focus of the governance model. Also, a formal process devoted to improving IT-business alignment maturity has been used effectively by many organizations.

Shared risks, responsibilities, rewards/penalties (Strong partnership of business and IT leaders)—This approach drives the business and IT communities toward a more partnership-oriented operating model where the responsibility for IT decisions is jointly made by business and IT management and accountability for IT investment results is shared by the business and IT communities. This alternative requires a shared perception of value and trust and is highly dependent on the prevailing organizational culture and its perception of contribution to business value.

Steering committees

- Strategic: senior executives setting "long term" direction
- Tactical: middle management planning
- Operational: day-to-day decisions
  The steering committee approach vests IT decision-making responsibility within a cross-functional body of executive management typically comprised of senior business executives and IT management. Generally considered a "best practice" in the management of IT decisions, the roles and membership of executive steering committees are usually a good indicator of how IT is valued in the organization. The role of an executive IT steering committee should include:
- Clearly stating the business role of IT in the organization
- Identifying the linkages (alignment) between the organization's strategic vision and IT's vision
- Establishing the principles for investing in IT and defining the methodologies and processes by which an IT investment may be made, e.g., presentation of IT investment proposals before the steering committee, demonstrating that the benefits of an IT investment can clear corporate "hurdle rates"
- Establishing ethical guidelines and policies that guide the selection of IT alternatives and investments
- Establishing architectural principles and standards that will guide the selection and deployment of specific technologies
- Establishing goals and measurements for assessing the impact of IT investment decisions

Steering committees, given their wide implementation in many organizations, will be discussed in more detail later in this chapter.

Value Measurement   (Formal assessment and review of IT's contributions to business strategies and infrastructure)—This is covered in Chapter 14—Assessing the Value of IT.

In summary then, governance alternatives can be grouped into three general categories:

1. *Governance based on organizational structure*—these forms of governance are enabled through organizational reporting relationships and responsibilities assigned to the different roles and functions embodied in those relationships. Examples of organizational structure-based governance from the preceding list of governance alternatives include:

   - Organization
   - CIO/CEO reporting relationship
   - Steering committees
   - Liaison
   - Location

2. *Governance based on processes*—these forms of governance are enabled through formal business and IT procedures, policies, and systems that the members of the organization must (or should) follow to make decisions about IT. Examples of process-based governance from the proceding list include:

   - Budget
   - Career cross-over
   - Communication/negotiation
   - Partnership/alliance management

- Value measurement
- Project approval (IT investment) process
- Education/cross-training

3. *Governance based on human relationships*—these forms of governance are enabled through the interpersonal relationships between the members of the organization including the organization's culture, perceptions of partnership, power, value and trust. These governance alternatives are not always embodied in formal documentation. Examples of relationship-based governance include:

- Shared risks, responsibilities, rewards/penalties
- Partnership/alliance management
- Communicate/market/negotiate
- Competitive enabler/driver

No one governance alternative is better than any other. The challenge for today's IT management is the judicious selection of alternatives from each of the three groups that best accomplishes the objective of making *informed* organizational decisions about IT.

▪▪▪ Forms of Governance and Leadership Roles in Cross-Functional Initiatives

One of the challenges faced by IT management is the transition from a local or proprietary infrastructure to more global standards that enable the organization to achieve strategic objectives that have worldwide reach. This inevitably places corporate IT management in conflict with local business units that have developed technologies that meet local (business) environmental needs.

Infrastructure transitions—for example, the implementation of an ERP system with global reach, the implementation of a global management reporting system, or the replacement of proprietary technology standards with industry standards—have profound implications for effective IT governance. Infrastructure transitions are hard to justify on purely economic benefits and often require substantial cooperation and resources from organizations that are skeptical about the benefits of moving away from proprietary technologies. Exacerbating the problem is the fact that the existing local technology infrastructure must still operate while the new global infrastructure is being put in place and tested. Additional global governance considerations are described later in this chapter.

Corporate mergers and acquisitions place similar demands on IT. How to effectively and efficiently consolidate the organizations is a vital concern. Naturally, this is also a daily activity confronting large multi-business unit firms whether their organizational structure is central, decentral, or federal (see Chapter 8—Organizing IT).

Many IT organizations "govern" these cross-functional initiatives by assembling either a steering committee, SWAT team, COC/COE, or a matrixed project team that is composed of individuals from the corporate IT organization and IT representatives from the affected business units. Corporate management runs it. This cross-functional team is typically responsible for establishing the architecture of the new IT infrastructure and designing the plan for its rollout. In this structure the managers from the business units continue their reporting relationship to their business units. Corporate managers interpret the business and IT strategy and provide guidance to the business unit representatives who must then implement the new infrastructure according to corporate mandates. This form of IT governance ensures that the leadership role of corporate management is to determine the strategy and design of IT infrastructure for the organization. It also defines the role of business unit IT management as the implementers of the (mandated) corporate design—that is, it is a very "top-down" style of management and governance. This form of governance also requires corporate management to evaluate the effectiveness of the business unit representatives with respect to their ability to implement the corporate objectives. The drawback to this form of governance—also called a "thick matrix"[9] is that the leadership roles almost always result in organizational conflict due to the competing interests of corporate management and representatives from the business units.

Another form of governance adopted by organizations to manage cross-functional initiatives is one in which corporate IT management acts in a role of providing guidance and assistance to the business units for adopting global infrastructure changes. In this form—called a "thin matrix"[9]—local business unit management has substantial flexibility with respect to interpreting corporate direction and making decisions about implementation approaches. Business unit management still, however, has the responsibility for making the appropriate level of investment to achieve the corporate objectives. The advantage of this form of governance is that it attains higher buy-in and cooperation on the part of business units, with the potential drawback that decisions may be delayed due to the need for consensus building. This form of governance works especially well in organizations whose cultures favor consensus building as a form of decision-making rather than the directive style of the "thick matrix."

A third form of governance for cross-functional initiatives is relatively new and recognizes the fact that organizations have to increasingly cope with geographically dispersed (and scarce) human resources and intellectual capital, but purposeful change to technology across the enterprise must still be effected for sound business reasons. The knowledge of these human resources (i.e., IT professionals) is the essential engine of innovation and organizational change. This third form—called a "strategic community"[9]—relies on the cultural and professional affinities of a community of IT professionals in the business and corporate organizations to manage the complexities of cross-functional initiatives in a collaborative fashion that emphasizes knowledge sharing among business unit managers. In this form of governance, the role of corporate IT management becomes one of defining strategy and facilitating and sponsoring (in some cases, providing funding and some level of infrastructure for communications) the community. Early experience with this form of governance has shown promising results, especially in the community's willingness to take a more prospective view of cross-functional issues rather than merely react to them in response to a corporate directive. This form of governance also appears to have a greater capacity to handle problems that are less well structured than the other forms of governance as the knowledge-sharing mechanisms lead to adaptive rather than reactive behaviors on the part of the individuals who comprise the community. Table 11-2 summarizes these forms of governance and their characteristic leadership roles.

TABLE 11-2 Forms of Governance and Leadership Roles[9]

Leadership role	Thick matrix	Thin matrix	Strategic community
Corporate headquarters	Designing and mandating strategy	Providing guidance	Defining strategy, providing sponsorship, and facilitating the community
Business unit manager	Ensuring compliance with corporate mandates	Interpreting corporate advisories and making decisions	Sharing knowledge and providing feedback to corporate headquarters

Steering Committees

As discussed earlier in this chapter, establishing steering committees is considered a "best practice" governance mechanism for making decisions regarding organizational investment and use of IT. Many large organizations have adopted executive steering committees at different organizational levels (e.g., "Global IT Steering Committee" to address investment in and use of IT for initiatives having enterprise-wide scope; divisional steering committees that address investment and use of IT at business unit level; and so on) with varying degrees of success.

What makes some IT steering committees successful while others seem to merely muddle along, mired in indecision? Let's first examine membership on the steering committee as an important critical success factor. Effective IT steering committees membership should include:

- The business executive committee (CEO, CFO, COO, Chief Marketing Officer, etc.)
- The CIO
- The Chief Technology Officer (CTO) if the organization separates CIO and CTO roles
- Divisional business heads
- The head of Information Systems and/or head of Networking

Membership in the IT steering committee is also an important indicator of the organizational value executive management places on IT. If the steering committee lacks significant membership from the business executive committee or the senior business unit management it will not have the organizational authority to make decisions regarding IT that are enforceable across the enterprise (e.g., cross-functional initiatives, common architectures, IT standards). The organizational credibility of the steering committee is highly dependent on having the right membership as well as the right members. (see "Steering Committees in Action" sidebar). Participants should possess relevant knowledge about what is happening internally and externally with regards to their organization and IT. They should be recognized as credible leaders with good connections throughout the organization. They should have formal authority and the managerial skills associated with planning, organizing, and controlling IT-business initiatives. Naturally the tactical and operational steering committees should define their membership based on the decisions that they are to make.

Aside from membership, what other factors are critical to the success of an IT steering committee? IT managers should consider the following factors when proposing or establishing a steering committee:

Bureaucracy Focus on the reduction/elimination of the "bureaucratic barriers" to expedite opportunities to leverage IT. This is essential to harness and utilize the IT advantage, since technologies are ever changing and traditionally "bureaucracy" has been considered as an impediment rather than a facilitator for progress and an aid in the implementation of change.

Career Building Opportunities for participants to learn and expand responsibilities. Since learning is a process in continuum and more responsibilities come with more knowledge, proper management, enhancement, and growth of careers should be focused upon. It goes a long way in not only helping participants to learn more but also to shoulder more responsibilities, take bold and educated decisions and calculated risks, and grow with the organization.

Communication Primary vehicle for IT and business discussions and sharing knowledge across organizations. The importance of communication cannot be overemphasized or undermined, especially in the field of IT and business where perceptions are usually off the mark more often than not and expectations are unreal when it comes to the effect, utilization, and impact of IT in business. The members of the steering committee should be responsible for communicating the activities of the group to their respective organization.

Complex Decisions   Do not get involved in "mundane" areas. Decision-making is a process in itself and complex decisions take time and analysis. But there is a tendency to get lost or too involved in the process of analyzing the pros and cons of a particular decision. These are "mundane" areas and are best avoided to enable swift decision-making, which could make a huge difference to an organization and its business. Naturally this is relative to the level/complexity of the decisions being made by the group (e.g., strategic, tactical, operational).

Influence/Empowerment   Authority to have decisions carried out. What good are decisions that are made if they cannot be executed, acted upon, or implemented? The one who makes the decisions is most influential on the direction the organization is going to take and the extent to which it will utilize opportunities. When there is a responsible figure within the organization to make decisions and to involve others so they will act on them, someone with empowerment to take decisions and to enforce authority, the result is the difference between the success and failure of those decisions.

Steering Committees in Action—Some "Real-World" Examples

Organizations are successfully employing IT steering committees to address different aspects of IT governance. Some of the notable examples of successful IT steering committees are:

USAA   United Services Automobile Association is a highly successful niche provider of insurance, financial services, and personal lifestyle enhancement services to its base of current and former U.S. armed forces officers and their families. USAA is known for its exceptional customer service, its integrity, and the loyalty of its customer base. USAA is also widely regarded as a leader in the use of IT as an enabler of business transformation. In the late 1980s USAA established several coordinating mechanisms to govern decisions regarding the use and deployment of IT. Among these were:

- An IS Council chaired by the CEO that met every quarter to review current Information Systems Division business plans and review current projects
- An Architecture Review Board to promote understanding of the Information Systems Division's business plans with the senior business systems division heads
- Multiple Executive Steering Committees for Systems headed by the senior vice president of each division with primary responsibility for developing a multi-year IT plan for their respective divisions. These committees prioritized systems development projects, approved modifications to existing systems, and determined systems budgets and timeframes
- Systems Working Groups (nine of them) located in multiple divisions that included middle managers from IT and business. These groups monitored maintenance to existing systems and developed quarterly schedules for maintenance.[22]

Citigroup   One of the world's leading financial services firms and an aggressive proponent of the use of technology for competitive advantage, Citigroup has established two committees with somewhat overlapping functions in its Consumer Banking Division that meet quarterly to provide IT governance:

- A Global Consumer Council, chaired by the senior vice president of marketing and including the firm's senior marketing managers and the senior IT officer
- A Global Consumer Technology Group, chaired by the senior IT officer and including the senior IT managers from around the firm as well as the senior vice president of marketing

Each group meets either back-to-back or sometimes holds joint sessions. It is their responsibility to reach joint decisions about technology and business that are informed by each other's unique perspectives of the market and the needs of Citigroup and its customers.[5]

Baxter International   A leading distributor of medical supplies to healthcare organizations throughout the world, Baxter established a global IT steering committee of senior business and IT executives that focuses on enterprise-wide initiatives such as Baxter's launch of a global Enterprise Resource Planning (ERP) effort in the late 1990s. This effort was focused on integrating multiple business processes in the areas of finance, logistics, and order management. To ensure success for this massive effort, the global steering committee assumed the following roles:[23]

- Made decisions on change management that examined how much change the organization could accept versus project deadlines
- Set clear milestones for the project
- Monitored the project's progress against deadlines and other milestones
- Provided direction to teams responsible for specific functional implementation (e.g., order processing)

Low-Hanging Fruit/Quick Hits   Immediate changes carried out when appropriate. Wisdom lies not just in effecting and implementing long-term change but also in recognizing opportunities for small, quick changes that could be effective and facilitate the realization of the organization's vision and objectives. Many decisions just do not demand "analysis-paralysis."

Marketing   Vehicle for "selling" the value of IT to the business. As with communication, marketing is another function that the steering committee has to adopt to "sell" the value of IT to the business organization. Even if the value of IT is realized and understood, adoption of IT in traditional terms would probably not be possible until it is aggressively promoted across the organization.

Objectives, Measurements   Formal assessment and review of IT's business contributions. IT does have its inherent value—an assessment and review of the contributions of IT to the organization in business terms helps keep the objectives and goals in perspective. It aids in the process of marketing IT's contribution across the business, primarily to its business partners. Additionally, the steering committee should have clearly defined objectives that are regularly measured and assessed.

Ownership/Accountability   Responsible/answerable for the decisions made. The steering committee members should be capable of accepting responsibility and should know that they are accountable for the same. This acts as a reinforcement of faith in their ability and elevates them to high regard and respect in the organization. The steering committee, not an individual or business unit, owns the decisions made.

Priorities Primary vehicle for selecting what is done, when, and how much resource to allocate (see the section that follows). Prioritizing is a key element of success. Knowing what, when, and how a resource should be allocated to different projects is a critical component of effective decision making. Being capable of prioritizing needs for allocation of resources is one of the most important success factors of a steering committee.

Relationships Partnership of business and IT. In continuation with *communication* and *marketing*, relationship building is critical for the success of a sound understanding and a sense of partnership among business and IT. Relationship also helps foster better understanding of each other's point of view and helps change wrong perceptions.

Right Participants Cooperative, committed, respected team members with knowledge of the business and IT. The right team makes all the difference. It would be difficult to realize objectives if a team is in place but the right participants are missing. Commitment and mutual respect must form an integral part of any team to succeed.

Share Risks Equal accountability, recognition, responsibility, rewards, and uncertainty. Being committed also means that team members are willing to share the "good" and the "bad" that comes along with making decisions. This approach dilutes risk and makes it more manageable and also enforces a strong sense of team spirit among the committee members.

Structure, Facilitator Processes and leadership to ensure the right focus. A story is told about the hay cutters in the forests of Africa. They blindly cut away trees, while the team leader climbs the tree to see if they are going in the right direction. If they are not, he shouts, "Wrong way, wrong way…!" Leadership plays this critical role and provides focus to help the team adapt to a certain process which helps achieve set goals and objectives.

In summary, steering committees are one of the more effective implementation of IT governance for making organizational decisions about investing in and deploying of IT. Before creating and empowering a steering committee, the IT manager needs to take into consideration the many factors that may influence the effectiveness of the committee that have been discussed in this chapter.

Prioritizing Projects

One of the most fundamental examples of IT governance is making decisions about project priorities. Which projects should be funded? How should risk be considered in making decisions about project priorities?

Some straightforward process guidelines are helpful in addressing these fundamental questions:

- Consider *all* projects
- Group projects based on:

   1. **Necessity, Opportunity, Desirability.** One technique for performing this grouping is by evaluating the *business issues* the projects are supposed to address against two criteria (see Figure 11-1):
   2. **Impact on the organization.**
   3. **Likelihood of occurrence.** Projects that address business issues with high organizational impact and that are most likely to occur should receive initial attention from the steering committee.

▪▪▪▪▪▪▪▪▪▪▪▪ FIGURE 11-1 Scenario Planning Grid.

Impact on Firm

	High	Medium	Low
High	High priority		
Medium		Medium priority	
Low			Low priority

Probability of Occurrence (vertical axis label)

4. **Risk.** One technique for classifying and grouping projects according to risk uses classifications of "high," "medium," or "low" risk within categories of organizational impact, development effort, technology, and organizational capability (see Figure 11-2).[12] For example, a project that was characterized by significant changes to business rules, employed emerging technology, and was proposed to take over two years to implement within an organization that had a poor track record of implementing large complex projects would be classified as "high" risk.

▪▪▪▪▪▪▪▪▪▪▪▪ FIGURE 11-2 Risk Level Criteria.

	Organizational Impact	Development Effort	Technology	Organizational Capability
High	• Significant change to business rules • Complex business processes • Multiple organizations involved	• Development/ system integration cost > $10 million • Over 2 years in development	• Emerging • Unproven • New for firm	• Immature organization • Uses the ad-hoc processes • Organizational track record suggest inability to mitigate risk
Medium	• Moderate changes to business rules • Medium complexity	• Up to 29 staff years • $2–$10 million • 1–2 years in development	• Proven in industry or at organizational level • New to organization	• Maturing organization • Reasonable level of success
Low	• Insignificant or no change in business rules • Low complexity	• Under 10 staff • Under $2 million • Under 1 year in development	• Standard proven organizational technology	• Mature organization • Strong track record • Stable organization

Source: SIM, Washington State Government.

Organizational capability is one of the most important categories of this risk classification technique as it tends to make clear the organizational practices that enhance *commitment* by business to a project versus mere participation.

An alternative method that can be employed for grouping projects by levels of risk examines three sources of risk: market risk, technology risk, and organizational risk.[10] Market risk looks at sources of project risk that are related to the external environment such as the size and scope of the markets being addressed by the project, knowledge of customer needs, the regulatory environment, the reaction of competitors and so forth. Technology risk examines those intrinsic sources of risk that emerge from uncertainty about the technology, liabilities that may accrue to the organization from using a particular technology, lack of standards, etc. Organizational risk focuses inward on issues such as the project's fit with the organization's capabilities, the cost of the project, the scope of organizational change required, etc. (see Figure 11-3).

5. **Resource demands.**   projects should be grouped by the human (e.g., intellectual), computing (e.g., computer equipment, software, networking, information storage), logistical (e.g., travel, office facilities, housing), and financial resources required (e.g., software licenses, capital investment) to implement the project.

6. **Anticipated return.**   projects should be grouped by their projected value (see Chapter 14—Assessing the Value of IT).

▪▪▪▪▪▪▪▪▪▪▪ **FIGURE 11-3** Risk Profiling.

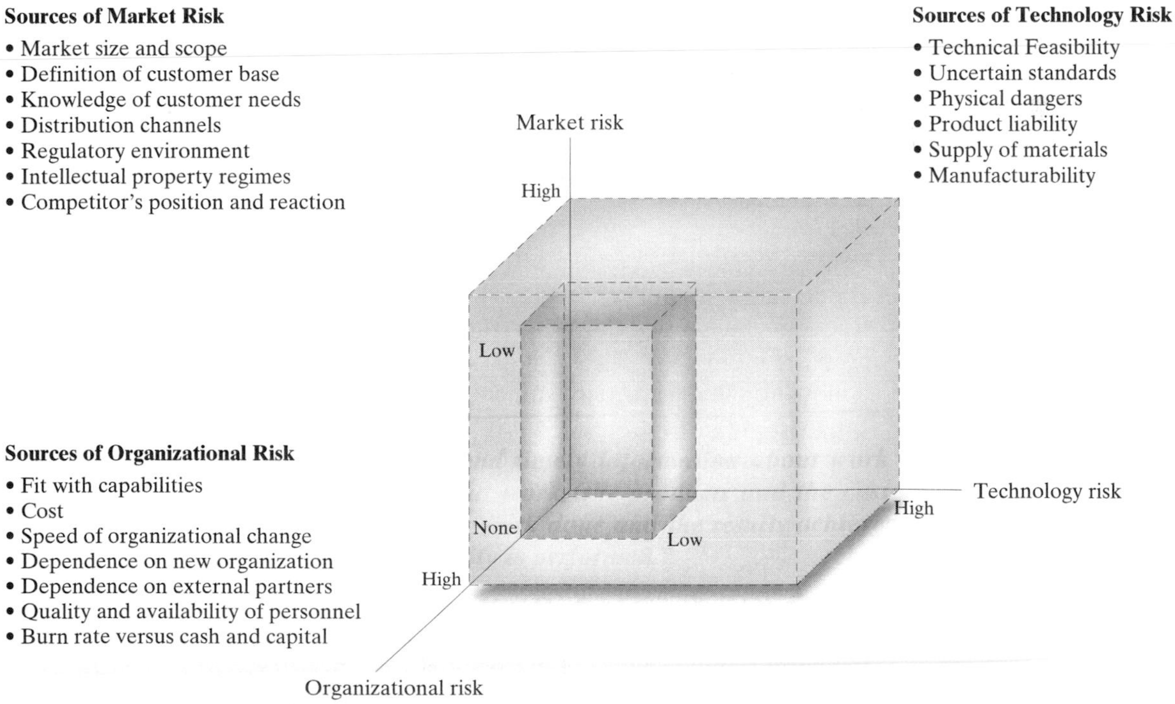

Sources of Market Risk

- Market size and scope
- Definition of customer base
- Knowledge of customer needs
- Distribution channels
- Regulatory environment
- Intellectual property regimes
- Competitor's position and reaction

Sources of Technology Risk

- Technical Feasibility
- Uncertain standards
- Physical dangers
- Product liability
- Supply of materials
- Manufacturability

Sources of Organizational Risk

- Fit with capabilities
- Cost
- Speed of organizational change
- Dependence on new organization
- Dependence on external partners
- Quality and availability of personnel
- Burn rate versus cash and capital

Source: Kaplan, R. and Norton, D., *The Strategy Focused Organization.* Harvard Business School Press (2001).[10]

Priority should be given to those projects having characteristics of:

1. Highest impact on the firm[13]
2. Highest likelihood of occurrence
3. Lowest combined attributes of risk (regardless of risk assessment method employed)
4. Least amount of resources demanded
5. Highest anticipated return

Mitigating Risk

Techniques that should be considered to mitigate or manage risk can be grouped according to whether the risk is market, development, organizational, or technology-related. These may include:

TECHNOLOGY RISK MITIGATION

- Having subject matter experts (SMEs) or consultants available for consultation or project management in situations of unfamiliarity with the technology
- Establishing an emerging technology scanning organizational function to address issues related to or the application of new technology
- Employing technology that is already known and used in the organization (with the implication that it meets organizational technology standards or guidelines)
- Performing pilot projects or "proof of concept" studies before full-scale rollout
- Attending conferences and reading professional journals (e.g., *Sloan Management Review, MIS Quarterly, Communications of the ACM*, etc.)
- Maintaining membership in professional societies (e.g., Society for Information Management)
- Implementing professional certification/study programs
- Participating in master's degree or master's certification programs

DEVELOPMENT RISK MITIGATION

- Modularizing projects (phased rollout)
- Employing project management with prior experience in the functional or technology area
- Establishing a development life cycle methodology and standards for IT applications and infrastructure
- Reducing the scope of projects (functional areas addressed or number of requirements)
- Following a "best practices" model for software engineering (e.g., the Software Engineering Institute's *Capability Maturity Model* ®; also staying current by browsing relevant literature and attending conferences and seminars

ORGANIZATIONAL RISK MITIGATION

- Secure executive sponsorship from business communities
- Joint accountability of business and IT management for project results
- Early and continuous involvement of business stakeholders in projects
- Establish a formal change management program for initiatives, including formal "usability testing" procedures and training on new business processes
- Establish formal communications channels up, across and down the business and IT organizations

- Establish formal and well-understood (by business and IT) processes for initiating, developing, testing, accepting and introducing new technology and applications into the production environment (including documentation)
- Establish formal escalation processes for identifying problems and raising them to the attention of the appropriate level of management

MARKET RISK MITIGATION

- Reduce the initial scope of geographic coverage of the application or project (e.g., initial rollout is in the U.S. or the EU (European Union) instead of a global rollout)
- Employ SMEs or consultants for expert advice in situations where there is regulatory risk (e.g., compliance with FDA or EPA regulations)
- Documentation and formal sign-off on customer (or end-user) requirements (if the "market" is internal to the organization
- Establish a customer "knowledge base" containing relevant facts and other information about the customer(s) and the dynamics of the market they are part of

▪▪▪ Global Considerations and IT Governance

IT organizations in the 21st century must develop governance mechanisms that accommodate the global environment in which their companies will increasingly operate. Transnational strategies are a fact of life for major companies today. Drucker emphasizes the importance of globalization and its impact on every organization today in his statement that "no institution can survive, let alone succeed, unless it measures up to the standards set by the leaders in its field, anyplace in the world."[14] IT has become the principal means by which organizations have implemented strategies for globalization, primarily because IT neutralizes the effect of geographical distance and time. Through its time/distance neutralizing effect, IT also has the power to shift labor markets in knowledge-intensive industries (e.g., the growing use of offshore application development companies, offshore customer call centers, or General Electric's stated objective of "follow the sun application development" processes). Without IT, none of this is possible in a meaningful sense.

In addition to the obvious benefits of reducing the impact of time and distance, IT also allows organizations to share knowledge and information on a global scale and in a *timely* fashion. Twenty-first century organizations are profoundly information and knowledge-based, with information being the "glue" that cements together the processes and people that make organizations run effectively.[15] True competitive advantage in the 21st century is increasingly dependent on an organization's ability to create and use new knowledge to develop new products or services, not the products or services themselves. Business and IT management must be able to think and act globally (e.g., where to locate the next customer call center or distribution center), regionally (how the organization can exploit particular regional advantages in South America or Asia) and locally (e.g., what local distribution channels are available for the organization's products and what local regulations must be adhered to).

What IT governance mechanisms, then, should be considered to support transnational strategies? Addressing that question first requires that IT management understand the types of global strategies and the special demands these strategies place on IT governance. One framework for categorizing international strategies describes them as falling into four basic types or business forms[16] (see Figure 11-4):

▪▪▪▪▪▪▪▪▪▪▪ **FIGURE 11-4** Global Characteristics of International (Exporter), Multinational, Multilocal, and Transnational or Metanational Companies.

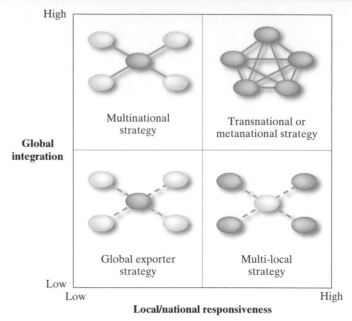

Source: Daniels, J. and Caroline, N., in J. Luftman, ed., *"Competing in the Information Age: Strategic Alignment in Practice."* Oxford University Press (1996).

Global Exporter   This form of international strategy characterizes organizations that typically expand overseas in search of new markets, usually by employing agents or trading partners to market and distribute their products in different geographic markets. Country nationals from the home office typically staff local offices and distribute products that are homogeneous—i.e., there is typically no local manufacturing of products. Most, if not all, corporate decision-making as well as value chain activities such as R&D, sales, service, and manufacturing is concentrated in the home office location. Customers of global exporters are treated the same whether they are global or local customers. High levels of integration and a sharing of common culture are strong characteristics of global exporters, with frequent communication between the local offices and headquarters being the norm. The principal basis of competition for the global exporter is taking advantage of production scale economies. IT, if used at all, is supported from the parent company.

Multinational   This form of international strategy tends to evolve from the global exporter form, with the organization typically moving sales and service functions and, ultimately manufacturing functions, to various country locations. The multinational organization usually retains tight control over the value chain activities that have been distributed. The home office tightly controls most functions, although some product development functions may be distributed to take advantage of local competencies. IT is controlled centrally from corporate headquarters, although some service might be supported locally. Like the global exporter, multinational products tend to be homogeneous, with allowance for some customization to meet the demands of local markets. Innovations generated by local offices are quickly harvested for incorporation into the headquarter's knowledge base, as the basis of competition for this strategy is sharing innovations that are generated by the headquarters organization. Headquarters typically plays a dominant role in governance by setting standards and policies, but local organizations have significant autonomy with regard to establishing processes to meet the demands of local customers. The multinational company services local customers via its national organizations, although their ability to service global customers is done only with difficulty.

Multilocal   These strategies focus on the need for responsiveness to local markets, with national organizations having a high degree of flexibility and decision-making autonomy to customize products and services for local needs. Value chain activities such as R&D, product development, manufacturing, sales, and service tend to be highly duplicated in each country, with the consequence that global customers find expenses of doing business with multilocals to be high due to integration costs. Headquarter's governance in this business form is weak, as the demands of local offices take precedence over headquarter's need for consistency in policies or procedures. Communication between different local offices is less likely than in either the global exporter strategy or the multinational strategy form, making the sharing and harvesting of knowledge for overall organizational benefit much more difficult than for the other international strategies. IT is typically decentralized or federated.

Transnational or Metanational   Strategies that can be truly characterized as global leverage the benefits of the other international strategies with none of the attendant drawbacks. Global companies implement process and technology architectures that reap the benefits of mass customization—low cost and local responsiveness. These companies are highly networked so that they can "do business anyplace" while being able to share knowledge and information between headquarters and between national organizational units. Decisionmaking in global organizations is based on centers of competence rather than on headquarters or local organizations; i.e., decisions are based on expertise rather than on the basis of organization form or location. The global organization supports local as well as global customers equally well. IT is distributed and shared across the organization, typically organized in a federal or N-Tworked.

What IT governance mechanisms, then, are most applicable to each of these international business strategies? As IT governance is concerned with the locus of decision-making power regarding the use of IT and the processes for making these decisions, the mechanisms of IT governance for international strategies will tend to reflect the forms of decision-making authority for each of these strategies and the need for standardization of process and communication between headquarters and local organizational entities. The IT governance mechanisms will also reflect the level of importance each international business strategy places on:

- The requirement for communication between the national ("local") offices and headquarters
- The requirement for communication between local offices
- The requirement for sharing information and knowledge between local offices
- The requirement for standardization of operations among local offices
- The need for local responsiveness

Based on our preceding discussion of each of the forms of international business strategy, we can summarize the likely IT governance mechanisms by the forms of international strategy in Table 11-3:

TABLE 11-3 IT Governance Mechanisms for International Strategy Types[16]	
International strategy type	*IT governance mechanisms*
Global exporter	• Centralized IT organization structure • Common architecture and applications established by headquarters • Technology standards and policies dictated and enforced by headquarters • Budgets established by headquarters for local organizations • Cost justification the basis for investment in IT
Multinational	• Mostly central with some federalized or hybrid IT organization structure • Corporate CIO and local office CIO/heads of IS • Common IT architecture for shared services and "common" functions such as e-mail, telecommunications network, etc. • Steering/architecture committees at corporate and local levels for decisions regarding IT investments • Business value justification for investment in IT
Multilocal	• Decentralized or Federal IT organization structure • Application investment decisions made by local offices to meet local market requirements • Minimal headquarters IT staff—focus on support of shared services (e.g., e-mail) • Minimal to low requirements for sharing information or applications between local offices • Local office CTO or CIO
Transnational/Metanational	• Federal or networked IT organization structure • High requirement for integration and sharing of information and knowledge among all organizational units • Centers of excellence (COEs) • Architecture committees with headquarters and local representation

▪▪▪▪▪▪▪▪▪

▪▪▪ IT Governance and Vendor Management

The Do's and Don'ts of Vendor Management

Do:

- Establish a vendor management team.
- Monitor service levels and end-user satisfaction.
- Track the service/product market and the vendor's place in it.
- Continually renegotiate contracts (with appropriate legal help).
- Keep business units accountable and involved.
- Think ongoing relationship—not just one-time transaction.
- Use the vendor's expertise to suggest solutions.

> ## *Don't:*
>
> - Try to manage a vendor without adequate expertise available (legal, HR, etc.).
> - Ignore the need to establish service level agreements.
> - Fail to establish firm accountability and metrics for performance.
> - Understaff the vendor management function.
> - Rely *solely* on the vendor's expertise.
> - Forget to keep an eye on vendor reputation and profitability.
>
> *Source:* Adapted from Meta Group.

If we consider that governance is fundamentally about the structure, form, and process of decisionmaking regarding the organizational use of IT, the forms of IT governance related to vendor management (see the "Do's and Don'ts of Vendor Management" sidebar) are typically centered around the management processes involved with identifying and selecting a vendor, contracting for services, monitoring vendor performance against the contract, and contract renegotiation (including contract termination and vendor deselection). These processes are very similar, except for their scope and the level of decisionmaking involved, regardless of whether the vendor is selling hardware, software, or services. There will be more discussion of this later in the chapter (also, see Chapter 8—Organizing IT).

Vendor Selection Once the decision has been made by IT management to use the services or products of an external vendor, and these services or products have been identified, the next important decision that IT management must make is which vendor services to use. In large organizations this decision may involve tens of millions of "hard dollar" costs associated with it over time frames that extend five or more years (e.g., licensing an ERP package). Large organizations with sizeable IT organizational budgets may have the governance mechanisms in place for vendor selection that involves the engagement of a neutral "informed buyer"[17] (usually a management consulting firm) selected by senior IT management to identify qualified vendors based on experience in similar situations. The informed buyer will typically use a Request for Proposal (RFP) as a governance mechanism to solicit and compare contract bids from qualified vendors (see the "Picking an Outsourcing Vendor" sidebar). Final vendor selection is typically done through the governance mechanism of a vendor selection committee which, for large contracts (e.g., the selection of an enterprise-wide ERP system) may include the CIO, CFO, a senior representative from the corporate legal organization, a senior representative from the purchasing organizations, and other key stakeholders, as appropriate. For vendor products or services that run into millions of dollars, the final decision as to the choice of vendor, however, should be shared among IT and business executives. The decision analysis worksheet in Figure 11-5 provides an excellent vehicle for assessing vendors. The first step is to identify product/service objects (e.g. skills, references, reputation, support, flexibility). Next, the relative importance of the objectives (weights) can be assigned. Each vendor is assessed and assigned a weight average. The vendor with the highest total weighted score is the best choice.

Contracting for Services The contract between the organization and the vendor is the principal governance mechanism of vendor management. Depending on the scope of services being provided by the vendor, the size (dollar amount) of the contract, and the number of organizations affected, the development of the contract is typically done by specialists in the IT organization with the active assistance of the

▪▪▪▪▪▪▪▪▪▪▪ FIGURE 11-5 Decision Analysis Worksheet

Decision Analysis Worksheet

DECISION STATEMENT:																												

(ALTERNATIVES table with columns A through M, each having SC and WT SC subcolumns, OBJECTIVES with WT column. Blank data rows and TOTAL WEIGHTED SCORE row at bottom.)

legal department. Large IT organizations have established organizational functions that facilitate the development of IT vendor contracts for business units within the organization as well as for the IT organization itself. In general, the facilitation of vendor contracts is a governance function that improves coordination between the organization and the vendor.

In developing a contract to license software from a vendor, IT management should consider the following as important elements to include in the contract:

- The right to assign the software license to a new corporate entity resulting from a merger, consolidation, acquisition, or divestiture
- The right to use the software for the benefits of a business unit formerly within your corporate organization that has been sold
- The right to assign the software license to, or allow the software to be used by, an outside entity if you outsource your data processing operations
- The right to make and own derivative works (i.e., code changes, translations, adaptations) based upon the software
- The right to port the software to any platform supported by the vendor at no or minimum charge
- A license that permits unlimited use within your corporate organization (i.e., "enterprise-wide" licenses)
- In situations other than enterprise-wide licenses, the right to transfer the software to other equipment and operating systems at no cost
- In situations other than enterprise-wide licenses, the right to use the software for the benefit of other entities (e.g., parent, subsidiary, division) within your corporate organization at no cost
- In situations other than enterprise-wide licenses, the right to transfer the software license to an existing entity (e.g., parent, subsidiary, division) within your corporate organization at no cost
- Limited liability for breach of your obligations under the software license agreement
- Prohibition against devices in the software that control your compliance with the software license

- The right to customize the duration of the software acceptance period
- The right to define software acceptance as occurring only upon your written notice
- Specific remedies for vendor's nonperformance
- Incentives to licensors to reward the performance in providing services
- Remedies for consequential damages that you suffer
- Use of your own form in place of the licensor's form for licensing contracts
- Contractually defined differences between:

    - Enhancements, releases, versions, etc., that you receive by subscribing to software support
    - Those the vendor insists are a new product requiring a new license

- Vendor's responsibility to meet the cost of procuring alternative third-party support if the vendor fails to provide adequate and timely service
- A cap on future maintenance prices
- Permission to exempt individuals, employees, contractors from signing documents that acknowledge confidentiality of software or bind them to terms of the license
- Avoidance of partial payments to vendors based on check points
- Contractual assurances regarding forward compatibility of software which changes in operating systems
- Contractual assurances regarding forward compatibility of software which changes in hardware
- Contractual assurances regarding forward compatibility of software which changes in other software from the same vendor

Contract Monitoring   This important IT governance mechanism, considered a core IT competency by some researchers,[17] is concerned with protecting the concerns of the business. It is needed to ensure that vendors—and the organization itself—fulfill their contracted obligations. This aspect of governance should also be concerned with monitoring the vendor's performance against accepted industry benchmarks of quality and service levels and preparing periodic reports to IT management on the performance of vendors against these metrics. Service level agreements (to be discussed in Chapter 13—Measuring, Reporting, and Controlling) along with incentives and penalties provide an excellent vehicle for managing these criteria.

Contract Renegotiation   This governance mechanism is associated with the processes that are initiated as a result of an event in contract monitoring that signals either:

- Contract expiration
- A material breach in contract by the vendor that may result in contract termination or renegotiation (e.g. poor performance, security lapses, criminal activity)
- A major change in the organization's management or industry (e.g., bankruptcy or merger on the part of the organization or the vendor)
- A significant change in the price for the same vendor services
- New technology

In any of the above cases, this process addresses the requirement to continually realign the need for the vendor's services with the services provided by that particular vendor.

In circumstances that are sufficient to warrant consideration to terminate the relationship with the vendor, IT management will need to repeat the process of vendor selection. IT management also needs to be especially careful and seek legal counsel before terminating a contract for "material breach" as this implies the existence of contract monitoring mechanisms that have been agreed to by both parties prior to the execution of the contract, as discussed above.

Vendor Relationship Development An emerging form of IT governance for vendor management that looks beyond the formal contractual relationship between the organization and the vendor. The use of steering committees, previously discussed, is an effective vehicle to build and manage the relationship. These steering committees generally take two forms:

1. Periodic (at least annual) meetings between senior IT management and key vendor management to identify how to derive additional business value from the current relationship. This involves the sharing of strategic objectives and plans by both parties and a growing relationship of trust between the principals. The potential of tying increased vendor revenue to the realization of specific incremental business value and benefit is a powerful incentive to most vendors to share plans and ideas, and add to the knowledge base of the vendor's client (the organization).
2. "Vendor councils" comprised of senior vendor representatives that convene periodically at the behest of senior IT management to address an issue of interest to the organization (e.g., an area of emerging technology). This is an opportunity for IT management to obtain insight on the issue of concern from a panel of experts from the vendor organizations in a non-competitive fashion (i.e., free consultation). Moreover, the insights obtained will be in the context of the fact that the vendor already works with the IT organization—they know the issues of greatest concern to the business and to IT management. It also provides the vendors with the opportunity to gather insight and intelligence about the organization they are servicing and to strengthen the mutual perception of shared values and common understanding so essential to long-term viable relationships.

▮▮▮ Outsourcing Considerations

Effective exploitation of IT in the 21st century requires IT managers to understand which IT competencies are essential to their organization's ability to respond to environmental changes and to exploit IT for competitive advantage. Competition in the 21st century demands that IT management consciously identify and nurture "core" IT competencies that have strategic impact (enable or drive competitive advantage in an organization's products and services).[19] Similarly, "non-core" IT competencies (e.g., applications development and support for back office processes, help desk) are being identified that do not help an organization differentiate its core products and services. There simply is no room in an IT organization for competencies that cannot be exploited for competitive advantage.[25]

The Do's and Don'ts of Picking an Outsourcing Vendor

Do:

- Ask for and check references and exercise due diligence.
- Assess the culture of your outsourcing partner.
- Evaluate multiple options—both suppliers and approaches.
- GET IT IN WRITING!
- Metrics matter—use them.

▪▪▪ Outsourcing Questions To Address

- Varying degrees of outsourcing – which is right for our organization?
  - None
  - Total
  - Partial – What to keep versus what to outsource? Who/how select?
- Emotion – How can someone else do it better, cheaper, faster?
- Cost – Is it ever worthwhile if we do not save money?
- Risk – Can it be quantified? minimized?
- Relationship – Can an outsourcing vendor really be my partner, or do they always have a different agenda? How govern?
- Length of fixed outsourcing engagement & renewal options?
- One versus multiple vendors?
- What about our people? How should we manage change?

- Open the kimono as much as possible.
- Pick an outsourcing partner with a strong partner network.

Don't:

- Buy on price alone.
- Overlook the reference-checking process.
- Use a price contract without considering the long-term consequences.
- Forget to provide for contingencies.
- Communicate via committee.
- Ever hand over project management.
- Rely on marquee references.
- Single-source.
- Let your head be turned by goodies.

With outsourcing arrangements becoming a familiar operating model for IT organizations (currently 82 percent of U.S. companies practice some form of selective outsourcing[18]), what governance mechanisms need to be considered by IT management? The governance mechanisms discussed in the previous section under vendor management apply to outsourcing arrangements as well, with a change in emphasis given to the scale and scope of outsourcing arrangements (many run into tens or hundreds of millions of dollars per year). A complete, objective, business-based assessment of the pros and cons is essential for any outsourcing consideration. The outsourcing questions that must be addressed are in the sidebar.

The first, and perhaps most important, aspect of governance as it relates to outsourcing is the decision itself to outsource. When should a firm outsource and when should it not (see Figure 11-6)? Ideally, organizations should strongly consider an arrangement with a transaction partner to handle IT functions that are both non-core competencies (see earlier discussion) and not critical to the success of the organization. Transaction partnering describes relationships that embrace ERP vendors, application service providers ("ASPs"), as well as mainstream outsourcing arrangements. Note that "ASPs" are different from traditional outsourcers:

- ASPs provide data center facilities, bandwidth, computer and storage capacity with varying degrees of administrative management to organizations to run applications. Clients are essentially responsible for all applications management. ASPs essentially enlarge the organization's existing IT infrastructure capability.

▪▪▪▪▪▪▪▪▪▪ FIGURE 11-6 Insource or Outsource?

		Yes	No
Core competency	Yes	Organization focus (Do it!)	Reassess (Why?)
	No	Strategic alliance (or hire, buy)	Transaction partner (ERP, ASP, outsource)

Yes   No

Critical success factor

- Outsourcing firms, on the other hand, may take over the data center facilities, bandwidth, computer and storage capacity and will assume administrative management and application development and management functions.

What Should an RFP for an Outsourcing Vendor Contain?

We suggest that IT managers consider the following format as a guideline for preparing an RFP for outsourcing services.

1. Objectives and Scope

2. Background
    2.1   background information
    2.2   information technology environment
    2.3   desired information technology environment

3. Technology Vision

4. Services Requested
    4.1   processing
    4.2   technical support
    4.3   database administration
    4.4   customer service help desk
    4.5   network services
    4.6   application development and maintenance
    4.7   data backup and recovery
    4.8   disaster recovery
    4.9   data security
    4.10 termination assistance
    4.11 accounting/administration
    4.12 account support
    4.13 other

5. Transition/Migration Services

6. Performance Requirements
    6.1   processing
    6.2   network services
    6.3   customer satisfaction
    6.4   customer service/help desk
    6.5   application maintenance

7. Resources
  7.1 physical resources
  7.2 personnel/human resources
  7.3 current information technology costs

8. Requirements for Vendor Proposal
  8.1 transmittal letter
  8.2 executive summary
  8.3 technical proposal
  8.4 personnel/human resources
  8.5 personnel transition
  8.6 pricing proposal
  8.7 vendor qualifications

9. General Terms and Conditions for Proposal
  9.1 Schedule
  9.2 Conditions For Proposal Acceptance

10. Proposal Evaluation
  10.1 procedures
  10.2 site visits
  10.3 evaluation criteria

Source: Transition Partners.

Organizations should perform inhouse the IT functions that are both core competencies and critical to the success of the organization. Core competencies and critical success factors/functions will differ among organizations, but in general these organizationally focused IT functions will be those that are ***critical*** to the organization's:

- Day-to-day operation
- Ability to competitively differentiate itself
- Ability to deliver value to its partners and customers
- Ability to innovate

Organizations should consider a strategic alliance arrangement in situations where the IT functions are not considered to be a core competency but are critical to the organization's success. In this situation, the organization should consider either hiring or buying the resources and/or skills needed to meet the requirements expressed as critical success factors. An example of this arrangement might be one where an organization contracts for the creation and operation of a telecommunications network that is critical to the operation of its business, but has determined that these competencies are not core to its business value proposition.

Lastly, in situations where the IT functions under consideration are a core competency but are not critical to an organization's success, the organization needs to reassess their role in the organization and their contribution to the organization's value proposition. Even though they may be considered to be a core competency, the organization may wish to consider other arrangements for IT functions that clearly have no critical role in contributing to the organization's success.[26]

One last caution: organizations should be aware that a decision to outsource the IT function in total seems to be almost irreversible. Once the IT function has been outsourced, the overwhelming evidence is that it is almost impossible to insource these functions again.

TABLE 11-4   Determinants of Partnership (Adapted from Henderson and Venkatraman[20])

	Partnerships	*Transactional relationships*
Mutual benefits	• Financial • Risk sharing • Innovation	• Financial (at best)
Commitment	• Shared goals • Incentives • Contracts	• Focused on completing the transaction
Predisposition	• Shared attitudes • Trust	• "What's in it for me?"
Shared knowledge	• Task • Domain • Culture	• None required except that required to complete the transaction
Distinctive competencies and resources	• Physical assets • Skills • Specialized knowledge	• Skills • Specialized knowledge
Organizational linkage	• Information • Process • Social	• None
Duration	• Potentially long-term	• Short-term

▮▮▮▮▮▮▮▮▮

Critical Success Factors

The term "Critical Success Factor" (CSF) has been used several times in this text, but what exactly does the term mean? One short and simple definition of the term is *"the thing(s) an organization MUST do to be successful."*[27] How does that definition translate into the management of IT organizations? One context for employing CSFs is described in Chapter 2—IT Strategy as part of the SWOT analysis exercise. The "Strengths" component of the SWOT analysis asks the analyst to identify the distinctive competencies (the things that make the organization unique or competitively different) and CSFs for the organization.

Some examples of CSFs as part of a SWOT exercise might be:

- Unique understanding of customer needs
- Customer information integrated across all divisions and available online
- Expert knowledge of Federal EPA regulations for the chemical industry
- Financial transaction processing cost lowest in the industry
- Customer perception of honesty and integrity

CSFs are important because they force management to focus on the processes, measurements, and initiatives that are vital to organizational success.

Particular attention should be paid to the vendor selection process and to the RFP and its review given the potential scope and impact of an outsourcing arrangement on IT processes, infrastructure and staff, and the likely size of the outsourcing contract. Structuring an RFP for outsourcing services also becomes more critical than an RFP for other vendor arrangements, given the issues of staff transition and the number of employees potentially affected by the outsourcing arrangement. See the "What Should a RFP for an Outsourcing Vendor Contain?" sidebar for helpful guidance on building an outsourcing RFP.

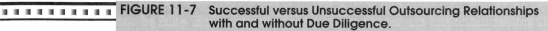

FIGURE 11-7 Successful versus Unsuccessful Outsourcing Relationships with and without Due Diligence.

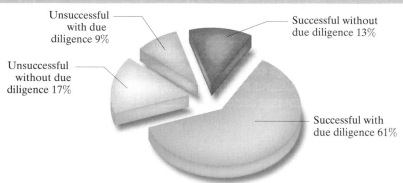

Unsuccessful with due diligence 9%

Successful without due diligence 13%

Unsuccessful without due diligence 17%

Successful with due diligence 61%

Source: International Data Corporation and Technology and Business Integrators, Inc.

To be effective, outsourcing relationships should be treated as partnerships or joint venture agreements instead of mere transactional relationships. To illustrate what we mean by a transactional relationship, imagine the sequence of events that takes place in the purchase of gasoline at a filling station. It doesn't matter to the purchaser of the gasoline who services his or her automobile. It also doesn't matter if the purchaser obtains the gasoline from a station on the Interstate or from one down the block, as long as the price is right! Transactional relationships are short-term and generally influenced by the price of the service. In a partnership relation, however, the identity of the individual (or corporate entity) is of utmost importance to the purchaser. An example of a "partner" relationship is typically found between an individual and their personal healthcare provider. It becomes vitally important (especially in crisis situations) that this relationship be continuous (i.e., long-term), trusting, and strong.

The reason for approaching an outsourcing relationship as a form of partnership has much to do with the characteristics and desired outcomes of a partnership versus a transactional relationship—see Table 11-4.[20] This partnership is also applicable in improving the relationship of IT and business, as discussed in Chapter 12.

One of the most important early aspects of IT governance with regard to establishing an outsourcing relationship is the process known as due diligence. Due diligence is the process of examining the financial underpinnings of a corporation as one of the first steps in a large-scale IT purchase, with the goal of understanding risks associated with the relationship. Issues that could be reviewed include corporate capitalization, material agreements, litigation history, public filings, intellectual property, and IT systems. Due diligence is also an important prerequisite for establishing a relationship of trust—one of the hallmarks of a partnership. Evidence compiled from industry surveys[21] reveals compelling evidence that outsourcing relationships without due diligence tend to be less successful than those in which the appropriate level of due diligence was performed on the vendor (see Figure 11-7).

Another governance consideration for outsourcing arrangements regards the use of "evergreen" clauses in vendor contracts. Vendors know that information technology professionals don't manage contracts very well. Vendors are also aware that the turnover ratio of CIOs, CEOs, and account managers involved in originally negotiating the outsourcing contract tends to be fairly high. As a result, many contracts contain an evergreen clause. This clause provides for the automatic extension of the agreement if the vendor is not notified by a predetermined future date. When challenged about the clause, the vendor usually responds by stating that it "just makes things easy." IT managers should, as a firm rule, never agree to evergreen clauses in outsourcing contracts. Similar to the evergreen clause are statements that inhibit the client from seeking bids from other vendors. These statements should be reviewed and removed.

Lastly, IT management should include remedies for poor performance in outsourcing contracts. Poor performance typically represents more than half of all reasons for terminating or renegotiating outsourcing contracts. IT management should incorporate governance mechanisms into outsourcing contracts that will address remedies for poor performance such as:

- Credits for performance shortfalls
- Two-party dispute resolution
- Third-party arbitration
- Termination remedies
- Litigation
- "Prenuptial" agreement describing how to easily end the relationship

In summary, IT governance is the procedural "glue" for IT decision making in organizations. IT governance is also a reflection of what the organizational culture values as important and who will make decisions about these things. Poor IT governance often reflects deeper cultural and strategic alignment issues and will hamper an organization's ability to deploy information technology as an enabler to change. Poor governance models are the typical result of organizational cultures that do not value IT.

IT management needs to be keenly aware of how governance works in their organizations. They should also work continuously with executive management and their business counterparts to establish the mechanisms and practices that enable sound governance and, ultimately, informed decisions about IT investments.

REVIEW QUESTIONS ▪▪▪▪▪▪▪

1. Describe the principles of IT governance and its importance to a company.
2. What are the major organizational symptoms of poor governance?
3. Describe some alternative forms of governance and their advantages and drawbacks.
4. Why is governance important to effective management of cross-functional initiatives?
5. Is governance important in creating an effective e-business? Why?
6. Describe the primary leadership roles and responsibilities in IT governance.
7. What are the primary roles of an IT steering committee?
8. Who should be part of an IT steering committee and why?
9. What is IT management's role in an IT steering committee?
10. What techniques might an IT steering committee use to prioritize projects?
11. What considerations regarding IT governance come into play when addressing international or global strategies?
12. What governance mechanisms are most commonly employed in managing vendor relationships?
13. Describe the decision-making process when considering outsourcing arrangements.
14. Describe remedies for poor performance that might be included in an outsourcing arrangement.

DISCUSSION QUESTIONS ▪▪▪▪▪▪▪

1. What forms of IT governance does your organization employ?
2. Have you observed any symptoms of poor IT governance in your organization? What are they?
3. Does your organization have an IT steering committee? What is its role and responsibilities? Who sits on the steering committee?
4. How does your organization prioritize projects?
5. How does your organization evaluate project risk?
6. How does your organization de-escalate troubled projects?[11]
7. How will your organization make decisions about its international IT functions?
8. What mechanism does your IT organization have in place regarding vendors? How well do they work?
9. How are outsourcing decisions made in your organization? By whom?
10. What do you believe might be the most important considerations in structuring an outsourcing agreement for your organization?

AREAS FOR RESEARCH ▪▪▪▪▪▪▪

1. Read the sections of Weill and Broadbent's book on leveraging the new infrastructure that address issues of IT governance.[5] What forms of IT governance that are addressed in this book do you believe would be most applicable to your own organization? Why?

2. Read Kaplan's and Norton's book on the use of balanced scorecards and their use as a governance mechanism.[10]

3. Using Kaplan and Norton's book as a guide, define your IT organization's criteria for success for each of the balanced scorecard dimensions and three measures in each dimension that would support these criteria for success.
4. Read Luftman's paper on the concept of strategic alignment maturity and the role governance plays in alignment.[3]
5. Based on the concepts embodied in the strategic alignment maturity model (see Chapter 3), how would you characterize (i.e., what maturity level) your orga-

nizational maturity with respect to its IT governance practices? Why? What are the implications for your organization of this level of IT governance maturity?
6. Read "Business as a Contact Sport" by Richardson, Vidauretta, and Gorman.[24] Which of the 12 principles of managing business relationships do you feel are most important to your organization? Which are not? What would you do to emphasize the principles that aren't being followed?

CONCLUSION ▪▪▪▪▪▪▪

This chapter has discussed the concept of IT governance as the organizational mechanism for making decisions about the use of information technology. This chapter has also underscored the importance of IT governance as a required component for the effective use of IT as an agent of business transformation and an enabler of business value. The concept of the IT steering committee as an IT

governance "best practice" has been discussed and some approaches for prioritizing projects that are based on sound business principles have been reviewed. Lastly, we addressed IT governance with respect to the growing globalization of business and governance mechanisms that organizations need to initiate in order to manage vendor relationships.

REFERENCES ▪▪▪▪▪▪▪

[1] Henderson, J. C. and Venkatraman, N., "Strategic Alignment: Leveraging Information Technology for Transforming Organizations," *IBM Systems Journal*, 32(1), 1993.

[2] InfoWorld, *True Value of IT*, April 2001.

[3] Luftman, J., "Addressing Business-IT Alignment Maturity," *Communications of the Association for Information Systems*, December 2000.

[4] Schein, E., "Three Cultures of Management: The Key to Organizational Learning," *Harvard Business Review*, *Sloan Management Review*, 38(1), Fall 1996.

[5] Weill, P., Broadbent, M., *Leveraging the New Infrastructure*, Harvard Business School Press, 1998.

[6] Venkatraman, N., "Five Steps to a Dot-Com Strategy," *Sloan Management Review*, Spring 2000.

[7] Hartman, A., Sifonis, J., *Net Ready—Strategies for Success in the E-conomy*, McGraw-Hill, 2000.

[8] Hutt, M., Stafford, E., Walker, B., and Reingen, P., "Defining the Social Network of a Strategic Alliance," *Sloan Management Review*, Winter 2000.

[9] Storck, J., Hill, P., "Knowledge Diffusion Through 'Strategic Communities.'" *Sloan Management Review*, Winter 2000.

[10] Kaplan, R., Norton, D., *The Strategy Focused Organization*, Harvard Business School Press, 2001.

[11] Keil, M., "Cutting Your Losses: Extricating Your Organization When a Big Project Goes Awry," *Sloan Management Review*, Spring 2000.

[12] Seattle State Government, SIM.

[13] Keene, P., *The Process Edge*, Harvard Business School Press, 1997.

[14] Drucker, P., *Management Challenges for the 21st Century*, HarperCollins, 1999.

[15] Davenport, T., *Information Ecology*, Oxford University Press, 1997.

[16] Daniels, John L. and Caroline, N., "Building Global Competence," in Luftman, J. (ed.) *Competing in The Information Age*, Oxford University Press, 1999.

[17] Feeny, D., "Core IS Capabilities for Exploiting Information Technology," *Sloan Management Review*, Spring 1998.

[18] Lacity, M. (University of Missouri), Willcocks, L., Feeny, D. (Oxford University) and Hirschheim, R. (University of Houston), December 1997.

[19] Rockart, J., Earl, M., and Ross, J., "Eight Imperatives for the New IT Organization," *Sloan Management Review*, Fall 1996.

[20] Henderson, J., Venkatraman, N., "Plugging into Strategic Partnerships: The Critical IS Connection," *Sloan Management Review*, Spring 1990.

[21] International Data Corp., and Technology and Business Integrators, Inc.

[22] Harvard Business School Case Study 9-188-102, *United Services Automobile Association*, Rev. September 23, 1993.

[23] Information Week, *CIO Forum: Lessons from ERP*, September 14, 1998.

[24] Richardson, T., Vidauretta, A., and Gorman, T., *Business as a Contact Sport*, Alpha Press, 2001.

[25] Diromualdo, A., "Strategic Intent for IT Outsourcing," *Sloan Management Review*, Summer 1998.

[26] Feeny, D., *Ibid*.

[27] Luftman, J., *Competing in the Information Age—Strategic Alignment in Practice*, ed. by J. Luftman, Oxford University Press, 1996.

IT Business Communications

"Knowledge may give weight, but accomplishments give luster, and many more people see than weigh."
—EARL OF CHESTERFIELD

"If you once forfeit the confidence of your fellow citizens, you can never regain their respect and esteem. You may fool all of the people some of the time; you can even fool some of the people all the time; but you can't fool all of the people all of the time."
—ABRAHAM LINCOLN

"I hate quotations. Tell me what you know."
—RALPH WALDO EMERSON

Preview of Chapter

One of the six components of the strategic alignment maturity assessment (discussed in Chapter 3—Strategic Alignment Maturity) is *communications*. The ability of the IT function and the business functions to communicate with each other is an important element that affects all of the other components. Partnership maturity is enhanced by effective communications. The enablement of communications is among the most important reasons for choosing from among the governance alternatives. The ability of IT to demonstrate the value of IT is dependent on the ability to communicate those values. Likewise, the effective communication of information between IT and the business functions is key to maintaining or improving the maturity of the organization's IT scope and architecture and making the best choices in regards to the IT organization's skills needs. It is high on the list of enablers and inhibitors to alignment.

This chapter will provide an overview of the important attributes of business-IT communications. Some background of the research that exists in support of the importance of communications will also be discussed. The significance of providing a learning environment (one which facilitates and encourages knowledge sharing) will be stressed, and some effective approaches to communication used by organizations will be presented.

What we will examine in this chapter:

- ■ Why is communications such an important factor in achieving alignment?
- ■ Why is understanding of the business by IT crucial to communications?
- ■ Why is it necessary for business partners to understand IT?
- ■ Why is communication so important in developing partnership?
- ■ What are some methods that can be used to improve communication?

▪▪▪ The Importance of Communication

Communication is the foundation of most, if not all, human activities. People (and even animals) would be unable to exist in groups if it were not for the ability to communicate with others. Communication, or the lack thereof, is a core component of relationships, whether they are professional or personal. Most readers may recognize this basic premise about communication, but understanding alone does not result in the ability of organizations to achieve competitive advantage or alignment among the IT function and the business functions. Organizations must understand how to make communication *effective*.

"Effective communications is the central lifeline of any organization. It is the vehicle for driving change, shaping expectations, and rallying workers around core purposes and common message."[1]

The ability of an organization to enable and sustain an environment in which effective communication takes place can be an important factor in the success of the organization. Communication and its factors are part of the *social dimension* of alignment. According to Reich and Benbasat,[2] the study of alignment consists of two distinct dimensions—the study of strategies, structure, and planning; and investigations of the actors involved. The studying of strategies, structure, and planning has been discussed in Chapters 2 and 3. Studying the actors involved in organizations focuses on the values, communications, and the understanding of each other's domains by the business and IT functions. These are our stakeholders.

These two dimensions of alignment are the *social* dimension and the *intellectual* dimension, respectively. The social dimension focuses on the "level of mutual understanding and commitment to business and IT mission, objectives, and plans by organizational members."[3] It is this factor that is addressed by improving communication. A second factor of the social dimension is that of *shared domain knowledge*. This factor is included in the attributes that are addressed in the strategic alignment maturity assessments communication component.

Communication in organizations is easy to take for granted, but it is important to keep a focus on the significance of communication. Even those companies that provide consulting services to businesses to assist them in improving alignment can go astray (see "Gartner, Align Thyself" sidebar).

Gartner, Align Thyself[4]

Gartner is one of the most influential IT research and consulting companies in the world. In the late 1990s, this firm found itself suffering from a lack of communications between its IT and business functions. Its own CIO and others estimate this cost the company millions of dollars a year. The poor morale that resulted from an almost complete lack of communications was another symptom of misalignment. There was no clearly understood decision-making or budget-setting process.

▪▪▪ Guidelines for Communicating

Many of the elements of communication during times of change are important even in less dynamic environments. During times of significant change, communications becomes especially important. The management of change was covered more fully in Chapter 10—Management of Change. In *Leading Change*,[5] John Kotter suggests the following key elements for effective communications of vision:

1. **Simplicity.** The use of jargon and "technobabble" must be avoided or eliminated. The relationship of the goals of the business strategy to the IT function or IT strategies to business functions needs to be expressed in language that is understandable by all of the parties involved. For example, when asked, "What time is it?" IT personnel should avoid describing how the watch is built.

2. **Metaphor, Analogy, and Example.** A verbal example is worth a thousand words. Describing an outcome or a view of the results to come can capture more support than a detailed description of the path to get there.

3. **Multiple Forums.** Communication can take many forms. Examples include meetings of various sizes, memos, newsletters, e-mail, Web sites, etc. All of these are appropriate.

4. **Repetition.** Important information may need to be delivered multiple times to be received correctly or to become firmly implanted in the minds of the receivers. *Communication* implies a sender and a receiver. If the information is not received, it has not been communicated.

5. **Leadership by Example.** Communication does not only occur with the visible transmission of information. The unspoken or unwritten messages received by actions of executives and managers can carry equal or greater information to other functions. The behavior of the person or function communicating a vision can convey a message that may destroy the chances of achieving a goal if it is inconsistent with the formal communication.

6. **Explanation of Inconsistencies.** Not all plans are without unknowns. These unknowns can appear to be inconsistencies within the communication being delivered. These inconsistencies should be addressed as part of the communication plan, lest they undermine the credibility of all the communication.

7. **Give and Take.** Communication does not or should not occur in one direction. Adjusting communication or the vision being communicated as a result of feedback can be a powerful factor in the success of the communication.

▪▪▪ Why IT Must Understand the Business

Communication is based on a complex linguistics structure. More simply, a language is used to enable people to speak with one another. People can use many means to communicate, (e.g., mime, sign language, drum beats, Morse code) but the use of a verbal language (e.g., English, Chinese, French, Russian) has been accepted for centuries as the most effective means of communication. To facilitate mutual understanding, people must use the same (or common) language. While this notion oversimplifies the situation in business, the idea of using a common language is easily shown to be necessary for effective communication.

Without a common language, the people exchanging information may not understand the communication. Even when using a common base language, misunderstandings can still occur if different dialects are used. Imagine conversations between "Brits" and Americans, in which the language has a common base but slang, idioms, and provincial terms are very different. In New York City, everyone knows the subway, but for Londoners, it is the "underground"; for Bostonians, it is the "T"; and for Washingtonians, it is the "Metro." The British have their own vocabulary where terms such as *bumpershoot*, *water closet*, *lorry*, and *apples and pears* all have meanings that many Americans aren't familiar with (see "Sample Glossary of British/American Slanguage" sidebar).

Sample Glossary of British/American Slanguage[6]

British	*American interpretation*
Apples and pears	Stairs
Banger	Sausage
Bathroom	Room with bathtub
Bonnet	Front hood of automobile
Braces	Suspenders
Bumpershoot	Umbrella
Chips	French fries
Flat	Apartment
Football	Soccer
Loo	Toilet
Lorry	Truck
Pants	Women's underwear
Subway	Pedestrian underpass
Suspenders	Garter belt
Trousers	Men's pants
Underground or tube	Subway, Metro, "the T"
WC or Water closet	Bathroom with toilet

American	*British interpretation*
Apples and pears	Fruit
Banger	Mallet or gavel
Bathroom	Toilet
Bonnet	Headpiece
Braces	Teeth retainer
Bumpershoot	–
Chips	Potato chips
Flat	Tire puncture
Football	American Football
Loo	–
Lorry	–
Pants	Men's trousers
Subway	Train runs underground
Suspenders	Holds up men's pants
Trousers	Men's pants
Underground or tube	Basement, sewer tunnel
WC or Water closets	–

In situations where IT and business personnel exchange information, an interpreter may be employed or each participant must learn the language of the other. Otherwise, participants in an information exchange will receive blank stares; similar to people attempting to converse in languages not understood by all. When financial analysts and managers begin discussing their requirements for business systems, terms like tax swaps, derivatives, investment options, portfolios, tranches, foreign currency exchanges, etc., often cause IT professionals to think that the business people are not speaking in English. Naturally, the numerous IT acronyms and technical terms cause the same problems for the business-oriented people.

Learning the business aspect of the organization that IT supports is equivalent to studying the language and customs of the customers in foreign countries that IT would intend to visit. Just like learning foreign languages, in some cases these studies will be more challenging than in other cases. Just as studying the customs and dialects of Great Britain would be easier for Americans than understanding Chinese or Russian; customer service issues would prove easier to understand than more complex financial operations or pharmaceutical research issues.

The more complex the challenge, the more it is necessary to understand the business. Communication can only be accomplished when there is common understanding of the material, requirements, and instruction that surround the activities that will be affected by IT systems. Another benefit of being knowledgeable about the business is that IT may recommend technologies that can improve the business process. Understanding the business will increase the opportunities of IT to find ways to improve productivity, reduce delays in sharing information, and provide the means to improve responsiveness to customers and other business partners.

As a corollary, understanding of the language used by business partners will enable the IT staff to build, install, and maintain systems with fewer misinterpretations and errors. The IT members of any cross-functional team will be able to better communicate with their business counterparts because they can discuss their work in business terms that will be readily understandable. With this said, it should be clear that this is not a one-way street. If it is good to have IT staff learn and understand the business, it would be equally beneficial for the business partners to learn more about IT terms, processes, activities, and requirements.

The "Sample Glossary of Financial Terms" sidebar illustrates some very common financial terms. IT is often asked to develop financial systems to perform financial valuations for the firm. The IT development team should be familiar with the financial terms to enable the development of error-free financial systems. As financial transactions become more complex, IT development teams will need to keep up with the increasing complexity of financial transactions; for example, learn and understand newer terms like derivatives, tax swaps, and tranches. The lack of understanding of the business that is supported by information systems increases the possibility that programming errors will be made. As IT managers, it would be prudent to make sure all staff become intimately familiar with the business they support in order to reduce the risk of misinterpretations and miscommunications.

Sample Glossary of Financial Terms[7]

Bearer Bonds In the past, usually every 6 months, bond owners would take a scissors to the bond, clip out the coupon, and present the coupon to the bond issuer or to a bank for payment. Those were "bearer bonds," meaning the bearer (the person who had physical possession of the bond) owned it. Today, many bonds are issued as "registered," which means even if you don't get to touch the actual bond at all, it will be registered in your name and interest will be mailed to you every 6 months.

Bond When a bond (an interest-bearing certificate) matures, the issuer redeems the bond and pays you the face amount. The purchaser may have paid $1000 for the bond 20 years ago and has received interest on that amount every six months for the last 20 years. The matured bond is now redeemed for $1000.

Treasuries The U.S. Treasury Department periodically borrows money and issues IOUs in the form of bills, notes, or bonds ("Treasuries"). The differences are in their maturities and denominations. Treasuries are auctioned. Short-term "T-bills" (Treasuries) are auctioned every Monday. The four-week bill is auctioned every Tuesday. Longer term bills, notes, and bonds are auctioned at other intervals. Treasury notes ("T-Notes") and bonds pay a stated interest rate semi-annually and are redeemed at face value at maturity. Exception: Some 30-year and longer bonds may be "called" (redeemed) at 25 years.

U.S. Savings Bonds Historically, Treasuries have paid higher interest rates than EE Savings Bonds. Savings bonds held five years pay 85 percent of five year Treasuries. However, in the past few years, the floor on savings bonds (4 percent under current law) has been higher than short-term Treasuries. So for the short term, EE Savings Bonds actually pay higher than Treasuries, but are non-negotiable and purchases are limited to $15,000 ($30,000 face) per year.

Zero Coupon Bond A zero-coupon bond has no coupons and there is no interest paid. But at maturity, the issuer promises to redeem the bond at face value. Obviously, the original cost of a $1000 bond is much less than $1000. The actual price depends on: a) the holding period — the number of years to maturity, b) the prevailing interest rates, and c) the risk involved (with the bond issuer).

▪▪▪ Why Is It Important for Business Partners to Understand IT?

From an IT organization point of view, it is equally important for the business functions to understand the language and terminology used by the IT function. If only the IT function alone were encouraged to learn their partners' activities, that would limit the possible improvement in communication and could prove to be a handicap to communication. Business must learn the language of IT to be equipped to converse in a language familiar to IT developers. Understanding IT can enhance communication by reducing the confusion that many business people have regarding technology. IT is well-known for having many acronyms, special terms, special meanings for common terms, and even different definitions for identical terms. (See the "Sample Glossary of Web Services Terms" sidebar.)

Sample Glossary of Web Services Terms[8]

SOAP Provides a way for applications to communicate with one another over the Internet, independent of platform. SOAP relies on XML to define the format of the information and then adds the necessary HTTP headers to send it.

UDDI A Web-based distributed directory that enables businesses to list themselves on the Internet and discover one another. It is comparable to a traditional phone book's yellow and white pages.

Web services A standardized way of integrating Web-based applications using open standards such as XML, SOAP, WSDL, and UDDI over an IP backbone.

Web Services Description Language (WSDL) An XML-formatted language used to describe a Web service's capabilities as collections of communication endpoints that can exchange messages. WDSL, developed jointly by Microsoft and IBM, is the language used by UDDI.

XML A specification developed by the World Wide Web Consortium to tag data.

If business partners are unfamiliar with these terms, they are likely to be confused in conversations where these terms are used. It would be more effective to have business partners know the meaning of some of these terms, much as IT is expected to understand the business terms. An alternative is for IT to avoid using terms that the business will not comprehend. Business people need not be technologists. They are interested in what/how IT can enable or drive enhancements to the business. If both groups learned all of the special terms, slang, and acronyms used by the other group, their communication would be greatly improved. In a true partnership, each group must contribute to that conversation—having a common language enables that partnership.

Understanding of business language and processes by IT, and an understanding of IT language and processes by the business functions, become crucial building blocks for developing a mutual understanding. The five basic elements to this foundation are: 1) understanding the language of their partner, 2) understanding the responsibilities and jobs of their partner, 3) understanding the requirements and information needs of their partner, 4) understanding the current capabilities of their partner, and 5) understanding the opportunities for improvement (potential) of their partner. It would seem that accomplishing all of the objectives on this list is a formidable task, but keep in mind it is not a requirement for each party to be a resident expert in the other's work. Having a rudimentary understanding of the five elements will improve communication and will lead to a better mutual understanding of the other's job and role. With mutual understanding, an organization can achieve a higher level of maturity and alignment. In the next section, mutual understanding is discussed as a driving force.

Developing Partnership Through Mutual Understanding

Two of the six attributes of the communications maturity assessment deal with the mutual understanding of the IT and business functions. The mutual understanding (which results from both the business functions understanding the world of IT and the IT function understanding the business world) increases *partnership* in achieving the goals of the organization. This is the same partnership model used to improve the relationship with external partners discussed in Chapter 11.

Henderson[9] describes two styles of relationships that have been described by various researchers—a *transactional* style of relationship and a *partnership* style of relationship. The transactional style refers to relationships defined by rules, policies, and procedures. Contractual relationships are the best example of this. The partnership style of relationship implies risk sharing, a longer time frame for exchanges, and the need to establish a range of mechanisms that monitor and execute the operations of the partnership. According to Henderson, this style of relationship consists of two dimensions: Partnership in Context (PIC), and Partnership in Action (PIA).

Partnership in context consists of the factors that affect the beliefs of the members of a relationship in the longevity, stability, and interdependence of the relationship. Partnership in action describes the factors that affect the day-to-day working relationship—the ability of the partners to affect the outcome of the relationship through influence over decision making.

▪▪▪▪▪▪▪▪▪▪▪ **FIGURE 12-1**   Six Determinants of Partnership.

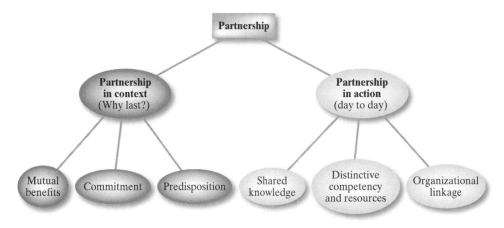

Source: Henderson, John C., *Plugging into Strategic Partnerships: The Critical IS Connection*, Sloan Management Review, Spring 1990.

Figure 12-1[10] describes the factors that make up the components of partnerships. Partnership in context describes why the members of a relationship think the relationship should last. Members of a lasting partnership believe that the mutual benefits achieved are greater than what could be achieved independently. Mutual benefits may be financial (revenue generation, cost reduction, business objective attainment), efficiency (quality and process improvement), or intangible (improved work life). Commitment reflects the shared desire for a partnership to be maintained. Shared goals and incentives to achieve those goals as partners also affect commitment. Finally, predisposition refers to the perceptions that exist prior to the partnership starting. These preconceived positions are often difficult to alter. Trust and attitude are key factors that affect this.

The determinants of partnership in action are shared knowledge, mutual dependency of distinctive competencies and resources, and organizational linkage. Shared knowledge relates to the need for the partners in a relationship to understand the others' role and what they do. This implies a linkage between mutual understanding and the other attributes of the communications maturity (e.g., knowledge sharing, organizational learning, and liaison(s) effectiveness). A partnership's mutual dependence on distinctive competencies and resources highlights the importance of understanding the need for each side of a partnership. The business functions must understand the importance of the success of IT in achieving the business goals, while the IT function must understand the importance of the business functions and their staff in achieving success with IT projects. The ability of IT and business functions to understand the *linkages* between each other, and for these linkages to be two-way, also affects the success of the partnership. For example, the more frequently decision making involves both groups of the partnership, the more likely it is that a good partnership exists.

The Road to Partnership

Henderson's research points to the following actions that organizations can take to creating effective partnerships:[11]

1. Education.   Skills transfer and training are important approaches to improving the understanding among IT and the business, especially in those areas where tasks are interrelated or dependent on each other. General education about the overall organization is also important. All members of a partnership should understand the important concepts and skills needed and contributed by other members of an organization. Finally, the need to understand the culture and social factors at play in a partnership can also be addressed through education.

2. **Joint Planning.** Joint planning is necessary for several reasons. First, it is an important process for developing an understanding of the mutual benefits through negotiation and agreement. The planning process itself is an educational vehicle. Joint discussions involving business and IT staff result in an exchange of information and knowledge. As discussed in the chapters on processes and strategy, planning is an ongoing and iterative process.

3. **Measurement and Control.** The benefits of a partnership must be recognizable by the organization's members for a sustainable commitment. The ability to identify and measure the benefits is therefore important to be able to judge whether the benefits are achieved. Naturally, all stakeholders must understand and agree to the objectives of the measurements selected. Benchmarking is one important method of creating effective measures. This provides an excellent vehicle for assessing the organization in comparison to others in the same firm, same industry, and exemplars across all industries. Measurement of benefits is described more completely in Chapters 13—Measuring, Reporting, and Controlling and in Chapter 14—The Value of IT.

4. **Effective Use of Teams.** Cross-functional teams are another way of improving the effectiveness of a partnership (and thereby improving communication maturity). Teams create an environment that fosters knowledge exchange, similar to joint planning. Teams also improve the understanding of the interrelationships between functions, and can help "normalize" cultural factors through the social exchanges that occur in team processes. Personal exchanges among different organizations lower information barriers that might exist otherwise. Teams can also contribute a level of stability in dynamic organizations. Reactions to rapid changes in an organization's environment can be faster when cross-functional teams are in place than when traditional organizational structures are used. Thus, teams can provide a more stable organization structure in dynamic environments.

5. **Multilevel Human Resource Strategy.** The actions described above should not be limited to any particular level of personnel in an organization. Partnerships must exist at all levels of the organization. Mutual understanding must exist between executives as well as nonmanagement personnel.

6. **Technology.** An interesting outcome of the pervasiveness of technology is that technology itself can play a major role in sustaining and improving partnerships. The ability to effectively exchange information, collaboration techniques and tools, and the measurement of benefits are all enhanced through the use of technology. Organizations that understand this and make use of technology are more likely to achieve stronger partnerships between IT and the business functions.

▪▪▪ Organizational and Global Culture

Organizational culture as well as cultural differences between organizations and countries can affect the effectiveness of communications in organizations.[12] The hidden messages in communications, or even actions that are taken without thought to messages being sent, can be more important than the intended message. The "Where's the Bus" sidebar provides one such example.

Where's the Bus?[13]

> *"...one German company needed to cut costs. Managers believed that the communications regarding the rationale were adequate. However, in their cost-cutting mode, they decided not to replace an old company bus that shuttled employees from the lowest level of a huge parking lot up to headquarters. At the same time, executives were receiving their new cars. In Europe, executive cars are very important status symbols, and each one received a new Mercedes."*
>
> *"Everything else that happened around the cost-cutting—articles, speeches about "being in it together"—was useless. All employees remembered was that the cost-cutting hit them (their bus was discontinued) and the executives got their cars. Morale (and employee support for cost containment) sank."*
>
> —CHARLENE MARMER SOLOMON,
> *COMMUNICATING IN A GLOBAL ENVIRONMENT*

The cultures of some regions of the world receive written communications more positively, while others view personal forms of communications as preferable. Managers need to take these factors into account when deciding how best to disseminate information. Even in cultures where non-written communication is preferable, written communication maintains a supporting role. Written communication is much more effective in addressing ambiguity, preventing misunderstandings, and identifying ownership and accountability.

▪▪▪ Addressing Communication Effectiveness

Galbraith[14] identified various mechanisms for increasing communication across business units. The six most pertinent are:[15]

1. **Direct Communication.** This describes communication among business and IT executives that is *direct*, such as ad-hoc meetings, electronic mail, and written communication.
2. **Liaison Roles.** The responsibility for communication among IT and business functions is delegated to individuals who facilitate the communication channels among business and IT functions.
3. **Temporary Task Forces.** The creation of project teams that exist for the duration of a specific project provides a mechanism for more effective communication flow.
4. **Permanent Teams/Committees.** These are also known as steering committees. This style of organizational structure as an answer to improving communication was discussed in Chapter 11—IT Governance. Although this technique for improving communication has become popular, "successful steering committees are difficult to find, and few firms know what to expect from their steering committees or what roles these committees should play in governing IT management."[16] Despite this comment, the study by Karimi, et al. found that the presence of steering committees did enhance the alignment within an organization. Luftman's[17] maturity assessment research further supports this.
5. **Integrating Roles.** This technique assigns a leader from an outside function to manage a team. For example, an IT person might lead a business quality team.
6. **Managerial Linking Roles.** This technique is similar to the matrix organization structure. Communication needs are addressed through the use of a product manager role.

Here are some sample approaches for each of these mechanisms:

Direct Communications Each activity across IT and its business partners differs in complexity, requirements, and importance. Direct communications should reflect this range of situations. For each activity, consideration should be given to determine the best vehicle and audience. For many day-to-day activities, e-mail is increasingly the most effective communication vehicle. Telephone calls are still made between people who look for a more interactive conversation. Where more complex issues are discussed and a wider audience needs to participate, telephone conferencing or video conferencing is employed. More groupware technologies are being adopted where the use of networked PCs, Web sites with shared storage, and electronic chalkboards are utilized. Virtual classrooms are being deployed and these can assist in conducting virtual meetings with greater interaction between participants. Rounding out the spectrum of direct communication options are: ad-hoc meetings, formal meetings, and traveling to meet with partners, clients, and vendors. It is important that consideration is given to provide the right level of interaction. A meeting of all project members in multiple sites might be an unnecessary cost if video conferencing or a virtual Web meeting could be held instead. It would be ineffective to have an introductory kick-off meeting between a new multisite project team with their business analysts using a noninteractive communications method.

Liaison Roles Are important in situations where business and IT are unable to devote sufficient time to working with each other. The liaison agent becomes a surrogate facilitator in assisting business and IT to join and work together. A liaison agent is not an interpreter! There is no replacement for requiring IT and business to understand one another. And there is no substitution for direct communication among IT and business representatives. The liaison agent must get IT and business stakeholders together and make sure that each group is providing the kind of participation needed for a successful development and deployment of business systems. The liaison role has become increasingly important because an effective liaison drives improvement in the quality of the product by reducing errors and therefore reducing the necessity of having tasks redone.

Temporary Task Forces Have become instrumental in many organizations for successfully completing business systems. Only when people from both IT and business are dedicated to a single project can the project team hope to be effective. The task force creates a central focus for each participant. Without this focus the daily distractions of their normal work would make the team members ineffective. Communication among task members improves because they share common goals and objectives. While it is common for each task force member to have a different agenda, these will be more closely aligned because it is unlikely that task members would want the project to fail.

Permanent Teams or Committees Are an effective means of providing stability. Steering committees, comprised of appropriate members from IT and business organizations to oversee IT and business projects, provide a mechanism for making improved long-term decisions. The introduction of an empowered permanent committee means that a legitimate formal process will exist, and decisions will more likely be made in the best interests of the firm. The communication among the members of the committee and those that make requests from the committee results in decisions that are much improved compared to those decided in a vacuum. IT decisions that are made in the best interests of the firm move IT toward a higher level of strategic alignment within the firm.

Integrating Roles Is similar to providing cross training to IT and business personnel. Sarah Jackson once said, "Before you criticize someone, walk a mile in their shoes. That way, if they get angry, they'll be a mile away—and barefoot." Having the experience to know what the other person needs to do often provides a refreshing perspective. One may find the job is not easy, so the switch is not permanent, but it will enlighten and thus improve the ability to more effectively work together. Rotating IT and business people between the two areas is a popular approach to broadening perspectives of the firm's staff.

Managerial Linking Roles Are often used to facilitate multiple/different priorities and agendas. Using a matrix structure, team members are provided guidance by multiple supervisors. While it is argued that working for two or more bosses can be quite troubling, if it is managed well, the workers are better assisted by superiors who are well versed in the respective subject matter. The workers can have their questions answered by those supervisors most likely to provide correct answers. Again the means of communication are improved because these workers have access to the right people. In prior situations, IT workers were often not allowed to discuss their project work with business managers unless their IT supervisors were involved. This change in reporting relationship means that now the IT workers have direct communication with their IT and business managers. This approach is most often used where IT and the business are most comfortable with each other on a partnership level.

Tips and Techniques

Understanding that communication is important is a start. As mental health professionals say, "Understanding that a problem exists is the first step to healing." There are a number of tactics for improving communication among IT and business organizations. First, leading business journals will often describe the problems, experiences, and solutions attempted in other organizations. Journals related to IT management frequently publish CIO and CEO experiences in addressing these insights. Learning from others' trials and tribulations is one way of preventing or recognizing the same problems in one's own organization.

For example, earlier in the chapter (See "Gartner, Align Thyself" sidebar) the difficulties Gartner faced were discussed. Communication needed to be improved in order to rectify the problems of financial losses and deteriorating employee morale. To do this, the CIO introduced what was called "project-based budgeting."[18] This process consisted of three advisory councils that involved business and IT leaders from around the world. The proposal process required that project sponsors tie project goals to corporate strategies. This process resulted not only in better alignment between business and IT, but also between different business units, by increasing the communications of the parties involved in prioritizing projects.

Too Much Communication?[19]

Tom Dolan, the CIO of Cablevision in 1995, needed to improve his organization's image. He attempted to do this by "branding" the IT organization—it was named Meta4 and communications about the organization and its efforts were increased. One method was the use of a scrolling CNN-like ticker line at the bottom of a Web-based tool that provided the reporting of metrics about IT to executives in addition to a five-minute video about IT projects. The video ran as a "commercial" on large-screen TVs in the executive suite that is used for functional areas to display operational metrics. However, executives began to wonder if the time and money spent on the commercial and the ticker would have been better spent on delivering on promised projects.

A study of the business-IT alignment within the Canadian Forces organization was conducted, reviewing issues surrounding communication and knowledge sharing.[20] The major finding of this study was that shared domain knowledge is critical in increasing the level of communication among IT and administration managers (the Canadian Forces equivalent of business managers).

Training of administration managers in IT and their inclusion in IT projects was recommended to address some of the deficiencies in the area of shared domain knowledge. Similarly, administration and IT officers were encouraged to take both business and IT courses. A recommendation was also made to establish steering groups to create more direct communications between the heads of IT and other branches of the Forces. Weekly IT information sessions were also suggested.

Sometimes, things go wrong and action is necessary to get things back on track. It has been suggested "two out of every three people have a hostile relationship with at least one person with whom they work."[21] When this occurs at higher levels of management, the results can impact the entire organization. It can create a division in an organization's culture at lower levels. It is important to recognize that personal relationships are at the core of effective communication, and the same tools must be brought to bear in business life that are used in personal life (see "Resolving Differences" sidebar). Healthy personal relationships between individuals in the organization are healthy for the organization as a whole as well.

Resolving Differences[22]

Stephen Covey, best known for his book *The Seven Habits of Highly Effective People*, writes frequently about personal relationships practices to follow in order to be effective at building partnerships. He has said that empathy, the practice of first seeking to understand and then to be understood, and synergy, arriving at a creative third alternative to a problem, are two important skills for maintaining partnerships:

"The skills of empathy and synergy are especially important in relationships such as partnerships and stakeholder relations. In any ongoing relationship, you need to practice these two skills constantly. ... You can experience synergy that comes from sincere empathy if both parties seek a creative, win-win third alternative to two opposing positions."

It is sometimes necessary to implement *formal* communication programs. Lucent Technologies implemented such a program specifically to address organizational alignment, community building, and operational effectiveness as part of a major IT project.[23] In the development of this program, the project leaders differentiated between two types of communication—*push communication* and *pull communication*. *Push communication* occurs when information is disseminated to the organization without being requested by the receivers of the information. *Pull communication* occurs when information is requested and normally implies the immediate availability of the information.

The project leaders at Lucent concluded that a balance between push and pull communication was necessary to effectively address the three objectives of the communication program. Community building was addressed primarily through push mechanisms, as the information that fosters this response is usually not critical to daily activities.

Communication to improve organizational alignment revolves around strategy and direction, thereby focusing the decision-making and managerial processes. A mix of push and pull communication was used to address the improvement of alignment. Push information was used to disseminate strategic direction information, and pull mechanisms for delivery of project status and measurements.

Operational efficiency is related to daily decision-making and management. Information that can be detailed and customizable is most effective in achieving this goal, so pull communication is most effective.

The Personal Factor

This chapter has stressed the organizational view of communications; the focus has been primarily on generic factors or structures that can address improving the effectiveness of communication within organizations. However, the chapter began by stating that communication is the foundation of *human* activities. This must be understood by IT as well as business personnel in the daily communications that occur. The ability to draw upon special techniques useful for maintaining personal relationships should not be dismissed.

Communication Style[24]

Communication can make or break a career, build or destroy a marriage, even begin or end a war. It is perhaps the most important thing we do. If we have a problem at work, we say it is a communication problem. If we have a problem in a relationship, we say it is a communication problem. But we typically don't know how to fix these problems, and we often don't know what caused the problem.

How to Talk Your Way Out of Trouble   Communication style is concerned with how you say what you say. This is an important distinction to make because people do not respond to what is said (the actual words). Rather, they respond to how something is said—the style or manner in which the words are used.

If you can control communication style, then you can control the outcome of most interactions. But in order to do this, you must keep this one essential thought in mind:

Each person expects the other person to communicate exactly as he or she communicates   We expect the other person to sound as we sound, and when these expectations are not met or when people communicate in a style that is inconsistent with past expectations, communication conflict exists (see the "How to Talk Your Way into Success" sidebar). It is the management of this conflict that leads to control, and subsequently, personal and professional success.

If you can control communication style, you can control the outcome of most interactions   While delivered here in a humorous fashion, a serious analogy of the business relationship and marriage relationship can be made. For example:

- You should talk to your business partners every day whether you want to or not.
- Compromise and negotiation are important factors in sustaining a partnership.
- It can be more painful and more work to break up than it is to stay together.
- Everybody involved is happier if the partnership is stable and happy.
- It is easier to achieve your goals and vision through *joint* planning and work.
- Never enter a relationship with another party without the knowledge and acceptance of your other partners.

How to Talk Your Way into Success[25]

Leaders persuade and influence others to accept ideas, to follow, and to take action. Thus, communication becomes the essence of leadership. Without effective communication, leadership does not exist.

Communication style refers to your encoding processes. It deals with how you say what you say.

The message then travels through some channel to reach the eyes and ears of a receiver, who goes through a reverse process to interpret the message. The receiver decodes the message by engaging in his or her own selecting and sorting process. When all of this is done, the best that we can hope for is that the receiver now has a similar idea reconstructed. The receiver then provides feedback, which gives you information about how your message was interpreted.

This reconstruction process is complicated by the fact that meanings are derived from each person's past experiences and individual perceptions of the world.

Communication is, indeed, a very complex process. Style of communication is but one aspect of the process, but *it is the one element that we have the most control over, and it is the means by which we get others to do willingly what we want them to do.*

It is imperative that all business partners maintain clear and honest communication. Trust and reputation is a premium that cannot be jeopardized for small immediate gains. The history of the world is littered with examples of mistrust and dishonesty that have sometimes taken centuries to undo. Sadly, there is mistrust in many parts of the world that may never be undone. The failure of large IT projects due to poor or nonexistent communications can create an environment in which it is difficult to build (or rebuild) trust and open communications. Communication is only worthwhile when the parties believe the communication has value and benefits both sides. If either party believes that the other party is not dealing in good faith, the best that can happen is that the party ignores the communication. The worst that can happen includes plotting revenge in project failure, working towards undermining other projects, and looking to break off all relationships (the ultimate divorce) between the parties.

In human interactions, reputation and integrity go hand in hand. Reputation may take a lifetime to build but can be destroyed by a single misfortune. Communicate problems and issues with your partners upfront. Telling them why you are dissatisfied with their efforts usually plays better than seeking to go around them or undermining their efforts. This would be a major step in demonstrating true honest communication and could establish a closer relationship.

▮▮▮ What Are the Best Methods to Improve Communications?

The strategic alignment maturity model assessment process can reveal opportunities for improving education and knowledge levels of the firm in IT and business arenas. The use of the assessment model can enable IT managers to learn the current extent of IT staff knowledge of their work and the work of their business counterparts. This leads to the discovery of areas that need improvement. Once areas of weakness are determined, active effort can be initiated to reduce the information or knowledge gap.

Knowledge sharing is a key element of communication. As previously discussed, cross training of individuals in both the business and IT would allow for staff to better understand language, activities, requirements, methods, objectives, and tools. Companies can introduce classes that both business and IT staff can jointly attend or have them geared to introductory material for each group. The business can introduce rotation programs where IT staff would work in the business areas and business staff can join IT project teams where both would learn new skills in an area where they formerly had no experience. The tour of duty could range from six months to two years, depending on the staff flexibility the firm has available.

It should not be surprising to find that business and IT staff need to learn more about their own areas, as well as those of their counterparts. IT has many tools available to them to enhance the cross training and sharing of information and knowledge, and technologies are improving all the time. This means that over the next few years or in the next few months, there will be new products and services available to the enterprise to enhance communication.

An example of an emerging technology today is the introduction of a Group Decision Support System (GDSS). See Figure 12-2, where the GDSS is illustrated. The GDSS is available now because of the advances in teleconferencing tools. Network bandwidth, television cameras, Web cams, laptop terminals, etc. have matured to allow for communication to be coordinated between multiple sites with multiple participants. The GDSS uses PCs or laptops for communication purposes. Each participant logs into the session and each participant can be identified or remain anonymous, according to the plan of the session moderator. The session moderator handles the interactions of the sessions and directs the discussion as a moderator would without GDSS. The session moderator can use large public screens for presentations and all the participants see the presentation simultaneously at all sites.

▪▪▪▪▪▪▪▪▪▪▪▪ **FIGURE 12-2** Models for Group Decision Support.

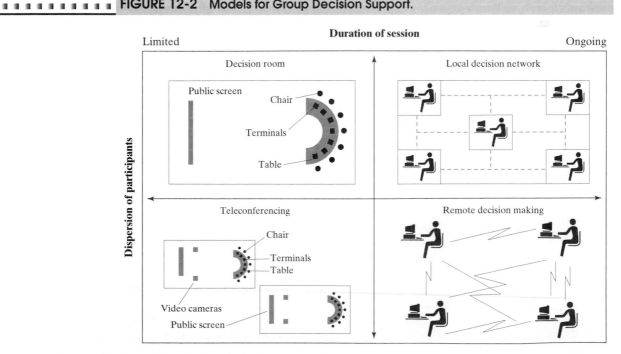

For the many companies that have already used the system or beta tested it, the following lessons have been learned:

GDSS can increase the number of ideas generated during a divergent process. This may be explained though the use of individual PCs and laptops. In a regular group meeting, everyone needs to communicate one at a time. Using GDSS, each participant can enter his or her ideas without having to wait for another respondent to answer. All participants can enter their thoughts and this can be shared to all participants via the session moderator.

Meeting participants will be active rather than passive, increasing energy and group focus. Because each participant can enter their ideas at the same time, they are more spontaneous and if they are more spontaneous, they will feel more motivated to be an active participant.

Anonymity is a continuous rather than discrete variable. This is to say that when a session moderator chooses to allow each participant to remain anonymous, the participation is from the entire group. In a general meeting session, participants are individuals and their participation occurs as discrete ideas and comments, restricted by their fears of how others might perceive them and their status in the organization.

Anonymity encourages GDSS participants to evaluate ideas more objectively. Whether the ideas come from the CEO or an entry level staffer, in an anonymous GDSS session, the ideas are evaluated on the basis of merit. In a general meeting, the CEO or CIO comments may have greater weight than others and therefore the ideas may not be evaluated solely based on merit.

Anonymous constructive criticism using GDSS improves the quality of ideas generated. This is a reverse perspective of the previous lesson. If the ideas come from an unidentified source, the criticism will not be limited by who generated the idea. The improvement of the idea can be done collaboratively without the fear of intimidation that would be found in a general meeting session.

GDSS may increase buy-in to the final result of the group effort. This again is based on an anonymous session structure. Since there isn't pressure to accept the ideas of just the few individuals with power, there will more satisfaction because all the ideas were addressed on merit. If the group accepts the result, no large set of individuals can feel the results were predetermined or forced upon them.

As the technology improves, effective GDSS meetings may be held on individual desktops.

Another important aspect is to jointly manage the communication between the business and IT. The senior management team must lead by example and foster strong communication between the CIO and other executives. Steering committees were also mentioned as a good vehicle to promote communication, especially if the committee becomes a permanent one. A permanent steering committee will be seen as a long-term commitment to alignment of the goals for both IT and the firm. The CIO and the steering committee must have true power to make improvements, and they both need to be heard as well as be good listeners in order to make a difference.

Many companies have been working on improving communications within the firm and building their strengths in knowledge sharing. In the "State Street Corporation" sidebar, State Street looked for ways to improve their IT-business relationship with some success. Many more companies will have to do the same if they wish to be competitive.

State Street Corporation: Building IT-Business Knowledge Sharing[26]

In 1998 John Fiore was promoted to CIO of State Street. His first three years as CIO was spent guiding the IT organization through the Euro conversions, Y2K, and considerable growth in the business. For 2001, his main goal has been to be the driving force behind "One State Street" (a term to describing how IT can work with the business to offer clients a singular view of the firm, suggesting a seamless face.)

Fiore feels strongly that the IT organization must, "...work hand in hand with the business to support the business. It's a partnership, we bring our expertise to the table and their business people bring their expertise to the table..."

To share this expertise across the enterprise,

> *"the CIO staff put together a series of focus groups with IT members from across State Street. These groups identified best practices in common areas of interest such as development processes, life cycle methodologies, application architecture, professional development, systems management, testing, and help desk management. These focus groups marked the beginning of the process of bringing people into the IT community. Now these groups have become institutionalized as the organization has evolved."*

This is an example of how the creation of several ad hoc IT-business committees was done so successfully that it became a permanent fixture in the corporate landscape.

State Street was also successful in creating infrastructure services to individual businesses. While changing the culture of the IT organization, the CIO staff worked hard to ensure these mechanisms were always linked back with the business leadership.

The use of liaison agents, task forces, cross-functional project teams, and direct communication are all necessary for effectively promoting good communication. All of these vehicles are fundamental in providing many outlets for IT and the business to talk, e-mail, meet, and share their ideas. It was mentioned previously that the marketplace has been introducing many new tools, such as groupware, instant messaging, Web cams, Web conferencing, electronic whiteboards, etc. to facilitate better communication. New products continue to appear, incrementally improving upon the available existing products. The wide use of cellular phones means that everyone can be connected throughout the workday. If a problem arises, everyone on the project can be reached and a joint teleconference could be set up in literally minutes when necessary. The use of new technologies and new ways of organizing workers, teams, and workflow ensure that the opportunities for improved communication exist.

Lastly, measurement and control must be widely used and the results must be communicated to everyone. Communicating how work and performance are measured is important because IT and the business need to understand the firm's priorities and how close they are to achieving those priorities. Measurements must focus on evaluating how the priorities are being reached. The results of measurement must be able to reflect on the successes or failures of IT and the business activity. Success or failure in an effective firm does not lay blame on a single area, department, or group. Success and failure are the result of team efforts and if IT and the business agree with that statement, then a partnership might actually exist between the two parties. Refer to the discussion on measurement in Chapter 13—Measuring, Reporting, and Controlling.

▪▪▪ What Is the Priority in Improving IT Communication?

In the beginning of this chapter, it was stated that communication was a foundation, or at least a fundamental building block, of human activity. It was also mentioned that effective communication was a central lifeline of any organization. A corporation today would not exist long if they had poor internal or poor external communication. Therefore, it is most likely there is decent, even good communication within the firm. The focus must be on where there can be improvements.

The strategic alignment maturity assessment model has several attributes that are affected by the level of communication. Results from conducting an assessment will be a good starting point in discovering opportunities for improvement. Refer to the strategic alignment maturity model assessment in Chapter 3—Strategic Alignment Maturity.

Training is often an important aspect that has quick payback and is most effective in reducing errors and waste. The discussion of training issues was included in Chapter 9—Human Resources Considerations.

The firm also needs to continually scan new technologies and products that can boost communication effectiveness among the business and IT staff. Pilot projects should be established to test products out in actual work situations. Purchase decisions should not be based on vendor claims and sales hype, but on results done using the firm's staff, working on the firm's project, and in the firm's corporate environment. With new products being introduced monthly, products to test must be chosen wisely and be piloted by experienced cross-functional teams. Refer to the discussion of similar efforts in Chapter 7—Managing Emerging Technologies.

Finally, this chapter has examined the importance of building partnerships though mutual understanding. Mutual understanding is also assisted by trust and integrity. Without these ingredients, there cannot be a partnership. Respect for the leader is the building block; the leader's example will lead subordinates in gaining respect for the organization. Leadership and building partnerships were discussed in Chapter 4—The Role of the CIO.

REVIEW QUESTIONS ▪▪▪▪▪▪▪

1. What is the importance of having good communication between IT and the business?
2. What are the key elements for effective communication of vision?
3. Why does communication between people require a common language?
4. How does cross training or cross education improve communication?
5. What are the benefits to the firm when business people understand IT better?
6. Why is partnership important to the firm?
7. What are the determinants of partnership?
8. Which actions did Henderson suggest are important to creating effective partnerships?
9. What mechanisms did Galbraith identify as increasing communication between business units?
10. In what ways can the firm improve business and IT communication? Explain.

DISCUSSION QUESTIONS ▪▪▪▪▪▪▪

1. What are some of the ways that organizations of which you are aware try to improve communication?
2. If trust is lost, what are the ways people can repair their relationship?
3. If trust is lost within the firm, what can the organizations within the firm do to repair their relationships?

Are there differences between how people handle the repair versus how an organization handles the repair?
4. What can a firm do to improve the education levels of their staff? What is the role of IT or business process certifications? Should continuing education and cross training be required?

5. What are the negative implications and issues when firms attempt to cross train their business and IT staffs?

6. What products should be developed in the future to support improved business—IT communication?

AREAS FOR RESEARCH ▪▪▪▪▪▪▪

1. Review the works of some of the key contributors to knowledge sharing (Nonaka, etc.)
2. What are the specific areas of the strategic alignment maturity model that help assess the level of communication between the business and IT?
3. What are the specific areas of the strategic alignment maturity model that help assess the level of education of the business and IT staffs?

4. What educational programs are available in your firm or firms of which you are aware? Discuss their goal and then discuss their effectiveness in achieving that goal.

CONCLUSION ▪▪▪▪▪▪▪

This chapter began by focusing on the importance of communication. It is an important element in assessing the alignment maturity level and is ranked high on the list of enablers/inhibitors to alignment. The firm is a complex organism that relies on communication to send messages to its staff, and needs its staff to work harmoniously with each other. Without effective communication, the firm would eventually die. The relationship between people within IT and in the business arena must be improved and cultivated to enable the development of mutual understanding that can lead to true partnership.

There were some simple basic concepts that should be emphasized. A common language is necessary for effective communication. Both IT and the business side have complex vocabularies. Communication can be drastically improved if IT and business both learn each other's jobs, requirements, methods, objectives, and languages. Both sides would then be empowered to make suggestions and offer assistance to one another.

The chapter also addressed the importance of communication as a part of effective leadership. Communication style, leading by example, honesty, trustworthiness, integrity all are important ingredients in getting heard. Flaws in any one of those ingredients can be disastrous to effective communication. Every member of the firm must be committed to improving communication so that it is effective and continuous.

REFERENCES ▪▪▪▪▪▪▪

[1] Solomon, Charlene Marmer, *Communicating in a Global Environment*, Workforce, November 1999.

[2] Reich, Blaize Horner, Denbasat, Izak, *Factors That Influence the Social Dimension of Alignment Between Business and Information Technology Objectives*, MIS Quarterly, March 2000.

[3] Reich, B.H., Benbasat, I., *A Model for the Investigation of Linkage Between Business and Information Technology Objectives"*, in J. C. Henderson and N. Venkatramam (editors), *Strategic Management of Information Technology* Volume 1. London: JAI Press, Inc. (1994).

[4] Ferranti, Marc, *Gartner, Align Thyself*, CIO, Nov. 15, 2001.

[5] Kotter, John P., *Leading Change,* Cambridge, MA: Harvard Business School Press, 1996.

[6] *http://www.slanguage.com*

[7] *http://www.cobeconet.com* and *http://www.invest-FAQ.com*

[8] *Computerworld*, June 24, 2002, Vol. 36, no. 26, pg. 29.

[9] Henderson, John C., "Plugging into Strategic Partnerships: The Critical IS Connection," *Sloan Management Review*, Spring 1990.

[10] *Ibid.*

[11] *Ibid.*

[12] Solomon, Charlene Marmer, *Communicating in a Global Environment*, Workforce, November 1999.

[13] *Ibid.*

[14] Galbraith, J. R., *Organization Design*, Reading, MA: Addison Wesley, 1977.

[15] Reich, Blaize Horner, and Denbasat, Izak, *Factors That Influence the Social Dimension of Alignment Between Business and Information Technology Objectives*, MIS Quarterly, March 2000.

[16] Karimi, Jahangir, Bhattacherjee, Anol, Gupta, Yash P., and Somers, Toni M., "The Effects of MIS Steering Committees on Information Technology Management Sophistication," *Journal of Management Information Systems*, Fall 2000.

[17] Luftman, J., "Assessing Business-IT Maturity," *"Communications of The Association for Information Systems,"* December 2000.

[18] Ferranti, Marc, "Gartner, Align Thyself," *CIO*, Nov. 15, 2001.

[19] Viscasillas, Stephanie, "Brand IT," *CIO*, Jan. 15, 2002.

[20] Hartung, Sharon, Reich, Blaize Horner, and Benbasat, Izak, "Information Technology Alignment in the Canadian Forces," *Revue Canadienne des Sciences de l'Administration*, Dec. 2000.

[21] Covey, Stephen, "Rebuilding Relationships," *Incentive*, January 2000.

[22] Covey, Stephen, "Resolving Differences," *Incentive*, July 1999.

[23] Carr, David C., and Folliard, Karen A., "How to Implement a Successful Communication Program: A Case Study," *Bell Labs Technical Journal*, July-September 1999, Vol. 4, Issue 3.

[24] McCallister, Linda, *Say What You Mean, Get What You Want*. New York: John Wiley & Sons, 1994—as summarized by MeansBusiness, Inc. at *www.meansbusiness.com*

[25] *Ibid*.

[26] Woodham, Richard and Weill, Peter, *State Street Corporation: Evolving IT Governance,* The Center for Information Systems Research at the MIT Sloan School of Management, 2002.

CHAPTER 13

Measuring, Reporting, and Controlling

"It is Drucker's first law of statistics that you can always get all the information except what you need."[1]

—PETER F. DRUCKER

Preview of Chapter

While other chapters discuss the role of CIOs and how they organize and manage IT, this chapter will focus on how management (IT and business) can be kept informed of the activity and progress of the IT organization. The demand from business has always been to expect that its technology is operating effectively and efficiently. Therefore, management must be aware of how the IT organization is meeting business expectations, as well as how "favorably" the IT organization performs in relation to other IT organizations (e.g., competitors in the same industry, exemplars). Without the ability to measure or compare IT activity, the enterprise would not be able to gauge how well IT is performing or whether IT is meeting the demands of the firm.

Information Technology as a business entity is comparatively young. While the other business entities (functional business units such as marketing, accounting, R&D) were introduced a century or more ago, IT has only entered its fifth decade, still unsure of its place in the enterprise. Of course, the need for IT is readily accepted by the other business entities; however, there are some who question whether IT belongs as a business partner or as just another service provider. This chapter will discuss measurements other than value, and how they can be used to monitor and control the activity of IT, so that IT can improve its performance in delivering and meeting commitments. The important question of the "value of IT" will be addressed in the next chapter.

What we will examine in this chapter:

- The importance of measurement
- What and how to measure
- Quality and efficacy of measures

■ Reporting to different audiences

■ Controlling IT through effective service level agreements(SLAs)

■ Negotiating a service level agreement

■ Making SLAs work—metrics

■ Introducing internal SLA to the firm

■ Using SLAs to measure external vendors and internal suppliers

■ SLA myths

■ Who owns measurements

■ What to do with the measurements

■ When measurements should be done

■ Whether the enterprise can succeed with or without measurements

▪▪▪ Introduction

Why measure? That seems like a simple question. Is the answer simple as well? Organizations want to measure so that they know how effectively and efficiently their Information Technology areas are performing. Other chapters in this book have described the importance of understanding the firm's priorities, and the need to align their activities to promote reaching those goals. But IT must not only learn how well they are doing in aligning their activity to accomplish the firm's goals and but also determine how close they are to achieving those goals.

The challenge is choosing what and when to measure. In the next chapter, it will become apparent that financial measures will be able to demonstrate the value of IT, but financial measures do not provide an indication of how well the processes are being performed and how they can be enhanced. Is the process meeting the needs of the business partner? Is the process operating at its optimum level? Is the process often nonfunctional or inoperable? To answer these questions, the organization must apply measures and find out which measures are important in determining the effectiveness of each process. More important is the need to apply the measurements to take specific action to improve performance. Later in this chapter there will be examples of approaches that firms may apply to improve their measurement strategies.

▪▪▪ IT—Necessary or Necessary Evil?

A profile of American IT organizations by the Metagroup in 1997 showed about 30 percent of IT organizations were "frozen in the past," where IT was managed as a cost, still mainframe-based with long development lead times, and without a flexible structure. Another 55 percent of the IT organizations were "in the abyss." There, spending was growing but IT was not managed as an investment; distributed computing was growing with uncontrolled complexity, and strategic work content was low. Only 10 percent of IT organizations were competitive. In this case, spending was under control; the portfolio was being managed; and development was effective while strategic content was high. The remaining 5 percent were in the "leading" category. Here spending was managed as an investment, packaged-based solutions played a key leveraged role, and sourcing was also leveraged. The IT organization had a market-ready mindset. This means that less than a fifth of the United States IT organizations have begun to realize their full potential.

▮▮▮▮▮▮▮▮▮▮▮ FIGURE 13-1   Why Is There IT?

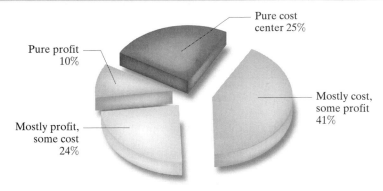

Source: Gartner Group.

In Figure 13-1, the Gartner Group surveyed a large cross section of major U.S. firms and one question asked of business leaders was, "Is your IT organization a cost center or profit center?" The results were not encouraging to IT managers. One quarter of the respondents thought that IT was a cost to bear versus only 10 percent that considered IT as a real moneymaker. Of the remaining respondents, 41 percent answered that IT was mainly a cost, while 24 percent saw that IT provided more profit than cost. In an optimistic view, over one-third of business leaders saw that IT provides opportunities for profit and strategic advantage. But almost two thirds of the business leaders saw IT as costing more than its benefits.

Even with this discouraging news, business leaders agree that technology has added a great benefit to the business. With the advanced technology that has been introduced into the office, it is recognized that this technology has helped office workers to become more productive and the business to be more profitable. In Figure 13-2, in a survey performed by *InformationWeek*, a resounding 97 percent of 300 IT and

▮▮▮▮▮▮▮▮▮▮▮ FIGURE 13-2   Productivity Study of IT and Business Executives.

**Do productivity gains translate into a
more profitable business?**

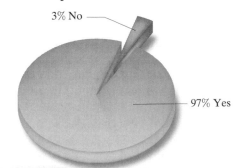

**Then why don't we get recognition
for our contribution?**

Source: InformationWeek research productivity study of 300 IT and business executives.

business leaders say that productivity gains translate into a more profitable business. So why isn't there a link between the successful additions of technology to the business and the contribution of IT to the organization? Is it because IT fails to measure their contribution and the services that they provide? Is productivity the wrong place to look?

▮▮▮ Measuring IT

In 1997, Dr. Luftman was quoted in *Information Week* as saying, "Far too often, IT is not measured in business terms, but in technology terms. Many IT people talk about MIPS installed, response times, function points, disk storage, and systems availability—these are not the kind of things business people focus on."[2] For the past four decades, the majority of performance measurements in IT have been either financially oriented or based on technological measures. Examples of various indicators for measuring overall IT performance are: IT expenditures as a percent of revenue, IT expenditure per employee, revenue per IT dollar, total IT expense budget versus actual (and by area within IT), total IT capital budget versus actual, and employees supported per IT employee. (For a more complete list, see Figure 13-3)

Information Technology managers are under increasing pressure to evaluate and justify the contribution of IT expenditures to the productivity, quality, and competitiveness of the organization. IT assessments are not well established and recent studies show that more research is needed.[3] Frequently, IT is used without a full understanding of its applicability, effectiveness, or efficiency. IT managers often lack the tools they need to decide if they are accomplishing the right activities.[4]

In Figure 13-4, a partial list of doubts, disillusionments, and disappointments with IT activity has been compiled from surveys of major businesses over the past decade. These statistics demonstrate the negative image of IT in many firms. Business units can exhibit a lack of respect for the way IT carries out their responsibilities, or worse, the business units can believe that IT is not optimizing their strengths in getting projects done. What can be done to demonstrate that IT is working effectively? What will demonstrate that IT is working rapidly and accurately? How can anyone tell if IT is on time and on budget? The next section explains why it is important to measure appropriately.

▮▮▮ The Importance of Measurement

IT has established itself as an organization, vital to major enterprises throughout the world. However, in many surveys (as shown in Figure 13-4), there are continuing questions from the business community. The business wants to know whether the IT organization is being run effectively and efficiently. They also want to identify opportunities for improving the effectiveness and efficiency of IT. If asked what is the difference between effectiveness and efficiency, one of the simplest answers is that effectiveness is doing the right things and efficiency is doing things the right way. Both reduce waste in time and money. To discover whether you are doing the right things the right way, the IT organization must begin by measuring what it is doing.

Several examples of IT measurements are shown in Figure 13-3. Some simple quantitative measures are expenditures per employee, budget versus actual, costs per MIPS, etc. Other measures are more complex or must be done over a period of time

- Percent of employees in support, management, maintenance, and development roles
- Percent of IT spending on legacy systems including cost by system
- Percent of requests serviced by users
- Percent of service level compliance
- Percent of software applications on current release
- Percent of spending on top business priorities (moving the business forward)
- Percent of time spent on testing
- Percent of user participation by project
- Percent projects on time, on budget, met user requirements
- Return on investment by project
- Revenue per IT dollar
- Rework cost: internal cost of rework across all IT processes
- Total IT capital budget versus actual
- Total IT expense budget versus actual (and by area within IT)
- Training hours both per IT employee and by skill level

Overall—qualitative measures

- IT yield: ratio of projected value of IT projects to actual benefits attained
- Sales revenue generated by IT initiatives
- Span of control
- User satisfaction survey of applications
- User satisfaction survey results
- User service level agreements

Network:

- Cost per device or local area network (LAN) port
- LAN hardware, management cost per LAN port
- LAN ports supported by LAN administrator
- Mean time to get project or modification implemented
- Mean time to repair
- Network availability percent
- Network response time
- Percent utilization by line segment

Data Center:

- Average response time
- Cost of service per user
- Costs per MIPS or combined power rating
- Installed release level of software compared with industry available release
- Memory, disk utilization statistics
- Percent system availability
- Percent utilization per server
- Total on-time delivery percentage
- Turn around time for key batch jobs

(continues on the next page)

(e.g., sales revenues generated by IT initiatives, overtime per month by skill level, cost of quality, cost of cancelled projects and system failures). Measurements that reflect schedules and project dependencies include percent of projects on time, on budget, backlog in months and number of requests, and backlog costs. There are other measures that are not quantitative, but are qualitative, requiring interpretation (e.g., surveys of user satisfaction of systems and applications, IT yield: ratio of projected value of IT projects to actual benefits attained). Yet all of these measurements alone do not adequately describe IT performance sufficiently to determine if IT performance is efficient or effective (See the "Single Snapshot versus a Series of Measures" sidebar).

▪▪▪▪▪▪▪▪▪▪▪ **FIGURE 13-3** **Sample Current IT Measurements. (continued)**

Overall IT—quantitative measures
- Average tenure
- Average time positions are open
- Backlog aging: the projected dollar value of work beyond 30, 60, and 90 days
- Backlog cost: the total dollar value of all work waiting to be completed
- Backlog in month and number of requests
- Call volume or problems reported by application and root cause
- Cost of quality: cost of cancelled projects and system failures
- Cost per function point
- Number of modifications to package software
- Employees supported per IT employee
- Hardware, software, services, staff, overhead, supplies as a percent of total IT budget
- IT employee satisfaction survey results
- IT expenditures as a percent of revenue
- IT expenditures per employee
- IT turnover (by reason)
- Number of changes to design
- Number of errors or defects per module
- Number of incident reports
- Number of internal promotions
- Number of lines of code reused
- Number of open positions
- Number of telecommuters
- Number of user requested changes per project
- Number of user stored queries
- Number of users requesting access to tools
- On-time completion rate of function point
- Overtime per month by skill level
- Percent development/support costs
- Percent IT budget increase/decrease
- Percent of applications that are custom compared with package software
- Percent of applications under service level agreements
- Percent of areas using formal methods and processes
- Ratio of contractors to employees

▪▪▪▪▪▪▪▪▪▪▪ **FIGURE 13-4** **Why IT Gets No Respect!**

IT blunders and black holes

- A full *one-third* of the IT money was essentially wasted (*No real–or even a negative–return*).
- More than *one half* of projects either *fail* or experience major cost *overruns*.
- Only *10%* were on *time* and on *budget*.
- More than *one third* of the attempts to implement major software *packages fail*.
- *71% cannot say* whether IT is delivering *value* for money.
- *38%* say IT is "…only *moderately* well in *alignment* with business objectives…"

**Companies are making the same mistakes
over and over again!**

Source: The Standish Group, *Fortune, Forbes*, Braxxon Technology, Global Investment Technology, Lientz & Rea.

A Single Snapshot versus a Series of Measures

Peter Drucker said in an interview in 1988, "Few people learn that the most meaningful information in social and economic matters is [found] within ranges and not in precise figures."[5] Is the importance of measurement found in the numbers that are recorded? No, frequently the direction or trend of change can be more significant. These measurements and others would help by being indicators of progress in a point of time and the direction of progress over a span of time. A literal snapshot of any performance cannot describe efficiency or effectiveness. However, a series of snapshots over a period of time can be a necessity for a worthwhile study.

Here is an example to illustrate this: IT measures service outages for a recently installed Web application on a monthly basis. Over a six-month period, the numbers of hours lost in a month to service outages were 7.2, 6.0, 20.0, 5.1, 4.3, and 3.9. What could one conclude? It appears that the service outages are declining over time. What is the significant of the third reading of 20.0? Without the other measurements, there could have been an assumption that the Web application had a serious problem, yet in view of the other readings, one sees that the third reading was an unusual occurrence and there may be reasonable explanations for this particular result.

Simply put, single measurements are one dimensional, whereas a series of measurements can often tell a complete story.

The need is clear that managers must identify a better way to measure the performance of their own organizations. Many managers have developed their own unique measures to use as an indicator of performance, but most of these measures are either not helpful or worse, misleading to their senior executives.[6] Other IT managers are looking at the incongruity of the goals of IT and the strategic goals of the enterprise. What is apparent is that many IT organizations are not measuring their performance by what success they were bringing to the company. Rather, they were looking at how well they were doing in adopting and using technology for their own area.

Measuring a process and discovering trends become important steps in determining efficiency and effectiveness. (See the "Measuring Projects Iteratively" sidebar). An improving trend can indicate an improvement of efficiency. For example, if processing policy applications through a computerized underwriting system for an insurance company continues to fall from 3.2 days to 2.9 days over a one-year period, it would indicate that the process is becoming more efficient. Effectiveness can also be improved when measurement is done over a span of time: for example, the monitoring of readings will enable management to take corrective action when the indicators are not moving in the expected direction.

Measuring Projects Iteratively

Project management has developed over decades of iterative processing and scheduling. The integration of Pert and Gantt charts to the scheduling process has greatly enhanced the effectiveness of the development process by improving the predictability of completion dates. Dependencies or conflicts with shared resources are now routinely taken into account and schedules are adjusted to offset bottlenecks.

> Development of PC software tools such as the network version of Microsoft Project have continued to improve project management and enable the project plan to be shared across the enterprise. When there are any delays, the project plan can be immediately updated and altered to reflect the delay. The project managers can take immediate steps to correct the variance or extend the project schedule. Project managers and their supervisors can monitor the project and be able to know if the project is ontime and onbudget. If there are variances, the managers will know why.

Using an iterative approach, continuous improvement will enable IT to improve the quality and effectiveness of its processes. For example, in the area of application development, continuous measurement will enable management to detect cost and time overruns. (See the "Measuring Projects Iteratively" sidebar).

▮▮▮ What and How to Measure

The relevance of the measurement is a key to being successful in assessing IT. But how does one decide what is relevant? In Figure 13-3, there are over 60 different measurements that are available to apply quantitatively and qualitatively. Most of the measurements on the long list can be measured easily because they are often tangible, numerical measurements. But both IT and the business need to be able to measure business impact, customer relationships, internal organization impact, investment impact, and value chain impact. It becomes important to document when changes occur and when processes are altered. The results of the changes should be reflected by changes in the measurement. All changes are not good; some changes mandated by regulation, such as additional reporting, may cause a reduction in efficiency, while elimination of unnecessary reporting might improve efficiency. But in either case, it is crucial to know how the processes are changing between any measurements, and any changes in the results need to be explained.

Researchers Myers, Kappelman, and Prybutok have studied the assessment of IT and claim that managers often disagree about what are ideal metrics. If there were an agreed set of metrics to measure the success of IT, there would be universal adoption of the standards. Although there is no ideal set of measurements, it is important to recognize that whatever the metrics are, there should be an agreed set of objectives among IT and business partners. There are some measurements that are good or better than others. Although there are measures that machines could statistically calculate or accountants could manually count that will lead to precision, it is vital that nonquantitative measures be considered as well. The need for new nonquantitative measurements is driven by the central theme that IT should be an enabler or driver of business improvement. But these intangible measures, opinions, and satisfaction indexes are measures that are subjective in nature. It is these measurements that are difficult and sometimes impossible to do.

▮▮▮ A 10 Step Approach to Developing Measurements

To resolve this issue of finding the right measures to use, the authors have developed an approach that can be adopted by any firm that wants to measure IT performance. Before examining this approach, let's review what has been discussed in previous chapters. The main objective of measurement, discussed in Chapter 12, is to communicate the progress or lack of progress in promoting the accomplishment of the firm's goals. In Chapter 2 and 3 it was explained that all organizational units should be aligned. The alignment maturity assessment has been used to measure IT-Business alignments. In

Chapter 4, the role of the CIO was detailed. The CIO is the driving force in developing, implementing, and monitoring IT activities. In Chapters 5 and 6, the IT processes were discussed, and it would be these processes that need to be measured. In Chapter 7, it was shown that how the firm manages new technologies becomes a critical issue as more and more companies are seeking to enable drive business change using new hardware, software, tools, etc. Chapters 8 and 11 presented a discussion of how IT is governed and organized. How IT is governed and organized will greatly impact how the measurements are done and who should be responsible for them. And lastly, in Chapters 9 and 10 the discussion focused on skills of IT staff and how those skills greatly affect it's ability to succeed. A skilled staff is necessary for managing change and improving the process over time. It is readily seen that developing exceptional measurements will require knowledge, cooperation, and communication from both IT and the business to succeed.

Step 1: Teams need to be established for each of the 38 IT processes. Members from both the business and from IT need to be recruited to assist in this process. All 38 processes will be reviewed and analyzed, and a plan will be established for each. The CIO and their senior management should be a part of each and every committee. Review the steering committee section in Chapter 11, IT Governance for success factors. (Warning: Make sure the business and IT staffs are given the appropriate amount of time to participate in these meetings. It is expected that the time spent on these processes will be significant.)

Step 2: Each committee will meet and define the goals of each IT process as their first objective. Those goals should all align with the objectives of the firm and across each process. The business and IT people will have unique perspectives and it will require a strong facilitator to ensure a common understanding and creation of compromise that both the business and IT can accept. (Warning: What IT does best in this process may not be the most important aspect or goal in the IT process. The goal should be to always permit the firm to succeed in meeting its strategic goals.)

Step 3: Once the goals for each IT process are identified, the next problem is to identify critical success factors (See Chapter 6 for more discussion of CSF.) For each of the goals, there may be one or more critical success factors that can point to successes, failures, and/or the direction of the performance of the IT process in reaching goals. (Warning: Determining critical success factors can be challenging. Some critical success factors are not obvious and some that seem obvious do not make sense under stronger scrutiny.)

Step 4: Guidelines now need to be established to measure if, and to what degree, the critical success factors have been met. Analysts and managers from both the business and IT should look at multiple measurements and test them under actual production situations. (Warning: This may be the most time-consuming part of the process. Validation of measurements should prove they make sense, are reasonable to perform, and mean what the measurements are intended mean.)

Step 5: Once the measures are set and have been tested, a complete pilot should be done and the members of the team should jointly participate in the pilot. Managers should work with the analysts to interpret the results of the pilot and to either concur with the results or initiate revising the measurements to correct any of the issues or problems raised. (Warning: Make sure the measurements do measure what is intended and that the results are significant. Once measurements are adopted, they are difficult to eliminate later, even if they offer meaningless numbers.)

Step 6:   When the pilot is completed successfully and the results tendered are deemed acceptable, the recommendation to apply these measurements should be raised to senior management for their endorsement. The CIO may want to be the one to propose the measurements to the senior management group. Naturally, different measurements are more appropriate for different levels or governance steering committees. Considerable time should be spent on ensuring that the right level of complexity is focused on. These measurements become the foundation for service level agreements (SLA's). The CIO can then champion the adoption to the respective steering committee. (Warning: all presentations made to adopt these measures should focus on how they will improve the firm's opportunity to reach the firm's goals. If the focus is purely on value, this may not be the best approach. For demonstrating the value of IT, see Chapter 14, which explores the value of IT.)

Step 7:   Upon approval of the senior management begin implementation of the new measures. Make sure that business people and IT staff understand why these measurements are meaningful. Publish results of the measurements as often as possible. (Warning: these measures can raise concerns from staff and could lead to lower morale, paranoia, even anger and mistrust. Open communication may be essential to making this program positive.)

Step 8:   Analyze results; review the results with appropriate partners. Work with partners to look for fixes and improvements in the processes and measures, as needed. This process should be on-going. (Warning: Constantly look for ways to improve the IT process and the overall measurement process. Look to incorporate new technologies whenever possible.)

This approach can fit any size company and can work within any environment to accomplish specific strategic goals and IT process improvements. Its major downside is that it requires complete cooperation and input from the staff. Consultants can participate in the process but it does require IT and business people to describe their roles and their goals. The senior management will still be required to explain the objectives of the firm in very specific terms.

Here are a few examples of the measurement process:

Process	Strategic Goal	C S F	Measurement
Data Planning	Facilitate reuse	Create common models	# common object
	Provide security	Create secure databases	# data break-ins
Recovery Planning	Recover from outage	Develop and test plan	Percent services available
Software Procure	Reduce cost	Negotiate pricing	Percent discount/ user
Staff Performance	Improve attendance	Collect data on abs	Trend of attend.
	Improve productivity	Collect data on stat	Compare/ productivity
Production	Monitor prod vs. schedule	Maintain schedules	# and percent late

For every one of the 38 IT processes, measurements can be designed to show trends of how each area is meeting their business goals.

Benchmarking Works Well with the Measurement Process

Is developing benchmarks essential for the monitoring of projects? Will future iterations of a project require the same benchmarks? Does creating benchmarks have an undisputable benefit? These issues are raised because the question, "should benchmarks be established?" must be answered. Benchmarks are necessary because they are important indicators and milestones, and often serve as beginning points for the measurement process. In Figure 13-5, initial benchmark process steps are illustrated. The benchmarking process has a five-stage lifecycle similar to many other development processes.

However, it is important to note that this process often requires that benchmarks be recalibrated and sometimes replaced by more than one set of new benchmarks. Some benchmarking techniques require a continuous method. As shown in Figure 13-6, the continuous benchmarking method requires measures to be constantly reviewed as a part of an iterative process. This commits the organization to a continuous improvement program where the expectation is that change will happen and the organization must be prepared to upgrade itself and its benchmarks. Measurement is but one of seven steps in the continuous benchmarking approach. The other steps in the process (i.e., define, prioritize, invest, contract, finance, and deliver an implementation) are just as important in the creation of effective benchmarks as the actual measurement.

In the figure, the benchmark process spans multiple processes and therefore multiple measures are employed. Because measurements can be skewed or misinterpreted, the choosing of appropriate measures is of the utmost importance, and that discussion is in the next section. The focus should be on identifying opportunities to improve all IT 38 processes.

Quality and Efficacy of Measures

Measurement can be skewed to demonstrate a particular condition or can be manipulated to reflect an inaccurate situation. In Chapter 14—Assessing the Value of IT, there will be discussion of the manipulation of ROI and other financial measures that can lead to misleading results. Measurements are often best when they forecast trends. The analysis of trends may be more informative because it is far more difficult to manipulate direction when a consistent approach in measurement is used. The interpretation of measurement is crucial to gaining correct insight as to what the measurement really indicates. Remember, measurement in this chapter is being used to determine whether performance is effective or efficient. And in Chapter 14, measurement will be used to determine if the performance is rewarding.

Quality of Measures

Peter B. B. Turney said,

"You need accurate and timely information about work done (the activities) and the objects of that work (the products and the customers). Performance measures describe the work done and the results achieved in an activity. They tell how well an activity is performed."

Does Improved Quality Reduce Cost?

"It used to be a common belief that improved quality meant higher cost. This seemed reasonable. Doesn't improved quality mean more inspectors, more rework, more costly warranties, and the like?"

▪▪▪▪▪▪▪▪▪▪ **FIGURE 13-5** The Five Stage Benchmarking Life Cycle.

Benchmarking process steps

Planning
- Identify what is to be benchmarked
- Identify comparative companies
- Determine data collection method and collect data

Analysis
- Determine current performance "gap"
- Project future performance levels

Integration
- Communicate benchmark findings and gain acceptance
- Establish functional goals

Action
- Develop action plans
- Implement specific actions and monitor progress
- Recalibrate benchmarks

Maturity
- Leadership position attained and practices fully integrated into process

Source: Robert C. Camp and *www.apqc.org.*

▪▪▪▪▪▪▪▪▪▪ **FIGURE 13-6** The Iterative Process for Benchmarking.

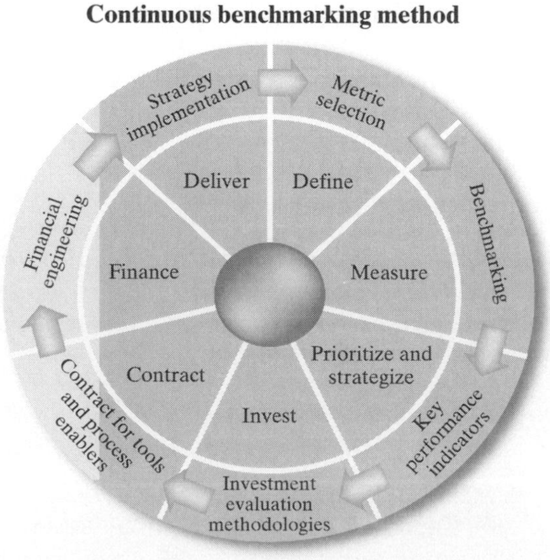

Continuous benchmarking method

Strategy implementation · Metric selection · Benchmarking · Key performance indicators · Investment evaluation methodologies · Contract for tools and process enablers · Financial engineering

Deliver · Define · Measure · Prioritize and strategize · Invest · Contract · Finance

Source: Dataquest, Gartner Group.

> *"How wrong we were. It's poor quality that costs money (and loses customers). Poor quality is doing a job more than once. It's wasting materials. It's having costly systems to keep track of defective parts. It's paying salaries for hordes of inspectors. It's incurring the cost of warranties and customer returns. And it's suffering the anger of disgruntled customers."*
>
> *"Improving quality is a sure way to reduce cost. Do it right, the first time."*[7]

In the "Quality of Measures" sidebar, Peter B. B. Turney makes the point that good quality can also be a significant indicator of good performance. Mr. Turney supplements the earlier definition, "Effectiveness is doing the right things and efficiency is doing things the right way," with "Quality is doing it right the first time." IT is most effective and efficient by doing the right things, the right way. But a description of high quality IT performance should be completing the process effectively, efficiently, the first time out. If there is little need for rework, repairs, or replacement, there can be a convincing argument that high quality magnifies the effectiveness and efficiency.

Certainly, high quality can improve the bottom line. Parasuraman, Zeithaml, and Berry (1985) listed the dimensions of service quality (or "determinants") as:

- **Reliability.** Consistency of performance and dependability; service performed right the first time;
- **Responsiveness.** Willingness/readiness of employees to provide service in a timely manner (promptness);
- **Competence.** Possession of the required skills/knowledge to perform the service;
- **Access.** Approachability and ease of contact; convenient hours and location;
- **Courtesy.** Politeness, respect, consideration, and friendliness of contact personnel;
- **Communications.** Keeping stakeholders informed in language they understand and listening to them. For example, business partners who are not technical will have difficulty understanding technical jargon yet they have the best knowledge of the products, services, and clients that the firm has. Engaging the business partners and learning what they know will improve the final product and increase the level of quality.
- **Credibility.** Trustworthiness, believability, honesty; having the customer's best interests at heart;
- **Security.** Freedom from danger, risk, or doubt;
- **Understanding/Knowing the Customer.** Making the effort to understand the customer's needs; and
- **Tangibles.** Physical evidence of the service, including facilities, personnel appearance, tools or equipment, etc.[8]

Here are more examples of the measurement process to reflect the importance of quality:

Process	Strategic Goal	C S F	Measurement
Asset Management	Maintain inventory Secure inventory	Create equip. list Secure inventory	Match asset/list # equip lost
Problem Control	Report problems Initiate action	Log problems Resolve problems	Call volume Customer survey

The determinants should be reviewed as a checklist of factors that may be appropriate and selected as critical success factors. Once the CSF is determined, measures must be tested to ensure that the CSF can be properly monitored for completion.

In the above examples, improvement in the quality of the execution of the process will reduce calls and losses in time, money, and equipment. Measurement will properly show the improvement and will justify any incremental costs. With many asset management processes, ones that are lax and poorly run often show huge losses, as people have the opportunity to literally walk away with company property. While costs appear to increase when more care is taken, the overall improvement will provide more than adequate payback.

Barry Myers, Leon Kappelman, and Victor Prybutok summarized their paper on *"A Comprehensive Model for Assessing the Quality and Productivity of the Information Systems Function,"* this way:

"The progress towards the development of a comprehensive framework for IT assessment is significant, yet a lot of work remains to be done. What are the dimensions of IT success that should be assessed? The dimensions critical to the success of the IT functions are:

1. *service quality*
2. *system quality*
3. *information quality*
4. *use*
5. *user satisfaction*
6. *individual impact*
7. *work group impact, and*
8. *organizational impact*

What are the measures for assessing the performance of the IT function in each dimension? This work provides everything needed to create comprehensive IT assessment systems. The existing models of IT success were updated to include emerging IT success dimensions of service quality and work group impact and provide a comprehensive method for organizing the various measures for IT success."[9]

Summarizing their research, they have created a roadmap of sorts to determine the criteria for selection of factors that will lead to an accurate assessment of IT performance. The eight dimensions listed and to integrate with external environmental variables as well as organizational variables. But the algorithms for selecting the appropriate dimensions and measures have yet to be developed, and how each manager will select the appropriate success dimension for each given their organizational and environmental context is still unknown. These researchers say that more research is needed in this field to study measurements and learn how various factors will interact with each other before anyone can establish a better model.

So these researchers believe that they have built a framework to assess IT success. The eight dimensions should be used as a checklist for appropriate strategic goals of an IT process. Each IT process has different combinations of critical dimensions and the larger processes might require use of all eight dimensions. To properly organize the various measures for each dimension, each dimension must be questioned to be assure that an effective assessment of the process can be achieved.

This is an example of the how the measurement process can be questioned:

Process	Strategic Goal	C S F	Measurement
Financial Perf:	Information quality:		
Vendor tracking	Administer vendors	Create vendor database	# vendors
	Track vendors	Monitor vendors actions	# transactions

- What are the necessary components to be measured here?
- Aren't there many intangible measures that deal with financial performance and satisfaction?

▪▪▪▪▪▪▪▪▪▪▪ **FIGURE 13-7** Matching the Needs of the Users with the Level of Reporting.

Types of IT reporting

Source: Anthony, R. N. *Planning and Control Systems: A Framework for Analysis*, Cambridge, MA: Harvard University Press (1965)

- How does satisfaction apply to the financial performance criteria?
- What are the appropriate dimensions to be added?

Use of the above questions will lead to defining a better selection of factors and measurements that will aid in producing effective models.

Reporting in IT

Audiences of IT Reports

Reports are products of applications. End users frequently receive reports as a consequence of the mountainous number of applications that are in production everyday. In this chapter, the reports present the performance indicators that have been previously discussed. These reports can be a summary or the detail, or a composite of a summary, detail, and projection of IT performance measurements. The report will differ by the audience and intent of the process. They review the service levels that the different steering committees agreed to.

In Figure 13-7, the chart illustrates the fact that reports can be tailored to the needs of the IT or business group. Although the majority of the reporting of performance measures is directed towards the operational managers group, the other three categories all benefit from a different view of the performance measures report.

For example, there are operational managers who work in both IT and in the various functional business units. Their interest in performance measures will differ by functional group because of their individual responsibility. The operational managers in IT will be keenly interested in network response times, system availability, backup measures, and maintenance schedules. The operational managers in human resources will want to know application availability of the human resource applications, especially where there may be Web access or intranet access to update the human resource databases. There will be database administrators, who will want to know statistical information on the use of the human resource databases for tuning and performance.

In fact, all the operational managers in each functional area have their own set of applications and databases that must be measured and reported on.

Every measurement process has a reporting process that is attached to it:

Process	Strategic Goal	C S F	Measurement
Data planning	Facilitate reuse	Create common models	# common object
	Provide Security	Create secure databases	# data break-ins
	Report new data	Create libraries w/ objts	Distribute report

Every IT process has one or more reporting objectives.

For knowledge and data workers, their interest would not be in the same statistics that the operational managers are reading. This group would need a different view of the same measures. For example, data workers in sales and marketing would like to know which sales locations could not transmit their data. In other words, they are not looking for how long the systems were inaccessible, but they need to identify which sales locations could not send in all of their data. They might have to project what the missing data would be if the system had not failed. It is still the same system performance information but from a different view.

For middle managers, their interest would include system availability as well as what locations were affected by the outages, but they would want to look at patterns of disruption. They seek opportunities to keep the problem from happening in the future and they would be looking for ways to improve the situation on a permanent basis. By examining the report on the pattern of outages on an historical basis, they might be able to determine if there is a physical hardware problem or a software issue. They may discover that the system may need tuning or replacement. This requires analysis and data compiled over a period of months with interpretations performed by both IT and business analysts to assist these managers.

Other middle managers will be looking to compare performance results of systems against competitors, business partners, and members of other industries. Reports of performance will allow managers to make decisions to fine tune systems, request minor and major fixes to existing systems, and to recommend new systems. Again, these reports are based on information gathered by IT but viewed in different perspectives with different derived products.

As for senior managers and executives, their requirements for reporting may differ greatly from the previous groups. Senior managers with responsibility for planning will want information on what IT is delivering and then compare those results to the strategic plans of the firm and to the deliverables that their competitors are preparing. The senior managers are often looking for ways to gain strategic advantage as well as attempting to close any competitive gaps with the competition. While senior executives (including the CIO) are certainly interested in ensuring optimal daily performance, they are the ones charged to provide competitive advantage with the tools and processes that IT has to offer. See Chapter 4—The Role of the CIO and Chapter 6—Planning-related IT Processes for the challenges of senior executives managing IT. The CIO has the most prominent role in the measurement processes and must, along with authorized deputies, participate in the development of the appropriate measurements of IT processes.

Variety in Reporting

Reports come in all shapes and sizes, differing in level of detail and timeframes. Some reports will require historical detail and will be of data accumulated over many months and even years. These reports will serve those managers who are seeking to find trends and patterns. It is this information that assists planners, developers, and strategists to develop projects that will need to be justified by the interpretation of the reports. It is this fact that elevates the importance of designing clear and understandable reports, so that interpretation of the reports is easy to do.

Some reports, as shown in Figure 13-8, are based on statistical data generated overnight or over a short period of time. These reports are useful to operational managers, technical managers, help desk managers, etc. These reports are designed to assist managers in determining quick repairs to systems when there are outages. Each report has different characteristics depending on what message the report is trying to relay and to whom the report is written. This is an important advantage since wide reporting differences can be a challenge.

Imagine how difficult it would be if reports were limited in versatility. Analysts would be struggling to understand how to read the reports that operational managers use or vice-versa. Would either worker have an advantage over the other in understanding the situation? Fortunately, this is not a question to answer here, but it leads to the next section, where we ask how can we better control IT?

Controlling IT

Using measurement to gauge performance is important. Monitoring the measurements is important to ensure that the performance is at acceptable levels. But what if the actual performance is declining or is at unacceptable levels? This leads to the third important task, controlling the IT processes and ensuring the performance is satisfactory. In the past decade, many businesses have introduced the service level agreement as a way to formalize the IT services.

What is a Service Level Agreement (SLA) (see Chapter 5)? Services for an agreed cost are the basis of any service level agreement. A service agreement is a contract (formal and legal bargain) between interested parties. It must be a fair bargain or one side will not want to fulfill it. The expectation of services must be a clear one. If the contractor does not understand what the buyer (or purchaser) wants, it would be almost impossible to have the agreement fulfilled, except by sheer luck. The contractor should spend time with the purchaser to understand the current level of service that the buyer is receiving. The buyer needs to identify what changes they want to see, as well as the current level of effort.

In the next sections, the topics will focus on using a Service Level Agreement as the way to monitor and control performance of both internal and external service providers.

▮▮▮▮▮▮▮▮▮▮▮▮ **FIGURE 13-8** Sample Online System Response Time Report.

Region	Transactions	Average second	Less than 1 second	Less than 2 seconds	Less than 5 seconds	Less than 10 seconds	More than 10 seconds
California	682,254	1.2	54.2%	90.7%	99.5%	99.9%	0.1%
Freeport	1,137,683	1.0	65.8%	93.5%	99.6%	99.9%	0.1%
Indiana	214,999	1.5	56.5%	85.4%	98.4%	99.3%	0.7%
Northwest	683,365	1.0	67.0%	93.8%	99.4%	99.9%	0.1%
Southwest	490,749	1.9	32.9%	65.0%	92.5%	97.1%	2.9%
Midwest Claims Center	197,861	1.1	64.5%	91.0%	99.2%	99.8%	0.2%
Midwest Premium Home Office	428,721	0.3	94.5%	98.0%	99.6%	99.8%	0.2%
Total	3,835,632	1.1	62.7%	89.5%	98.6%	99.5%	0.5%

Average Window: 1 hour and 13 minutes
Total response time incidents: 1
Slow response time percentage: 0.07%

The Elements of an Effective Service Level Agreement

Controlling performance of IT services to ensure that the needs of the business are met is difficult; that is why the business has often introduced a legal agreement to secure the provision of IT services. However, any contract or service level agreement not well written is not effective and does not protect the business. In Figure 13-9, the seven leading best characteristics of effective service level agreements are shown.

First, IT should provide a clear expectation of benefits and services that will be provided to the business partner at a delivered cost. Managing expectations is a very difficult but important task. Expectations, like opinions, are subjective, and can vary widely, depending on the issues. As mentioned earlier, IT executives have one level of expectation of their work and responsibilities to the business and business executives have a different perspective. Who is right? Maybe they are both a little right and both a little wrong, but since the business often funds the IT groups, the businesses appear to have the bigger say. The sponsor often has the right to decide what they are willing to pay for. IT should not decide what should be important to the business and what is not, since they would tend to place a greater emphasis on what they do well rather than what may be best for the enterprise. It then becomes imperative for IT to ensure that they learn the needs of their business counterparts.

Secondly, IT must specify in clear, distinct terms the complete services, the service providers, and where the services will be performed. To produce an effective service level agreement is to create realistic and achievable performance goals. The service expectations must be clearly spelled out and they must be easily measured and monitored, as well as being verifiable when questioned. SLAs provide the means that will be used to measure the quantity and quality of the service and the frequency that the monitoring will take place. The owner of the process must remain within the firm, even if the entire process is outsourced. In addition, the service level agreement should have clear enforcement rules and consequences for not meeting obligations. The service level agreements should also outline bonuses and incentives for delivery of services beyond the stated minimums and should be clear as to what the bonuses would be for each degree of service provided beyond the criteria.

Third, IT needs to include a set of measurements that can be agreed upon that will effectively measure the outcome of the benefits and services provided and that will adequately determine the performance of the contractor. Not only should the measurement process be clear; the process should also be flexible to change easily when new demands are brought to bear upon the original process. As emerging technologies get adopted, the measurements should reflect any productivity gains that arise. Measurements should also reflect any changes to the measurement process as well.

▪▪▪▪▪▪▪▪▪▪▪▪ **FIGURE 13-9 Seven Characteristics of Highly Effective Service Level Agreements.**

The best characteristics of a good service level agreement should be:

1. Based on current "user" expectation, not history or what it used to be like.
2. Each service level agreement should be defined by location, function and service type.
3. The agreement uses benchmarks and baselines for measuring performance.
4. The agreement specifies minimums, penalties, and incentives.
5. The agreement specifies reports and tracking tools to be monitored in order for the performance of the contractor to be assessed.
6. The agreements are not too few, yet not too many, so that it is not overly complex while not so simple as to be ignored; and
7. The agreement gets adjusted periodically to reflect changes in the technology or the process.

Fourth, IT must maintain a set of monitors that will use the measures set forth earlier to ensure that proper measurement of performance is taken, and to ensure that the adequacy of the contractor can be determined. Monitoring is an important accompaniment to measurement. Monitoring is the first step in determining the adequacy of the service provider and whether the expectations of benefit and service are matched up. The one responsible for monitoring should also be identified. When someone is not designated to monitor, quite often no one will do it. IT and their business partners should share the monitoring as a way to take joint responsibility.

Fifth, IT must add a set of enforceable penalties and rewards in the contract so that the performance of the contractor will not be left to chance. Enforcement is another important complement to measurement and monitoring. Without the ability to enforce the service agreement, there would be little need to monitor or measure the events. Without the threat of penalties or the lure of rewards, contractor behavior will be difficult to alter in a positive manner. The penalties should be severe enough that the contractor will want to fulfill his obligation under the contract, but not so severe that it would cause his bankruptcy. A balance of awards that encourages the timely completion of the contract should also accompany the penalty clause.

The final two characteristics are equally important. IT must have contracts that are simple but not so vague that they can be ignored. Contracts that are vague become impossible to enforce because the vagueness of the language can provide many excuses for noncompliance. Likewise, IT must be assured that the agreement continues to evolve over time so that it continues to be viable, because needs and technologies are guaranteed to change. As technologies improve, measuring the process might become more accurate or may allow more things to be measured. The service agreement should be open to amendment, if it can be shown that the set of measurements should be updated to reflect improved technologies. The contract should be flexible to adopt the improvements without having to renegotiate the entire bargain. Keep in mind, the measurements must be balanced to business and IT objectives, and agreed to by all stakeholders.

In summary, all service level agreements need to establish these five areas: 1) expectation, 2) measurements, 3) monitoring, 4) enforcement, and 5) renewal/renegotiation. If even one of these five areas is overlooked, the service level agreement could easily become unmanageable. See the "Negotiating a Service Level Agreement" sidebar for tips from the Cutter Consortium 10.

Negotiating a Service Level Agreement

A number of outside consulting organizations are advising their clients on how to negotiate reliable service level agreements. The Cutter Consortium provided the following note.

Act on the following five tips to revamp your current SLA program and when drafting your next agreement:

- **Get a Baseline:** Gather as much quantitative historic data as possible on the prior performance of the service to help set realistic, attainable service level agreements. Always expect to adjust your settings down the road.
- **Define Responsibility:** Identify who is responsible for measurement, how is it to be done, and who fixes problems. Match responsibilities to job titles so that they're not dropped during staff turnover. Draft penalty clauses for nonperformance, as well as bonuses for service levels met.
- **Allow for Modifications:** New applications, new technologies, or changes in the organization can have an impact on network demands and performance expectations. Outline a process in advance for amending the SLA resulting from anticipated changes or unrealistic expectations.

- **Ensure Reports Are in Terms Anyone Can Understand:** Department managers, consultants, and end-users need to read SLA reports to make changes at the line-of-business level. Go for a user-friendly format that limits the technical jargon.
- **Don't Forget the End-User Experience:** Performance indicators for separate components may seem on track, but the cumulative performance of these interdependent metrics may add up to sluggish application delivery. If end-users complain that the process is too slow, listen and work to identify the problem.

See Figure 13-10, where an example case study for developing an effective SLA is illustrated.

Source: http://www.cutter.com[10]

Making SLAs Work—Metrics

Service level metrics are an important element of the service agreement. Without measurement, it would be difficult to assess the adequacy of the vendor and his activity. The SLA is basically a written document that is to define the expectation of the parties in agreement. If the parties negotiate the agreement in good faith, it should be representative of all the parties' expectations of benefits and services.

Here is a partial list of examples of service level metrics:

- Application availability
- Average application response time
- Number of application crashes per unit of time
- Average throughput
- Network availability and bandwidth
- Server availability
- Elapse time to repair hardware failure
- Mean time between server failure
- Number of operating system failures per unit of time
- Number of middleware failures per unit of time
- Number of production jobs not completed during the batch night shift

To illustrate the implementation of these examples, refer to Figure 13-10, a case study on introducing outsourcing to a firm's payroll operation. IT and finance jointly managed the payroll. The IT department was responsible for the payroll system while the payroll unit was responsible for data entry and maintenance. In the case study, the implementation team selected a number of measures to monitor the activity of the vendor. The team could have chosen other measures and questions remain whether better choices could have been made.

Each measurement reflects an indicator commensurate with an activity. The issuance of correct checks, forms, and reports is an important requisite of the process. Having the system up and running keeps the productivity of the staff at peak levels and it, too, is an indicator of optimal results. There were other measures that could have been used and still could be included today. They could have introduced cost per transaction (in this case, calculated the cost per employee for the year by number of employees and pay periods). They could have surveyed employee satisfaction with the vendor's system. Also, they could have looked at the training costs per employee. All of these additional measures would have provided a broader look at the effectiveness of the outsourcing process.

▪▪▪▪▪▪▪▪▪▪▪▪ **FIGURE 13-10** Corporation Case Study.

The XYZ Corp. Case Study—Part 1

In mid-1998, the XYZ Corp. was facing a crisis. Their business office was losing staff, they had not completed the Y2K upgrade to their payroll system, and there were going to be changes in the compensation schedule of their sales force that they had not yet addressed. The XYZ Corp. had investigated two avenues. The first was to hire new staff, bring in a number of consultants, and attempt to upgrade the existing system to handle both Y2K and the changes to the compensation system. The other alternative was to outsource the payroll area to a nationally known vendor. The vendor had thousands of existing clients, many of them were the same size, and there were even one or two companies that were competing against them in the same industry.

The questions that were raised in the senior management meetings revolved around the large start-up cost, migration of the existing data, and the loss of control of the payroll. The President was advised by the CFO and the CIO that outsourcing the payroll system offered the best chance of success in handling the Y2K issue as well as handling future changes to the compensation plans. Convinced that this was the right direction, the XYZ Corp. went ahead with the outsourcing project.

The XYZ Corp. created two teams to address the outsourcing initiative. The first team was created to develop the contract specifications and handle the legal and financial issues. The second team was responsible for identifying the plan for measuring, monitoring, and enforcing the contract provisions. The additional responsibility of keeping the contract up-to-date was also assigned to the second team.

The first team assembled a cross functional team of analysts, lawyers, payroll administrators, Human Resource staff and an outsourcing consultant to develop a contract and Service Level Agreement between the vendor and the XYZ Corp. The vendor provided sample contracts that were used in prior situations with other firms. The team used that framework but wanted to craft an agreement that would be customized to XYZ Corp. environment and had specific instructions to include options to change the agreement from time-to-time when compensation plans changed and when reporting needs changed.

The first team also waited for the second team to complete their analysis before finalizing the SLA. The second team also assembled a cross-functional team of payroll administrators, human resource staff, business analysts, and IT systems analysts. The second team needed to review the entire payroll process as it was being done and they examined how the process could be improved. The team needed to recommend how the process can be measured, what were the expected deliverables (besides payroll checks, there are governmental reporting, W-2, W-4, 1099, et al.), and explain what the governmental penalties for non compliance are? The team was also asked to list what are the possible changes to the system that may be asked for in the future.

(continues on the next page)

Using Service Level Agreements to Measure External Vendors

The discussion of service level agreements centers on how SLAs provide an important guide to measuring IT processes against specific criteria. Service level agreements can be created for two distinct situations. One situation would be a legal contract that will bind an external vendor and the firm that engaged the services. The other would be using SLAs to measure services performed by internal units of the firm for internal customers within the firm.

The external SLA will explicitly state the level of service expected, how the measurements will be taken, and who the responsible external parties will be. In addition, it must include: identification of the internal responsible parties and owners; identification of the monitors of the performance; identification of the methods to mediate and renew the contract provisions; and the incentives, penalties and provisions for the enforcement of the contract. In this external arrangement, a vendor provides the service by supplying outsource services to the business.

The service level agreement becomes the tool to manage vendor relationships. In Chapter 11—IT Governance, this area was discussed in detail under the section titled "Vendor Management."

▪▪▪▪▪▪▪▪▪▪▪ **FIGURE 13-10 (continued)**

The XYZ Corp. Case Study—Part 2

When the second team completed its first phase, the first team used those findings to complete the Service Level Agreement. The XYZ Corp. now had its payroll performed by an outside vendor. Although the first team's job was complete, the second team's next phase was critical. They worked with the vendor to migrate existing payroll data from XYZ Corp.'s old system to the new one. There were numerous data errors that had to be corrected as well as many missing data elements that had to be completed. The complexity of the different compensation plans had to be translated into understandable terms and entered into the new system. Many special reports were required to explain who, why, and how much compensation was owed under the current plans and identification of the exceptions was a daunting task. The task was completed several weeks past the scheduled project date.

The decision to run in parallel was made by project leaders of both firms, to reduce the risk of disaster. They choose to run through the first quarter of 1999, so that W-2's could be verified and compared for both the new and old payroll systems. Training of the remaining staff was initiated. The vendor provided the training in using the vendor system to add, maintain, and change employee information and compensation data. System training was done both on site as well as at the vendor's training centers.

The second team went into its third phase, introducing metrics and monitoring the vendor performance. The checks were being produced and were sent out to the appropriate people. There were several instances of glitches where direct deposit was rejected and paper checks were issued in lieu of the direct deposit. There were also instances of incorrect deductions taken, and commissions calculated incorrectly, but over 95% of the checks in the first month of transition were correct.

The second team then introduced the following metrics:

- Percentage of incorrect checks issued
  - Incorrect deductions
  - Incorrect salary
  - Incorrect commission
  - Incorrect payment method

- Percentage of incorrect reports issued
  - W-2's that are wrong
  - W-4's that are wrong
  - 1099's that are wrong
  - reports filed late

- System processing delays
  - System downtime
  - System not responsive or slow
  - Network failure
  - System failure

Using Service Level Agreements to Measure Internal Resources

Not all outsourcing arrangements are with external vendors. Working with internal business partners and IT requires SLA's.Iin Figure 13-11, Texas Instruments showed how SLAs can improve the relationship between IT and the business, yet there are risks that include exposing the weaknesses in the IT organization. If the IT organization cannot perform the processes they are contracted to do, they run the risk of being outsourced to external vendors who can do the job right.

The SLA in this situation is used to explicitly state the level of service expected, how the measurements will be taken, and who the responsible internal parties will be. Not unlike the external SLA, a well written internal service level agreement will specify the services that will be provided, the timeframe that they will be provided in, as well as the specific quantities and levels of quality required for the service. In addition, it must include: identification of the internal responsible parties and owners; identification of the monitors of the performance; and identification of the methods to mediate and renew the contract provisions.

The XYZ Corp. case Study—Part 3

The payroll team was downsized to reflect the change in organizational structure. The remaining payroll team had the responsibility of maintaining payroll records and monitoring the payroll process through the metrics shown above. IT staff was made available to the payroll unit to collect and process the metrics for the unit.

After successfully completing the parallel testing phase, the W-2's were correct except for a handful of complex cases which needed to be done manually. Senior management was very pleased with the result and was relieved in knowing that the vendor's system was already Y2K compliant. The case could have ended here but additional events occurred in the latter half of 1999.

The following additional issues arose during the year. Another change to the compensation plan would be needed for the second year in a row. The IRS requested that the 2000 W-2's be provided by electronic mail filing. The current submission of the W-2's by magnetic tape would still be accepted for 1999 but that everyone should expect it to be mandatory in 2000. These changes also affected the handling of 1099's and any other correspondence with the IRS. The state in which XYZ Corp. resided also announced that it required all companies to provide the state with a list of all new hires in order for the state to track down deadbeat dads. A newly passed state law provided the state the ability to locate and garnish the wages of deadbeat dads.

The vendor spoke to all of their clients and assured them that all of these changes mandated by the IRS and government authorities will be addressed. The vendor had thousands of clients affected by the same changes and had already begun work in upgrading their systems to handle these changes. XYZ Corp. seemed to have been rewarded in moving to this vendor, where the initial high costs and maintenance charges were offset by what it would have cost them to upgrade their old system (not only for Y2K but for all the additional government regulation changes.)

There were additional charges that arose from the change in the compensation system, but there were not additional charges for mandated changes by the IRS or for local and state government changes. The second team continually monitored the performance of the vendor and found that the vendor mostly performed as stipulated in the contract. There were only some instances where there were improper deductions being made, but these were quickly addressed in the next payroll cycle.

Overall, this implementation of the outsourcing project was a successful one. The designers of the process were from a cross section of the company, both IT and the business were actively involved, and they anticipated changes in the future and contracted for those changes. The monitoring of the measurements was important because it quickly alerted management when fixes were necessary and they were done.

In essence, to create the proper SLA, the firm is required to determine every aspect of the IT process, from quality, quantity, and timeliness of delivery to measuring, monitoring, and enforcing the process. Service level agreements are contracts that bind two or more internal parties to a specific agreement—the contractor or provider of the service and the receiver or client of the service. In an internal arrangement, Information Technology is the provider and the business is the client.

Internal outsourcing can provide an incentive for both the business and IT to work closely together to improve the firm's position. Because there will be additional scrutiny of the work that each unit will produce, there will be added incentive to succeed.

SLA Myths

Service level agreements are an important step in managing expectations of business partners, defining measures, and ensuring contractor behavior; however, some misconceptions exist that should be clarified. First, "service level metrics do make a service level agreement" is often untrue. Service level metrics provide measures or indicators

▪▪▪▪▪▪▪▪▪▪▪ **FIGURE 13-11** Texas Instruments, Inc.: Service Level Agreements and Cultural Changes.[11]

In December 1996, Jodie Ray, then CIO of Texas Instruments discussed the introduction of Service Level Agreements (SLAs) to the firm:

"We started reengineering IT in 1994 but we struggled with how to partner with the businesses. We needed a good communications tool. Service Level Agreements help business people articulate their needs and focus Information Systems and Services (IS&S) on returning business value."

Implementing SLAs causes radical reorganization and a paradigm shift for many of the staff of IS&S. Deneese Gibson, IS&S Controller, said:

"When we really got into it, we realized that just looking at data communications was still selling things, not services. If we really wanted to be true to the concept of Service Level Agreement, we couldn't think in terms of data communications, but rather of supplying communications from the desktop to their destination."

The thoughts from the business sector also changed. Larry Dix, Systems Manager, Semiconductor Group explained:

"The main difference SLAs make is that they place an upper limit on how much we spend on IT. If core IT can't deliver the services for less, we'll buy them from someone else. We don't care if we buy our services internally or externally, but we want to stop spending so much on IT."

After three years of hard work and negotiation, Texas Instruments began achieving favorable financial results. As important as achieving monetary gains, IT and the business found that they were able to build better relationships. Bonnie Lawson Wagner, Manager, SLA Portfolio Management stated:

"SLAs are not a quick fix to close IT's credibility gap with the business units, I do believe, however, they are an important first step in achieving improved customer satisfaction, customer intimacy and moving toward a customer driven approach in delivering IT services."

By early 1997, Pallab Chatterjee was named CIO and Senior Vice President of the Semiconductor Group. He noted that he was committed to continuing the efforts to increase the impact of the IT organization on the business bottom line:

"Service Level Agreements used internally is a proactive way of making business alignment happen."

Source: Ross, J. W., "Case Study: Texas Instruments, Inc.: Service Level Agreements and Cultural Change," Center for Informational Systems Research, Sloan School of Management, Massachusetts Institute of Technology (1997).

of performance. But monitoring and enforcement are necessary to ensure that an agreement is fully complied with and executed properly. As a quick example, if you went on a diet and then purchased a scale, you provided yourself the means to measure your weight. But unless you actually put yourself on the scale, looked at the dial, and adjusted your food intake to reflect your weight goals, you did not measure the success of your diet.

Secondly, "service level agreements will make users happy" is another falsehood. Although there are many good things that users should like about a service level agreement, a service level agreement will not necessarily improve the current process, and there are no guarantees that the vendor will fulfill the agreement. There is solace in knowing that if the contractor is unable to fulfill the contract, there will be penalties, but everyone should prefer that the agreements be met.

Third, "service level agreements will result in higher service levels" is again often wrong. When going from an unwritten statement to a written statement, the level of required performance is lower than what is normally provided to allow some slack. This is not to say that a service level agreement will always deliver a subaverage performance, but it is usually true that contractors will fight for a lower expectation, to ensure themselves some slack in the agreement.

Fourth, "Penalty clauses in a service level agreement will guarantee service levels" can be false. Enforcement of the penalty clauses are important factors in modifying contractor behavior, as long as the penalty clause is not so severe as to cause the contractor to file for bankruptcy.

Finally, "service level agreements are not necessary when outsourcing IT functions" is untrue. When contractors outside of the firm are providing service, it is paramount to ensure that you have a well-defined service agreement with the contractor. Although there are some consumer protection laws available to cover contract work, a firm needs to ensure that there is a clear contractual agreement between parties.

▪▪▪ Remaining Issues of IT Controls

Who Owns Measurements

This is an often-disputed topic. The following questions commonly appear:

- Who should own measurement?
- Is measurement a process that should be owned by the people doing the measurement or is it a corporate asset or cost?
- Is this question similar to who should own payroll?
- Should the owners of internal processes that are being measured simply own it?
- Does it even make a difference?

Yes, ownership indicates a level of responsibility. It also can mean that the possessors would have the ability to monitor and manipulate their own reports. From an auditing perspective, no one should be able to do that. If the area is financially important, there would be independent oversight. That is why the payroll department is a centralized activity, monitored to assure that on an accounting basis they report and pay the staff with utmost propriety. The payroll department is a separate unit in most organizations and they reside within a financial organization where they have their own separate budget. When measurement of the payroll department is required, it is often done by another corporate unit within the financial organization. In other areas, measurement is done in large part by internal units, often reporting on their own processes.

These questions are then raised:

- Who should be responsible for performing surveys, developing satisfaction indexes, and building strategic process maps?
- Who will arrange meetings with senior staff to design, implement, and monitor measurements?
- Who should pay for it all?

This is the crux of the issues that many companies face. Some companies have created a special unit to do this, but there is no consensus as to whether it belongs in IT, finance, HR, or some other corporate function, such as quality control. The controversy does not end there, but the answer often must be decided between the CEO, COO, CFO, and CIO. They must decide how and who will own and pay for the measurement, monitoring, and feedback (reporting) process. Many times the process can only be effective if it is a corporate mandate. The enterprise must find ways of funding the measurement process without penalizing the individual units. If the enterprise is unable to do this, then the measurements, monitoring, and enforcement will never get done.

What to Do with the Measurements

There is always continuous improvement in the development of measurements. Remember that the early primary measures have been financial ones. They were the easiest to facilitate because they were both tangible and easy to gather in quick order. Numerical analysis of spending, gross sales, and department expenditures were used to create the first indicators (return to Figure 13-3 for the examples of IT measures). Now, there are expanded measurable indicators that include more difficult measures, such as customer satisfaction surveys, employee satisfaction surveys, user satisfaction of application surveys, management opinion surveys, etc. These measures are difficult to gather and require some expertise in setting up scales and interpreting meaning of the responses. Nonetheless, many designers of the performance monitors prefer using these new measures. They continue their efforts in various research areas to combine many of these measures, both tangible and intangible, into a comprehensive package of measures. Why?

Simply, IT needs to establish a report card for its performance. IT wants to be able to know how it is doing. Financial measures are poor indicators of performance because they reflect past, not present, performance, and they are unlikely indicators of future performance. The time lag between profits from products, the development cycles, and the like, means that there can be no current measures of the effectiveness of IT. Moreover, they also fail to accurately convey IT's role in the financial picture. To create a more accurate picture, surveys are done to improve the collection of intangible data. This intangible data is extremely complex to deal with. Although the concept of using surveys is simple, there still exists the issue of how do you interpret them and, when you have completed interpreting them, how can you combine them with other survey results? It is not easy to determine the relative importance of one question versus another. How does customer satisfaction with one process get measured against dissatisfaction with another process? More complex would be the question of relating two different dissatisfactions by two different business partners in two different areas. Again in numerical measures, when they involved money, the scale was based on dollars, and the dollar was easily scalable across the entire firm. When dealing with opinion surveys and satisfaction indexes, there isn't a simple set of benchmarks or rulers to enable a consistent comparison. This requires expertise in developing standards in interpreting results from surveys, distinguishing the differences both quantitatively and qualitatively. Creating effective and understandable benchmarks will be the most challenging task of all.

Here is an example of the necessity of interpreting the measurement process:

Process	Strategic Goal	C S F	Measurement
Problem Control	Report problems Initiate action	Log problems Resolve problems	Call volume Customer survey
Data Planning	Facilitate reuse Provide security	Create common models Create secure databases	# common object # data break-ins

The issue of these examples is:

1. Do the business partners surveys truly reflect the ability of problem control to solve problems or initiate actions? Are call volume, length of call, and number of repeat calls better indicators? How are these interpreted?
2. Does the number of objects in a library indicate extensive reuse? If it were possible to count number of accesses to the library, would that be easier to interpret?

After you are able to produce these measures, what would you do with them and how could they be used? Continuing the analogy of IT seeking their own report card, compare this to a student's report card; in this case, it is often the student's parents that would make the most use of the report card. So also in the case of IT—it would be the senior executives of the firm's business managers and the senior IT executives who will benefit most from seeing those report cards on measures. The business needs effective objective methods to decide on questions such as, how much to budget on future spending within IT, or to outsource or insource, or arrange for more training, or hire more staff, or contract for more consultants.

There are many questions that can be answered if senior management knows the current status and effectiveness of their IT organization. The IT organization would be able to address issues or weaknesses discovered through measurement and work towards building on strong competencies, too. Measurement represents a vital and necessary part of effective administration of IT. It means that with effective measurement of both tangible and intangible activities, financial and nonfinancial indicators would be able to project a meaningful barometer of the performance of IT; where it has been, where it is now, and the direction it is traveling in.

In Figure 13-12, performance measures are listed for a specific objective, to improve efficient order management. These performance measures are quantifiable and the results will be easy to interpret. The measurement should be done periodically so that the progress or trend of the activity will hopefully demonstrate improvement in the service.

In Figure 13-13, a similar set of performance measures is listed for customer management. Many of these measures are similar to the same gauges used by popular customer relationship management (CRM) programs to determine how well IT and the business are performing in keeping their customers satisfied.

This is an example of how the measurement process can be applied to customer management:

Process	Strategic Goal	C S F	Measurement
Service mktg	Administer custs Initiate new svcs	Meet custs needs Report new reqmt.	# sales to cust # new cust

▪ ▪ ▪ ▪ ▪ ▪ ▪ ▪ ▪ ▪ ▪ **FIGURE 13-12 Performance Measures for Efficient Order Management.**

- Short order lead times
- In-stock availability
- Order accuracy
- Access to order status information
- Response time to customer inquires

▪ ▪ ▪ ▪ ▪ ▪ ▪ ▪ ▪ ▪ ▪ **FIGURE 13-13 Performance Measures for Efficient Customer Management.**

- Lower inventory carrying cost
- Reduced human intervention
- Greater order accuracy
- Improved production planning/forecasting based on demand
- Lower order administration
- Lower number of complaints
- Improved customer decision-making based on preferences
- Increased number of automatic restocking customers
- Lower stock-out occurrences

When Measurements Should Be Done

Deciding when to measure is not an easy question to answer because it is so dependent on the measurement. There are no standard frequencies and/or stable intervals. Ideally some measures can be done continuously, but those are generally of the hardware statistical variety, such as system and network availability, bandwidth and hardware capacity. Some measures are doable on a daily basis, such as daily transactional volumes, online sales, and e-mail delivered. Some measures are only available on a weekly or monthly basis, such as man-hours worked, projects installed, monthly or weekly sales totals, user requests, or error reports. Many of the important measurements from satisfaction and opinion surveys do not have a set interval, or they are only offered semiannually or annually.

If the answer, "it should be done when it should be done" is unsatisfactory, then the better answer is that, "it should be done consistently and repeatedly." Some measurements will have intervals that will be longer than one would hope for a report card of a business unit; but report cards are only distributed at the end of a school's reporting period. Note that not every school has even a midterm report card. The focus of having measurements, done on a consistent and repeated basis, means that IT will be graded periodically.

The Difference Between Monitoring and Simply Measuring IT

There is always continuous improvement in the development of measures. Remember that the early primary measures have been strictly discontinuous single measures. With the improvement of technology, IT can provide continuous monitoring of these measurements. Why? Simply, IT needs a more visible map of where it needs to go. IT also wants to be able to show how it is doing and what will need improvement or fine tuning. To enable a better, more accurate picture, many steps are needed to improve the collection of intangible data, like assessing the impact on the user and ascertaining what the users really need. This intangible data is extremely complex to deal with. Although the premise is simple, the execution is difficult and there are issues of how to interpret, when to complete interpreting, and how to combine them with the other intangibles.

If there isn't measurement, is the firm more likely to fail at improving itself? Can the CIO accomplish the main goal of adding value to the firm using IT? These form the next question.

Can the Enterprise Succeed Without Measurement?

In Figure 13-14, a Forrester Research study shows that 57 percent of companies they surveyed cannot justify investments because they don't know how to measure customer profitability. This inability to measure is reducing their effectiveness.

How can these companies use IT effectively if they cannot determine if their activities are meeting strategic goals?

Certainly, measurement and analysis are not the lone enablers of success. But without service level agreements, the firm cannot control outsourced processes well. Even once the measuring benchmarks have been decided, the monitoring must be enabled to ignite active management. Can any company succeed when it is unable to develop new and improved, efficient and effective processes? The answer is "No," but not because it cannot continue to do business as usual, but because it cannot survive in today's competitive "information society." Creating new and improved processes that are efficient and effective is what enables the firm to meet its strategic goals. Without meeting its strategic goals, how long can a company survive today?

▪▪▪▪▪▪▪▪▪▪▪ **FIGURE 13-14** Results from a Business Planning Survey.

Little customer-focused business planning

- Only 42% of companies prepare a business case for their CRM project.
- Only 45% have centralized CRM responsibility
- 57% can't justify investments because they don't know how to measure customer profitability
- Only 10% measure ROI

**How can the business keep their customers
without effectively using IT?**

**And if they don't measure it, can they even know
when they are using IT effectively?**

How Does the Enterprise Benefit from Measurement?

Measurement is necessary to improve performance. Performance is related to effectiveness, efficiency, and quality, and to understand if a process is effective, efficient, or of high quality, it must be measured and compared to other similar processes. This can be done through benchmarking, trend analysis, satisfaction surveys, and many other measurement processes. Measurement is an integral part of monitoring project performance. Project management tools can continuously monitor project activities and schedules. Managers can be alerted to project difficulties early enough to often repair the problems before they cause a project delay. Measurement is also important in determining if vendors and internal suppliers are performing to service level agreements. All of these aspects explain the importance of measuring, monitoring, and analyzing performance.

In today's information age filled with new technologies, it is still paramount that all units within a business must be working toward the same strategic goals of the firm. Therefore, the best course to travel is the one that will work toward strategic alignment with the firm. The alignment maturity assessment provides both a measurement and and benchmark for firms to apply.

CIOs are responsible for organizing and managing IT. The answer to the question, "How does the CIO keep informed of the activity and progress of the IT organization over the span of each day (or even week or month)?" is simply that they need a report card to do this. The CIO must be aware of how the IT organization is meeting business expectations, as well as how effectively the IT organization performs in relation to others in the industry. Without the CIO's ability to measure or compare, the enterprise would be unable to gauge how IT is performing or whether IT is meeting the demands of the firm. Now whether it is in the form of 10 step development of internal measurements, or some other form of benchmarking, it will have to be developed by the firm itself. It must be customized and fitted to the firm's culture, industry, financial standing, size, and maturity.

It becomes the responsibility of the CIO to derive benefit from these measurements. The CIO needs to ensure that feedback is engineered back into the IT units so that improvements can be made where there is weakness and advantage can be gained where there are strengths. Efficiency and effectiveness of IT can both be improved when the results of measurement are properly interpreted and there are effective changes made to processes and activities. The CIO needs to use the report cards to demonstrate these trends to his business partners, to encourage spending when it is needed, to illustrate trends (both good and bad) where they are apparent, and to aid in focusing other departments in strategic issues.

REVIEW QUESTIONS ■ ■ ■ ■ ■ ■ ■

1. What are the major components of measurement that can be used to measure performance of Information Technology?
2. Why are financial measures often not good indicators of performance?
3. Why are nonquantifiable measures of performance better indicators than quantifiable measures? What intangible items would be evidence of effective performance indicators?
4. Return on investment (ROI) has always been a main focus of financial analysts. What intangible benefits of Information Technology are often difficult to quantify for this measurement?
5. Some say that the progress towards building a comprehensive framework for IT assessment has begun, but may never finish. Explain.
6. How would you suggest a company begin to develop performance measures for their Information Technology function?

DISCUSSION QUESTIONS ■ ■ ■ ■ ■ ■ ■

1. Why aren't many measures sufficient to evaluate the effectiveness and level of performance that Information Technology provides?
2. Does your company have an effective set of tools to measure the performance of Information Technology? Has it been published or otherwise communicated? What are its main components and measures?
3. What do you think are Information Technology's distinctive competencies?
4. Does your IT function have systemic competencies? What are they? How are they measured?
5. What do you think are the main weaknesses in evaluating the performance of Information Technology? Is your company better or worse than average when evaluating IT?

AREAS FOR RESEARCH ■ ■ ■ ■ ■ ■ ■

1. Read CobiT 3rd Edition, "Management Guide," "Framework" and "Control Objectives" released by the CobiT Steering Committee and the IT Governance Institute 07/2000.
2. Read Barry L. Myers, Leon A. Kappelman, and Victor R. Prybutok's "A Comprehensive Model for Assessing the Quality and Productivity of the Information Systems Function: Toward a Theory for Information Systems Assessment." *Information Resources Management Journal*, 10(1), pgs. 6–25.
3. Read Peter B.B. Turney's "Activity-Based Management—ABM puts ABC Information to Work", *Management Accounting*, 01/1992, pgs. 20–25.

CONCLUSION ■ ■ ■ ■ ■ ■ ■

This chapter has discussed the concept of measurement. The chapter started with long lists of what can be measured. Within those lists, there were measures that could easily be done; they were tangible, numerical measures. There were measures that machines could statistically calculate or accountants could manually count. A new 10 step process was introduced to enable the firm to build their own measurement model and customize it to their environment. It would be difficult but the gains would be tremendous. The addition of benchmarking creates more measures. Service level agreements have also helped identify significant additional measures and encourage continuous monitoring of many IT processes. While measurement of financial activities as well as hardware and transactional functions have dominated the previous decades, it is clear that the intangible and nonquantifiable measures have become more important in the new "informational society." But these intangible measures, opinions, and satisfaction indexes are measures that are subjective in nature. It is these measurements that are difficult, and in some cases even impossible, to do. Yet many of those indicators may be the most important indicators to measure. These intangible measures are more meaningful because they are not numerical abstractions of nonessentials. Customer satisfaction, staff abilities, technology leadership, and product focus are more indicative of measures of competence in Information Technology than response times, transaction cycles, MIPS, and so forth.

Today, there is greater focus on aligning Information Technology with the business and insuring that IT assists its business partners to meet the firm's strategic goals. While progress towards building this comprehensive framework continues at a slow pace, these measures are beginning to gain acceptance in many major corporations and enterprises in both the United States and abroad. Many companies have begun to measure their Information Technology effectiveness with these new concepts and have found success already. Companies that begin to gain strategic advantage over their competitors because of these new concepts will find that they will be unable to keep these advantages for long unless they make continuous improvement to their processes though effective use of measurement, monitoring, and enforcement.

REFERENCES ▪▪▪▪▪▪▪

[1] Umbaugh, Robert E., "Peter F. Drucker on MIS Management," in *Handbook of MIS Management*, 2ed., (1988) p. 66.

[2] Violino, Bob, "Return on Investment: The Intangible Benefits of Technology Are Emerging as Most Important of All," in *Information Week (6/30/97)*, p. 37.

[3] Myers, Barry L., Kappelman, Leon A., and Prybutok, Victor R., "A Comprehensive Model for Assessing the Quality and Productivity of the Information Systems Function: Toward a Theory for Information Systems Assessment," in *Information Resources Management Journal* (10[1]–1997), pp. 6–25.

[4] Davis, G. B., and Hamann, J. R., "In-Context Information Systems Assessment: A Proposal and an Evaluation," in *Information Systems Assessment: Issues and Challenges* (1988), pp. 283–296.

[5] Umbaugh, Robert E., "Peter F. Drucker on MIS Management," in *Handbook of MIS Management*, 2ed. (1988), pp. 67–69.

[6] Quinn, J. B., and Baily, M. N., "Information Technology: Increasing Productivity in Services," in *Academy of Management Executive, 8(3)* 1994, pp. 28–48.

[7] Turney, Peter B. B., "Activity-Based Management," in *Management Accounting* (January 1992), pp. 20–25.

[8] Parasuraman, A., Zeithaml, V. A. and Berry, L. L., "A Conceptual Model of Service Quality and Its Implications for Future Research," in *Journal for Marketing, 49(4)* 1985, pp. 41–50.

[9] Myers, Barry L., Kappelman, Leon A., and Prybutok, Victor R., "A Comprehensive Model for Assessing the Quality and Productivity of the Information Systems Function: Toward a Theory for Information Systems Assessment," in *Information Resources Management Journal (10[1]–1997)*, pp. 6–25.

[10] Cutter Consortium in *Network Magazine* (Issue #6, 21 March, 2000).

[11] Ross, J. W., "Case Study: Texas Instruments, Inc.: Service Level Agreements and Cultural Change," Center for Informational Systems Research, Sloan School of Management, Massachusetts Institute of Technology (1997).

CHAPTER 14

Assessing the Value of IT*

"The past forty years have seen dramatic advances in the technology of information processing, and its widespread adoption bears testimony to the advent of the 'information society.' However, the economic implications of this transition remain to some degree obscure, since there is little evidence that the new technology has led to clear improvements in productive efficiency." [1]

—GEOFFREY M. BROOKE

Preview of Chapter

This chapter examines vehicles for demonstrating the financial contribution of IT to its business partners. Other chapters in this book have explained the processes that are performed within IT, and the way IT and the firm measures those performances. Those measures are mainly used to guide, manage, and control the IT processes. The focus of this chapter is on today's most valuable financial measures: real options, portfolio valuation of IT projects, and activity-based management. These approaches will assist IT in demonstrating its financial value to the organization. This chapter also relates to Chapter 11—IT Governance by providing financial tools to assist management in setting IT priorities.

What we will examine in this chapter:

- Importance of assessing IT value
- Traditional financial measures to show value
- Applying an improved financial measure—options
- Evaluating a portfolio of IT investment projects
- Activity-based management
- The difference between showing value and simply measuring it
- Leveraging the assets of IT for competitive advantage
- How IT governance is a shared responsibility
- How the enterprise can benefit from these processes

* Special thanks to Professor Tim Koeller of Stevens Institute of Technology.

Other chapters discussed developing and governing IT strategies for enabling and driving business strategies. These strategies will provide value to the business. The purpose of this chapter is to discuss how IT can measure and demonstrate the contribution of these strategies to the business and with the business.

▪▪▪ Introduction

While delivering competitive advantages to the organization is important, these added strengths are meaningless unless the business managers of the firm can readily see the value. The business must make effective use of IT, learning to use IT as an asset. But how can the business do this if they are unaware of the abilities and strengths of IT? As Robert Kaplan and David Norton wrote in 1992, "What you measure is what you get. Senior executives understand that their organization's measurement system strongly affects the behavior of managers and employees."[2] This suggests that effectively measuring the performance of IT can change behavior of the business managers in their relationship with IT.

In the previous chapter, we measured the activity of IT in many ways. What is the difference here? Howard Rubin says,

"Information systems input (investments in tools, techniques, people, environment, architecture, the workplace) has no meaning unless it is connected to business outcomes (improved quality, shorter cycle times, new services, increased shareholder value, enhanced customer satisfaction and so on). Good metrics answers the question: What is the value of (add here any technology you like) to the business? Effective measurement programs take concerns in both IS and the business as their basis."[3]

He suggests that IT must evolve by adding business-oriented measurement to its current set of measurements. It is only after having business oriented metrics that IT will have the ability to demonstrate value to their business managers. In fact, the responsibility for demonstrating these business value measurements should be shared by both IT and business executives.

Asking ten IT executives how they demonstrate the value of IT to the business would likely evoke ten different responses. However, the pressure is increasingly great for IT to show its value to the firm. This chapter will describe both traditional and more innovative ways of demonstrating business-oriented measurements of the value of IT.

▪▪▪ Traditional Financial Approaches

ROI, Residual Income, and Economic Value Added of an Individual Investment

The measurement method known as Return on Investment (ROI) is widely cited as a technique for assessing the value of IT investments (e.g., see Lewis and Koller (2001)[4] and Violino (1997)[5]). The ROI method was developed in the early twentieth century at Dupont Powder Company as an effective way of allocating investment funds within a manufacturing firm comprised of a number of functional activities (e.g., manufacturing, selling, purchasing) each of which is viewed as an investment center. ROI is generally calculated as net earnings from operations (earnings after deducting the depreciation expense but before deducting interest expense) divided by net assets (defined as total assets less goodwill, other intangible assets, and current liabilities).

In those early years the ROI method was used at Dupont and other firms (e.g., General Motors) to complement extensive top-management insight concerning the technological and market conditions within which the firm's operating divisions conducted their business. After World War II, with the rise of diversified corporations and ever more decentralized decision making, the ROI measure became a popular metric used by top management to evaluate the performance of divisions and their managers. This use of the ROI method often led to its manipulation by managers attempting to show enhanced short-term results. See Figure 14-1 for examples of ROI calculations for two major corporations in different industries.

For example, a division manager can increase the ROI ratio by increasing its numerator (operating income) or by decreasing its denominator (the division's investment base). This manipulation could occur if management avoids profitable opportunities capable of earning ROI's in excess of the corporation's cost of financial capital, but which fail to exceed the current average ROI of the division. Actions that are taken solely to increase the short-term ROI can thus substantially compromise the evaluation, and achievement, of the corporation's strategic initiatives. For example, Lewis and Koller cite a recent survey in which 59 percent of a set of ROI analyses of Internet technology projects resulted in positive returns. This unrealistically high percentage is attributed in part to the firms' efforts to justify expected profits from investments in the developing technology. Assessing the results after the implementation might show a very different result. What was the lesson learned?

▪▪▪▪▪▪▪▪▪▪▪▪ **FIGURE 14-1 Sample ROI Calculations.**

Based on the financial statements of 2001, the sample ROI of the firm was as follows:[6]

General Motors Corporation (GM)

(In Millions)
Total Income Available for Interest Expense = 16,397.0
Total Assets = 303,100.0
Current Liabilities = 63,156.0
Other intangibles = 7,622.0

Return on Investment (ROI) = **Total Income Available for Interest Expense**
(Total Assets – Current Liabilities – Other Intangibles)

$$= \frac{16,397.0}{303,100.0 - 63,156.0 - 7,622.0}$$

$$= .07195 \text{ or } 7.2\%$$

Microsoft Corporation (MSFT)

(In Millions)
Total Income Available for Interest Expense = 11,525.0
Total Assets = 59,257.0
Current Liabilities = 11,132.0
Other intangibles = 0.0

Return on Investment (ROI) = **Total Income Available for Interest Expense**
(Total Assets – Current Liabilities – Other Intangibles)

$$= \frac{11,525.0}{59,257.0 - 11,132.0 - 0.0}$$

$$= .2395 \text{ or } 23.95\%$$

The limitations of the ROI analyses are well known and led to the development of the residual income and economic value added techniques. Briefly, residual income is very similar to the economist's measure of excess profit. It is the difference between a division's (or other activity's) reported operating income and the financial opportunity cost of the division's investment base. The latter component is the product of the investment base and a risk-adjusted cost of financial capital for the division. The residual income measure will always be increased by investments earning rates of return above the cost of capital, promoting congruence between operating management and the firm's wealth goals, and eliminating the kind of potentially dysfunctional manipulation possible under the ROI method.

However, despite its relative advantages over the ROI method, the residual income technique received little attention from firms until it was extended and revived as the "Economic Value Added" (EVA) concept in the early 1990s by the Stern Stewart consulting firm. The EVA concept uses recent developments in corporate finance, especially the capital asset pricing model, to identify the cost of capital for a specific division or business unit. The EVA method also attempts to remove distortions to the investment decision created by the Generally Accepted Accounting Practices (GAAP) required for external financial reporting. Perhaps the most noteworthy of these distortions involves expenditures that, viewed from an economic value perspective, should be capitalized and amortized over time, but which must be expensed under GAAP. This distortion of economic value is especially evident for intangibles such as intellectual property, research and development, customer, brand, and market development, and enhancement of worker productivity. Kaplan and Atkinson (1998)[7] have shown that long-term EVA and ROI will be overstated under GAAP as compared with the true economic value of the investment. This result is obtained because the expensed investments in these intangibles, made in the early years of the investment's economic life, are not amortized in later years. Put simply, GAAP overstates operating income and understates the investment base relative to an economic treatment of the investment activity, in which investments in intangibles would be capitalized in the early years of the investment and amortized in subsequent years.

This inconsistency between firms' treatment of investment projects from an internal economic value perspective and from the external reporting perspective of financial accounting is one reason for the lukewarm reception of the EVA method.[8] This unfortunate result has been observed despite increased pressures on firms from external financial markets to more effectively manage their portfolios of capital investments to the benefit of stockholders. As Kaplan and Atkinson have suggested, managers' difficulties in effectively addressing these pressures may result from limited abilities to consider, and incorporate, the risks accompanying investment projects, including investments in IT. Overall, these methods are imprecise. The projects that are funded are often those that shout the loudest.

Discounted Cash Flow Analysis (and Extensions) of an Individual Investment

The ROI and residual income (or EVA) methods, though relatively easy to implement, share the limitation that they do not explicitly reflect the economic circumstances of an investment project over its lifetime. For example, none of the previous methods can readily accommodate subsequent investment outlays, or uneven cash flows, that may arise during the project's economic life. Capital budgeting methods, including the Net Present Value (NPV) technique, permit the firm to choose between alternative investment opportunities to advance the market value of the firm under these types of conditions. By allocating its resources among such opportunities on a long-term basis, discounted cash flow methods avoid some of the short-term myopia of ROI calculations. However, they are not without their own limitations. An example of the NPV method of capital budgeting and some of its limitations are described in Appendix 14A.

Defining the Concepts of Net Present Value and Modified NPV

Net Present Value is an approach used in capital budgeting where the present value of cash outflow is subtracted from the present value of cash inflows. When the NPV is greater than zero, it is assumed that the transaction is favorable. If the NPV is zero or less, then it is considered unfavorable. This financial calculation is often used to analyze the expected effective rates of return for expenditures made. Appendix 14A shows a sample calculation.

The major limitation of the standard NPV calculation is that it is done initially with fixed rates of interest based on the best guess at the time of the original calculation. These calculations would be greatly improved as updated rates of interest became known and the volatility of the rates was reduced.

Modified NPV is a ratio of present value of the inflows to the present value of the outflow. The modified NPV will usually be greater than the standard NPV because it will include the interest earned during the deferral period. See Appendix 14B.

The standard NPV method faces a potentially difficult problem when new information about the investment project is acquired during its economic lifetime, and uncertainty about its cash flows is reduced. The NPV technique developed as a method for evaluating projects based on their measurable cash flows, but not on their intangible strategic benefits to a firm's competitive position. To be fair, discounted cash flow techniques were originally designed to value passive investments in financial securities, reflecting the relatively passive nature of a firm's creditors and stockholders. In contrast to this static perspective, the strategic management of investments, including IT investments, has necessarily concerned itself with the dynamics of competitive position. New information provided to management as a project unfolds affords managers the flexibility to alter original strategies concerning the project so as to exploit newly developing opportunities, or to avoid developing losses.

▪▪▪ Activity-Based Management Measures

Activity-based costing provides the input to enable the activity-based management process to assess the performance of work in an area and therefore assist management in making decisions. See the "Defining the Concepts of ABC and ABM" sidebar for an explanation of activity-based costing and activity-based management. It provides managers with useful information they need regarding the contribution that each customer makes to overall profitability. With this information, managers will be able to identify what projects will maximize performance and prove to be a good strategic addition when implemented.

Defining the Concepts of Activity-Based Costing (ABC) and Activity-Based Management (ABM)

Activity-based costing is a methodology that measures the cost and performance of activities, resources, and cost objects. Resources are assigned to activities, and then activities are assigned to cost objects based on their use.

Activity-based management is defined as a discipline that focuses on the management of activities as the route to improving the value received by the customer and the profit achieved by providing this value. This discipline includes cost driver analysis, activity analysis, and performance measurement. Activity-based management draws on ABC as its major source of information.[20]

Studies show that 20 percent of all customers provide virtually all the profits of a company. Another 60 percent break even and the remaining 20 percent only reduce the bottom line. Would a company benefit from knowing which companies were in each percentile, and could they actually gain an advantage, if they knew?[21]

How does ABC work? A company evaluates the resources, processes, and money required to produce a product or a service. If the IT help desk were to be studied, the first step would be to establish the activity centers and activities. The ABC team must identify all the activities within the help desk, such as installing software or routing a call to a technician. Once the activities are established, the ABC team then needs to determine the parts of each activity that cost money. There can be hidden details that may be taken for granted, such as the cost of each phone call made in response to the original call. The key here is to delineate the components of fixed, variable, and hidden costs. These costs can then be associated with each activity that becomes the basis of determining the cost driver (or unit of output that is used to calculate the cost of each activity.) So each type of call to the help desk would have different cost drivers based on the service requested. Once every activity is categorized and its cost drivers computed, the ABC analysis can evaluate the overhead and operating expenses by linking costs to customers, services, products, and orders.[22] The most important contribution of this model is to inform managers what processes really cost and provide a basis of maximizing profitability by encouraging profitable processes and discouraging unprofitable activities. This method is compared to other value methods in Figure 14-11 found later in this chapter.

While ABC and ABM have grown in popularity and many major companies and organizations, such as IBM, Kraft Foods, NASA, and Blue Cross and Blue Shield of Florida[23] have adopted this model, there has been growing concern that this model does not entirely satisfy sufficient analysis of all IT processes and activities. Companies began searching for a different implementation of ABC for the IT area.

▪▪▪▪▪▪▪▪▪▪▪ **FIGURE 14-2** Mapping IT Investment Characteristics to Financial Call Option Characteristics.

IT investment	Options model variable	Call option
PV of IT project's assets to be acquired	PV (assets to be acquired)	Stock price
IT expenditure needed to acquire the assets	PV (expenditure)	Exercise price
Decision deferral period	t	Time to expiration
Time value of money	r_f	Risk free interest rate
Risk of IT project's assets	σ^2	Variance of return or stock

Source: adapted from Luehrman, T. A., *Capital Projects as Real Options: An Introduction*, Harvard Business School Teaching Note (1994).

▪▪▪ Applying Traditional Approaches in a New Way

Real Options

Discounted cash flow analysis was originally developed to determine the value of a static financial security, such as a bond or equity instrument. However, discussion to this point has suggested the inadequacies of this method when valuing strategic investment proposals (including those for IT projects) having dynamic, strategic characteristics. The following describes why the theory and analysis of real options is a more appropriate method for valuing such investments. One example of the relevance of an options approach to an IT investment decision is in our analysis of the option to abandon a project.

Many IT managers are aware of the future strategic options (e.g., cost savings, new products/services, and markets) that may evolve from current investment projects even if they are uncertain about the eventual dollar amounts resulting from these options. However, lacking a clear grasp of the fundamentals of real options valuation (a field normally mastered by financial specialists), these managers are generally unable to exploit the power of this method, and to more fully and appropriately align their IT investments with the financial valuation of their firm. Fortunately, Luehrman (1998a)[9] has provided an excellent explanation of this somewhat esoteric topic. In the balance of this section the key elements of his explanation will be summarized. Following his example, it is assumed that the decision to pursue an investment project can be deferred for a period of time.

An opportunity to create an IT investment at some future time is similar to the financial concept of a call option. This is an option (but not an obligation) for the decision maker to buy an asset (e.g., a financial security) by paying a given amount on or before a certain point in time. If a financial call option could be identified that is very similar to the IT investment being considered, then the market value of that financial call option, determined in a well-defined and efficient security market, would provide a good approximation of the value of the opportunities expected from the IT investment. Since finding such a similar financial security is unlikely, real options analysis attempts to build one.

This is done by mapping five characteristics of the investment opportunity onto five corresponding characteristics of a financial call option. The call option that is being

▪▪▪▪▪▪▪▪▪▪▪ **FIGURE 14-3**   Decision Tree Analysis Versus Real Option Analysis.

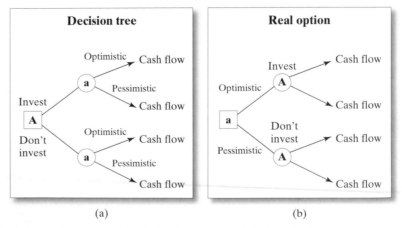

(a)   (b)

Source: adapted from Luehrman, T. A., *Capital Projects as Real Options: An Introduction*, Harvard Business School Teaching Note (1994).

described is a "European" call; an option that can be exercised only at the date of expiration.[10] Figure 14-2 shows this mapping of characteristics. The present value of the investment's assets to be acquired or developed corresponds to the stock price of the call option. The investment expenditure corresponds to the exercise price of the call option. The length of time before the investment decision must be made corresponds to the length of time until the option expires. The risk concerning the investment project's cash flows corresponds to the standard deviation of the return to the security. The cost of capital is the risk-free rate of interest.

The value of the option to defer the investment derives largely from the reduction in uncertainty that will occur by deferring the decision. That is, up to the time when the investment must be made the decision maker is able to acquire evolving information about the wisdom of making the investment, primarily as expected future cash flows become known with greater certainty, but also as intangible benefits of the investment are brought into clearer view and measurement. Thus, the static NPV method and the flexible options approach to this situation will yield equivalent results only when the investment decision cannot be deferred.

Luehrman (1998a)[9] has provided a simple way of representing the two sources of value derived from a real option. The first is the interest income that can be earned on the investment funds during the deferral period. The second results from the decision maker's ability to react to changing uncertain conditions during the deferral period by altering investment decisions to the firm's benefit. Simple examples of this representation of the two sources of value derived from a real option appear in Appendix 14B.

Trigeorgis[11] suggests that decision tree analysis (DTA) is a technique capable of accounting for a firm's revisions of its strategies and operations under uncertainty. Briefly, management is considering a sequence of decisions, each of which depends on uncertain future events that can be described probabilistically, where probabilities are derived from past information or from future information that can be obtained at some cost. Management will choose the alternative that maximizes its risk-adjusted NPV.

A simple example of DTA is in Appendix 14C. The example illustrates how Decision Tree Analysis (DTA) can extend NPV analysis by explicitly considering the relationship between decisions made over time and conditional on previous decisions. It also permits the analyst to amend standard NPV calculations to incorporate the value of options to alter (e.g., abandon) subsequent decisions. However, Trigeorgis notes that DTA suffers from a number of practical and conceptual limitations. First, the complexity of the decision tree can increase rapidly with increases in the number of managerial decisions, and with decisions that must be made more frequently than was suggested in the simple example above. Second, the use of a constant discount rate in NPV calculations is incorrect in problems involving a sequence of decisions and options concerning the use of assets. These options can, for example, reduce the risk of a project after a point in time, and should be reflected in a lower cost of capital. Finally, nothing in DTA requires the analyst to emphasize, or even consider, the options available to managers to amend their strategic plans as they unfold over time.

Luehrman (1994)[12] has provided a simple way to contrast the general class of discounted cash flow analysis (including DTA) with an options approach. As shown in Figure 14-3a, a decision tree analysis of discounted cash flows is based on the assumption that managers will make an investment decision and then wait to observe its results. In many important instances, however, managers can wait until some uncertainty is resolved before the investment decision must be made, as shown in Figure 14-3b. The case shown in Figure 14-3a is not an option, while the case shown in Figure 14-3b is an option, and efficient capital markets will value the two cases differently. A simple example of DTA with an option to abandon is in Appendix 14D.

Real Option Valuation of an Individual Investment

The expressions for the modified NPV and cumulative volatility permit the valuation of a European call option using the Black-Scholes model for options valuation. This model provides a dollar value for the option, based on the five factors shown in Figure 14-2.

As an example, consider an IT project that was seeking capital funding of $3 million in return for which the firm expects to receive assets with a present value of $2.7 million. While the assets are risky with a standard deviation of 40 percent per year, the firm is able to defer the investment decision for three years. The project would have been initially turned down because the NPV was less than zero (actually the traditional NPV calculation would yield −$300,000.00). Using the three year European call option with the Black-Scholes model, the calculation of the real option value would be done as follows:

$$\text{Modified NPV} = \$2.7 \text{ million} / [\$3 \text{ million} / (1.05)^3] = 1.042 \text{ or approx. } 1.04$$

$$\text{Cumulative volatility} = (.40)\left(\sqrt{3}\right) = .693 \text{ or approx. } .70$$

(Using the table in Figure 14E-1) the Black-Scholes determinant is approximately 28.8 percent.

$$\text{Value of real option} = \$2.7 \text{ million} \times 28.8 \text{ percent} = \$777,600$$

Therefore, using the European call option calculation, the model suggested that because of the heavy volatility the projected variance of the asset risk could be over $777,600. The variance does not suggest that the project is definitely worthwhile; on the contrary, it is saying that it was not, at this point, but with better information later, it may be. The option to revisit this project is what makes the project worth doing because the variance suggests it may be profitable and the cost for looking at it three years from now is low enough for the investment of a pilot project to make sense.

This example is, of course, fairly simplistic, and potential problems with the real options approach can arise. For example, real options analysis uses much of the same data, present in spreadsheet form, that are used to conduct NPV analyses. However, the explicit incorporation of the uncertainty associated with real options, as reflected in cumulative volatility, theoretically adds a new element to the capital budgeting problem. This element could be addressed if methods such as sensitivity analysis were added to consider alternative "what if" scenarios concerning the value of the term $\sigma\sqrt{t}$. In addition, many corporate investment decisions are complex, especially if they require the analyst to consider expected interdependencies and synergies among investment projects and related options. This method is compared to other value methods in Figure 14-9 found later in this chapter. Finally, Housel et al. (2001)[13] have suggested that the real options approach, like the other financial methods previously discussed, suffers from the limitation that it is based on cash flow projections, but that IT investments (e.g., in support of core corporate processes) often do not result in easily measured cash flows. That is, the evaluation of IT investments typically includes only those financial items that the firm systematically records and reports; for example, the tangible cost of the investment, increased revenues, and cost savings. Little or no account is taken of other, less easily measured strategic objectives, including how the investment can improve less tangible outcomes such as business processes, marketing and customer service, or the firm's competitiveness.

▪▪▪▪▪▪▪▪▪▪ **FIGURE 14-4** "Tomato Garden" of IT Investment Project.

Modified NPV of IT investment project

| | Out of the money | **1.0** | In the money |
| | | | |

Cumulative volatility of IT investment Project

$(\sigma \sqrt{t})$

Low

VI. Invest never	I. Invest now
V. NPV < 0, modified NPV < 1: Doubtful investments: *Probably never invest*	II. NPV > 0, modified NPV > 1: *Exercise option early or maybe now*
IV. NPV < 0; Modified NPV < 1: IT project requires active development: *Maybe invest later*	III. NPV < 0; Modified NPV > 1 because option to wait is valuable given high volatility. *Probably invest later*

High

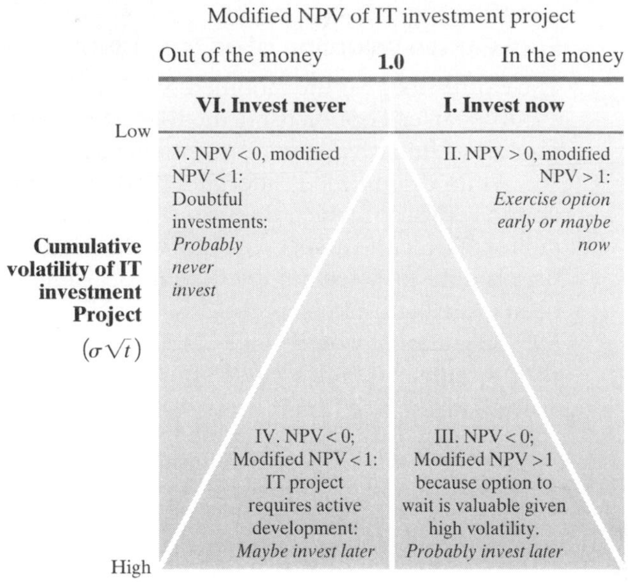

Source: adapted from Luehrman, T.A., 1998b "Strategy as a Portfolio of Real Options," *Harvard Business Review*, September-October (1998).

However, Parker, Benson, Trainor (1988)[14] and others have shown that aspects of information economics can be brought to bear on this shortcoming of traditional financial analyses of investment projects.[15] Buss (1983)[16] describes a framework in which investment projects are ranked (as a high, medium, or low priority) for each of four criteria: financial benefits, intangible benefits, technical importance, and fit with business objectives. Each of these criteria would, in turn, be comprised of relevant elements. For example, Buss suggests that intangible benefits could include such elements as improving client service, speeding up decision making, improving the quality of information, and standardizing manual processes. Each element would be scored for an IT investment project and the total score derived for "intangible benefits" would be added to the total score for "financial benefits" (based on its own relevant elements, e.g., ROI), for "technical importance" and for "fit with business objectives". The sum obtained across the four criteria would be used to compare the IT investment against competing projects.

As reported by Semich (1994),[17] Oracle Corporation developed a similar decision model in which financial investment criteria are combined with an information economic analysis of the intangible benefits and risks associated with investments in IT. Briefly, their method consists of the following steps:

Create a committee of stakeholders affected by the IT investment, including IT managers and business unit managers.

Define intangible benefits of the IT investment that are agreed to by the committee; for example, more flexible and efficient budgeting, improved decision analysis, improved information request responsiveness.

Define intangible risks associated with the IT investment; for example, slow response to system change, risk of poor integration with existing systems, staff resistance to a new system.

Establish weights to the relative importance of the tangible benefits (the financial result), the intangible benefits, and the intangible risks of the IT investment.

Estimate on a scale of zero to five the likelihood of each benefit and risk being observed.

Multiply each likelihood estimate by the weight established for that factor and add up the products. The investment alternative that results in the greatest sum is the preferred alternative.

While these methods obviously depend on a number of subjective evaluations, they complement financial methods, including real options analysis, to the extent: 1) that they build consensus among the participants in IT investment decisions, and 2) that they couple financial calculations with intangible benefits and risks, aspects of strategic concern. Thus, rather than propose the real options approach as *the* preferred means of evaluating IT investments, use it in combination with these methods of incorporating intangibles and of building consensus among the stakeholders within the organization.

Luehrman (1994, 1998b)[12, 18] has shown that the two elements of value afforded by a real option can be effectively represented in a graphical "tomato garden" format. (See Figure 14-4) The vertical axis of this diagram represents a project's cumulative volatility $\left(\sigma\sqrt{t}\right)$ and the horizontal axis represents its modified NPV. As shown in Figure 14-4, the space occupied by this "garden" can be segmented into distinct regions according to a project's standard NPV, modified NPV, and cumulative volatility. For each region it is possible to characterize the appropriate investment strategy in a fairly simple, intuitive manner.

This framework can also be used to examine dynamic changes in appropriate investment strategies. For example, as time passes the term t used to calculate both the modified NPV and cumulative volatility will become smaller because the deferral period has decreased. A lower value for t should result in a smaller cumulative volatility and a smaller modified NPV, assuming that none of the other four key variables have changed. Within Figure 14-4, this investment project will move up and to the left. Thus, a project formerly located, say, in region III, suggesting that the investment should probably be deferred, could now find itself in region IV, where it has become somewhat less promising.

Luehrman has suggested other uses of this framework, including the evaluation of investment projects with more complex real options. However, the key feature of his approach is unchanged: Options analysis of real investments forces the decision makers to realistically consider their decisions in line with the financial valuation of the firm. This evaluation of investment projects requires an understanding of the strategic options available to the firm, and managers who will incorporate the value of these options in their analyses.

For example, at the beginning of this section, an IT project was seeking capital funding of $3 million. The project would have been initially turned down because the NPV was less than zero (actually −$300,000.00). Using the European call option calculation, the model suggests it may be profitable and the cost for looking at it three years from now is low enough for the investment to make sense. Using Figure 14-4, the project would be in region III, because it has a negative NPV, a positive modified NPV, and it has a high volatility. At the end of each year the project is reviewed to see if any of the factors have changed. By the end of three years the volatility will approach zero and the project will either move to area VII or I. If it goes to area I, then it will be approved for completion. If it is in area VII, it will be terminated, and the loss will be limited to the pilot and maintenance of the project. The benefit of this process is the limit of risk on the downside and the elevation of many upside projects to evaluate. The potentials are outstanding while your risk exposures are limited, and that is a good deal!

Techniques such as Rapid Application Development (RAD) that break projects down into smaller (three to six month) deliverables (chunks) take advantage of the options approach. For example, the evaluation team might agree to go forward with a project. At the end of the first deliverable (three to six months), the team can assess the options of whether to deploy the first part, expand it to a second part, or abandon it. If it is deployed, the organization can immediately obtain the benefits of the function provided. If the option for expanding the project with a second function set is selected, the evaluation team should prioritize what will be included. After the second part is deployed the team can again assess whether to deploy, expand, or continue with additional function. This approach has an additional benefit in that it helps manage the demand to change requirements that occurs during development. If a requirement change occurs, it should be deferred to a subsequent release. Effective prioritization of function to include in a release will provide a faster payback as compared to the traditional approach that waits for an entire project to be complete before it is deployed.

Evaluating a Portfolio of IT Investment Projects

A SIM (Society for Information Management) International Working Group on "Managing the IT Investment Portfolio" (2001)[19] emphasized the need for organizations to adopt a portfolio management process in assessing and managing their "IT landscapes." This process would ensure that:

1. IT investment proposals are understood in terms of expected business outcomes, the efforts needed to reach those outcomes, and the risks involved in achieving the outcomes.
2. IT investments will advance the value of the firm.
3. the risks associated with IT investments are in line with the business's acceptable risk profile.
4. IT investments are aligned with business strategies.

Luehrman's "tomato garden' is consistent with the concept of a portfolio of investment projects undertaken by a firm. The financial theory of portfolio selection indicates that the risk-return profile of a portfolio of securities can be improved by

▪▪▪▪▪▪▪▪▪▪▪▪ FIGURE 14-5 The Three Phases of Managing an IT Investment Portfolio.

Strategic management of a porfolio of IT investment

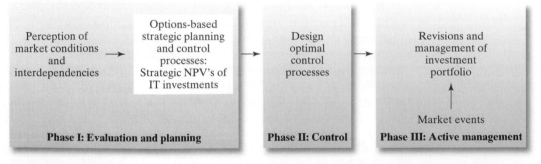

Source: adapted from Trigeorgis, L., *Real Options: Managerial Flexibility and Strategy in Resource Allocation*, MIT Press (1996).

recognizing interdependencies among the individual elements of the portfolio, particularly statistical correlations between their returns. Luehrman's simple diagram captures the value and uncertainty associated with a collection of real investment projects, where each project falls into a decision region defined by its relative value and uncertainty. It also permits the analyst to address potential interdependencies among projects.

This portfolio aspect of the "tomato garden" has been addressed by Trigeorgis somewhat more formally. He provides a framework within which a firm may undertake the valuation of investment projects using the real options approach and recognize the strategic mix of the interdependent projects. Briefly, his framework requires that investment planning, control measures to monitor project performance, and incentive schemes should all be tied to the objective of maximizing the firm's value. A key element of this objective is the requirement that sources of strategic value such as real operating options, competitive interactions, interdependencies among investments, and growth opportunities should be incorporated. His framework is based on the following concepts:

1. The objective of value maximization refers to a broad measure of NPV
2. Strategic NPV = Traditional NPV of expected cash flows + Value of operating options from flexible management + Investment interaction effects
3. Strategic management of investments requires the management of a collection (or portfolio) of future investment opportunities and options
4. Appropriate control targets are necessary for the effective implementation of a value-maximizing (strategic NPV) approach

Figure 14-5 describes the three phases of Trigeorgis' framework. Phase I emphasizes the valuation and planning of strategic investments. During this phase possible interdependencies, synergies, and future opportunities from projects should be considered, along with related operating options. During Phase II control targets are set that are consistent with continuous value maximization, and during Phase III the firm engages in the active, flexible management of individual investment projects, including decisions about which operating options to exercise, or about what newly developing options should be considered. This last phase is developed more fully in Figure 14-5. In keeping with Luehrman's "tomato garden" framework, the active management of a portfolio of IT investment projects will require periodic monitoring and nurturing of their changing position in the landscape of the "garden." That is, over time projects' modified NPV's and cumulative volatilities may change, as we noted earlier. Consequently, the active management of IT investments indicated in Phase III of Trigeorgis' strategic management framework will require reevaluations of options and of the strategic relevance of IT investments, as well as the development of promising projects. Figure 14-5 offers a simple representation of some of the elements of those reevaluations.

Trigeorgis's "strategic management framework" clearly offers an improvement of the methodologies used to conduct the evaluation of investment projects. Its acknowledgment that the firm is managing a portfolio of projects, among which may exist potentially significant interdependencies and synergies (e.g., cost reduction, existing market expansion, and the development of new markets), is much closer to the firm's goal of value maximization than are traditional, static financial calculations. Furthermore, this framework provides a fairly general context within which to consider the evaluation of real options, a realistic element of a firm's strategic management. Thus, the incompatibility between traditional NPV valuation methods and a firm's strategic planning activities can be overcome. Finally, implicit in Trigeorgis' framework is the well-known requirement that operating and investment decisions made by functional managers (e.g., IT managers) be aligned with the realities of the possible investment outcomes, real options, and organizational controls recognized by the firm's top management. Trigeorgis' framework is sufficiently general to incorporate, for example, the kinds of evaluation methods suggested by Buss and the Oracle Corporation as noted earlier, in which intangible benefits and risks are considered as part of the investment decision. These methods should help align the perceptions of IT managers and of business managers concerning the interdependencies and synergies of a proposed portfolio of IT projects. With this alignment in place, the strategic value of the firm's collection of IT investments along with the firm's value should be enhanced.

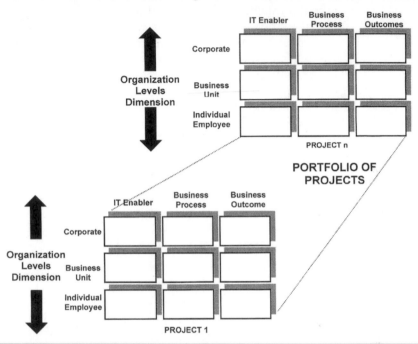

FIGURE 14-10 TVO Framework: IT Governance Process that Accesses a Portfolio of IT Projects.

Figure 14.10 represents the governance processes, in combination with the application of portfolio management. The complete TVO process combines the use of portfolio management, options, and the value management governance process. Each project/opportunity is identified, and compared against all projects/opportunities from the perspective of the entire organization, business, unit, and individual employee. Those that best meet the overall priorities of the firm are selected. Those projects that have been selected are broken down into manageable pieces and implemented using an options approach. The C.R. England Trucking project in Figure 14.9 was compared against other opportunities in the corporate portfolio of choices. The business and IT executives on the governance team selected it based on an assessment using a dashboard similar to Figure 14.6.

Hence, using Figure 14.6 as a vehicle to prioritize and select Project1, Project2, Project3, Project4, and Project5, in concert with Figure 14.9, which breaks down each project into corporate value, business unit value, and individual employee value, while having business members of the governance process (see Chapter 10, IT Governance) assess the overall business outcome and business changes, and IT members of the governance process assess the information technology necessary to drive/enable the changes, are all occuring simultaneously. The IT and business governance team (as described in Chapter 10) will use the above during strategy formulation to select and allocate resources; during project execution to evaluate and monitor the projects progress; and after the project is deployed to assess the attainment of value. Naturally, Figure 14.10 can be expanded to include customers/clients and external partners as appropriate.

By applying the TVO process your organization can help ensure that:

1. IT and business management work together to identify and ensure the attainment of the benefits. This relationship is essential to mature IT-business alignment.

2. The organization moves from a pure cost center perspective, where the TCO approach is a best practice, to one emphasizing value creation (i.e., a profit center perspective). Strategic financial and other methods for evaluating IT investments under uncertainty (e.g., real options, information economics) need to be applied.

3. Managers evaluate and coordinate a collection, or portfolio, of projects with an effective IT governance process, that includes IT and business leaders sharing accountability.

This approach enables a more effective allocation of resources by allowing the participants to better understand the problems and opportunities that exist across organizations. Another benefit is a better understanding of how these projects can be leveraged across organizations, thus facilitating the integration of IT and the processes they enhance to the entire firm. This method is compared to other value methods in Figure 14-11 later in this chapter.

While the preceding has looked at financial business measures, other management researchers have been looking into other measures that will demonstrate the value of IT and continue to enhance the entire enterprise.

Defining the Concepts of Total Cost of Ownership (TCO) and Total Value of Ownership (TVO)

Total cost of ownership implies that the acquisition cost of materials is only a portion of the true cost of a product or process. For example, the TCO of a personal computer would include the original purchase cost of the hardware, software, and peripherals plus the cost for maintenance, as well as any and all technical support costs. Some argue that training costs should be considered as well, to distinguish those products with steep learning curves.

Total value of ownership differs from TCO in that it considers the benefits of competing products or processes instead of just focusing on their individual costs. It is a comparative measure that asks the individual to judge the merits of the added benefits against the higher TCO for two competing products; for example, the desktop PC versus a notebook/laptop PC. Basing a purchase decision on just the TCO, the desktop PC would be usually less expensive and it would most likely be chosen. Using TVO, one would need to determine the value of mobility for the individual workers. If end users would be able to use the notebook for fieldwork or at home, it could be considered that the benefits outweigh the additional TCO of the units. For IT processes, see Value Management Framework.

A variation that has begun to gain wide acceptance is a hybrid model that has taken the concept of the total cost of ownership (TCO) model (see the "Defining the Concepts of TCO and TVO" sidebar) and placed it within the ABC framework. Companies have successfully applied the best features of both models by using the TCO in-depth approach, and basing it on the concepts of ABC. This approach determines the total costs associated with the acquisition and subsequent use of a given item or service from a given supplier. TCO allows one to measure, manage, and reduce the costs of Information Technology while improving the overall value of IT investments over the life of the IT assets.[24]

TCO was developed to understand the cost of owning and using IT assets over their useful life. It draws primarily from two types of resources, people and technology. TCO provides a comprehensive view of what it actually costs to provide computing capabilities to the enterprise, establishing a baseline that can be measured (usually expressed in terms of cost per user and/or cost per client, e.g. connected via network) and can be provided to management in an understandable format. There are many cost drivers within a TCO analysis, some of which overlap with traditional ABC drivers (such as FTEs (full-time employees), messages, trouble tickets, etc.) In a typical distributed environment, the following are common cost drivers and/or impact cost: number of platforms supported, number of operating systems supported, number of locations, size of locations, response time requirements, resolution time requirements, availability/reliability of network, and software application version control.

One can readily see that TCO is a virtual subset of an ABC implementation, focusing on IT events with the goal of establishing the true cost of IT assets and IT applications. When many different IT functions and processes of an enterprise are analyzed through a TCO analysis, the following enterprise concerns can be addressed:

- Provide predictable costs and level budgets
- Determine which IT resources can be applied to the firm's core mission
- How to determine the current costs and services of IT operations
- How to increase service levels at an affordable cost
- How to track or recognize actual on-going IT costs
- How to find a cost-effective way of improving IT expertise
- How to determine the most effective implementation strategy to improve effective and efficient delivery of IT services[25]

TCO provides an organization with the ability to measure IT investments and manage the cost and quality of the services received. Specifically, TCO provides insight and measurement into the direct costs incurred to provide the IT utility to the desktop and opportunities for improvement through pinpointing inefficiencies in technology and business practices.

ABC, ABM, and TCO are just some of the ways that the firm can evaluate the cost of business processes and activities. They are widely accepted in accounting and management. There are many more measures and methodologies that have been developed. Figure 14-6 contains a list of resources available to obtain additional detail about these and other various value methodologies.

Perhaps more important than focusing on cost is the need to look at the Total Value of Ownership (TVO) of a firm's IT investments. Traditional accounting and financial measures may no longer be enough. Too often the focus is on tangible, easy-to-quantify benefits. Less obvious, and often difficult-to-measure, benefits must also be included. IT is typically not well positioned to identify many of these benefits. Indeed, these managers are often unable to ensure that the expected business changes (e.g., business process modifications) advanced to justify IT projects actually derived benefits from the projects. Three key differentiating features of a TVO approach recognize that:

1. IT and business management must work together.
2. The firm needs to move from a pure cost center perspective, where the TCO approach is a best practice, to one emphasizing value creation (i.e., a profit center or investment center perspective).
3. Managers must evaluate and manage a collection or portfolio of projects.

The measures introduced in this chapter enable IT to reduce risk and select projects that fit. Knowing what is profitable, what is not, and what is worth doing over the long term translates into an effective message that IT will want to share with the business. It is this message that IT must convey to the other divisions of the firm. Total Value of Ownership (TVO) needs to be considered. This leads to the next important topic of the Value Management Framework and how the firm can leverage the assets of IT to improve competitiveness.

FIGURE 14-7 Where to Find More Information on Methods and Measures.

Resources for more methodologies

Applied information economics
Uses scientific and mathematical methods to evaluate the IT investment process. **www.hubbardross.com**

Balanced scorecard
Integrates traditional financial measures with three other key performance indicators: customer perspectives, internal business processes and organizational growth, learning and innovation. **www.bscol.com, www.aquent.com**

Economic value added
Calculates "true" economic profit by subtracting the cost of all capital invested in an enterprise–including the technology–from net operating profit. **www.sternstewart.com**

Economic Value Sourced
Quantifies the dollar values of risk and time and adds these into valuation equation.
(Select the Products and Services page and then Initiatives-Business Value Consulting.) **www.metagroup.com**

Portfolio management
Manages IT assets from an investment perspective by calculating risks, yields, and benefits. **www.metricnet.com, www.metagroup.com**

Real option valuation
Values corporate flexibility above all else; tracks "assets in place" and "growth options" to present the widest array of future possibilities. (Enter "real option valuation" in the search field.) **www.pwcglobal.com**

▪▪▪ Leveraging the Assets of IT for Competitive Advantage

The discussions to this point have considered the financial evaluation of IT investments, the importance of pursuing investments that add value to the organization, and the relevance of the investments to the organization's strategic management objectives. In discussing the determination of the value derived from these investments the emphasis has been on financial value, or valuation. However, it is appropriate to consider "value" more broadly. An expanded use of the term provides additional insight and detail concerning some of the issues addressed by the "information economics" approaches discussed earlier, in which intangible benefits and risks of IT investments are considered. It also sheds further light on the possible workings of Trigeorgis' strategic management framework.

The value management approach and examples that follow provide organizations seeking an IT-leveraged path to competitiveness with a model that can help to identify improvements in customer-focused processes. It is based on Cathy Curley's early research that was sponsored by IBM's Advanced Business Institute. The first two examples are shown in Figure 14-8. Frito Lay had the business objective of increasing its market share of salty snacks. To meet this objective managers recognized the need to change the processes (this effort can be comprised of traditional business process enhancements, major business transformations, business cost reductions, quality improvements, or new business model experimentation) used for pricing and defining the mix of products for its delivery routes. The technologies that enabled these process changes were the use of a new hand-held device, the network to transmit information, and an Executive Information System (EIS) to report sales status.

The second example is McGraw-Hill's recognition of the need to provide college professors with the ability to customize textbooks for their courses. This required changes to the entire book-producing process. The information technology necessary to support these changes included an online repository of text that can be accessed by

FIGURE 14-8 Examples of Applying the Value Management Framework.

Value management framework

Frito Lay

| **IT enabler:** Hand-held computer Network EIS | ⬅ | **Business process:** Product pricing and mix for route sales | ⬅ | **Business outcome:** Market share increase |

McGraw-Hill Textbook Publishing

| **IT enabler:** PC front-end Integrated database | ⬅ | **Business process:** Textbook production | ⬅ | **Business outcome:** Flexibility customization |

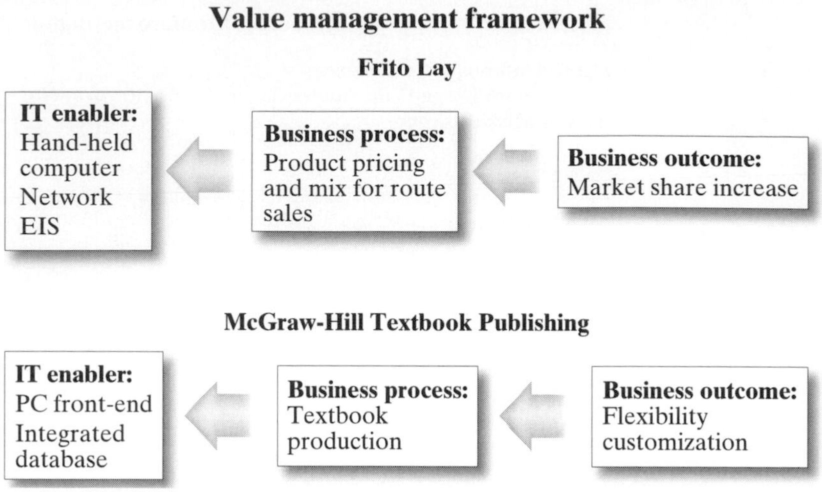

professors using an easy-to-use PC interface. Today, Pearson and other leading publishers also have a similar effective vehicle for customizing textbooks.

In these examples the business objectives and value were initially defined. The business processes that would be affected were then identified. A business executive sponsor and business champions were committed to the success of these objectives and process changes. The information technology was selected to best enable the process changes, that is, to generate the greatest value to the business.

The preceding approach, when applied with the appropriate business stakeholders, also helps address the frequently discussed productivity paradox. By focusing on the business processes that will need to change to enhance the business, the organization will recognize that it is not the information technology alone that brings the benefits. IT can only enable and drive changes to the business processes that result in value.

Also, the evaluation should take into account all potential stakeholders, including individual employees, departments and business units, the entire enterprise, and partners and customers. Considerations such as the quality and functionality of the project must be included. Adding these considerations to the previously discussed examples of Figure 14-8, Figure 14-9 illustrates an expanded value management framework used by C.R. England Trucking. This example began with a definition of the business objectives and value. The business processes that would be affected were then identified. A business executive sponsor and business champions were committed to the success of these objectives and process changes. The information technology was selected to best enable the process changes that added to the value of the business. The major difference in this example is that the business value, business process changes, and information technology necessary to achieve the business outcome are evaluated for the individual truck drivers, the group of truck drivers, and the firm as a whole. This method is compared to other value methods in Figure 14-10, later in this chapter.

It is important to note that the business process can be broken down or reduced to the activity level. This will permit the additional application of ABC, as discussed earlier.

▪▪▪▪▪▪▪▪▪▪▪ FIGURE 14-9   The Application of the Expanded Value Management Framework.

Expanded value management framework

C.R. England & Sons, Trucking

	IT enabler	Business process	Business outcome
Individual	Satellite communications	Message sequencing	Efficient mileage
Work group	Decision support system	Load matching	Improve profit load
Business unit	Executive information system	World-class management super goals	World-class customer service

▪▪▪ How IT Governance Is a Shared Responsibility

IT and business managers need to work together to evaluate and manage a collection, or portfolio, of IT projects. Can both IT and other business managers share equally in the evaluation of the portfolio of projects? The answer should be "*Yes*." It is important to recognize that the ultimate value of the project(s) will not come from the technology alone, but from how the business applies the technology to change the respective business process. The changes cannot be "owned" by the IT project team but must be "owned" by a business sponsor and champion. The roles played by the business sponsor and champions are critical to the success of the project and the attainment of the benefits.

The combined application of real options, value management, and portfolio analysis as tools, metrics, and indicators enables IT management and business management to act cooperatively in steering the business in the correct direction. Each process has good merits on its part. Real options enable the business to reduce financial risks, value management leverages IT assets, and the portfolio analysis and valuation enables IT to view all of its activity in light of strategic, financial, customer, and growth perspectives. All become important factors in IT decision making that should not be done by either IT or the business separately.

Figure 14.6 provides a "dashboard" approach to capturing these elements of the IT portfolio. As shown, this hypothetical portfolio consists of four IT projects. The expected benefit of each project is represented by its value, including benefits identified through information economic analyses and the potential value of the most likely strategic options associated with the project.

Critial IT projects are identified by the "Must Do" column (e.g. government regulation, keep up with competitors, Y2K). Expected project risk is represented by the standard deviation of the IT asset's returns, and reflects the probabilities of the project's technical and business success. The cost of the developing each project option is also a necessary element of this "dashboard" approach, and could be derived using TCO and information economic analyses. A risk free discount rate of 6% is used to calculate each project's value.

Project Name	"Must Do" (Years,t)	Time to expiration of option	PV of IT Projects Assets ($M)	IT Project Cost ($M)	Project Risk (Standard Deviation: σ)	Conventional NPV	Value-to-cost Metric	Volatility Metric $\left(\sigma\sqrt{t}\right)$
Project 1		2	40	37	.35	3	1.21	.495
Project 2		1	40	43	.25	-3	0.99	.250
Project 3		2	40	43	.45	-3	1.05	.636
Project 4	Regulation	0	40	37	-	3	1.08	0

It is important to note that this "dashboard" view of the firm's IT projects is not a static construct, but may exhibit changes over time as options are exercised, as intangible benefits and costs change, and as expected probabilities and volatilities are revised in light of evolving technical and business knowledge. These changes should be considered as the firm manages its IT investment portfolio in alignment with the firm's strategic objectives. The review and prioritization of the portfolio should be done by a team of business and IT executives, as described in Chapter 11, IT Governance.

▪▪▪ How the Enterprise Can Benefit from These Processes

The importance of the models introduced in this chapter is apparent when the work of IT to add value to the business is considered. But it is important to note that all of the models represent an ongoing process that continues to evolve and change. These processes must evolve and change with the business. Today, it is still paramount that all units within a business work toward the same strategic goals of the firm. Therefore, the best course to travel is the one that will lead in the strategic direction of the firm. Both academic and business management consultants seriously debate how to find the actual course because there isn't a meaningful single set of tools to use. However, it appears to make sense that some combination of financial measures, nonfinancial measures, and partnerships leveraging IT assets will help guide managers to do the right thing. Gauging numerical, financial, tangible, and intangible characteristics of activities to form an understandable analysis will be a great challenge. In most organizations, the CIO and the senior business executives must be able to do this together in order to reach a sensible and effective outcome.

The CIO's most important job will be to encourage all staff to embrace the idea of the practices introduced here. The CIO must ensure that everyone participates. Everyone needs to review the results of enhanced measurement and models, and succeed in leveraging the assets of IT. It is for the staff of the CIO to utilize the results of enhanced measurement to effect change in the organization. As was discussed earlier in Chapter 4 on Leadership, the CIO is but one person who is far more effective when inspiring improvement as opposed to looking over everyone's shoulder. The benefits from leveraging IT must be shown through demonstrating its value and taking steps to continually make the unit, department, company, and enterprise better as a whole.

REVIEW QUESTIONS ▪▪▪▪▪▪▪

1. How do real options reduce the risk of IT investments?
2. Why are return on investment (ROI) financial measures not often good indicators of performance?
3. Since ROI has always been a main focus of financial analysts, what intangible benefits of Information Technology are often difficult to quantify for this measurement?
4. How does managing a portfolio of IT investments compare to looking individually at IT projects? Explain the concept of the activity-based costing.

5. What are the differences between activity-based costing and activity-based management?
6. How can total cost of ownership become a subset of activity-based costing? Explain.
7. Would you suggest a company begin to develop/adopt multiple value methodologies to manage their Information Technology function? Explain.

DISCUSSION QUESTIONS ▪▪▪▪▪▪▪

1. Why aren't business and financial measures sufficient to value the effectiveness and level of contribution that Information Technology provides?
2. Does your company have an effective set of tools to measure the value of Information Technology? Has it been published or otherwise communicated? What are its main components and measures?

3. What do you think are Information Technology's distinctive competencies?
4. Does your IT function have systemic competencies? What are they? How are they measured?
5. What do you think are the main weaknesses in finding value in Information Technology? Is your company better or worse in evaluating IT?

AREAS FOR RESEARCH ▪▪▪▪▪▪▪

1. Read Robert S. Kaplan's "Introduction to Activity Based Costing," in *Harvard Business Review*, September 22, 1998.

2. Read Peter B. B. Turney's "Activity-Based Management—ABM puts ABC Information to Work," *Management Accounting*, 01/1992, pgs. 20–25.

CONCLUSION ▪▪▪▪▪▪▪

This chapter has discussed the concept of value. But many business managers do not understand or appreciate the opportunities that IT can provide the enterprise. Researchers and CIOs of the most successful firms have determined that the most effective way of assessing and demonstrating value is through leveraging IT. While traditional accounting of financial activities as well as hardware and transactional functions have dominated the previous decades, it is clear that the intangible and nonquantifiable measures have become more important in the new "informational society." The reason for the need for new applications of the traditional methods is their importance in measuring the business relevance of IT activities.

This chapter focused on five major value methods to assist in assessing and demonstrating the value of IT. Each method has virtues that have enabled them to be successfully used to augment illustrations of the benefits of Information Technology to senior executives and other business leaders. To summarize the strengths and weaknesses of these concepts see Figure 14-10. Enhanced measures improve the means of identifying cost and aid in leveraging the assets of IT. As a result, measures like the "activity-based costing" and the "portfolio of IT investments" now include components such as cost drivers, activity drivers, resource drivers, innovation, risk, and/or IT alignment. These intangible measures are more meaningful because they are not numerical abstractions of nonessentials. Customer satisfaction, management of risk, technology leadership, and product focus, are also more indicative measures of competence in Information Technology than response times, transaction cycles, MIPS, etc.

Today, there is greater focus on aligning Information Technology with the business and ensuring that IT assists its business partners to meet the firm's strategic goals. Leveraging Information Technology to achieve competitive advantage is an important goal for the CIO, CFO, COO, and CEO. The CIO must have the support of the CEO and the other senior executives in order to be effective in delivering value to the business. This was discussed at length in Chapter 2—Strategic Alignment. While progress toward building this comprehensive framework continues at a slow pace, these practices are beginning to gain acceptance in many major corporations and enterprises in both the United States and abroad. Many companies have begun to measure their Information Technology with these new concepts and are experiencing success.

FIGURE 14-11   **Summary of Value Processes.**

	Methodology	Strengths	Weaknesses
Return on Investment (ROI), Economic Value Added (EVA)	Analysis of financial statement data.	Simple numerical result.	Easy to manipulate. ROI can lead to contradictory or misleading results.
Real options	Conversion of IT investments into a financial concept similar to a call option.	Provides a straight forward analysis of strategic investment proposals allowing effective comparisons among both long term and short term projects. Reduces risks by permitting deferral of final commitment of funds until long term projects have reduced their uncertainty.	Requires effective skills in mapping investment opportunities into options categories while carefully defining their characteristics. Requires good judgment in risk analysis.
Portfolio valuation	Builds a framework in which investment planning, control measures that monitor project performance and incentive schemes, should all be tied to maximizing the firm's value. It is assumed that the firm will recognize the strategic mix of interdependent IT projects in evaluating them.	Assesses the interdependence of IT projects and seeks to ensure that the projects are aligned with business strategies. Ensures that the risks associated with IT investments are in line with the business view of acceptable risk.	Continuous monitoring of IT projects must be done and re-evaluations require active management of all IT investments. Needs committed and active business and IT management.
Activity-based management	Measures cost and performance of activities, resources and cost objects. Based on their use, looks to ensure that both value to the customer and profit to the firm is actually what is happening.	The model informs managers what processes really cost and provides a basis for maximizing profitability by encouraging profitable activity and discouraging nonprofitable ones.	Not as effective in evaluating strategic processes. Requires effective skills in determining hidden costs and determining how costs can be allocated between interdependent processes.
Information economics	Evaluates intangible costs, benefits and risks as complements to financial valuation results.	Improves IT investment decisions by explicitly addressing intangibles. Helps build consensus among IT stakeholders concerning investment strategies.	Relies upon subjective methods of weighting intangibles vs. financial investment criteria.

Appendix 14A

▪▪▪▪▪▪▪ Traditional Capital Budgeting ▪▪▪▪▪▪▪
Net Present Value Calculations for an IT Investment

The traditional statement of the NPV method of capital budgeting is expressed as:

$$\text{NPV} = \sum_{t}^{T} E(c_t) / (1 + r_j)^t - I$$

where $E(c_t)$ is the cash inflow from the investment project expected to arrive at year t, I is the current investment outlay required to begin the project, T is the number of years of the project's economic life, and r_j is the risk-adjusted discount rate (cost of capital) appropriate to the project, which is the sum of a risk-free interest rate (usually on three-month Treasury bills) and a risk premium compensating the firm's owners for the risk of the project. It is generally assumed that the firms are averse to risk. Investment projects that are within the same line of business as the firm and are no more or less risky than the firm's ongoing projects should be discounted at the firm's average cost of capital, calcu-lated from the rates of return required to satisfy the debt and equity sources of the funding that supports the firm's activities. Investment projects with above-average risk (e.g., introduction of a new technology to increase market share) require a value for r_j in excess of the firm's average cost of capital. The cap-ital asset pricing model of corporate finance has been suggested as a basis for determining the required rate of return for an investment project (r_j) as a function of its risk. The firm is assumed to opti-mize the expected returns from investment projects, given the risk of those projects.

Fama (1977)[26] has shown that the present value of a future net cash inflow is its current expected value, as discounted at the rate r_j, where the discount rate is known and deterministic over time. Any uncertainty about the present value of cash inflows results from uncertainties about the cash flows through time.[27]

Appendix 14B

▪▪▪▪▪▪▪ Examples of Two Sources ▪▪▪▪▪▪▪
of Value Derived from a Real Option

Luehrman (1998a)[9] has provided a simple way of representing the two sources of value derived from a real option. The first source is the interest income that can be earned on the investment funds during the deferral period. This value can be measured as the present value of the investment expenditure, or in financial terms as the present value of the option's exercise price, where the expenditure is discounted at the risk-free rate of interest (r_f):

$$\text{PV(expenditure)} = \text{Expenditure}/(1 + r_f)^t$$

where t is the number of time periods during which the investment expenditure can be deferred. To calculate a form of the NPV of the investment, Luehrman suggests using the ratio of the investment asset's value (in present value terms) to its cost PV(expenditure above). Or,

$$\text{modified NPV} = \text{PV(assets to be acquired)}/\\\text{PV(expenditure)}$$

where the modified NPV may be greater than or less than one in value. This modified NPV will gen-erally exceed the standard NPV result because it includes the interest income earned during the deferral period.[28]

As noted above, the second source of value contributed by the real option results from the decision maker's ability to react to changing uncertain conditions during the deferral period by altering investment decisions to the firm's benefit. Uncertainty is measured in real options analysis as the cumulative volatility of the investment's future value, $\sigma\sqrt{t}$, where σ is the standard deviation of the investment's return per unit of time and t denotes the number of time periods in the deferral period. Note that the standard deviation is denominated in the same units (dollars) as the value of the future assets. Technically speaking, uncertainty is more properly measured as a variance per period, σ^2. The expression $\sigma^2 t$ would show the cumulative volatility of the asset's future value during the t periods in the deferral period, but this expression is difficult to interpret; that is, the meaning of dollars squared is not obvious. The square root of this expression, shown as $\sigma\sqrt{t}$, returns this metric to readily understood dollars.[29]

Appendix 14C

▪▪▪▪▪▪▪▪ Decision Tree Analysis ▪▪▪▪▪▪▪▪ of an IT Investment

As a simple example of DTA, consider the case of an IT manager presented with an opportunity to develop a system at an initial pilot cost of $200,000.[30] This system is expected to enable the firm to generate useful information about customer preferences for some of the firm's products, and to use that information to create new products and markets. After a three-year pilot period, the firm will determine whether the new system is worth continuing, based on the solution of a number of technical and business problems. If so (there is a 30 percent probability that the effort will be continued), the firm will expand the system's development by making an additional investment of $6 million. It is estimated that the probability that the expanded system will be highly useful in enhancing operating performance is 20 percent, resulting in cash inflows of $16 million beginning in Year 5. It is estimated that the probability that the expanded system will be moderately useful in enhancing operating performance is 60 percent, resulting in cash inflows of $8 million beginning in Year 5. It is estimated that the probability that the expanded system will result in low usefulness in enhancing operating performance is 20 percent, resulting in cash inflows of –$200,000 beginning in Year 5. The risk-adjusted cost of capital is 10 percent.

Figure 14C-1 describes the decision tree for this case. Squares represent decision nodes for management, and circles represent points in time when states of nature are revealed to management. Present value amounts are indicated in italics at decision nodes. To determine the optimal decision at any point in time the analyst should start at the end of the decision tree and work backwards. Starting at Year 5 the expected present value of cash inflows is:

$$E_5(\text{PV}) = .20(\$16M) + .60(\$8M) + .20(-\$200K)$$
$$= \$7.96 \text{ million.}$$

Discounting backward to Year 4:

$$E_4(\text{PV}) = \$7.96M/(1.10) = \$7.2 \text{ million.}$$

Discounting again to Year 3 we can obtain the NPV by subtracting out the $6 million investment required at that time:

$$E_3(\text{NPV}) = \$7.2M/(1.10) - \$6M = \$540,000,$$

and to arrive at the decision point in Year 0:

$$E_0(\text{NPV}) = [(.30)(\$540K) + (.70)(0)]/ (1.10)^3 - \$200K = -\$74,000.$$

Thus, the expected NPV of this project is –$74,000, which would lead to its rejection by management. As Trigeorgis has noted, however, real-world managers who can exploit asymmetric outcomes of the DTA through flexible operations may find this project to be worthwhile. For example, flexibility can exist in the firm's ability to abandon the project at some point during the life of the project if its abandonment value exceeds the NPV of subsequent cash flows.

▮▮▮▮▮▮▮▮▮▮▮ **FIGURE 14C-1** **Illustration of the Decision Tree Example.**

Decision tree of an IT investment

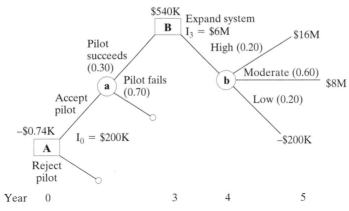

Source: adapted from Trigeorgis, L., *Real Options: Managerial Flexibility and Strategy in Resource Allocation*, MIT Press (1996).

Appendix 14D

▮▮▮▮▮▮▮ **Present Value Calculations** ▮▮▮▮▮▮▮
for an IT Investment with the Option to Abandon

Following Trigeorgis, we can expand this simple case to consider the option to abandon, and to consider expected cash flows in Years 6 through 15 following the implementation of the fully-developed system. Figure 14D-1 shows the expanded decision tree. The probabilities of market success in Years 6 to 15 have been added on the right side of the tree. Management estimates that if the new system results in high market usefulness in Year 5, then the probabilities of high, moderate, and low usefulness in Years 6 to 15 are 60 percent, 30 percent, and 10 percent, respectively. If the new system results in moderate market usefulness in Year 5, then the probabilities of high, moderate, and low usefulness in years 6 to 15 are 10 percent, 80 percent, and 10 percent, respectively. If the new system results in low market usefulness in Year 5, then the probabilities of high, moderate, and low usefulness in Years 6 to 15 are 10 percent, 30 percent, and 60 percent, respectively. In any of the Years 6 to 15 management expects net cash inflows of $3 million if the system results in high market usefulness, $1 million per year if the system results in moderate market usefulness, and –$1 million per year if the system results in low market usefulness. The firm

has the option to abandon the investment at the end of Year 15 for an expected salvage value of $2 million. The firm may also abandon the project at the end of Year 5, at which time the salvage value is expected to be $3 million, derived in part from the proceeds of the sale of the customer information gathered up to that time. A detailed description of the cash flows associated with this investment project is provided below.

Information acquired up to the end of Year 5, especially related to the probabilities of success in Year 5, can be used to revise its IT investment decisions. For example, if at the end of Year 5 it appears likely that the system will enjoy only low success, then the firm may decide to abandon the project since the expected value of continuing after Year 5 is $800,000, as shown below, which is less than the $3 million disposal value available at Year 5. The flexibility afforded the firm in this case should be valued along with the static NPV calculation indicated in Figure 14C-1 previously. If abandonment is chosen in this case, the value of the low branch in Figure 14D-1 (b_3) emanating from node b changes from –$0.2M (as in Figure 14C-1) to (–$1M + $3M) = $2M. The NPV calculation at Year 5 would then be:

█ ■ ■ ■ ■ ■ ■ ■ ■ ■ ■   **FIGURE 14D-1**   Illustrating the Decision Tree Example with Options.

Decision tree of an IT investment with an option to abandon the project

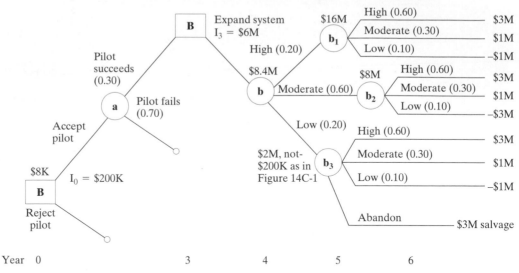

Year   0   3   4   5   6

Source: adapted from Trigeorgis, L., *Real Options: Managerial Flexibility and Strategy in Resource Allocation*, MIT Press (1996).

$E_5(NPV) = (.2)(\$16M) + (.6)(\$8M) + (.2)(\$2M)$
$= \$8.4$ million

instead of the value of \$7.96 million obtained without considering the option to abandon the project in Year 5. The present value of flexibility in this case is:

$(.30)(\$8.4M) - \$7.96M)/(1.10)^5 = \$82,000$

Furthermore, the NPV of the project at Year 0 would be the sum of the static NPV derived earlier (−\$74,000) plus the present value of the option to abandon (\$82,000), for an overall NPV of \$8,000. That is, the project, which originally resulted in a negative NPV, now becomes desirable when the value of the abandonment option is incorporated into the analysis.

Based on the values discussed in the chapter, the expected annual cash flows in Years 6 to 15, conditional on high, moderate, and low success in Year 5, are:

$E(inflow; high success in Year 5)$
$= (.6)(\$3M) + (.3)(\$1M) + (.1)(-\$1M) = \$2M$

$E(inflow; moderate success in Year 5)$
$= (.1)(\$3M) + (.8)(\$1M) + (.1)(-\$1M) = \$1M$

$E(inflow: low success in Year 5)$
$= (.1)(\$3M) + (.3)(\$1M) + (.6)(-\$1M) = \$0M$

Thus, discounting back to Year 5 and including the salvage value expected in Year 15:

$E_5(Year 6 to 15 flows; high success in Year 5)$
$= \sum^{10} \$2M/(1,10)^t + \$2M/(1.10)^{10} = \$13$ million

$E_5(Year 6 to 15 flows; Moderate success in Year 5)$
$= \sum^{10} \$1M/(1.10)^t + \$2M/(1.10)^{10} = \$7$ million

$E_5(Year 6 to 15; low success in Year 5)$
$= \sum^{10} \$0/(1.10)^t + \$2M/(1.10)^{10} = \$800,000$

If we include the cash inflow expected for Year 5 with these expected values we can derive the expected cash inflows beginning in Year 5, conditional on high, moderate, or low success in Year 5:

$E_5(Years 5 to 15; high success in Year 5)$
$= \$3M + \$13M = \$16$ million

$E_5(Years 5 to 15; moderate success in Year 5)$
$= \$1M + \$7M = \$8$ million

$E_5(Years 5 to 15; low success in Year 5)$
$= -\$1M + \$800K = -\$200,000.$

These values are consistent with the expected cash inflows at Year 5 shown in Figure 14D-1.

Trigeorgis notes that a simple NPV focus on the expected value of cash inflows as of the end of Year 5, given information available at Year 0 (=(.2)(\$13M) + (.6)(\$7M) + (.2)(\$800K) = \$7M > 0) misses the point of flexible operations undertaken by this firm. The firm in this case has the flexibility (and option) to wait until the end of Year 5 before it must decide whether to implement the system at that time. At time period 0 the *only* decision facing the firm is whether to undertake the pilot investment.

Appendix 14E

Black-Scholes Values for a European Call Option

Sharpe et al. (1999) have reported that the Black-Scholes formula for estimating the value of a European call option V_c is:

$$V_c = N(d_1) \, PV(\text{assets to be acquired}) - N(d_2) \, (PV(\text{expenditure})/e_f^{rt})$$

where

$$d_1 = [\ln(\text{modified NPV}) + (r_f + 0.5 \, \sigma^2) \, t] / \sigma\sqrt{t}$$

$$d_2 = [\ln(\text{modified NPV}) + (r_f - 0.5 \, \sigma^2) \, t] / \sigma\sqrt{t}$$

and where $N(d_1)$ and $N(d_2)$ are the probabilities that outcomes of less than d_1 and d_2, respectively, will occur in a normal distribution possessing a mean of zero and standard deviation of one. The following table (See Figure 14E-1), adapted from Luehrman (1998a), gives the Black-Scholes values expressed as a percentage of the investment's underlying asset value and schedule of the distribution.

FIGURE 14E-1 Partial Listing of Black-Scholes Values.

Black-Scholes value table

	Modified NPV									
	0.90	0.92	0.94	0.96	0.98	1.00	1.02	1.04	1.06	1.08
0.05	0.0	0.1	0.3	0.6	1.2	2.0	3.1	4.5	6.0	7.5
0.10	0.8	1.2	1.7	2.3	3.1	4.0	5.0	6.1	7.3	8.6
0.15	2.2	2.8	3.5	4.2	5.1	6.0	7.0	8.0	9.1	10.2
0.20	4.0	4.7	5.4	6.2	7.1	8.0	8.9	9.9	10.9	11.9
0.25	5.9	6.6	7.4	8.2	9.1	9.9	10.9	11.8	12.8	13.7
0.30	7.8	8.6	9.4	10.2	11.1	11.9	12.8	13.7	14.6	15.6
0.35	9.8	10.6	11.4	12.2	13.0	13.9	14.8	15.6	16.5	17.4
0.40	11.7	12.5	13.4	14.2	15.0	15.9	16.7	17.5	18.4	19.2
0.45	13.7	14.5	15.3	16.2	17.0	17.8	18.6	19.4	20.3	21.1
0.50	15.7	16.5	17.3	18.1	18.0	19.7	20.5	21.3	22.1	22.9
0.55	17.7	18.5	19.3	20.1	20.9	21.7	22.4	23.2	24.0	24.8
0.60	19.7	20.5	21.3	22.0	22.8	23.6	24.3	25.1	25.8	26.6
0.65	21.7	22.5	23.2	24.0	24.7	25.3	26.2	27.0	27.7	28.4
0.70	23.6	24.4	25.2	25.9	26.6	27.4	28.1	28.8	29.5	30.2
0.75	25.6	26.3	27.1	27.8	28.5	29.2	29.9	30.6	31.3	32.0

Cumulative volatility (row labels on left)

Source: adapted from Luehrman, T. A., 1998a, "Investment Opportunities as Real Options: Getting Started on the Numbers," *Harvard Business Review*, July-August 1998.

REFERENCES ▪▪▪▪▪▪▪

[1] Brooke, Geoffrey M., "The Economics of Information Technology: Explaining the Productivity Paradox," in *CISR WP No. 238* (April 1992), Center for Information Systems Research, Sloan School of Management, Massachusetts Institute of Technology.

[2] Kaplan, Robert S., and Norton, David P., "The Balanced Scorecard—Measures That Drive Performance," in *Harvard Business Review*, no. 92105 Jan.-Feb. 1992.

[3] Rubin, Howard, "Measure for Measure," in *ComputerWorld*, 1992.

[4] Lewis, D. and M. Koller, M., "ROI: Little More than Lip Service." *Internet Week*, October 1, 2001.

[5] Violino, B., "ROI: The Intangible Benefits of Technology Are Emerging as the Most Important of All." *Information Week*, June 30, 1997.

[6] Published Annual Financial Statements of General Motors Corporation and Microsoft Corporation, as of December 2001.

[7] Kaplan, R. S. and Atkinson, A. A. *Advanced Management Accounting*, 3rd edition. Upper Saddle River, NJ: Prentice Hall, 1998.

[8] This inconsistency is also observed in the difference between a firm's reported accounting income and its residual income (or EVA).

[9] Luehrman, T. A. 1998a. "Investment Opportunities as Real Options: Getting Started on the Numbers." *Harvard Business Review*, July-August, 1998.

[10] An "American" call option may be exercised at any time prior to expiration; the valuation of American call options is more complex than the case of European call option, and is not discussed in this book.

[11] Trigeorgis, L. *Real Options: Managerial Flexibility and Strategy in Resource Allocation*. MIT Press, 1996.

[12] Luehrman, T. A. *Capital Projects as Real Options: An Introduction*. Harvard Business School Teaching Note, 1994.

[13] Housel, T. J., El Sawy, O., Zhong, J. J. and Rodgers, W. "Measuring the Return on Knowledge Embedded in Information Technology." *Proceedings*, 22nd International Conference on Information Systems: 97–106, 2001.

[14] Parker, M. M., Benson, R. J. and Trainor, H. E. *Information Economics: Linking Business Performance to Information Technology*. Englewood Cliffs, NJ: Prentice Hall, 1988.

[15] The balanced scorecard approach is also valuable as a means of identifying key nonfinancial aspects of strategy. See, for example, Kaplan, R. S. and D. P. Norton, "The Balanced Scorecard (Measures that Drive Performance." *Harvard Business Review*, January-February, 1992.

[16] Buss, M. D. J. "How to Rank Computer Projects." *Harvard Business Review*, January-February, 1983.

[17] Semich, J. W. "Here's How to Quantify IT Investment Benefits." *Datamation*, January 7, 1994.

[18] Luehrman, T. A. 1998b. "Strategy as a Portfolio of Real Options." *Harvard Business Review*, September-October, 1998.

[19] SIM International Working Group 2001. *Managing the IT Investment Portfolio: Final Report*.

[20] Miller, John A., *Implementing Activity-Based Management in Daily Operations*. New York: John Wiley & Sons, pp. 11–13.

[21] *http://www.offtech.com.au/abc/How_ABC_Works.html*

[22] Chutchian-Ferranti, Joyce, "Activity-Based Costing." *Computerworld*, (1997).

[23] Based on case studies by Carreon, David, "IBM Sales Force Benefits from Automation with ABC,"; Haedicke, Jack, "ABC a Key Enabler for ECR,"; Walters, Jeff; Rattan, Pat; Smith, Steve; and Webster, Dr. Douglas, "ABC at NASA's Lewis Research Center,"; and Boardman, Lee, "Blue Cross and Blue Shield of Florida Subsidiaries Insure Profitability Using ABC." *http://www.bettermanagement.com* (2002).

[24] Based on the presentation of Booz-Allen & Hamilton, prepared by Turner, Deborah K. and Repczynski, Ann R., "Total Cost of Ownership: The Secret of ABC for Information Technology," *http://www.bettermanagement.com* (2001).

[25] *Ibid.*

[26] Fama, E., "Risk-Adjusted Discount Rates and Capital Budgeting Under Uncertainty." *Journal of Financial Economics* 5, No. 1: 3–24. 1977.

[27] Myers and Turnbull (1977) have indicated that an investment project's true riskiness depends on factors such as the time pattern and growth rate of its expected cash flows and the methods by which investors revise their expectations about these cash flows. If a project's riskiness cannot be assumed constant in the periods of its economic life, then different costs of capital should be used in those time periods, not a single discount rate as suggested by the standard NPV calculation. See Myers, S. C. and Turnbull, S., "Capital Budgeting and the Capital Asset Pricing Model: Good News and Bad News." *Journal of Finance* 32, No. 2: 321–33, 1977.

[28] This definition of modified NPV is somewhat similar to the profitability index associated with the standard NPV model: profitability index = PV (cash inflows)/PV (investment).

[29] As a practical matter a value for σ can be estimated in a number of ways. The firm could use the standard deviation of its stock price over the past few years as a rough approximation to σ. This approach assumes that past volatility of the firm's productive asset values

have been reflected in its stock price. A second alternative would require some benchmarking of the volatility of returns to similar investments in the firm's past, or in other firms. A third approach would be to use Monte Carlo simulation applied to the project's expected cash flows to simulate a probability distribution function and σ.

[30] This case is similar to one presented by Trigeorgis. See Trigeorgis, L. *Real Options: Managerial Flexibility and Strategy in Resource Allocation*. MIT Press. 1996.

FURTHER REFERENCES ▮▮▮▮▮▮▮

Myers, S. C., "Using Simulation for Risk Analysis" in *Modern Developments in Financial Analysis* (S. C. Meyers, ed.), Praeger, 1976.

Sharpe, W. F., Alexander, G. F. and J. V. Bailey, *Investments*, 6th Edition. Upper Saddle River, NJ: Prentice Hall, 1999.

Thatcher, M. E. and Oliver, J. R., "The Impact of Technology Investments on a Firm's Production Efficiency, Product Quality, and Productivity." *Journal of Management Information Systems* 18, No. 2: 17–45, 2001.

Index